INSTRUCTOR'S MANUAL TO ACCOMPANY

LITERATURE

INSTRUCTOR'S MANUAL TO ACCOMPANY

LITERATURE

An Introduction to Fiction, Poetry, Drama, and Writing

TENTH EDITION

X. J. Kennedy

Dorothy M. Kennedy

Dana Gioia

PEARSON
Longman

New York   Boston   San Francisco
London   Toronto   Sydney   Tokyo   Singapore   Madrid
Mexico City   Munich   Paris   Cape Town   Hong Kong   Montreal

ACKNOWLEDGEMENTS

"Buck It" by Jerald Bullis. Reprinted by permission of the author. "Introduction to Poetry" from *The Apple That Astonished Paris*, poems by Billy Collins. Copyright © 1988 by Billy Collins. Reprinted by permission of The University of Arkansas Press. "Women at Fifty" by Andrea Hollander Budy, from *House Without a Dreamer*. Copyright © 1993 by Andrea Hollander Budy. Reprinted by permission of the author. "Introduction to Poetry" from *Another Kind of Travel*, poems by Paul Lake. Copyright © 1988 by Paul Lake. Reprinted by permission of the author.

Vice President and Editor-in-Chief: Joseph P. Terry
Executive Marketing Manager: Ann Stypuloski
Senior Supplements Editor: Donna Campion
Electronic Page Makeup: Grapevine Publishing Services, Inc.

Instructor's Manual to Accompany *Literature: An Introduction to Fiction, Poetry, Drama, and Writing*, Tenth Edition.

Copyright © 2007 by X. J. Kennedy, Dorothy M. Kennedy, and Dana Gioia

All rights reserved. No part of this book may be reproduced in any manner whatsoever without permission, except in the case of brief quotations embodied in critical articles and reviews. Printed in the United States.

ISBN: 0-321-46176-2

1 2 3 4 5 6 7 8 9 10—DOC—09 08 07 06

Contents

POETRY

WRITING

Preface

We've always found, before teaching a knotty piece of literature, that no preparation is more helpful than to sit down and discuss it with a colleague or two. If this manual supplies you with such a colleague at inconvenient hours, such as 2:00 A.M., when there's no one in the faculty coffee room, it will be doing its job.

This manual tries to provide exactly that sort of collegial conversation—spirited but specific, informal but informed. We offer you a sheaf of diverse notes to supply—if you want them—classroom strategies, critical comments, biographical information, historical context, and a few homemade opinions. These last may be wrong, but we set them down to give you something clear-cut with which to agree or disagree. Candor, we think, helps to enliven any conversation.

The manual includes:

- Commentary on every story, poem, and play presented in the text, except for a few brief poems quoted in the text as illustrations;
- Additional classroom questions and discussion strategies;
- Thematic Indices at the beginning of the "Fiction" and "Poetry" sections.

PLAN OF THE BOOK

There is a plan to *Literature*, but the book does not oblige you to follow it. Chapters may be taken up in any sequence; some instructors like to intersperse poetry and plays with stories. Some may wish to teach Chapter 25 on "Myth and Narrative" immediately before teaching *Oedipus the King*. Many find that "Imagery" is a useful chapter with which to begin teaching poetry. Instructors who prefer to organize the course by theme will want to consult the detailed thematic indices.

If, because you skip around in the book, students encounter a term unknown to them, let them look it up in the Index of Terms on the inside back cover. They will be directed to the page where it first occurs and where it will be defined and illustrated. Or have them look it up in the Glossary of Literary Terms at the back of the book.

In the poetry chapters, the sections titled "For Review and Further Study" do not review the whole book up to that moment; they review only the main points of the chapter. Most of these sections contain some poems that are a little more difficult than those in the body of that chapter.

FEATURES OF THIS EDITION

The tenth edition of *Literature* incorporates many changes. We have revised this edition with the simple aim of bringing in useful new features and selections without losing the best-liked material. We have been guided in this effort by scores of instructors and students who use the book in their classrooms. Teaching is a kind of conversation—between instructor and student, between reader and text. Revising *Literature*, we try to help keep this conversation fresh by mixing the classic with the new, the familiar with the surprising.

Casebooks on Major Authors and Literary Masterpieces

We have made substantial changes in our casebooks in this new edition. There are now nine casebooks—four of which are new. We continue to include substantial special chapters on five major authors (Flannery O'Connor, Emily Dickinson, Langston Hughes, Sophocles, and William Shakespeare), and we now supplement those author studies with four new casebooks on popular works frequently used by students for critical analyses or research papers. Our new literary masterpiece casebooks cover three works of fiction (Edgar Allan Poe's "The Tell-Tale Heart," Charlotte Perkins Gilman's "The Yellow Wallpaper," and Alice Walker's "Everyday Use") and one long poem (T. S. Eliot's "The Love Song of J. Alfred Prufrock"). These special chapters present a variety of material—biographies, photographs, critical commentaries, and statements by the authors. Our aim has been to provide everything a student might need to begin an in-depth study of each author or work.

Illustrated Shakespeare

Reading Shakespeare can be intimidating to students who have never seen a live production of one of his plays. (Unfortunately, today most American teenagers have never seen any live professional production of spoken drama—by Shakespeare or anyone else.) What is a college instructor to do?

The new edition of *Literature* presents three plays by Shakespeare—*Othello*, *Hamlet*, and *A Midsummer Night's Dream*—in a new illustrated format featuring dozens of production photos. We have endeavored to illustrate every major scene in each play as well as most of the major characters. This new approach helps students visualize the action of the plays. It also helps break up the long blocks of print to make the text less intimidating.

For today's visually oriented students, *Literature*'s new format should represent a breakthrough in accessibility.

Latin American Poetry Chapter

The unique bilingual chapter on Latin American Poetry introduced in the last edition proved very popular. Using excellent Spanish-language poems, this chapter provides students with the opportunity to experience poetry in a different language (and English translation) and to see how literature represents and illuminates a different cultural experience. We have revised the chapter slightly to give greater emphasis to Mexican poetry. Students are also introduced to the role of surrealism in Latin American poetry with an image from Frida Kahlo and words from César Vallejo and Olga Orozco. This important chapter will not only broaden most students' knowledge of world poetry, it will also recognize the richness of Spanish-language poetry in the literature of the Americas—a very relevant subject to today's multicultural classrooms. The bilingual selections may also give your Spanish-speaking students additional chances to shine in class.

Glossary of Literary Terms

The comprehensive Glossary of Literary Terms at the back of the book has been retained by popular demand from the previous editions. It includes every term highlighted in boldface throughout the text as well as other important terms—over 350 entries in all—providing a clear and accurate definition usually with cross references to related terms. The purpose of the glossary is to provide for students a single accessible reference to all key literary terms.

New Stories, Poems, and Plays

The Fiction section includes 11 new stories, bringing the total number to 66. (There are also 31 pieces of critical prose.) We have added several new stories to broaden and update our coverage. New selections that deepen our international and multicultural coverage are Octavio Paz's "My Life with the Wave," Helena María Viramontes's "The Moths," Alice Munro's "How I Met My Husband," Dagoberto Gilb's "Look on the Bright Side," and Yiyun Li's award-winning "A Thousand Years of Good Prayers."

Other additions show contemporary American masters at their peak performance, such as Anne Tyler's "Teenage Wasteland" and Tobias Wolff's "A Rich Brother." A few familiar classic stories have also been added, including Eudora Welty's "A Worn Path" and O. Henry's "The Gift of the Magi." (O. Henry's classic story provides a great opportunity to teach students about irony.) We have also included Flannery O'Connor's fascinating last story, "Parker's Back," a strikingly timely tale about both tattoos and religious fundamentalism.

We've kept Leo Tolstoy's harrowing novella *The Death of Ivan Ilych* because of the impassioned requests of several instructors. Also retained by popular demand is Kurt Vonnegut's mordant satire "Harrison Bergeron," a contemporary science-fiction classic that has become a classroom favorite. Vonnegut's story helps maintain our coverage of popular fictional genres—a long-standing interest of this anthology. The current edition contains classic examples of the Gothic tale (Gilman, Poe), the adventure story (London, Crane), science fiction (Vonnegut, Le Guin), as well as Magical Realism (García Márquez, Paz, Borges). These selections combine with traditional realist and modernist stories to demonstrate the full range of the short story's possibilities.

In the Poetry section we proudly provide the most extensive selection of poems found in any comparable book in the field—over 500 poems in the new edition. We have added 58 new poems to the book—to freshen the selections, update our coverage of contemporary work, and broaden our ambitious Latin American poetry chapter.

We have streamlined our unique bilingual chapter on Latin American Poetry, with added focus on contemporary Mexican poetry, while continuing to offer the masterworks of Sor Juana, Pablo Neruda, Jorge Luis Borges, and Octavio Paz.

We have also added a fascinating casebook on T. S. Eliot's popular but challenging poem "The Love Song of J. Alfred Prufrock." It includes interesting critical excerpts as well as early reviews of the poem which demonstrate to students the slowness and difficulty of building a literary reputation.

We have freshened the casebooks on Emily Dickinson and Langston Hughes with new poems, and added a provocative new selection by Aimee Mann in the chapter on "Song." Many other fine new poems have been added from the writers Gwendolyn Brooks, Andrea Hollander Budy, E. E. Cummings, Marisa de los Santos, Rita Dove, Paul Laurence Dunbar, Alice Fulton, Jane Hirschfield, Suji Kwock Kim, Ted Kooser, David Lehman, Shirley Geok-lin Lim, April Lindner, Heather McHugh, Ogden Nash, Lorine Niedecker, Jacqueline Osherow, Kenneth Rexroth, Charles Simic, Larissa Szporluk, Amy Uyematsu, Gina Valdés, William Carlos Williams, Christian Wiman, Bernice Zamora, and many others. We also continue to include comic poems amid the lofty classics. Why? Students love them, and a little lightness helps make poetry less intimidating

Our Drama section has been substantially and stylishly revised. Our aim has been to make this section much more accessible and immediate to students, many of whom have had little or no personal experience with live theater. Our biggest innovation has been to create the "Illustrated Shakespeare." You will notice the changes immediately. The major scenes in all three Shakespeare plays are now illustrated with striking production photos—dozens of them. Many other new photos have also been added to the Drama section.

We have also brought back—by popular demand—the Dudley Fitts and Robert Fitzgerald translations of Sophocles. These classic plays are now complemented by the addition of Rita Dove's contemporary version of the Oedipus myth, *The Darker Face of the Earth*, which is set on a plantation in the ante-bellum American South. We have also added a short but powerful scene from Christopher Marlowe's *Doctor Faustus* to the section on tragedy as well as new critical material on Shakespeare. There are now 19 critical commentaries on the dramatists in the extensive casebooks on both Sophocles and Shakespeare.

New Writing Material

All of the writing material in the tenth edition of *Literature* is either new or radically revised. Writing instruction has always been an important focus of this book. Because today's students need a more concise, visual, and schematic approach than did the previous generation, we have streamlined every aspect of our extensive coverage so that students can easily find useful and accessible information—in outline form wherever possible.

Every thematic chapter of Fiction, Poetry, and Drama includes a new WRITING EFFECTIVELY section that has four elements—WRITERS ON WRITING, which personalizes the composition process; WRITING ABOUT ——, which discusses the specific topic of the chapter; a WRITING CHECKLIST, which provides a step-by-step approach to composition and critical thinking; and a WRITING ASSIGN-MENT and MORE TOPICS FOR WRITING, which provide a rich source of ideas for writing a paper. These features are designed to make the writing process easier, clearer, and less intimidating.

We now have eight full writing chapters at the end of *Literature* to provide comprehensive coverage of the composition and research process. Two of these chapters—"Keeping a Journal" and "Writing an Essay Exam"— are entirely new. All of the other chapters have been substantially revised for clarity and accessibility. We strove to simplify the text but not dumb it down. Clarity and concision are never out of place in a textbook, but condescension is fatal. One of our chief aims has been to make the information and structure of the writing chapters more visual for today's Internet-oriented students. Instructors will note how information that appeared in prose paragraphs in earlier editions now appears in outline or checklist form.

We have reprinted and annotated 15 complete student papers, including a research paper, to provide models for critical writing. (There are also two card reports and a review.) Each paper focuses on a work or author in the book and often provides a close reading that emphasizes specific elements of the work's structure and meaning.

We also now show many samples of student work-in-progress as a way of illustrating the writing process. We include, for example, a step-by-step presentation of how students can develop topics, generate ideas, and formulate a strong thesis, and we show how an early draft is revised into a more precise final version. We include sample brainstorming notes and other pre-writing techniques, to provide students with a more helpful and systematic account of the writing process. We have also integrated the concept of developing a cogent literary argument (with attention to thesis, purpose, audience, support, and organization) throughout the writing chapters.

Critical Approaches to Literature

Chapter 50, "Critical Approaches to Literature," has proven to be a popular feature of the last few editions of *Literature*. It contains three selections for every major critical school—thirty selections in all. The critical excerpts have been carefully chosen both to illustrate the major theoretical approaches and to be accessible to beginning students. The critical selections focus on literary works found in the present edition. Among the new critical excerpts are examinations of works by Zora Neale Hurston, Franz Kafka, and a piece by Camille Paglia on William Blake. Taken together with the many commentaries in the casebooks and WRITERS ON WRITING feature, *Literature* now includes a total of 135 critical excerpts. This expanded coverage gives *Literature* both more depth and greater flexibility for instructors who prefer to incorporate literary theory and criticism into their introductory courses.

MyLiteratureLab

MyLiteratureLab is a Web-based state-of-the-art interactive learning system designed to accompany *Literature* and help students in their coursework. It adds a new dimension to the study of literature with Longman Lectures—evocative, richly illustrated audio readings along with advice on how to read, interpret, and write about literary works from our roster of Longman authors (including X. J. Kennedy). This powerful program also features Diagnostic Tests, Interactive Readings with clickable prompts, film clips of selections in *Literature*, sample student papers, Literature Timelines, and our Avoiding Plagiarism and Research Navigator™ tools. For a detailed guide to *MyLiteratureLab*, please turn to page xxi of this manual.

STATISTICS ON POETRY

The tenth edition of *Literature* includes over 500 whole poems. In case you wish to teach a poet's work in greater depth than a single poem affords, these 25 poets are the most heavily represented (listed by number of poems):

Emily Dickinson	21
Langston Hughes	17
Robert Frost	13
William Shakespeare	8
William Carlos Williams	8
W. B. Yeats	8
Alfred, Lord Tennyson	7
Walt Whitman	7
W. H. Auden	6
William Blake	6
E. E. Cummings	6
Thomas Hardy	6
John Keats	6
John Donne	5
Gerard Manley Hopkins	5
Elizabeth Bishop	4
Gwendolyn Brooks	4
T. S. Eliot	4
George Herbert	4
A. E. Housman	4
Edna St. Vincent Millay	4
Edwin Arlington Robinson	4
William Stafford	4
Wallace Stevens	4
William Wordsworth	4

There are three poems each by Buson, Billy Collins, Wendy Cope, Robert Graves, Robert Herrick, Ben Jonson, Omar Khayyam, Philip Larkin, Sylvia Plath, Alexander Pope, Ezra Pound, Alastair Reid, Adrienne Rich, Theodore Roethke, and John Updike. Many other poets are represented doubly.

Texts and Editorial Policy

Spelling has been modernized and rendered American, unless to do so would change the sound of a word. Untitled poems are identified by their first lines, except for those that have titles assigned by custom ("The Twa Corbies"). The poems of Emily Dickinson are presented as edited by Thomas H. Johnson.

It would have been simpler to gloss no word a student could find in a desk dictionary, on the grounds that rummaging through dictionaries is good moral discipline; but it seemed best not to require the student to exchange text for dictionary as many as thirty times in reading a story, poem, or play. Glosses have been provided, therefore, for whatever seemed likely to get in the way of pleasure and understanding.

The spelling *rime* is used instead of *rhyme* on the theory that rime is easier to tell apart from *rhythm*.

Additional Teaching Resource

Ask your Longman representative for our *Teaching Composition with Literature: 101 Writing Assignments from College Instructors*, a collection of proven writing exercises based on selections from the book contributed by dozens of teachers from across North America.

A Note on Live Readings

Many find that, for drumming up zeal for poetry, there is no substitute for a good live poetry reading by a poet whose work students have read before. Anyone who wants to order a live poet is advised to visit the Web site of Poets and Writers <www.pw.org> and use their online directory of writers to get information about inviting a poet to visit your college or university. Not all poets give stirring performances, of course, so ask your colleagues on other campuses for suggestions, lest you get stuck with some mumbling prima donna.

If you want the poet to visit classes or confer with student writers, be sure to specify your expectations ahead of time. Some poets, especially media figures whose affairs are managed by agents, will charge for extra services; less-known visitors grateful for a reading are often pathetically happy to oblige (they may even walk your dog). All poets, if they are to do their best for you, need an occasional hour of solitude to recharge their batteries.

With a Little Help from Our Friends

If we have described this manual as a 24-hour teacher's lounge, we are pleased to report how many interesting colleagues have stopped in to chat. We receive a steady stream of letters on *Literature* from instructors throughout North America and abroad. Sometimes they disagree with our comments; more often they add new information or perspective. Frequently they pass on stories about what works or does not work in their classrooms. Much of this information is simply too good not to share. We have, therefore, supplemented our own comments with hundreds of comments from instructors (always properly credited to their authors).

Thanks

Two fine writers helped prepare material appearing in the new edition. April Lindner of Saint Joseph's University in Philadelphia, Pennsylvania, served as associate editor for the writing section. Using her extensive teaching experience in both literature and composition, she not only developed materials with the editors for this book but also tested them in her classroom. Meanwhile, Michael Palma scrupulously examined and updated every chapter from the previous edition. His deep knowledge of literature and crisp sense of style keeps the new edition fresh, informed, and accessible. Ongoing thanks also go to Diane Thiel of the University of New Mexico, who originally helped develop the Latin American poetry chapter in the previous edition, and to Susan Balée, who contributed to the chapter on writing a research paper.

Ellen Mease, a professor of drama at Grinnell College, not only provided good counsel on the Drama section but also wrote the extensive entry on Shakespeare's *A Midsummer Night's Dream.* Ongoing thanks to Daniel Stone, Robert McPhillips, Cheryl Clements; Lee Gurga; Nan LaBoe; Richard Mezo; Jeff Newberry; Beverly Schneller; Janet Schwarzkopf; Theresa Welford; and William Zander for help with this book.

Many instructors, most of whose names appear in this manual, generously wrote us with their suggestions and teaching experiences. Other instructors are noted in the introductory remarks to the textbook itself. We thank them all for their pragmatic and informed help. We are grateful to Donna Campion at Pearson Longman and to Dianne Hall for their formidable effort and good will in managing the design and production of the manual. Finally, we would like to thank Mary Gioia, whose remarkable planning and editorial skills kept this manual in running order despite its erratic drivers.

On Teaching Literature

We'll close with a poem. It is by Billy Collins, from his collection *The Apple That Astonished Paris* (University of Arkansas Press, 1988), and it sets forth an experience that may be familiar to you.

INTRODUCTION TO POETRY

I ask them to take a poem
and hold it up to the light
like a color slide
or press an ear against its hive.

I say drop a mouse into a poem
and watch him probe his way out,
or walk inside the poem's room
and feel the walls for a light switch.

I want them to waterski
across the surface of a poem
waving at the author's name on the shore.
But all they want to do
is tie the poem to a chair with rope
and torture a confession out of it.

They begin beating it with a hose
to find out what it really means.

As you might expect, Billy Collins, a past U.S. Poet Laureate, is himself a professor of English—at Lehman College of the City University of New York.

May this manual help you find ways to persuade your students to set aside rope and hose and instead turn on a few lights.

XJK, DMK, and DG

Guide to

myliteraturelab™

*W*here literature comes to life!

http://www.myliteraturelab.com

Introduction

Welcome, instructors, to *MyLiteratureLab*, a specially configured interactive Web site for users of Kennedy/Gioia's *Literature* series. If you and your students are using the Interactive Edition of *Literature*, your book includes an access code that lets you use the Web site at no additional charge. In the front of the book you and your students will find a chart with all the media resources on the site, listed by author, which correspond to specific selections in the book. Additionally, throughout the text there are marginal icons designating which authors and selections have corresponding materials on the site.

For help in using *MyLiteratureLab* in your course, this Instructor's Manual includes listings of available resources by author, on a chapter-by-chapter basis, and in the relevant entries on each selection.

If you have used *The Craft of Literature* CD-ROM that accompanied previous editions, please note that all the resources on the CD (and more) are now available at *MyLiteratureLab*.

If you are not using the Interactive version of Kennedy/Gioia *Literature* and are interested in using *MyLiteratureLab*, visit **http://www.myliteraturelab.com** to find out how you and your students can access the site.

Features

This brief guide highlights the main benefits and features of *MyLiteratureLab*. You may refer to the Instructor Resource section of *MyLiteratureLab* for a more extensive Faculty Teaching Guide.

- *Video clips of the authors*—X. J. Kennedy and Dana Gioia—introduce most chapters with suggestions for approaching the chapter's content.

- *Film and audio clips* of stories, poems, and plays.

- *Longman Lectures*—Longman's award-wining authors, including X. J. Kennedy, discuss popular literary works in ten-minute illustrated lectures designed to help students find a way "in" to a literary selection and then write about it.

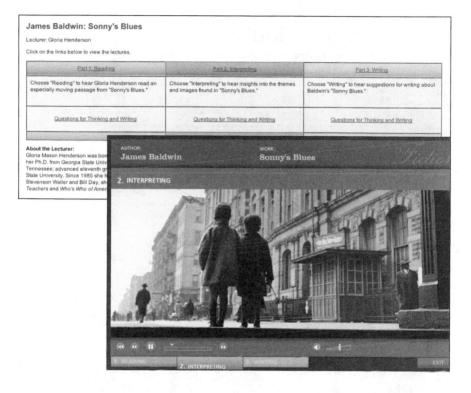

- *Interactive Readings*— with hyperlinked text, give insight into the work's craft elements and provide study questions to illuminate the meaning.

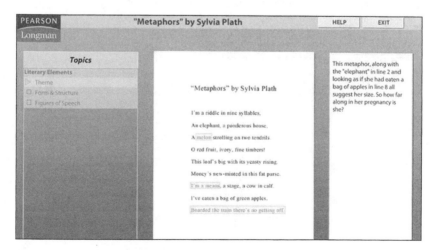

- *Interactive Writing Guidance*—step-by-step explanations and student exercises that support writing a paper, from generating ideas to developing a thesis to organizing a literary argument.

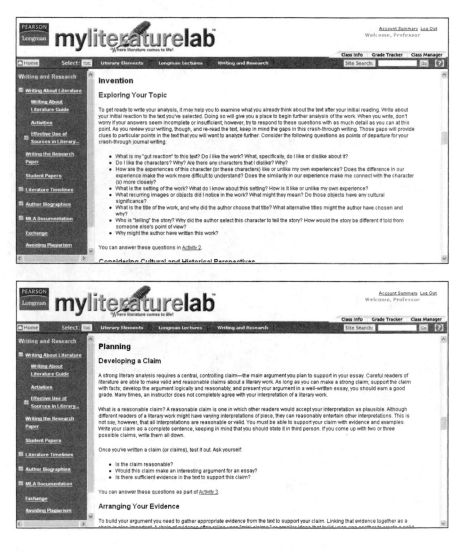

- *Interactive Guidance on Acknowledging Sources*—helpful tutorials and exercises for students to learn how to acknowledge sources and to understand and avoid plagiarism.

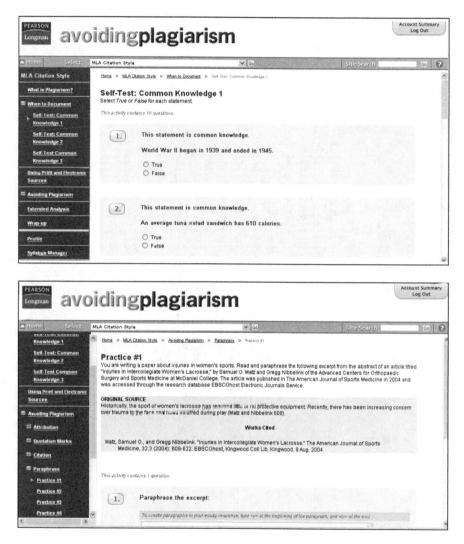

- *MLA Documentation*—explanations, examples, helpful links for students to learn about and use MLA documentation.

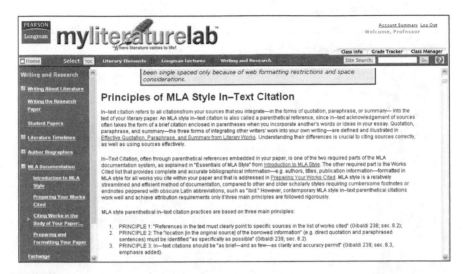

- *Research Navigator*—extensive help on the research process and access to four reliable, useful databases (**EBSCO** Academic Journal and Abstract Database, *New York Times* Search by Subject Archive, **"Best of the Web"** Link Library, and *Financial Times* Article Archive).

- *Sample Student Papers*—papers on selections found in the book.

> Raz 1
>
> Katherine Raz
>
> Professor Lopez
>
> English 210
>
> 3 March 200X
>
> Point of View in Alice Walker's "Everyday Use"
>
> Alice Walker is making a statement about the popularization of black culture in "Everyday Use." The story involves characters from both sides of the African American cultural spectrum, conveniently cast as sisters in the story. Dee/Wangero represents the "new black," with her natural hairdo and brightly colored clothing. Maggie remains traditional: the unchanged, unaffected bystander. Nowhere in the dialogue do Walker's characters directly mention their feelings about the Americanization of African tradition.

Using MyLiteratureLab *in Your Course*

You can use *MyLiteratureLab* to help build student interest.

- *MyLiteratureLab* helps make literature come alive. Audio and video clips and Longman Lectures encourage student interest —not only from hearing a poem read expertly or seeing a professional production of a story or play, but also by opening the door to the ways literature can be interpreted.

- *MyLiteratureLab* helps create a theatrical experience. Approximately half of today's college freshmen have never seen a live professional play, and the clips shown here give them the flavor of live performance.

- *MyLiteratureLab* gives background material and critical essays that allow students an opportunity to study an author, selection, or critical theory in depth.

- *MyLiteratureLab* offers X. J. Kennedy's and Dana Gioia's informal comments on how literature can enrich a student's life (see "Why Literature Matters" on the opening screen), as well as video clips of them reading their own poetry.

MyLiteratureLab helps students read and interpret.

- *Chapter Introductions* offer reinforcement of the discussions given in the book. The video and text introductions by X. J. Kennedy and Dana Gioia succinctly cover the related chapter in the book's content.

- *Interactive Readings* give practice in understanding the craft topic in the text's chapter. It takes students line by line through a story, poem, or scene from a play, giving them guidance about what is "happening" in the selections as well as asking them questions about the craft.

- *Longman Lectures* include words and images to contextualize and enrich the content of each lecture. Each lecture is organized into three parts: reading, interpreting, and writing, all supported with writing prompts. The three-part structure encourages students to read and interpret the work more thoughtfully and spark ideas for research and writing.

- *Student Papers* can be used as models. Students are also asked to read the papers critically and answer questions about them, helping to sharpen their own rhetorical skills.

You can use *MyLiteratureLab* to supplement and enrich your assignments.

- Every major section of *MyLiteratureLab* is supported with pedagogy. Students don't just watch a video clip and then turn to something else. Critical thinking questions accompany every element.

You can incorporate *MyLiteratureLab* into your course in a number of ways.

- *As homework*—to reinforce the content covered in class and in the anthology.

- *In class*—to promote discussion and provide alternative ways of covering the syllabus.

- *For research assignments*—to get students started on researching an author or a work via the Background and Critical Essays sections and with the very useful Researcher Navigator tool.

- *For independent study.*

You can access *MyLiteratureLab* to best suit your needs.

- A special section on the site just for Kennedy/Gioia users lets you access the resources of *MyLiteratureLab* via the Kennedy/Gioia table of contents.

- You can also use the content on *MyLiteratureLab* through its "regular" access. Entering the site in this way gives you immediate access to Diagnostics, Interactive Readings, Longman Lectures, and Writing and Research content including Research Navigator.

- Available in Course Compass, Web CT, and Blackboard course management systems.

Author Index

MLL *MyLiteratureLab* Resources

FICTION

James Baldwin	*Sonny's Blues*: Longman Lecture ▪ Biography, Critical Archive, Bibliography
T. Coraghessan Boyle	*Greasy Lake*: Critical Essay
Raymond Carver	*Cathedral*: Longman Lecture ▪ Biography, Critical Archive, Bibliography
Willa Cather	*Paul's Case*: Video, Audio, Critical Essay ▪ Biography/Photos, Critical Archive, Bibliography
John Cheever	Biography, Critical Archive, Bibliography
Kate Chopin	*The Storm*: Longman Lecture, Interactive Reading, Student Paper, Critical Essay ▪ Biography, Critical Archive, Bibliography
William Faulkner	*A Rose for Emily*: Critical Essay *Barn Burning*: Video(2), Audio(2), Critical Essay(2) ▪ Biography/Photos, Critical Archive, Bibliography
Gabriel García Márquez	Biography, Critical Archive, Bibliography
Charlotte Perkins Gilman	*The Yellow Wallpaper*: Critical Essay ▪ Biography, Critical Archive, Bibliography
Nathaniel Hawthorne	*Young Goodman Brown*: Longman Lecture ▪ Biography, Critical Archive, Bibliography
Ernest Hemingway	*A Clean, Well-Lighted Place*: Critical Essay ▪ Biography, Critical Archive, Bibliography
Zora Neale Hurston	*Sweat*: Longman Lecture, Interactive Reading
Shirley Jackson	*The Lottery*: Interactive Reading, Critical Essay
James Joyce	*Araby*: Longman Lecture, Interactive Reading, Critical Essay ▪ Biography, Critical Archive, Bibliography

William Shakespeare	*Hamlet, Prince of Denmark*: Critical Essay *A Midsummer Night's Dream*: Critical Essay *Othello*: Video, Audio, Interactive Reading, Student Paper, Critical Essay ▪ Biography/ Photos, Critical Archive, Bibliography
Sophocles	*Antigonê*: Longman Lecture ▪ *Oedipus*: Longman Lecture ▪ Biography, Critical Archive, Bibliography
Tennessee Williams	Biography, Critical Archive, Bibliography
August Wilson	*Fences*: Longman Lecture ▪ Biography, Critical Archive, Bibliography

Chapter Guide

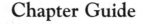 # *MyLiteratureLab* Resources

Fiction

Reading a Story

Chapter Introduction to Reading a Story
Video Introduction to Reading a Story
    Dana Gioia
Background
    John Updike
Interactive Reading
    John Updike, *A & P*
Critical Essays
    What Makes a Short Story Short?, by Norman Friedman
    Irony and Innocence in John Updike's "A & P,"
        by Lawrence Jay Dessner
Student Essay
    Why Sammy Really Quits, by Peter A. Smith

Point of View

Chapter Introduction to Point of View
Video Introduction to Point of View
    X. J. Kennedy
Background
    James Baldwin
Longman Lecture
    James Baldwin, *Sonny's Blues*
Critical Essay
    Faulkner's "A Rose for Emily," by James M. Wallace

Character

Chapter Introduction to Character
Video Introduction to Character
    Dana Gioia
Background
    Raymond Carver
    Katherine Anne Porter

Audio Clip
    Henry Fonda introduces *The Jilting of Granny Weatherall*
Video Clip
    The Jilting of Granny Weatherall
Longman Lecture
    Raymond Carver, *Cathedral*
Interactive Reading
    Katherine Mansfield, *Miss Brill*
Critical Essays
    Internal Opposition in Porter's "Granny Weatherall," by Joseph Wiesenfarth
    Alienation in "Miss Brill," by Robert L. Hull
    Flat and Round Characters, by E. M. Forster

Setting

Chapter Introduction to Setting
Video Introduction to Setting
    X. J. Kennedy
Background
    Amy Tan
Longman Lecture
    Kate Chopin, *The Storm*
Interactive Reading
    Kate Chopin, *The Storm*
Critical Essays
    *Acting Like Fools: The Ill-Fated Romances of "At the 'Cadian Ball" and
        "The Storm,"* by Lawrence I. Berkove
    Boyle's "Greasy Lake" and the Moral Failure of Postmodernism,
        by Michael Walker
Student Essay
    *Rising Feminist "Storms": Sexuality and Desire in Kate Chopin's
        "The Storm,"* by Amy Mendenhall

Tone and Style

Chapter Introduction to Tone and Style
Video Introduction to Tone and Style
    Dana Gioia
Background
    William Faulkner
Audio Clip
    Henry Fonda introduces *Barn Burning*
Video Clip
    Barn Burning
Critical Essays
    Survival Through Irony: Hemingway's "A Clean, Well-Lighted Place,"
        by Annette Benert

Reading "Barn Burning," by Hans H. Skei
Style, by Hallie Burnett

Theme

Chapter Introduction to Theme
Video Introduction to Theme
    X. J. Kennedy

Symbol

Chapter Introduction to Symbol
Video Introduction to Symbol
    Dana Gioia
Interactive Reading
    Shirley Jackson, *The Lottery*
Critical Essays
    Social Evil: "The Lottery," by Lenemaja Friedman
Student Essay
    To Stay in Omelas, by Anthony P. Iannini

Critical Casebook: Flannery O'Connor

Background
    Flannery O'Connor
Longman Lecture
    Flannery O'Connor, *A Good Man Is Hard to Find*
Interactive Reading
    Flannery O'Connor, *A Good Man Is Hard to Find*

Critical Casebook: Three Stories in Depth

EDGAR ALLAN POE'S "THE TELL-TALE HEART"
Background
    Edgar Allan Poe
Video Clip
    Edgar Allan Poe, *The Tell-Tale Heart*
Longman Lecture
    Edgar Allan Poe, *The Tell-Tale Heart*
Critical Essays
    Poe's "The Tell-Tale Heart," by E. Arthur Robinson

CHARLOTTE PERKINS GILMAN'S "THE YELLOW WALLPAPER"
Background
    Charlotte Perkins Gilman
Critical Essay
    What Cure for the Madwoman in the Attic?, by John Sutherland

ALICE WALKER'S "EVERYDAY USE"
Background
    Alice Walker
Longman Lecture
    Alice Walker, *Everyday Use*
Student Essay
    Analyzing Point of View in Alice Walker's "Everyday Use," by Katherine Raz

Stories for Further Reading

AMBROSE BIERCE'S "AN OCCURRENCE AT OWL CREEK BRIDGE"
Background
    Ambrose Bierce
Video Clip
    An Occurrence at Owl Creek Bridge
Critical Essay
    Something Uncanny: The Dream Structure in Ambrose Bierce's
    "An Occurrence at Owl Creek Bridge," by Peter Stoicheff

WILLA CATHER'S "PAUL'S CASE"
Background
    Willa Cather
Audio Clip
    Henry Fonda introduces *Paul's Case*
Video Clip
    Paul's Case
Interactive Reading
    Willa Cather, *Paul's Case*
Critical Essay
    What Really Happens in Cather's "Paul's Case," by Michael N. Salda

ANTON CHEKHOV'S "THE LADY WITH THE PET DOG"
Background
    Anton Chekhov

KATE CHOPIN'S "THE STORM"
Longman Lecture
    Kate Chopin, *The Storm*

GABRIEL GARCÍA MÁRQUEZ'S "THE HANDSOMEST DROWNED MAN
    IN THE WORLD"
Background
    Gabriel García Márquez

NATHANIEL HAWTHORNE'S "YOUNG GOODMAN BROWN"
Background
    Nathaniel Hawthorne
Longman Lecture
    Nathaniel Hawthorne, *Young Goodman Brown*

Zora Neale Hurston's "Sweat"
Background
    Zora Neale Hurston
Interactive Reading
    Zora Neale Hurston, *Sweat*

James Joyce's "Araby"
Background
    James Joyce
Interactive Reading
    James Joyce, *Araby*
Longman Lecture
    James Joyce, *Araby*
Critical Essay
    The Ironic Narrator in James Joyce's "Araby," by Janice E. Patten

Bobbie Ann Mason's "Shiloh"
Longman Lecture
    Bobbie Ann Mason, *Shiloh*

Joyce Carol Oates's "Where Are You Going, Where Have You Been?"
Background
    Joyce Carol Oates
Longman Lecture
    Joyce Carol Oates, *Where Are You Going, Where Have You Been?*

Tim O'Brien's "The Things They Carried"
Longman Lecture
    Tim O'Brien, *The Things They Carried*

Poetry

Reading a Poem

Chapter Introduction to Reading a Poem
Video Introduction to Reading a Poem
    X. J. Kennedy
Background
    Robert Browning
    Adrienne Rich
Audio Clip
    My Last Duchess
Longman Lecture
    My Last Duchess
Interactive Reading
    "*Out, Out—,*" by Robert Frost

Critical Essays
> Frost's " 'Out, Out—,'" by Gloriana Locklear
> *Structure and Meaning in Browning's "My Last Duchess,"* by Joshua Adler
> *Yeats's "The Lake Isle of Innisfree": Images of Dark Desires,*
>   by Scott C. Holstad

Student Essay
> *A Feminist Reading of Browning's "My Last Duchess,"*
>   by Artavia Lineszy-Overton

Listening to a Voice

Chapter Introduction to Listening to a Voice
Video Introduction to Listening to a Voice
>   Dana Gioia

Background
>   William Blake

Audio Clip
>   *The Chimney Sweeper*

Longman Lectures
>   Wilfred Owen, *Dulce et Decorum Est*
>   William Butler Yeats, *The Lake Isle of Innisfree*

Interactive Reading
>   Wilfred Owen, *Dulce et Decorum Est*

Critical Essays
> *Fact and Symbol in "The Chimney Sweeper" of Blake's "Songs of Innocence,"*
>   by Martin K. Nurmi
> *"Dulce Et Decorum Est"—A Dramatist's Point of View,* by Troy M. Hughes
> *Robinson's "Luke Havergal,"* by Ronald E. McFarland

Words

Chapter Introduction to Words
Video Introduction to Words
>   X. J. Kennedy

Background
>   Billy Collins
>   E. E. Cummings
>   John Donne

Audio Clip
>   *anyone lived in a pretty how town*

Longman Lectures
>   Billy Collins, *The Names*
>   John Donne, *Batter my heart, three-personed God, for You*
>   Lewis Carroll, *Jabberwocky*

Interactive Reading
>   Lewis Carroll, *Jabberwocky*

Critical Essays
> Thomas Hardy's "The Ruined Maid," Elsa Lanchester's Music-Hall, and
> the Fall into Fashion, by Keith Wilson
> Carroll's "Jabberwocky," by Karen Alkalay-Gut
> Anyone's Any: A View of Language and Poetry Through an Analysis of
> "anyone lived in a pretty how town," by James Paul Gee

Saying and Suggesting

Chapter Introduction to Saying and Suggesting
Video Introduction to Saying and Suggesting
> Dana Gioia

Interactive Reading
> Richard Wilbur, Love Calls Us to the Things of This World

Critical Essays
> "Kubla Khan": The Poet in the Poem, by Geoffrey Little
> From Cold War Poetry, by Edward Brunner

Student Essay
> Symbolic Language in Coleridge's "Kubla Khan," by Patrick Mooney

Imagery

Chapter Introduction to Imagery
Video Introduction to Imagery
> X. J. Kennedy

Background
> Gerard Manley Hopkins

Video Clip
> Gerard Manley Hopkins, Pied Beauty

Longman Lecture
> John Keats, Bright star! would I were steadfast as thou art

Interactive Reading
> Theodore Roethke, Root Cellar

Critical Essays
> Seeing "Pied Beauty": A Key to Theme and Structure, by Amy Lowenstein
> Some Observations on Elizabeth Bishop's "The Fish,"
> by Ronald E. McFarland
> Roethke's "Root Cellar," by George Wolff

Figures of Speech

Chapter Introduction to Figures of Speech
Video Introduction to Figures of Speech
> Dana Gioia

Background
> Sylvia Plath
> William Shakespeare

Audio Clip
   William Shakespeare, *Shall I compare thee to a summer's day?*
Longman Lecture
   Robert Burns, *Oh, my love is like a red, red rose*
Interactive Reading
   Sylvia Plath, *Metaphors*
Critical Essays
   Shakespeare's "Sonnet 18" ["Shall I compare thee to a summer's day?"],
      by Robert H. Ray
   Shakespeare's "Sonnet 18" ["Shall I compare thee to a summer's day?"],
      by Mark Howell
   "Metaphors," by Karen Alkalay-Gut
   Atwood's "You fit into me," by Jes Simmons
Student Essay
   Shakespeare's Eternal Summer, by Laura Todd

Song and Sound

Chapter Introduction to Sound
Video Introduction to Sound
   X. J. Kennedy
Background
   Alfred, Lord Tennyson
Audio Clip
   The splendor falls on castle walls
Longman Lecture
   Edward Arlington Robinson, *Richard Cory*
Interactive Reading
   William Butler Yeats, *Who Goes with Fergus?*
Critical Essays
   A Re-examination of "Richard Cory," by Charles A. Sweet, Jr.
   Cosmic Irony in Wordsworth's "A Slumber Did My Spirit Seal,"
      by Warren Stevenson
   Rhetorical Figures in Yeats's "Leda and the Swan,"
      by Barbara Edwards-Aldrich
Student Essay
   Playing Upon Words [On Updike's "Recital"], by Bryan C. Smith

Rhythm

Chapter Introduction to Rhythm
Video Introduction to Rhythm
   Dana Gioia
Background
   Dorothy Parker
   Gwendolyn Brooks

Video Clip
  Jack Lemmon reads *Résumé*
Interactive Reading
  Gwendolyn Brooks, *We Real Cool*
Critical Essays
  Creating the Blues ("Dream Boogie"), by Steven C. Tracy
  On *"We Real Cool,"* by James D. Sullivan
Student Essay
  The Tides of "We Real Cool," by Juli Grace

Closed Form

Chapter Introduction to Closed Form
Video Introduction to Closed Form
  X. J. Kennedy
Background
  Robert Frost
  Edna St. Vincent Millay
Video Clip
  Edna St. Vincent Millay, *What lips my lips have kissed, and where, and why*
Longman Lectures
  Robert Frost, *Acquainted with the Night*
  The Theme of Love in Shakespeare's Sonnets
Interactive Reading
  Dylan Thomas, *Do not go gentle into that good night*
Critical Essays
  The Making of a Poem: Dylan Thomas's "Do not go gentle into that good night," by Oliver Evans
  Clerihews, by Israel Shenker
Student Essay
  Analysis of Edna St. Vincent Millay's "What lips my lips have kissed, and where, and why," by Stephanie Willson

Open Form

Chapter Introduction to Open Form
Video Introduction to Open Form
  Dana Gioia
Background
  E. E. Cummings
Audio Clip
  Buffalo Bill 's
Interactive Reading
  Walt Whitman, *Cavalry Crossing a Ford*
Critical Essays
  Cummings's "Buffalo Bill 's," by Thomas Dilworth
  Whitman's Theme in "Cavalry Crossing a Ford," by Dale Doepke
  "Easter Wings," by Joan Klingel Ray

Student Essay
> *The Emotional Response of Forché's "The Colonel,"* by Michelle Brown

Symbol

Chapter Introduction to Symbol
Video Introduction to Symbol
> X. J. Kennedy

Interactive Reading
> Wallace Stevens, *Anecdote of the Jar*

Critical Essays
> *Frost's "The Road Not Taken": A 1925 Letter Comes to Light*,
> by Larry Finger
> *Stevens's "Anecdote of the Jar": Art as Entrapment*, by A. R. Coulthard
> *The God-Curst Sun: Love in "Neutral Tones,"* by James Hazen

Poetry and Personal Identity

Longman Lecture
> Sylvia Plath, *Lady Lazarus*

Recognizing Excellence

Longman Lecture
> Elizabeth Bishop, *One Art*

Casebooks: Emily Dickinson and Langston Hughes

Background
> Emily Dickinson
> Langston Hughes

Longman Lectures
> Emily Dickinson, *Because I could not stop for Death*
> Langston Hughes, *The Weary Blues*

Casebook: T. S. Eliot's "The Love Song of J. Alfred Prufrock"

Student Paper
> *The Existential Anguish of J. Alfred Prufrock*, by Patrick Mooney

Poems for Further Reading

GWENDOLYN BROOKS'S "THE MOTHER"
Background
> Gwendolyn Brooks

Longman Lecture
> Gwendolyn Brooks, *The Mother*

SAMUEL TAYLOR COLERIDGE'S "KUBLA KHAN"
Background
  Samuel Taylor Coleridge
Audio Clip
  Kubla Khan
Critical Essay
  "Kubla Khan": The Poet in the Poem, by Geoffrey Little

ROBERT FROST'S "MENDING WALL"
Background
  Robert Frost
Longman Lecture
  Mending Wall

SEAMUS HEANEY'S "DIGGING"
Longman Lecture
  Digging

JOHN KEATS'S "ODE ON A GRECIAN URN"
Background
  John Keats
Audio Clip
  Ode on a Grecian Urn
Student Essay
  John Keats's "Ode on a Grecian Urn": Dissolving into the Moment,
    by Michelle Brown

MARY JO SALTER'S "WELCOME TO HIROSHIMA"
Longman Lecture
  Welcome to Hiroshima

WILLIAM SHAKESPEARE'S "THAT TIME OF YEAR THOU MAYST IN
    ME BEHOLD"
Longman Lecture
  That time of year thou mayst in me behold [Sonnet 73]

X. J. Kennedy and Dana Gioia Read Their Poems

X. J. Kennedy
  For Allen Ginsberg
  Snowflake Soufflé
  Nude Descending a Staircase
  In a Prominent Bar in Secaucus One Day

Dana Gioia
  California Hills in August
  Summer Storm
  Unsaid
  Money

Drama

Reading a Play

Longman Lecture
  Susan Glaspell, *Trifles*

Critical Casebook: Sophocles

Background
  Sophocles
Longman Lectures
  Antigonê
  Oedipus the King

Critical Casebook: Shakespeare

Chapter Introduction to Shakespeare
Background
  William Shakespeare

Othello

Video Introduction to *Othello*
  X. J. Kennedy
Audio Clip
  Excerpt from a 1944 recording of Paul Robeson's *Othello*
Video Clip
  Excerpt from a performance of *Othello* starring William Marshall,
    Ron Moody, and Jenny Agutter
Interactive Reading
  Othello, Act V, Scene ii
Critical Essay
  Impertinent Trifling: Desdemona's Handkerchief, by Harry Berger, Jr.
Student Essay
  A *Guiltless Death: The Unconsummated Marriage in* Othello,
    by K. A. Goodfellow

Hamlet

Longman Lecture
Critical Essay
  Gertrude's Willow Speech: Word and Film Image, by Hanna Scolnicov

A Midsummer Night's Dream

Longman Lecture
Critical Essay
  Shakespeare's A Midsummer Night's Dream, by Robert Fleissner

The Modern Theater

Background
    Henrik Ibsen
Longman Lecture
    Henrik Ibsen, A *Doll's House*

Plays for Further Reading

Background
    Arthur Miller
    Tennessee Williams
Longman Lecture
    Arthur Miller, *Death of a Salesman*

New Voices in American Drama

Chapter Introduction
Video Introduction
    Dana Gioia
Background
    David Hwang
    August Wilson
Longman Lecture
    August Wilson, *Fences*
Critical Essays
    Saying Goodbye to the Past: Self Empowerment and History,
       by Douglas Anderson
    The Sound of a Voice: *David Hwang*, by Gerald Rabkin
    The Expressionistic Devices in Death of a Salesman,
       by Barbara Lounsberry

FICTION

Stories Arranged by Type and Element

If you prefer to teach a *different* story to illustrate an element of fiction—to discuss style, say, with the aid of "Cathedral" or "A Good Man Is Hard to Find" instead of the examples in the chapter on style—you will find the substitution easy to make. Many choices are at your disposal in Chapter 12, "Stories for Further Reading," and other stories in the book lend themselves to varied purposes. The following list has a few likely substitutions. If you teach other elements of fiction (e.g., humor, fantasy) or specific genres, you will find some nominations here.

FABLE, PARABLE, AND TALE

STORIES INCLUDED IN CHAPTER
- The Appointment in Samarra
- The Camel and His Friends
- The North Wind and the Sun
- Godfather Death
- Independence

OTHER SUGGESTED STORIES
- The Handsomest Drowned Man in the World
- My Life with the Wave
- The Parable of the Prodigal Son
- The Tell-Tale Heart

PLOT

STORY INCLUDED IN CHAPTER
- A & P

OTHER SUGGESTED STORIES
- Barn Burning
- The Five-Forty-Eight
- The Gift of the Magi
- How I Met My Husband
- Look on the Bright Side
- The Lottery
- An Occurrence at Owl Creek Bridge
- A Rose for Emily
- Saboteur
- The Story of an Hour

POINT OF VIEW
First Person Narrator as Central Character

SUGGESTED STORIES
- A & P
- Araby (*mature narrator recalling boyhood view*)
- Cathedral
- Greasy Lake
- The House on Mango Street
- How I Met My Husband
- Look on the Bright Side

POINT OF VIEW (Cont.)
The Moths
My Life with the Wave
No One's a Mystery
A Pair of Tickets
The Prophecy
The Yellow Wallpaper

First Person Narrator Not the Protagonist

STORIES INCLUDED IN CHAPTER
A Rose for Emily
Sonny's Blues

ANOTHER SUGGESTED STORY
The Ones Who Walk Away from
Omelas

Third Person, All-knowing Narrator

SUGGESTED STORIES
The Gift of the Magi
A Good Man Is Hard to Find
The Handsomest Drowned Man in
the World
The Man to Send Rain Clouds
The Rocking-Horse Winner
The Storm
The Things They Carried
Where Are You Going, Where Have
You Been? (*paragraphs 1–13*)

Third Person, Limited Omniscience
(Narrator Seeing into One Major Character)

STORIES INCLUDED IN CHAPTER
Teenage Wasteland
A Worn Path

OTHER SUGGESTED STORIES
Barn Burning
The Five-Forty-Eight
The Gospel According to Mark
Interpreter of Maladies
The Jilting of Granny Weatherall
The Lady with the Pet Dog
Miss Brill
An Occurrence at Owl Creek Bridge
The Open Boat
Parker's Back
Revelation
Shiloh
The Story of an Hour
A Thousand Years of Good Prayers
To Build a Fire
Young Goodman Brown

Objective or "Fly-on-the-Wall" Point of View

SUGGESTED STORIES
The Chrysanthemums
A Clean, Well-Lighted Place
(*paragraphs 2–75*)

CHARACTER

SETTING

TONE AND STYLE

Stories Included in Chapter	Other Suggested Stories
Barn Burning	Cathedral
A Clean, Well-Lighted Place	Girl
	A Good Man Is Hard to Find
	Greasy Lake
	I Stand Here Ironing
	The Jilting of Granny Weatherall
	Look on the Bright Side
	The Open Boat
	A Rose for Emily
	The Tell-Tale Heart
	The Things They Carried
	Where Are You Going, Where Have You Been?
	A Worn Path
	Young Goodman Brown

IRONY

Stories Included in Chapter	Other Suggested Stories
The Gift of the Magi	The Appointment in Samarra
Saboteur	The Camel and His Friends
	Dead Men's Path
	The Gospel According to Mark
	Happy Endings
	How I Met My Husband
	The Jilting of Granny Weatherall
	The Lottery
	An Occurrence at Owl Creek Bridge
	The Open Boat (*irony of fate*)
	The Rocking-Horse Winner
	A Rose for Emily
	The Storm
	The Story of an Hour
	The Tell-Tale Heart
	To Build a Fire

SYMBOL

Stories Included in Chapter	Other Suggested Stories
The Chrysanthemums	Araby
The Lottery	Cathedral
No One's a Mystery	A Clean, Well-Lighted Place
The Ones Who Walk Away from Omelas	The Gospel According to Mark
	Greasy Lake (*the lake itself*)
	The Handsomest Drowned Man in the World
	The Jilting of Granny Weatherall
	The Moths
	My Life with the Wave
	The Open Boat
	Parker's Back

SYMBOL (Cont.)
A Rose for Emily
Sweat
The Tell-Tale Heart
The Yellow Wallpaper
Young Goodman Brown

OTHER ELEMENTS AND GENRES

FANTASY AND THE SUPERNATURAL
The Appointment in Samarra
Godfather Death
The Gospel According to Mark
The Lottery
The Metamorphosis
My Life with the Wave
The Ones Who Walk Away from Omelas
The Rocking-Horse Winner
Young Goodman Brown

HUMOR
A & P
Greasy Lake
Harrison Bergeron
How I Met My Husband
Independence
Look on the Bright Side

MYTH, FOLKLORE, AND ARCHETYPE
The Appointment in Samarra
Godfather Death
The Lottery
Where Are You Going, Where Have You Been?
Young Goodman Brown

SCIENCE FICTION
Harrison Bergeron
The Ones Who Walk Away from Omelas

Stories Arranged by Subject and Theme

In case you prefer to teach fiction according to its subjects and general themes, we have provided a list of stories that may be taken up together. Some instructors who arrange a course thematically like to *begin* with Chapter 6, "Theme," and its four stories.

ART, LANGUAGE, AND IMAGINATION
    Cathedral
    Everyday Use
    The Gospel According to Mark
    The Jilting of Granny Weatherall
    The Ones Who Walk Away from Omelas
    Parker's Back
    Sonny's Blues
    The Yellow Wallpaper

CHILDHOOD
    Araby
    Girl
    The House on Mango Street
    The Rocking-Horse Winner

COMING OF AGE, INITIATION STORIES
    Araby
    Barn Burning
    Battle Royal
    Greasy Lake
    How I Met My Husband
    The Moths
    No One's a Mystery
    Paul's Case
    The Prophecy
    Where Are You Going, Where Have You Been?

DEATH
    The Appointment in Samarra
    Dead Men's Path
    The Death of Ivan Ilych
    A Family Supper
    Godfather Death

A Good Man Is Hard to Find
The Gospel According to Mark
The Jilting of Granny Weatherall
The Moths
The Open Boat
A Rose for Emily
Sweat
To Build a Fire

DEFIANCE OF FATE
The Appointment in Samarra
Godfather Death
The Open Boat
A Worn Path

DISABILITIES
Cathedral
Shiloh

DIVINE REVELATION
The Gospel According to Mark
Parker's Back
Revelation

EPIPHANIES AND ILLUMINATIONS
Araby
Greasy Lake
Interpreter of Maladies
Miss Brill
The Moths
A Pair of Tickets
The Parable of the Prodigal Son
Revelation
The Story of an Hour
(*See also* DIVINE REVELATION)

FACING ONE'S OWN DEATH
The Death of Ivan Ilych
The Five-Forty-Eight
A Good Man Is Hard to Find
The Gospel According to Mark
The Jilting of Granny Weatherall
An Occurrence at Owl Creek Bridge
The Open Boat
To Build a Fire

FAMILIES
Barn Burning
Everyday Use
A Family Supper

A Good Man Is Hard to Find
The House on Mango Street
Interpreter of Maladies
I Stand Here Ironing
The Jilting of Granny Weatherall
The Metamorphosis
The Moths
A Pair of Tickets
The Parable of the Prodigal Son
The Rich Brother
The Rocking-Horse Winner
The Storm
Teenage Wasteland
A Thousand Years of Good Prayers

FATHER-CHILD RELATIONSHIPS
Barn Burning
A Family Supper
The Metamorphosis
A Pair of Tickets
The Parable of the Prodigal Son
The Storm
A Thousand Years of Good Prayers

FRIENDSHIP AND CAMARADERIE
A & P
Araby
Cathedral
Greasy Lake
The Open Boat
The Prophecy
The Things They Carried

GENERATION GAPS
A & P
Araby
A Family Supper
Girl
Greasy Lake
I Stand Here Ironing
The Moths
Teenage Wasteland
A Thousand Years of Good Prayers
Where Are You Going, Where Have You Been?

HOLDING A JOB, WORK
A & P
A Clean, Well-Lighted Place
The Five-Forty-Eight
Interpreter of Maladies

LONELINESS
  The Chrysanthemums
  A Clean, Well-Lighted Place
  The Five-Forty-Eight
  How I Met My Husband
  Miss Brill
  The Moths
  Paul's Case

LOVE AND DESIRE
  A & P
  Araby
  The Chrysanthemums
  Happy Endings
  How I Met My Husband
  Interpreter of Maladies
  The Jilting of Granny Weatherall
  The Lady with the Pet Dog
  My Life with the Wave
  No One's a Mystery
  Parker's Back
  Shiloh
  The Storm
  The Story of an Hour

MACHISMO AND SEXISM
  A & P
  The Five-Forty-Eight
  Greasy Lake
  Sweat
  A Thousand Years of Good Prayers

MAGIC AND THE OCCULT
  The Appointment in Samarra
  Godfather Death
  The Rocking-Horse Winner
  Young Goodman Brown

MARRIAGES (THE GOOD, THE BAD, AND THE UGLY)
  Cathedral
  The Gift of the Magi
  Happy Endings
  Interpreter of Maladies
  No One's a Mystery
  Shiloh
  The Storm
  The Story of an Hour
  Sweat
  A Thousand Years of Good Prayers
  The Yellow Wallpaper

MOTHER-CHILD RELATIONSHIPS
Everyday Use
Girl
I Stand Here Ironing
Interpreter of Maladies
The Jilting of Granny Weatherall
The Moths
A Pair of Tickets
Revelation (*the "ugly girl" and her mother*)
The Rocking-Horse Winner
Teenage Wasteland

MULTICULTURAL PERSPECTIVES
Battle Royal
Dead Men's Path
Everyday Use
A Family Supper
The House on Mango Street
Independence
Interpreter of Maladies
Look on the Bright Side
The Man to Send Rain Clouds
The Moths
A Pair of Tickets
The Prophecy
Sonny's Blues
Sweat
A Thousand Years of Good Prayers
A Worn Path

MURDER
A Good Man Is Hard to Find
The Gospel According to Mark
A Rose for Emily
The Tell-Tale Heart
Sweat

NATURE
The Man to Send Rain Clouds
The Open Boat
The Storm
To Build a Fire

PRIDE BEFORE A FALL
Barn Burning
Dead Men's Path
The Five-Forty-Eight
Revelation

RACE, CLASS, AND CULTURE
   Barn Burning
   Battle Royal
   Dead Men's Path
   Everyday Use
   The Gift of the Magi
   The House on Mango Street
   How I Met My Husband
   Independence
   Look on the Bright Side
   The Man to Send Rain Clouds
   The Moths
   A Pair of Tickets
   Revelation
   The Rich Brother
   Sonny's Blues
   Sweat
   A Thousand Years of Good Prayers
   A Worn Path

SIBLINGS
   Everyday Use
   The Metamorphosis
   A Pair of Tickets
   The Parable of the Prodigal Son
   The Rich Brother
   Sonny's Blues

THE STRENGTH OF OLD PEOPLE
   The Jilting of Granny Weatherall
   The Moths
   A Worn Path

VICTIMS AND VICTIMIZERS
   Battle Royal
   The Five-Forty-Eight
   A Good Man Is Hard to Find
   Saboteur
   Sweat
   The Tell-Tale Heart
   Where Are You Going, Where Have You Been?
   The Yellow Wallpaper

WAR
   An Occurrence at Owl Creek Bridge
   The Things They Carried

THE WISH TO LEAVE EVERYTHING AND RUN AWAY
   The Chrysanthemums
   A Family Supper

Stories Students Like Most

At the end of the book is a short student questionnaire. This form solicits each student's opinion about his or her reactions to the book. The editors read and save each completed questionnaire they receive. These candid student responses often help improve the anthology from edition to edition.

These student responses are interesting in their own right, but they also add perspective on what really happens in the classroom. The stories students prefer often differ sharply from those that instructors rate most highly. Instructors can learn a great deal by remembering how younger readers find certain selections both exciting and illuminating that may seem overly familiar to seasoned teachers.

Here are the top stories from previous editions chosen by a large sample of students over the past four years.

FAVORITE STORIES *(Student Choices in Rank Order)*

1. William Faulkner, "A Rose for Emily"

2. Franz Kafka, *The Metamorphosis*

3. Shirley Jackson, "The Lottery"

4. Edgar Allan Poe, "The Tell-Tale Heart"

5. T. Coraghessan Boyle, "Greasy Lake"

6. Charlotte Perkins Gilman, "The Yellow Wallpaper"

7. Jack London, "To Build a Fire"

8. John Updike, "A & P"

9. Flannery O'Connor, "A Good Man Is Hard to Find"

10. John Cheever, "The Five-Forty-Eight"

Let us add one cautionary footnote: Kafka's *The Metamorphosis* polarizes students (not necessarily a bad thing). It not only ranks second among student favorites, it is the overwhelming first choice among stories students dislike.

FICTION

A story even shorter than the one about the last person in the world and her doorbell appeared in a letter to the editor of the *Times Literary Supplement* for January 16, 1981. "Unluckily," writes Hugh R. Williams, "I cannot remember the source." He offers it as the briefest ghost tale ever discovered:

> Before going to bed one night, a man put his wig on the bedpost. In the morning it had turned white.

Suggestion for an assignment in writing a story: Write another supernatural tale that ends with the revelation of something inexplicable. It need not be so brief, but keep it within two paragraphs.

1
Reading a Story

For a second illustration of a great detail in a story, a detail that sounds observed instead of invented (besides Defoe's "two shoes, not mates"), you might cite a classic hunk of hokum: H. Rider Haggard's novel of farfetched adventure, *She* (1887). Describing how the Amahagger tribesmen dance wildly by the light of unusual torches—embalmed corpses of the citizens of ancient Kor, left over in quantity—the narrator, Holly, remarks, "So soon as a mummy was consumed to the ankles, which happened in about twenty minutes, the feet were kicked away, and another put in its place." (Pass down another mummy, this one is guttering!) Notice the exact specification "in about twenty minutes" and the unforgettable discarding of the unburned feet, like a candle stub. Such detail, we think, bespeaks a tall-tale-teller of genius. (For this citation, we thank T. J. Binyon's review of *The Private Diaries of Sir Henry Rider Haggard* in the *Times Literary Supplement*, 8 Aug. 1980.)

When you introduce students to the *tale* as a literary form, you might point out that even in this age of electronic entertainment, a few tales still circulate from mouth to ear. Ask them whether they have heard any good tales lately (other than dirty jokes).

FABLE, PARABLE, AND TALE

W. Somerset Maugham, THE APPOINTMENT IN SAMARRA, page 4

Maugham's retelling of this fable has in common with the Grimm tale "Godfather Death" not only the appearance of Death as a character, but also the moral or lesson that Death cannot be defied. Maugham includes this fable in his play *Sheppey* (1933), but it is probably best known as the epigraph to John O'Hara's novel *Appointment in Samarra* (New York: Random, 1934).

Students may be asked to recall other fables they know. To jog their memories, famous expressions we owe to Aesop ("sour grapes," "the lion's share," "dog in the manger," and others) may suggest the fables that gave them rise. At least, the fable of the hare and the tortoise should be familiar to any watcher of old Bugs Bunny cartoons.

Aesop, THE NORTH WIND AND THE SUN, page 5

Aesop's fables are still so familiar to many students that they may be tempted to treat them condescendingly as "kids' stuff." His fables are also so compact that they seem slight. It may help students initially to point out that in classical times the notion of a special literature for children as opposed to other groups did not exist. Aesop told his stories to a mixed audience probably consisting mostly of adults. It might even be interesting to ask a fundamental question such as whether a story is necessarily different if it is directed toward adults or children.

Most fables involved animals endowed with human traits of character and consciousness. We have deliberately chosen a fable that endows astronomical bodies—the sun and the moon—with character traits to demonstrate the range of imaginative possibilities open to the fabulists. (The Bidpai fable that follows provides a more conventional example of the animal tale.) Any student interested in pursuing the effect of such cosmic fables on contemporary literature might want to investigate two books by Italo Calvino—*Cosmicomics* (1965) and *t zero* (1967)—whose characters include planets, physical forces, and mathematical ideas.

Bidpai, THE CAMEL AND HIS FRIENDS, page 6

Bidpai's Sanskrit fables remain little known in English, but they occupy an important place in Asian literature—from Turkey and Iran to Indonesia and India. Translations and adaptations abound in the East as extensively as Aesop's fables do in the West.

The *Panchatantra*, or *Five Chapters*, was intended as a sort of moral textbook. The frame-tale presents a learned Brahmin teacher who used animal tales to instruct his students, the three amazingly dimwitted sons of a king. (Remedial education, it appears, is nothing new.) The moral code espoused by the fables is consistently practical rather than idealistic. Shrewdness and skepticism, they suggest, are necessary traits for survival in a world full of subtle dangers. The foolishly trusting camel in the fable reprinted here finds out too late that his "friends" have fatal designs—not bad advice for members of a royal family or anyone else to learn.

Chuang Tzu, INDEPENDENCE, page 8

Chuang Tzu's parables are famous in Chinese culture, both as works of intrinsic literary merit and as pithy expressions of Taoist philosophy. Parables are important literary genres in traditional societies. They reflect a cultural aesthetic that appreciates the power of literary artistry while putting it to the use of illustrating moral and religious ideas. Clarity is a key virtue in a parable or moral fable. Its purpose is not merely to entertain but also to instruct.

Chuang Tzu's celebrated parable suggests the uneasy relationship between philosophy and power in ancient China. It was not necessarily a safe gesture to decline the public invitation of a king, and the refusal of employment could be construed as an insult or censure. Chuang understands that the only safe way to turn down a monarch is with wit and charm. He makes his moral point, but with self-deprecating humor.

In his indispensable book *Essentials of Chinese Literary Art* (Belmont, CA: Duxbury, 1979, p. 46), James J. Y. Liu of Stanford University comments on the sly rhetoric of this parable:

> Instead of solemnly declaring that worldly power and glory are all in vain, Chuang Tzu makes us see their absurdity by comparing them to a dead tortoise. At the same time, life unburdened with official duties is not idealized, but compared to the tortoise dragging its tail in the mud.

The *Tzu* following Chuang's name is an honorific meaning *master*. The philosopher's historical name was Chuang Chou. The Chinese surname is conventionally put first, so Chuang is the proper term to use for the author.

This parable was a favorite of the Argentinean writer Jorge Luis Borges, who was fascinated by the Chinese fabular tradition.

Jesus's "Parable of the Prodigal Son" (Luke 15: 11–32) is found in the chapter on "Theme." It may be interesting for students to compare the differing techniques of these two classic parables from different traditions.

Jakob and Wilhelm Grimm, GODFATHER DEATH, page 9

For all its brevity, "Godfather Death" illustrates typical elements of plot. That is the main reason for including it in this chapter (not to mention its intrinsic merits!). It differs from Updike's contemporary "A & P" in its starker characterizations, its summary method of telling, its terser descriptions of setting, and its element of magic and the supernatural. In its world, God, the Devil, and Death walk the highway. If students can be shown these differences, then probably they will be able to distinguish most tales from most short stories.

"Godfather Death" may be useful, too, in a class discussion of point of view. In the opening pages of Chapter 2, we discuss the ways in which this tale is stronger for having an omniscient narrator. If you go on to deal with symbolism, you may wish to come back to this tale for a few illustrations of wonderful, suggestive properties: the magical herb, Death's underground cave, and its "thousands and thousands" of flickering candles.

This is a grim tale even for Grimm: a young man's attentions to a beautiful princess bring about his own destruction. In a fairy tale it is usually dangerous to defy some arbitrary law; and in doing so here the doctor breaks a binding contract. From the opening, we know the contract will be an evil one—by the father's initial foolishness in spurning God. Besides, the doctor is a thirteenth child—an unlucky one.

Possible visual aids are reproductions of the "Dance of Death" woodcuts by Hans Holbein the younger. Have any students seen Ingmar Bergman's film *The Seventh Seal*, and can they recall how Death was personified?

Anne Sexton has a sophisticated retelling of "Godfather Death," in which the doctor's guttering candle is "no bigger than an eyelash," in her *Transformations* (Boston: Houghton, 1971), a collection of poems based on Grimm. "Godfather Death" is seldom included in modern selections of fairy tales for children. Bruno Bettelheim has nothing specific to say about "Godfather Death" but has much of interest to say about fairy tales in his *The Uses of Enchantment* (New York: Knopf, 1976). Though Bettelheim's study is addressed primarily to adults "with children in their care," any college student fascinated by fairy tales would find it stimulating.

PLOT

THE SHORT STORY

John Updike, A & P, page 14

Within this story, Sammy rises to a kind of heroism. Despite the conventional attitudes he expresses in the first half of the story (his usual male reactions to girls in two-piece bathing suits, his put-down of *all* girls' minds: "a little buzz like a bee in a glass jar"), he comes to feel sympathy for the girls as human beings. He throws over his job to protest against their needless humiliation, and in so doing he asserts his criticism of supermarket society, a deadly world of "sheep" and "houseslaves" whom dynamite couldn't budge from their dull routines. What harm in a little innocent showing off—in, for once, a display of nonconformity?

Sammy isn't sophisticated. He comes from a family of proletarian beer drinkers and thinks martinis are garnished with mint. His language is sometimes pedestrian: "Really, I thought that was so cute." But he is capable of fresh and accurate observations—his description of the way Queenie walks on her bare feet, his comparison of the "clean bare plane" of her upper chest to "a dented sheet of metal tilted in the light." (Could Sammy be capable of so poetic an observation, or is this Updike's voice?)

Carefully plotted for all its seemingly casual telling, "A & P" illustrates typical elements. The *setting* is clear from Updike's opening paragraph ("I'm in the third checkout slot . . . with my hand on a box of HiHo crackers"). Relatively long for so brief a story, the *exposition* takes up most of the story's first half. Portraying Queenie and the other girls in loving detail, this exposition helps make Sammy's later gesture of heroism understandable. It establishes, also, that Sammy feels at odds with his job, and so foreshadows his heroism. He reacts against butcher McMahon's piggishness: "patting his mouth and looking after them sizing up their joints." *Dramatic conflict* arrives with the appearance of Lengel, the manager, and his confrontation with the girls. Lengel catches Sammy smiling—we can guess the clerk is in for trouble. Crisis and climax are practically one, but if you care to distinguish them, the *crisis* may be found in the paragraph "I thought and said 'No' but it wasn't about that I was thinking," in which Sammy hovers on the brink of his decision. The *climax* is his announcement "I quit"; the *conclusion* is his facing a bleaker future. The last sentence implies not only that Sammy will have trouble getting another job, but that if he continues to go through life as an uncompromising man of principle, then life from now on is going to be rough.

In "A & P" and the fairy tale "Godfather Death," the plots are oddly similar. In both, a young man smitten with a young woman's beauty makes a sacrifice in order to defend her from his grim overlord. (It is far worse, of course, to have Death for an overlord than Lengel.) If this resemblance doesn't seem too abstract, it may be worth pursuing briefly. The stories, to be sure, are more different than similar, but one can show how Updike is relatively abundant in his descriptions of characters and setting and goes more deeply into the central character's motivation—as short-story authors usually do, unlike most writers of tales.

For a good explication of this story, see Janet Overmeyer, "Courtly Love in the A & P," in *Notes on Contemporary Literature* for May 1972 (West Georgia College, Carrollton, GA 30117).

Updike himself reads this story and five others on *Selected Stories*, a set of two audiotape cassettes (169 minutes) produced by Random House (ISBN 0–394–55040–4). This is a crisp, dry reading that brings out the humor of "A & P."

MLL *MyLiteratureLab Resources.* Photographs and biographical information for Updike. Interactive reading, student paper, and critical essay for "A & P."

WRITERS ON WRITING

John Updike, WHY WRITE?, page 20

Although John Updike is probably the most prolific novelist-critic active in American letters, he has written surprisingly little about his own creative process. Perhaps he has been so busy examining the work of other writers that his critical attention has been mostly focused outward. A certain native reticence, however, must also surely be at play. His 1975 essay "Why Write?" is therefore a key document in understanding his artistic perspective.

The passage excerpted is an elegant defense of imaginative writing as a special means of human communication not reducible to an abstract message. Art's indirection, silences, and complexity are essential to its essence. "Reticence is as important a tool for the writer as expression," Updike asserts. Genuine writing is "ideally as ambiguous and opaque as life itself."

2
Point of View

For other illustrations of the relatively scarce second-person point of view, see Richard Hugo's poetry collection *31 Letters and 13 Dreams* (New York: Norton, 1977): "In Your Fugitive Dream," "In Your War Dream," "In Your Young Dream," and others. These poems also appear in Hugo's collected poems, *Making Certain It Goes On* (New York: Norton, 1984).

William Faulkner, A ROSE FOR EMILY, *page 28*

Over the past years whenever we have polled college students about their favorite short stories, Faulkner's "A Rose for Emily" has usually ranked first. The story has immense appeal to students for its memorable title character, brooding atmosphere, and eerie surprise ending. It is also a story that immediately rewards rereading and study. After knowing the ending, one discovers details in virtually every paragraph that anticipate the conclusion—the poison, the smell, the vanished suitor, to mention only a few.

The style of "A Rose for Emily" is unusually conventional for Faulkner. There are no elaborate periodic sentences or stream-of-consciousness narration. The simple and direct style reflects the particular speaker Faulkner chose to tell the story. The unnamed narrator is a townsman of Jefferson, Mississippi, who has for some years watched Emily Grierson with considerable interest but also respectful distance. He openly describes his perspective as average; he always uses *we* in the story, never *I*. His tone and manner are informed but detached, and surprisingly cool given the horrific conclusion. He mixes his own observations with town gossip to provide a seemingly reliable view of Jefferson's opinion of Miss Emily. (The story would be radically different if it were told from Emily Grierson's point of view.)

While the narrator notes and reports many things about Miss Emily's history and personality, he is not the man to analyze or ponder their significance. The careful reader, however, soon understands several important factors affecting her. Miss Emily's father has somehow kept her down—dominating her life and driving away suitors. She also has difficulty accepting loss or change. She will not, for example, initially admit that her father has died or let the doctors or the minister dispose of the body. Miss Emily seems starved for affection and emotionally desperate enough to risk censure from the town when she takes Homer Barron as her lover. At the end the reader also sees her determination in killing Barron, though her motives are open to question. Did she want to exact revenge for his apparent refusal to marry her? Or did she want to keep him with her forever?

The genre of the story is Gothic—more precisely, Southern Gothic—which may be another factor in its popularity. Gothic fiction tries to create terror and suspense and is usually set in isolated old houses, castles, or monasteries, populated by mysterious individuals. Typical Gothic devices include locked rooms, ancient servants, dusty chambers, and decayed mansions—all properties found in "A Rose for Emily." Usually taking place in the interior spaces of sinister buildings, Gothic fiction also thrives on cultivating an oppressively claustrophobic atmosphere of disturbing mystery and implicit evil. This story provides a good introduction to the genre for students, and compared to another Faulkner story like "Barn Burning," it demonstrates how powerfully genre can shape an author's work.

Students will want to make sure of exactly what happens in the story. From the detail that the strand of hair is *iron-gray*, it appears that Emily lay beside Homer's body recently, long after it was rotten; she probably lay beside it many times, for her pillow is clearly indented. Just as she had clung to her conviction that her father and Colonel Sartoris were still alive, she had come to believe that Homer Barron had faithfully married her, and she successfully ignored for forty years all the testimony of her senses. The conclusion of the story is foreshadowed by Emily's refusal to allow her father to be buried, by her purchase of rat poison, by the disappearance of Homer Barron, and by the pervasive smell of decay. In fact, these foreshadowings are so evident it is a wonder that, for those reading the story for the first time, the ending is so surprising. Much of the surprise seems due to the narrator's back-and-forth, unchronological method of telling the events of the story. We aren't told in proper sequence that (1) Emily buys poison, (2) Homer disappears, and (3) there is a mysterious odor—a chain of events which might immediately rouse our suspicions. Instead, we hear about odor, poison, and disappearance, in that order. By this arrangement, any connection between these events is made to seem a little less obvious.

Having satisfied their natural interest in the final horror of the story, students can be led to discuss why "A Rose for Emily" isn't a mere thriller. Why (they may be asked) is the story called "A Rose"? No actual rose appears in it. Perhaps Emily herself is the white rose of Jefferson (like the heroine of *The White Rose of Memphis*, a novel by Faulkner's grandfather). But the usual connotations of roses will apply. A rose is a gift to a loved one, and the whole story is the narrator's tribute to Emily.

But, some may object, how can anyone wish to pay tribute to a decayed old poisoner who sleeps with a corpse? The narrator patiently gives us reasons for his sympathy. As a girl, Emily was beautiful, a "slender figure in white," fond of society. But her hopes were thwarted by her domineering father, whose horsewhip discouraged suitors from her door. Her strength and pride vanquished all who would invade her house: the new Board of Aldermen who tried to collect her taxes, the Baptist minister sent to lecture her on her morals, the relatives from Atlanta who eventually departed. "It is important," Ray B. West writes, "to realize that during the period of Emily's courtship the town became Emily's allies in a contest between Emily and her Grierson cousins, 'because the two female cousins were even more Grierson than Miss Emily had ever been'" ("Atmosphere and Theme in Faulkner's 'A Rose for Emily,'" *Perspective* [Summer 1949]: 239–45).

Emily's refusal to recognize change is suggested in the symbol of her invisible watch (paragraph 7), with its hint that she lives according to a private, secret time of her own. Her house seems an extension of her person in its "stubborn and coquettish decay" (2). Now it stands amid gasoline pumps, refusing, like its owner, to be part of a new era. The story contains many such images of stasis: when Emily confronts the aldermen, she looks bloated, "like a body long submerged in motionless water"—a foreshadowing, perhaps, of the discovery of Homer's long-guarded dust.

Some have read the story as an allegory: Homer Barron is the crude, commercial North who invades, like a carpetbagger. Emily, with her faithful ex-slave, is the Old South, willing to be violated. In an interview with students at the University of Virginia, Faulkner played down such North-South symbolism. "I don't say that's not valid and not there," he said, "but . . . [I was] simply writing about people." (The whole interview in which Faulkner discusses this story, not very helpfully, is in *Faulkner in the University*, Frederick Gwynn and Joseph Blotner, eds., UP of Virginia, 1959.)

Still, it is clear that Emily, representing an antebellum first family, receives both Faulkner's admiration and his criticism for resisting change. "The theme of the story," according to C. W. M. Johnson, "can be stated: 'If one resists change, he must love and live with death,' and in this theme it is difficult not to see an implied criticism of the South" (*Explicator* VI [No. 7] May 1948: item 45). But Faulkner's criticism, Ray B. West, Jr., feels, is leveled at the North as well. West makes much of the passage in which Faulkner discerns two possible views of Time (55). If, for the South, Time is "a huge meadow which no winter ever quite touches," then for the North it is a mere "mathematical progression" and "a diminishing road." West would propose, for a statement of the story's theme: "One must neither resist nor wholly accept change, for to do either is to live as though one were never to die; that is, to live *with* Death without knowing it" (*Explicator* VII [No. 1] Oct. 1948: item 8).

Studying "A Rose for Emily" may help prepare students for Faulkner's "Barn Burning" (Chapter 5), whose central character, the son of a sharecropper, is Colonel Sartoris Snopes. "A Rose for Emily" is clearly in the tradition of the Gothic story, for it has a crumbling mansion, a mysterious servant, and a hideous secret. For comparison, one might have students read Poe's "The Tell-Tale Heart," if they don't know it already: another story of madness and murder, but told (unlike "A Rose") from the point of view of the mad killer.

For a valuable discussion of the story's point of view, see John Daremo, "Insight into Horror: The Narrator in Faulkner's 'A Rose for Emily,'" in Sylvan Barnet, ed., *A Short Guide to Writing about Literature*, 5th ed. (Boston: Little, Brown, 1985). A more superficial view of the story is expressed in this limerick by a celebrated bard, Anonymous:

> Miss Emily, snobbish and cranky,
> Used to horse around town with a Yankee.
> > When she'd wake up in bed,
> > With the dust of the dead,
> She would sneeze in her delicate hanky.

Faulkner's story resembles a riddle, argues Charles Clay Doyle of the University of Georgia. The resemblance lies not so much in the story's structure or rhetoric "as in the tricky way it presents clues, clues that tell the truth but at the same time mislead or fail to enlighten. The pleasure of discovery experienced by readers of the story resembles the pleasure we take in learning the answer to a riddle: we are astonished that the solution, which now seems so obvious, so inevitable, could have eluded us." Furthermore, Doyle finds an allusion to a well-known riddle in Faulkner's final description of Emily's chamber: Homer's "two mute shoes and the discarded socks." The riddle is, "What has a tongue but can't speak?" (Answer: a shoe.) Taking the phrase *mute shoes* to echo the riddle, Doyle thinks the shoes a pair of silent witnesses who, in their way, resemble the narrator himself, who shows us the truth but does not state it outright ("Mute Witnesses: Faulkner's Use of a Popular Riddle," *Mississippi Folklore Register* 24 [1990]: 53–55).

Years ago, Joanna Stephens Mink of Illinois State University, Normal, divided her class into several groups and conducted a mock murder trial of Emily Grierson, which ended, after spirited debate, with an acquittal of Miss Emily by reason of insanity. For Professor Mink's full account, see "We Brought Emily Grierson to Trial" in *Exercise Exchange*, Spring 1984: 17–19. Inspired by her example, Saul Cohen of County College of Morris in New Jersey later tried a similar experiment. In this instance, enough suspicion was raised about the actions of Miss Emily's servant to create reasonable doubt, leading to a straight acquittal. Professor Cohen's account appears in *Exercise Exchange* for October 1990.

> **MLL** *MyLiteratureLab Resources.* Photographs, biographical information, bibliography, and critical overview for Faulkner. Critical essay on "A Rose for Emily."

Anne Tyler, TEENAGE WASTELAND, page 35

For more than forty years, Anne Tyler has been writing a series of remarkable novels that explore the mysteries, and often the miseries, of love and family relationships. Among her short stories, "Teenage Wasteland" stands out for the shrewdness, the humor, and ultimately the sadness with which it explores similar themes. With its presentation of conflicts and misunderstandings between teenagers and their parents, it is a story that students will identify with, and one that should make for some very lively class discussions. Don't assume that students will reflexively identify with Donny and fault Daisy; young adults may feel that they see right through him and turn out to be among his harshest critics. Opinions may run the entire gamut—from a belief that Donny is crying out for the help that would have saved him if only he had had more caring and understanding parents, to the assumption that Daisy has done all she possibly could in dealing with an intractable child. Freud once famously described the bringing up of children as one of three "impossible professions." Anyone who has ever tried to raise a child will understand what he meant; so will anyone who has ever read "Teenage Wasteland."

Here are some possible answers to the questions given at the end of "Teenage Wasteland." Other answers, of equal merit, may occur to you and your students.

QUESTIONS

1. *From whose point of view is the story told? How would you characterize the method employed—omniscient, limited omniscient, or objective?* The point of view employed is that of limited omniscience. The entire story is narrated

from the perspective of Donny's mother, Daisy Coble. Through this technique we are given a heightened sense of her feelings—her confusion, frustration, and helplessness—as she attempts to reach her son and deal with his ever-worsening situation.

2. *What is the significance of the opening paragraph of the story?* The story's opening seems to suggest that Daisy holds to her memories of her sweet, adorable, innocent child, whose needs she could meet and whose problems she could deal with, before he morphed into this sulky and uncommunicative stranger. (One can almost imagine her and Matt beaming at their newborn child and thinking on some level that "We haven't made any mistakes yet, we still have the chance to be wonderful parents and raise a happy, well-adjusted son.") But reread paragraph 101 for a sense of how these memories may have been modified in light of recent events.

3. *Daisy is extremely self-conscious and concerned about how others view her. Find instances of this trait in the text. How does it affect her approach to raising her children?* As early as paragraph 3, we see that "It shamed her now to sit before this principal as a parent, a delinquent parent, a parent who struck Mr. Lanham, no doubt, as unseeing or uncaring." In paragraph 8, when she and Matt sit in Mr. Lanham's office a second time, she is heavily focused on her and her husband's personal appearance and seems convinced that the principal regards them as "failures." She is clearly very insecure; instead of acting consistently and firmly according to a deeply held set of beliefs, she conforms herself to others' assumptions and expectations. As a result, she wavers, backtracks, and shifts direction in dealing with Donny. Not only does she spread her own confusion outward, she also opens herself to manipulation, as shown, for example, in paragraphs 61–63.

4. *Daisy's attitude toward Cal undergoes frequent and at times rapid changes. Find examples in the text. What does she seem to think of him by the end of the story?* On first meeting Cal, Daisy seems a little put off by his hair and clothing and the loud rock music playing in his house—all attempts, she senses, to "relate" to teenagers in a superficial way. She takes a more sympathetic view of him in light of Donny's apparent improvement in school (fueled also, no doubt, by Cal's relieving her of the burden of helping Donny with his studies). She is persuaded by him to take a more indulgent view of Donny (paragraphs 36–42) and to dismiss the concerns of Donny's history teacher (paragraphs 53–55). She is jealous of Cal's influence over Donny and later exasperated by his constant making of excuses for the boy no matter what he does. In the end, she appears to regard him—accurately, no doubt—as an irresponsible fraud who has at best done Donny no good, and has in all likelihood helped—with her own unconscious complicity—to worsen the situation.

5. *How does the portrayal of Donny's sister, Amanda, help to clarify the larger concerns of the story?* Amanda's fleeting appearances in the story communicate the fact that her needs are being neglected (paragraphs 5 and 32) as Daisy involves herself more and more thoroughly—and ineffectively—in Donny's situation (similarly, the shadowy presence in the story of Daisy's husband, Matt, reinforces our sense of him as remote and unhelpful). In paragraph 14, Daisy

wonders whether her relative neglect of Donny when Amanda was a baby may have contributed to his present problems, which suggests that she may now be trying, at Amanda's expense, to redress the balance. At the end of the story, "Donny's sister seems to be staying away from home as much as possible." Opposite ways of dealing with the two children seem to have led, sadly, to similar outcomes.

6. *Would you describe Tyler's presentation of Daisy as satirical or sympathetic? Can it be both at once? Explain.* There are strongly satiric elements in "Teenage Wasteland." Matt, Donny, and especially Cal behave foolishly and/or self-servingly just about all of the time. While Daisy's is a more nuanced characterization, her insecurity and indecisiveness make her appear somewhat ridiculous at times, and, in common with many parents of her generation, her dread of stunting her children by over-disciplining them leads to an often absurd tolerance and laxity. But, just as we have all immediately followed some stinging observation about a friend with "But he means well" or "She has a good heart," Tyler shows us Daisy's genuine love for Donny and her anguish as she sees him slipping away from her; to simply dismiss her as a fool would be to deprive the story of a good deal of its human richness. In the end, we are left feeling sad and sympathetic, not smugly superior.

James Baldwin, SONNY'S BLUES, page 43

The narrative structure of "Sonny's Blues" is more complex and interesting than it may seem at first glance. The story reads so smoothly that it is easy to overlook the fact that it begins *in medias res*. "Sonny's Blues" opens with the title character's arrest for the sale and possession of heroin; it ends in a jazz club with the older brother's ultimate understanding and acceptance of Sonny. This linear narrative is interrupted, however, by a long flashback that describes the uneasy earlier relation between the brothers. Since their parents are dead when the story opens, we meet the father and mother only in the flashback. The mother is the central moral figure of the story. Her last conversation with the narrator ultimately becomes a crucial part of his impetus to reconcile with Sonny. (The other, more immediately compelling motivation is the death of the narrator's small daughter from polio: "My trouble," the narrator confesses, "made his real.") When the narrator promises to take care of his kid brother, his mother warns him it will be hard. She has seen enough of the world's trouble to be fatalistic. "You may not be able to stop nothing from happening," she tells him, before adding, "But you got to let him know you's *there*." In one sense, "Sonny's Blues" is essentially the story of the narrator's slow, difficult process of living up to the promise he gave his mother.

The basic conflict of the story, which is—it is essential to remember—*the older brother's story,* is the narrator's inability to understand and respect the life of the younger brother he so clearly loves. Baldwin carefully establishes the brothers as opposites. The narrator is a cautious, respectable family man. He teaches math and is proud of his professional standing. Living in a Harlem housing project, he consciously protects himself from the dangers that surround him. Notice how intensely he appears to dislike Sonny's friend, the drug addict, when he encounters him in the school courtyard at the beginning of the story.

However, the narrator is also compassionate, and it is important to see, in the same episode, how quickly he recognizes and responds to the addict's battered humanity. That gesture prefigures his reconciliation with his brother. Sonny, by contrast, is a romantic artist who is not afraid of taking risks to pursue the things he desires. His passion for music makes him impatient with everything else. He drops out of school. In his brother's view he is "wild" but not "hard or evil or disrespectful."

The outer story of "Sonny's Blues" is the title character's rehabilitation from drug addiction, reconciliation with his estranged brother, and recognition as a jazz pianist. The inner story is the narrator's spiritual and emotional growth into a person who can understand his younger brother's unorthodox, but nonetheless valuable, life. There should be no doubt that Baldwin, the former boy preacher, saw the narrator's inner growth as in some sense religious. The final scene in the nightclub ends with a religious vision of the blues. Listening to the group leader, Creole, play, the narrator says:

> He hit something in all of them, he hit something in me, myself, and the music tightened and deepened, apprehension began to beat the air. Creole began to tell us what the blues were about. They were not about anything very new. He and his boys up there were keeping it new, at the risk of ruin, destruction, madness, and death, in order to find new ways to make us listen. For, while the tale of how we suffer, and how we are delighted, and how we may triumph is never new, it always must be heard. There isn't any other tale to tell, and it's the only light we've got in all this darkness.

That passage not only offers as good an explanation of the blues and jazz as one is likely to find anywhere; it speaks cogently on the purpose of all art. It is worth having students pause over it. The final scene of "Sonny's Blues" is set in a dark, smoky nightclub, and its lyric quality marks a noticeable shift in tone from the realistic narrative style that preceded it. As the closing episode gains force along with the music it describes, it becomes a kind of vision for the narrator. In intellectual terms (for, after all, the narrator is a reflective math teacher), the vision brings him to a deep understanding of the human importance of art and the terrible cost of its creation. In emotional terms, his comprehension of jazz is inseparable from his sudden and profound understanding of Sonny's identity and motivations as an artist.

Unless the reader can accept the narrator's capacity for this transforming insight, the story is flawed by the sudden change of tone. Several critics have expressed their problem with the conclusion. They feel that Baldwin's authorial voice has replaced the narrator's. As Joseph Featherstone said in an initial review of *Going to Meet the Man*, the volume in which "Sonny's Blues" first appeared:

> The terms seem wrong; clearly this is not the voice of Sonny or his brother, it is the intrusive voice of Baldwin the boy preacher who has turned his back on the store front tabernacles but cannot forget the sound of angels' wings beating around his head. (*New Republic*, 27 Nov. 1965)

> [reprinted in Kenneth Kinnamon's "Twentieth Century Views" collection, cited below]

On one level, Featherstone's criticism makes sense. The tone of the final scene is elevated and religious. It is quite unlike the narrator's opening voice. However, a reader, wrapped up in the power of the final scene, is entitled to respond that the entire story up until then exists to justify this passage. "Sonny's Blues" is not merely the story of the narrator's experiences; it is the tale of his inner transformation. The final scene is the demonstration of the older brother's spiritual growth which his earlier experiences of death and loss have motivated. In understanding and accepting Sonny, he has enlarged his soul enough to understand Sonny's music, too.

There is a large, interesting body of criticism on James Baldwin's work. Kenneth Kinnamon's "Twentieth Century Views" critical collection, *James Baldwin* (Englewood Cliffs, NJ: Prentice Hall, 1974) remains extremely useful. John M. Reilly's cogent sociological essay, "'Sonny's Blues': James Baldwin's Image of Black Community," will be interesting for students writing on the story. Sherley Anne Williams's "The Black Musician: The Black Hero as Light Bearer" examines the metaphoric role of the musician in Baldwin's work, with special attention given to "Sonny's Blues." Bruce Bawer's insightful overview of Baldwin's fiction, "Race and Art: James Baldwin," in his critical collection *The Aspect of Eternity* (St. Paul, MN: Graywolf, 1993), will be very useful for students planning a paper on the author. Bawer surveys Baldwin's career in a biographical context and candidly evaluates the strengths and weaknesses of the novels. Quincy Troupe's *James Baldwin: The Legacy* (New York: Simon, 1989) contains memoirs, tributes, and appreciations by fellow writers, including Maya Angelou, William Styron, Toni Morrison, and Chinua Achebe. Carolyn Wedin Sylvander's *James Baldwin* (New York: Ungar, 1980) also provides a reliable survey of the author's work, though her discussion of "Sonny's Blues" is brief.

Before students plunge into the secondary material on Baldwin, however, they should be encouraged to read the author's own essays. Baldwin was one of the finest essayists of his time, and there is no better introduction to his work than the title piece in *Notes of a Native Son*, Baldwin's passionate memoir of his Harlem youth.

MLL *MyLiteratureLab Resources*. Biographical information and bibliography for Baldwin. Longman Lecture, critical overview, and excerpts about "Sonny's Blues."

Eudora Welty, A WORN PATH, page 64

Eudora Welty's name would be sure to appear on any list of the greatest American short story writers of the twentieth century. "A Worn Path," one of her most celebrated stories, shows her artistry at its height. While constantly advancing the plot and creating a unique and memorable central character, she achieves the vividness, the precision, and at times even the rhythms of poetry at its best. Death is everywhere in the story's landscape—dead trees, dead weeds, dead cornstalks, the dead birds in the hunter's game sack—and the threat of death hangs constantly over Phoenix Jackson and her quest. The title itself evokes both of the tale's principal emphases, the frequency with which she undertakes this journey, and the exhaustion ("worn" as in "worn out") that she meets and conquers with her steadfastness of spirit.

Here are some possible answers to the questions given at the end of "A Worn Path." Other answers, of equal merit, may occur to you and your students.

QUESTIONS

1. *What point of view is used in this story? Explain your answer.* The point of view is that of limited omniscience. Everything is seen from the perspective of the central character, Phoenix Jackson. Welty does not, of course, confine herself to the vocabulary of her point-of-view character, who has, after all, no formal education, but she does render all of the events and the sense impressions of the story essentially as they present themselves to that character. For example, she refers only to "the big building" (paragraph 69) and "the document that had been stamped with the gold seal and framed in the gold frame" (paragraph 70); this is the extent of Phoenix Jackson's awareness of these things, and this therefore is the extent to which they are described to us.

2. *What is the significance of the old woman's being named Phoenix?* Mythologically, the phoenix is a beautiful, lone bird that lives in the Arabian desert; it spontaneously combusts every five hundred years or so and is then regenerated out of its own ashes, thus functioning as a symbol of long life and even immortality. Phoenix Jackson, whose dignity and perseverance confer a great beauty upon her, is basically a lone figure as she moves among the other characters in the story. The wintry landscape through which she moves is a desert of sorts. She achieves a kind of regeneration of will and purpose each time she must go to the city for her grandson's medicine, and she allows no obstacle to defeat or even deflect her in the fulfillment of that purpose.

3. *Welty presents Phoenix's dreams and hallucinations as if they were as real as everything else she encounters. What does this technique contribute to the story's effect?* We are told that "a bush caught her dress" (paragraph 7), not that her dress got caught on the bush's thorns; we are told that "a little boy brought her a plate with a slice of marble cake on it" (paragraph 15) as if it were really happening; when she thinks she sees a ghost (paragraphs 22–24), we don't learn what it really is until she does. Welty has locked us into Phoenix's point of view and we see everything from her perspective, just as she sees it. Through this technique, her sense of her reality is made extraordinarily real and immediate to us.

4. *How would you characterize the way Phoenix is viewed and treated by the white people she meets? Does their behavior toward her give you any indication of where the story is set and when it takes place?* No one is hostile or abusive to her, and she is even helped by the people she encounters—the hunter helps her up, the lady on the street ties her shoes when asked to, and the nurse at the doctor's office gives her a nickel. At the same time their treatment of her is more condescending than respectful: everyone calls her "Granny," not "Ma'am" or, in the nurse's case, "Mrs. Jackson." The hunter finds her quite amusing, makes complacently demeaning assumptions about her intentions (paragraph 48), and repeatedly tells her what to do as if he were speaking to a child. Even without corroboration, all of this would suggest that the story is set in the pre-1960s South, as is corroborated by details within the text: the city is identified as Natchez (paragraph 61) and Phoenix was already too old for schooling at the time of "the Surrender" (paragraph 90) of the Confederacy in April 1865.

5. *In paragraph 52, Phoenix laughs at the black dog "as if in admiration." What does she admire about him, and what does this attitude tell us about her?* As she herself says, what she admires about the dog is that "He ain't scared of nobody. He a big black dog." Phoenix may not be very big, but she displays similar characteristics, as shown by her response when the hunter insultingly points his gun at her and asks, "Doesn't the gun scare you?"

6. *"With her hands on her knees, the old woman waited, silent, erect and motionless, just as if she were in armor" (paragraph 85). Is the comparison at the end of this sentence just a striking visual image, or does it have a larger relevance?* Surrounded on all sides by obstacles—poverty, racism, forgetfulness, age and physical decline, the winter landscape with its dangers both real and hallucinatory—Phoenix Jackson *is* in armor, an armor compounded of her tenacity, determination, and love for her grandson.

WRITERS ON WRITING

James Baldwin, RACE AND THE AFRICAN AMERICAN WRITER, page 70

Baldwin was an essayist of genius—forcefully intelligent, penetratingly insightful, and passionately consumed with pursuing his ideas to their inevitable conclusions. He wrote extremely well on most topics he addressed, but none so completely engaged his creative powers as himself. "One writes out of one thing only," he remarked, "one's own experience." Baldwin's talent for seeing both sides of an issue is never so apparent than in his autobiographical writing since he alternately views his own life as both representative and singular. One sees this open-minded ability—indeed what John Keats called "negative capability"—to embrace opposites in this excerpt from Baldwin's "Autobiographical Notes," in which the author examines the many imaginative sources of a writer.

3
Character

Katherine Anne Porter, THE JILTING OF GRANNY WEATHERALL, page 76

"I spend my life thinking about technique, method, style," Katherine Anne Porter told her friend and fellow novelist Glenway Wescott. "The only time I do not think about them at all is when I am writing." Marked by scrupulous and fastidious craft, by adherence to the highest standards of achievement, her fiction, including the novel *Ship of Fools*, fills less than a thousand pages. In her autobiographical statement for *Twentieth-Century Authors* (1942), Porter said, "As for aesthetic bias, my one aim is to tell a straight story and to give true testimony."

With its frequent excursions into the rambling consciousness of its dying protagonist, "The Jilting of Granny Weatherall" may not always be "a straight story" in terms of undemanding linear narrative, but it is certainly "straight" in the larger sense of fidelity to the realities of human nature and experience, the "true testimony" that the rest of her comment refers to. Its emotional power lies largely in its presentation of the complexities of emotion, in our understanding that no matter how much Granny Weatherall feels that her life has turned out better than it would have with George, and no matter how much the details of the story support her judgment, her jilting remains a raw, painful, irreducible fact that has, in its way, shaped the rest of her life. In paragraph 28, Granny thinks: "Don't let things get lost. It's bitter to lose things." Her own awareness of, and refusal to confront, the larger application of this insight is shown in her very next thought: "Now don't let me get to thinking, not when I am tired and taking a little nap before supper."

Here are some possible answers to the questions at the end of "The Jilting of Granny Weatherall." Other answers, of equal merit, may occur to you and your students. Other questions may occur as well.

QUESTIONS

1. *In the very first paragraph, what does the writer tell us about Ellen (Granny Weatherall)?* That Ellen Weatherall is feisty, accustomed to having her way, and unwilling to be treated like the sick old woman she is, all comes through the story from the start.

2. *What does the name of Weatherall have to do with Granny's nature (or her life story)? What other traits or qualities do you find in her?* Granny has "weathered all"—unrequited love, marriage, the birth of five children, early widowhood, backbreaking labor, "milk-leg and double pneumonia," the loss of her favorite

daughter, and the frustrations of old age. Her victories over adversity have made her scornful of her daughter Cornelia, who seems to her weak and inadequate. Granny is tough and inclined to hold a grudge. She has never forgiven the man who jilted her. So overweening is her pride, in fact, that at the moment of her death, when she wants a sign and fails to perceive one, she decides she will "never forgive."

3. *"Her bones felt loose, and floated around in her skin, and Doctor Harry floated like a balloon" (paragraph 6). What do you understand from this statement? By what other remarks does the writer indicate Granny's condition? In paragraph 56, why does Father Connolly tickle Granny's feet? At what other moments in the story does she fail to understand what is happening, or confuse the present with the past?* Granny is very ill, her sense of reality distorted by lengthening periods of confusion. The story quite convincingly ushers Granny Weatherall by fits and starts into an altered state of consciousness preceding death. Granny's weakened grasp on reality is again apparent: when the doctor "appeared to float up to the ceiling and out" (paragraph 7); when "the pillow rose and floated under her" and she thought she heard leaves, or newspapers, rustling (8); when she pondered her impossible plans for "tomorrow" (17 and 26) in her belief that she could, if she wanted to, "pack up and move back to her own house" (24); in the distortions that creep into Granny's sense of the passage of time (28, 29, 36, 37, 42, 43, 50, 56, and 57); when she feels the pillow rising again (29); in Granny's sporadic inability to hear (31 and 32); in her belief that there are ants in the bed (40); in Granny's occasional inability to speak clearly enough to be understood (40 and 53); when Granny has hallucinations in which she confronts her daughter Hapsy (41, 50, and 60); in the doctor's "rosy nimbus" (51); in Granny's failure to comprehend that Father Connolly is not tickling her feet but administering the last rites of the Catholic Church (56). (In the anointing of the sick, formerly known as Extreme Unction, the priest makes a sign of the cross with oil upon the eyes, ears, nose, mouth, hands, and feet of the person in danger of death, while praying for his or her soul.)

4. *Exactly what happened to Ellen Weatherall sixty years earlier? What effects did this event have on her?* George, the man she was to marry, had failed to show up for the wedding. This blow to Ellen's pride had left permanent scars even though Ellen had subsequently lived a full and useful life. It is hard to say whether her exacting, imperious, unforgiving ways resulted from the jilting—or caused it!

5. *In paragraph 49, who do you guess to be the man who "cursed like a sailor's parrot"? In paragraph 56, who do you assume is the man driving the cart? Is the fact that these persons are not clearly labeled and identified a failure on the author's part?* The most likely guess about the man who "cursed like a sailor's parrot" is that he was John, the man Ellen eventually married. Presumably John had always loved her and was angry because she had been so deeply hurt. The identity of the man driving the cart is more nebulous. Was he George? John? A confused amalgam of the two? That the reader remains unsure is not a fault in the story. The dreamlike haze surrounding the man's identity beautifully reflects Granny's loosening hold on reality.

6. *What is "stream of consciousness"? Would you call "The Jilting of Granny Weatherall" a stream of consciousness story? Refer to the story in your reply.* The story's point of view is one of selective omniscience. The events are reported in the third person by a narrator who can see into Granny Weatherall's mind. When Granny is lucid, the story proceeds in tidy chronological order. In the story's most interesting passages—especially in paragraphs 17–18 and 24–31—Porter uses stream of consciousness with great skill to present the randomly mingled thoughts and impressions that move through Granny's dying mind. By fragmenting Granny's thoughts, by having her shuttle back and forth between reality and fantasy, by distorting her sense of the passage of time, the author manages to persuade us that the way Granny experiences dying must be nearly universal.

7. *Sum up the character of the daughter Cornelia.* Cornelia, evidently the oldest of Granny's children, is a dutiful daughter—a fact resented by her cantankerous mother (10). Granny feels demeaned by her knowledge that Cornelia often humors her to keep peace. And, like mothers everywhere, Granny regards her daughter as far less competent than herself. Cornelia is tenderer, less tough than Granny. She weeps beside the deathbed. The old woman fails to appreciate her daughter's care and compassion because she scorns her own need of them.

8. *Why doesn't Granny's last child, Hapsy, come to her mother's deathbed?* Hapsy, the youngest child and her mother's favorite, died young. Paragraph 41 suggests that she may have died giving birth to a son.

9. *Would you call the character of Doctor Harry "flat" or "round"? Why is his flatness or roundness appropriate to the story?* A "flat" character, the doctor is little more than a prop in this account of Granny's dying. There is no reason for him to be more than that, for it is Granny's life and death that we are meant to focus on.

10. *How is this the story of another "jilting"? What is similar between that fateful day of sixty years ago (described in paragraphs 29, 49, and 61) and the time when Granny is dying? This time, who is the "bridegroom" who is not in the house?* Before talking about the final paragraph, why not read aloud to your students the parable of the wise and foolish virgins (Matthew 25:1–13)?

Then shall the kingdom of heaven be likened unto ten virgins, which took their lamps, and went forth to meet the bridegroom.

2   And five of them were wise, and five were foolish.
3   They that were foolish took their lamps, and took no oil with them:
4   But the wise took oil in their vessels with their lamps.
5   While the bridegroom tarried, they all slumbered and slept.
6   And at midnight there was a cry made, Behold, the bridegroom cometh; go ye out to meet him.
7   Then all those virgins arose, and trimmed their lamps.
8   And the foolish said unto the wise, Give us of your oil, for our lamps are gone out.

9   But the wise answered, saying, Not so; lest there be not enough for us and you: but go ye rather to them that sell, and buy for yourselves.

10 And while they went to buy, the bridegroom came; and they that were ready went in with him to the marriage: and the door was shut.

11 Afterward came also the other virgins, saying, Lord, Lord, open to us.

12 But he answered and said, Verily I say unto you, I know you not.

13 Watch therefore; for ye know neither the day nor the hour wherein the Son of Man cometh.

Evidently, the bridegroom whom Granny awaits at the end of the story is Christ. When he does not appear, she feels jilted for a second time. Why doesn't he come? Why does Granny not receive the sign she asks for? Is it because her pride is so overweening ("I'll never forgive it") as to keep her from salvation? Is it because of her refusal to stay prepared for death (18)? Or did she receive her sign (the last rites of the Church) and merely fail to perceive it? Students may object to the apparent grimness of the ending. Some of them are likely to insist that Granny gets worse than she deserves, that Porter has allowed her symbolism to run roughshod over her humanity. Divergent opinions may spark a lively discussion.

11. *"This is the story of an eighty-year-old woman lying in bed, getting groggy, and dying; I can't see why it should interest anybody."* How would you answer this critic? Such a critic will be hard to convince. But perhaps discussion can show that the story is remarkable for its condensation of a long life into a few pages. How does it feel to die? All of us find the question interesting, and Porter answers it. Although Edith Wharton has argued in *The Writing of Fiction* (New York: Scribner, 1925) that it is not the nature of a short story to develop a character, "The Jilting of Granny Weatherall" certainly makes character its central concern. We finish the story persuaded that we know Ellen Weatherall very well indeed—better than she knows herself.

Here is a bleak reading of the story for possible discussion: For sixty years Ellen Weatherall has suppressed the memory of George, the man she loved, who jilted her. She prays not to remember him, lest she follow him down into the pit of Hell (29). If she remembers him, she herself will be damned—yet she remembers him. She longs to see him again (42), imagines him standing by her deathbed (30). In the end she beholds the pit: a darkness that will swallow up light. For the sake of a man, she has lost her soul.

But is the story so grim an account of one woman's damnation? It seems hardly a mortal sin to remember a person and an event so crucial in one's life; damnation seems undeserved. We sense that the author actually admires Granny's defiance in blowing out the light at the end. To say the least, the story is splendidly ambiguous.

"The Jilting of Granny Weatherall" lent itself effectively to the PBS television film series *The American Short Story*, obtainable on videotape or DVD for classroom viewing from Library Video Company at <www.libraryvideo.com>. Anyone interested in writing for television might care to see Corinne Jacker's excellent script, reprinted in *The American Short Story*, Volume 2 (New York: Dell, 1980), together with a revealing interview with the scriptwriter on the problems of adapting "Granny"—such as a dearth of physical action in the present—and Carolyn G. Heilbrun's short critical essay on the Porter story.

Porter's familiarity with illness and the threat of death may have been drawn from memory. As Joan Givner recounts in her biography, *Katherine Anne Porter* (New York: Simon, 1982), Porter had to struggle for years against bronchial troubles and tuberculosis. Defiantly, she endured to age ninety.

 MyLiteratureLab Resources. Photographs and biographical information for Porter. Video clips, audio clips, and critical essay for "The Jilting of Granny Weatherall."

Katherine Mansfield, MISS BRILL, page 83

Like many practitioners of the modern short story, Katherine Mansfield frequently uses small details and seemingly trivial incidents to suggest a sense of a character's entire life. We might borrow James Joyce's term "epiphany," applied to the way in which a small gesture may lead to a revelation of or insight into character, in discussing Mansfield's "little sketch." (In fact, in the situation of its protagonist and her sense of herself, "Miss Brill" calls to mind "Clay" and "A Painful Case," two of the stories in Joyce's masterful collection, *Dubliners*.) In the second half of the story, Miss Brill herself undergoes two such revelations, with far different reactions and consequences. Her own sense of oneness with her fellow concert-goers, in which her assumptions about their pettiness and absurdity is replaced by a larger human sympathy, is quickly undercut by her awareness of her own pettiness and absurdity in the eyes of others.

The narrative point of view in "Miss Brill" is interesting: third-person, selective omniscience. The narrator is detached from the characters but can also see events through the eyes of the protagonist. This narrative strategy allows the reader to experience the action inwardly with the emotional intensity of Miss Brill, but it does not limit itself to only the exact words and ideas that the protagonist would use (as a first-person narrative would). At times Mansfield's narrative style could be called stream of consciousness since it often portrays the title character's interior monologue and the momentary play of thoughts and images on her mind. But the author alternates these stream of consciousness techniques with a more Flaubertian selective omniscience. A close examination of Mansfield's opening paragraph will reveal how both methods co-exist in the story. In classroom discussion you might explore whether students identify more strongly with "the hero and heroine," whose cruel comments Miss Brill overhears, or with the title character. This line of questioning could be used to explore how the reader's sense of identification colors his or her sense of a fiction work.

Here are some possible answers to the questions given at the end of "Miss Brill." Other answers, of equal merit, may occur to you and your students.

QUESTIONS

1. *What details provide insight into Miss Brill's character and lifestyle?* Miss Brill lives frugally, alone in a small room, eking out a meager living by teaching English and reading the newspaper aloud to an invalid gentleman four afternoons a week. She seems happy with her lot even though her daily activities are drab by most standards and her pleasures are small ones. Her well-worn fur delights her, and an almond in the Sunday honey-cake is cause for rejoicing.

2. *What is the point of view in "Miss Brill"? How does this method impove the story?* "Miss Brill" is written with selective omniscience: from the third-person viewpoint of a nonparticipant, but one who sees events through the eyes of the story's protagonist. In paragraph 5, Miss Brill notices that there is "something funny" about her fellow park sitters: "They were odd, silent, nearly all old, and from the way they stared they looked as though they'd just come from dark little rooms or even—even cupboards!" (That she might look the same to them never enters her head—until she is forced to see herself as others see her.) Because we as readers experience the day's happenings from the perspective of Miss Brill, we come to understand and to sympathize with the sweet old dear, even going along with her sudden view of herself as an actress in a play performed every Sunday. To an intense degree we share her dismay and hurt when she overhears herself called a "stupid old thing" and her furpiece ridiculed as "exactly like a fried whiting."

3. *Where and in what season does Mansfield's story take place? Would the effect be the same if the story were set, say, in a remote Alaskan village in the winter?* In the opening paragraph Mansfield makes clear that Miss Brill is in the *Jardins Publiques* and, therefore, somewhere in France: in a small town, it seems, since the Sunday band concert is a big feature of local life. In paragraph 6 we learn that the sea is visible from the park. We also know that the season is autumn. Miss Brill has taken her fur out of its box for the first time in a long while. The trees are covered with "yellow leaves down drooping" (6). A chill in the air foreshadows the chill of Miss Brill's dashed spirits at the end of the story.

4. *What draws Miss Brill to the park every Sunday? What is the nature of the startling revelation that delights her on the day this story takes place?* Because she lives on the fringes of life in her small French town, Miss Brill regards her solitary Sundays in the park as the highlight of her week. Here, watching the people who come and go and eavesdropping on their conversations, she feels a connection with her fellow human beings. The smallest details about them excite her interest. She comes to feel herself one of them, an actor in life's drama. So caught up does she become in the sudden revelation that all the world's a stage and that she, like everyone else, has a part to play, that she has a mystical experience. In her mind, she merges with the other players, and "it seemed to Miss Brill that in another moment all of them, all the whole company, would begin singing" (10).

5. *Miss Brill's sense of herself is at least partly based on her attitudes toward others. Give instances of this tendency, showing also how it is connected with her drastic change of mood.* Early in the story (paragraph 5), her reaction to some of her fellow concert-goers is a bit condescending, which enables her to feel somewhat superior—which is highly ironic in light of subsequent developments. At paragraphs 9 and 10, just before her disillusionment, she feels herself to be at one with the rest of the audience, an equal participant in what she thinks of as the significance and beauty of the event. Then, when she discovers how she really appears to at least some of the others present, it is this cruel epiphany that shatters her happiness and even her sense of herself.

6. *What explanations might there be for Miss Brill's thinking, in the last line of the story, that she "heard something crying"?* Miss Brill, who loves her fur as if it were

a living pet or companion, is probably capable of thinking it was that "little rogue" she heard crying over the cruelty of the young couple in the park. It's possible, too, for the reader to believe that Miss Brill actually does hear a sound and that the "something crying" is herself. Perhaps she has, as Eudora Welty surmises in "The Reading and Writing of Short Stories," suffered a defeat that "one feels sure . . . is forever" (*Atlantic Monthly*, Feb.–Mar. 1949).

 MyLiteratureLab Resources. Interactive reading and critical essay for "Miss Brill."

Tobias Wolff, THE RICH BROTHER, page 86

Discussing this story with your students and seeing how they react to the personalities of Pete and Donald—which brother do they relate to and which one do they reject, and why?—should provide an interesting insight into how young people currently feel about such things as success, materialism, spirituality, and the larger purposes of life. But you should be careful not to let such discussions, fascinating as they may be, overwhelm or distort Tobias Wolff's story. It is clear enough that Pete is far from being a wholly admirable character: he is extremely materialistic and rather hard-hearted; the concept of *schadenfreude*, the taking of a (perhaps self-justifying) pleasure in the failures and misfortunes of others, is introduced in the second paragraph, and later in the story (paragraphs 61–64) Pete heartily endorses the concept. Like Dr. Sloper in Henry James's *Washington Square*, he takes a great satisfaction in being in the right, even at the expense of the needs and feelings of others.

But Bertrand Russell remarks somewhere that if one party to an argument is wrong, that doesn't necessarily prove that the other one is right; and so we should bear in mind that Pete's being a limited and unsatisfactory soul does not automatically confer moral superiority upon Donald. Donald may talk a good spiritual game, and he can be impulsively generous, but he is also laughably inept and almost boundlessly naïve; it isn't clear that the family to whom he gave the farm's groceries were even in need, and one needn't be as cynical as Pete to see right through the vagueness and the grandiosity of Webster. Wolff is not a nineteenth-century Russian novelist, and if Donald is a holy fool, the emphasis in the phrase should fall heavily on the noun. (Similar tendencies toward idealizing a character—or at least taking his self-assessment at face value—will probably be shown by students in appraising Sammy, the narrator of John Updike's "A & P.")

It is all but impossible to discuss this story without raising the question "Who is really 'The Rich Brother'?" To respond as Hemingway might have, "Pete—he has more money," is obviously flip and unsatisfactory. But it seems equally glib, if not fatuous, to settle for "Donald—he's rich in spirit." If it doesn't sound unduly cynical, we might float the suggestion that if Donald is the richer one, it is because (thanks to Pete's sense of brotherly obligation or psychological need) he can live in Pete's Darwinian universe without being exposed to its risks. For all the superficial differences between the two brothers, in some fundamental ways they are strikingly similar: each is pig-headed to the point of incorrigibility and smugly convinced of his superiority to the other.

Here are some possible answers to the questions given at the end of "The Rich Brother." Other answers, of equal merit, may occur to you and your students.

QUESTIONS

1. *Are the brothers in the story developing characters or static ones? Does either of them undergo a change, or do we simply learn more about their established personalities as the story proceeds?* There are shadings and complexities, and one or two revelations along the way, but both brothers are basically static characters who conform throughout the story to the descriptions of them given at the beginning. Even the conclusion is not an epiphany or a breakthrough: Pete's need to take care of Donald has already been shown by his taking the long drive to get him, and his attitude in the last paragraph feels much more like resignation than revelation.

2. *What point of view does Wolff employ in this story? Do Pete's perceptions of Donald seem fundamentally sound to you, or is it necessary to go beyond them for a more objective appraisal?* The point of view employed is limited omniscience, and the point-of-view character is Pete. Everything is seen from, and colored by, his perspective. Even though we are given a rich sense of Donald's character, he is presented entirely from the outside. Nonetheless, even acknowledging that Pete's view of his brother is jaundiced, there isn't much that Donald says or does that would contradict or significantly undercut that view.

3. *Donald tells Pete that "you don't have any purpose in life. You're afraid to relate to people who do, so you make fun of them. . . . You're basically a very frightened individual."* Do you agree with this analysis or not? Explain. Webster certainly deserves Pete's scorn, and perhaps Donald does as well, but scorn as zealous and pervasive as Pete's does have something defensive about it. His vigorous acquisitiveness and his dream of being blind and cared for by Donald (see question 5) would seem to provide some substantiation of Donald's analysis here.

4. *Do you believe Donald's claim that Pete tried to kill him when they were children? Why or why not?* According to some views, Pete's comment that "Mom was in a state every time you burped" (paragraph 100) establishes the truth of Donald's claim, but such an interpretation strikes us as a wild inflation of normal sibling rivalry and resentment at feeling like the less favored child. Pete may be insensitive and competitive, but nothing else in the story suggests that he is vicious or violent, let alone fratricidal. And Donald is somewhat dramatic. In all likelihood, the truth lies somewhere in between, probably closer to Pete's version.

5. *In one of Pete's dreams he is blind and dependent on Donald to take care of him. Does Pete really need Donald? If so, for what?* Donald certainly needs Pete, as much as he hates to admit it, and the dependency does appear to be mutual, as much as Pete would hate to admit it. What does he need Donald for? Moving from the most Pete-like to the most Donald-like response, we might say: (1) to feel superior to him; (2) to help Donald as a way of proving to himself that he's not completely selfish; (3) to get from Donald the sense of a larger purpose and spiritual dimension that are otherwise missing from his life.

6. *Near the end of the story, Pete wants to know what Donald means when he says "I don't blame you." What do you think he means?* Moving this time from the most Donald-like to the most Pete-like view, we offer these possibilities: (1) "I am a true Christian who doesn't hold a grudge"; (2) "I know you can't help being what you are"; and (3) "Playing the moral superiority card is my way of proving to both of us that I'm better than you—and maybe driving you a little crazy in the process."

7. *Could this story have been called "My Brother's Keeper"? Explain.* The obvious allusion is to the story of Cain and Abel in Chapter 4 of the Book of Genesis. "I do not know. Am I my brother's keeper?" is Cain's reply, after he has killed Abel, to the Lord's question, "Where is your brother?" (see the last sentence of "The Rich Brother"). Clearly, in his awareness that he will go back for Donald, Pete recognizes that he is compelled to be his brother's keeper, a fact that he sees as his cross, but one that others might see as his redemption.

Raymond Carver, CATHEDRAL, page 98

In a relatively brief time after its first appearance in the *Atlantic Monthly* in 1981, Raymond Carver's "Cathedral" became an acknowledged classic of American fiction. Widely anthologized, frequently analyzed, and almost universally admired, the short story perfectly blends the compressed and understated qualities of Minimalism with the lyrical emotionalism of realists like Sherwood Anderson. It also portrays in a credible way a positive transformation of character. Initially a man of petty prejudice and small worldview, the narrator grows in humanity and understanding as the story develops. Few contemporary stories have such a cogently uplifting effect.

According to Raymond Carver, "None of my stories really happened, of course. But there's always something, some element, something someone said to me or that I witnessed, that may be the starting place." In her introduction to *Carver Country*, Carver's widow, the poet Tess Gallagher, makes clear that a great many of the details of "Cathedral" were rooted in an actual experience. Carver was uneasy when a blind man Gallagher knew came for a visit, and Carver became jealous of the man's relationship with her. As interesting as these facts may be, in the end, of course, they matter less than their reworking into an independent artistic pattern, an entertaining narrative that communicates movingly about attitudes and relationships.

On the surface, "Cathedral" is a simple story told flatly by a narrator of limited awareness, both of himself and of others. His misgivings about the visit, rooted in his lack of experience with the blind, are clearly spelled out in paragraphs 1, 5, 9, and 17; the fact that his perceptions are veiled by unexamined assumptions is shown further in paragraphs 31 and 44. His blundering attempts at small talk lead to increased discomfort (25), and it seems to be a combination of thoughtlessness and the wish to cover over the awkward situation that impels him finally to turn on the television set.

Throughout, his wife demonstrates a much more relaxed attitude, seeing Robert not as an abstraction or the representative of an alien group, but as an individual, a valued friend and former colleague—so much so, in fact, that in some ways she seems to have an easier and more intimate rapport with him than she does with her own husband. The narrator initially reacts with jealousy and resentment at his seeming exclusion from this closeness; but as the story proceeds, he slowly achieves an emotional breakthrough.

Students have phrased the story's theme in different ways: "Barriers tend to break down when people try to communicate with one another," and "Even those not physically blind sometimes need to be taught to see," and "Stereotypes render sighted people blind to the common humanity we all share." Obviously, the story itself is much more effective and affecting than any possible statement of its theme.

For a writing topic, a student might be asked to read D. H. Lawrence's "The Blind Man" (in *Complete Short Stories*, Volume 2 [Penguin Books]) and compare the characters of the blind man and the sighted man with the similar pair in "Cathedral."

Tami Haaland of Montana State University has provided a critical analysis of "Cathedral" for inclusion in this manual:

The unnamed narrator of "Cathedral" is a man confined—intellectually and emotionally. He thinks he knows things, but he is intentionally labeling and limiting. His first words, "the blind man," show this tendency, and his subsequent comments indicate his desire not to move beyond his most superficial impressions or his tendency to stereotype ("I wasn't enthusiastic about his visit. He was no one I knew. And his being blind bothered me").

"Cathedral" presents a succession of psychological and spiritual openings brought about because the narrator is repeatedly thrown out of his comfort zone. He can either accept new information (understanding that blind men have beards, for instance) or find a way to block the information. The culmination comes in the final scene, where he "didn't feel like [he] was inside anything." Perhaps Carver recalled the story of Tiresias and Oedipus: the blind man observes more than the seeing man, and when the seeing man becomes symbolically blind at the end of the story, his world opens up.

The narrator in "Cathedral" is intent on stopping up his senses. He doesn't want to know any more than he has to, so it seems appropriate that he watches television, drinks, eats, and smokes pot through much of the story. The blind man, Robert, joins him, but for the narrator this binge seems to be a daily pattern. The emphasis on drinking, eating, and smoking early in the story (drinking is one of their "pastimes") alleviates some of the tension between husband and wife as well as the narrator's discomfort in having "the blind man" in his home. During the meal, the narrator begins to refer to Robert by his name instead of "the blind man." This marks the beginning of a change in the narrator.

Initially, the narrator seems surprised that other people have experiences and perceptions that are different from his. He even remarks on word choice that he finds unusual: "my wife's word, inseparable." It is also "beyond [his] understanding" that Robert was never able to see his wife and that the wife could never be seen by her husband. This remark implicitly invites comparison to the narrator and his wife. How much does he really see of her? Does he understand her at all? Does he try? Only a few lines later he sees her pull into the driveway with Robert: "She was still wearing a smile. Just amazing." Apparently he sees something in her that he didn't expect. When she looks at him a moment later, he says, "I had the feeling she didn't like what she saw."

It would be interesting to trace imagery and language associated with sight through this story. The wife is uptight too, like her husband, but her primary concern is that her husband will misbehave. This fear becomes evident very early after the three of them are together in the living room. The narrator asks which side of the train Robert sat on, and she reacts by saying, "What a question." Robert shows himself to be more open than either husband or wife.

In the last scene, Robert takes on a kind of fatherly role, encouraging the narrator to explain and eventually draw the cathedral. A key statement here comes after the narrator attempts to describe and explain: "I guess I don't believe in it. In anything. Sometimes it's hard." This admission seems to be the psychological or spiritual reason for the narrator's limitations. He has no faith, not even in himself. A few lines later he says, "But I can't tell you what a cathedral looks like. It just isn't in me to do it. I can't do anymore than I've done." He then confesses that, "My legs felt like they didn't have any strength in them." He is exhausted, empty, and his preconceptions no longer seem to be in the way. He also believes that he is incapable of continuing the conversation on cathedrals.

Apparently Robert sees his potential and encourages the narrator to start drawing. It's as if he is coaxing a child through a difficult project. The cathedral could be seen as a symbol of faith both in its function as a place of worship and also in the way that it was built by successive generations, many of whom would never see the finished structure. The narrator doesn't see his finished structure either, though he knows that it as well as his sense of not being contained was "really something." It is as if the narrator has developed a new sensibility, an emotional and intellectual openness that he didn't have before.

In my experience, students often don't get the ending. They react much like the wife who steps into the scene and finds it bizarre that these two men sit side by side, their hands linked, drawing a cathedral on a paper bag.

MLL *MyLiteratureLab Resources.* Biography, critical overview, and bibliography for Carver. Longman Lecture on "Cathedral."

WRITERS ON WRITING

Raymond Carver, COMMONPLACE BUT PRECISE LANGUAGE, page 109

This excerpt from Carver's "On Writing" is both an explicit announcement of his literary aims and an implicit defense of his minimalist aesthetic, which at the time of writing was being hotly debated by critics. Carver insists that the imaginative endeavor "to write about commonplace things and objects using commonplace but precise language" is not a retreat from fiction's greater ambitions since the author still tries to evoke "immense, even startling power." Notice the names that Carver invokes—Vladimir Nabokov, Isaac Babel, Guy de Maupassant, Henry James, and Evan Connell (the last is the author of two classic contemporary American novels, Mrs. *Bridge* and Mr. *Bridge*). Carver places his own imaginative enterprise in the great tradition of Realist fiction (all his names but Nabokov are major Realists). Finally, Carver asserts that the sort of writing he practices is hard to do well—a statement subsequently proved by his many less talented and less scrupulous imitators.

QUESTIONS FOR DISCUSSION

1. What does Raymond Carver's statement tell us about the qualities he prizes in literature? About his personal writing habits?

2. Consider "Cathedral." How does it show that this writer practices what he advocates?

4
Setting

Kate Chopin, THE STORM, page 115

Kate Chopin wrote "The Storm" at a single sitting in July 1898. Its four adult characters had previously appeared in "At the 'Cadian Ball," written in 1892 and published in *Bayou Folk* (1894), Chopin's first collection of short fiction. The earlier story recounts the relationship of Calixta and Alcée and the circumstances that led to their marriages.

The setting of "The Storm" provides its most powerful unifying element. The raging storm initiates the plot by trapping Bobinôt and Bibi at Friedheimer's store and providing Alcée with an excuse to seek shelter at the home of his former lover, Calixta. Setting and plot reinforce each other. The storm not only affects the situation of each character, it also reflects the tempestuous inner states of Alcée and Calixta, who find themselves unexpectedly alone. Their passionate adultery is supremely satisfying—the classic Chopin touch that so outraged her contemporaries. No wonder she never published the story in her lifetime. The frank depiction of sexual passion in "The Storm" (especially in terms of the woman's desire and enjoyment), the complete lack of remorse or guilt on the part of the adulterous lovers, and Chopin's apparent acceptance of the situation put it well beyond the limits of what was acceptable a century ago.

Present-day students will not be shocked or outraged by the story in the way that Chopin's contemporaries would have been, but they may still vigorously debate both the behavior of the lovers and Chopin's own intentions, particularly in terms of the story's very last sentence. Is that last sentence ironic? If so, at whose or what expense—the lovers themselves, the betrayed spouses, the institution of marriage?

Any discussion of the setting should not overlook the story's cultural milieu: the French Catholic bayou country of Louisiana. This region was not Chopin's native territory. She was born an Irish American in St. Louis and went to New Orleans at nineteen. She sees the milieu, therefore, with the relative objectivity of an outsider who is nonetheless rooted by family and children. Part of the special charm of her fiction is its careful depiction of this exotic local culture so different from the rest of the South.

QUESTIONS FOR DISCUSSION

1. *What causes Calixta's infidelity?* Her husband loves her, in his way. He buys a can of shrimp because he knows she likes it. He stands in awe of her scrupulous housekeeping, but he seems to know nothing of her sensuality. We're told that after he buys the shrimp, he sits "stolidly." It is this stolidness, perhaps, that has prevented his ever having plumbed his wife's passionate nature.

2. *Doesn't Calixta love her husband?* She does, apparently: She worries about him and her son when the storm comes up. She seems genuinely glad to be reunited with them when they come home. But passions, Chopin seems to say, cannot be denied. Their force is equal to that of a storm, and the marriage bed is not the likeliest place for the release of that force. Indeed, the author hints that marriage and sexual pleasure are incompatible in Parts IV and V of the story, where Alcée urges his absent wife to stay away another month and where we learn that for Clarisse, "their intimate conjugal life was something which she was more than willing to forgo for a while."

 MyLiteratureLab Resources. Biography, critical overview, and bibliography for Chopin. Longman Lecture, interactive reading, student essay, and critical essay for "The Storm."

Jack London, To Build a Fire, page 119

Like other American fiction writers at the end of the nineteenth century and the beginning of the twentieth—among them Stephen Crane, Frank Norris, and Theodore Dreiser—Jack London expressed a Naturalistic viewpoint in his presentation of man as a creature pitted against and often dwarfed by the forces of nature. Like Ernest Hemingway for a later generation, London gave his work what many considered an extra dimension by living the adventurous life that he described in his fiction. Having endured the winter of 1897–1898 in a cabin in the Klondike, he felt that the individual battling against nature was capable of a nobility that was denied to the anonymous masses toiling in the great cities.

The point of view in "To Build a Fire" is that of an omniscient narrator who can see into both the man's mind and the dog's. The namelessness of the human character seems simultaneously to make him a representative of all humanity in his fight against nature's relentless assault and to emphasize his—and consequently our—insignificance in the face of such overwhelming odds. Skillfully, London builds up almost unendurable suspense, and our hopes, like those of the protagonist, are kept alive almost until the end. But once we have been told how limited the man's perceptions are (third paragraph), a sense of foreboding is created that will only grow stronger as the story proceeds and we are forced to come to terms with his fatally foolhardy assumptions.

London lavishes upon the setting the amount of detail usually reserved for a story's characters. The arctic weather functions as if it were a character, a malignant adversary doing battle with the man. Detail is piled upon detail as the struggle is gradually lost. The frost on the man's face, the numbing of his extremities and exposed skin, his confusion, and finally, his inability to use his frozen fingers to keep his feeble fire going or even to kill the dog—all of these lead up to and into the drowsy calm that signals his end.

Along the way the man makes us aware of the fatal mistakes he has made, the most serious no doubt being his decision to venture alone into the wilderness. Underestimating his adversary, he fails to ascertain the temperature and to cover his face. Finally, suffering from mental confusion, he gets his feet wet and then builds a fire in the wrong place. By that time it is too late to rectify what has gone wrong. The dog, protected by his instincts, survives.

The theme of the story, that our struggle against nature is a vastly unequal one that leaves little or no margin for error, is clearly dramatized. But the descriptive power of the text, in its almost overwhelming vividness, provides an excellent opportunity to remind students that, aside from all questions of larger thematic significance, one of the primary functions of literature has always been to recreate and record the textures of life and to convey the *feeling* of an experience to those who have not had it for themselves. The brilliance of London's achievement at this level is undeniable.

A videocassette of "To Build a Fire," with Orson Welles reading the entire text of the story, is available from Library Video Company at <www.libraryvideo.com>.

Frivolous writing assignment, perhaps for doing in class: retell this story in 500 words, from the dog's point of view.

T. Coraghessan Boyle, GREASY LAKE, page 130

It is rebellious adolescence in general that Boyle describes in his opening paragraph; but he's also talking about the late 1960s, when adolescents were in plentiful supply, "bad" behavior was much admired, and "courtesy and winning ways went out of style." In 1967, when the American attack on Khe Sanh (mentioned in paragraph 7) took place, Boyle himself was nineteen years old. We can only guess that that's about the year in which "Greasy Lake" is set. Not only the epigraph but also the title of the story come from that bard of a slightly later era, Bruce Springsteen, whose first album appeared in 1973.

Are Digby and Jeff really "bad"? Well, no, and neither is the narrator. They're just engaging in the kind of behavior they think is expected of them (1, 3, 4). When, on the night of the story, their rebellion backfires, throwing them into a grimmer world than they had bargained for, they feel revulsion. As is clear at the end, they have had enough of being "bad." Like the boy in James Joyce's "Araby," they have grown up painfully. (For other stories of a young man's initiation into maturity, see "A & P" and "Barn Burning." A young woman who is similarly initiated, or seems about to be, appears in "Where Are You Going, Where Have You Been?")

That the narrator of "Greasy Lake" grows and changes during his adventures is apparent from the two views of "nature" he voices, one in paragraph 2 and one in paragraph 32. Early in the story, "nature" was wanting "to snuff the rich scent of possibility on the breeze, watch a girl take off her clothes and plunge into the festering murk, drink beer, smoke pot, howl at the stars, savor the incongruous full-throated roar of rock and roll against the primeval susurrus of frogs and crickets." By the end of the story, these swinish pleasures have lost their appeal. When, at dawn, the narrator experiences the beauties of the natural world as if for the first time, he has an epiphany: "This was nature."

Students can have fun demonstrating how Greasy Lake is the perfect setting for Boyle's story. Like the moral view of the narrator (at first), it is "fetid and murky, the mud banks glittering with broken glass and strewn with beer cans and the charred remains of bonfires. There was a single ravaged island a hundred yards from shore, so stripped of vegetation it looked as if the air force had strafed it" (2). The lake is full of "primordial ooze" and "the bad breath of decay" (31).

It also hides a waterlogged corpse. Once known for its clear water, the unlucky lake has fallen as far from its ideal state as the people who now frequent its shores have fallen from theirs. (If you teach the chapter on symbol, hark back to Greasy Lake once more.)

Still, in its way, Greasy Lake is a force for change. Caught trying to rape the girl in the blue car, the narrator and his friends run off into the woods and into the water. Waiting in the filthy lake, the narrator is grateful to be alive and feels horror at the death of the "bad older character" whose body he meets in the slime. His growth has begun. When at the end of the story, two more girls pull into the parking lot, the subdued narrator and his friends are harmless. Cold sober and bone tired, they know they have had a lucky escape from consequences that might have been terrible. Also, the narrator knows, as the girls do not, that Al is dead, his body rotting in the lake. He won't "turn up"—except perhaps in the most grisly way. It is this knowledge and the narrator's new reverence for life that make him think he is going to cry.

Students might enjoy spelling out the change in the narrator's outlook. By what hints does Boyle show us that some time has elapsed since the events of the fateful night? Surely the story displays little admiration for the narrator's early behavior, which he now regards with sarcasm, as when he says, "Digby wore a gold star in his right ear and allowed his father to pay his tuition at Cornell" (3), or when he speaks of "new heights of adventure and daring" (6). Other ironic remarks abound, showing his altered view. The maturity the narrator acquired that night seems to have been permanent.

Critics have cited Boyle as a writer socially and politically disengaged; but satire, he points out, can be corrective. "It can hold up certain attitudes as being fraudulent, and in doing that suggest that the opposite might be an appropriate way to behave. And I hope that if my work is socially redemptive, it is in that way" (interview with David Stanton in *Poets & Writers*, January/February 1990). Surely "Greasy Lake," a story some readers find shocking, is socially redemptive.

In a letter to the editor of the *New York Times Book Review* (February 27, 2000), Boyle took issue with a critic who had thought "Greasy Lake" to be about characters in a popular song:

> The story itself was inspired by Bruce Springsteen's song "Spirit in the Night" and employs an epigraph from that song, but it is not . . . "about its characters." As anyone who has read the story will know, the characters and situations are wholly invented. I see "Greasy Lake" as a kind of riff on the song, a free take on its glorious spirit.

Candace Andrews of San Joaquin Delta College argues that, while on the surface "Greasy Lake" seems merely to recount the misadventures of a nineteen-year-old delinquent, a careful reading will show that much of the story retells the narrator's experience in Vietnam—"It is a tale of a young man who has been to war and back." For a writing assignment, she had her students list every reference or allusion to war, and she told them, "Then bring your 'research' together into some kind of coherent statement which supports the idea that the narrator is a Vietnam veteran." We do not believe, ourselves, that Boyle's several references to war necessarily require the narrator to be an ex-GI. He would have followed the war news and come to feel that the war was senseless violence—like the action out at Greasy Lake on a Saturday night. When he tells us (in paragraph 40) that he and

Digby looked at the girl "like war veterans," we take that to be a metaphor: he too feels a sort of battle fatigue. However, you may care to check out Professor Andrews's provocative theory for yourself. What do your students think of it?

MLL
MyLiteratureLab Resources. Critical essay on "Greasy Lake."

Amy Tan, A Pair of Tickets, page 137

"A Pair of Tickets" is a story of self-discovery—born in pain but eventually resolved in joy. Pain unites characters from different countries and decades. The narrator's still-fresh sorrow at her mother's death, the mother's abiding despair at losing her twin daughters on the war-torn road to Chungking, and the daughters' ache at losing their mother not once, but twice (first as babies in 1944 and then again as adults after they learn their mother is dead) are all caused by the same tragic historical circumstance and its far-reaching consequences. Joy, however, eventually links June with her two half-sisters. Acknowledging what they have lost, they find that much remains.

Here are some possible answers to the questions given at the end of "A Pair of Tickets." Other answers, of equal merit, may occur to you and your students.

QUESTIONS

1. *How is the external setting of "A Pair of Tickets" essential to what happens internally to the narrator in the course of this story?* "A Pair of Tickets" is a story that grows naturally out of its setting. June's journey to China is one of both external and internal discovery. Finding China, she also finds part of herself. Tan announces the theme at the end of the first paragraph: "I am becoming Chinese." China becomes a spiritual mirror for the narrator, just as her glimpse of her half-sisters' faces provides a living mirror of her own and her late mother's face. One might say that "A Pair of Tickets" is the story of Americanized June May Woo (born, as her passport says, in California in 1951) becoming Jing-mei Woo by discovering her ethnic and cultural roots in her ancestral homeland.

2. *How does the narrator's view of her father change by seeing him in a different setting?* Although June's mother haunts the story, her father is also a quiet, important presence. As the title says, this story is about a *pair* of tickets. June's seventy-two-year-old father, Canning Woo, accompanies her on the trip to China. He is returning after four decades. He is June's physical and psychological link with the homeland, as well as her living link with the family history that she (like most children) only half knows. His revelations teach her about both her mother and herself. Seeing him in China, June gets a glimpse of his past, what he was like as a young man before she was born. "He's a young boy," she observes on the train to Shenzen, "so innocent and happy I want to button his sweater and pat his head."

3. *In what ways does the narrator feel at home in China? In what ways does she feel foreign?* June is Chinese American, which means that she experiences the two cultures from both the inside and the outside. Just as going to China helps her understand how she is Chinese, it also reminds her how much she has been

shaped by America. She understands Mandarin Chinese but cannot speak it well. She does not know the Cantonese of her relatives or her father's Mandarin dialect. Although she is purely Chinese in ancestry, not only her clothes betray her American upbringing—she is also too tall. "I stand five-foot-six," June observes, "and my head pokes above the crowd so that I am eye level only with other tourists." And yet she physically resembles her half-sisters, realizing at the end of the story: "And now I also see what part of me is Chinese. It is so obvious. It is my family. It is in our blood."

4. *What do the narrator and her half-sisters have in common? How does this factor relate to the theme of the story?* She and her half-sisters share a biological and spiritual link to their common mother, and through her they share a bond to one another. "Together we look like our mother," June observes. "Her same eyes, her same mouth." Their fates are interrelated, as reflected by their names. In China, June asks her father the meaning of her Chinese name, Jing-mei, and he interprets her name to signify the younger sister who is the essence of the other lost daughters. As she discovers on meeting them, she does share their essence—they are all daughters of the same mother.

5. *In what ways is the story interesting because it explores specifically Chinese American experiences? In what other ways is the story grounded in universal family issues?* Although "A Pair of Tickets" is saturated in Chinese history and culture, and its plot reflects a situation unlikely to be repeated in other contexts, it also explores nearly universal themes of self-discovery, cultural awareness, and family history. One might say that Tan's broader theme is dual identity—an especially relevant theme for many Americans who come from immigrant families. Tan explores this quintessentially American experience with humor, compassion, and imagination.

Wayne Wang's 1993 film version of *The Joy Luck Club* will probably disappoint most of Tan's readers as much as it did movie critics. The subject matter is so interesting that it carries the film along, but Wang sentimentalizes and sensationalizes the story into a sort of Asian American soap opera. The final episode (drawn from "A Pair of Tickets") is condensed and simplified. The *pair* of tickets is, alas, reduced to a single passage: June flies to China alone, and poor Canning Woo gets left in the States. The film may nonetheless be useful to students who need help in visualizing the American and Chinese milieus of the story. Under pressure, one might assign a particularly movie-struck student the task of comparing and contrasting the movie's version of "A Pair of Tickets" to the original story.

MLL *MyLiteratureLab Resources*. Biography, critical overview, bibliography for Tan.

WRITERS ON WRITING

Amy Tan, SETTING THE VOICE, page 150

Tan's 1989 essay on the relation between finding her authorial voice and remembering her mother's "broken" English provides a fascinating glimpse into the relationship between life and art. It also highlights the issue of audience. An artist's strategy of literary creation necessarily includes the image of his or her ideal reader. The act of imaginative identification has often been problematic for minority or immigrant writers. Should they address their own communities, or should they try to reach a mainstream that may be ignorant of their particular experiences? Such writers must often imagine an audience that does not yet exist and hope their work summons it into being. Tan's immensely popular books have done just that by creating a huge diverse audience of readers. This passage describes how Tan gradually developed the distinctive style for the stories that made up *The Joy Luck Club*.

5
Tone and Style

This celebrated story is a study in contrasts: between youth and age, belief and doubt, light and darkness. To the younger waiter, the café is only a job; to the older waiter, it is a charitable institution for which he feels personal responsibility. Of course, he himself has need of it: it is his refuge from the night, from solitude, from a sense that the universe is empty and meaningless, expressed in his revised versions of the Hail Mary and the Lord's Prayer. The older waiter feels kinship for the old man, not only because the waiter, too, is alone and growing old, but because both men are apparently atheists. Willing to commit suicide, the old man (unlike his pious daughter) evidently doesn't think he has any immortal soul to fear for. Robert Penn Warren is surely right in calling Hemingway, at least in this story, a religious writer. "The despair beyond plenty of money, the despair that makes a sleeplessness beyond insomnia, is the despair felt by a man who hungers for the sense of order and assurance that men seem to find in religious faith, but who cannot find grounds for his faith" ("Ernest Hemingway," in Warren's *Selected Essays* [New York: Random, 1951] 80–118). What values are left to a man without faith? A love of cleanliness and good light, of companionship, of stoic endurance, and above all, of dignity. (Another attempt to state the theme of the story is given at the beginning of Chapter 7.)

At the heart of the story is the symbol of the café, an island of light and order surrounded by night and nothingness. Contrasting images of light and darkness begin in the opening paragraph: the old man, not entirely committed either to death or to life, likes to sit in the shadow of the leaves. Every detail in the story seems meaningful: even, perhaps, as L. Rust Hills points out, "the glint of light on the soldier's collar . . . an attribute of sexual potency" (*Writing in General and the Short Story in Particular* [Boston: Houghton, 1977] 85).

The story has been much admired for Hemingway's handling of point of view. The narrator is a nonparticipant who writes in the third person. He is all-knowing at the beginning of the story: in the opening paragraph we are told how the old man feels, then what the waiters know about him. From then on, until the waiters say "Good night," the narrator remains almost perfectly objective, merely reporting visible details and dialogue. (He editorializes for a moment, though, in observing that the younger waiter employs the syntax of "stupid people.") After the waiters part company, for the rest of the story the narrator limits himself to the thoughts and perceptions of the older waiter, who, we now see, is the central character.

It is clear all along, as we overhear the conversation of the two waiters, that Hemingway sides with the elder's view of the old man. The older waiter reveals himself as wiser and more compassionate. We resent the younger man's abuse of the old man, who cannot hear his "stupid" syntax, his equation of money with happiness. But the older waiter and Hemingway do not see things identically—a point briefly discussed in the text in a comment on the story's irony.

A small problem in reading the story is to keep the speakers straight. Evidently it is the younger waiter who has heard of the old man's suicide attempt and who answers the questions at the beginning of the story.

Jan Hodge of Morningside College has written to contest our interpretation. He offers an interesting revisionist reading of the text:

> I was a bit taken aback by your note [on paragraphs 20 and 21] that "The younger waiter says both these lines. A device of Hemingway's style is sometimes to have a character pause, then speak again—as often happens in actual speech." This may be the case, though I don't know of any instances offhand in his writing where there is not some kind of indication when this is what is happening, or where context wouldn't make it clear that the same speaker speaks successive lines, each enclosed in quotation marks.
>
> As I read the story, the young waiter speaks the first of the lines in question here, and the older waiter the second. This would be consistent not only with their respective characters, but with conventionally alternating lines of dialogue in the rest of that section *if* . . . and herein lies the critical problem, paragraphs 39–42 read in your text:
>
> "You can't tell. He might be better off with a wife."   *[clearly the older waiter]*
> "His niece looks after him."
> "I know. You said she cut him down."
> "I wouldn't want to be that old. An old man is a nasty thing."
>   *[clearly the young waiter]*
>
> But the words "You said she cut him down" must be spoken by the young waiter, because the older waiter has told him that earlier. The passage makes perfect sense if the lines are adjusted this way:
>
> "You can't tell. He might be better off with a wife."   *[older]*
> "His niece looks after him. You said she cut him down."   *[young]*
> "I know."   *[older]*
> "I wouldn't want to be that old . . ."   *[young]*
>
> I haven't checked the critical record recently, but many years ago a student doing a research paper on this story ran across an article on the passage which argued (as I recall, though I can't swear to it) that the compositor had slipped, and that the manuscript has the dialog as in the second version above. Voila! All difficulties vanish.

Hemingway's device of assigning two successive speeches to the same character without identifying him (paragraphs 20–21 and probably 32–33) has given rise to much confusion among readers—also to twenty or more scholarly articles on the correct reading of the story. David Kerner's "The Foundation of the True Text of 'A Clean, Well-Lighted Place'" settles the question. Demonstrating that the device appears many times in Hemingway's novels and stories, Kerner suggests—with evidence—that Hemingway may have learned it from Turgenev or Joyce (*Fitzgerald/Hemingway Annual* [1979]: 279–300). Later, Kerner examined manuscripts of books Hemingway saw through press and found thirty-eight clear instances of the device ("The Manuscripts Establishing Hemingway's Anti-Metronomic Dialogue," *American Literature* 54 [1982]: 385–96).

How original Hemingway's style once seemed may be less apparent today, after generations of imitators. Ford Madox Ford described the famed style: "Hemingway's words strike you, each one, as if they were pebbles fetched fresh from a brook" (introduction to *A Farewell to Arms* [New York: Modern Library, 1932]). Students may be asked to indicate some of the more prominent pebbles: the repetitions of such words as *night, light, clean, late, shadow, leaves,* and (most obviously) *nada.* The repetitions place emphasis. Students may be asked, too, to demonstrate whether Hemingway's prose seems closer to formal writing or to speech. It might help to have them notice the preponderance of one-syllable words in the opening paragraph of the story and to compare Hemingway's first paragraph with that of Faulkner's "Barn Burning." Faulkner's second sentence is a 117-worder, clearly more recondite in its diction (*dynamic, hermetic*). Most of Hemingway's story is told in dialogue, and usually we notice that a character *said* (unlike Faulkner's characters, who often *whisper* or *cry* their lines).

Frank O'Connor comments adversely on the Hemingway style:

> As practiced by Hemingway, this literary method, compounded of simplification and repetition, is the opposite of what we learned in our schooldays. We were taught to consider it a fault to repeat a noun and shown how to avoid it by the use of pronouns and synonyms. This led to another fault that Fowler christened "elegant variation." The fault of Hemingway's method might be called "elegant repetition." (*The Lonely Voice* [Cleveland: World, 1963])

This criticism may be well worth quoting to the class. From "A Clean, Well-Lighted Place," can students see what O'Connor is talking about? Do they agree with him?

In a preface written in 1959 for a selection of his stories that did not materialize as a book, Hemingway congratulated himself for his skill at leaving things out. In his story "The Killer," he had left out Chicago; in "Big Two-Hearted River," the war. "Another time I was leaving out good was in 'A Clean, Well-Lighted Place.' There I really had luck. I left out everything. That is about as far as you can go, so I stood on that one and haven't been drawn to that since" ("The Art of the Short Story," *Paris Review* 79 [1981]: 100).

Hemingway himself had reason to empathize with the older waiter. "He was plagued all his adult life by insomnia and in sleep by nightmares," notes biographer Carlos Baker (*Ernest Hemingway: A Life Story* [New York: Scribner, 1969] viii–ix).

MLL *MyLiteratureLab Resources.* Biography, critical overview, and bibliography for Hemingway. Critical essay for "A Clean, Well-Lighted Place."

William Faulkner, BARN BURNING, page 160

"Barn Burning" makes an interesting contrast to "A Rose for Emily." Whereas the earlier story (first collected in 1931) is written in a realist mode with Gothic elements, "Barn Burning" (1939) shows Faulkner in his Modernist mode—not opaque but richly textured and subtly nuanced. There are many ways to contrast the two stories, but one interesting way for students is to discuss how the different narrative points of view help shape radically different styles and effects.

The unnamed narrator of "A Rose for Emily" speaks in a public voice; he intends to represent the town's collective and considered view on Miss Emily Grierson. His style is lucid, measured, informed, and detached. "Barn Burning," however, is narrated from an objective third person point of view that enters the main character Sarty's mind. The objective external view is, therefore, constantly mixed with the confusion and emotions of a boy undergoing terrible stress. The narrator is not constrained to describe things only in the boy's limited vocabulary but can examine and represent his innermost thoughts and feelings. The narrator also helps the reader understand the boy's situation better than the character himself does.

The protagonist of "Barn Burning" is a poor ten-year-old boy with the unusual and very Faulknerian name of Colonel Sartoris Snopes (called Sarty by his family). His father, Abner Snopes, is a primitive and vengeful man who divides the world into two opposing camps—blood kin ("us") and enemies ("they"). He is the poor, ignorant, and vicious patriarch of an impoverished family. (Significantly, Faulkner gives Ab several features that link him on an associative level with the devil, as Edmond Volpe demonstrates in his discussion of "Barn Burning" in the section on "Critical Approaches to Literature.") The main psychological story of "Barn Burning" is Sarty's growing awareness of his father's depravity and the boy's internal struggle between blood loyalty to his father and a vague but noble ideal of honor suggested by the aristocratic Major de Spain. The boy loves his father but he also understands his immoral destructiveness. Sarty sees himself as an individual different from his father and kinfolk. By the end of the story he has achieved a difficult and tortured moral independence from his father.

From the opening paragraph, we can tell that the tone of the story will be excited and impassioned—at least in the moments when we see through Sarty's eyes. Even his view of canned goods in the general store (where court is being held) is tinged with intense emotion. Fear, despair, and grief sweep over Sarty because his father is on trial as an accused barn burner.

The boy's wonder and dismay are conveyed in a suitably passionate style. Whenever Sarty is most excited, Faulkner's sentences grow longer and more complex and seem to run on like a torrent. The second sentence of the story is a good illustration, as is the sentence in which Sarty jumps out of the way of Major de Spain's galloping horse and hears the barn going up in flames (at the climax of the story, the long sentence in paragraph 107). A familiar student objection is that Faulkner embodies the boy's feelings in words far beyond a ten-year-old's vocabulary—especially one who can't even read, as we learn about Sarty in the opening paragraph. You might anticipate this objection by making clear that a story about a small boy, even when the story is presented largely in terms of his own perceptions, need not be narrated by the boy himself; nor does the author need to confine himself within the limit of the boy's ability to comprehend and to express what he observes and feels (refer to the discussion of the quotation from *As I Lay Dying* at the beginning of the chapter). "Barn Burning" is told by an omniscient narrator who, much of the time, gives us the viewpoint of the main character.

Now and again, the narrator intrudes his own insights and larger knowledge. At times Faulkner rapidly shifts his perspective from outside Sarty's mind to inside it. Two such shifts take place in a sentence in paragraph 7 ("For a moment . . ."), in which, first, we get the boy's thoughts and then an exterior look at his crouched figure ("small for his age . . . with straight, uncombed, brown hair and eyes gray and wild as storm scud"), followed by a return to the boy's perceptions. In the paragraph telling how Ab Snopes's "wolflike independence" impressed strangers (25), Faulkner makes a judgment far beyond the boy's capacity. In paragraph 26, the narrator again separates his view from the boy's to tell us what Sarty would have thought if he were older—"But he did not think this now." The narrator is again clearly in evidence in the story's last two paragraphs.

Lionel Trilling wrote a good defense of the style in this story: the complexity of Faulkner's rhetoric reflects the muddlement and incompleteness of the boy's perceptions and the boy's emotional stress in moving toward a decision to break away from father and family (*The Experience of Literature* [New York: Holt, 1967] 745–48). He is perplexed and innocent, and we realize that somehow he loves his terrible father. In the next-to-last paragraph, Sarty's impressions of his father's war service are set beside the grim truth—which only the father (and the narrator) could know. Wayne C. Booth comments on this passage: "We can say with some confidence that the poignancy of the boy's lonely last-ditch defense of his father is greatly increased by letting us know that even that defense is unjustified" (*The Rhetoric of Fiction* [Chicago: U of Chicago P, 1961] 308).

If you teach "Barn Burning" together with "A Rose for Emily" (Chapter 2) to demonstrate that point of view, remember that "Barn Burning" is the more difficult story. You may want to take up "A Rose for Emily" first and to spend a little while getting students into the universe of Faulkner. Any brief discussion of the Civil War and its effects will help prepare them for "Barn Burning." Though her perch in society is loftier, Miss Emily, like Ab Snopes, is fiercely proud and capable of violent revenge, and she too holds herself above the law. As with Miss Emily, Snopes is characterized in part through the symbolic use of details. The neat, "shrewd" fire (paragraph 26) reflects his cautious nature; his weapon of revenge, fire, is to be "regarded with respect and used with discretion." The rug that he soils and then ruins is emblematic of the social hierarchy that he defies and that he refuses to make amends to. His deliberately dirtied boots communicate his contempt for his employer as well as his own dirtiness of spirit. Clearly, Faulkner's impressions of both Snopes and Miss Emily are as complex as his feelings about the South itself.

"A Rose for Emily" also introduces the legend of Colonel Sartoris, war hero, mayor, and first citizen, whose fame and influence linger. Coming to "Barn Burning," students may then appreciate the boy hero's given name. Addressing the boy (in 10), the Justice foreshadows the story's conclusion: "I reckon anybody named for Colonel Sartoris in this country can't help but tell the truth, can he?" Truthfully, Sarty warns Major de Spain that his father is going to burn the major's barn; in so defying Ab, Colonel Sartoris Snopes rises to his namesake's nobility. (But, according to Frederick R. Karl, the line from Sartoris to Snopes is not one of simple degeneration. Karl points out that Colonel Sartoris "uses his power for white supremacy, harasses and even murders carpetbaggers, and makes certain that Negroes lose the vote. He . . . is a power-hungry, politically obsessed individual whose will is law. He establishes a dynasty, and its elements, while high and grand, are little different from the dynasties at the middle level established by Will Varner and at the lower levels by the Snopeses" [*William Faulkner: American Writer*, New York: Weidenfeld, 1989].)

Question 1 directs the student to paragraph 107, a crucial passage that repays close attention. From the roar Sarty hears, and from the detail that the night sky is "stained abruptly," it is clear that Ab Snopes and Sarty's older brother succeed in setting fire to de Spain's barn. We had long assumed that, although a total of three shots ring out, the barn burners get away, for they turn up in a later volume of Faulkner. But Joseph L. Swonk of Rappahannock Community College, North Campus, persuades us that the outcome is grimmer. Sarty cries "Pap! Pap!"—then trips over "something," looks back, and sobs "Father! Father!" "I contend," says Professor Swonk, "that he tripped over the bodies of his father and brother, that he was looking backward at the bodies, and that his shift from 'Pap' to 'Father' was eulogistic. Furthermore, he continues in this manner: '*Father. My Father* . . . He was brave! . . . He was! He was in the war!'" Now referring to his father in the past tense, Sarty is delivering a final tribute over Ab's corpse.

"Barn Burning," to place the story in the chronicles of Yoknapatawpha County, is a prelude to the Snopes family history later expanded in Faulkner's trilogy *The Hamlet* (1940), *The Town* (1957), and *The Mansion* (1959); in fact, a heavily revised version of "Barn Burning" forms the first chapter of *The Hamlet*. At the conclusion of "Barn Burning," Sarty Snopes turns his back on his father and his clan; so, in the trilogy, the primary figure is Flem, Sarty's brother, who remains. Meeting Flem Snopes, whose father Ab is still well known as a barn burner, Jody Varner in *The Hamlet* says dryly, "I hear your father has had a little trouble once or twice with landlords."

"Barn Burning" was adapted for television by Horton Foote for the PBS television series *The American Short Story* and stars Tommy Lee Jones. It is available on videocassette and DVD from Library Video Company at <www.libraryvideo.com>. A paperback, *The American Short Story*, Volume 2 (New York: Dell, 1980), includes short scenes from Horton Foote's television script based on Faulkner's story.

For a stimulating attack on Faulkner's style, see Sean O'Faolain, *The Vanishing Hero* (Boston: Little, Brown, 1957) 101–3, 111–12, 133. Charging that Faulkner can't write plain English because "his psyche is completely out of his control," O'Faolain cites lines of Faulkner that he thinks rely on pure sound instead of sense ("the gasoline-roar of apotheosis") and complains that Faulkner needlessly uses "second-thought words" ("He did not know why he had been compelled, or anyway needed, to claim it"; "This, anyway, will, shall, must be invulnerable"). In O'Faolain's view, when Faulkner begins a sentence with "I mean," it is a tipoff that he doesn't know what he means and won't know until he says it. O'Faolain's objections might make for a provocative class discussion.

 MyLiteratureLab Resources. Photographs, biographical information, bibliography, and critical overview for Faulkner. Video clips, audio clips, and critical essays on "Barn Burning."

IRONY

O. Henry, THE GIFT OF THE MAGI, page 174

This classic tale by the master of irony is easily the most popular and beloved of his many stories, since it combines his favored surprise ending—familiar also from such stories as "The Cop and the Anthem" and "The Ransom of Red Chief"—with a sentimental glow and a wholehearted endorsement of the beauty of young love. Sophisticated students may groan a bit at the archness of some of the writing and the contrivance of the plot, but they will probably be touched in spite of themselves by its portrait of an immensely appealing and devoted young couple.

Here are some possible answers to the questions given at the end of "The Gift of the Magi." Other answers, of equal merit, may occur to you and your students.

QUESTIONS

1. *How would you describe the style of this story? Does the author's tone tell you anything about his attitude toward the characters and events of the narrative?* Clearly, O. Henry does not hold with those who feel that the best style is a transparent medium between author and reader. His writing constantly calls attention to itself by its hyperbole, allusiveness, and chattiness; the style invites this scrutiny not only indirectly but even overtly, as in paragraph 18. Like a miniature Fielding or Thackeray, the author interposes himself between the material and the reader in such a way that his genial tone and his controlling presence reassure us that all will be well in the end.

2. *What do the details in paragraph 7 tell you about Della and Jim's financial situation?* Here's an opportunity to get students to do a bit of interpretive reading. We've just been told in paragraph 6 that "Twenty dollars a week doesn't go far." Even with no other guide to monetary values a century ago, we can conclude from that fact that an $8 flat is not a very sumptuous residence. And even though some grades of pier-glass (a long, narrow mirror usually set between windows) can be expensive, it is suggested here that a pier-glass in an $8 flat is of rather shoddy quality.

3. *O. Henry tells us that Jim "needed a new overcoat and he was without gloves" (paragraph 25). Why do you think Della didn't buy him these things for Christmas instead of a watch chain?* Presumably for the same reason that your mother doesn't want a blender for Mother's Day. As paragraph 6 points out, she wants to buy him a gift that would be "fine and rare and sterling—something just a little bit near to being worthy of the honor of being owned by Jim." It must be something precious and extravagant enough to convey her feelings for him, not something merely functional, however much in need of it he might be.

4. *"Eight dollars a week or a million a year—what is the difference? A mathematician or a wit would give you the wrong answer" (paragraph 34). What, in your*

view, is "the wrong answer," and why is it wrong? What might the right answer be? A mathematician might talk about the differences in purchasing power, comfort, and security between the two amounts; a wit might counter the adage "Money can't buy happiness" with the equally stale rejoinder, "No, but it sure helps." The right answer might be that those who have less take it less for granted, and value what they have—including each other—that much more.

5. What is ironic about the story's ending? Is this plot twist the most important element of the conclusion? If not, what is? The obvious irony is that what they sold to buy one another's gifts made those gifts worthless from a practical standpoint. But the larger theme—or the larger irony, if you prefer—is that those gifts were of much greater value as expressions of the depth and selflessness of their love for each other.

Ha Jin, SABOTEUR, page 178

This bitter political story depicts how an unjust system gradually corrupts its innocent victims—or to quote W. H. Auden, "Those to whom evil is done / Do evil in return." The protagonist, Mr. Chiu, is a gentle man of strong personal integrity but seemingly no passionate political views. His malicious arrest, which is a vicious joke by two railroad policemen, puts him in a difficult and painful ethical dilemma. If he lies about his innocence and signs a phony confession—thereby denying the gross misjustice done to him—the police will let him go. If he refuses to lie, he will continue to be punished. Mr. Chiu initially refrains from endorsing the official lie at considerable personal cost. Only when he has been weakened by a relapse of hepatitis and dismayed by the public torture and humiliation of his lawyer, does Mr. Chiu reluctantly agree to sign the false confession. His rage at the injustice he has suffered and his impotence in preventing it lead him to seek revenge the only way he can—a murderous plan that is not only disproportionate, but also one that eventually punishes the guilty and innocent alike.

Jin's story contains irony upon bitter irony. Mr. Chiu's honeymoon ends in jail. The police are the perpetrators of injustice. The innocent Mr. Chiu must pretend to be guilty to be set free. A man with no crimes must sign a confession. The ultimate irony is that by falsely claiming to be a saboteur, Mr. Chiu secretly becomes one. It is a sign of Jin's talent that these ironies emerge naturally—and usually surprisingly—from the narrative.

Jin's story reminds us of how pervasively irony is used in political fiction, especially works written in Communist societies. As the work of such disparate writers as Milan Kundera (Czech), Mikhail Bulgakov (Russian), Solwomir Mrozek (Polish), and Ha Jin demonstrate, a sense of irony helps in presenting the painful distance between the noble aims of the revolutionary worker societies and the often brutal realities. "In China," Jin has commented, "I still have the feeling that evil very often prevails and the good suffer." Jin's story also reminds us that irony is not necessarily a comic device, but can be a very dark, indeed tragic instrument. There is nothing funny about Mr. Chiu's humiliations, punishments, or murderous revenge.

WRITERS ON WRITING

Ernest Hemingway, THE DIRECT STYLE, page 186

Hemingway was internationally famous during his lifetime, and he gave many interviews. He talked expansively about travel, sports, food, politics, and personalities, but he usually became evasive when asked about his own work. He was almost entirely silent on his immensely influential style. This passage from Edward Stafford's "An Afternoon with Hemingway," therefore, is especially valuable to students of the writer's work. Connoisseurs of literary journalism may enjoy Stafford's old style of interviewing, which has now been almost entirely replaced by the *Paris Review* question-and-answer format. The 1964 publication date may seem confusing, Hemingway having died in 1961; the interview was conducted in the late fifties, but Stafford did not publish it until after the novelist's death.

Hemingway's remarks are particularly interesting because he relates his style to his creative process. Hemingway wrote and revised his work in three stages—pencil, typescript, and proof. At each stage he consciously worked on conveying the "feeling or emotion" he wanted in each scene. Note, too, how Hemingway mentions that a writer needs to present the different sides of a story without judging. (His view here recalls John Keats's theory of "negative capability" as the mark of a particular kind of literary artist.)

6
Theme

Instructors who wish to teach all the stories in the book according to themes (not just the stories in this chapter) will find suggestions in this manual in "Stories Arranged by Subject and Theme" (pp. 9–16).

Stephen Crane, THE OPEN BOAT, page 191

It may interest students to know that "The Open Boat" is based on Crane's own experience of shipwreck, but they may need some discussion to realize that factuality does not necessarily make a story excellent. Newspaper accounts may be faithful to the fact, but few are memorable; on the other hand, fine stories are often spun out of imagined experience—as was Crane's novel *The Red Badge of Courage*, a convincing evocation of the Civil War by a writer who was born six years after it ended.

For what reasons is "The Open Boat" a superb story? Its characters are sharply drawn and believable; captain, cook, oiler, and correspondent are fully realized portraits, etched with great economy. Crane deeply probes the mind of his primary character, the correspondent, from the point of view of limited omniscience. The author knows all, but he confines his report to what he sees through the correspondent's eyes.

The story seems written with intense energy; students will find many phrases and figures of speech to admire. In a vigorous simile, Crane conveys the motion of the boat and a sense of its precarious balance: "By the very last star of truth, it is easier to steal eggs from under a hen than it was to change seats in the dinghy" (paragraph 31). In the same passage, a man changing places in the boat picks himself up and moves his body as carefully as if he were a delicate piece of china. One way to get students to sense the degree of life in a writer's style is to have them pick out verbs. In the opening sentence of Part II (21): "As the boat *bounced* from the top of each wave the wind *tore* through the hair of the hatless men, and as the craft *plopped* her stern down again the spray *slashed* past them." Building suspense, Crane brings the men again and again within sight of land and then drives them back to sea. He aligns enemies against them: sharks, the ocean current, the weight of water that sloshes into the boat and threatens to swamp it. The climax of the story—the moment of greatest tension, when the outcome is to be decided—comes in paragraph 204, when the captain decides to make a run through the surf and go for shore.

The situation of having one's nose dragged away before he can "nibble the sacred cheese of life" (70, 143) is a clear instance of irony of fate, or cosmic irony. (These slightly ponderous terms are defined as briefly as possible in the Glossary of Literary Terms.) Crane, who sees Fate as an "old ninnywoman" (70), knows that the rain falls alike on the just and the unjust. There is no one right way to state the theme of this rich story, but here are some attempts by students, each with some truth in it:

The universe seems blind to human struggles.

Fate is indifferent, and it doesn't always reward the brave.

It's an absurd world; only people are reasonable.

This theme (however it is stated) may be seen also in the symbol of the giant tower (204) and Crane's remarks on what it suggests: "The serenity of nature amid the struggles of the individual," a presence not cruel or beneficent or treacherous or wise. Students who like to hunt for symbols sometimes want to see the boat as the universe, in which man is a passenger. A case can be made for reading the story in this way. But everything in the story (ocean, waves, shark, beach, lighthouse), however full of suggestions, is first and foremost a thing concrete and tangible.

Although the secondary theme of comradeship is overtly expressed only in paragraph 43 ("the subtle brotherhood of men that was here established"), it informs the entire story. Until they quit the boat, the men are willing to spell one another at the oars; and even in the water, the captain still thinks of the correspondent's safety. The word "heroism" remains unspoken, but it is clearly understood: in "The Open Boat," a hero seems to be one who faithfully does what needs to be done. All four men thus qualify for the name.

Remembering the scrap of verse by Victorian bard Caroline Norton (179), the correspondent finds himself drawn into sympathy with any sufferer who, like himself, has to die in a remote place. The sentimental lines give rise to a feeling that, under the circumstances, seems heartfelt and real. In their time, the stormy life and dashing Byronic ballads of Caroline Norton (1808–1877), granddaughter of Richard Brinsley Sheridan, attracted wide notice. (James Joyce mentions another poem of hers in "Araby," paragraph 23.)

For its view of people as pawns of nature, Crane's story has been classified as an example of American naturalism. Clearly, "The Open Boat" also has elements in common with more recent fiction and drama of the absurd: its notion of Fate as a ninny, its account of Sisyphean struggles in the face of an indifferent universe. For critical comment on these aspects of the story, see Richard P. Adams, "Naturalistic Fiction: 'The Open Boat,'" *Tulane Studies in English* 4 (1954): 137–47; and Peter Buitenhuis, "The Essentials of Life: 'The Open Boat' as Existentialist Fiction," *Modern Fiction Studies* 5 (1959): 243–50.

The late William Maxwell, a novelist and for many years a *New Yorker* fiction editor, was once asked in an interview, "As an editor, in deciding whether or not to read a story how much weight do you place on the first sentence?" "A great deal," Maxwell replied. "And if there is nothing promising by the end of the first page there isn't likely to be in what follows. . . . When you get to the last sentence of a [story], you often find that it was implicit in the first sentence, only you didn't know what it was." Asked for his favorite opening lines in fiction, Maxwell's first thought was of "None of them knew the color of the sky," from "The Open Boat" ("The Art of Fiction," *Paris Review* 82 [December

1982]). Students may be asked what this first line reveals. (That the sea compels the survivors' whole attention.) How does the final sentence in the story hark back to the first?

Alice Munro, HOW I MET MY HUSBAND, page 208

Alice Munro's ingeniously plotted story would make an interesting alternative selection to use in the discussion of plot in "Reading a Story" (Chapter 1). The development in the plot of this story reflects the young narrator's growing awareness of how love and infatuation operate. "How I Met My Husband" would also work well in a discussion of "Point of View" (Chapter 2). Munro's story shows how even a sensible and observant narrator can misjudge people and events, especially when she is involved in the action. Munro is masterful in portraying Edie's opinions of her neighbors and employers. Edie is a richly realized narrator—engaging, complex, and human. At fifteen she is, ironically, too smart to appreciate how innocent she still is. She does not yet understand the sexual feelings she experiences. Previously in control of most social situations, she stumbles through this comic romance mostly in embarrassed confusion. Finally, the story cunningly demonstrates the power of the title as a literary device. By calling her story "How I Met My Husband," she invites the reader to expect that this weirdly mismatched and overtly doomed infatuation between Edie and Chris Watters might actually work out.

Here are some possible answers to the questions given at the end of "How I Met My Husband." Other answers, of equal merit, may occur to you and your students.

QUESTIONS

1. *How would you judge Edie as a narrator? Do we feel she is being objective about the people and events she describes? Take one character or incident and comment on her depiction of it.* Edie is smart and sensible for her age, but she has a highly critical kind of intelligence and is apt to find fault with most people. She generally keeps her mouth shut in situations, but as a narrator, she speaks candidly to the reader. An amusing illustration of Edie's narrative "objectivity" is her treatment of the gossipy Loretta Bird. Edie views Loretta Bird with delightful disdain and constantly comments on the hypocrisy or pretension behind everything Loretta Bird says. Her candor might be less agreeable if she was not equally candid in confessing her own failings. She readily admits how many dumb things her young self did or said simply because she could not think of anything better. Her narration may be subjective, but it is not overtly self-serving.

2. *How does Munro present Chris Watters as a character? What do we know about him?* The important thing for students to realize is that we see Chris Watters through Edie's eyes. When she first meets him, Watters seems poised and charming. He flirts with her so suavely that at first she does not understand he is flirting. Nonetheless, she is affected by his compliments. ("I wasn't even old enough then to realize how out of the common it is, for a man to say something like that to a woman . . . for a man to say a word like *beautiful*.") She begins to

fall in love with him without at first admitting it openly in her narrative, and she observes him with the obsessive attentiveness that characterizes sexual attraction. When his unglamorous fiancée, Alice Kelling, arrives, Edie does not waver in her affection. Observing Watters and his fiancée together, she senses that he has little attraction left for the woman. Her infatuation with Watters leads her (and probably the reader) to excuse the lapses in his character. Edie is utterly sympathetic to his flight (in both senses of the word) from the apparently unsuitable Alice Kelling. It is not until long after Watters has flown away, and Edie realizes that he is not going to write (and by implication, never going to see her again), that the reader begins to appreciate how untrustworthy he was. We actually know very little about Watters (except his exciting profession) beyond what Alice and Edie tell us, and both women have a vested interest in him.

3. *Does the story have a climax? If so, when does it occur?* Students may find this a surprisingly difficult question. Many of them will say the climax of the story occurs in the final paragraph when Edie starts dating Mr. Carmichael, the mailman. That moment may be the story's unexpected conclusion, but the climax occurs a few pages earlier, when the women in the story are having dinner and after Chris Watters has flown away. Trouble erupts when Edie admits to being "intimate" with the pilot. That uproarious scene is the moment of greatest tension, when the real outcome of the story is being decided. Edie's public humiliation pushes her into maturity, and her fervent loyalty to her errant airman will prove sadly misplaced, even though she does not fully understand its effects for some time. Mrs. Peebles protects her from the worst of the gossip by getting rid of Alice Kelling and keeping Edie on as help, but the key events that will affect Edie's future life have now been set in place.

4. *What effect does Munro achieve by titling her story "How I Met My Husband"? Isn't that title misleading?* Munro's title is both accurate and misleading. Edie indeed tells the story of how she met her husband, but he is probably not the character the reader at first assumes she will marry. If the title is a trick, it is a brilliant and insightful one, because by assuming that Chris Watters will eventually marry Edie, the reader shares Edie's own romantic illusions. We tend to give Watters the benefit of the doubt when, in retrospect, we see he was only a charming cad. Notice how Munro keeps other eligible males out of the first three quarters of the story. We—like Edie—have nowhere to fasten our romantic assumptions except on this exotic pilot (exotic to Edie, that is: "I only knew he wasn't from around here" is how she describes him from their initial meeting. That may not sound like much to us, but to a fifteen-year-old farm girl, her words connote a world of mystery). Munro's teasing title, therefore, is a psychological ploy that makes readers identify more closely with the narrator's emotions than they themselves initially realize. Munro's story is a good example for students of how a work's title is an essential part of the text and contributes to its total meaning.

There is an excellent interview with Alice Munro in Volume 3 of *Short Story Criticism* (Detroit: Gale, 1989). This useful volume, which will be found in most large libraries or online, also contains excerpts from reviews and essays on Munro's short fiction.

Luke 15:11–32, The Parable of the Prodigal Son, page 220

The original setting of this famous parable may help clarify its principal theme. Jesus has been preaching in the towns and villages along the road to Jerusalem. He has attracted great crowds, including many disreputable people whom Jewish religious leaders would traditionally have avoided or spurned. The Pharisees (strict practitioners of Jewish dogma) and the Scribes (doctors of religious law) express shock that Jesus would be willing to receive and even dine with sinners (not to mention tax collectors). In Luke 15, Jesus answers their criticism with three parables: the lost sheep, the lost coin, and the prodigal son. These parables implicitly preach compassion and concern for sinners. The righteous, Jesus implies, don't reject sinners; they seek to bring them back to virtue.

Most parables from the Gospels have a slightly abstract quality. Short, simple, and allegorical, they illustrate their morals through exemplary but deliberately generalized characters and action. The characters in "The Parable of the Prodigal Son," however, feel like individual human beings. We experience their motivations, emotions, and thoughts. The parable reads like a short story. The philosopher George Santayana called it "a little masterpiece."

The human theme of the parable might be summarized as "genuine virtue includes the power to forgive" or "true goodness requires love and compassion, not just outward virtue." The elder son has led an outwardly virtuous life, but when his erring brother returns home, he cannot put aside his jealousy to greet him. He resents his father's joy as well as his brother's behavior. His external righteousness has not nourished his heart: he feels neither joy nor compassion. The father, however, rejoices in the younger son's safe return. Santayana thought that the parable also had a psychological theme: "There is more joy in finding what was lost than there would be in merely keeping it."

We tend to remember this parable as the story of the younger son. (Its traditional title, "The Parable of the Prodigal Son," surely contributes to this overly narrow focus.) However, the parable is more richly complex; it is, as the opening line tells us, the story of two brothers: "A certain man had two sons." In his excellent commentary on the Gospel, *Saint Luke* (London: Penguin, 1963), G. B. Caird points out that the loving and generous father has actually lost both sons, "one in a foreign country, the other behind a barricade of self-righteousness. The elder contrived, without leaving home, to be as far away from his father as ever his brother was in a heathen pigsty. Both brothers are selfish, though in totally different ways" (p. 182). The theme of the parable would be less dramatically presented if we did not see (and probably feel some sympathy with) the older brother's uncharitable reaction to the prodigal's return.

The father refuses to be drawn into an argument with his older son. When the son complains to him, he answers with, to quote G. B. Caird again, "the gentlest of rebukes": "Son, thou art ever with me, and all that I have is thine. It was meet that we should make merry, and be glad: for this thy brother was dead, and is alive again; and was lost, and is found."

It may be worthwhile to point out a few memorable details along the way. Ask for someone to define the word *prodigal*. You will be surprised how few students know what it means. (On second thought, maybe you won't be surprised.) You may want to point out that tending pigs—unclean animals, according to Jewish belief—was a horribly degrading job for the younger son. You may also wish to store up the prodigal's phrase, "I will arise and go to my father" in your memory for the next time you teach William Butler Yeats's "The Lake Isle of Innisfree." Yeats's poem begins, "I will arise and go now, and go to Innisfree," and the poet intends a biblical echo to let us know that his return to this spot is no mere weekend holiday. Finally, you might want to point out how the image of killing "the fatted calf" has become a traditional symbol for extravagant and joyful feasting. (Students in the Boston area may recognize it as the name of a local restaurant.)

A good writing exercise is to ask students to retell the parable from the older brother's perspective. Can they present his version of the story without losing the original theme? (For a comic retelling of the parable from just this slant, see Garrison Keillor's satiric skit, *The Prodigal Son*.)

Another version of the prodigal son's story occurs in Rainer Maria Rilke's novel, *The Notebooks of Malte Laurids Brigge* (1910). Rilke's powerful retelling of the parable appears as the last few pages of the book, and it can be easily understood by someone who has not read the rest of the novel. (In the German-speaking world, his parable is frequently anthologized separately.) In Rilke's version, the younger brother is "a man who didn't want to be loved," a person who could not bear the weight and responsibility of another's affection. A savvy student could write an excellent term paper on comparing Rilke's parable to the Gospel original.

Kurt Vonnegut, Jr., HARRISON BERGERON, page 221

"Harrison Bergeron" is a story that tends to divide teachers. Many instructors like Vonnegut's science fiction satire immensely, but a vocal minority of college instructors consider "Harrison Bergeron" too boisterously direct. Students, however, usually find the story powerful and provocative. They consistently rate it among their favorite works. (Science fiction remains one of the few literary genres truly popular among students.) Whenever we have dropped the story from the anthology, letters pour in asking for its reappearance.

We suspect that the gap between some instructors and students reflects differences between high literary culture and popular literary culture. By the Olympian standards of Chekhov's "The Lady with the Pet Dog" or John Cheever's "The Five-Forty-Eight," Vonnegut's gutsy satire is no deathless masterpiece. Its humor is elementary, and its characters are flat. Vonnegut's style has neither the evocative conciseness of a Hemingway nor the lyrical resonance of a Porter.

But to catalogue what Vonnegut is *not* misses what he *is*—a contemporary satirist who uses science fiction conventions to frame his iconoclastic ideas. Vonnegut's roots are in science fiction. Viewed from the vantage of that genre, the particular qualities of "Harrison Bergeron" become more obvious. One particularly interesting classroom use for the story is as a platform for examining the idea of genre. Have students compare it to a classic, realist story like "Araby" or "Paul's Case" and enumerate the differences in style, structure, setting, and characterization.

Science fiction short stories are more concerned with exploring ideas than with careful portrayal of psychological and social reality. The classic sci-fi short story makes a few changes in technology and then speculates on their social, political, psychological, or moral implications. The purpose is not to predict the future, but to explore the possible consequences of present trends abetted by future technology. In "Harrison Bergeron" Vonnegut explores the idea of a futuristic society which has developed the technology to enforce an extreme version of social equality at all costs. Vonnegut's story belongs to a long tradition of anti-utopian satire usually called dystopian fiction. (Modern dystopian fiction developed out of Menippean satire, which emphasizes ideas and employs loose form, a tradition that includes Jonathan Swift's *Gulliver's Travels* and François Rabelais's *Gargantua and Pantagruel*.) Among the best known dystopian literary works are George Orwell's *1984*, Aldous Huxley's *Brave New World*, Eugene Zamyatin's *We*, and Anthony Burgess's *A Clockwork Orange*, but there are countless other anti-utopian novels, stories, films, and television shows. Describing all sorts of possible nightmare futures proved one of the late twentieth century's favorite pastimes.

The theme of "Harrison Bergeron" strikes most students with great force, and they can usually summarize it one way or another. "Down with mediocrity and conformity" is one common answer, or "Individual excellence involves risk." A more elegant and comprehensive statement of the story's themes might be: "By attempting to enforce equality too vigorously, society risks penalizing excellence." Vonnegut's story objectifies the well-known American distrust of intellectuality, and it exaggerates this prejudice to an insane degree. Some students may read the story remembering how in high school or junior high they were ridiculed by classmates for showing interest in ideas or learning. Vonnegut imagines a society so dedicated to a perverse concept of equality that it condemns absolutely all excellence, including good looks, physical grace, and imagination. The story is probably best seen as a fable. It certainly has a moral: don't be afraid to excel. As in most fables, rounded characterization is unnecessary to its purpose.

Until Vonnegut began to reach a wide general audience in the 1960s, his following was mainly limited to science fiction fans—but he has insisted that his work is not confined to science fiction. In an essay, "Science Fiction," for the *New York Times Book Review* (September 5, 1965), he said that until he read the reviews of his first novel, *Player Piano* (New York: Delacorte, 1952), he had not thought of himself as a science fiction writer. "I supposed that I was writing a novel about life, about things I could not avoid seeing and hearing in Schenectady, a very real town, awkwardly set in the gruesome now. I have been a sore-headed occupant of a file drawer labeled 'science fiction' ever since, and I would like out."

There is little criticism on Vonnegut's short stories. What exists can mostly be found in Gale Research's *Short Story Criticism*, vol. 8 (Detroit: Gale, 1991). There are many excellent books and articles on Vonnegut's novels. *The Vonnegut Statement*, edited by Jerome Klinkowitz and John Somer (New York: Delacorte, 1973), is a lively anthology of criticism of Vonnegut's work by various hands. Vonnegut's most interesting commentator, however, may be the author himself. A thick book of interviews, *Conversations with Kurt Vonnegut*, edited by William Rodney Allen (Jackson: UP of Mississippi, 1988), contains a great deal of interesting biographical and literary material. *Harrison Bergeron* was filmed in 1995. Directed by Bruce Pittman and starring Sean Astin, Andrea Martin, and Christopher Plummer, the film is available on videotape.

WRITERS ON WRITING

Kurt Vonnegut, Jr., THE THEMES OF SCIENCE FICTION, page 226

Kurt Vonnegut has spent much of his career telling the literary world that he is not a science fiction writer. He realizes that a genre label keeps a writer from serious critical attention. (Both he and Ursula Le Guin have suffered from such critical stereotyping.) And yet Vonnegut's literary roots are indisputably in science fiction, and his best novels—most notably *Cat's Cradle* (1963) and *Slaughterhouse Five* (1969)—grow out of the genre's enlivening traditions without being limited by its narrower conventions. In Vonnegut's voluminous published interviews, these two passages best represent his interest in using the possibilities of science fiction to describe the technologically dependent modern world. He also discusses the ghettoization of science fiction writers by the literary establishment.

7
Symbol

John Steinbeck, THE CHRYSANTHEMUMS, page 231

John Steinbeck was a writer whose best work came relatively early in his career. His later work—much of it ambitiously allegorical fiction or literary journalism—has tended to obscure his genuine achievement. In the second half of the 1930s, however, Steinbeck published in quick succession his greatest works of fiction: *In Dubious Battle* (1936); *Of Mice and Men* (1937); *The Long Valley* (1938), a collection of stories that includes "The Chrysanthemums"; and his masterpiece, *The Grapes of Wrath* (1939). With great feeling for his characters and often intense emotional impact, he shows us the lives of hard-working people whose desire for fulfillment are balked by custom and circumstance, by powerful economic forces that thrive upon their exploitation, and, at times, by their inability to comprehend their own longings.

Elisa is a complex study in frustration. She is a strong, intense woman with far more energy than she can put to use: we learn at the outset that "even her work with the scissors was over-eager, over-powerful" and that her house is "a hard-swept looking little house, with hard-polished windows." Trapped under a "grey-flannel fog" that encloses the valley like a lid on a pot, she works behind a symbolic barrier: a wire fence "that protected her flower garden from cattle and dogs and chickens" and that also protects her from the wider world. Custom denies her and her restless energy the adequate outlets that men enjoy. She cannot buy and sell cattle as Henry does. She cannot drift about the countryside mending utensils as the traveling repairman does, though his unfettered lifestyle powerfully appeals to her. "That sounds like a nice kind of a way to live," she declares on meeting him. "I wish women could do such things," she tells him later, and adds, "I can sharpen scissors, too. . . . I could show you what a woman might do." But she will never be given such an opportunity.

Besides her frustration at the passive role thrust upon her, Elisa is thwarted because her considerable gifts for nurturing—her "planting hands"—have little value in the wider world. The remarkable chrysanthemums are richly symbolic of her feminine talents. Yet the practical and shortsighted Henry, because the flowers are not a cash crop, says, "I wish you'd work out in the orchard and raise some apples that big." The traveling repairman feigns an interest in the chrysanthemum shoots for his own gain and then throws them on the road and saves the pot. In the sight of the flower pot's contents discarded in the road, Elisa sees the end of her brief interlude of hopes and dreams.

Mordecai Marcus, in his critical commentary, sees Elisa's flowers as substitutes for the children she (now thirty-five) was apparently unable to have ("The Lost Dream of Sex and Childbirth in 'The Chrysanthemums,'" *Modern Fiction Studies* 11 [1965]: 54–58). The suggestion is not unlikely; according to Elizabeth

E. McMahan, however, "it does not necessarily have anything to do with a longing for children" ("'The Chrysanthemums': A Study of a Woman's Sexuality," *Modern Fiction Studies* 14 [1968]: 453–58).

Given to speaking in impassioned poetry ("Every pointed star gets driven into your body"), Elisa is further thwarted by having to live a life devoid of romance. Although kind and considerate, Henry is dull. When he tries to turn a compliment, the best he can do is, "Why—why Elisa. You look so nice!" When pressed for details, he says: "You look strong enough to break a calf over your knee, happy enough to eat it like a watermelon."

Though crafty and unkempt, the repairman has a touch of the poet. He can describe a chrysanthemum as "a quick puff of colored smoke." Elisa's short-lived belief that he values her flowers (and by extension, recognizes her womanliness) releases in her a long-pent eroticism for which the repairman is ill prepared. He changes the subject.

Elizabeth McMahan finds a "purification ritual" in the scene that follows. Elisa "felt shame after her display of passion before the stranger. Now she cleanses herself before returning to her husband, the man to whom she should lawfully reach out in desire," punishing herself with the abrasive pumice until her skin is "scratched and red."

Elisa's battle with her stifled sexuality is conveyed in detail ("her hand went out toward his legs in the greasy black trousers. . . . She crouched low like a fawning dog"). William R. Osborne demonstrates that Steinbeck, in revising the story, heightened Elisa's earthiness and the sexual overtones of her encounter with the repairman (*Modern Fiction Studies* 12 [1966]: 479–84). The revised version as it appeared in *The Long Valley* (New York: Viking, 1938) is the text used in this book.

In the end, Elisa tries to satisfy her spiritual and erotic cravings by asking Henry if they might order wine with their dinner. "It will be enough if we can have wine. It will be plenty." It isn't enough, of course, and she cries "weakly—like an old woman"—she who had briefly thought herself strong. Her new interest in prize fights, in the spectacle of blood-letting she had formerly rejected, manifests Elisa's momentary wish for revenge on men: her desire to repay them for her injured femininity. At least, this is the interpretation of Marcus and of McMahan. Alternatively, one may see in this curiosity about the violence of the boxing ring a woman's envy of the opportunities given to men to work off their aggressions and frustrations in socially acceptable ways.

If your students are familiar with *Of Mice and Men*, you may encourage them to make connections between Elisa's situation and those of the many stunted characters—whether physically, mentally, or emotionally—in that classic novella. A particularly apt comparison, of course, is with Curley's wife, who speaks movingly of the loneliness and confinement of her life and complains, "Seems like they ain't none of them cares how I gotta live." One may also discuss Elisa in terms of George, the protagonist of *Of Mice and Men*, who also—albeit on a much more profound level—responds to the ruin of his dreams by resigning himself to being swallowed up in the emptiness and meanness of spirit all around him.

The story and the novella also bear comparison on a technical level, in that both are attempts by Steinbeck to confine himself to the objective point of view, presenting his characters, as far as possible, from the outside only, and allowing us to deduce what is taking place within them. Steinbeck acknowledged that *Of Mice and Men* was a formal experiment, an attempt to write a work that was simultaneously narrative fiction and playable drama. (Not surprisingly, the work has been successfully adapted as a play, film, TV drama, and opera.) "The Chrysanthemums" also illustrates the objective point of view, or "the fly on the wall" method. After some opening authorial remarks about the land, Steinbeck confines himself to reporting external details. Although the reader comes to share Elisa's feelings, we do not enter her mind; we observe her face and her reactions ("Elisa's eyes grew alert and eager"). This cinematic method of story-telling seems a hardship for the author only in paragraph 109, when to communicate Elisa's sadness he has to have her whisper aloud.

Like his early model, D. H. Lawrence, Steinbeck is fond of portraying people swept up by dark forces of the unconscious. (A curious book for additional reading: Steinbeck's early novel *To a God Unknown* [New York: Viking, 1933], which shows the influence of both Lawrence and Robinson Jeffers.) "The Chrysanthemums" invites comparison with Lawrence's "The Blind Man," which also conveys a woman's struggle for intellectual survival while living with a mindless husband on a farm. Henry Allen is no match, though, for Lawrence's impressive Maurice. If the two stories are set side by side for evaluation, Lawrence's may well seem (in our opinion) the deeper and more vivid. Though finely perceptive, "The Chrysanthemums" has something methodical about it, as if the young Steinbeck were deliberately trying to contrive a short-story masterpiece. But this is to dissent from the judgments of Mordecai Marcus, who thinks it indeed "one of the world's great short stories," and of André Gide, who in his *Journals* finds it in a league with the best of Chekhov (Vol. IV [New York: Knopf, 1951] 79).

Shirley Jackson, THE LOTTERY, page 239

Shirley Jackson's famous story shocks us. By transferring a primitive ritual to a modern American small town and by making clear in passing that the same ritual is being carried out in surrounding towns, the author manages to create in us a growing sense of horror over what is happening. Very early—in paragraphs 2 and 3—she mentions the stones that have been gathered in preparation for the day's events. Not until much later in the story does the importance of the stones begin to dawn.

Students might be asked to sum up the rules of Jackson's lottery, which are simple and straightforward. The male head of each household—or, if he is absent, another representative of the family—draws a slip of paper out of a big black box. One householder pulls out a piece of paper that has a black circle crudely penciled on it. Each member of his family is then obliged to participate in a second drawing. This time the unlucky recipient of the black circle is stoned to death by the other townspeople, including the members of his or her own family. Whatever justification might ever have existed for the ritual has long since been forgotten. The people simply accept the proceedings as an annual civic duty, the up-to-date version of an ancient fertility ritual ("Lottery in June, corn be heavy soon").

What is spine-chilling in Jackson's story is the matter-of-factness with which the ritual is carried out. Each June the townspeople assemble to murder one of their neighbors. The discrepancy between ordinary, civilized, modern behavior and the calm acceptance of something as primitive as human sacrifice gives "The Lottery" a terrible power. Among the story's many ironies, some of the most notable are:

1. *The point of view*. An objective narrator tells the story, remaining outside the characters' minds, yet the narrator's detachment contrasts with the attitude of the author, who presumably, like the reader, is horrified. That the day's happenings can be recounted so objectively lends them both credence and force.

2. *The setting*. The beauty of the June day is out of keeping with the fact that what takes place on the town green is a ritual murder.

3. *The misplaced chivalry*. Though women can be stoned to death in these yearly proceedings, they are whenever possible protected from having to take part in the general drawing (paragraph 13).

4. *The characters*. The townspeople are perfectly ordinary types, "surveying their own children, speaking of planting and rain, tractors and taxes" (3). Mr. Summers is in charge because he "had time and energy to devote to civic activities" (4). Old Man Warner is a stickler for tradition. Neighbors chat amiably. Children play. All are grateful that the proceedings will be over in time for them to enjoy their noon meal.

As a matter of course, even the small son of the victim is given some stones to throw at his mother. That is perhaps the most horrifying detail of all.

The story's very outrageousness raises questions about unexamined assumptions in modern society. Do civilized Americans accept and act upon other vestiges of primitive ritual as arbitrary as the one Jackson imagines? Are we shackled by traditions as bizarre and pointless as the lottery in Jackson's story? What determines the line between behavior that is routine and that which is unthinkable? How civilized in fact are we?

In *Private Demons: The Life of Shirley Jackson* (New York: Putnam 1988), Judy Oppenheimer gives a good account of the story's genesis. Jackson wrote "The Lottery" in 1948 while pregnant with her third child. She had been reading a book on ancient customs of human sacrifice and had found herself wondering how such a rite might operate in the village of North Bennington, Vermont, where she lived.

Peter Hawkes of East Stroudsburg University finds an obstacle to teaching "The Lottery" in that many students think its central premise totally unrealistic and absurd. How, they assume, can this story have anything to do with me? Hawkes dramatizes the plausibility of the townspeople's unswerving obedience to authority. With a straight face, he announces that the Dean has just decreed that every English teacher give at least one F per class to reduce grade inflation, passes around a wooden box, and tells students to draw for the fatal grade! "While I pass the box around the room, I watch carefully for, and indirectly encourage, the student who will refuse to take a slip of paper. When this happens, I ask the class what should be done. Invariably, someone in the class will say that the person who refused to draw deserves the F. Hearing this, the student almost always draws." See Hawkes's account in "The Two Lotteries: Teaching

Shirley Jackson's 'The Lottery'" (*Exercise Exchange*, Fall 1987). We would expect a class to greet this trick with much skepticism! But what if you were to try it on them *before* assigning the story?

In teaching freshman composition, Doris M. Colter of Henry Ford Community College reports terrific success with this story. She starts with the question, "What characteristics of human nature does Jackson's story reveal?" Her students' responses serve as thesis statements for thousand-word essays. Students have to quote from the story itself and must bolster their theses by citing current news stories, films and TV programs, fiction, and any other evidence. One obvious thesis statement, "Rational people can act irrationally," drew a torrent of evidence showing that latent evil lurks in people you wouldn't suspect, perhaps in every one of us (one bright student even cited Conrad's "Heart of Darkness"). Even more stimulating was the thesis "What is fair is not always right" or "Doing things the right way doesn't always mean doing what is right." Jackson's observation rang true: "The people had done it so many times that they only half listened to the directions." Students recalled moments when they had vacuously recited words (prayers, the Pledge of Allegiance) or performed by rote, not thinking about the commitment they were making. One student recalled her own marriage vows, though the marriage had ended in divorce.

More controversial, Colter found, was the thesis, "'The Lottery' is a scathing parody of the Biblical story of redemption." Tessie, like Jesus, might be viewed as a sacrificial lamb whose death will save the community. The names of the characters carry religious connotations. *Delacroix* means "of the cross"; *Adams* connotes the first man. Colter remarks, "Jackson's words—'Steve Adams was in the front of the crowd of villagers, with Mrs. Graves beside him'—are suggestive, at least subliminally, of a close association between the first sinner and the consequences of that sin." If these interpretations seem farfetched, perhaps they didn't seem so to the members of one Michigan school board who thought Jackson's story blasphemous and banned a textbook in which it appeared.

Jackson once remarked that in writing "The Lottery" she had hoped "to shock the story's readers with a graphic demonstration of the pointless violence and general inhumanity in their own lives" (quoted by Lenemaja Friedman, *Shirley Jackson* [New York: Twayne, 1975]). For class discussion: What is the point of Jackson's comment? Is it true? In our own society, what violent behavior is sanctioned? How are we comparable to Jackson's villagers? Don't we too casually accept the unthinkable?

"The Lottery" invites comparison with Hawthorne's "Young Goodman Brown": in each, an entire community is seen to take part in a horrifying rite.

Yet another interpretation is possible. Jackson ran into parental opposition when she announced her intention of marrying fellow Syracuse University student Stanley Edgar Hyman, and some of her housemates warned her of the perils of living with a Jew. Shocked by these early run-ins with anti-Semitism, Jackson once told a friend (according to Judy Oppenheimer) that "The Lottery" was a story about the Holocaust.

There are dangers, of course, in reading more meaning into the story than it will sustain. Jackson herself, in *Come Along with Me* (New York: Viking, 1968), insists that we accept the story at face value. Be sure to read through the excerpt at the end of the chapter that shares Jackson's impressions of readers' responses to her story.

MyLiteratureLab Resources. Interactive reading and critical essay on "The Lottery."

Elizabeth Tallent, No One's a Mystery, page 245

Elizabeth Tallent's story is a wonder of economy. Ask the class to list everything they can tell about the characters and the situation from just the first paragraph. All three main characters of the story are introduced in the first three sentences—the unnamed eighteen-year-old narrator who is having an adulterous affair, her lover Jack, and his wife. The description of the litter-filled pickup truck tells us many things about Jack. The tequila bottle says a great deal both about Jack and his under-the-legal-drinking-age lover. We also note that Jack's wife drives a Cadillac. And we even know that country music is playing on the tapedeck. (We later learn what Rosanne Cash song is playing.)

The form of "No One's a Mystery" is mostly a conversation between two lovers. The narrative conflict is inseparable from their difficult situation. Jack is married to someone else, but the narrator fantasizes about marrying him. There is also an unstated but significant difference between their ages. The lovers recognize these conflicts—how could they not?—but each tries to mollify the problems in a different way. The narrator, who is younger and more optimistic, imagines their life together if Jack divorces his wife; she deals with the problems romantically by removing them. Jacks softens the conflict by poking fun at their affair. He satirizes both the girl's fantasy and himself. He jokingly predicts that in two years she won't even remember the name of "that old guy" in "the filthy dirty pickup truck."

Underneath the banter, however, seems to be real affection beyond sexual infatuation. Both lovers want—on some level—to believe the narrator's dream. By the last line of the story even Jack has temporarily entered the girl's fantasy of romantic escape. Tallent manages to depict the situation with an evocative complexity equal to the troubling circumstances. "No One's a Mystery" exemplifies how potent dialogue can be as a narrative technique.

Finally, it may be interesting to discuss the central symbol of "No One's a Mystery": the locked diary that Jack gives his lover on her birthday. This item not only provides the subject of their conversation, it also serves as the story's complex central image; a completed diary provides a day-by-day account of the past, but an empty diary reminds the owner of the still unwritten possibilities of the future. It is also provocative to note that this diary has a lock and that it was given on the girl's eighteenth birthday—the threshold of her adult life. This symbol so completely pervades the story that it would not be incorrect to describe the plot as the two lovers' differing versions of what this diary will ultimately contain.

Here are some possible answers to the questions given at the end of "No One's a Mystery." Other answers, of equal merit, may occur to you and your students.

Questions

1. How does Jack's present to the narrator, the "five-year diary with a latch and a little key," function symbolically in the story? The diary, described in the very first sentence of the story, clearly comes to symbolize the couple's relationship on a number of levels. A diary, especially one with a lock and key, is a place to keep one's most private thoughts. The narrator is having trouble opening it, suggesting that she is having trouble reaching her deepest feelings, because an open acknowledgment of the realities and the likely outcome of her situation would be almost unbearably painful to her. In fact, she is interrupted in her attempt to open it by the sudden appearance of her lover's wife. The fact that it is a five-year diary suggests what will happen to their relationship through the changes that time will bring, including the fact that as she matures and experiences more of life, she will suffer the loss of her illusions and the ability to maintain them.

2. What do we learn about Jack's marriage? Through what details are these insights communicated? He is obviously unhappily married, or he wouldn't be seeing someone else. He feels that his marriage is stale, at least in part because his wife is unimaginative and predictable (paragraphs 12–14); she is cautious (driving exactly the speed limit), while he is reckless (going at least eighty). They seem totally incompatible: she seems to be materialistic and concerned with appearances (her Cadillac), while he drives a "filthy dirty pickup truck" (paragraph 20) and has been wearing the same scuffed boots for the last two years. Though we are given no details or explanations, his comment that "It must have been a fast divorce" does seem to suggest that he feels trapped in his marriage, unable to get free of it.

3. What does each character's version of their future tell us about him or her? The narrator's versions of the entries she will make in the diary on each of her birthdays describe a beautiful, uncomplicated future for the two of them—a reminder that her current birthday is only her eighteenth and that she still has many hard lessons to learn about the limits of life's possibilities. Jack, somewhat older, is infinitely more skeptical, even cynical: to him, it seems inevitable that he will fail her or she will grow tired of him, or both; he first presents an alternative ending to their relationship, but even when he lets himself be drawn into her fantasies, he undercuts each of her imaginings with a less pleasant detail: "trying to finger-paint with caca," "a middle name she hates," "it's kind of a bittersweet smell."

4. The story ends with Jack's words, "if you want to know the truth." Do you think that the narrator does want to know the truth? Jack obviously feels that she doesn't. All of her hopes depend on his freeing himself from his marriage and marrying her, and since all the details and all of his comments undercut the likelihood of this happening, everything in the story seems to reinforce his view.

5. A quoted phrase can often take on new meanings in a new context. Consider the story's title: Is its application to the story literal or ironic? It could be argued that the narrator, out of a profound need to protect herself from the realities of her situation, is a mystery to herself; but Jack's—and, it would seem, the story's—unrelieved pessimism about the outcome of the relationship suggest that she is no mystery to him and that he is no mystery at all to himself.

Ursula K. Le Guin, THE ONES WHO WALK AWAY FROM OMELAS, page 248

Ursula Le Guin's "The Ones Who Walk Away from Omelas" may be the most unusual story in the book in its relation to the conventions of storytelling. It does not describe the actions of a particular character or small group of characters. It has no plot or protagonist in the usual sense. A skeptical critic of old-fashioned taste might even claim that it is not truly a short story—a fiction, yes, but not a story. Le Guin's central character is an imaginary society. Her plot is a survey of the civilization that leads up to a single shocking revelation. Yet this unusual work has been recognized as a small classic from the beginning. It won a Hugo (science fiction's most prestigious award) after its first magazine appearance, and it has been frequently anthologized in both science fiction and mainstream anthologies.

"The Ones Who Walk Away from Omelas" seems only slightly less unusual when seen in the context of science fiction. The story belongs to a standard genre of science fiction that presents an imaginary civilization in order to criticize some aspect of our own culture, and yet even when viewed against such science fiction conventions, Le Guin's story is an unusually plotless, subtly ironic, and intellectually complex piece. This story's genre is often called utopian fantasy (after Thomas More's 1516 *Utopia*), though some readers might claim that she actually describes a dystopia, a conspicuously flawed society. (Some famous dystopian fictions would include George Orwell's *1984*, Aldous Huxley's *Brave New World*, and Anthony Burgess's *A Clockwork Orange*.) In fact, Le Guin's story borrows elements from both the utopian and dystopian traditions. Le Guin's narrator fervently wants to believe that Omelas is a perfect society; the narrator intends the story to be a utopian vision. The reader, however, sees the horrifying moral compromise at the center of the society, and, as the story's title suggests, the author also sees Omelas as a covert dystopia.

Le Guin's story is overtly disturbing—and all the more so because the narrator blithely accepts the undeserved suffering that shocks the reader. Her penetrating parable raises the same ethical issue as Dostoyevsky's famous tale of "The Grand Inquisitor" from *The Brothers Karamazov*: would it be morally acceptable to purchase universal happiness at the cost of injustice to one innocent child? Le Guin appears to say that no society should rest on such injustice. Surely, it is not coincidental that by the time the narrator tells this story, the happy civilization of Omelas has apparently ceased to exist. In this detail, Le Guin suggests perhaps that Omelas has rotted from within and that any civic or cultural achievements purchased at such a price could not endure.

Although Le Guin admits she knew *The Brothers Karamazov*, she claims in a note on this story, in her collection *The Wind's Twelve Quarters* (New York: Harper, 1975), that she got the idea for the story from William James's essay "The Moral Philosopher and the Moral Life."

Two dominant symbols in "The Ones Who Walk Away from Omelas" deserve discussion. The first is the city of Omelas itself, "bright-towered by the sea." What does Omelas symbolize? At the very least, it suggests the dream of human happiness. ("They were not simple folk, you see," the narrator tells us, "though they were happy.") The citizens of Omelas are "Joyous!" as well as "mature, intelligent, passionate adults whose lives are not wretched." To the narrator at least, Omelas represents a happiness no longer possible in a cheerless time. In a moral sense, however, Omelas symbolizes the hidden compromises that prosperous societies must make. "It is the existence of the child, and their knowledge of its existence," the narrator claims, "that makes possible the nobility of their architecture, the poignancy of their music, the profundity of their science."

The unforgettable symbol of Le Guin's story, however, is the filthy, feeble-minded child locked in the dark cellar. The symbolic significance of this pathetic figure and its grim setting ramifies in many directions. The child is imprisoned in the basement of "one of the beautiful public buildings of Omelas." It is the hidden injustice on which the city is built. The child symbolizes all the evil that citizens in a society must learn to accept without question in order to enjoy their own position. "They all know that it is there, all the people of Omelas," the narrator assures us. The child does not suffer because the good citizens of Omelas are ignorant: it suffers because the citizens are willing to trade its "abominable misery" for their peace, pleasure, and prosperity. Although the child is universally known, it is also kept out of sight. In psychological terms, the child symbolizes the horrible knowledge the conscious mind wishes to repress in order to maintain its happiness.

Students planning to write on Le Guin's story might compare it to Dostoyevsky's powerful "The Grand Inquisitor" (*The Brothers Karamazov*, Volume I, Book 5, Chapter 5). How does Le Guin's parable differ from Dostoyevsky's? How does her work resemble his? Le Guin's other fiction will also provide fruitful areas for research. Her finest work is her novels, especially *The Left Hand of Darkness* (1969), *The Lathe of Heaven* (1971), and *The Dispossessed* (1974). (Her "Earthsea" trilogy of novels for young adults is also superb.) *The Dispossessed* would be a particularly interesting book to compare and contrast to "The Ones Who Walk Away from Omelas" because the novel presents two radically different societies, each with conspicuous strengths and weaknesses that puzzle the narrator, who wrestles with the ethical issue of which to consider superior.

MLL *MyLiteratureLab Resources.* Student essay on "The Ones Who Walk Away from Omelas."

WRITERS ON WRITING

Shirley Jackson, BIOGRAPHY OF A STORY, page 253

Shirley Jackson's commentary is appealingly coy in its refusal to interpret her celebrated story or even to tell us what she had in mind when she wrote it—why should she, after all, limit our responses to the dimensions of her achievement? It is also very interesting to discover that when "The Lottery" first appeared, it was not greeted with the universal acclaim that it now enjoys; it should be pointed out, however, that despite his confession of failure to fully understand the story, Harold Ross wrote to Jackson's husband shortly after its publication to say that "it was a terrifically effective thing, and will become a classic in some category." The last sentence of Jackson's comment, while it may make us laugh out loud on first reading, is ultimately as disturbing in its implications about human nature as "The Lottery" itself.

8
Evaluating a Story

The purpose of this chapter is not to have students judge whether a story is good or bad. What we hope to foster is increased self-consciousness among students about the criteria by which they evaluate literary works. So often beginning students have difficulty in articulating their reactions beyond "I liked it" or "I didn't like it." This chapter explores some basic approaches to evaluating a story by understanding what the work tries to accomplish and the means by which the author proceeds. It then challenges the student to observe that process attentively and to articulate a response based on some modestly consistent principles. It also provides students with a specific work of fiction to ponder and discuss so that the chapter does not become merely an exercise in abstraction. Ultimately, the chapter preaches no particular set of aesthetic values since there are many ways to approach literature. Instead, it stresses the importance of careful observation, analysis, and articulation in all attempts at literary evaluation.

Yiyun Li, A THOUSAND YEARS OF GOOD PRAYERS, page 262

Students may find the protagonist of this quiet but powerful story to be a somewhat remote, exotic figure, but many will be able to relate to the clash between old-country and old-school parents and their assimilated children, and everyone will identify with the wary dance of tensions, assumptions, and misperceptions between parent and adult child. (The theme of culture clash in this story is of particular importance to the author, as can be seen by comparing the daughter's remarks in paragraph 104 with the excerpt from Yiyun Li's autobiographical essay that follows the story.) And as alien as Mr. Shi might seem on the surface, he bears a striking resemblance to a famous and quintessentially American character—Willy Loman in Arthur Miller's *Death of a Salesman*. Like Willy, Mr. Shi can survive only by maintaining comforting illusions about himself and the meaning of his life, and he seems condemned to express his love and hopes for his daughter in ways that complicate their relationship and increase the tension between them.

Here are some possible answers to the questions given at the end of "A Thousand Years of Good Prayers." Other answers, of equal merit, may occur to you and your students.

QUESTIONS

1. *Early in the story, the author says of Mr. Shi that "it is never his habit to talk about the past" (paragraph 13). Why do you think that is?* We all have things in our past that we could wish were otherwise, and there are many different ways of

coping with unpleasant or uncomfortable memories, ranging from one extreme—obsessively revisiting painful experiences in the hope of understanding them differently and coming to terms with them—to the other—sealing such experiences away and avoiding them as much as possible. In evading confrontation with his own unhappy memories, Mr. Shi tends toward the latter approach; he is not especially reflective by nature, and, perhaps more important, he is the product of a culture that emphasized conformity, secrecy, and blind obedience over independence of thought and openness of feeling.

2. *What qualities about Mr. Shi's friend "Madam" make her particularly appealing to him?* Consciously, he admires her for her verve and her energy, for a youthfulness that belies her age (paragraph 13), and for her apparent ability to immerse herself happily in the present moment and in the beauty of the world around her, which makes him think that she "must have been shielded from life's unpleasantness" (paragraph 36)—just as he feels he has tried to do for his wife and daughter (when in fact a good part of what he tried to shield them from was the truth about himself). Unconsciously, perhaps part of her appeal to him is the language barrier: denied access to her past and her real feelings, he can make comforting assumptions about her without fear of having his illusions shattered; and he can unburden himself to her without later worrying that he may have revealed too much.

3. *Mr. Shi says to his daughter, "Talking is telling people how you feel about them, and inviting them to tell you how they feel about you" (paragraph 57). Is this really what he does when he talks to her?* It is and it (mostly) isn't. After making that comment, he says, "You're my daughter and I want you to be happy." But most of the time, without realizing it, what he says to her has less to do with the realities of her personality and her life than it does with his predetermined assumptions about her, about what happened in her marriage, about the proper role of women and of wives, and about life in general.

4. *What is the significance of the story's title?* In paragraphs 37–40, Mr. Shi quotes a Chinese saying to Madam and glosses it with: *"There's a reason for every relationship, that's what the saying means."* Since a thousand years of good prayers are called for to bring about a good father-daughter relationship, he adds: *"Of course, there's a reason for a bad relationship, too—I must be praying halfheartedly for a thousand years for the daughter"*—a comment that is quite characteristic of Mr. Shi, in that he appears to accept his share of responsibility for the situation while completely avoiding the real issues involved.

5. *Do you think that Mr. Shi really loves his daughter? Give the reasons for your answer, with details from the text.* This question should provoke a lively class discussion, and some students will no doubt use Mr. Shi's outburst in paragraph 102 to answer in the negative. But feelings can still be genuine and profound even when they coexist with insensitivity, intolerance, and incomprehension. Part of his anger may lie in the fact that, in a similar situation, rather than indulging his personal feelings the way that she has done, he sacrificed his happiness for family and propriety's sake. You can be disappointed in your children and even angry at them without ceasing to love them dearly.

6. *At paragraph 17 Mr. Shi thinks that "America makes him a new person." In what ways does he seem like a new person? In what ways does he not? After confronting the realities of his life, is he truly a new person at the end of the story?* The full statement is: "America makes him a new person, a rocket scientist, a good conversationalist, a loving father, a happy man." Most interestingly, the statement seems to imply that he was not any of those things before coming to America, although at one time or another in the story he claims to have always been each of these things except a good conversationalist. He is certainly more open and forthcoming than he ever was in China, but as we see at the very end of the story, he can go only so far in this direction, even with himself, without completely destroying the image of himself that he needs to preserve.

7. *How do you think the author wants you to feel about Mr. Shi after you have read the story?* The confidence and assurance of youth, joined with a contemporary climate of intolerance for weakness and failure, may produce some harsh judgments of Mr. Shi among your students, but it should be clear from the tone and the details of the story that the author wants us to feel sad for the desperate means by which Mr. Shi keeps his sense of self intact, and sympathetic to someone who—like all of us, but perhaps more than most of us—is the helpless prisoner of his time, his place, and his own personality.

WRITERS ON WRITING

Yiyun Li, WHAT I COULD NOT WRITE ABOUT WAS WHY I WAS WRITING, page 271

In this excerpt Yiyun Li provides us with a unique glimpse into the mind and feelings of a young Chinese girl in the early 1990s. Deeply distrustful of a brutal and dishonest government and of a system designed to crush every atom of genuineness and individuality, Li alternated between "daytime bravado" in her circumspect but daring criticism of that system and night-time terror at the thought of what it might do to her in retaliation. Though she shared the storeroom every night with girls from "the group who believed their only future was to go to America," she "did not consider [her]self one of them"—quite ironically, since in all likelihood Li was the only one of them who ultimately had the chance to live the "American dreams" that made life bearable for the others. Like Mr. Shi's daughter in "A Thousand Years of Good Prayers," Li associated her native language with evasion, secrecy, and deceit, and turned to English as a language in which one could speak freely and thus, in effect, become a different person. What moved her to tears upon first hearing a tape of Don McLean's 1971 smash hit "American Pie" was not only the sadness of the song itself and the sadness in the singer's voice, but also the need to hope for love and change even in the face of hopelessness and silence.

9
Reading Long Stories and Novels

Leo Tolstoy, THE DEATH OF IVAN ILYCH, page 280

"Beyond any doubt," said Tolstoy's biographer Henri Troyat, writing of *The Death of Ivan Ilych*, "this double story of the decomposing body and the awakening soul is one of the most powerful works in the literature of the world." Completed in 1886, when its author was fifty-seven, this short novel stands relatively late in Tolstoy's literary career. *War and Peace* had appeared in 1863–1869, *Anna Karenina* in 1875–1877. Still to come were *The Kreutzer Sonata* (1889) and *Resurrection* (1899–1900). Tolstoy undertook *The Death of Ivan Ilych* as a diversion from writing his earnest sociological treatise *What Then Must We Do?*—a work that few readers have preferred. Apparently, however, he became deeply involved in the story, for he toiled over it for nearly two years. It was to be (he told a correspondent) an account of "an ordinary man's ordinary death." This irony is stressed in the opening words of Part II: "Ivan Ilych's life had been most simple and most ordinary and therefore most terrible"—a sentence that the poet Randall Jarrell called one of the most frightening in literature.

Tolstoy based details of his story upon actual life: his memories of the agonizing death of his brother Nikolai, whom he dearly loved, and a description of the final illness of one Ivan Ilych Mechnikov, public prosecutor of the Tula district court, which he had heard from Mechnikov's brother.

Jarrell's essay, "Six Russian Short Novels" (reprinted in his posthumous collection, *The Third Book of Criticism* [New York: Farrar, 1965]), supplies further insights. Ilych is a man whose professional existence—being absurd, parasitic, irrelevant, and (to take a term from Sartre) unauthentic—has swallowed up his humanity and blinded him to the real. A life so misled is terrible, more to be dreaded than "real, serious, all-absorbing death." Revealingly, Jarrell quotes from Tolstoy's autobiographical *Confessions*, in which the author tells how he felt himself, like Ivan Ilych, shaped by society into an artificial mold, encouraged in his "ambition, lust of power, selfishness." Tolstoy himself had experienced a season of grave illness; it had given him time to reflect on his life (before his conversion to Christianity) and to find it meaningless. In his *Confessions*, Tolstoy also tells of the death of his brother, who "suffered for more than a year, and died an agonizing death without comprehending what he had lived for, and still less why he should die." Some of the details in *Ivan Ilych* are believed to have been taken from Tolstoy's memory of his brother's struggles against disease and a futile search for a cure.

More clearly perhaps than any other modern writer, Tolstoy succeeds in raising an ordinary man to tragic dignity. As one critic observes, writing not of Tolstoy's story but of the nature of tragedy, "To see things plain—that is *anagnorisis*, and it is the ultimate experience we shall have if we have leisure at the point of death. . . . It is what tragedy is ultimately about: the relaxation of the unthinkable." This statement, from *Tragedy* by Clifford Leech (London: Methuen, 1969), seems closely applicable. Only when Ivan Ilych accepts the unthinkable truth that his life has been lived in vain can he relinquish his tightfisted grip on life, defeat pain, and, on the brink of death, begin to live. Whether or not we accept Tolstoy's religious answer, the story compels us to wonder what in our own life is valuable—what is authentic beyond petty, selfish, everyday cares.

Tolstoy's subtle, complex history of a spiritual awakening may take a while to sink in. When she dealt with the story in class, Dr. Edna H. Musso of Daytona Beach Community College found her students' reaction to it "so lackluster" that she decided that they didn't like the story. The dissenters made a fair case. "[Ilych's] life was so drawn out," wrote one student, "that I was almost relieved when he finally died." In the end, however, the class voted by a margin of two to one that the story should remain in the book. Most students felt that "the interpersonal relationships are true to life" and decided (as one put it) that "it will wake somebody up to see their own life paralleling Ivan's."

Embedded in Ivan's story is another story: Praskovya's story, equally convincing as a study of character development. This insight comes to us from Nancy Adams Malone of Mattatuck Community College, who writes:

> *Question: How does the girl described in paragraphs 68–70 as "attractive, clever" and "sweet, pretty" turn into the appalling woman we meet at the beginning of the story?* To a twentieth-century reader, it's a story as startlingly recognizable as Ivan's own. Praskovya's story begins in paragraph 72 with her first pregnancy. Like any thoughtless, well-meaning, ignorant young couple of our own time, they are not prepared for a change in emotional balance. The successful bride turns into an insecure woman rather suddenly. She's worried about losing her looks, she needs reassurance that her husband still loves her—in short, paragraph 73. Like many other young husbands, Ivan is dismayed by the new whiny, tearful, demanding wife, and does the natural (not the necessary) thing: he retreats. This move naturally increases the insecurity and the demands, a predictably vicious circle. . . .
>
> Paragraphs 80–81 show another recognizable pattern: the family moves, and although the husband may be absorbed in his work, the wife has been uprooted from whatever emotional supports she has had earlier, family or friends or both. Money troubles, of course, don't help. And two children died. Even in a century that didn't expect to raise all its children (as we do), this loss couldn't help being an emotional wound. Paragraph 82 shows how Ivan dealt with all these troubles: "His aim was to free himself more and more from unpleasantness . . . by spending less and less time with his family." Without making any kind of point of it, Tolstoy shows clearly how Ivan contributes to his wife's emotional and spiritual deterioration.

Here are some possible answers to the questions given at the end of *The Death of Ivan Ilych*. Other answers, of equal merit, may occur to you and your students.

QUESTIONS

1. *Sum up the reactions of Ivan's colleagues to the news of his death. What is implied in Tolstoy's calling them not friends, but "nearest acquaintances"?* "The first

thought of each of the gentlemen in that private room was of the changes and promotions [Ivan's death] might occasion among themselves or their acquaintances" (paragraph 5). Then, after these selfish hopes, they thought of their boring duties: to attend the funeral, to visit Ivan's widow (paragraph 18). Tolstoy suggests Ivan had no true friends but only "so-called friends" (18) and "nearest acquaintances" (19).

2. *What comic elements do you find in the account of the wake that Peter Ivanovich attends?* Comic elements include the Church Reader with his imperious tone (paragraph 24), Peter Ivanovich's struggles with the rebellious springs of the couch (33, 37), and his longing to escape to a card game—fulfilled at the end of Chapter I. The widow haggles over the price of a cemetery plot (33–35) and utters the great comic lines (in 40) congratulating herself on enduring Ivan's screams.

3. *In Tolstoy's description of the corpse and its expression (paragraph 27), what details seem especially revealing and meaningful?* See paragraph 27, especially the statement that the corpse's expression contains "a reproach and a warning to the living."

4. *Do you think Tolstoy would have improved the story had he placed the events in chronological order? What if the opening scene of Ivan's colleagues at the law courts and the wake scene were to be given last? What would be lost?* Tolstoy's arrangement of events seems masterly. We see from the first the selfish, superficial circle of colleagues among whom Ivan lived and his rather obtuse, querulous, self-centered wife. As the story unfolds, we follow Ivan's progress from total absorption in his petty affairs to his final illumination. We begin with an exterior view of the context of Ivan's society and end with one man, all alone, confronting eternity.

5. *Would you call Ivan, when we first meet him, a religious man? Sum up his goals in life, his values, and his attitudes.* Ivan seems a usual, sensual man, able to minimize his feelings of guilt (paragraph 59). His life centers in the official world, and he believes it should flow "pleasantly and properly" (82). "The pleasures connected with his work were pleasures of ambition; his social pleasures were those of vanity" (108).

6. *By what "virtues" and abilities does Ivan rise through the ranks? While he continues to succeed in his career, what happens to his marriage?* Ivan performs his official duties with "exactness and incorruptible honesty" (81). He is decorous and rule-abiding, wields power objectively and does not abuse it (65). As he succeeds in the world, his marriage deteriorates (82), and it improves only when Ivan and his wife see little of each other (98).

7. *"Every spot on the tablecloth or the upholstery, and every broken window-blind string, irritated him. He had devoted so much trouble to arranging it all that every disturbance of it distressed him" (paragraph 104). What do you make of this passage? What is its tone? Does the narrator sympathize with Ivan's attachment to his possessions?* Ivan's excessive concern with every spot on the tablecloth seems part of his fussy overemphasis on material possessions. Tolstoy is sug-

gesting, of course, that Ivan's insistent worldliness goes together with a neglect for the welfare of his soul.

8. *Consider the account of Ivan's routine in paragraph 105 ("he got up at nine . . .").* *What elements of a full life, what higher satisfactions, does this routine omit?* Ivan's routine (paragraph 105) omits love, worship, and any profound involvement with his friends and family. His social consciousness is confined to a little chat about politics; his interest in art and science to a little chat about "general topics." Ivan devotes himself only to superficial courtesies and appearances—to maintaining "the semblance of friendly human relations" without any deeper fondness or compassion.

9. *What caused Ivan's illness? How would it probably be diagnosed today? What is the narrator's attitude toward Ivan's doctors?* The illness might be diagnosed as cancer of the abdomen complicated by falling off a ladder while hanging curtains. (The fall is casually described in paragraph 99.) Tolstoy detested physicians and implies (in paragraphs 115–120, 128, 152–153) that Ivan's doctors are know-nothings. In 247, Ivan submits to an examination that he sees as "nonsense and pure deception," like the speeches of certain lawyers to whom he had listened as a judge. The "celebrated specialist" (258–259) seems a quack.

10. *In what successive stages does Tolstoy depict Ivan's growing isolation as his progressive illness sets him more and more apart?* See especially paragraphs 308–311. (Tolstoy's story has a theme in common with Thomas Mann's *The Magic Mountain*: the sick and the healthy are races set apart.)

11. *What are we apparently supposed to admire in the character and conduct of the servant Gerasim?* From our first meeting with him, Gerasim radiates generosity, warm sympathy, and cheerful acceptance of God's will. All men shall come to death, even Ivan Ilych, he affirms (in 50). Gerasim is the good peasant, faithful and devoted, willing to sit all night holding his master's legs (285).

12. *What do you understand from the statement that Ivan's justification of his life "prevented his moving forward, and it caused him most torment of all"? (paragraph 346).* By his reluctance to acknowledge that his life "was not all the right thing" (as he finally admits in paragraph 348), Ivan is hindered in his advance toward enlightenment.

13. *What is memorable in the character of Ivan's schoolboy son? Why is he crucial to the story? (Suggestion: look closely at paragraphs 349–350.)* Ivan's son, though only briefly sketched, is unforgettable. Early in the story (in 48), Peter Ivanovich finds in his eyes ("tearstained" from genuine grief) "the look . . . of boys of thirteen or fourteen who are not pure-minded." As in all masturbators (according to popular lore), "terribly dark shadows showed under his eyes" (268). Yet it is the schoolboy, alone among Ivan's immediate family, who loves Ivan and feels sorry for him. By kissing his father's hand (349), the boy brings on Ivan's illumination.

14. *What realization allows Ivan to triumph over pain? Why does he die gladly?* It is revealed (in paragraph 350) that although Ivan's life has been futile, he still

can set it right. "He whose understanding mattered" (351) now understands him. Able to love at last, Ivan feels sorry not for himself but for his wife and son. When at last he is willing to relinquish the life to which he has desperately clung, death holds no fear.

15. *Henri Troyat has said that through the story of Ivan Ilych we imagine what our own deaths will be. Is it possible to identify with an aging, selfish, worldly, nine-teenth-century Russian judge?* Randall Jarrell seems right in his observation that "we terribly identify ourselves with" Ivan Ilych. "Ivan Ilych's life has been a con-ventional falsehood; *The Death of Ivan Ilych* is the story of how he is tortured into the truth. No matter how alien they may have seemed to him to begin with, in the end the reader can dissociate neither from the falsehood, the torture, nor the truth: he is Ivan Ilych."

Franz Kafka, THE METAMORPHOSIS, *page 317*

Few works of fiction have attracted more critical commentary than Franz Kafka's *The Metamorphosis*. This troubling, mysterious story leaves few readers unmoved, and the tale is a regular favorite among students, who generally find its night-marish premise and tight family focus gripping. Teachers rarely have trouble get-ting students to talk about the story; the challenge is to keep the classroom dis-cussion from becoming entirely impressionistic. Kafka has a famously strange effect on readers: they tend to project their own concerns and obsessions into his stories. While it may be impossible to come to one conclusive reading of *The Metamorphosis*, that impossibility should not prevent readers from working toward careful and consistent readings.

Originally issued as a separate volume in 1916, *The Metamorphosis* is a par-ticularly interesting work to examine because it is the longest piece of fiction that Kafka completed and published during his lifetime. (All three of his novels are in some sense unfinished, and all were published posthumously.) Although the obsessively self-critical Kafka considered the work "imperfect almost to its very marrow," *The Metamorphosis* shows his literary artistry at its most ambitious, powerful, and assured.

To what genre does *The Metamorphosis* belong? One can legitimately describe it as a long short story or a short novel. German readers would gener-ally consider it a novella (a fictional tale of intermediate length), a form they see as one of their central literary traditions, practiced by such masters as Heinrich Von Kleist, E. T. A. Hoffmann, and Hermann Hesse. Famous novellas include Thomas Mann's *Death in Venice*, Henry James's *Daisy Miller*, and Leo Tolstoy's *The Death of Ivan Ilych*. In America, there is no distinct tradition of the novella—despite the missionary efforts of James—so our critics usually consider *The Metamorphosis* a long short story. In any event, both terms imply an extended narrative that combines the concentrated focus of a short story with the novel's insistence on following a course of action to its end. A novella—unlike a novel—almost inevitably centers on a single character (e.g., Gregor Samsa, Ivan Ilych) in the same way that most short stories do, but the author need not compress the narrative into a few exemplary incidents; there is room for the story to unfold more fully. *The Metamorphosis* plunges us into the con-sciousness of its protagonist, Gregor Samsa, in the way a novel might. There is no sense that Kafka is curtailing the narrative at any point. Instead, the story unfolds at its own deliberate pace.

The instructor may want to point out the overall structure of the story, which is unique in Kafka's fiction. *The Metamorphosis* is divided into three equal sections. Many critics have noticed that this structure resembles a three-act play. In his introduction to *The Complete Stories of Franz Kafka* (New York: Viking, 1983), John Updike observes that in each "act," "the metamorphosed Gregor Samsa ventures out of his room, with tumultuous results." The British scholar Ronald Gray elaborates how each section ends with a climactic moment:

> In the first, Gregor Samsa awakens to the realisation that he has turned into an insect and emerges from his bedroom to be driven back by his infuriated father. In the second, he tries to accommodate himself to his absurdly hideous predicament . . . again, a brief sally into the living room is repulsed by the father, this time even more violently, as he pelts Gregor with apples. In the third, Gregor comes out while his sister is playing the violin, entranced by the music which seems to be the "food" he has so long been unable to find, but a third attack drives him back to die alone and untended. . . . After Gregor's death they turn with relief to the happier life that now awaits them. (Reprinted in *Franz Kafka's The Metamorphosis* in Harold Bloom's "Modern Critical Interpretations" series.)

Although Gray is wrong in citing a third "attack" on Gregor (he returns the last time to his room unmolested—at least physically), he does clarify the basic structure of the story. Heinz Politzer offers a more schematic structure in his *Franz Kafka: Parable and Paradox* (Ithaca, NY: Cornell UP, 1966): "The first part shows Gregor in relation to his profession, the second to his family, and the third to himself." This structure does not become annoying, Politzer claims, "because the three parts are united by Gregor's fate, which is and remains an enigma."

The long list of questions at the end of the story is designed to focus students on interesting aspects of the plot and situation they may have overlooked in their initial reading. Considering these narrative details may suggest themes and interpretations that may not have initially occurred to them.

Here are some possible answers to the questions given at the end of *The Metamorphosis*. Other answers, of equal merit, may occur to you and your students.

QUESTIONS

1. *What was Gregor's occupation before his transformation? How did he come to his particular job? What keeps him working for his firm?* The question of Gregor's employment is crucial to understanding the story. Gregor works as a traveling salesman—a situation he dislikes. He wants to quit his job, but the pressure to support his family and pay off his bankrupt father's business debts keeps him trapped in his career. Gregor's boss holds the father's debts, so his job reinforces his sense of obligation to his family. The influential Kafka scholar Walter H. Sokel has observed that *Schuld*, the German word for *debt*, also means *guilt* in German. The symbolism of its double meaning has not been lost on Freudian and Marxist critics. Both family debts and family guilt force Gregor into intolerable employment.

2. *When Gregor wakes to discover he has become a gigantic insect, he is mostly intent on the practical implications of his metamorphosis—how to get out of bed, how to get to his job, and so forth. He never wonders why or how he has been changed. What does this odd reaction suggest about Gregor?* The only fantastic element present in *The Metamorphosis* is its opening sentence. After that unexplained event, the subsequent action unfolds in a bizarrely realistic fashion. Perhaps the strangest detail of all is Gregor's matter-of-fact acceptance of his transformation into a monstrously large insect. He never wonders why or how he has been changed from a young man into vermin. Although he worries about a great many other things, he accepts his new situation absolutely. This narrative detail is surely part of what gives Kafka's tale its uniquely brooding mystery. For some unstated reason, Gregor acknowledges the inevitability of his fate. Establishing why Gregor and his family so naturally accept his transformation into a despicable creature is central to any interpretation of the story. (See comments on question 10 for some common interpretations of Gregor's metamorphosis.)

3. *When Gregor's parents first see the gigantic insect (paragraph 25), do they recognize it as their son? What do their initial reactions suggest about their attitude toward their son?* Although Gregor's parents are horrified to see his new shape, they never doubt that the huge insect is their son. They do not, for instance, fear that some supernatural monster has occupied their son's room. They instinctively recognize the vermin as Gregor. The mother's first reaction seems to be horror or—some critics claim—deep shame. His father is angry and then starts to weep. The family is already publicly embarrassed that Gregor appears to have barricaded himself in his room and has missed his business trip. The suspicious chief clerk from his office has arrived to check on him. Kafka never explains why the parents recognize their transformed son, but the implication seems to be that his new monstrous form manifests something latent in the old Gregor. What that characteristic is has become the crux of most critical debates.

4. *How does each family member react to Gregor after his transformation? What is different about each reaction? What is similar?* Each of the family members acts differently to him although they all feel ashamed of his condition. His sister initially shows the most concern for him. Her loving care sustains him, and when she abandons him (in Part III), he loses his grip on life. Gregor's mother is full of sympathy for her son but, old and asthmatic, she is ineffective in helping or defending him. Gregor's father lacks all compassion for his son's situation. He mercilessly drives Gregor back into his room the first two times he emerges. He resents having to work again, and subsequent events suggest that he had earlier been exploiting his son by forcing Gregor to pay off the family debts.

5. *What things about Gregor have been changed? What seems to have remained the same? List specific qualities.* While Gregor has undergone a complete physical metamorphosis, he changes very little mentally—at least at first. He is still beset by all his usual worries. Gradually, however, Gregor seems to regress. He accepts his own ineffectiveness and passivity; he also accepts his own monstrous unworthiness and repulsiveness. He becomes childlike in his complete dependence on

his family, whereas earlier he had supported them. He not only becomes filthy but slowly loses any shame about his squalid condition. Eventually, he even accepts his own death. "His own belief that he must disappear was, if anything, even firmer than his sister's" (paragraph 89). He has no resentment for his family; he thinks of them "with deep emotion and love." Monstrous and dying, he remains an obedient son.

6. The Metamorphosis *takes place entirely in the Samsa family apartment. How does the story's home setting shape its themes?* Except for the final scene, all of *The Metamorphosis* takes place in the Samsa family apartment. This claustrophobic setting underscores the domestic nature of the story. Kafka's psychological and mythic focus is on the family—especially the relationship between child and parents. It is worth noting that the two Samsa children have Christian names—Gregor and Grete—whereas Mr. and Mrs. Samsa lack first names. In fact, the parents are usually called by the archetypal names of *Father* and *Mother*. (Curiously, although Kafka himself was Jewish, he makes the Samsas Christian—notice the reference to Christmas and how the family makes a sign of the cross over Gregor's dead body; the story suggests Christian as well as Jewish readings.) As Gregor hides in his room, he listens to his family. He becomes a passive witness to their lives. Some critics feel that the central action of the story involves the family more than Gregor; his transformation is only the catalyst to their drama. It might be worth asking the class if they agree or disagree with this emphasis.

7. *What family member first decides that they must "get rid" of the insect? What rationale is given? In what specific ways does the family's decision affect Gregor?* Gregor's sister ultimately decides that "we must try to get rid of it" (paragraph 80). Her attitude has gradually changed from one of solicitous concern to hostility. She does not refer to Gregor by name; he is now an *it*. "I refuse to utter my brother's name in the presence of this monster," she declares. At this point Gregor starts to lose his human identity. She argues that they have been mistaken to think that this creature is her brother. Why? If this were Gregor, she maintains, "he would've realized a long time ago that it's impossible for human beings to live with a creature like that, and he would've left on his own accord" (paragraph 85). Gregor, in other words, would not have added to the family burden but would have eased it. His role, she implies, is that of a provider, not an embarrassing dependent. The sister's announcement provides a turning point in the story. Already weak and injured, Gregor declines into death.

8. *How does the family react to Gregor's death?* When the charwoman announces that Gregor is dead, the parents rush out of bed to check the evidence in their son's room. "Well," says Gregor's father, "now thanks be to God." They cross themselves, but only Grete shows some sympathy. "Just look how thin he was," she observes. When Gregor's mother invites her daughter to sit beside them in their bedroom, Mrs. Samsa already has "a sad smile." When they finally emerge from the bedroom, they appear to have been crying, but their grief is short-lived. They are openly relieved that Gregor is gone. They soon appear more vigorous and determined. They make plans for the future. When the charwoman disposes of the body, she is grinning. The family is now openly confident and affectionate for the first time.

9. *Does Grete change in the course of the story? If so, how does she change?* One of the strangest features of *The Metamorphosis* is its closing paragraph. Having lost their only son, the Samsas undergo a quiet transformation into a secure and loving family. The final image is quite unexpected. The parents notice Grete becoming "more vivacious." In spite of all their recent troubles, "she had blossomed into a pretty and shapely girl." It is time, they decide, "to find her a good husband." Immediately after Gregor's unceremonious funeral, they are already planning a marriage. At least one critic has claimed that the title, *The Metamorphosis*, refers to Grete rather than Gregor; she has been transformed from a girl into a young woman. Her transformation brings the promise of new life while Gregor's brought only death.

10. *In what ways is Gregor's metamorphosis symbolic?* The chief concern in interpreting *The Metamorphosis* with students is to read Kafka's story as symbolic rather than allegorical. Kafka resists conventional interpretation; no one tightly consistent reading will fit all the facts of the tale. Part of Kafka's particular genius was in creating seemingly allegorical situations (as in *The Castle* and *The Trial*) that refuse to fall into neat patterns. Allegory's central technique—like Kafka's—is the extended metaphor, but whereas allegory consistently equates the metaphor with a specific meaning, Kafka's metaphors suggest multiple interpretations. The thrill and mystery of reading Kafka's fiction is the sense that one is always on the brink of understanding everything followed by the discovery of some new fact that changes or contradicts one's own theory.

There are a great many interpretations of Gregor Samsa's metamorphosis. One inarguable observation is that his transformation is horrible. He has become a huge insect that everyone finds disgusting; he himself is ashamed of his new form and hides when his sister enters his room to feed him. One can read the entire story as an extended metaphor, an anti-allegory that no single interpretive key will unlock, in which Gregor's metaphorical identity as a revolting insect becomes literally true. This line of inquiry stills begs the question of *why* Gregor became an insect. Kafka's text is famously silent on this crucial point; it can only be approached by implication. The two most common interpretations are that Gregor's transformation is a *retribution* for some unstated crime (whether it is his own crime, his father's, his family's, or society's, depends on the critic's orientation) or that his change reflects a *wish fulfillment* on his part to abandon his job and be cared for by his family (whether this is a self-asserting wish for freedom or a shameful regression to childhood also depends on the critic's approach).

There is an immense amount of commentary available on *The Metamorphosis*. Harold Bloom's "Modern Critical Interpretations" series contains a volume of essays on the story, *Franz Kafka's The Metamorphosis* (New York: Chelsea, 1988). This compilation includes particularly interesting essays by Martin Greenberg, Stanley Corngold, Ronald Gray, and Walter H. Sokel. For a general study of the author, Erich Heller's *Franz Kafka* (Princeton: Princeton UP, 1974) remains a fine short introduction. Page for page, however, Walter H. Sokel's pamphlet *Franz Kafka* (New York: Columbia UP, 1966) is probably the best introduction in English; moreover, it provides a compelling psychological reading of *The Metamorphosis*. Roy Pascal's *Kafka's Narrators* (Cambridge UP, 1982) provides an extremely insightful discussion of how the impersonal narrator of *The Metamorphosis* submerges the reader in Gregor's consciousness in subtle and unexpected ways.

Students curious to know exactly what sort of bug poor Gregor became should consult Vladimir Nabokov's lively *Lectures on Literature* (New York: Harcourt, 1980). Nabokov, who was not only a magisterial novelist but also a renowned entomologist, explores the nature of the *"ungeheures Ungeziefer"* (Kafka's German phrase for Gregor's new shape, which can be translated either as *gigantic insect* or *monstrous vermin*). No one has been able to identify precisely what sort of insect Kafka had in mind—a mystery that almost certainly was the author's intention. Nabokov, however, discusses what sort of bug he was not. Gregor, Nabokov resolves, was definitely not, as some readers often assume, a cockroach. Not all critical issues in Kafka are, it appears, beyond resolution. An interesting half-hour video cassette of Vladimir Nabokov (played by Christopher Plummer) analyzing *The Metamorphosis* is available from Library Video Company at <www.libraryvideo.com>.

One final note: an intriguing tribute to Kafka, one that sums up the powerful appeal of his stories, is that of the dramatist Vaclav Havel, former president of Czechoslovakia:

> In Kafka I have found a portion of my own experience of the world, of myself, and of my way of being in the world. I will try . . . to name some of the more easily defined forms of this experience. One of them is a profound, banal, and therefore utterly vague sensation of culpability, as though my very existence were a kind of sin. Then there is a powerful feeling of general alienation, both my own and relating to everything around me, that helps to create such feelings; an experience of unbearable oppressiveness, a need constantly to explain myself to someone, to defend myself, a longing for an unattainable order of things. (From a lecture on Kafka delivered at Hebrew University in Jerusalem in April 1990; *New York Review of Books,* September 27, 1990.)

Has the mind of Gregor Samsa ever been more concisely or more accurately described? For a writing assignment, students might be given a copy of Havel's remarks and asked to show, by referring to particulars in the story, how they apply to *The Metamorphosis*.

 MyLiteratureLab Resources. Biography, critical overview, and bibliography for Kafka.

WRITERS ON WRITING

Franz Kafka, DISCUSSING *THE* METAMORPHOSIS, page 348

What would a reader give for a *Paris Review* interview with Franz Kafka? There are so many unresolved issues about both his life and his work. The closest one will ever come is Gustav Janouch's *Conversations with Kafka,* a book-length memoir of the short-lived author by a young friend and admirer who knew him in Prague.

Janouch's father worked with Kafka at the Workmen's Accident Insurance Institution and introduced his literary son to his colleague. Kafka soon became the boy's mentor. As Janouch records, Kafka was masterfully evasive about interpreting his work. His unguarded comments to the young Gustav about the autobiographical elements in *The Metamorphosis* are the closest the author ever came to discussing the personal origins of the novella. Janouch also intimately portrays the anguished self-doubt Kafka felt about his own work.

Be advised that there are two editions of *Conversations with Kafka*. The later edition (New York: New Directions, 1971) is by far the better one because it contains a great deal of material accidentally dropped from the first version.

10
Critical Casebook:
Flannery O'Connor

Flannery O'Connor is generally acknowledged as one of the greatest American fiction writers of the last century—a reputation that rests mostly on her emotionally powerful, incisively drawn, and exuberantly original short stories. Although her prose style is lucid and accessible, her fiction is by no means easy going. The stories violate the usual standards of good taste—presenting violence, racism, madness, deceit, despair, and sexual perversity—and challenge the reader's worldview. She is at once the darkest satirist and brightest religious visionary in modern American fiction. Students may find her initially troubling, perhaps even infuriating, but few contemporary writers so deeply reward study and discussion.

If you think Flannery O'Connor's Southern world is likely to strike your students as remote and unfamiliar, you might begin by telling the class a little about it. Should your library own a copy of Barbara McKenzie's book of photographs, *Flannery O'Connor's Georgia* (Athens: U of Georgia P, 1980), by all means bring it in and show it around. McKenzie recalls John Wesley's remark in "A Good Man Is Hard to Find," "Let's drive through Georgia fast so we won't have to look at it much," and supplies a series of pictures of some "oppressive" landscapes. Besides, there is a stone marker announcing Toomsboro, a town whose name foreshadows the ending of "A Good Man Is Hard to Find," and a glimpse of a pig parlor of which Mrs. Turpin of "Revelation" might have been proud.

An essay worth quoting aloud is Alice Walker's sympathetic tribute, "Beyond the Peacock: The Reconstruction of Flannery O'Connor," *In Search of Our Mothers' Gardens* (New York: Harcourt, 1983). "She was for me," declares Walker, "the first great modern writer from the South," and she praises O'Connor for not trying to enter the minds of her black characters, not insisting on knowing everything, on being God. "After her great stories of sin, damnation, prophecy, and revelation, the stories one reads casually in the average magazine seem to be about love and roast beef."

O'Connor's *Collected Works* has been accorded the honor of appearing in the Library of America series. This volume, along with three works of O'Connor criticism, was reviewed by Frederick Crews in the April 26, 1990, issue of the *New York Review of Books*. Crews has interesting things to say about O'Connor's debt not only to New Criticism, but also to Edgar Allan Poe and Nathanael West. He offers insight as well into what he calls her "stern fanaticism" and her "twisted feelings about segregation."

FLANNERY O'CONNOR'S FICTION

A GOOD MAN IS HARD TO FIND, page 358

Without some attention to its Christian (specifically, Catholic) assumptions, this story won't make much sense to students, who might mistake it for a tale of meaningless violence. Their seeing what O'Connor is driving at depends on their reading with great care the conversation about Jesus between the Misfit and the grandmother, and the account of the old woman's epiphany and death (paragraph 137).

Who is the central character? Clearly, the grandmother. This is her story from beginning to end, the story of her long overdue moral and spiritual growth. She causes things to happen; the Misfit merely reacts to her. She persuades the family to depart from the main road to see the old plantation. She causes the accident by letting the cat out of the basket. She dooms the family when she recognizes the Misfit. Her final gesture incites the Misfit to murder her.

O'Connor loves to pick unlikely, ordinary people and show how, by the sudden and unexpected operation of God's grace, they are granted the possibility of sanctity. In "A Good Man Is Hard to Find" the nitwit grandmother dies loving (and presumably forgiving) the Misfit. In "Revelation" the smug Mrs. Turpin is blessed with a vision of salvation. In the course of "A Good Man Is Hard to Find," the grandmother grows and changes. At first, she seems a small-minded biddy, selfish or at least self-centered, capable of stupid remarks like "Oh look at the cute little pickaninny!" (18) and "People are certainly not nice like they used to be" (36), capable of blaming Europe for "the way things were now" (45), of regretting that she hadn't married Mr. Teagarden "because he was a gentleman and had bought Coca-Cola stock when it first came out" (27).

In the end, when we are told that "her head cleared for an instant," the grandmother becomes newly perceptive. She reveals—and offers to the Misfit— her vast, compassionate heart. We have no reason to doubt the Misfit's shrewd remark, "She would have been a good woman . . . if it had been somebody there to shoot her every minute of her life." In slaying her, the Misfit has done her a tremendous favor: he has made a martyr of her. For one moment just before she dies, the old lady doubts Jesus, or at least feels forsaken: "Maybe he didn't raise the dead" (134). It is an understandable reaction, after the colossal shock she has undergone: she knows that her family has been massacred. But this moment of confusion passes. In O'Connor's Catholic worldview, the grandmother is headed straight to heaven for her final Christ-like act of love the moment before she dies. She realizes that there is a chance that the Misfit will repent, and she reaches out to him lovingly, as though he were a child. By this time, she already knows that the Misfit's gang has murdered her son and daughter-in-law and all the children. The Misfit may be a ruthless murderer, but that doesn't prevent her from loving him and hoping for his redemption. Symbolically, in death the old woman's body lies with legs in the form of a cross, a look of childlike sweetness on her face. The Misfit, naturally, is glum, having just declined a chance for his own salvation.

The scene at Red Sammy's Barbecue is no mere filler. It tightens the suspense and enforces the hint that the much talked-about Misfit is bound to show his face. In his highway signs, Red Sammy boasts of his uniqueness: NONE LIKE FAMOUS RED SAMMY'S. He considers himself a hard-to-find good man. In calling him a good man (36), the grandmother first introduces the theme. The barbecue proprietor agrees with her, even declares, thinking of how many bad characters are on the loose these days, "A good man is hard to find" (44). In the end, the title leaves us thinking: yes, a good man (a saint) certainly is hard to find. We find, at the end, a serenely good woman whose salvation has been achieved only through traumatic suffering and the amazing arrival of grace.

An insightful and outspoken student might wonder about the appropriateness of imposing Catholic terms of redemption on all these Southern Protestants. (That the eight-year-old is named John Wesley suggests that the family is at least nominally Methodist.) The story may draw other objections as well. O'Connor's use of familiar racist epithets will outrage some African American students unless they see that O'Connor is only reporting faithfully how the characters think and talk, not condoning it or thinking that way herself. This will be a problem, too, in teaching "Revelation" (and most Faulkner novels and *Huckleberry Finn*).

For O'Connor's own reading of this famous story, see her critical comments following the stories in this chapter. Her interpretation will certainly startle many students reading the story for the first time. If you choose to consider O'Connor's comments in class, it may be worth asking how authoritative a writer's interpretation of her own work is. Are there limitations or inherent biases in a writer's self-assessments? According to the intentional fallacy, we cannot uncritically accept an author's statement of intended meaning, because the author is unable to see his or her own work objectively. An author necessarily sees the finished work through the veil of the original intent, with the possibility of projecting onto the text meanings that were intended but that have not been realized and therefore are not communicated to any other reader through the text itself. Still, knowing an author's conscious intentions may help point a reader in the right direction—at least in general terms.

In an incisive essay on Flannery O'Connor, Clara Claiborne Park points out that while O'Connor may have objected to readers' attempts to reduce her stories to literal meanings or themes, she herself tended to do so in her own commentaries on the stories. Despite their excellence, the stories, when so reduced, may be faulted as oversimplified fables of Christian salvation through suffering. "A Good Man Is Hard to Find" seems vulnerable to this charge. Park observes: "As incursions of grace through arson and through murder and through sudden stroke become familiar to the point of predictability, all moral ambiguity evaporates, leaving the stories that puzzled us all too clear" (*Rejoining the Common Reader*, Chicago: Northwestern UP, 1991). A question for class discussion is: can O'Connor be defended against this charge? (Perhaps she intends no ambiguity.) Evidence of the story's depth and complexity can be found in a volume containing critical essays by various hands, *A Good Man Is Hard to Find*, edited by Frederick Asals (in the series "Women Writers: Texts and Contexts," New Brunswick: Rutgers UP, 1993).

[MLL] *MyLiteratureLab Resources*. Biography, critical overview, and bibliography for O'Connor. Longman Lecture on "A Good Man Is Hard to Find."

REVELATION, page 368

"People talk about the theme of a story," Flannery O'Connor wrote, "as if the theme were like the string that a sack of chicken feed is tied with. They think that if you can pick out the theme, the way you pick the right thread in the chicken-feed sack, you can rip the story open and feed the chickens. But this is not the way meaning works in fiction. . . . A story is a way to say something that can't be said any other way, and it takes every word in the story to say what the meaning is" ("Writing Short Stories," *Mystery and Manners: Occasional Prose*, selected and edited by Sally and Robert Fitzgerald [New York: Farrar, 1980]).

"Revelation," a beautifully plotted story, builds slowly to its crisis or turning point: Mary Grace's assault on Mrs. Turpin in the doctor's office or, more specifically, the moment when she declares, "Go back to hell where you came from, you old wart hog." The climax we take to be Mrs. Turpin's challenge to God, "Who do you think you are?"; and the conclusion, her shocked acceptance of the final revelation—the vision of the bridge to heaven.

Significantly, the book that strikes Mrs. Turpin and shatters her view of herself is called *Human Development*. Even the hogs are fat with meanings. They resemble Mrs. Turpin, who is overweight, with eyes small and fierce, and whom Mary Grace calls a wart hog. In her perplexity, Mrs. Turpin is herself like the old sow she blinds with the hose. Her thoughts about pigs resemble her thoughts on the structure of society, "creating a hierarchy of pigs with a pig astronaut at the top"—Josephine Hendin writes in *The World of Flannery O'Connor* (Bloomington: Indiana UP, 1970). Mrs. Turpin gazes into her pig parlor "as if through the very heart of mystery." As darkness draws near—and the moment of ultimate revelation—the pigs are suffused with a red glow. Contemplating them, Mrs. Turpin seems to absorb "some abysmal life-giving knowledge." What is this knowledge? Glowing pigs suggest, perhaps, the resurrection of the body. As Sister Kathleen Feeley says in her excellent discussion of this story, "Natural virtue does as much for fallen men as parlor treatment does for pigs: it does not change their intrinsic nature. Only one thing can change man: his participation in the grace of Redemption" (*Flannery O'Connor: Voice of the Peacock* [New Brunswick: Rutgers UP, 1972]).

Epiphanies, O'Connor finds, are imminent in the drabbest, most ordinary life. She makes the doctor's waiting room the setting for prophecy, and makes a pigpen the doorstep of beatitude. Mrs. Turpin, bigoted and smugly self-congratulatory, seems an unlikely recipient for a revelation direct from God; yet even she is capable of accepting such a revelation and of being transformed and redeemed by it. Like Malamud's Angel Levine, Mary Grace, a pimpled Wellesley girl with emotional difficulties, seems an unlikely messenger of the Lord. But Mary Grace—an agent of redemption, as her name indicates—announces herself as a kind of biblical prophet: with "churning face," she goes into a trance. Her eyes change color, and Mrs. Turpin knows that the girl is about to utter some profundity meant for Mrs. Turpin alone.

Like the handwriting on the wall, Mary Grace's utterance is baffling and mysterious. Sorely troubled, Mrs. Turpin revolves it over and over in her mind all afternoon. She knows from Whom the message came: "What do you send me a message like that for?" (paragraph 179), and her impulse is to defend herself, to argue back at God. Her irate challenge to the Almighty, "Who do you think you are?" is exactly the question God is asking *her*. God replies immediately: He is Lord of all creation, whose natural world "burned for a moment with a transparent intensity." He is the giver of life and of death, as Mrs. Turpin realizes when she sees Claud's truck, whose driver and passengers at any moment could be destroyed. Then, in the final revelation, God shows her exactly who *she* is:

just another sinner, whose pride in her virtues must perish in eternal light. For Mrs. Turpin, the hard road toward sainthood lies ahead.

"I like Mrs. Turpin as well as Mary Grace," said O'Connor in a letter to a friend. "You got to be a very big woman to shout at the Lord across a hogpen. She's a country female Jacob. And that vision is purgatorial" (letter to Maryat Lee, May 15, 1964, in *The Habit of Being: Letters of Flannery O'Connor*, ed. Sally Fitzgerald [New York: Farrar, 1979] 577).

Joyce Carol Oates, in a comment on "Revelation," finds the story intensely personal. Mary Grace is one of those misfits—"pathetic, overeducated, physically unattractive girls like Joy/Hulga of 'Good Country People'"—of whom the author is especially fond. "That O'Connor identifies with these girls is obvious; it is *she*, through Mary Grace, who throws that textbook on human development at all of us, striking us in the foreheads, hopefully to bring about a change in our lives" ("The Visionary Art of Flannery O'Connor," in *New Heaven, New Earth* [New York: Vanguard, 1974]). In a survey of fiction, Josephine Hendin also stresses O'Connor's feelings of kinship for Mary Grace. As the daughter of a genteel family who wrote "distinctly ungenteel books," O'Connor saw herself as an outsider: "She covered her anger with politeness and wrote about people who did the same." In "Revelation," Mary Grace's hurling the book is an act of violence against her mother, for whom Mrs. Turpin serves as a convenient stand-in ("Experimental Fiction," *Harvard Guide to Contemporary Writing* [Cambridge: Harvard UP, 1979]).

One of the last stories Flannery O'Connor finished, "Revelation" appeared in her posthumous collection *Everything That Rises Must Converge* (New York: Farrar, 1965). Walter Sullivan believes that Mrs. Turpin's vision of the bridge of souls, with its rogues, freaks, and lunatics, is the author's vision of humanity and her favorite cast of characters. The story stands as "a kind of final statement, a rounding off of her fiction taken as a whole" ("Flannery O'Connor, Sin, and Grace," in *The Sounder Few: Essays from the Hollins Critic*, ed. R. H. W. Dillard, George Garrett, and John Rees Moore [Athens: U of Georgia P, 1971]).

At least one African American student has reacted angrily to "Revelation," calling it the "most disgusting story I've ever read" and objecting to "the constant repetition of the word *nigger*." This is a volatile issue and involves a genuine concern. If possible, the matter should be seriously addressed in class rather than ignored or brushed aside. No one would assume that because *Othello* depicts several murders, it therefore endorses murder, but in these sensitive times some students will take the occurrence of racial epithets in a story as proof of racism on the part of the author. Thus, you might begin by pointing out—or better, lead the students to point out—that while the word appears frequently in the dialogue and in Mrs. Turpin's interior monologues, O'Connor does not employ it when speaking in her own voice: her depiction of the reflexive racism of her characters does not constitute an endorsement of racism. The use and repetition of the word *nigger* will inevitably create an uncomfortable atmosphere in class and will wound the feelings of African American students; such usage is to be found in much literature of the past, as witness the constant controversy over *Huckleberry Finn*. But literature must be given the scope to tell the truth about human experience including its uglier manifestations, however painful the truth may sometimes be. We cannot properly come to terms with the endemic racism of America's past (and present) by euphemising it out of our collective memory. It seems rather ironic, to say the least, that we should insist—quite rightly—that our culture is profoundly racist and at the same time seek to suppress classic works of literature for their accurate depiction of that racism.

 MyLiteratureLab Resources. Biography, critical overview, and bibliography for O'Connor.

PARKER'S BACK, page 382

"Parker's Back" is a fitting coda to Flannery O'Connor's life work in that, like so many of her finest fictions, it concerns itself with a flight from—and ultimate submission to—the relentless power of saving grace. As mentioned earlier, students schooled in and comfortable with the prevailing tendencies of contemporary American short fiction may initially have a hard time with O'Connor for a number of reasons, one of which is the "Southern grotesque" element in her fiction. Another, of course, is the all-pervading religious sensibility in her work; as her fellow Southern novelist Madison Jones has observed, "O'Connor is one of only a tiny few Southern writers who survived—with strong faith intact—the rapid diminishment after World War II of the older vision . . . a fundamental assumption that individual human beings are participants in the mystery of a universal drama of good and evil directed by some kind of divinity beyond man's understanding" ("O'Connor and Current Fiction," *Flannery O'Connor: In Celebration of Genius*, ed. Sarah Gordon [Athens, GA: Hill Street P, 2000]). Yet another of the difficulties that she presents, and far from the least of them, is the cool detachment, even steeliness, of her approach to her graceless protagonists. As Fred Chappell points out in the same volume, "O'Connor is cooler than [Baudelaire, Mark Twain, Poe, and other 'masters of the sardonic']. Icy disdain pervades her pages, and she is as religiously pitiless as Virgil admonishes Dante to become as he guides the trembling poet through the horrors of the Inferno" ("Vertigo"). That O'Connor herself was neither unaware of nor uncomfortable with this tendency in her work is clear from another passage in her essay "The Grotesque in Southern Fiction":

> It's considered an absolute necessity these days for writers to have compassion. Compassion is a word that sounds good in anybody's mouth and which no book jacket can do without. It is a quality which no one can put his finger on in any exact critical sense, so it is always safe for anybody to use. Usually I think what is meant by it is that the writer excuses all human weakness because human weakness is human. The kind of hazy compassion demanded of the writer now makes it difficult for him to be anti-anything. Certainly when the grotesque is used in a legitimate way, the intellectual and moral judgments implicit in it will have the ascendancy over feeling.

Lack of grace in O'Connor's characters usually manifests itself in one of two forms: her protagonists may be either smug and self-assured, like the grandmother in "A Good Man Is Hard to Find" or Mrs. Turpin in "Revelation," or else stricken and floundering, like O. E. Parker in "Parker's Back." We could say that both types are on display in this story, since Sarah Ruth Cates fits quite neatly into the former category. It is important to realize that, despite her all-encompassing religiosity, Sarah Ruth is far from being a role model or spiritual guide. According to Stephen Sparrow in "The Ultimate Heresy: The Heartless God in 'Parker's Back,'" "Sarah Ruth has embedded herself in the off-putting and dismal prospect of a policeman God; a vengeful God. Banished from her mind is the God of the Gospels. Gone is the Good Shepherd . . . or the Prodigal Father who cannot resist loving the wayward son after his U turn." A similar point is made in a sermon preached by Father Paul Yerger of the Orthodox Church in 2004, a sermon which, interestingly enough, took "Parker's Back" as its text: " . . . something attracts him to Sarah Ruth; he is hungry for something: to love something greater than himself, to partake of beauty and glory and mystery, like the tattooed man he saw at the fair. But when he tries in his own way to put on Christ, to give her his whole self, his whole body, his back that he could not see, he is rejected. The deepest longings of his heart find no place in her religion." And O'Connor herself made the point in a letter just nine days before her death: "Sarah Ruth was the heretic—the notion that you can worship in pure spirit." In telling Parker that God "don't *look*. He's a spirit. No man shall see his face" (paragraph 185), she rejects the Incarnation, one of the central mysteries of the Christian faith.

Parker is no heretic. He has no false beliefs, since he has no beliefs at all. He has been in flight from religion from an early age: "He began to drink beer and get in fights. His mother wept over what was becoming of him. One night she dragged him off to a revival with her, not telling him where they were going. When he saw the big lighted church, he jerked out of her grasp and ran. The next day he lied about his age and joined the navy" (paragraph 20). His hatred of his given names can be easily explained by their oddity and their propensity to provoke ridicule, but a on a deeper level the meanings of those names are emblematic of his rejection of faith: Obadiah is the name of an Old Testament prophet, and it means "servant of God"; Elihu (the more common spelling) is one of Job's comforters, and his name signifies "my God is he."

It is a measure of how far Parker is from understanding the varieties of religious experience or even the nature of his own wife that he can for even a moment entertain the notion that she will be pleased by the tattoo of Christ on his back. From their first meeting, "Vanity!" and "Idolatry!" have been among her favorite exclamations. "They were married in the County Ordinary's office because Sarah Ruth thought churches were idolatrous. Parker had no opinion about that one way or the other" (paragraph 72)—no opinion, and no insight either, just as he has shown no real insight into her feelings and attitudes throughout their relationship: at times "he had a suspicion that she actually liked everything she said she didn't" (paragraph 2); he "did not for a minute think that she didn't like the tattoos" (paragraph 17); "it was plain to Parker after he had visited three times that she was crazy about him" (paragraph 67).

Thus we can see that Parker's indifference to the finer points of religious belief is part of a much larger indifference to just about everything beyond himself and his immediate needs and gratifications. We learn early on that he has had involvements with a number of women (from which he seems to have formed the impression that he is devastatingly irresistible) and that he has no intention of ever getting married. He is very much a creature of the moment: "Long views depressed Parker. You look into space like that and you begin to feel as if something were after you, the navy or the government or religion" (paragraph 36). His existence has been a series of impulsive actions—he fled from religion to the navy, then fled from the navy, and so on—and he has thrashed his way blindly through his life. He is out of touch with his own inner needs and discontents, and nothing has ever touched that part of himself but the tattooed man at the fair and his own subsequent pursuit of tattoos: "Parker had never before felt the least motion of wonder in himself. Until he saw the man at the fair, it did not enter his head that there was anything out of the ordinary about the fact that he existed. Even then it did not enter his head, but a peculiar unease settled in him. It was as if a blind boy had been turned so gently in a different direction that he did not know his destination had been changed" (paragraph 19).

Thereafter, Parker's life plays out a cycle of restlessness, the acquisition of a new tattoo, satisfaction with it for a month or so, and then the repetition of the pattern. It is interesting to observe, however, that despite the seemingly static nature of this procedure, there is some subtle but steady movement taking place throughout. As we see in paragraph 22, his tattoos progress from inanimate objects (anchors and crossed rifles) through animals (a tiger, a panther, a cobra, hawks) to humans (Queen Elizabeth II of Great Britain and her husband, Prince Philip—which demonstrates as well as anything could O'Connor's contention that "He did not care much what the subject was as long as it was colorful"); the final step in this progression is, of course, his leap from the human to the divine with the tattoo of Christ on his back. Also, all of his previous tattoos have been where he could see them; in having his back tattooed for Sarah Ruth, he shows that he has broken free of the limits of his self-preoccupation by reaching out to another, which foreshadows his leap to the acceptance of Christ. Just as he has incorporated his previous tattoos into his spirit ("It was as if the panther and the lion and the serpents and the eagles and the hawks had penetrated his skin and lived inside him in a raging warfare" [paragraph 21]), so too the acceptance of Christ on his back signifies his acceptance of Christ into the very core of his being—as is further signified by his pronouncing, at Sarah Ruth's insistence, his full name.

Finally, we can see an upward progress within Parker not only in his seeking the Christ tattoo for Sarah Ruth, but also in the development and refinement of his motivations in doing so. At first it was "urgent that he get exactly the right one to bring Sarah Ruth to heel" (paragraph 80). Following his accident with the tractor and the resulting "burning bush" ("and if he had known how to cross himself he would have done it"), he seems concerned to find one that she will not, in spite of herself, be able to resist—though in the end it is Parker himself who cannot resist the "all-demanding eyes" on his back. After the barroom fight leads him to examine his soul for the first time in his life, he determines that "she would at least be pleased. It seemed to him that, all along, that was what he wanted, to please her" (paragraph 151). From wishing to subjugate her to his will, to wanting to give himself over to her wishes, his feelings toward Sarah Ruth parallel his feelings toward Christ, and thus prefigure his salvation.

The Stephen Sparrow essay quoted above is worth consulting in its entirety. The text can be found online at *Comforts of Home*, a site dedicated to Flannery O'Connor (http://mediaspecialist.org).

—*Michael Palma*

 MyLiteratureLab Resources. Biography, critical overview, and bibliography for O'Connor.

FLANNERY O'CONNOR ON WRITING

EXCERPT FROM "ON HER OWN WORK": THE ELEMENT OF SUSPENSE IN "A GOOD MAN IS HARD TO FIND," page 396

O'Connor's comments come from a reading she gave in 1963, remarks reprinted in her posthumous critical collection *Mystery and Manners* (New York: Farrar, 1969), 107–14.

Southern students, she had learned, tended to recognize the grandmother as exactly like one of their own relatives, "and they knew, from personal experience, that the old lady lacked comprehension, but that she had a good heart." When her head clears for an instant, the grandmother

> realizes, even in her limited way, that she is responsible for the man before her and joined to him by ties of kinship which have their roots deep in the mystery she has merely been prattling about so far. At this point, she does the right thing, she makes the right gesture. I find that students are often puzzled by what she says and does here, but I think myself that if I took out this gesture and what she says with it, I would have no story.

It is important to note O'Connor's warning against equating the Misfit with the devil. Instead, in her view, this murderous criminal is a potential saint gone terribly wrong. She even claims that the grandmother's gesture, "like the mustard seed, will grow to be a great crow-filled tree in the Misfit's heart" and redeem him. Can we accept O'Connor's statement that "in this story you should be on the lookout for such things as the action of grace in the grandmother's soul, and not for the dead bodies"?

Frederick Asals points out in a fruitful critical reading that it remains hard to ignore all those dead bodies. In Asals's view, no other O'Connor story sets up such extreme tension between matters sacred and profane, between comedy and violence. See *Flannery O'Connor: The Imagination of Extremity* (Athens: U of Georgia P, 1982), 142–54.

ON HER CATHOLIC FAITH, page 398

O'Connor's brief statement on her faith is extraordinarily revealing. To say that her self-description avoids conventional Catholic pieties is an understatement. The Church itself, she maintains, is part of the burden a Catholic bears only because one believes in the divinity of Christ. The key statement is her explanation why her violent and grim stories are never bitter: "You have to cherish the world at the same time you struggle to endure it."

EXCERPT FROM "THE GROTESQUE IN SOUTHERN FICTION": THE SERIOUS WRITER AND THE TIRED READER, page 399

O'Connor's remarks about "the serious writer" and "the tired reader" constitute a brilliant defense of real literary artistry in an age that mostly demands light entertainment. Now decades later—in the literary era of Oprah Winfrey—O'Connor's tough-minded and commonsensical stance seems more relevant than ever. She insists that storytellers aim for their art to be a "redemptive act." Art seeks to transform its audience, not merely to entertain it. Such art, O'Connor states, does not come without cost. The cost to the writer is the requirement "to operate at the maximum of his intelligence and his talents." The cost to the tired reader is to wake up and pay attention. There was nothing middlebrow about O'Connor's aesthetic; she aimed high and expected her readers to do the same.

QUESTIONS

1. What is Flannery O'Connor's opinion of book clubs? Explain her remark on this subject in the second paragraph.

2. Does O'Connor condemn people who want fiction to leave them "lifted up"? What is her attitude toward them?

3. By what means can writers write the great novels of the future?

CRITICS ON FLANNERY O'CONNOR, pages 402–409

We have presented a selection of critical perspectives on O'Connor to supplement the three statements she made on her own work. (She was a formidably lucid explicator of her own methods.) The four articles excerpted on her work by literary critics provide different perspectives. **Robert H. Brinkmeyer, Jr.,** offers a reader-response analysis of O'Connor's complex relation to her readers. **J. O. Tate** provides a historical analysis of the factual sources of O'Connor's memorable character, the Misfit, in "A Good Man Is Hard to Find." (We even reproduce the original newspaper article O'Connor saw in 1952 that inspired the story.) **Mary Jane Schenck** deconstructs the same story. **Kathleen Feeley** contrasts Sarah Ruth's narrowness of spirit with her husband's openness to mystery, and thus redemption, in "Parker's Back."

11
Critical Casebook: Three Stories in Depth

Edgar Allan Poe ❖ The Tell-Tale Heart
Charlotte Perkins Gilman ❖ The Yellow Wallpaper
Alice Walker ❖ Everyday Use

Edgar Allan Poe, THE TELL-TALE HEART, page 413

In *The Uses of Enchantment*, the celebrated study of the psychological dimension of fairy tales, Bruno Bettelheim maintains that people who read fairy tales to children should not talk to them about what the stories mean. Thus, it could be argued that a story such as Poe's "The Tell-Tale Heart" is not meant to be picked apart and subjected to analysis. XJK remembers that once, after a class had read a Poe tale, a wonderful controversy broke out when someone complained, "this story doesn't really say anything." Everyone tried to sum up the story's theme, he reports, but failed miserably, and at last decided that there is a place in literature for stories that don't say anything in particular, but supply their readers with memorable nightmares and dreams. Many a writer of horror stories might summarize his or her intentions in the famous words of Joe the fat boy in Charles Dickens's *The Pickwick Papers*—"I wants to make your flesh creep"—and leave it go at that.

On the other hand, "The Tell-Tale Heart" must have something more than a good scare going for it to have attracted the attention of so many critics over the years. Daniel Hoffman, for instance, in his highly personal and deeply stimulating *Poe Poe Poe Poe Poe Poe Poe* (1973), sees the old man as a father-figure, even a Father-Figure, and suggests that in striking at his eye "the young madman strikes, symbolically, at his sexual power." Hoffman also says that the narrator "is full of the praise of his own sagacity, a terrible parody of the true sagacity of a Dupin or a Legrand. For what he takes to be ratiocination is in fact the irresistible operation of the principle of his own perversity, the urge to do secret deeds, have secret thoughts undetected by the otherwise ever-watchful eye of the old man."

This and other demonstrations of the narrator's imbalance come at the very beginning of the story, and they provide the context in which we will evaluate everything else that he says and does. The teller of Poe's tale is a classic unreliable narrator. The narrator is not deliberately trying to mislead his audience; he is delusional, and the reader can easily find the many places in the story where the narrator's telling reveals his mistaken perceptions. His presentation is also deeply ironic: the insistence on his sanity puts his madness on display. The first paragraph alone, brief as it is, should provide fertile ground for students sent to find evidence of his severe disturbance. From there, you can lead the class into a discussion of the subsequent manifestations of his madness—his perception of the old man's eye as a thing in itself, independent of its admittedly benevolent possessor; his extreme attention to details and matters that others could find insignificant; his fixation on a single objective for an insanely long period of time; his need to flaunt his brilliance, even if only to himself, by inviting the police into the house, and so on.

Is it his own heart that the narrator hears at the end, as Hoffman and others have suggested, or is it the wholly imaginary manifestation of his own guilty conscience? No one can say for certain, and perhaps no one should. As suggested above, the claim that the story contains no larger meaning represents one extreme of possible responses, but it may be an equally extreme response in the opposite direction to impose a strict—and potentially reductive—interpretation upon every last detail. At least some of the story's considerable power lies in the fact that we can't explain everything away.

Instructors should note that there are two student essays and a sample card report on this story included in the chapter "Writing About a Story." You may want to suggest that students review any or all of this material.

"The Tell-Tale Heart" was adapted for television in the PBS television series *The American Short Story*, and is available on videocassette. Additionally, an A & E biography of Edgar Allan Poe is also available on videocassette.

IDEAS FOR WRITING

1. As students love creative writing assignments, you might consider giving them the chance to rewrite this story using a different narrator. This will give them a much better sense of what Poe was talking about in "The Tale and Its Effect"; they will see how a writer's choices add up to either a successful or an unsuccessful narrative.

   Edgar Allan Poe paid very careful attention to the technical details of his stories. He knew that craft led to effects, so he planned every detail of his stories from theme to character to point of view. As Daniel Hoffman shows, "The Tell-Tale Heart" wouldn't be half as effective without the madman himself as its narrator. Indeed, its climax would not occur without that point-of-view choice. An omniscient narrator in this case might reveal the mysteries that give the story its power (the idea that the dead man is in fact the narrator's father, as Hoffman suggests; the paranoia of the narrator would also be moot for an omniscient voice).

2. Terror and humor are sometimes not far apart. Students can certainly tell stories of times they were terrified (about to be spanked, perhaps, for a childhood infraction), yet their seemingly inappropriate response was laughter.

   Flannery O'Connor noted that one of the great influences on her own writing was Edgar Allan Poe's stories. She echoed him in the creation of bizarre characters and also in his use of the grotesque—mixing elements of humor with moments of horror. A stolen wooden leg, for example, is both hilarious and horrendous. In Poe's story, the paranoid narrator of "The Tell-Tale Heart" is likewise amusing—in the way he "thrusts" his head into the room of the sleeping victim, for example. One can imagine him caricatured in a skit on *Saturday Night Live*.

3. Father and son relationships in Poe's stories are virtually never good. Sons want to kill fathers and fathers want to kill sons, either explicitly or implicitly. Poe felt himself to be a victimized son, first of David Poe, who abandoned him, his mother, and his sister; and later of John Allan, his oppressive foster father. Biographical information works well in understanding relationships among characters in Poe's stories.

MLL *MyLiteratureLab Resources.* Photographs, biographical information, critical overview, bibliography for Poe. Video clips and critical essays for "The Tell-Tale Heart."

EDGAR ALLAN POE ON WRITING

THE TALE AND ITS EFFECT, page 417

This early review of Nathaniel Hawthorne's tales serves to highlight one of Poe's favorite critical theories, that of "unity of effect." The idea, however, was not a new one: it was originally propounded by Aristotle in his *Poetics*. According to Aristotle, a good story (or play) has a "unity of action" achieved by presenting the reader with a complete and ordered set of actions, or incidents, all of which are designed to produce a particular "effect" on the reader, and no one of which can be left out without disjointing the artistic whole.

Poe is talking about the same thing in both this review of Hawthorne's *Twice-Told Tales* and in "The Philosophy of Composition." To achieve the maximum effect on the reader, the artist's creation needs to be short, something that can be read in one sitting—in other words, a short prose tale or a poem. Poe's literary criticism distinguished him in his own day as much as his tales and poems did. He was the first person to define the short story as a distinct literary form and to outline its component parts.

A useful exercise for students is to look for "unity of effect" in Poe's own tales and poems. You can decide whether he has met his own criteria in statements such as, "If his very initial sentence tend not to the out-bringing of this effect, then [the writer] has failed in his first step." See if the first sentences of these tales by Poe measure up to his strict rules for creative writers.

Creative Assignment Idea. For a more creative assignment, ask students to write their own short story with an eye to "unity of effect." To structure the task, give students several elements that must be integral to the story—for example, "a black cat"; "an atmosphere of terror, disgust, or hilarity"; "an orphan"; "an abandoned warehouse"; "a silver flute." You can add or subtract elements as you like, but such an assignment is sure to appeal to the more creative among your students.

ON IMAGINATION, page 418

The notion of combining beauty and deformity—"combinable things hitherto uncombined"—suggests a quality to be found in stories by both Edgar Allan Poe and Flannery O'Connor. That quality is "the grotesque," where humor and horror go hand-in-hand, as do beauty and deformity ("A beautiful dead woman," Poe's subject of choice, suggests the combination of beauty and deformity—the beauty is necessarily deformed by the decomposition of the corpse.)

Again, Poe's ideas here are influenced by Aristotle's *Poetics*. Aristotle believed there was nothing new under the sun, but originality could be achieved by new combinations of already extant elements. In this way, "the range of Imagination is unlimited." A nearer influence, however, was probably Samuel Taylor Coleridge, the English Romantic poet. The Romantics believed fervently in the imagination as a "vital" quality of the creative mind. This imagination can look upon fixed and dead objects, dissolve their fixities and "generate . . . a form of its own," an organic whole recreated from disparate parts. In the fourteenth chapter of his *Biographia Literaria* (1817), Coleridge writes that the "synthetic" power of the imagination "reveals itself in the balance or reconciliation of opposite or discordant qualities: of sameness, with difference; of the general, with the concrete; the idea, with the image. . . . "

What Poe shared with Coleridge was a tendency to abuse substances (alcohol for Poe, opium for Coleridge) to achieve these effects of heightened imagination. In the case of O'Connor, intense religious belief heightened her imagination and also her belief that average readers needed strong and violent imagery to awaken them to the reality of their plight in a fallen world—the necessity of struggling for salvation on a daily basis.

THE PHILOSOPHY OF COMPOSITION, page 418

Poe wrote this essay to explain how he composed his poetic masterpiece, "The Raven." He wants to counter the idea of the poet as an "artiste" who works only when inspiration strikes, and then in a "fine frenzy" of "ecstatic intuition." On the contrary, Poe describes the poet as an architect who carefully selects every incident, character, and metrical device with which he will build his poem. The effect he produces may be magical, but the actual work of creating the effect is rational and painstaking.

A very conscious craftsman, Poe's essays on composition belie the biographical image of him as a drunken madman, scribbling away without forethought or design.

Assignments. (1) Can you apply Poe's philosophy of composition to one of his tales or poems? In particular, look for instances of beauty and deformity and extremity of atmosphere (e.g., paranoia in "The Tell-Tale Heart"). (2) What poetic devices does Poe use to good effect in his prose compositions?

Critics on "The Tell-Tale Heart," pages 419–423

Daniel Hoffman, The Father-Figure in "The Tell-Tale Heart"
Scott Peeples, "The Tell-Tale Heart" as a Love Story
John Chua, The Figure of the Double in Poe

Daniel Hoffman's psychological reading of "The Tell-Tale Heart" will help students see below the story's surface and into its fascinating subtext. His penetrating analysis of a fictional character—the story's narrator—may allow students to see this favorite story in an entirely different light.

In "'The Tell-Tale Heart' as a Love Story," **Scott Peeples** follows Hoffman's suggestion that the old man is a father-figure and states that "the story invites us to find a method to the narrator's madness, to locate the logic beneath the insanity." Peeples makes a particularly interesting point about the death watches, the insects in the wall, who rhythmically knock their heads against the wood as part of their mating ritual, connecting the term *watch* both to the timepiece (and the narrator's obsession with timekeeping) and a vigil for the dying, and—somewhat more distantly—connecting the mating ritual with the love that the narrator professes to feel for the old man.

As Hoffman and others have done, **John Chua** in "The Figure of the Double in Poe" suggests that in his fiction Poe may be working through his own tangled relationship with his foster-father, John Allan. Chua also points out that in his reviews and critical writings Poe expressed his disdain for didactic and moralistic purposes in literature, emphasizing instead the aesthetic dimension and "a concentrated effect on or emotional response from the reader." In Chua's view, it can be argued that "the protagonist and the antagonist are moral equals" and even that "the two characters could well be the same person."

Charlotte Perkins Gilman, The Yellow Wallpaper, page 424

"The Yellow Wallpaper" is now such a famous short story that it is interesting to recall how recently it was rescued from oblivion. The facts behind the original creation of the tale and its modern rediscovery are worth recounting. Gilman completed the story in 1890 after the breakup of her first marriage. Based on her own experience with depression and the debilitating effects of her medical treatment for the condition, "The Yellow Wallpaper" was written, she later claimed, to "save people from being driven crazy." Gilman sent the story to William Dean Howells, then the most influential critic in American fiction. Admiring it, he sent the story to Horace Scudder, the editor of the *Atlantic Monthly,* who turned it down on the basis of its stark and unsettling contents. As Howells later commented, it was "too terribly good to be printed" there. When the story was published in *New England Magazine* in 1892, it stirred up a minor controversy. Howells later reprinted it in his 1920 anthology, *The Great American Short Stories.* For the next fifty years the story remained out of print. In 1973, the Feminist Press reissued it as a separate pamphlet with an admiring afterword. Six years later, Sandra Gilbert and Susan Gubar discussed it in their pioneering feminist study, *The Madwoman in the Attic* (1979). Soon thereafter, "The Yellow Wallpaper" became one of the most widely discussed texts in feminist criticism of American literature.

"The Yellow Wallpaper" lends itself to many different readings, but most obviously it invites—some critics might say *demands*—a feminist approach. Gilbert and Gubar explore the rich subtext of the story. The narrator is not only physically imprisoned in her comfortable, airy room; she is spiritually and intellectually confined in a patronizing male world that reduces her to childish dependency. Whatever critical approach one adopts, the important thing is not to simplify Gilman's complex and richly ambiguous narrative.

The first issue for students to deal with is the narrative situation. "The Yellow Wallpaper" is told by a woman undergoing a nervous breakdown. She suffers visions and is plagued by obsessions. Forbidden to write by her concerned but patronizing husband, she secretly jots down her thoughts and experiences. Her prose is conspicuously anxious and disconnected. Not only is the narrator unreliable, her reports are complicated further by the untrustworthy behavior of her husband and his sister, who take care of her. With good but misguided intentions, they talk down to her, and much of what they say appears to be deliberately misleading. A chief irony of the story is that the further the narrator sinks into madness the more clearly she understands the hypocrisy and paternalism of her keepers. Nothing anyone says in the story can be accepted uncritically.

A good way to acclimatize students to the uncertainty of the narrative situation is to ask them to recount everything they know about the room the narrator shares with her husband in the rented mansion. (The husband, however, has also selected the room because it has another bedroom nearby that he can move into if need be.) The narrator initially describes it as follows:

> It is a big, airy room, the whole floor nearly, with windows that look all ways, and air and sunshine galore. It was a nursery first and then playroom and gymnasium, I should judge; for the windows are barred for little children, and there are rings and things in the walls.

No one in the story ever questions that the room was once a nursery, but as later details pile up (the striped wallpaper, the bolted-down bed, the stairway gate), the alert reader wonders if it was not really once a genteel cell for an affluent lunatic. Like many other things in the story, a pleasant surface covers an authoritarian reality. Students should be encouraged to examine every aspect of this story with equal care and skepticism.

Another question to ask students is, who is the woman the narrator sees in the wallpaper? If this were a supernatural tale, the reader might eventually assume that it was a ghost or demon who inhabited the yellow wallpaper, and there are overtones of the macabre in Gilman's story. However, Gilman—like Poe before her—uses the outward narrative forms of Gothic and supernatural fiction to explore uncomfortable psychological territory. The woman imprisoned in the wallpaper is the narrator's double, probably the parts of her being confined and repressed by her suffocating life. Only as the narrator sinks into madness do her own inhibitions drop sufficiently that she can liberate these forbidden or unacknowledged aspects of her psyche.

In "The Yellow Wallpaper," Gilman uses the traditional figure of the *doppelgänger* (a German term that, translated literally, means "double-goer") in an original, feminist way. In Romantic literature the double usually represented an evil self that had broken free of the dominant, moral, conscious self. The evil double often battles the "real" self for control of the person's life. In Gilman's story, the repressed self that is finally liberated also wants to take over the narrator's life, but the double is neither obviously evil nor morally dangerous. Once free, the double seems to merge into the narrator. "I wonder if they all come out of the wallpaper as I did?" she suddenly comments. Although the narrator's outer life is crumbling, she is achieving a new authenticity in her inner life. Robert Louis Stevenson's classic *doppelgänger* story, *The Strange Case of Dr. Jekyll and Mr. Hyde*, was published with immense acclaim in 1886—only four years before Gilman wrote "The Yellow Wallpaper." One wonders if Gilman knew it. She seems to take Stevenson's conventional moral themes and revise them radically from a feminist perspective.

Finally, students may want to explore the complex central image of Gilman's story, the yellow wallpaper. The "repellent, almost revolting," "smouldering unclean" yellow wallpaper resists neat allegorical interpretation; it is a troubling, changing symbol of the forces that haunt, imprison, and torment the narrator. At first its "bloated curves and flourishes" seem to have no shape, but gradually the obsessively observant narrator starts to comprehend its shape. In a probing essay, "Feminist Criticism, 'The Yellow Wallpaper,' and the Politics of Color in America" (*Feminist Studies* 15:3 [Fall 1989]), Susan S. Lanser compares the narrator's analysis of the wallpaper to deciphering the text of her own imprisoned female identity:

> The narrator is faced with an unreadable text, a text for which none of her interpretative strategies is adequate. . . . But from all this indecipherability, from this immensely complicated text, the narrator—by night, no less— finally discerns a single image, a woman behind bars, which she then expands to represent the whole.

Students wishing to write on Gilman may want to read her feminist utopian novel, *Herland* (1915), which describes a trio of American men visiting an all-female country. Gilman was, first and foremost, a writer on social issues. Even her champions concede that none of her other short stories is up to the level of "The Yellow Wallpaper." *Herland*, a novel of ideas, shows Gilman at her best—it is a radical, progressive questioning of the traditional assumptions of her age. They may also wish to consult Carol Farley Kessler's interesting long essay on Gilman's life and work in *Modern American Women Writers* (New York: Scribner, 1991).

Two stories in this book could provide students with particularly interesting topics to compare and contrast with "The Yellow Wallpaper." Poe's "The Tell-Tale Heart" uses Gothic conventions and an unreliable narrator to depict the consequences of a mental breakdown; William Faulkner's "A Rose for Emily" provides interesting parallels to Gilman's story, as Faulkner's mad Emily Grierson is trapped in an old house by different sorts of male presences.

"The Yellow Wallpaper"/Charlotte Perkins Gilman, a volume devoted to "The Yellow Wallpaper" and edited by Thomas L. Erskine and Connie L. Richards, appeared in 1993 from "Women Writers: Text and Context," a series of casebooks about short fiction from Rutgers University Press. It includes historical documents and critical commentaries on the story. Additionally, Professor Charlotte Rich edits the *Charlotte Perkins Gilman Newsletter* out of SUNY College at Cortland (Cortland, New York 13045). The newsletter is also available online at <http://web.cortland.edu/gilman>, as are numerous Gilman Web sites and

resources. Check a search engine for the most recent addresses. Also of interest, University of New England in Portland, Maine, hosted the fourth International Gilman Conference in June 2006.

 MyLiteratureLab Resources. Biography, critical overview, and bibliography for Gilman. Additional prose and poetry excerpts by Gilman. Critical essays on "The Yellow Wallpaper."

CHARLOTTE PERKINS GILMAN ON WRITING

WHY I WROTE "THE YELLOW WALLPAPER," page 435
WHATEVER IS, page 436
THE NERVOUS BREAKDOWN OF WOMEN, page 437

Gilman's "Why I Wrote 'The Yellow Wallpaper'" and "The Nervous Breakdown of Women" appeared in her monthly magazine *The Forerunner*, which she published—and wrote the entire contents of—from 1909 to 1916. According to Gilman's biographer, "Reading through these issues, one gets a sense of Gilman's virtuosity, of the range of her interests and attitudes. . . . The overriding commitments reflected in the magazine were to the belief in the rights of women and the superiority of a collective social order" (Ann J. Lane, *To Herland and Beyond: The Life & Work of Charlotte Perkins Gilman* [New York: Pantheon, 1990] 278). One can see the commitment to women's rights in both these short pieces. Despite the artistry of "The Yellow Wallpaper" and the story's symbolic and psychological richness (perhaps the "embellishments and additions" she alludes to?), her account of the story's origins is focused exclusively on practical and didactic concerns. "The Nervous Breakdown of Women" is remarkable for the force and directness of its style, for its sympathy and understanding, and especially for its central insight, that while men have been supported and sustained by women throughout history, everything that women have accomplished has been achieved in the face of objections and opposition from men. Gilman's poem "Whatever Is" shows similar commitments in its rueful awareness that Truth must always fight a long, uphill battle against the dull weight of tradition and received opinion.

CRITICS ON "THE YELLOW WALLPAPER," pages 438–442

Juliann Fleenor, GENDER AND PATHOLOGY IN "THE YELLOW WALLPAPER"
Sandra M. Gilbert and Susan Gubar, IMPRISONMENT AND ESCAPE: THE
    PSYCHOLOGY OF CONFINEMENT
Elizabeth Ammons, BIOGRAPHICAL ECHOES IN "THE YELLOW WALLPAPER"

In an excerpt from their groundbreaking study *The Madwoman in the Attic,* **Sandra M. Gilbert and Susan Guar** emphasize Gilman's feminist focus on the marginalization, isolation, and silencing of women, along with her awareness that freedom from these confinements can be brought about only by women themselves in acts of self-empowerment. Combining a biographical and feminist approach, both **Juliann Fleenor** and **Elizabeth Ammons** make use of Gilman's own experiences to illuminate aspects of "The Yellow Wallpaper." Fleenor concentrates on Gilman as wife and mother, Ammons on Gilman's childhood relationships with both her parents, and both conclude that the obstacles to women's freedom and fulfillment are not only men but also those women who allow themselves to be defined and limited by traditional assumptions regarding a woman's "place."

Alice Walker, Everyday Use, page 443

"Everyday Use" is a genuinely funny story ("Ream it out again," the mother says as she tries to learn her daughter's new name, and she keeps—possibly with tongue in cheek—slipping the new name in throughout the story) with serious undertones. Narrated by the mother, whose wry good sense contrasts vividly with her older daughter's pretensions, the story highlights not only a generation gap, but a contrast between two sharply different attitudes toward the idea of heritage.

Dee, having suddenly discovered that old quilts and dashers are potentially interesting decorations, accuses her mother and sister of not understanding their heritage because they fail to appreciate the artistic value of such objects. However, she herself is so divorced from her heritage that she does not know which member of the family made the dasher. It may be true, as Dee accuses, that Maggie and her mother don't "understand" their heritage—at least not in an intellectual way. The story suggests, however, that by using the quilt, and by having learned the traditional skills passed from generation to generation required to make one, Maggie, the homely, uneducated sister, knows more about her African American heritage than does Dee (Wangero). Maggie and her mother *live* their cultural heritage; they are nourished by it through everyday use and versed in the craftsmanship needed to pass it on to future generations.

That the mother loves Dee is clear. Although she's aware of the unattractive elements in Dee's nature, her dream of Dee showing her appreciation for her mother on a television show reveals wistfulness: the older woman longs for Dee to return her love. Instead, Dee is scornful. "You ought to try to make something of yourself, too, Maggie," she says as she departs, as if she herself were a superior being, to be emulated. Dee, in spite of her education, has never learned to imagine how she appears to others.

"Everyday Use" is an accessible story for students that explores powerful issues. Although the setting is specifically African American, the themes of family identity, intergenerational conflict, cultural heritage, and self-esteem are universal. The basic narrative situation—the educated daughter returning on a family visit to criticize her mother and stay-at-home sister—is also particularly relevant to many college students, and most students find it interesting to see this situation from the mother's perspective. Do your African American students like this story, or are they offended by it? Do any of them feel that the story reinforces undesirable stereotypes? Do any of your black students side with Dee, who is trying so hard to leave poverty and ignorance behind? If the black students in your class are willing to be drawn out on this subject, the discussion might be lively and valuable.

William Scurrah of Pima Community College in Tucson, Arizona, developed with his students a provocative revisionist reading of "Everyday Use." If one views Mama as an unreliable narrator, it changes the reader's view of Dee:

> First person narrators are not necessarily to be believed (not so much on the facts they describe, but on the perspective they bring to those facts) just because it's their words printed on the page. To *whom*, for example, is Mama speaking? One student pointed out that the audience couldn't be, say, her neighbors, for they would not need to be told what Mama could do (e.g., kill hogs and butcher bull-calves)—only people for whom such activities were unfamiliar would need to have them described. And is Mama bragging? Why do people brag? Is she talking to herself? Is she imagining herself on television, on that program she envisioned at the beginning of the story, explaining to that video world her way of life? Is so, what is the irony in that?
>
> By the end of the period, some students were energized ("I always thought this story was so dumb, but it isn't!"), others were upset ("We've just ruined my favorite story!"). But none of us, including me, was taking the story, or the author, at face value anymore.

Scurrah's skepticism on Mama's reliability as a narrator provides a provocative way of analyzing a story that is deceptively simple on the surface.

Students wanting critical perspectives on Walker should consult *Alice Walker: Critical Perspectives Past and Present* (New York: Amistad, 1993), edited by Henry Louis Gates, Jr., and K. A. Appiah, which collects a representative cross-section of reviews, essays, and interviews with the author.

MLL   *MyLiteratureLab Resources.* Biography, critical overview, and bibliography for Walker. Longman Lecture, student paper on "Everyday Use."

ALICE WALKER ON WRITING

THE BLACK WOMAN WRITER IN AMERICA, *Interview by John O'Brien,* page 449

REFLECTIONS ON WRITING, *Interview by William R. Ferris,* page 451

John O'Brien's interview with Alice Walker was conducted in 1973, the year in which "Everyday Use" was published in book form. In speaking of the situation of the black woman writer, Walker quite rightly complains of any emphasis—whether on biographical details or on interactions with white culture—that takes away attention from the work itself. She also calls for work "that exposes the *subconscious* of a people, because the people's dreams, imaginings, rituals, legends, etc. are known to be important, are known to contain the accumulated collective reality of the people themselves"—a prescription that is very applicable to "Everyday Use" itself. Two decades later, in her conversations with William R. Ferris, Walker made further comments that bear directly on the story, touching on quilting as one of the "art forms that were not necessarily recognized as art forms" which gave generations of black women one place to fulfill that human need to "to create."

CRITICS ON "EVERYDAY USE," pages 453–460

Barbara T. Christian, "EVERYDAY USE" AND THE BLACK POWER MOVEMENT
Houston A. Baker and Charlotte Pierce-Baker, STYLISH VS. SACRED IN "EVERYDAY USE"
Elaine Showalter, QUILT AS METAPHOR IN "EVERYDAY USE"

The themes discussed by Walker in the interviews excerpts are also prevalent in the critical pieces on "Everyday Use" that we have presented here. **Barbara T. Christian**'s historical critical approach explores the political and cultural background of the period when Walker wrote "Everyday Use." She points out that, despite being a participant in and beneficiary of the social revolution of the 1960s, Walker took a realistic view of society and of the male excesses of the Black Power movement, and refused to dismiss the dignity of her foremothers and the richness of their culture. **Houston A. Baker and Charlotte Pierce-Baker** contrast the synthetic cultural values of the progressive Dee (Wangero) with the authenticity of the tradition carried on by her mother and sister. Following their lead, **Elaine Showalter** also provides some interesting historical background on the unique place of quilting in the aesthetic heritage of black women.

12
Stories for Further Reading

Chinua Achebe, DEAD MEN'S PATH, page 462

Chinua Achebe is the senior eminence of English-language African fiction. His first novel, *Things Fall Apart* (1958), almost immediately achieved classic status, and his subsequent books have only reinforced his reputation. Achebe's literary sensibility is rooted in British Realist fiction, and he stands unapologetically in the tradition of George Eliot, Joseph Conrad, E. M. Forster, and even—despite the evident differences of themes and settings—Jane Austen. Part of the pleasure of reading Achebe surely comes from his penetrating social intelligence and capacity for realistic psychological portrayal. He is also masterfully concise. (His short novels brilliantly depict broad canvases just as this very short story tells a great deal about Nigerian society.) Achebe's great innovation is to bring these Austen-like qualities to the complex and turbulent world of post-colonial West Africa. His forms feel familiar but his content is strikingly new and historically significant. Achebe directly addresses social and political issues in his work, but he never puts his fiction in the service of a particular ideology.

"Dead Men's Path" enacts in miniature one of the central themes of Achebe's novels—the clash between modern European ideas and traditional African values, progressive international standards and deeply rooted local custom. The story's protagonist, Michael Obi, is a well-educated, forward-thinking idealist with a passion for "modern methods." Quite intelligent and undoubtedly dedicated to education, Obi is more comfortable in abstract thought than in facing the complexities of real life. He doesn't notice unspoken feelings; for example, his wife's considerable disappointment upon learning that the other teachers are all unmarried. His view of the world is rational and therefore incapable of fully understanding the parts of life ruled by emotion, intuition, or custom. Obi looks down on the older headmasters of the Mission schools. Note how Achebe subtly undercuts Obi in the opening paragraphs. Only twenty-six, the newly appointed headmaster appears much older with his "stoop-shouldered" posture and "frail" build.

Achebe's story was first published in 1953 just as the newly independent nations of Africa were making their first strides towards modernization. Michael Obi represents the new African, the progressive who hopes to rebuild his society. The tragic histories of most post-colonial African nations in the latter half of the twentieth century reveal how prescient Achebe's diagnosis of modernization was. No standardized international idea of progress could be imposed on traditional African societies without terrible cost and probable failure.

Names are often significant in Achebe's fiction. Michael Obi's name demonstrates his divided heritage. Michael is a Christian baptismal name of

European heritage. (Remember, Obi works for "Mission" schools—as did Achebe's father, who was a devout Christian.) Obi, by contrast, is an African name. His name itself embodies the cultural conflict he is about to enter.

Having introduced his protagonist and set up the narrative premise, Achebe focuses his story on a single incident—Obi's attempt to close the footpath that the locals believe is used by dead and unborn souls to enter the village. Obi uses rational, progressive arguments in discussing the matter with the village priest (who, ironically, seems both more rational and more open-minded than the ideological headmaster). "What you say may be true," admits the priest, adding "but we follow the practices of our fathers." The results of Obi's idealistic obstinacy ultimately prove disastrous for both the school and his own career.

An interview with Chinua Achebe covering a variety of topics, including Achebe's view on what is uniquely African about his role as an artist in the community, is available on audiocassette tape from American Audio Prose Library.

Anjana Appachana, THE PROPHECY, page 465

Anjana Appachana's "The Prophecy" is in one sense a conventional coming-of-age story—a vivid account of a seventeen-year-old college student's unwanted pregnancy and her attempts to solve her dilemma. Appachana's setting, a conservative Indian women's college, gives the story an unconventional and slightly exotic feel for an American audience. Although accessible to non-Indian readers, "The Prophecy" revels in local color. In the opening scene, for example, Appachana employs several Anglo-Indian and Hindi words—*scooterwallah*, *paan*, *beedi*, *Memsahib* (all of these words are glossed in the book). It will be worth dwelling on the use of these terms in class. What does Appachana gain by using them?

The opening scene also leads us to the house of Chachaji, the astrologer. This incident sets the story firmly in Indian society, where astrologers are frequently consulted before important decisions. The visit to Chachaji's also provides the story with its title. It will provide an interesting topic for class discussion to compare his prophecies for Amrita with the actual outcome described in the final two paragraphs.

The critic K. C. Nambiar reviewed Appachana's first collection of short stories, *Incantations* (1991), for the Indian periodical *Hindu*, commenting that the author was "an unbiased and perceptive observer of the fast changing face of India's urban scene, especially the generation of young women in their twenties." That remark certainly applies to "The Prophecy," which dramatizes the generational gap in attitudes between the two college-age friends and their parents. Although many of the incidents in the story could easily have happened in contemporary America, it may be worthwhile to have students list those things that would be less likely to occur here. This exercise will not only illuminate the story's particular social commentary, it will also clarify how fiction can often strike a universal chord while being most culturally specific in its depiction.

Margaret Atwood, HAPPY ENDINGS, page 476

Margaret Atwood's "Happy Endings" is a representative as well as an unusually engaging example of post-modern metafiction. Like much metafiction, it makes no attempt to make the reader believe in the verisimilitude of the narrative but instead overtly and exuberantly explores the nature of narrative structure. The author sets up the simple situation in one short line, "John and Mary meet." Then she asks the obvious narrative question, "What happens next?"

The bulk of the story consists of six mutually exclusive or minimally overlapping "endings" to the story. Despite the story's title, most of the endings are *not* "happy." Only the first alternative is unconditionally blissful. The second involves suicide, the third includes a triple murder, the fourth presents a tidal wave that kills thousands, the fifth depicts mortal illness. By now even the dimmest reader will begin to suspect that the piece's title was ironic.

Atwood is making several points through her multiple endings. First is that there is something unconvincing and inauthentic about most narrative endings. Second, all human endings are ultimately the same—we all die. Mortality is the central fact of human existence. Finally, Atwood suggests that "Beginnings are always more fun," possibilities are more pleasant than actualities. A sure sign of Atwood's literary talent is her ability to communicate these often disturbing, slightly abstract themes in such an accessibly comic way. Her humor may be dark, but it is genuine. Grim as the narrative often is in parts, "Happy Endings" nonetheless has fun with the conventions of storytelling in a way most readers can appreciate.

Ambrose Bierce, AN OCCURRENCE AT OWL CREEK BRIDGE, page 479

"Bitter Bierce" was what his contemporaries called him, and as both man and writer he earned the title. In life, he seems to have quarreled with and become estranged from everyone he ever met, including his wife and sons. In literature, he is still best known for *The Devil's Dictionary*, among whose acid definitions are: "History: an account mostly false, of events unimportant, which are brought about by rulers mostly knaves, and soldiers mostly fools" and "Marriage: the state or condition of a community consisting of a master, a mistress, and two slaves, making, in all, two."

But "An Occurrence at Owl Creek Bridge" remains Bierce's most popular piece of writing. One reason for its enduring popularity is, of course, the surprise ending. Yet this story affects the reader on a deeper level than those of some of Bierce's clever contemporaries, such as Frank L. Stockton's "The Lady or the Tiger?" One reason for the story's greater expressive power is certainly Bierce's superior artistry. Another must surely be his evocation of life, in all of its splendor and its "blessings," through the heightened senses of a man about to die. Here as elsewhere in his work, life turns out to be a cruel cheat in the end; but here much more than elsewhere, he makes clear, in vivid and sensuous detail, why we cling to it so desperately.

QUESTIONS FOR DISCUSSION

1. *What has brought Peyton Farquhar to the brink of hanging?* Incited by the Federal Scout, he has apparently tried to burn down Owl Creek Bridge, which is in the hands of the Union Army.

2. *One student, after reading Bierce's story, objected to it on the grounds that the actions of the Federal Scout (paragraphs 9–17) are not believable. "Since when do military men dress up like the enemy and incite civilians to sabotage?" was her question. How would you answer it?* One possible answer might be that Farquhar, "a slave owner and like other slave owners a politician," has managed in his own way to engineer damage to the enemy and so has become a marked man. A believer in "at least a part of the frankly villainous dictum that all is fair in love and war" (8), Farquhar is lured into a fatal trap by someone in the enemy camp who assents to the same view.

3. *Are you surprised by the story's conclusion? Can you find hints along the way that Farquhar's escape is an illusion? At what point in the story does the illusion begin?* Bierce lays in enough hints to make most readers accept the surprise ending, though they may want to reread the story just to make sure. In paragraph 5, though Farquhar makes a conscious effort to think about his wife and children, he has already begun to experience an alteration in his sense of time. Recall the old general belief that at the moment of death we see our whole lives pass by again in a flash. As soon as an escape plot forms in Farquhar's mind (6), the sergeant moves off the plank and the noose tightens around the doomed man's neck. Since we know from the ending that the rope does not break, what happens to Farquhar after the flashback (8–17)—except for the physical sensations of hanging—has to be a fast-moving hallucination in the mind of a dying man.

Bierce has planted clues that this is so. With "superhuman" effort Farquhar manages to free his bound hands. His senses are "preternaturally keen and alert" (20). His ability to dodge all the bullets fired at him seems miraculous. The forest through which he walks is unfamiliar and menacing; the stars above him are "grouped in strange constellations"; he hears "whispers in an unknown tongue" (34). Soon "he could no longer feel the roadway beneath his feet" (35). His wife greets him with "a smile of ineffable joy" (36)—then he is dead.

4. *From what point of view is "An Occurrence at Owl Creek Bridge" told?* In the third person by a nonparticipating narrator able to see into Farquhar's mind.

5. *At several places in the story Bierce calls attention to Farquhar's heightened sensibility. How would you explain those almost mystical responses to ordinary stimuli?* They are the out-of-body sensations of a dying man. Much has been written about such experiences in the popular press. For some interesting, serious comments on the subject see Elisabeth Kübler-Ross, *On Death and Dying* (New York: Macmillan, 1969). Dr. Ross quotes the testimony of persons who, after being declared clinically dead, were resuscitated. Some reported finding themselves floating in space, gazing down upon their own bodies.

6. *Where in Bierce's story do you find examples of irony?* There is irony in the contrast between the understated title and the extravagant style of the narrator. Ironic, too, is the mention of Farquhar's belief that "all's fair in love and war"— a belief shared by the Federal Scout who lures Farquhar to his capture and death. Verbal irony occurs in "Death is a dignitary who when he comes announced is to be received with formal manifestations of respect, even by those most familiar with him" (paragraph 2), and "The liberal military code makes provision for hanging many kinds of persons, and gentlemen are not excluded" (3). Students may find other examples as well.

7. *Do you think the story would have been better had Bierce told it in chronological order? Why or why not?* In defense of the way the story is told, we'd argue mainly that Bierce's use of flashback heightens the suspense created by the opening scene on the bridge.

A topic for writing: Compare this story with Borges's "The Gospel According to Mark." Both stories deal with men on the brink of death and their inner experiences.

A famous French film adaptation of "Owl Creek" won an Academy Award in 1964 for best short subject and was later used by Rod Serling for a *Twilight Zone* episode. It has almost no dialogue and is available on DVD and videocassette from Library Video Company at <www.libraryvideo.com>.

MLL   *MyLiteratureLab Resources.* Photographs and biographical information for Bierce. Video clip and critical essay on "An Occurrence at Owl Creek Bridge."

Jorge Luis Borges, THE GOSPEL ACCORDING TO MARK, page 485

Jorge Luis Borges, who considered himself primarily a poet, is almost certainly the most influential short story writer of the last half century. His mix of fantasy and realism was the catalyst to the Latin American literary "boom" of magical realism. His use of nonfiction forms—like the essay, book review, or scholarly article—as vehicles for the short story not only inspired experimental writers of metafiction, it also helped challenge, among literary theorists, the traditional distinctions between fiction and factual writing. Writers as diverse as John Barth, Italo Calvino, Gabriel García Márquez, John Updike, Thomas Disch, Donald Barthelme, J. G. Ballard, Michel Foucault, and Angela Carter all reflect Borges's influence.

Many Borges stories—including "The Gospel According to Mark"—operate simultaneously on two levels. The surface of the story usually offers a conventional narrative, often with a surprise ending. Borges's masters in fiction were traditional storytellers like Robert Louis Stevenson, Rudyard Kipling, and G. K. Chesterton. (He was also particularly fond of mystery and supernatural tales.) Borges frequently employed old-fashioned narrative devices borrowed from their work, but he was equally fascinated by the literature of mysticism and the occult, not only the Christian and Jewish traditions but also the Islamic and Chinese. From these mystics and metaphysicians, he developed an obsession for speculating on secret patterns in reality. For Borges, the search for hidden significance was not a literary game; it was an essential undertaking, part of humanity's attempt to uncover God's plan, and the temporal world's means of understanding eternity. Not surprisingly, one of Borges's favorite modern writers was Kafka.

Borges's fascination with hidden significance leads to a consciously constructed second level of meaning in many of his stories, in which surface details can be discovered to have secret implications. The amazing thing about Borges's stories is the sheer density of meaning the careful reader will find embedded in the text. One need not catch or understand all these hidden clues to appreciate his stories, but discovering them does enrich one's experience. They are not trivial details, but the individual threads to a complex pattern of expression.

"The Gospel According to Mark" is an example of how tightly interwoven Borges's symbolic subtext can be. In this story, his main technique is irony, the traditional way of saying one thing while meaning another. Virtually everything that happens in the story has an ironic significance. The questions addressed below elucidate some, but by no means all, of the ironic underpinnings of this haunting story.

QUESTIONS FOR DISCUSSION

1. *What is about to happen to Baltasar Espinosa at the end of this story?* If students don't understand Borges's surprise ending—the point, that is, where the overt and ironic narratives meet—they will not be able to figure anything else out. Most students will catch the ending at once—Baltasar Espinosa is about to be crucified by the Gutre family. However, it may be worth asking this basic question to make sure no one misses it.

2. *How old is Espinosa? What is ironic about his age?* Espinosa is thirty-three, the age at which Jesus is traditionally thought to have been crucified.

3. *What is the background of the Gutre family? How did they come to own an English Bible? Why is it ironic that they own this book?* Like America, Argentina is a country populated largely by immigrants. (Borges himself was a mixture of English, Italian, Jewish, Uruguayan, and Argentinean stock.) The Gutre family are the descendants of Scottish immigrants, but they have lived on the Argentinean pampas so long that they have forgotten not only their English but even their ancestry. Their name is a corruption of the name *Guthrie*. Significantly, Borges links their Scottish ancestry to Calvinism, with its belief in absolute predestination. (In retrospect, Espinosa's sacrificial death seems fated.) The irony of their owning an English Bible is multiple: they cannot read; they know no English; they are seemingly ignorant of Christianity; they have forgotten their Scottish roots. However, there is, of course, a deeper irony. Although they have forgotten everything else, the Gutres have unconsciously maintained a Calvinistic sensibility that leads them to interpret the Gospel with absolute literalism.

4. *The narrator claims that the protagonist, Espinosa, has only two noteworthy qualities: an almost unlimited kindness and a capacity for public speaking. How do these qualities become important in the story?* Espinosa's two qualities seal his fate. His gift for public speaking makes his renditions of the Gospel particularly effective to the illiterate Gutre family. He even rises to his feet when reading the parables. His unlimited kindness makes Espinosa a perfect Christ figure—the gentle man who sacrifices himself to redeem others. (One can find significance in virtually all of Espinosa's other attributes, as listed in the first paragraph.)

5. *When Espinosa begins reading the Gospel of Saint Mark to the Gutres, what changes in their behavior does he notice?* Once Espinosa begins reading the Gospel, he suddenly makes an intense connection with the Gutre family. Until then conversation had proved difficult. They treat him with ever-greater respect and follow his orders. He catches them talking about him respectfully, but he does not understand the significance of their change in behavior until too late.

6. *What other action does Espinosa perform that earns the Gutres' gratitude?* Espinosa helps treat the Gutre girl's injured pet lamb. (Borges's choice of that symbolic animal is surely not coincidental.) The family seem to consider his intercession miraculous, although Espinosa does not understand their reaction. There is a consistently ironic gap between what he notices in their behavior and what their actions really signify. It is a good exercise to have students list as many ironic episodes or situations as possible.

7. *Reread the last paragraph. Why is it ironic that the Gutres ask Espinosa's blessing and the daughter weeps?* The irony is that the three people asking his blessing are about to murder him. The weeping girl is both one of his assassins and a Mary (or, perhaps more appropriately, a Mary Magdalene) figure crying at the crucifixion.

8. *Why do the Gutres kill Espinosa? What do they hope to gain?* The Gutres kill Espinosa to achieve salvation. The father questions Espinosa quite explicitly on that point the morning before his execution. For obvious reasons, old Gutre is particularly anxious to know if the soldiers who executed Christ were also saved.

9. *Is the significance of Espinosa's death entirely ironic? Or does he resemble Christ in any important respect?* The central question in interpreting Borges's story is whether it merely depicts a grotesquely ironic misunderstanding or rather suggests a deeper religious vision. Whatever one's conclusions, it is certain that Borges had a lifelong fascination with the idea of Christ and redemption. Some of his best stories, like "Three Versions of Judas" and "The Circular Ruins," explicitly concern the Incarnation. Borges never used the Christian mythos carelessly. A narrowly ironic reading of "The Gospel According to Mark" is easy to make. It is an ironic horror story in which the protagonist unwittingly creates the conditions for his own ritual murder. Read this way, the story is quite satisfactory—like a superior episode of *The Twilight Zone*. The story, however, also allows a deeper, though still ironic religious reading. Here, too, Espinosa is an unwitting Christ-figure, but one understands him not to represent real Christianity but a shallow parody of it. He is a Christ without divinity, a figure whose teaching lacks moral weight and whose death will save no one. When quizzed by the Gutre father about particular points in the Gospel, Espinosa asserts things he does not believe in order to save face. His theology is "a bit shaky," and so he answers other questions without examining their logical or theological consistency. In his bewildered way, Espinosa enjoys the authority of his divine position, but he neither understands nor deserves it. He is a well-meaning sham, quite unable to comprehend that the Gutres (whom he unmaliciously, but also un-Christianly, considers beneath him) might take matters of salvation seriously. He is a dilettante unsuitably cast in the role of a deity. Although he seems to accept his death meekly (we do not know for sure what follows his realization), he has only the outward features of a redeemer. His dabbling in the divine has not only destroyed him, it has morally corrupted his followers. Espinosa may be a Christ-figure, but he is no Christ.

Students wishing to do a paper on Borges might profitably compare "The Gospel According to Mark" with Borges's ingenious tale "Three Versions of Judas." For more sophisticated students, a comparison between "The Gospel According to Mark" and Flannery O'Connor's "A Good Man Is Hard to Find" could be an absorbing project. Both stories end in senseless murders, and both depict complex and heretical reaction to the Gospels. A 75-minute video interview with Borges, *Profile of a Writer*, is available on video cassette.

Willa Cather, PAUL'S CASE, page 489

"Paul's Case" may put you in mind of several other intractable "cases" in modern American fiction, for example, the title character of Nathanael West's *Miss Lonelyhearts* or Tommy Wilhelm in Saul Bellow's *Seize the Day*. Both protagonists move us by their zeal to live meaningfully in a world of callousness and easy accommodations, and both appall us with their idiotic choices and almost willed self-destructiveness. If you have ever tried teaching either of these short novels, you will have realized the difficulty of leading students to understand the complexities of the characters and the themes, especially when most of their questions begin with "Why doesn't he just . . . ?"

Such youthful frustration is surely appropriate. There would be something freakish about young people embracing middle-aged defeat and disillusion. But with an adolescent protagonist such as Paul, a teacher might assume a greater degree of understanding and sympathy in students' responses—and perhaps be surprised at their hostility toward or even rejection of Paul. Perhaps it isn't too surprising: imagine for a moment how students would react to him if he were one of their classmates. And remember that it is much easier to sympathize with Paul as a fictional character than it would be to deal with him as one of your own students.

Even within the context of the fiction, it is a tribute to the depth of Cather's art and insight that she has not made it easy for us. What Paul aspires to be, is, from any mature perspective, hollow and superficial. What he rejects, however unglamorous it may be, is not on its face hateful. The reactions of his teachers and even his father to Paul's behavior are not harsh or punitive; just about everyone, including his fellow ushers as they sit on him until he has calmed down, seems to want to help. And he is, after all, a thief and an unrepentant one at that—a fact that will no doubt be seized upon by students seeking justification for their dislike of him.

QUESTIONS FOR DISCUSSION

1. *What is it about Paul that so disturbs his teachers? Recall any of his traits that they find irritating, any actions that trouble them. Do they irritate or trouble you?* The boy's dandyism, his defiance, and his unconcealed contempt disturb his teachers beyond all reason. They also disturb many readers, who find a discrepancy between their own negative feelings about Paul and the fondness Cather seems to feel toward him. The school principal and Paul's art teacher are able to muster sympathy for the boy (paragraphs 7–8), but they don't claim to understand him.

2. *What do the arts—music, painting, theater—mean to Paul? How does he react when exposed to them? Is he himself an artist?* Oddly, when he hears a concert, it's "not that symphonies, as such, [mean] anything in particular to Paul" (11). The romance and beauty in the air excite him to hysteria. He reacts in the same way to fine food and wine, good clothes, a lavishly decorated room. For all his

sensitivity, he is not an artist, and he doesn't respond to art as an artist would. It's the *idea* of art and beauty, the pleasure they afford his senses, that evoke a response in him. In *Willa: The Life of Willa Cather*, Phyllis C. Robinson points out that Paul "may have had the sensitivity of an artist but, unlike his creator, he was without discipline, without direction and, saddest and most hopeless of all, he was without talent." In that fact lies his private tragedy.

3. *In what different places do we follow Paul throughout the story? How do these settings (and the boy's reactions to them) help us understand him, his attitudes, his personality?* Cather shows us Paul in school, at home, in the art gallery, in the theater, and, finally, in the big city. Everywhere, he functions apart from the ordinary beings who surround him. Isolated and unhappy, Paul regards his aesthetic longings as evidence of his superiority to other human beings. Absence of hope and cool disdain for the ordinary ways of attaining wealth and finery and an invitation to New York drive him to one grand, suicidal fling in the beautiful, glamorous world where he imagines he belongs.

4. *Does Cather's brief introduction into the story of the wild Yale freshman from San Francisco (in paragraph 54) serve any purpose? Why do you suppose he and Paul have such a "singularly cool" parting? What is Cather's point?* In New York Paul expects to find wealthy persons of taste and temperament similar to his own. He finds instead the disappointing Yale student who, far from sharing Paul's reverence for beauty, seems to the boy hopelessly crass. Ironically, though he seems to have grown up with all the advantages Paul has lacked, this worldly student disappoints Paul as much as do his family and friends at home. Who could measure up to Paul's impossible standards? For the rest of his stay, Paul is content to observe his fellow guests from afar.

5. *Is Paul a static character or a dynamic one? If you find him changing and developing in the course of the story, can you indicate what changes him?* The only change in Paul's character during the story seems to be the fairly minor one mentioned in paragraphs 42–43. Once settled in at the Waldorf, he realizes he is no longer "dreading something." Is this change enough to justify our calling him a dynamic character? The change seems to signal in Paul a deepening involvement in an unreal world rather than any growth. We think he's a static character. His perceptions and values, and the actions that follow from them, remain unchanged.

6. *Comment on some of the concrete details Cather dwells on. What, for instance, do you make of the portraits of Washington and John Calvin and the motto placed over Paul's bed (paragraph 18)? Of the carnation Paul buries in the snow (paragraph 64)?* Paul's sensibilities recoil from all that is ugly, even ordinary. His room, featuring pictures of those austere and well-disciplined heroes George Washington and John Calvin, is hateful to him. Working-class Cordelia Street, where he lives, induces in him "a shuddering repulsion for the flavorless, colorless mass of every-day existence; a morbid desire for cool things and soft lights and fresh flowers" (19). By paragraph 64, after Paul has run away from New York, he realizes that fresh flowers do not stay fresh forever. He sees the parallel between "their brave mockery" and his own "revolt against the homilies by which the world is run" and characterizes both as "a losing game in the end." He dies like the flowers, his "one splendid breath" spent.

7. *What implications, if any, does the title "Paul's Case" have for this story? Is Paul mentally ill, or does Cather place the roots of his malaise elsewhere?* Robinson has this to say about Cather's view of Paul:

> As if to underscore her own intuition in regard to the story, Willa gave it the subtitle "A Study in Temperament," and to the modern reader the pathological attributes of Paul's malaise are more persuasive than the romantic aspects. Willa told George Seibel that she drew on two boys who had been in her classes for the character of Paul, but to others she confessed how much of her own hunger and frustration were embodied in the unhappy boy's flight from the drab reality of his daily life and in his instinctive reaching out for beauty.

In other words, we today tend to think Paul seriously disturbed, but apparently Cather didn't see him that way. In conflict with school, neighbors, and family, Paul seems to her an admirable victim. Cather often sticks up for the lonely, sensitive individual pitted against a philistine provincial society—as in her famous story "The Sculptor's Funeral."

"Paul's Case" was featured in the PBS television film series *The American Short Story*. It is available on video and DVD from Library Video Company at <www.libraryvideo.com>. Short scenes from the script of Ron Cowen's adaptation are included in *The American Short Story*, Volume 2 (New York: Dell, 1980), and invite comparison with the original.

A detailed plan for teaching "Paul's Case" is offered by Bruce E. Miller in *Teaching the Art of Literature* (Urbana, IL: NCTE, 1980). To get students involved in the story before they read it outside of class, Miller suggests reading passages from the early part of the story (before Paul flees to New York) and summarizing what happens, and then asking students how they'd imagine Cather would continue the story. He advises the instructor to show the class a few photographs of adolescent boys and to ask how closely the pictures reflect students' mental images of Paul. The point is to spark a discussion of Paul's complex character. Is he a cheat? A victim? A hero? Various opinions are likely to emerge, and students may come to see "that the different views of Paul are not necessarily incompatible with each other, and that Cather has accomplished the difficult feat of delineating a complex character who, though flawed, engages the reader's sympathy."

 MyLiteratureLab Resources. Photographs, biographical information, bibliography, and critical overview for Cather. Video clips, audio clips, and critical essay for "Paul's Case."

John Cheever, THE FIVE-FORTY-EIGHT, page 503

The power of this remarkable story comes from the depth and complexity of its two main characters. Cheever creates a cold, manipulative, egotistic figure in Blake. He is a man who is outwardly capable but inwardly empty. He understands with keen clarity the public behavior of people, but he has almost completely lost touch with the emotional needs that drive them. He is, to put the matter tersely, a heartless bastard. Cheever carefully explores the chilling details of his private life, but he never judges Blake. The genius of his presentation is to let Blake's character reveal itself in dozens of telling specifics—like the bookshelves he builds in the doorway between his and his wife's bedrooms or his inability in the Madison Avenue bar to remember Miss Dent's name. Blake is an unusual creation for Cheever. As William Peden pointed out in *The American Short Story: Continuity and Change 1940–1975* (Boston: Houghton, 1975), "Except for the sadistic organization man of the merciless 'The Five-Forty-Eight,' most of Cheever's nonheroes are essentially amiable men."

Cheever creates an equally complex and troubling character in Miss Dent. His presentation of her is dramatically masterful. At first, we see her only as a vulnerable, shy, and unstable young woman. She is "undistinguished in every way." However, as the story reaches its climax, her underlying strength and courage become evident. If one uses E. M. Forster's two categories of "flat" and "round" characters, Miss Dent is unquestionably a round character. Her behavior surprises us. Each action reveals something new about her. Blake—we are not surprised to observe—fails to understand the individuality and depth of her character. To him, she is a flat character, just another of the women he has picked deliberately "for their lack of self-esteem." He can see but not assimilate the unusual details of her life, like the piano squeezed into her small room with its Beethoven sonatas on the music rack.

"The Five-Forty-Eight" could easily have become pure melodrama. Imagine a bare-bones plot summary: abused and spurned secretary exacts revenge on heartless boss. Doesn't that sound like something from a soap opera like *The Young and the Restless* or *One Life to Live*? Melodrama, of course, is not all bad; it offers an emotional force and directness that subtler literary forms sometimes lack. Cheever borrows the narrative drive and gripping emotionalism of the mode while transcending its limitations largely through the richness of his two leading characters. The relatively simple plot acquires deep emotional resonance because both Blake and Miss Dent, despite their unusual and disturbing qualities, seem like genuinely real people.

"The Five-Forty-Eight" is told by an omniscient third-person narrator (who knows, for instance, why an unanswered phone is ringing in the Shady Hill station), but the narrator articulates the story mainly from Blake's perspective. We see Miss Dent only from the outside, but we follow Blake's inner life moment by moment. "The Five-Forty-Eight" is predominantly his story, even if Miss Dent comes to control events. Blake is an intelligent and observant, if utterly uncompassionate, man. Cheever's style reflects the quickness of Blake's mind as well as the cruel selfishness of his concerns. It is interesting to note how wonderfully Cheever evokes Blake's heightened consciousness on the train. Confronting the possibility of his own death, he sees everything beyond the train window with an almost lyric poignancy:

> Out of the window he saw the river and the sky. The rain clouds were rolling down like a shutter, and while he watched, a streak of orange light on the horizon became brilliant. Its brilliance spread—he could see it move—across the waves until it raked the banks of the river in dim firelight. Then it was put out. Help would come in a minute, he thought.

Extraneous description? No, the passage puts the reader in Blake's consciousness. We experience the nervous, silent, brooding moments with him. He worries that he may be killed. He remembers the horrifying dead bodies he saw in the war. He watches the daylight die and implicitly ponders his own mortality. Although the train ride with Miss Dent takes only a few pages, Cheever places us so vividly in Blake's mind that we, too, experience its awful duration.

The names of the characters are interesting. Neither is given a first name—only generic WASP-y surnames. Blake's lack of a first name suggests his lack of intimacy and amiability. He is curt, distant, and businesslike. "Miss" Dent always carries her formal title. Since the story is told largely from Blake's perspective (though in the third person), one might also surmise that the title reflects his wish to keep her at a safe distance. Indeed, Blake keeps most of the world at a considerable emotional distance. He thinks of his neighbors as Mr. Watkins and Mrs. Compton. There is also an appropriate symbolism in Miss Dent's name. She has been bruised and injured by life.

On the train, the balance of power shifts from Blake to Miss Dent. At the office she had been in Blake's power. He had used it to exploit, hurt, and discard her. Now, pressing a gun against his stomach, *she* exercises absolute power over him. She will also humiliate and discard him, but her actions, though tinged with insanity and desperation, fundamentally differ from his. Blake's cruel treatment of Miss Dent was unreflective and dispassionate. The encounter left so little impact on his hardened nature that he cannot even remember her name exactly when she begins to stalk him. For Miss Dent, however, her retaliation has a paramount importance. It provides her with the self-esteem that she hopes may lead her to sanity.

It would be easy for a reader who does not look too closely at the text to glamorize Miss Dent into a feminist heroine avenging the wrongs of her sex against a piggish male. That would be the melodramatic version of the story. In a manner a bit reminiscent of Flannery O'Connor, Cheever makes Miss Dent a much more uncomfortable heroine. While not perhaps insane, Miss Dent is deeply disturbed. She has visionary dreams and she considers herself clairvoyant; she even quotes the Book of Job as if she were God's messenger. She lives in almost complete isolation ("I have never had a true friend in my life"). Her letter to Blake begins, "Dear Husband." Yet out of this confusion arises a deep humanity and a frighteningly lucid self-knowledge. Miss Dent understands her own sickness better than the doctors. She needs love and self-esteem in a world that refuses her both.

The ending of "The Five-Forty-Eight" is especially powerful because it provides both narrative surprise and symbolic appropriateness. The journey that seemed to have begun in revenge ends in redemption. By sparing Blake's life, Miss Dent affirms her own compassion while also demonstrating the power that she could wield. She purges her spirit of the harm Blake did her (and Blake sees that she has been successful). She also seeks to disrupt Blake's life in a way that will make him realize how shallow, cruel, and loveless it is, although she understands that it may be impossible to reach his humanity in any genuine way. ("I really don't want to harm you, I want to help you, but when I see your face it sometimes seems to me that I can't help you.") Miss Dent is surely transformed by the encounter. A difficult but essential question for readers to ponder, however, is whether the incident will change Blake in any important way. In her study *John Cheever* (New York: Twayne, 1979), Lynne Waldeland writes that the matter-of-fact last line "leaves us believing that no rude awakening into an enlarged humanity has taken place for Blake." What do your students think?

Students wishing to write on Cheever might find it interesting to compare "The Five-Forty-Eight" to another of the stories first published in the same volume, *The Housebreaker of Shady Hill* (1958). Two excellent stories you might recommend are "The Country Husband" (which won the O. Henry Award in 1955, the same year that "The Five-Forty-Eight" won a Benjamin Franklin Award) and the title story, "The Housebreaker of Shady Hill." The protagonists of both stories are considerably more sympathetic men than Blake. Francis Weed, in "The Country Husband," also has a brush with death when his airplane makes a crash landing. An interesting paper might compare him to Blake. The title character of "The Housebreaker of Shady Hill" loses his job and begins to burglarize his wealthy neighbors to pay the bills. His excruciating moral consciousness makes a stark contrast to Blake's self-absorption. Both stories can also be found in *The Stories of John Cheever* (New York: Random, 1978), which is available in a Ballantine paperback.

Most of the best writing on Cheever is biographical. The body of criticism on his work remains relatively small. In addition to Lynne Waldeland's study, one might consult George W. Hunt's interesting *John Cheever: The Hobgoblin Company of Love* (Grand Rapids, MI: Eerdman, 1983). Hunt's book is an excellent appreciation of Cheever's artistry, and it subtly reveals the essentially religious nature of the stories. Scott Donaldson's *John Cheever: A Biography* (New York: Random, 1988) provoked complaints from the Cheever clan when it first appeared, but it remains indispensable. It is both well researched and well written. Equally useful is Donaldson's collection of Cheever's many interviews, *Conversations with John Cheever* (Jackson: U of Mississippi P, 1987).

For interested students, a 1979 PBS television adaptation of Cheever's story, directed by James Ivory with a screenplay by Terrence McNally, is available on DVD and videocassette.

 MyLiteratureLab Resources. Biography, critical overview, and bibliography for Cheever.

Anton Chekhov, THE LADY WITH THE PET DOG, page 512

Anton Chekhov's late stories mark a pivotal moment in European fiction—the point where nineteenth-century realist conventions of the short story begin their transformation into the modern form. The Russian master, therefore, straddles two traditions. On one side is the anti-Romantic realism of Maupassant with its sharp observation of external social detail and human behavior conveyed within a tightly drawn plot. On the other side is the modern psychological realism of early Joyce in which the action is mostly internal and expressed in an associative narrative built on epiphanic moments. Taking elements from both sides, Chekhov forged a powerful individual style that prefigures modernism without losing most of the traditional trappings of the form. If Maupassant excelled at creating credible narrative surprise, Chekhov had a genius for conveying the astonishing possibilities of human nature. His psychological insight was profound and dynamic. Joyce may have more exactly captured the texture of human consciousness, but no short story writer has better expressed its often invisible complexities.

It is an instructive irony that short fiction at the end of the twentieth century seemingly owed more to Chekhov than to Joyce or any other high-modernist master. In 1987, when Daniel Halpern asked twenty-five of the noted writers featured in his collection *The Art of the Tale: An International Anthology of Short Stories 1945–1985* (New York: Viking, 1987) to name the most crucial influences on their own work, Chekhov's name appeared more often than that of any other author. Ten writers—including Eudora Welty, Nadine Gordimer, and Raymond Carver—mentioned Chekhov. (James Joyce and Henry James tied for a distant second place with five votes each.) Chekhov's preeminent position among contemporary writers is not accidental; no other author so greatly influenced the development of the modern short story. As the late Rufus Matthewson once observed, Chekhov fully articulated the dominant form of twentieth-century short fiction: "the casual telling of a nuclear experience in an ordinary life, rendered with immediate and telling detail." Chekhov was the first author to consciously explore and perfect this literary method in his vast output of short stories.

Chekhov does not eliminate—or even minimize—plotting from his stories. He is masterful in creating narrative suspense. His plots, however, are usually highly compressed. Early in his career Chekhov had to write according to strict space limits (only one hundred lines of newsprint), and he learned by constant practice to eliminate all unnecessary elements from a story. What Chekhov offered instead was the luminous detail, a few significant particulars that summon up a character or scene. In a letter to his brother, Chekhov explained how by depicting the right external detail, he could evoke the inner state of a character or special quality of a landscape:

> When describing nature, a writer should seize upon small details, arranging them so that the reader will see an image in his mind after he closes his eyes. For instance: you will capture the truth of a moonlit night if you'll write that a gleam like starlight shone from the pieces of a broken bottle, and then the dark, plump shadow of a dog or wolf appeared. You will bring life to nature only if you don't shrink from similes that liken its activities to those of humankind.
>
> In displaying the psychology of your characters, minute particulars are essential. God save us from vague generalizations! Be sure *not* to discuss your hero's state of mind. Make it clear from his actions. Nor is it necessary to portray many main characters. Let two people be the center of gravity in your story: he and she. (Letter to Alexander Chekhov, May 10, 1886)

What seems most distinctive about Chekhov's mature stories is how the plot inevitably originates from the inner force of his characters. The story line never seems imposed for its own sake as it often does, for example, in the shorter works of Balzac or Hoffmann, which revel in narrative twists and surprise endings. One sees parallels to Chekhov in certain stories by Melville, Tolstoy, and Flaubert. Their main interests, however, lay in the novel, and they had no inclination to explore so fully or adventurously the potential of short fiction. Chekhov, by contrast, was obsessed with the form of the short story. Although he died at forty-four, and had careers in both medicine and theater, he wrote over eight hundred stories.

Chekhov's major innovation comes from realizing the psychological potential of the character-driven story by merging plot and protagonist. As the narrative develops, Chekhov allows the protagonist to change as well—subtly and credibly. There is perhaps no better representative of Chekhov's dynamic psychology than Dmitry Gurov, the protagonist of "The Lady with the Pet Dog," which Vladimir Nabokov called "one of the greatest stories ever written." Published with symbolic appropriateness in 1899, this story shows Chekhov (who would die within five years) reinventing the form for the twentieth century. In the case of this brief tale, Gurov undergoes a strange and winding course of emotional and moral growth that few readers would expect.

The opening section of the story deserves close attention. We first meet Gurov on the esplanade at Yalta where he is taking a holiday alone. An attractive man from the upper class, he has been trapped for years in a loveless arranged marriage. Not yet forty, he has already become an experienced seducer. His affairs always end badly, but he cannot resist starting new ones. His doomed adulteries have left him cynical and bitter. Chekhov presents Gurov in a mostly unfavorable light, emphasizing his manipulation, misogyny, and amorality, and yet the author refuses to simplify his protagonist into a stock villain. Gurov possesses contradictory impulses. His low opinion of women, for example, accompanies an inexplicable preference for their company. Nothing in the story's opening suggests the inner transformation that Gurov will undergo—more or less against his will—and the initially unfavorable view of his character ensures that the reader's attitudes will also need to be revised.

We don't really know Anna Sergeyevna, the lady with the pet dog, until her seduction. Before that decisive moment she is seen mostly from the outside. She is little more than a series of gestures, remarks, and generally understated reactions. She is a young, bored, upper-class married woman in Yalta for the first time. After "her fall," she bursts out with a passionate fit of repentance. Only then does the reader gets a glimpse of her inner life. Although still quite young, she—like Gurov—is also a creature of contradictions. She wants to be honest and pure, but she also craves excitement and adventure. She, too, is trapped in a suffocating marriage. Anna wants to experience more of life ("To live, to live!"). She has even faked an illness to escape on a holiday to the Black Sea resort. By the standards of Chekhov's day, she is hardly a model heroine.

When Anna Sergeyevna leaves Yalta, her affair has seemingly concluded. Chekhov then explicitly shows the reader what was suggested all along—to Gurov the romance had little emotional depth. He had not sought love but only the emotional excitement of an infatuation. He was not even attracted by anything particularly personal about the young woman, only by her obvious availability and the excitement of pursuit. The affair with Anna was merely "another episode or adventure in his life." Its demise leaves him "moved, sad, and slightly remorseful" but certainly not heartbroken. Returning to Moscow, he expects to forget her—more or less—in a month.

Now, midway in "The Lady with the Pet Dog," comes the quiet climax of the story. This quintessentially Chekhovian moment is so private and internal that it is easy to miss the first time one reads the story. Returning to his daily routine in Moscow, Gurov gradually realizes he is in love with Anna. As a result, he also recognizes that the separation between his external and internal lives has become intolerable. His family leaves him mostly irritated or bored. He especially loathes the vulgar male world he inhabits—"frenzied gambling, gluttony, drunkenness, continual talk always about the same things." The mention of "talk" is not unimportant. Gurov's loneliness does not seem primarily sexual, though that craving is part of it. He also feels the agonizing absence of anyone he can talk to meaningfully about the private realities of his life. He now resolves to visit Anna in her hometown—a dangerously bold thing to do by the social standards of this time. If he missteps, he could easily ruin both of their lives forever.

What follows Gurov's decision is both simple and remarkable. Arriving in the city of S—, Gurov eventually manages to meet the astonished Anna at the theater one night. They both admit that they are in love. She promises to meet him discreetly in Moscow. (It would be impossibly risky to meet in her own city.) Under the pretense of consulting a physician for "a woman's ailment," she travels to Moscow every few months for an assignation. Although they remain trapped in their marriages, the couple carve out a secret world of happiness and dream—futilely, Chekhov hints—of escape.

Their solution—to continue their adulterous affair in secrecy and deception—is simple, but by the standards of 1899, hardly admirable. Chekhov, however, presents it in remarkably neutral terms. Conventional morality plays no significant part in the story's conclusions. No one is censured. The couple seem, in fact, to enjoy the author's qualified sympathy. Chekhov, however, does not rail against hypocritical public standards as a reformist like Shaw or Ibsen might; he simply portrays the couple's situation. Perhaps even more interesting is his ultimate characterization of Gurov. The protagonist initially appears as a conventional literary seducer—handsome, urbane, calculating, and amoral—but Chekhov gradually reveals that his unattractive appetite for philandering is actually a misdirected hunger for something deeper. He craves intimacy, though he has mistaken sexual conquest for it. After almost dispassionately seducing Anna and ending the affair with seasoned skill, Gurov astonishes himself by finding love "really, truly—for the first time in his life." The cynical roué unwittingly finds a sort of redemption—but not in any of the ways Chekhov's audience would have easily understood or endorsed. Gurov does not repent his adultery and renounce Anna. Neither does he find the means to legitimize their relationship in marriage (an impossibility in the Russia of 1899). They simply continue to meet in secret. Only their furtive lives are, in a sense, redeemed, but at least their lives now touch something authentic. Readers today, especially students, might fail to understand how boldly this story moves to its conclusion.

Each of the story's major settings—Yalta, Moscow, and the unnamed provincial town—reveal something about the couple. The seaside resort of Yalta provides an almost anonymous place where both individuals can escape the restrictions of their repressive homes. It also serves as a romantic backdrop for their trysts. By contrast, Moscow is the social prison in which Gurov lives—locked in his loveless marriage and shallow friendships. Anna's city plays the same harsh role in her life. It represents the social order that confines her in unhappiness. At the end of the story, however, the couple recreate a small secret island of happiness in a Moscow hotel—a small room of private authenticity symbolically set against a metropolis of public convention. Inside its walls, the couple is happy, but, as Chekhov suggests in the final paragraph, it is a place they can never safely leave.

Students intending to write a paper on Chekhov's fiction should be steered toward Ronald L. Johnson's excellent survey, *Anton Chekhov, A Study of the Short Fiction* (New York: Twayne, 1993). It is a fine primer. The secondary literature on Chekhov is immense. Ronald Hingley's *A New Life of Anton*

Chekhov (New York: Knopf, 1976) remains useful, as does Edmund Wilson's 1952 essay "Seeing Chekhov Plain," which is collected in *A Window on Russia* (New York: Farrar, 1972). Ernest J. Simmons's *Chekhov* (Boston: Atlantic, 1962) is valuable, readable, compact, and rich in critical intelligence. Any student willing to write a long paper on Chekhov might want to read at least one of the plays as well. Most of Chekhov's stories have been reissued in Constance Garnett's translations by Ecco Press. See also *The Unknown Chekhov*, translated by Avrahm Yarmolinsky (New York: Farrar, 1954) for stories Garnett left out. The Norton Critical Edition of *Anton Chekhov's Short Stories* (New York: Norton, 1979), which contains thirty-four stories as well as some of Chekhov's wonderful letters, is also useful. V. S. Pritchett's *Chekhov: A Spirit Set Free* (New York: Vintage, 1988) provides a graceful and engaging biographical study by this notable English man of letters.

Kate Chopin, THE STORY OF AN HOUR, page 523

By all accounts, Oscar Chopin seems to have been, by the standards of the time, a loving and quite indulgent husband to his wife, Kate. "The Story of an Hour" is, of course, fiction, but underlying the key fourteenth paragraph are such facts as Chopin's marriage when she was only twenty, her giving birth to six children in the space of eight years, and the family's move from sophisticated New Orleans to the rural Louisiana Bayou—along with the fact that her writing career seems to have begun only after his early death. Both here and in "The Storm," Chopin presents her characters and situations without judging or moralizing. Instead, she dramatizes situations in which basically decent people find themselves in honest conflict between duty and desire, between one kind of love and another, situations in which they have strong and sincere feelings on both sides of the issue.

QUESTIONS FOR DISCUSSION

1. *Is Mrs. Mallard's sorrow at the news of her husband's death merely feigned? Try to account for her sudden changes of feeling.* Undoubtedly her grief is sincere. Caught within a conventional marriage, she has not realized the freedom she has been denied. Notice that her rush of new joy, her looking forward to a whole new life, begins when she observes that spring is bursting forth, too, in the natural world.

2. *Some stories—for instance, "An Occurrence at Owl Creek Bridge"—are noted for their surprise endings. How can it be claimed that "The Story of an Hour" has a triple surprise ending?* Surprise ending l: Mrs. Mallard realizes that her husband's death has left her unexpectedly happy. Surprise ending 2: Her husband is still alive. Surprise ending 3: She dies herself. "The Story of an Hour" has been criticized for having a rigged ending that strikes some readers as a cheap trick. But the convention is used here not merely for its shock value but also to illuminate Mrs. Mallard's repressed resentment against her husband.

MLL *MyLiteratureLab Resources.* Biography, critical overview, and bibliography for Chopin. Longman Lecture on "The Story of an Hour."

Sandra Cisneros, THE HOUSE ON MANGO STREET, page 525

Sandra Cisneros began as a poet, and "The House on Mango Street," the opening piece of her 1984 collection of the same name, achieves its principal effects
through techniques associated as much with poetry as with short fiction—
brevity, economy of style, and the use of detail, rather than narrative or statement, as the primary vehicle of theme. In this regard, "The House on Mango
Street" has much in common with Jamaica Kincaid's "Girl." You might also, if
you are familiar with it, be reminded of James Joyce's masterful "The Sisters,"
which, like the Cisneros and Kincaid selections, is the first story in the volume
in which it appears. Like Joyce, Cisneros presents her material through the eyes
and the sensibility of a very young first-person narrator; also like Joyce, Cisneros
employs a certain amount of indirection. This technique can make for a useful
exercise in close, interpretive reading. Ask the class whether the narrator is male
or female, and they will no doubt automatically assume the latter because the
author is a woman; then ask them what details in the story "prove" the point
(the narrator shares a bedroom with Nenny [end of paragraph 5], who is "my sister" [end of paragraph 1]). Ask them how old they think the narrator is, and why
they think so; you'll probably get a number of answers, but it will be interesting
to see if anyone points out the narrator's assumption, at the end of paragraph 5,
that, like the children, her parents *have* to share a bedroom because the house is
too small for them to have their own rooms.

But while "The Sisters" depends almost entirely on the reader's understanding the significance of things that the narrator does not, the young speaker
in "The House on Mango Street" is for the most part acutely aware of her situation and its larger implications. She knows that the new house represents both
a pause from, though not necessarily an end of, the rootlessness (and its consequent insecurity) that she and her family have experienced; it also represents
freedom from the restrictions that she and her family have had to endure,
restrictions that are focused in large part on the lack of privacy—having to be
careful not to make too much noise, having to hear about it when too much
noise is made, being unable to keep one's personal business to oneself, even
something so private as taking a bath. And even worse is the sense of what such
a lifestyle means in the eyes of others, as is vividly portrayed in paragraphs 6
through 10: when the nun from the narrator's school passes by the flat on
Loomis and says "You live *there*?," the narrator's internal reaction is: "The way
she said it made me feel like nothing."

Yet, brief as "The House on Mango Street" is, it does much more in its
eleven paragraphs than celebrate such things as striving, upward mobility,
and the fulfillment of the American dream. The dream that the narrator's
mother has spun and clung to is a dream of a very different house from the
small, cramped one on Mango Street, and so is the house that her father
talked about whenever he bought a lottery ticket. Although they recognize
that "the house on Mango Street isn't it," both parents seem to see the
house—whether truly so in their own minds or simply in an attempt to keep
their children's hopes alive—as a way station in the fulfillment of their
dreams, not as the end of the line, the outer limit of their real-life possibilities. But the narrator seems to have been around enough blocks—Loomis,
Keeler, Paulina, and others that she can no longer remember—to have
already grasped a sense of the limits of the American dream for people like

her and her family, people who don't win lotteries and whose dreams are destined to remain merely dreams: "I know how these things go."

Sandra Cisneros reads from her books, *The House on Mango Street* and *Woman Hollering Creek*, on audiocassette tape available from Random House Audio.

Ralph Ellison, BATTLE ROYAL, page 526

Ralph Waldo Ellison—his father named him after Emerson—was born in Oklahoma City in 1914, in a state without a history of slavery. In "Battle Royal," he transfers his protagonist to an unidentified town in the South. With the aid of a State of Oklahoma scholarship, Ellison attended Tuskegee Institute in Alabama. "Ellison has been everything," Langston Hughes once noted, "from shoeshine boy to first trumpeter in a jazz orchestra." In 1936 he moved to New York City to study sculpture and music composition. But befriended by Richard Wright, at the time working on the novel *Native Son*, Ellison was encouraged to become a writer. *Invisible Man*, which took Ellison seven years to write, clearly owes something to Wright's fiction: naturalism based on autobiography. Wright's work seemed too limited to realism, however, to suit Ellison, who said he wanted to introduce "imagination . . . a sense of poetry" to the fiction of black experience. (Ellison discusses his complex relationship with Wright in several places in his 1964 collection of essays, *Shadow and Act*—especially in his long interview with fellow novelist Richard G. Stein, which opens the volume.) In its portrait of the artist as a young man, Ellison's novel also seems more than fleetingly indebted to James Joyce.

In a 1963 interview with Ellison, Allen Geller asked whether the writer agreed with the advice of the dying grandfather in "Battle Royal." Does the old man advocate divorce from society—to go along with society on the surface only, while actually working to undermine it? Ellison replied:

> Not to act without it but act against it, to collaborate with its destruction of its own values. That's the way that a weak man, that weak old grandfather—physically weak, that is—found for dealing with a circumstance, but his grandson actually writes his memoirs. *Invisible Man* is a memoir of a man who has gone though that experience and now comes back and brings his message to the world. It's a social act; it is not a resignation from society but an attempt to come back and be useful. There is an implied change of role from that of a would-be politician and rabble-rouser and orator to that of writer. No, there's no reason for him to lose his sense of a social role. But I think . . . *Invisible Man*, his memoir, is an attempt to describe reality as it really exists rather than in terms of what he assumed it to be. ("An Interview with Ralph Ellison," *The Tamarack Review*, reprinted in *The Black American Writer*, vol. I: Fiction, ed. C. W. E. Bigsby [Baltimore: Penguin, 1971].)

Booker T. Washington (1856–1915), the founder of Ellison's alma mater, takes some hard satirical jabs in "Battle Royal" (and in the college memories in *Invisible Man*). Students may need to know that, although widely admired in his day as the nation's outstanding black leader and educator, Washington has been regarded more critically by later black intellectuals. In his autobiography, *Up from Slavery* (1901), Washington tries to show that black people's best hope for advancement lies in humility, self-improvement, and conciliation. Ironically, Ellison quotes a speech given by Washington in 1895 (paragraph 67 of "Battle Royal"), calling on blacks to cultivate friendship with the Southern white man. "In those pre-invisible days," the narrators tells us, "I visualized myself as a potential Booker T. Washington" (95).

The secondary literature on Ellison is immense, and most of it necessarily focuses on *Invisible Man*. A good place for students to begin is the author's most important critical collection, *Shadow and Act* (1964). For a lively short introduction to *Invisible Man*, see Barbara Christian's essay "Ralph Ellison: A Critical Study," in *Black Expression*, edited by Addison Gayle, Jr. (New York: Weybright and Talley, 1969). For a full-length study of Ellison's work, see Robert G. O'Meally's *The Craft of Ralph Ellison* (Cambridge: Harvard UP, 1980). O'Meally not only explores literary influences (Joyce, Faulkner, Hemingway, Richard Wright), but also demonstrates that in language and methods of storytelling, Ellison is really indebted to black folklore, sermon, and song.

 MyLiteratureLab Resources. Biography, critical overview, and bibliography for Ellison.

Gabriel García Márquez, THE HANDSOMEST DROWNED MAN IN THE WORLD, page 536

"Magic Realism" (*el realismo magical*) was a term first coined in 1949 by the Cuban novelist Alejo Carpentier to describe the matter-of-fact combination of the fantastic and the everyday in Latin American fiction. About the same time it was also used by European critics to describe a similar trend in postwar German fiction exemplified by novels such as Gunter Grass's *The Tin Drum* (1959). (The German art critic Franz Roh had employed the same term in 1925, but he applied it only to painting.) Magic Realism has now become the standard name for a major trend in contemporary fiction that stretches from Latin American works like Gabriel García Márquez's *One Hundred Years of Solitude* (1967) to *norteamericana* novels like Mark Helprin's *Winter's Tale* (1983) and Asian works like Salman Rushdie's *Midnight Children* (1981). In all cases the term refers to the tendency among contemporary fiction writers to mix the magical and the mundane in an overall context of realistic narration.

If the term "Magic Realism" is relatively new, what it describes has been around since the early development of the novel and short story as modern literary forms. One already sees the key elements of Magic Realism in *Gulliver's Travels* (1726), which factually narrates the fabulous adventures of an English surgeon. Likewise Nikolai Gogol's short story "The Nose" (1842), in which a minor Czarist bureaucrat's nose takes off to pursue its own career in St. Petersburg, fulfills virtually every requirement of this purportedly contemporary style. One finds similar precedents in Dickens, Balzac, Dostoyevsky, Maupassant, Kafka, Bulgakov, Calvino, Cheever, Singer, and others. Seen from an historical perspective, therefore, Magic Realism is a vital contemporary manifestation of a venerable fictive impulse.

The possibilities of storytelling will always hover between the opposing poles of verisimilitude and myth, factuality and fabulation, realism and romance.

If mid-century critics (like F. R. Leavis, V. S. Pritchett, F. W. Dupee, Irving Howe, and Lionel Trilling) almost exclusively favored the realist mode, their emphasis reflected their generation's understandable fascination with the immediate past. They still lived in the shadow of what Leavis called the "Great Tradition" of the psychological and social novel. This tradition encompassed (to expand Leavis's Anglophilic list a bit) Jane Austen, George Eliot, Henry James, Edith Wharton, Joseph Conrad, Virginia Woolf, D. H. Lawrence, Willa Cather, Ernest Hemingway, and early James Joyce. As the realistic novel confidently continued in the first decades of the century, it was all too easy to imagine that this particular line of development had decisively superseded the older pre-novelistic modes of storytelling. These London, Oxford, and New York critics would hardly have imagined that a radically different kind of fiction was being developed beyond their ken in places like Argentina, Colombia, and Peru. By the time García Márquez and his fellow members of "*el boom*" (the boom) in Latin American fiction came to maturity, the reemergence of the fantastic heritage in fiction seemed nearly as revolutionary as the region's politics.

As a young law student, García Márquez read Kafka's *The Metamorphosis*. It proved a decisive encounter, and the influence is not hard to observe in his early stories, which so often present bizarre incidents unfolding in ordinary circumstances. If Kafka reinvented the fable by placing it in the modern quotidian world, García Márquez reset it in the unfamiliar landscape of the Third World. If Kafka made spiritual issues more mysterious by surrounding them with bureaucratic procedure, his Colombian follower changed our perception of Latin America by insisting that in this New World visionary romanticism was merely reportage. García Márquez also had another crucial mentor closer at hand—the Argentinean master, Jorge Luis Borges. Only thirty years García Márquez's senior, Borges had quietly redrawn the imaginative boundaries of Latin American fiction. Almost single-handedly he had also rehabilitated the fantastic tale for serious fiction. Removing religion and the supernatural from any fixed ideology, he employed the mythology of Christianity, Judaism, Islam, and Confucianism as metaphysical figures. Paradoxically, he expressed his sophisticated fictions in popular rather than experimental forms—the fable, the detective story, the supernatural tale, the gaucho legend. He was the first great post-modernist storyteller, and he found an eager apprentice in García Márquez, who developed these innovative notions in different and usually more expansive forms.

Stripped of any magical dimension that the narrative invests them with, the realistic events of "The Handsomest Drowned Man in the World" could not be simpler or more mundane. A stranger's corpse washes ashore; the townspeople prepare it for a funeral, meanwhile making inquiries into the identity of the stranger and the circumstances of his death; all their efforts lead to no factual discoveries; in the end, they ritualistically return the body to the sea. Everything that gives the story depth and significance occurs above the level of these simple facts: the great beauty and the great size of the corpse; the seeming increase in its size even after death, so much so that it pops the buttons of the shirt that has been sewn for its funeral; and so on.

From the beginning of the story, every significant occurrence takes place in the perceptions of the townspeople, in their reactions to the sudden presence of the corpse among them, and in the feelings and actions that follow from those reactions. These effects begin almost immediately, when, in paragraph 2, "the men who carried him to the nearest house noticed that he weighed more than any dead man they had ever known" and "maybe the ability to keep on growing after death was part of the nature of certain drowned men."

Paragraphs 3 through 7 concern themselves with the effect that the dead man has upon the women of the village. To fully understand that effect, we must of course know something about what the village was like before the drowned man's sudden arrival on its shores, about its "stone courtyards with no flowers . . . on the end of a desertlike cape" and "the lonely look of other drowned men who came out of the sea [and] that haggard, needy look of men who drowned in rivers" (paragraph 3). This corpse has come from "faraway oceans and deep waters" to point out to them the contrast between the richness of life's possibilities and the poverty of their real lives. His size makes them aware of the smallness of their existence: "They could not find a bed in the village large enough to lay him on nor was there a table solid enough to use for his wake" (paragraph 4). They feel intuitively that the restlessness of the sea and the calm of the wind have something to do with his coming, and they sense that had he lived among them, the circumstances, both physical and emotional, of life in the village would have had to enlarge to accommodate what he represents to them. And his beauty makes them feel the drabness and pettiness of their existence, as they think about how embarrassed and self-effacing he would have been about his own size and awkwardness, deflecting their pettiness and meanness of spirit with his peacefulness and gentleness. So important have these feelings become to the women that when the men return empty-handed, having been unable to discover any facts about the dead man that might possibly threaten the symbolic value he has taken on, their reaction is: "Praise the Lord, . . . he's ours!"

The very next sentence tells us that "[T]he men thought the fuss was only womanish frivolity," and they immediately set about trying to dispose of this troublesome object as quickly as possible. But as the women stall and ultimately expose the dead man's face, the validity of their response is demonstrated by its being communicated to their men: "There was so much truth in his manner that even the most mistrustful men, the ones who felt the bitterness of endless nights at sea fearing that their women would tire of dreaming about them and begin to dream of drowned men, even they and others who were harder still shuddered in the marrow of their bones at Esteban's sincerity" (paragraph 9).

In the end, the previously flowerless village is festooned with flowers for Esteban's funeral, and the townspeople "also knew that everything would be different from then on, that their houses would have wider doors, higher ceilings, and stronger floors." The effect of the handsomest drowned man in the world has been transformative, and permanently so; it is magical, but it is also very real.

MLL *MyLiteratureLab Resources*. Biography, critical overview, and bibliography for García Márquez.

Dagoberto Gilb, Look on the Bright Side, page 540

In addition to being extremely entertaining, Dagoberto Gilb's "Look on the Bright Side" raises the interesting issue of the relationships among author, narrator, and reader. In reading poetry written in the first person, we usually begin with the assumption that the speaker is not only reliable—that his or her descriptions, attitudes, and conclusions are to be taken at face value—but also essentially interchangeable with the author. Despite the constant admonitions, in books such as this one, against that assumption, we tend to maintain it unless we are given reasons not to. Such reasons may range from the rueful callowness that informs Housman's "When I was one-and-twenty" to the full-blown megalomania, if not outright madness, of the Duke in Browning's "My Last Duchess."

In reading a story told from the first-person point of view, we realize that the narrator is a fictional character distinct from the author, but once again, until and unless we are alerted to the contrary, we tend to assume that the narrator's views and values are being endorsed by the author and passed on to us for our endorsement as well. Needless to say, there are some notable exceptions: from the beginning of Poe's "The Tell-Tale Heart," for instance, the narrator's hysterical tone and absurd claims tell us that he is not to be trusted. But, to take another example, we may have to read fairly far into Updike's "A & P" before we begin to suspect that not all of Sammy's assessments of himself and his own motivations are necessarily to be taken at face value.

The opening paragraph of Gilb's story—with its emphasis on self-respect, pride, and standing up for one's rights even when it isn't very practical—leads us to expect that our unnamed narrator will turn out to be an honest and righteous soul, an innocent underdog passed over and exploited by a system that is stacked against him. Admittedly, as the story unfolds, there are things that do reflect in his favor: he is laid off from his job; the customs officer at the border gives him a fair amount of uncalled-for attitude; and the judge in his case determines that the original rent increase, which set the story's entire sequence of events in motion, was inappropriate. But there are clues as early as the second paragraph that things aren't entirely the way that opening would suggest. "My wife told me to pay it and not have the hassle. She knew me better than this" hints that he might be motivated as much by stubbornness and contrariness as he is by principle (also, in paragraph 44 he acknowledges that neither the rent nor the living conditions were quite as intolerable as he makes them sound here). And his referring to his children as "our little why nots"—presumably an allusion to the chancing of unprotected sex that led to their conceptions—gives another insight into the complexities of the characterization.

Even the points in his favor tend to be undermined along the way. He has lost his job through no fault of his own, but he is not overzealous in trying to find another one. (Some might argue, along with the customs official, that this is not the best time for a man with a wife and three children to support to take his family on vacation.) The customs official is irritatingly condescending, but the narrator is smuggling four bottles of rum (and carrying a couple of joints in his wallet.) The verdict is in his favor, but vindication and a cut in the back rent are insufficient to him; as he has previously said, ". . . mostly it was the principle of the thing. It seemed to me if I had so much to lose for being wrong, I should have something equal to win for being right" (paragraph 60). He is emphatic about his rightness even when—or, perhaps, especially when—he is clearly not right: he doesn't deny, in paragraph 58, that he has a tax delinquency from a previous year (just as he acknowledges, in paragraph 83, that his application for a painting job "listed all this made-up experience I had"), but he obviously feels that the government has no right to deduct this debt from the large refund that he's been counting on, and he even feels that the government should cut him some slack because he works hard and isn't planning to flee the country: "The thing is, it's no use being right when the US Govt thinks it's not wrong."

Gilb writes with considerable wit and flair, and indeed there is something attractive about the energy and resilience of the narrator's personality, as reinforced by the title itself (it is in paragraph 82 that he supplies the story's title, when he says "You have to look at the bright side"). But even here, in the larger context, there is a troubling element: at this point in the story, he has sent his family to relatives in Mexico and is sleeping on a mattress on the floor of a bare apartment as he waits to be evicted. And despite the by now ritualistic emphasis on how these circumstances provide the perfect opportunity for a fresh start and that things will turn around soon, the end of the paragraph suggests that he may—and, given his previous arc, probably will—soon be sleeping in the back seat of his car.

The likelihood that the grimmest possibilities will come to pass is reinforced by the conclusion, as the narrator hangs around with an obviously deranged stranger, about whom, still looking on the bright side, he says, "Even if he was a little wired, he wasn't like the guy who was still rolling around under the tree or the one screaming at the top of his lungs." The very end, as the narrator "was getting used to the bench, even when I did catch that whiff of piss" is somewhat chilling in its implications: despite the title and the narrator's sense of himself, what we are left with here is not an indomitable spirit in the face of life's inevitable reverses, but a man readily accommodating himself to increasingly desperate circumstances that were easily avoidable, if not largely of his own making.

Nathaniel Hawthorne, YOUNG GOODMAN BROWN, page 548

"Young Goodman Brown" is Hawthorne's most frequently reprinted story and probably the most often misunderstood. Some initial discussion of the story's debt to American history may be helpful—most students can use a brief refresher on the Salem witchcraft trials, in which neighbor suspected neighbor and children recklessly accused innocent old women. The hand of the devil was always nearby, and it was the duty of all to watch for it. From Cotton Mather's *Wonders of the Invisible World* (1693), Hawthorne drew details of his imagined midnight Sabbath. In revealing to Brown the secret wickedness of all the people he knew and trusted, the story seems to illustrate the Puritan doctrine of innate depravity. Humankind was born tarred with the brush of original sin and could not lose the smudge by any simple ritual of baptism. Only the elect—the communicants, those who had experienced some spiritual illumination which they had declared in public—could be assured of salvation. Brown's unhappy death at the end of the story seems conventional: Puritans held that how one died indicated his chances in the hereafter. A radiantly serene and happy death was an omen that the victim was Heaven-bound, while a dour death boded ill.

The devil's looking like a blood relative may reflect another Puritan assumption. Taken literally, perhaps the resemblance between the devil and Brown's grandfather suggests that evil runs in Brown's family, or in the Puritan line as the devil asserts (18–19). Or that wickedness lurks within each human heart (as well as good) and that each can recognize it in himself, as if he had looked into a mirror. Of course, donning the family face may be one more trick of the devil: an attempt to ingratiate himself with Brown by appearing as a close relative. Hawthorne's great-grandfather, the witch trial judge, would have agreed that the devil often appears in disguise. The Salem trials admitted "spectral evidence"—testimony that the devil had been seen in the form of some innocent person. Spectral evidence was part of the case against Goody Cloyse, Goody Cory, and Martha Carrier—all named in Hawthorne's story, all of whom Judge John Hathorne condemned to death. For more on Puritan doctrines (and how they eroded with time), see Herbert W. Schneider's classic study *The Puritan Mind* (U of Michigan P, 1958). Of Hawthorne's tales and *The Scarlet Letter*, Schneider observes:

> [Hawthorne] did not need to believe in Puritanism, for he understood it. . . . He recovered what the Puritans professed but seldom practiced—the spirit of piety, humility, and tragedy in the face of the inscrutable ways of God. (262–63)

We realize that this story is often interpreted as highly ambiguous, highly ambivalent in its attitude toward Puritanism and the notion of innate depravity. But we read it as another of those stories in which the Romantic Hawthorne sets out to criticize extreme Puritanism and to chide the folly of looking for evil where there isn't any. In this regard, the story seems much like "Ethan Brand," in which the protagonist sets out to find the unpardonable sin, only to receive God's pardon anyway; and like "The Minister's Black Veil," in which Mr. Hooper makes himself miserable by seeing the world through a dark screen. (The latter is, admittedly, a more ambivalent tale: Hawthorne also finds something to be said in favor of that black veil and its wearer's gloomy view.) Brown's outlook has been tainted by dark illusion, conjured up, it would seem, by the devil's wiles.

Some students will take the devil's words for gospel, agree that "Evil is the nature of mankind," and assume that Brown learns the truth about all those hypocritical sinners in the village, including that two-faced Faith. One likely point of departure is the puns on *Faith* in Brown's speeches:

> "I'll cling to her skirts and follow her to heaven" (paragraph 5).

> "Faith kept me back awhile" (12).

> "Is there any reason why I should quit my dear Faith . . . ?" (39)

> "With Heaven above, and Faith below, I will yet stand firm against the devil" (46).

> "My Faith is gone!" (50)

What Faith does Hawthorne mean? Surely not Puritanism—in this story, hardly a desirable bedfellow. More likely Brown's Faith is simple faith in the benevolence of God and the essential goodness of humankind. Brown's loss of this natural faith leads him into the principal error of the Salem witch-hangers: suspecting the innocent of being in league with the devil. At first, Brown assumes that his Faith is a pretty little pink-ribboned thing he can depart from and return to whenever he feels like it. Brown believes he is strong enough to pass a night in the evil woods and then return to the bosom of his faithful spouse unchanged. Of course this conviction is blind pride, and it works Brown's ruin.

Why does Brown go out to the woods? Apparently he has promised the devil he will go meet him, but go no farther. By meeting the devil he has "kept covenant" (15). The initial situation—that Brown has a promise to keep out in the woods—is vague, perhaps deliberately like the beginning of a dream.

And was it all a dream? Hawthorne hints that the devil's revelations to Brown and the midnight Sabbath are all one grand illusion. When Brown staggers against the supposedly flaming rock, it proves cold and damp, and a twig that had been on fire suddenly drips cold dew. (We are indebted here to F. O. Matthiessen's discussion in *American Renaissance* [Oxford: Oxford UP, 1941] 284.) If we read him right, Hawthorne favors the interpretation that Brown dreamed everything ("Be that as it may . . ."). Leave it to the devil to concoct a truly immense deception.

Still, some ambiguity remains. As Hawthorne declared in a letter to a friend in 1854, "I am not quite sure that I entirely comprehend my own meaning in some of these blasted allegories." If what Brown saw at the witches' Sabbath really did take place, then his gloom and misery at the end of the story seem understandable. Some have read the story to mean that Brown has grown up to have a true sense of sin and therefore ends a good Puritan; he has purged himself of his boyish good cheer. But we find the morose Brown deluded, not admirable, and suspect that Hawthorne does too.

Students may not have met the term *allegory* in this book unless you have assigned the chapter "Symbolism," but some will know it already. Not only Faith can be seen as a figure of allegory, but Young Goodman Brown himself—the Puritan Everyman, subject to the temptation to find evil everywhere. For a class that has already begun symbol-hunting, "Young Goodman Brown" is a fair field. Among the more richly suggestive items are the devil's snaky staff or walking-stick (13), with its suggestions of the Eden snake and the serpentine rods of the Egyptian magicians (Exodus 7:8–12). When the devil laughs, it squirms happily (22). It works like seven-league boots, and its holder enjoys rapid transportation. The devil gives it to Goody Cloyse and then plucks Brown a fresh stick from a maple (38–41); when Brown grasps it in despair (51), it speeds him on to the unholy communion. Other symbolic items (and actions) include the forest—to enter it is to be led into temptation, and Brown keeps going deeper and deeper— the withering of the maple branch at the devil's touch (38), and the proffered baptism in blood or fire at the evil meeting (67).

But the richest symbol of all is Faith's lost pink ribbon that flutters to the ground, prompting Brown to conclude that Faith too is a witch who let fall her ribbon while riding on a broomstick to the midnight Sabbath. (Many students, unless you help them, will miss this suggestion.) Sure enough, when Brown arrives, Faith is there too. The ribbon, earlier suggesting youthful beauty and innocence, becomes an ironic sign of monstrous evil and duplicity. This terrible realization causes Brown to decide to follow the devil after all—even though, presumably, the fluttering ribbon was another diabolical trick. When Brown meets the real Faith once more, she is still all beribboned, as if she hasn't lost anything.

How to state the theme? Surely not "Evil is the nature of mankind" or "Even the most respected citizens are secretly guilty." That is what the devil would have us believe. A more defensible summing-up might be "Keep your faith in God and humankind" or "He who finds evil where no evil exists makes himself an outcast from humanity."

Compare this story with Shirley Jackson's "The Lottery." There, too, a whole town takes part in a blood-curdling rite—but in public, not clandestinely.

MLL   *MyLiteratureLab Resources.* Longman Lecture on "Young Goodman Brown."

Zora Neale Hurston, SWEAT, page 558

Hurston's stark tale of a bitter marriage turned murderous first appeared in the one and only issue of the Harlem arts journal *Fire!!* in November 1926. *Fire!!*, which carried the subtitle "A Quarterly Devoted to the Younger Negro Artists," presented some of the leading talents of the new generation, including Langston Hughes, Countee Cullen, and Arna Bontemps. "Sweat," with its use of authentic black dialect and folkways, its forthright presentation of harsh subject matter, and (to quote Alice Walker) its "sense of black people as complete, complex, *undiminished* human beings," makes it a representative work of the Harlem Renaissance.

QUESTIONS FOR DISCUSSION

1. *What importance does the setting of "Sweat" have to its action?* The story takes place mostly in a house on the outskirts of a small Florida town (which critics identify with Hurston's hometown of Eatonville). The isolation of Delia's home is essential to the plot. Its distance from town means that she has no protection there from Sykes's violence, just as its isolation ultimately gives Sykes no escape from his slow, painful death by snakebite. The setting is also important to the story's motivation. Delia has bought the house with her own hard work. Sykes wants to kill her for the house so that he can bring another woman home to it. The house also becomes a symbol to the otherwise disappointed Delia of what she has managed to accomplish in her hard, painful life. ("It was lovely to her, lovely.")

2. *What has Delia and Sykes's marriage been like?* Delia married out of love. Sykes, she believes, brought only lust to the union ("a longing after the flesh"). Two months after the wedding, he gave her the first of many brutal beatings. In town, he is notorious for beating her and she for surviving his savage assaults. Sykes has frequently disappeared to squander his irregular earnings while Delia has worked as a laundress to pay their bills. Delia's hard work wounds Sykes's masculine pride: it reminds him that he cannot support her. Sykes is now adulterously involved with Bertha. Delia is not surprised to discover that he is trying to kill her.

3. *What is the significance of the story's title?* Hurston's title describes Delia's existence. Trapped in a brutal, loveless marriage and getting no help from Sykes in supporting the two of them, Delia has almost nothing in her life except work. Defending herself against Sykes's threats, she summarizes her life as "Sweat, sweat, sweat! Work and sweat, cry and sweat, pray and sweat!" The title also suggests why Delia is deaf to Sykes's pleas at the end of the story: love and compassion have been sweated out of her.

4. *Is Delia right to let Sykes die at the end of the story?* This may be an uncomfortable question for students, but the point of Hurston's story is to make us con-

sider uncomfortable issues. It may be important to remind students that Delia is not responsible for Sykes's being bitten by the snake; he has fallen into his own trap. If she is guilty of anything, it is only of not trying to help her husband—a sin of omission rather than commission. There is little question that a jury would acquit her of any charge. If ever a woman could claim extenuating circumstances, it is Delia. The more interesting question is whether Delia is morally culpable. In this regard, Hurston seems to suggest that Sykes has made Delia a person callous enough to watch coldly her own husband die. The ending has led one critic, Robert Bone, in his *Down-Home: Origins of the Afro-American Short Story* (New York: Columbia UP, 1988), to call "Sweat" a self-indulgent "revenge fantasy." But most critics have agreed with Lillie P. Howard, who viewed "Sweat" as a complex moral investigation of a good woman in an extreme situation:

> Delia could have warned him, saved him, but she understandably does not. She has been hardened by his constant abuse and has built up a "spiritual earthworks" against him. Poetic justice has been rendered. (*Zora Neale Hurston* [New York: Twayne, 1980] 65)

What do your students think?

5. *How does the language of "Sweat" contribute to the story's effect?* There are two different levels of language employed in the story. Hurston presents the narration in sharp and evocative standard English, whereas the dialogue is written in the rural black dialect of her native Central Florida. Their constant alternation heightens the story's considerable nervous energy and suspense. The dialect also adds realism to the story: it evokes real people and a real region. Students sometimes experience some initial difficulty in reading dialogue in dialect because it looks different from conventional English. It is important to get them to hear it. You might ask the class why Hurston chose to write the dialogue in dialect. Would the story be different if the dialogue were written in standard American English?

A volume of critical essays dealing with "Sweat," edited by Cheryl Wall, is available from Rutgers UP (in its series dealing with short fiction, "Women Writers: Texts and Contexts"). Students planning to write on Hurston will find it helpful to read Laura M. Zaidman's comprehensive article on the author in *Dictionary of Literary Biography 86: American Short-Story Writers, 1910–1945*, edited by Bobby Ellen Kimbel (Detroit: Gale, 1989), which provides an insightful and highly readable introduction to her life and work.

Beverly Bailey of Seminole Community College in Sanford, Florida, has informed us that Hurston's hometown of Eatonville hosts an annual festival in her honor. In addition to music, crafts, food, and entertainment, there are also scholarly presentations. For information on the Zora Neale Hurston Festival see <http://www.zoranealehurstonfestival.com>. Prof. Bailey also recommends Steven Glassman and Kathryn Lee Seidel's *Zora in Florida* (Orlando: U of Central Florida, 1991), which Bailey calls "a fine study of the place that nurtured and inspired Hurston's work, the frontier wilderness of central Florida and the all-black town of Eatonville."

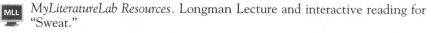 *MyLiteratureLab Resources.* Longman Lecture and interactive reading for "Sweat."

Kazuo Ishiguro, A FAMILY SUPPER, page 566

The novelist Kazuo Ishiguro has published only a handful of short stories, and "A Family Supper" certainly makes one wish he wrote more. Compressed, affecting, and evocative, this melancholy tale of homecoming radiates a dark, disturbing power. An estranged son returns to Japan from California two years after his mother's death. He finds his once formidable father a broken man—devastated by both the bankruptcy of his business and the death of his wife. The depth of the father's sorrow and regret are gradually revealed to be almost limitless. The son, who has recently left a failed romance in California, tries to sympathize, but his already strained relationship with his father remains awkward and formal. Both father and son seem genuinely to love one another, but their ability to express that affection in either words or actions is inadequate to the situation.

Death casts its shadow everywhere in this autumnal story, which is set near "the end of a sunny autumn day." There is not enough emotional warmth left within the family to light or warm the chilling blackness settling over the father's world. The evening grows darker as the story continues, finally leaving the three characters in a gloom so thick that the narrator can no longer see the outer world or recognize a photograph of his own mother in the inner world of his family home. The story ends in darkness and silence as father and son sit together in a quietly desperate formality.

Ishiguro has a notable, almost poetic gift for communicating what is not said. The central narrative suspense of "A Family Supper" is never overtly articulated—namely, that the father may be planning to poison himself along with his two children (the narrator and his sister). This terrifying possibility is repeatedly suggested by details in the story—especially the father's deep admiration for his dead business partner Watanabe, "a man of principle and honor," who killed his entire family in a sort of suicide ritual. Likewise, there is some doubt whether the death of the narrator's mother was truly an accident. The father suspects that it was suicide (although this theory may be a projection of his own obsession). Likewise, the particulars of the mother's poisoning given at the opening of the story prepare us for the possibility of unexpected death from food.

By the end of the story the unspoken dangers seem to have passed—at least for the children. The father concedes that Watanabe's suicide was a mistake, and he expresses hope that his son will stay in Japan, and comfort that his daughter may move back home after completing school. The father's half-hearted conviction that "Things will improve then," however, is illusory. The reader knows that the son will probably leave Japan, where he does not feel entirely comfortable. The sister also seems likely to go to America with her new boyfriend. The father's life will not improve. He will face more of the loneliness and regrets that seem already to have almost paralyzed him.

Students should have little trouble with this story. Although "A Family Supper" is deeply embedded in the particulars of Japanese culture, Ishiguro has deftly arranged the narration to explain every unfamiliar aspect as it appears (while simultaneously adding suspense by delaying full explanations of certain strictly narrative elements like the specifics of the deaths of both Watanabe and the narrator's mother). As a result, we find the story both credibly Japanese and universal—a family facing dissolution and ruin after terrible losses.

James Joyce, ARABY, *page 573*

Set in the city Joyce called "dear old dirty Dublin," "Araby" reveals a neighborhood so dreary that it seems no wonder a sensitive boy would try to romance his
way out of it. In paragraphs 1–3, details stack up tellingly, painting a scene of
frustration and decay. We see the dead-end street with an abandoned house at
its "blind end"; the boy's house where the priest had died, its room full of "musty
air" and "old, useless papers"; dying bushes, a rusty bicycle pump; a street of shadows and dark, dripping gardens lit by somber violet light. Still, the description is
not unrelievedly sad. Playing in the cold, the boys feel their bodies glow. From
"dark, odorous stables" comes the "music" of jingling harnesses. And for the boy,
Mangan's sister lends the street enchantment.

Most students won't need help to see that "Araby" is told by its main character. They may need class discussion, though, to realize that the narrator is a
man who looks back on his boyhood memories. One indication of the narrator's
maturity is his style. In the first paragraph, he remarks, in unboyish language,
that the houses, "conscious of decent lives within them, gazed at one another
with brown imperturbable faces." Besides, this mature storyteller is about to step
back and criticize his younger self: "her name was like a summons to all my foolish blood" (paragraph 4).

Mangan's sister, whose name is never told, seems an ordinary young woman
who summons her kid brother to tea. She is a vague figure: the boy glimpses her
from afar, sometimes while peering at her from shadow. John J. Brugaletta and
Mary H. Hayden suggest that the conversation in which the boy promises to bring
her a gift takes place only in his mind. Mangan's sister, they argue, may never have
set foot in the room where the priest died (6), into which the boy retreats to have
his visionary experience. In this musty shrine, his senses swoon. He clasps his
hands in an attitude of prayer, murmurs an incantation over and over (*O love! O
love!*), and conjures her face before him—"At last she spoke to me." Even the
spikes he sees her clasping are unreal, for they couldn't be there in the dead priest's
drawing room. In the end, at the bazaar, the image of Mangan's sister fades before
the physical presence of the banal, flirtatious English salesgirl who says, "O, I never
said such a thing." Neither did Mangan's sister say a word to the narrator that
bound him to his imagined promise ("The Motivation for Anguish in Joyce's
'Araby,'" *Studies in Short Fiction* [Winter 1978]: 11–17). Professor Roger Silver of
the University of Maryland takes issue with this interpretation. He writes:

> If one looks at the text, paragraph 6 ends with the narrator "murmuring: *O
> love! O love!* many times." Then Joyce begins a new paragraph, "At last she
> spoke to me." Why does this paragraph have to take place in the priest's room?
> I would think that some time has gone by, and the narrator has now met Man-
> gan's sister outside the house. Brugaletta and Hayden say that Mangan's sister
> doesn't answer the narrator when he promises to bring back something from
> the fair. That doesn't mean that the narrator is having a vision. After all,
> Joyce does mention in paragraph 9 that she spoke, and does have her say, "—
> it's well for you." We could still agree with Tindall that Mangan's sister sym-
> bolizes Ireland's Church and keep all the other religious symbolism.

The boy's daydreams of Mangan's sister are difficult to take seriously. Amid
barrels of pigs' cheeks, he carries her image in his mind as a priest carries a chal-

ice. He regards her with "confused adoration" and feels himself a harp on which she plays (5). From early in the story, the boy has projected a dazzling veil of romance over the commonplace. At the end, he realizes with shock that illusion has had him in thrall. Araby, the enchanted fair, turns out to be merely a drab charity bazaar where gimcracks are peddled, men count money, and a scatter-brained salesclerk makes small talk till the lights go out. The boy's intense anguish seems justified.

Nearly everything Joyce wrote has a thread of allegory, and "Araby" may be no exception. Making much of the identity of Mangan's sister, William York Tindall remarks: "Since [James Clarence] Mangan, one of Joyce's favorite poets, dedicated 'Dark Rosaleen,' his most famous poem, to his country, it seems likely that Mangan's sister is Ireland herself, beckoning and inviting." Tindall thinks the boy's frustrated quest is for Ireland's Church, toward which Joyce, too, felt bitter disillusionment. Rather than pursue Dark Rosaleen, the mature Joyce (and his protagonist Stephen Dedalus) chose exile. "Araby" makes a good introduction to *Portrait of the Artist as a Young Man*. (Tindall discusses the story in *A Reader's Guide to James Joyce* [New York: Noonday, 1959] 20.)

Araby, the bazaar with the "magical name," is paramount. Besides, the apple tree in the unkempt garden (2) hints of the tree in some lost Eden. Dublin, clearly, is a fallen world. Other items also suggest sterility and decay: the "blind" or dead-end street and its "uninhabited house . . . detached from its neighbors" (1); the dead priest's rusty bicycle pump (2). Counting coins on a tray like that used to serve communion, the men in paragraph 25 perform a little act with symbolic overtones. The darkening hall has seemed to the boy "a church after a service," and the two money changers are not driven out of the temple—they drive out the boy.

Elizabeth A. Flynn compares reactions to this story by twenty-six male and twenty-six female college students in "Gender and Reading," *College English* 45 (Mar. 1983): 236–53. Some men felt uncomfortable with the boy's solipsistic infatuation. Recalling similar experiences of their own, they had trouble attaining distance. Several men, Flynn reports, were harsh in their judgment on Mangan's sister. They saw the girl as manipulating the boy for her own ends: "just using him," "playing him along." Most of the women students made better sense of the story. They didn't condemn Mangan's sister, and they understood the ending. They recognized that as the lights of the bazaar go out, the boy passes a painful judgment on himself: he has been a vain fool. Some women saw him gaining from his experience. Freed from his delusion, he can now reenter reality. If your men students have trouble understanding the story, you might have them take a good look at the last line.

On the popular poem "The Arab's Farewell to His Steed," which the uncle remembers, Matthew A. Fike of the University of Michigan writes, citing an insight by Stanley Friedman: "Joyce's reference to this poem, a work notable for its sentimentality, directs attention to the main significance of 'Araby': the assault on sentimentality and illusion" (Friedman, *The Explicator* 24:5 [Jan. 1966], item 43). There seems more than a little resemblance between the boy's worship of Mangan's sister for "the white curve of her neck" and the Arab's devotion to his horse, with its "glossy neck." Ironically, the Arab's glamorized view of his steed contrasts with the awareness that Joyce's narrator achieves, or as Fike puts it, "The nomad never parts with his horse, but the boy abandons his illusion." (Thanks to Mr. Fike for prompting XJK to greater precision in his footnote on "The Arab's Farewell.")

MLL *MyLiteratureLab Resources*. Biography, critical overview, and bibliography for Joyce. Longman Lecture, interactive readings, and critical essay for "Araby."

Jamaica Kincaid, GIRL, page 578

"Girl" is the first story in Jamaica Kincaid's first book, *At the Bottom of the River*. As such, it might be seen—like Hemingway's "Indian Camp" in *In Our Time*—as a kind of keynote to the body of her work. It is also worth noting that the first half of the volume's dual dedications reads: "For my mother, Annie, with love."

The form of "Girl" is worth considering in class because its compact length makes it easy for students to see the parts and the whole simultaneously. The form of "Girl" can be reasonably viewed in at least two ways. It can be cogently argued that "Girl" is a character sketch rather than a short story. Kincaid does not—at least overtly—describe a significant action with its motivations and consequences. Instead she presents a memorable character (and deftly implies another) through a speech. If "Girl" is viewed as a character sketch, therefore, it must be considered a sketch of *two* people—mother and daughter. The story reminds us that a person need not be presented at length to be credibly characterized. The daughter has only two short and perhaps silent (but italicized) comments. Yet we see her life vividly rendered throughout her mother's torrent of advice.

Considered as a sketch in this fashion, "Girl" could conceivably be analyzed as one would analyze a poem, emphasizing such things as tone, voice, rhythm, and selection and placement of detail as vehicles and even components of meaning. From the most trivial of matters to the most significant, the recurring theme of the mother's advice is that there is one right way to do everything, and that way must be followed in order to avoid all of life's many dangers. (Again, one may draw a comparison with Hemingway.)

If "Girl" is viewed as a short story, however, then the mother's speech is itself the central action. Her motivations are almost self-evident—love, worry, and a conviction that traditional ways are best. Her speech to the girl even hints at the central conflicts in their relationship—the mother's desire for her daughter to be a lady and the girl's feeling of being unjustly criticized (not to mention being overwhelmed by so many orders all at once).

Without much difficulty, students (who may have heard from their own parents long lists of advice more or less similar in tone) will identify the speaker in "Girl" as a mother and the listener as her daughter. The mother's diatribe is interrupted only twice, when the daughter protests. (The italics leave it ambiguous whether the daughter responds aloud or merely mentally.) From the language, such as the names of foods (*dasheen, doukona*) and the details of daily life, we soon see that the setting is another country—the author's native Antigua, we might guess. The mother's words seem an accumulation of instructions repeated over many years. Her intent is to teach her daughter to measure up, to grow into a lady and not a "slut." Any deviation from her rules, the mother worries, may be a fatal step toward sluthood. Clearly, she sees a woman's role in life as traditionally restricted and restricting. But the mother is not merely delivering negative, binding orders; she tries to impart a whole body of traditional wisdom about the right way to do things. She offers her daughter the secrets of catching fish, avoiding bad luck, curing a cold (or a pregnancy), bullying a man, lovemaking, and making ends meet.

Some students, especially female students, will no doubt roll their eyes in recognition at the portrait of the mother and identify with the daughter, although they will grudgingly acknowledge that the mother is motivated by love and concern for her daughter's well-being. They may identify more directly with the mother—and find a greater depth and resonance in the text—if they perceive her to be also motivated, no doubt unconsciously, by self-concern as well: by the need to justify the choices and especially the sacrifices that she has made in her own life, and by the need to validate her own insights through their adoption by someone else.

The poet Cindy Milwe, who teaches at Santa Monica High School in Santa Monica, California, has contributed this note on teaching "Girl":

"Girl" never fails to engage teenagers and, despite its brevity, has proven useful in many classroom contexts. I have even used it with ninth graders as an introduction to *Romeo and Juliet*, with tenth graders as way into *A Doll's House*, and with seniors in a creative writing class to help them understand the notion of voice (focusing on the imperative nature of the piece and its almost relentless repetition).

Regardless of grade level, I have students read the story the night before and ask two good readers to be prepared the following day to read aloud (one as the mother and one as the daughter). During the in-class reading, I ask students to focus on the voices of these two characters and then I ask the following discussion questions:

1. What do we know about the mother and daughter? What don't we know? What can we infer? (For critical reading purposes and to facilitate a richer discussion, I will often have students jot down what they consider to be important lines from the text and then have them explain, in writing, what they are able to infer from those lines.)

2. What kinds of things is the mother trying to teach her daughter? Which commands and instructions seem particularly useful or problematic? Why?

3. Do you think she's a good mother based on the advice and warnings she offers? Why or why not?

4. Why is this story called "Girl" when the girl only "speaks" two sentences? What might Kincaid be suggesting about being a girl in general or about being a girl in this situation?

After talking about the story at length, I open up the discussion by asking students to share the various things they've learned about being a "boy" or a "girl" and from whom they've learned them. In a creative writing class, I ask students to make two columns on a piece of notebook paper and list the various "commands"—using the imperative—and the various "instructions" (using the repeated phrase "This is how to . . .") that they've heard from people in their own lives. They will then use these lists as preliminary notes to craft their own story with two voices, using "Girl" as a model.

Jhumpa Lahiri, INTERPRETER OF MALADIES, page 579

That Jhumpa Lahiri should have come out of nowhere to win the Pulitzer Prize with her first book seems less startling after one has experienced her work. "Interpreter of Maladies" catches the reader's attention from the very first sentence and never relaxes its hold until the end. Its quiet mastery is evident throughout, in the beautifully controlled writing, in the eye for vivid and telling detail, in the expert dialogue and sharp characterization, and especially in the wise and sympathetic portrayal of the complexities of the human heart.

QUESTIONS FOR DISCUSSION

1. *From whose point of view is the story told? How would you characterize the method employed—omniscient, limited omniscient, or objective?* The correct answer is, of course, *limited omniscient*. The method is not objective: we do not see everything from the outside as we would if we were present, but we are given insights into the unspoken thoughts and feelings of someone other than ourselves. The author has limited her omniscience in this story to Mr. Kapasi; it is his inner state that we are privy to, and everyone and everything else in the story is presented through his viewpoint.

2. *Mr. Das tells Mr. Kapasi (paragraph 20), "In a way we have a lot in common . . ." What does he mean by this? Do they in fact have much in common?* As a science teacher in a middle school who takes his classes to the Museum of Natural History in New York City, Mr. Das expresses a sense of kinship with Mr. Kapasi in his role as a tour guide. Also, although unknown to Mr. Das, both are the fathers of three children, and both are in less than totally satisfactory marriages. But beyond such superficial resemblances, everything in the text suggests the great differences between the two: Mr. Das is somewhat immature, quite unselfconscious, a bit crass, seemingly satisfied with his life and himself; Mr. Kapasi is older, a person of dignity and reserve, greatly concerned with his appearance and the impression he makes on others, who has established a life of comforting rituals to cope with his unhappiness in his marriage.

3. *What can we determine about the relationship of Mr. and Mrs. Das from the details given in the first few pages of the story?* The first clause of the very first sentence of the story is "Mr. and Mrs. Das bickered." Mrs. Das agrees to take their daughter to the toilet only after he points out that he gave Tina her bath the previous night: they do not freely assist and support each other as partners in a mutually loving relationship, but instead keep strict domestic accounts, as if each fears to be taken advantage of by doing more than the other. While Mr. Das is eager to enjoy the sights of the tour (though he derives more enjoyment from reading descriptions in his tour book, even when he is standing right in front of the thing being described), he makes no real effort to communicate that eagerness to his wife, who is clearly, behind her sunglasses, bored and apathetic. Their annoyed exchange over his supposed stinginess (paragraphs 46-48), as well as their readiness to act this way in front of a stranger, also shows the strains in their relationship.

4. *On one level, "Interpreter of Maladies" is about a clash of cultures. In what ways do the members of the Das family seem particularly American to Mr. Kapasi? How are these characteristics contrasted with Indian life and behavior?* Though Indian in appearance, Mr. and Mrs. Das dress like Americans and speak with American accents (unsurprisingly, as they were born and raised and have lived their entire lives in America). Their reactions to the monuments of their ancestral culture range from shallow to indifferent and are expressed in terms such as "neat" and "cool." They seem incapable of—and, except for a few perfunctory tries, uninterested in—disciplining their children, and in fact they seem to Mr. Kapasi more like children than parents: "it was hard to believe they were regularly responsible for anything other than themselves" (paragraph 45). As Mrs. Das later makes clear, they were thrown together from a very early age and allowed to explore and fashion their own relationship: "The things we did those Friday and Saturday nights, while our parents sat downstairs drinking tea . . . I could tell you stories, Mr. Kapasi" (paragraph 141). This is in sharp contrast to Mr. Kapasi's arranged marriage, with its total lack of physical joy and intimacy (paragraph 99).

5. *When Mrs. Das comments on Mr. Kapasi's responsibilities as an interpreter of maladies (paragraph 74), her remarks underline the importance of subjective perceptions. People don't usually change in the space of an afternoon, but our perceptions of them may shift profoundly, especially if we don't know them very well. How would you characterize and describe the separate stages of Mr. Kapasi's evolving feelings about Mrs. Das?* Through the first part of the story, Mr. Kapasi's impressions of Mrs. Das are, if not exactly contemptuous, then certainly condescending. He seems to see her as somewhat inappropriately dressed, and he notices that she is indifferent and a bit sullen, more interested in applying her nail polish than in observing the sights or even controlling her daughter's behavior. The first real shift in his view of her comes when she describes his job as an interpreter of maladies as "so romantic" (paragraph 61); not insignificantly, two paragraphs later he bites into the piece of gum she has offered him and "a thick sweet liquid burst onto his tongue": she has already provided him, as it were, with a taste of life's possibilities. By paragraph 79, he is flattered by her interest in his job and stirred by her use of the word "romantic" in connection with him; from that point, he builds an increasingly detailed fantasy of two soul mates, each trapped in a sterile marriage, who will ultimately reconnect and bond with one another, a bond that in his mind grows from friendship and shared amusements to incorporate, by paragraph 99, at least the hint of a physical dimension. In his loneliness he has fastened on her as his salvation from a life that he now regards as empty and sterile. After she tells him the story of Bobby's conception, his feelings toward her begin, at paragraph 145, to take a very different and decisive turn.

6. *Why does Mrs. Das tell Mr. Kapasi such intimate details about her life? How does she respond to his interpretation of her malady? How accurate, in your view, is his interpretation?* Having suffered for eight years, as she says, with a need to unburden herself, Mrs. Das is drawn to Mr. Kapasi because she is impressed by his skills as an interpreter of maladies; she sees him as sensitive, wise, and, above all, possessed of a healer's gifts (he is also no doubt an acceptable confidant because he is a stranger and they will never see one another again). With her revelation, she has punctured his fantasies of a soul mate and has diminished herself in his eyes.

"Mr. Kapasi felt insulted that Mrs. Das should ask him to interpret her common, trivial little secret" (paragraph 161). Struggling with his disillusionment and his sense of obligation to try to help, he seems not to realize how brusque, unsympathetic, and even offensive his question must sound to Mrs. Das, just as he seems not to realize that pain and guilt are not mutually exclusive feelings. Mr. Kapasi had sought romance and found squalor instead; Mrs. Das had sought understanding and received only judgment. In the end, one may feel sadness for both of them, each trapped in his or her limitations and each unable to give what the other needs.

D. H. Lawrence, THE ROCKING-HORSE WINNER, page 593

Students have no difficulty with the conventions of Realism, for it is the dominant narrative mode of the fiction and the films with which they are most likely to be familiar. Likewise, the popularity of J. R. R. Tolkien, J. K. Rowling, superhero comics, and the *Star Wars* movies, indicates that students are equally at home with the mode of Romance, especially fantasy. But they may find themselves uncomfortable with mixing the two, as in "The Rocking-Horse Winner," a fantastic story that takes great pains to create a generally realistic atmosphere and to have its characters respond to external stimuli in the ways that "normal" people would. They may be resistant to details such as the picking of winning horses through a frenzied and debilitating ride on a rocking-horse, especially when such things are central to the unfolding of the narrative. Thus it might be advisable at the outset of the presentation of "The Rocking-Horse Winner" to frame the discussion in terms of the conventions of Magic Realism. (See the discussion in this manual of García Márquez's "The Handsomest Drowned Man in the World" for an extended treatment of the subject.) Past a certain point, however, explanation is useless: one either accepts the conventions or does not.

"The Rocking-Horse Winner" has occasioned some superb criticism. Any student wishing to write on the story should read the excerpt from Daniel P. Watkins's penetrating economic analysis of the tale found in this anthology in "Critical Approaches to Literature." The poet W. D. Snodgrass has also written a brilliant essay on the subject, "A Rocking-Horse: The Symbol, the Pattern, the Way to Live," which examines the psychological and symbolic underpinning of "the perfect story by the least meticulous of serious writers." Originally published in the *Hudson Review* (Summer 1958), Snodgrass's essay has been widely reprinted and still represents one of the foundational articles in Lawrence studies.

A DVD of "The Rocking-Horse Winner" with a compelling 1950 film adaptation as well as a 20-minute short and other materials is available from the Library Video Company at <www.libraryvideo.com>.

QUESTIONS FOR DISCUSSION

1. *The family members in Lawrence's story harbor a number of secrets. What are they?* The mother's secret is that "at the center of her heart was a hard little place that could not feel love, no, not for anybody" (paragraph 1). Paul's secret is that,

by furiously riding his wooden rocking-horse, he is often able to predict which horses will win races. Bassett's secret, and Uncle Oscar's, is that they profit from Paul's predictions, even while the boy is on his deathbed. Their winnings are kept secret. Paul gives his mother 5,000 pounds but does it anonymously. The house itself whispers a secret, "There must be more money" (5, 6, 181). The three children hear the whisper, but no one talks about it.

2. *What motivates each main character? What sets Paul's quest apart from that of the others?* It is the desire for more money that motivates them all. Perhaps the most blatant evidence of the family's obsession with riches appears in Uncle Oscar's attempt to console his sister after her son's death: "My God, Hester, you're eighty-odd thousand to the good and a poor devil of a son to the bad" (244)—as if he were enumerating her assets and liabilities on an imaginary balance sheet.

Paul's frenzied pursuit of money differs from the greed of the others in that he wants wealth not for himself but for his mother. Clearly he hopes that, by being "luckier" than his father, he will win his mother's love and attention.

3. *Some details in Lawrence's story are implausible. What are they?* Those students who can appreciate Lawrence's particular blend of reality and fantasy will like "The Rocking-Horse Winner." A house that whispers is unusual, but even a hard-headed realist can probably accept it at least as a metaphor. That a boy can learn to predict the winner in a horse race by riding his rocking-horse is perhaps harder to believe.

4. *At what places in his story does Lawrence make use of irony?* Paul, intent upon stopping the whispers in the house, anonymously gives his mother 5,000 pounds as a birthday present. Ironically, his gift has the opposite effect. The whispers grow louder. Given his mother's insatiable greed for money, this result comes as less of a surprise to the reader than to Paul.

There is irony in the story's title. Paul, the rocking-horse winner, loses his life.

Ironic, too, are Paul's final words: "I *am* lucky" (241). In his mother's definition of luck, in paragraph 18 ("It's what causes you to have money"), Paul *is* lucky, of course—or was.

5. *In what sense may Paul's periodic rides on the rocking-horse be regarded as symbolic acts?* The single-minded frenzy with which Paul rides his rocking-horse parallels the intensity of the money-lust that dominates Paul's family. There is no joy in his riding, as there is no joy in his house.

6. *What is the theme of "The Rocking-Horse Winner"?* The love of money is destructive of all other love and even of life itself.

Bobbie Ann Mason, SHILOH, page 604

In reviewing Bobbie Ann Mason's *Love Life*, the critic Robert McPhillips summarizes the special appeal of her first book, *Shiloh and Other Stories* (1982). "In one volume," McPhillips observes, "Mason had populated a literary landscape almost as distinctive as Sherwood Anderson's *Winesburg, Ohio.*" He goes on to say:

Formerly ordered by the rhythms of farm life, these lives are now lived against the manufactured hum of television shows, rock and country music and MTV. Mason is at her best when evoking the confusion—sometimes comic and sometimes troubling—that this radical cultural upheaval creates in people who have lost touch with their past but who suddenly face a dizzying number of options—educational, occupational and sexual—from which they must try to piece together their present lives. (*New York Post*, 19 Mar. 1989.)

Although McPhillips was discussing the entire collection, he could have been specifically addressing the title story.

QUESTIONS FOR DISCUSSION

1. *"Shiloh" is told by a third-person narrator who observes both Leroy and Norma Jean Moffitt. Does the narrator present one character more deeply than the other?* Although the narrator appears initially to be impersonal, the story presents Leroy's thoughts and feelings more deeply than Norma Jean's. We see Norma Jean mainly from the outside. We follow her actions closely but don't always understand her motivations. Leroy's psychology is much more clearly presented—perhaps because he himself understands it. Having been partially crippled in a truck accident, Leroy has been forced to reexamine his life. He has discovered things about himself that his formerly busy schedule did not allow—his newfound passion for building things, for example, and his new appreciation for his wife. He also sees how much his hometown has changed. He seems to see his life up close for the first time. "He has begun to realize that in all the years he was on the road," Mason writes, "he never took time to examine anything. He was always flying past scenery."

2. *What role does the electric organ play in Norma Jean and Leroy's relationship? Does it in any way influence the breakup of their marriage?* Leroy enjoys his wife's obsession with the electric organ he bought her for Christmas. He loves the music, though he mainly uses it to drift off into his daydreams. For Norma Jean, however, the music unleashes her frustrations. She buys a "Sixties Songbook" and, playing through these old tunes, she feels dissatisfied with what she has done with her youth. "I didn't like these old songs back then," she tells her husband. "But I have this crazy feeling I missed something." Characteristically, Leroy cuts off the conversation. "You didn't miss a thing." In the background is the real hole in their life—their son, Randy, who died in infancy. They never speak about him, a silence that is symptomatic of the couple's inability to address and resolve the real issues in their marriage. The couple has had no other children. Possibly, motherhood and family life is one of the other things Norma Jean has missed and that might have offset her sense of having missed being young. Norma Jean's new smoking habit is surely also significant. Is it the sign of delayed adolescent rebellion in a woman approaching middle age?

3. *What does the story's title contribute to its meaning? Isn't the Shiloh battleground incidental to the couple's situation?* The trip to the Shiloh battleground becomes a symbol for the failure of the Moffitts' marriage. As the British writer Francis King observed in a review of *Shiloh and Other Stories*, when Leroy takes

Norma Jean "to the Civil War battlefield of Shiloh, she in effect, vanishes out of sight, leaving him with the desolating sense that, just as he never understood the inner workings of history that erupted in so much carnage, so he has never understood the inner working of the marriage that is now causing his own inner death" (*The Spectator*, August 20, 1983). Norma Jean's mother has urged them to visit the battleground as she did on her honeymoon. Now that Leroy is injured, he has warmed to the idea, but his notion that their aimless visit to Shiloh would remedy or improve their relationship reflects how poorly he understands his wife. Leroy has good intentions; he wants to improve their marriage. But he has grown so remote from his wife's inner life that his solutions—building a log cabin she does not want or having a picnic in Shiloh—have no connection to her still only half-realized aspirations.

[MLL] *MyLiteratureLab Resources.* Longman Lecture on "Shiloh."

Joyce Carol Oates, WHERE ARE YOU GOING, WHERE HAVE YOU BEEN?, page 613

Like many another celebrated work of fiction, Oates's story was inspired by an account of an actual event. As she has pointed out, the germ of the story was an article, "The Pied Piper of Tucson," which appeared in *Life* magazine in 1966. The article concerned a man in his twenties, dressing and acting like a teenager, who seduced (and sometimes murdered) young girls. Interesting as this fact may be, one should avoid overemphasizing it in presenting the story. For one thing, Oates used the article only as a starting point, and in fact she claims that she never finished reading it, so as to leave room for her imagination to do its work. For another, literature seeks not merely to record fact but to transform it by incorporating it into a larger, meaningful whole. Serious fiction—especially fiction like that of Oates, which is often drawn from violent and sensational occurrences—is at pains to dispute the journalistic cliché by probing the recesses of human nature to show that there is no such thing as "a senseless act."

QUESTIONS FOR DISCUSSION

1. *Describe Connie as you see her in the first few paragraphs of the story. In what ways is she appealing? In what respects is she imperceptive and immature?* Connie, Oates implies, is still growing and doesn't know whether to act "child-like" or "languid." Still discovering her identity, she behaves one way at home and another way elsewhere. Her mind is "filled with trashy daydreams," and the first caresses of love seem to her just "the way it was in movies and promised in songs."

2. *Describe the character of Arnold Friend. In what ways is he sinister? What do you make of his strangely detailed knowledge of Connie and her family, of his apparent ability to see what is happening at the barbecue, miles away? Is he a supernatural character?* Perhaps Arnold's knowledge was obtained merely by pumping Connie's friends for information and by keeping close watch on her house, and perhaps his reported vision of the barbecue is merely feigned for Connie's benefit. Much about

him seems fakery: his masklike face and "stage voice," his gilded jalopy, his artificially padded boots, his affecting the speech, dress, and music of the youth culture (although he is over thirty). Still, there are hints that he is a devil or a warlock. Perhaps Ellie Oscar, the "forty-year-old baby," is his imp or familiar; perhaps his bendable boot conceals a cloven hoof. He works a kind of magic: on first spying Connie he draws a sign in the air that marks her for his own. He threatens to possess her very soul: he will enter her "where it's all secret" and then, after the sex act, she will give in to him (paragraph 104). A charismatic person like Charles Manson, he seeks young girls to dominate.

3. *Why doesn't Connie succeed in breaking loose from Arnold Friend's spell?* She seems entranced, like a dazed and terrified bird facing a snake. Everything appears unreal or "only half real" (94). Like a practitioner of brainwashing, Arnold Friend denies reality: "This place you are now—inside your daddy's house—is nothing but a cardboard box I can knock down any time" (152). Arnold suggests that Connie's beating heart isn't real ("Feel that? That feels solid too but we know better") and soon she thinks her body "wasn't really hers either" (155). Perhaps some student will suggest that Connie really wants to give in to Arnold Friend—after all, she loves to flirt with danger and when Friend first looked at her in the parking lot, she looked back. But Connie's terror seems amply justified; Friend after all has threatened to kill her family unless she submits to him.

4. *What seems ironic in the names of the leading characters?* Friend is no friend; a more appropriate name for him would be Fiend. Ellie Oscar, like his first name, seems asexual. His last name suggests a trophy from the Motion Picture Academy—fitting for a media slave who keeps his ear glued to his transistor radio. His androgynous name perhaps recalls that of another assassin, Lee Oswald. Connie is a connee—one who is conned.

5. *What is the point of view of this story? How is it appropriate?* Limited omniscience, with the author seeing into only one character's mind. The author perceives more than Connie does and observes Arnold Friend and Ellie more shrewdly than Connie could observe them.

6. *Explain the title. Where is Connie going, where has she been?* She has been living in a world of daydreams, and now, at the end, she is going out into a sunlit field to be raped. In the beginning of the story we are shown that Connie lives mainly in the present; in the opening paragraph she sees "a shadowy vision of herself as she was right at the moment." She doesn't seem bothered by the ultimate questions asked in the title of the story. Arnold Friend answers the questions in paragraph 152: "The place where you came from ain't there any more, and where you had in mind to go is cancelled out." She has been nowhere, she is going nowhere—for in his view, there is no reality.

7. *What significance, if any, do you find in this story's being dedicated to Bob Dylan?* No doubt some of Dylan's music flows through Connie's mind, and some of Friend's repartee seems a weak-minded imitation of Dylanese: surreal and disconnected, as in his tirade to Ellie (133): "Don't hem in on me . . ." Arnold Friend bears a faint resemblance to Dylan: he has "a familiar face, somehow," with hawk-like nose and hair "crazy as a wig," and he talks with a lilting voice

"as if he were reciting the words to a song." His approach is "slightly mocking, kidding, but serious and a little melancholy" and he taps his fists together "in homage to the perpetual music behind him" (77). Joyce Carol Oates has remarked that Dylan's song "It's All Over Now, Baby Blue" (1965) was an influence on her story. Dylan's lyric addresses a young girl, Baby Blue ("My sweet little blue-eyed girl," Arnold calls Connie), who must make a hasty departure from home across an unreal, shifting landscape. A vagabond raps at her door, and she is told, "Something calls for you / Forget the dead you've left." Oates's title recalls a line from another Dylan song, "Mr. Tambourine Man": "And there is no place I'm goin' to."

In teaching this story to her students at the University of Georgia, Professor Anne Williams had "a couple of minor epiphanies." She has written to share them with us:

> "Ellie" may be a diminutive of "Beelzebub," lord of the flies. The story is certainly full of references to flies. I also noticed a series of comic allusions to various fairy tales, all of which, according to Bettelheim, concern the difficulties of coming to terms with adult sexuality:
> "Snow White" (in reference to the mother's jealousy over Connie's looks, so much like her own faded beauty [1–2]);
> "Cinderella" (the pumpkin on Arnold's car [36]);
> "Little Red Riding Hood" (here, there seems a fundamental structural parallel—and Arnold is described: "the nose long and hawk-like, sniffing as if she were a treat he was going to gobble up" [46]).

In spite of *hawk-like*, we agree that the description makes Arnold sound distinctly like a wolf. Professor Williams refers, of course, to Bruno Bettelheim's *The Uses of Enchantment* (New York: Knopf, 1976). Perhaps Oates's story might be taken up together with the Grimm tale "Godfather Death."

A film has been based on Oates's story: *Smooth Talk* (1987), directed by Joyce Chopra, with screenplay by Tom Cole. In an interview, Oates remarked that although she had nothing to do with making the movie, she respects the "quite remarkable" results. "The story itself is a Hawthornian parable of a kind, 'realistic' in its surface texture but otherwise allegorical" (interview with Barbara C. Millard, *Four Quartets*, Fall 1988). Is it, then, an account of a confrontation with the Devil, comparable with "Young Goodman Brown"?

 MyLiteratureLab Resources. Longman Lecture on "Where Are You Going, Where Have You Been?"

Tim O'Brien, THE THINGS THEY CARRIED, page 625

In 1987 Tim O'Brien published a wonderfully odd and powerful short story in *Esquire*, "How to Tell a True War Story." (It was reprinted in his 1990 collection, *The Things They Carried*.) In "How to Tell a True War Story," O'Brien mixes the techniques of memoir, literary criticism, and fiction to discuss how one conveys the grotesque atmosphere of the Vietnam War. Early in the story O'Brien's narrator observes:

A true war story is never moral. It does not instruct, nor encourage virtue, nor suggest models of proper human behavior, nor restrain men from doing the things they have always done. If a story seems moral, do not believe it. . . . You can tell a true war story by its absolute and uncompromising allegiance to obscenity and evil.

That artistic credo illuminates but does not entirely describe "The Things They Carried." This story includes the obscene, the immoral, and the improper, but it uses those darker elements to portray a certain harsh and uncomfortable sort of virtue. By incorporating the evil and the obscene, "The Things They Carried" transcends the rules of the genre that O'Brien proclaims—admittedly through the voice of a fictionalized narrator—in "How to Tell a True War Story."

O'Brien's style in "The Things They Carried" (and in several other works) is both distinctive and unusual. He builds the story out of a series of fragmentary portraits, and he shifts aggressively from one character to another. He relishes bold shifts in tone or setting. His diction is omnivorous—from the soothingly domestic to the gritty and bellicose. He often provides elaborate catalogues as if the reality of the Vietnam War could be described only by listing all the disparate persons, places, and things it brought together. On some level the entire story is a list—the things the platoon carry into combat. The bold juxtaposition of scenes and the evocative catalogues give O'Brien's story a strongly poetic quality, and his expressive effects are as often lyric as narrative.

The reader soon recognizes that "the things" these young men carry into battles are as often mental as material. Along with weapons, food, supplies, and personal effects, they also carry hope, fear, love, hate, and belief. Kiowa, for example, carries both his Christianity and his distrust of white men. These internal possessions are reflected by two physical objects—an illustrated New Testament given to him by his Sunday-school-teaching father, and his grandfather's hunting hatchet. Each of his fellow soldiers carries a similarly complex load of objects and obsessions.

The ending of "The Things They Carried" is especially suggestive. After Lavender's death, First Lieutenant Jimmy Cross burns his most precious possession—the letters and photographs from Marthe, a college girl back home. Destroying these physical objects represents an emotional change inside Cross. Burning letters he knows by heart and cherishes as his most intimate connection with the innocent world of home, Cross deliberately razes part of himself, a source of his own humanity. He seemingly destroys this part not out of anger but from both duty and resolve. He must become a stronger if narrower person to protect his men. He must distance himself from his own civilian identity to become a better combat officer. The incident is simultaneously grim, tender, and honest. Now Cross carries something else into combat—perhaps the heaviest burden of all—Lavender's death and the fate of his men.

O'Brien's story teaches itself in a classroom. One sure-fire approach is to ask students to list all the members of the platoon with their combat specialties and then add the most important things (internal and external) each carries into combat. Then ask what these things suggest about the person in question. A good writing assignment is to ask students what three things they would carry into combat and why. (Conscientious objectors can choose what they would carry into the Peace Corps.)

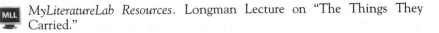 *MyLiteratureLab Resources.* Longman Lecture on "The Things They Carried."

Tillie Olsen, I STAND HERE IRONING, page 637

Both the slenderness of Tillie Olsen's body of published work and its heavily autobiographical dimension are factors in its remarkable concentration, consistency, and integrity. From the four long stories—including both this story and the brilliant and harrowing "Tell Me a Riddle"—that make up her first book, published when she was nearly fifty, to *Silences* (1978), part meditation and part commonplace book, her work has been distinguished by its originality of style and form, its passionate immediacy, and its examination of the ways in which economic and political forces, social expectations, and other pressures undercut and often stifle the drive toward self-expression and realization.

"I Stand Here Ironing" is a long dramatic monologue spoken by the mother of Emily, a talented nineteen-year-old. The narrator addresses an unidentified *you*, who is not physically present. The story, therefore, is an extended interior monologue, a mental rehearsal of what the mother might say to the person requesting an interview about the woman's daughter. From various details the reader assumes that this *you* is an educational counselor, teacher, or school psychologist. As it unfolds, the mother's monologue tells the story of her oldest daughter's life as well as her own difficult circumstances in managing with five children. She reveals Emily's gift for comedy but also her lack of success in school. The mother is especially skeptical of the advice that "experts" like *you* offer; their counsel generally causes more pain. "So all that is in her will not bloom," she notes fatalistically, "but in how many does it?"

QUESTIONS FOR DISCUSSION

1. *What is the point of view in "I Stand Here Ironing"? Who is the "you" in Olsen's story?* The story is told in the first person by the mother of a gifted young woman. The author never identifies the "you" in so many words. We can only deduce from internal evidence (in paragraphs 2, 50, 52) that the mother's interior monologue is in response to a call from a counselor or teacher—in college probably, because Emily is nineteen years old—requesting a conference with the mother. The narrator makes clear in paragraph 55 that she has no intention of going to see the caller.

2. *Briefly describe the circumstances into which Emily was born.* Emily's childhood was one of poverty and deprivation, perhaps best summed up by her mother in paragraph 55. That Emily was a child whose mother loved her fiercely is poignantly evident in paragraph 8: "She was a miracle to me, but when she was eight months old I had to leave her daytimes with the woman downstairs to whom she was no miracle at all."

3. *What are we to make of Emily's telling her mother not to awaken her the next morning even though she has midterms (53)?* By the time she is nineteen, her daughter is apparently over the terrible "goodness" the mother remorsefully recalls as characteristic of Emily when she was a little girl. Emily indicates that she will skip her midterms—not out of lighthearted laziness, however, but out of a sense of futility brought on by the uncertainties of modern life, the conviction that "in a couple of years . . . we'll all be atomdead." It is perhaps Emily's neglect of her school work that has occasioned the phone call from her teacher or counselor.

4. *Is there any justification for the mother's determination not to accept the invitation to come in and talk about her daughter?* The mother now realizes that whenever in the past she consulted "experts," their advice caused needless pain. She ignored her own common sense and breastfed her daughter on a rigid schedule because "the books" so decreed (6). "They" said Emily was ready for nursery school at age two (12). The mother, rendered helpless by her need to work for a living, therefore sent her daughter to nursery school. "They"—the people at the clinic—persuaded Emily's mother to send her to a convalescent home to recover from the measles (26). In retrospect the mother realizes her daughter would have been far better off at home. The best advice she ever received came from a man with no special credentials, who kindly entreated her to smile more when she looked at Emily. The happiest moments she remembers are those when, following her own instincts, she kept her children home from school even when they weren't really sick.

5. *What makes "I Stand Here Ironing" more than just a case study of a talented but deprived young woman? What besides the task at hand is suggested by Olsen's use of iron and ironing board in her story?* "I Stand Here Ironing" is enriched by the symbolism of iron and ironing board. The fervent plea that ends the story is the mother's hope that her daughter will know "that she is more than this dress on the ironing board, helpless before the iron." The iron here suggests fate, heredity, environment—all those forces that limit any individual's aspirations. The mother, who is herself an intelligent, perceptive, sensitive person, has been thwarted by poverty. Like mothers everywhere, she wants a better life for her child. This longing permeates the story. Indeed, her daughter at nineteen leads a very different life from her own at the same age.

6. *One student has called "I Stand Here Ironing" "a very modern story. It could have been written yesterday." What elements in the story support that assessment?* Though few people iron anymore and no one rides the streetcar, and in spite of its references to the Depression of the thirties and to World War II, Olsen's story strikes many a contemporary note. Single parents who have to entrust their children to inadequate day-care so that they can hold down jobs are less the exception now than they were when Olsen wrote her story. The author, by demonstrating that the thoughts of a housewife are fit matter for a story, has in a way written a feminist document. There is a sturdy insistence, too, on the part of the narrator-mother, that parents cannot be held eternally accountable for their children's inadequacies. "She has lived for nineteen years. There is all that life that has happened outside of me, beyond me" (3). Only now has popular psychology begun to concede as much. That sad little Emily, "a child of anxious, not proud, love," should have blossomed into a beautiful, popular comedienne—not trouble free, but at least functioning normally—says something important about the resilience of the human spirit.

Octavio Paz, MY LIFE WITH THE WAVE, page 642

Octavio Paz's fascinating "My Life with the Wave" (first collected in English in 1976 in the book *Eagle or Sun*) triumphantly defies easy classification. Depending upon the angle from which it is viewed, the piece can be seen as a Modernist parable, an erotic allegory, a Surrealist prose poem, or a Magical Realist short story. Each approach offers some insight—and may spur some interesting class discussion—but ultimately the story must be accepted on its own terms—alluring, troubling, and elusive.

The exposition is notably short and matter-of-fact. By the end of the first paragraph the wave has left the sea to follow her lover into town, and she has refused to leave him. Paz clearly has no interest in verisimilitude. He has unapologetically established the impossible premise—no scientific, supernatural, or mythic explanation is offered—and he now explores the consequences. Once the considerable difficulty of transporting the wave into the city is solved—which costs the narrator a year in prison—the pair begin a passionate love affair. At first their lovemaking is a sunlit sea of pleasure.

Slowly the relationship darkens. At the center of the problem is the unalterable differences between the two lovers who remain unknowable to one another. The narrator studies the wave earnestly. "But never did I reach the center of her being," he confesses. The wave exists beyond humanity. She, too, now finds her human lover unsatisfying. They alternate between love and anger. After the wave nearly drowns the narrator (for throwing away her fish, toward which he feels jealousy), he begins "to fear and hate her." He begins to visit an old girlfriend and plot an escape.

The ending of the story becomes a terrifying parable of sexual revulsion and cold-hearted revenge. The couple grow increasingly estranged. In winter he abandons her for a month and returns to find her frozen. There is no touch of compassion in the narrator. "I was unmoved by her weary beauty," he comments. Rather than warm her or return her to the sea, he sells her to a waiter who chops her into little pieces of ice to use in the restaurant.

What is one to make of Paz's compelling tale? It depends entirely on how one approaches the work. On a realistic level—if we accept its fantastic central premise—the story depicts a passionate but failed love affair that eventually becomes murderous. But few readers will entirely resist the urge to interpret the text symbolically. The key is probably to accept each meaning the story suggests without insisting on any one reading, though the temptation to read it as a dark allegory of male and female sexuality may be strong in many. Although cast as prose fiction, "My Life with the Wave" unfolds and resolves very much like a poem, and this compressed and evocative tale deserves to be read with the same care one would lavish on poetry.

The poet Diane Thiel, who teaches at the University of New Mexico, offers a provocative reading of Paz's story, which she sees as an allegory of the creative process. This interpretation both illuminates and justifies the story's disturbing conclusion.

Paz's "My Life with the Wave" has a many-layered nature which eludes immediate definition. Is it a love relationship the wave describes, or is it an aspect of himself? Is it memory? Or is it the muse, inspiration—which follows him from the sea, causes his imprisonment, and then is waiting for him on his return home, ready to toss him in many directions?

The wave is vested with human qualities (a voice, a body, feelings, and moods), and the speaker has a relationship with her which is both physical and emotional. The personification of the wave, along with bizarre physical details of her elemental nature (such as the speaker's hiding her in the water tank on the train, her "falling in a fine rain" into the engine to travel to his home) give the piece a surreal or magically real quality. A superficial reading might lead to the conclusion that the wave is merely a representation of a love relationship. The sensuous nature of the wave and the erotic and tempestuous relationship of the speaker with her support this impression. A closer reading, however, reveals some inconsistencies. The wave presents some non-human qualities. Her tempests, like those of the sea, are tied to the weather. She lacks the human center of mortality, and the vulnerability which comes from it.

The origin of this piece—its inclusion in *Aguila o Sol* (Eagle or Sun), a collection of prose poems which deals with the creative process—offers a useful clue to the deeper, possible meanings of the wave. The pieces in *Aguila o Sol* describe the artistic process as a physical, erotic encounter, sometimes violent. Paz's choice of a wave to depict the experience is an evocative one. As a writer, he struggles with the volatile demands of the Muse. It is a relationship which strikes a familiar chord with all writers. The wave will follow you home. You have no choice in the matter. It will come in search of you. You will do anything for this wave. Going to prison will not keep you from writing. But it is a tempestuous relationship—tortuous at times, because you may not know what the Muse requires.

The double metaphor—the creative process as a wave, and the wave as a person—is effective because it can describe the relationship with the Muse simultaneously on intellectual, emotional, and visceral levels. The erotic connotations are particularly effective because they heighten the intensity of the piece. Paz chooses a feminine noun (*la ola*) for his character, which requires the feminine pronoun in Spanish. The effect in the original language is somewhat subtler than the use of "she" in English. The translation strongly encourages one to initially read the piece as a description of a love relationship.

"My Life with the Wave" embodies many qualities of the prose poem (though this form itself, as a fusion of genres, often eludes definition). Paz's piece feels drawn by the drift of the unconscious, while simultaneously steeped in wry humor and the details of the everyday world—elements which are central to prose poetry. The piece develops around the image of the wave—from the gentle caress to a howling storm which calls up the monsters of the depths. These primordial images occur in stark contrast to the world of trains, police, apartments and ice buckets.

The final image of the wave, broken up to fill ice buckets, may be chilling, but it is also a clue to her identity. The ideas generated by the creative process become tortuous at times. One may have to leave the project for a while, in order to allow the inspiration to solidify into words. For the writer, inspiration can be a monster with which one must battle, until it is broken up into pieces—words, poems, stories. The fact that the speaker "sells" the wave further suggests her nature as Muse. Is the waiter the editor, who uses small shards of the product of inspiration to enrich the lives of readers, like chilled wine? It is an unfortunate fate—the wave of inspiration reduced to restaurant ice. One cannot truly capture the wave, Paz seems to suggest, only serve it in the tiniest of pieces.

QUESTIONS AND DISCUSSION TOPICS

1. "My Live with the Wave" is a fantastic story, but the plot still in some ways resembles a conventional human love affair. In what ways does the love story resemble a conventional romance between two humans?

2. Does Paz ever explicitly state why the wave left the sea? What details does he give to reveal her motivation?

3. How is the wave different from an ordinary woman? How is she similar?

4. Why does the narrator begin to love the wave?

5. When does the narrator cease loving her? Why do his feelings change so radically from earlier?

6. One critic has suggested that the theme of "My Live with the Wave" is the impossibility of sustained romantic or sexual passion. Defend or disagree with that statement.

7. Is the narrator justified in dispatching the frozen wave? Do his actions represent a symbolic murder or simply the final break-up between two lovers?

8. If the wave is a symbol, what symbolic associations does she suggest?

Leslie Marmon Silko, THE MAN TO SEND RAIN CLOUDS, page 646

"The Man to Send Rain Clouds" was—amazingly—Leslie Marmon Silko's first published story. Appearing in 1969 when the author was still in college, it shows her sensibility already fully formed. ("The Man to Send Rain Clouds" was later incorporated in Silko's *Storyteller* [1981], a miscellany of stories, memoirs, anecdotes, poems, and photographs that portray her native Laguna Pueblo in New Mexico.)

The compression of Silko's story is particularly noteworthy. In a few pages she sketches the complex cultural heritage of the Laguna Pueblo, which combines both tribal and Catholic elements. To the Laguna Indians, their tribal and Catholic rituals are not mutually exclusive. Over the centuries they have incorporated Christian elements into their native rites. To the local priest, however, their combination of "pagan" and Christian beliefs seems at first sacrilegious. (Indeed, a priest's involvement in their burial custom would be forbidden by strict Catholic protocol.)

The story centers on Leon's attempt to bury his grandfather in such a way as to guarantee that the rains will come for the pueblo. In order to perform the necessary ritual, Leon must obtain holy water from the parish priest. Father Paul does not want to cooperate because the dead man did not receive last rites and will not even have an orthodox Christian burial. This initial conflict could easily have been developed stiffly and abstractly. The characters, especially in so short a work, might have remained stereotypes. Silko's achievement in "The Man to Send Rain Clouds" is to create a small cast of credible people who reveal their inner character as the action unfolds. She never reduces her characters to ideological counters but develops them as feeling, thinking, and often surprising human beings. Silko does not lecture; she shows.

The gift of storytelling has been central to Silko's artistic mission. It also appears to be part of her heritage. In an interview with the German journalist Thomas Irmer, Silko claimed that storytelling is an essential part of pueblo tribal culture:

> The education of the children is done within the community, this is in the old times before the coming of the Europeans. Each adult works with every child, children belong to everybody and the way to teaching is to tell stories. All information, scientific, technological, historical, religious, is put into narrative form. It is easier to remember that way. So when I began writing when I was at the University of New Mexico, the professor would say now you write your poetry or write a story, write what you know, they always tell us. All I knew was my growing up at Laguna, recallings of some other stories that I had been told as a child. (Thomas Irmer, "An Interview with Leslie Marmon Silko" at <http://www.altx.com/interviews>)

Commenting on this story, the novelist Louis Owen admires its evocative compression and humanity:

> There is a wonderful beauty about the story, as clean and sparse as the New Mexican landscape where it's set. Like Hemingway at his best, Silko leaves almost everything out. . . . She presents a Pueblo world with simple and profound clarity—no sentimental posturing, no romantic lens filter, no explanation. She expects us to enter the terrain of the Pueblo worlds the same way the priest in the story does, through accommodation made with understanding and above all, respect. (Ron Hansen and Jim Shepard, eds., *You've Got to Read This* [New York: Harper, 1994])

Anyone particularly interested in this story will want to read *Storyteller*. For a fascinating portrait of Silko's early development, look at *The Delicacy and Strength of Lace* (St. Paul: Graywolf, 1985), which reprints her correspondence with the poet James Wright during the last eighteen months of his life.

A 1991 audio cassette tape of Silko reading from *The Almanac of the Dead*, her epic novel, and talking about a return to tribal values in the Americas is available from New Letters on the Air at <www.newletters.org>.

Helena María Viramontes, THE MOTHS, page 649

Through the voice of the unnamed protagonist-narrator of "The Moths," Helena María Viramontes provides a deft mixture of anger, frustration, and tenderness. It is hard to imagine the young person who will not find some point of contact with her. The overt reference may be to scarlet fever, but the word "rages" in the second line of the story sets a keynote for much of what is going on inside her. The first three paragraphs detail a litany of "whippings, . . . puberty, . . . my first lie," and the taunts of her sisters. She does not seem to fit into any of her assigned roles—she is not pretty or delicate or submissive; instead, she is "disrespectful and unbelieving" (paragraph 9), and in her resentment at being stigmatized just for being what she is, she lashes out. As she points out, she "even went so far" (paragraph 3) as to challenge her beloved Abuelita. But, unlike her taunting sisters, her martyr-like mother, and her furious and imperious father, Abuelita does not aggravate the situation by responding with defensiveness and hurt feelings. Rather, she shows patience, gentleness, and love: "My hands began to fan out, grow like a liar's nose until they hung by my side like low weights. Abuelita made a balm out of dried moth wings and Vicks and rubbed my hands, shaping them back to size. It was the strangest feeling. Like bones melting. Like sun shining through the darkness of your eyelids."

These are the same qualities that the young girl will later summon from within herself in her grandmother's time of need, but she must undergo a process of development before she arrives at that point. From early on, she is responsive to her grandmother's accepting and protective nature: "I always felt her gray eye on me. It made me feel, in a strange sort of way, safe and guarded and not alone. Like God was supposed to make you feel" (paragraph 4). Supposed to, but didn't: "I sat down on one of the pews. . . . After I cleaned my fingernails, I looked up at the high ceiling. I had forgotten the vastness of these places, the coolness of the marble pillars and the frozen statues with blank eyes. I was alone. I knew why I had never returned" (paragraph 7). Therefore, as the story's second sentence maintains, "it seemed only fair" that she should respond when Abuelita needed her help. She remains in this attitude—more than grudging, but less than spontaneously selfless—for a good part of the story, acknowledging that she never kissed Abuelita or her mother and that she apparently, without fully understanding why, wanted to upset her mother even further (paragraph 12).

Here is the story's turning point. The girl sits on the porch swing and dozes off, "repeating the words to myself like rosary prayers: when do you stop giving when do you start giving when do you. . . ." She awakens, at what may very well be the moment of her grandmother's death, to the setting sun (remember the earlier comparison to "sun shining through the darkness of your eyelids") and—in a remarkable passage describing the sun's transition from defiance to resignation, that "although endings are inevitable, they are necessary for rebirths"—she comes to her own moment of revelation. From there on, the tone is one of calm acceptance as she ministers to her grandmother's body in the same nurturing spirit that had characterized Abuelita's cooking and planting, culminating in the appearance of "the moths that lay within the soul and slowly eat the spirit up." Just as Abuelita's body and soul have released the moths at last, the narrator achieves a cathartic release of her anger and bitterness.

POETRY

Poems Arranged by Subject and Theme

This list sorts out and classifies most of the poems in the textbook. Besides subjects or themes, it includes some genres (i.e., elegies, poems of spring and other seasons).

How to Use This Information. Browse through this list and you will find many poems worth teaching side by side. This list will be particularly helpful to the instructor who wishes to organize a poetry course differently from the way the book is structured: to teach poetry not by the elements of poems, but by themes. However you prefer to organize your course, you will find this list a ready source of possible writing assignments.

For Writing Topics. You might have students read three or four poems in a group (say, those in the category "Apocalypse," or a few of your choice from "Coming of Age"), then ask them to reply, in a page or two, to the question, "What do these poems have in common?" Or, "How do these poets differ in their expressions of a similar theme?"

What follows is thorough but not exhaustive. We have left out some categories that sounded unpromising. Would you have cared that the book has four locomotive poems (by Dickinson, Stillman, Whitman, and William Carlos Williams) or three (by Yeats, Hollander, and Anonymous) about swans? Not all these themes and subjects are central to their poems, but all will be fairly evident.

ANGELS, DEVILS, GHOSTS, WITCHES, AND
ASSORTED MONSTERS

Anonymous	The Cruel Mother
Anonymous	The Three Ravens
Atwood	Siren Song
Bogan	Medusa
Budy	Snow White
Keats	La Belle Dame sans Merci
Martin	Taken Up
Orr	Two Lines from the Brothers Grimm
Poe	Annabel Lee
Robinson	Luke Havergal
Sexton	Her Kind
Simic	Fork
Yeats	The Second Coming

ANIMALS (BEAST AND BIRD)

Blake	The Tyger
Chesterton	The Donkey
Clare	Mouse's Nest

Collins	Care and Feeding
Frost	Design
Hall	Names of Horses
Hardy	The Darkling Thrush
Hollander	Swan and Shadow
Hopkins	The Windhover
T. Hughes	Hawk Roosting
Layton	The Bull Calf
Levin	Brief Bio
Lowell	Skunk Hour
Nash	The Panther
Ryan	Turtle
Smart	For I will consider my Cat Jeoffry
Tennyson	The Eagle
Wiman	Poštolka

APOCALYPSE

Dylan	The Times They Are a-Changin'
Frost	Fire and Ice
L. Hughes	Harlem [Dream Deferred]
L. Hughes	End
Levine	They Feed They Lion
Salter	Welcome to Hiroshima
Yeats	The Second Coming

ART

Auden	Musée des Beaux Arts
Blake	The Tyger
Cherry	Advice to a Friend Who Paints
Keats	Ode on a Grecian Urn
Morgan	The Master
Pastan	Ethics
Stevens	Anecdote of the Jar
W. C. Williams	The Dance

ASIAN EXPERIENCE / ASIAN POETRY

Basho	Heat-lightning streak
Basho	In the old stone pool
Buson	On the one-ton temple bell
Buson	The piercing chill I feel
Issa	Cricket
Issa	Only one guy and
Jin	Missed Time
Khayyam	Rubaiyat
Kim	Monologue for an Onion
Lim	Learning to love America
Lim	Riding into California
Li Po	Drinking Alone by Moonlight
Matsushita	Rain shower from mountain
Morgan	The Master

Moritake	The falling flower
Ozawa	War forced us from California
Salter	Welcome to Hiroshima
Satyamurti	I Shall Paint My Nails Red
Song	Stamp Collecting
Uyematsu	Deliberate
Wada	Even the croaking of frogs

BELONGING TO A MINORITY (see also BLACK EXPERIENCE, NATIVE AMERICAN LIFE)

Abeyta	thirteen ways of looking at a tortilla
Alarcón	The X in My Name
Cofer	*Quinceañera*
Dunbar	We Wear the Mask
Espaillat	Bilingual / Bilingüe
L. Hughes	Harlem [Dream Deferred]
L. Hughes	Ku Klux
L. Hughes	Theme for English B
Lim	Learning to love America
Lim	Riding into California
Olds	The One Girl at the Boys' Party
Osherow	Song for the Music in the Warsaw Ghetto
Reid	Speaking a Foreign Language
Trethewey	White Lies
Uyematsu	Deliberate
Valdés	English con Salsa

BLACK EXPERIENCE (see also BELONGING TO A MINORITY)

Brooks	Southeast Corner
Brooks	We Real Cool
Cullen	For a Lady I Know
Dunbar	We Wear the Mask
Hayden	Those Winter Sundays
Hayden	The Whipping
L. Hughes	As Befits a Man
L. Hughes	Dream Boogie
L. Hughes	Dream Deferred [Harlem]
L. Hughes	I, Too
L. Hughes	Ku Klux
L. Hughes	The Negro Speaks of Rivers
L. Hughes	Song for a Dark Girl
L. Hughes	Subway Rush Hour
L. Hughes	Theme for English B
Nelson	A Strange Beautiful Woman
Randall	A Different Image
Randall	Ballad of Birmingham
B. Smith	Jailhouse Blues
Stillman	In Memoriam John Coltrane
Trethewey	White Lies
Walcott	The Virgins

CARPE DIEM

Herrick	To the Virgins, to Make Much of Time
Horace	*Carpe Diem* Ode
Housman	Loveliest of trees, the cherry now
Marvell	To His Coy Mistress
Millay	Second Fig
Milton	How soon hath time
Shakespeare	O mistress mine
Waller	Go, Lovely Rose

CHILDHOOD (*see also* FATHERS AND CHILDREN, MOTHERS AND CHILDREN)

Bishop	Sestina
Blake	The Chimney Sweeper
Cleghorn	The Golf Links
Cummings	in Just–
Espaillat	Bilingual / Bilingüe
Frost	Birches
Grosholz	Listening
Hayden	The Whipping
Justice	On the Death of Friends in Childhood
Lawrence	Piano
Olds	The One Girl at the Boys' Party
Orr	Two Lines from the Brothers Grimm
Roethke	My Papa's Waltz
Simic	The Magic Study of Happiness
Stroud	Missing
Thiel	*Memento Mori* in Middle School
Thomas	Fern Hill
Trethewey	White Lies

CITY LIFE

Blake	London
Brooks	Southeast Corner
Brooks	We Real Cool
Dove	Silos
Eliot	The *Boston Evening Transcript*
Eliot	The Love Song of J. Alfred Prufrock
Eliot	The winter evening settles down
Ginsberg	A Supermarket in California
Hardy	The Ruined Maid
L. Hughes	Ballad of the Landlord
L. Hughes	Prayer ("Gather up")
Millay	Recuerdo
Swift	A Description of the Morning
Whitman	I Hear America Singing
Wilbur	Love Calls Us to the Things of this World
C. K. Williams	Elms
W. C. Williams	The Term
Wordsworth	Composed upon Westminster Bridge

COMING OF AGE

Cofer	Quinceañera
de los Santos	Perfect Dress
Espaillat	Bilingual / Bilingüe
Housman	When I was one-and-twenty
Milton	How soon hath time
Uyematsu	Deliberate

DEATH (*see also* ELEGIES)

Anonymous	Lord Randall
Anonymous	The Three Ravens
Anonymous	The Twa Corbies
Ashbery	At North Farm
Auden	Funeral Blues
Bensley	Last Haiku
Brooks	The Mother
Brooks	Southeast Corner
Ciardi	A Box Comes Home
Collins	The Names
Dickinson	Because I could not stop for Death
Dickinson	I heard a Fly buzz – when I died
Donne	Death be not proud
Dryden	To the Memory of Mr. Oldham
Frost	Birches
Frost	"Out, Out—"
Gunn	The Man with Night Sweats
Housman	To an Athlete Dying Young
Hudgins	Elegy for My Father, Who Is Not Dead
L. Hughes	As Befits a Man
Jonson	On My First Son
Justice	On the Death of Friends in Childhood
Keats	This living hand, now warm and capable
Keats	When I have fears that I may cease to be
Kooser	Carrie
Larkin	Aubade
Lennon/McCartney	Eleanor Rigby
Merwin	For the Anniversary of my Death
Owen	Anthem for Doomed Youth
Pastan	Ethics
Pinsky	ABC
Plath	Lady Lazarus
Poe	Annabel Lee
Ransom	Piazza Piece
Robinson	Luke Havergal
Roethke	Elegy for Jane
Rossetti	Uphill
W. J. Smith	American Primitive
Stevens	The Emperor of Ice-Cream
Stillman	In Memoriam John Coltrane
Tennyson	Break, Break, Break

Tennyson	Dark House, by which once more I stand
Tennyson	Tears, Idle Tears
Whitman	O Captain! My Captain!
Wordsworth	A Slumber Did My Spirit Seal

ELEGIES (*see also* DEATH)

Collins	The Names
Dryden	To the Memory of Mr. Oldham
Housman	To an Athlete Dying Young
Hudgins	Elegy for My Father, Who Is Not Dead
Jonson	On My First Son
Merwin	Elegy (*quoted in Scholes, "How Do We Make a Poem?"*)
Osherow	Song for the Music in the Warsaw Ghetto
Poe	Annabel Lee
Roethke	Elegy for Jane
Stillman	In Memoriam John Coltrane
Whitman	O Captain! My Captain!

FAITH, DOUBT, AND RELIGIOUS VISION

Arnold	Dover Beach
Bible	The Parable of the Good Seed
Brooks	the preacher: ruminates behind the sermon
Brutschy	Born Again
Dickinson	Because I could not stop for Death
Dickinson	Some keep the Sabbath going to Church
Donne	Batter my heart, three-personed God, for You
Donne	Death be not proud
Eliot	Journey of the Magi
Hardy	Hap
Herbert	Easter Wings
Herbert	Love
Herbert	The World
Hopkins	God's Grandeur
Hopkins	No worst, there is none
Hopkins	Pied Beauty
Hopkins	The Windhover
Hudgins	Elegy for My Father, Who Is Not Dead
Jarman	Unholy Sonnet: Hands Folded
Larkin	Aubade
Martin	Taken Up
Menashe	The Shrine Whose Shape I Am
Milton	How soon hath time
Milton	When I consider how my light is spent
Rossetti	Uphill
Sáenz	To the Desert
Wilbur	Love Calls Us to the Things of This World
Wordsworth	The World Is Too Much with Us
Yeats	The Magi
Yeats	The Second Coming
Zamora	Penitents

FAME

Dickinson	I'm Nobody! Who are you?
Dickinson	Victory comes late
Guiterman	The Vanity of Earthly Greatness
Keats	When I have fears that I may cease to be
Lehman	Rejection Slip
Shelley	Ozymandias

FAMILIES / PARENTS AND CHILDREN

Anonymous	The Cruel Mother
Bishop	Filling Station
Brooks	The Mother
H. Crane	My Grandmother's Love Letters
Espaillat	Bilingual / Bilingüe
Foley	Haiku ("Learning to Shave")
Grosholz	Listening
Gurga	Visitor's Room
Hayden	Those Winter Sundays
Heaney	Digging
Hecht	Adam
Hudgins	Elegy for My Father, Who Is Not Dead
Kees	For My Daughter
Kooser	Abandoned Farmhouse
Larkin	Home is so Sad
Lawrence	Piano
Olds	Rites of Passage
Orr	Two Lines from the Brothers Grimm
Phillips	Running on Empty
Pound	Salutation
Plath	Daddy
Roethke	My Papa's Waltz
W. J. Smith	American Primitive
Stroud	Missing
Uyematsu	Deliberate
Wilbur	The Writer
Wright	Autumn Begins in Martins Ferry, Ohio

FARM AND COUNTRY

Frost	Birches
Frost	"Out, Out—"
Frost	Stopping by Woods on a Snowy Evening
Hall	Names of Horses
Hardy	The Ruined Maid
Kooser	Abandoned Farmhouse
Layton	The Bull Calf
Stafford	The Farm on the Great Plains
Toomer	Reapers

FATE

| Anonymous | The Three Ravens |

Mann	Deathly
Millay	What lips my lips have kissed
Nelson	A Strange Beautiful Woman
Poe	A Dream within a Dream
Ransom	Piazza Piece
Robinson	Luke Havergal
Simic	My Shoes
Stafford	The Farm on the Great Plains
Stallworthy	An Evening Walk
Szporluk	Vertigo
W. C. Williams	El Hombre
W. C. Williams	Smell

LOVE AND DESIRE

Addonizio	First Poem for You
Anonymous	Bonny Barbara Allen
Anonymous	Lord Randall
Arnold	Dover Beach
Atwood	Siren Song
Bloch	Tired Sex
Bridges	Triolet
E. B. Browning	How Do I Love Thee? Let Me Count the Ways
Budy	Snow White
Burns	Oh, my love is like a red, red rose
Chaucer	Merciless Beauty
Cope	Lonely Hearts
Cope	*from* Strugnell's Rubaiyat
Cummings	somewhere i have never travelled
Dickinson	The Soul selects her own Society
Dickinson	Wild Nights - Wild Nights!
Donne	The Flea
Donne	A Valediction: Forbidding Mourning
Drayton	Since there's no help, come let us kiss and part
Fairchild	A Starlit Night
Frost	The Silken Tent
Glück	Mock Orange
Graves	Counting the Beats
Graves	Down, Wanton, Down!
Gunn	The Man with Night Sweats
Hardy	Neutral Tones
Hayden	Those Winter Sundays
Housman	When I was one-and-twenty
Jonson	To Celia
Keats	La Belle Dame sans Merci
Levertov	The Ache of Marriage
Lindner	Low Tide
Mann	Deathly
Marvell	To His Coy Mistress
McHugh	Language Lesson, 1976
Millay	What lips my lips have kissed

MAGIC AND VISION

MARRIAGE AND DIVORCE

MEDICINE

MOTHERS AND CHILDREN
Anonymous	The Cruel Mother
Bradstreet	The Author to Her Book
Grosholz	Listening
Lawrence	Piano
Lim	Learning to love America
Olds	The One Girl at the Boys' Party
Olds	Rites of Passage
Plath	Metaphors
Randall	Ballad of Birmingham
Stevenson	The Victory
Trethewey	White Lies

MUSIC
Atwood	Siren Song
Campion	Rose-cheeked Laura, come
L. Hughes	Song for a Dark Girl
L. Hughes	The Weary Blues
Osherow	Song for the Music in the Warsaw Ghetto
Stillman	In Memoriam John Coltrane
Whitman	I Hear America Singing

MYTH AND LEGEND (*other than poems in Chapter on "Myth and Narrative"*; *see also* SCRIPTURE AND APOCRYPHA)
Atwood	Siren Song
Keats	La Belle Dame sans Merci
Tennyson	Ulysses
Thiel	*Memento Mori* in Middle School
Yeats	Leda and the Swan
Yeats	Sailing to Byzantium
Yeats	Who Goes with Fergus?

NATIVE AMERICAN LIFE
Anonymous	Last Words of the Prophet ("Navajo Mountain Chant")
Erdrich	Indian Boarding School: The Runaways
Jeffers	Hands
Momaday	Simile

NATURE (*see also* ANIMALS, THE SEASONS)
Bishop	The Fish
Blake	To see a world in a grain of sand
Blake	The Tyger
Chesterton	The Donkey
Clare	Mouse's Nest
Dickinson	I taste a liquor never brewed
Dickinson	The Lightning is a yellow Fork
Dickinson	A Route of Evanescence
Frost	Desert Places
Hall	Names of Horses

Hardy	The Darkling Thrush
Hirshfield	Tree
Hollander	Swan and Shadow
Hopkins	Pied Beauty
Hopkins	Spring and Fall
Hopkins	The Windhover
Housman	Loveliest of trees, the cherry now
T. Hughes	Hawk Roosting
Joyce	All day I hear
Keats	To Autumn
Kim	Monologue for an Onion
Layton	The Bull Calf
Levin	Brief Bio
Lindner	Low Tide
Nash	The Panther
Reeser	Winter-proof
Roethke	Root Cellar
Rossini	Final Love Note
Ryan	Blandeur
Ryan	Turtle
Smart	For I will consider my Cat Jeoffry
Stafford	Traveling Through the Dark
Steele	Summer
Stephens	The Wind
Stevens	Anecdote of the Jar
Stevens	Thirteen Ways of Looking at a Blackbird
Teasdale	The Flight
Tennyson	The Eagle
Tennyson	Flower in the Crannied Wall
W. C. Williams	El Hombre
W. C. Williams	Smell
W. C. Williams	Spring and All
Wiman	Poštolka
Wordsworth	I Wandered Lonely as a Cloud
Wright	A Blessing
Yeats	The Lake Isle of Innisfree

OLD AGE (AND AGING)

Collins	Care and Feeding
Hardy	The Darkling Thrush
Larkin	Aubade
Shakespeare	That time of year thou mayst in me behold
Tennyson	Ulysses
W. C. Williams	To Waken an Old Lady
Yeats	Sailing to Byzantium
Yeats	When You Are Old

POVERTY

Alarcón	The X in My Name
Blake	The Chimney Sweeper

Cleghorn	The Golf Links
L. Hughes	Prayer ("Gather up")
Niedecker	Popcorn-can Cover

PRAISE AND EXALTATION

Blake	To see a world in a grain of sand
Burns	Oh, my love is like a red, red rose
Dickinson	I taste a liquor never brewed
Hopkins	God's Grandeur
Hopkins	Pied Beauty
Shakespeare	Shall I compare thee to a summer's day?
Tennyson	The splendor falls on castle walls
Whitman	I Hear America Singing
Whitman	Song of the Open Road
Wilbur	Love Calls Us to the Things of This World

PROTEST POEMS

Alarcón	The X in My Name
Auden	September 1, 1939
Blake	London
Ciardi	A Box Comes Home
Cleghorn	The Golf Links
Cullen	For a Lady I Know
Cummings	next to of course god america i
Dunbar	We Wear the Mask
Dylan	The Times They Are a-Changin'
L. Hughes	Dream Deferred
L. Hughes	I, Too
L. Hughes	Ku Klux
Levine	They Feed They Lion
Lim	Riding into California
McKay	America
Owen	Dulce et Decorum Est
Randall	Ballad of Birmingham
Rich	Aunt Jennifer's Tigers
Wordsworth	The World Is Too Much with Us

SCIENCE AND TECHNOLOGY

Eberhart	The Fury of Aerial Bombardment
Frost	Design
Martin	Taken Up
Reed	Naming of Parts

SCRIPTURE AND APOCRYPHA

Bible	Parable of the Good Seed
Chesterton	The Donkey
Hecht	Adam

THE SEASONS
Spring

| Frost | Nothing Gold Can Stay |

Housman   Loveliest of trees, the cherry now
W. C. Williams   Smell
W. C. Williams   Spring and All

Summer
Steele   Summer
Toomer   Reapers

Autumn
Hopkins   Spring and Fall
Keats   To Autumn
Longfellow   Aftermath
Robinson   Luke Havergal
Stephens   The Wind
Wright   Autumn Begins in Martins Ferry, Ohio

Winter
Bly   Driving to Town Late to Mail a Letter
Frost   Stopping by Woods on a Snowy Evening
Haines   Winter News
Hardy   The Darkling Thrush
Hayden   Those Winter Sundays
Niedecker   Popcorn-can cover
Reeser   Winter-proof

SPORTS
Fehler   If Richard Lovelace Became a Free Agent
Housman   To an Athlete Dying Young
Rexroth   Vitamins and Roughage
Stroud   Missing
Updike   Ex-Basketball Player
Whitman   The Runner
Wright   Autumn Begins in Martins Ferry, Ohio

TIME, THE PASSAGE OF (*see also* CARPE DIEM, OLD AGE)
Auden   As I Walked Out One Evening
Cummings   anyone lived in a pretty how town
Eliot   The Love Song of J. Alfred Prufrock
Hirshfield   Tree
Horace   *Carpe Diem* Ode
Housman   Loveliest of trees, the cherry now
Jeffers   To the Stone-cutters
Levertov   Ancient Stairway
Milton   How soon hath time
Pastan   Ethics
Shakespeare   Not marble nor the gilded monuments
Shakespeare   That time of year thou mayst in me behold
Shelley   Ozymandias
Stafford   The Farm on the Great Plains
Stroud   Missing
Yeats   Sailing to Byzantium

VIOLENCE

Eberhart	The Fury of Aerial Bombardment
Hayden	The Whipping
L. Hughes	Ku Klux
L. Hughes	Song for a Dark Girl
Orr	Two Lines from the Brothers Grimm
Owen	Dulce et Decorum Est
Randall	Ballad of Birmingham

WAR

Arnold	Dover Beach
Auden	September 1, 1939
Betjeman	In Westminster Abbey
Ciardi	A Box Comes Home
Cummings	next to of course god america i
Eberhart	The Fury of Aerial Bombardment
Jarrell	The Death of the Ball Turret Gunner
Kees	For My Daughter
Komunyakaa	Facing It
Lovelace	To Lucasta
Nemerov	The War in the Air
Osherow	Song for the Music in the Warsaw Ghetto
Owen	Anthem for Doomed Youth
Owen	Dulce et Decorum Est
Reed	Naming of Parts
Salter	Welcome to Hiroshima
Whitman	Beat! Beat! Drums!
Whitman	Cavalry Crossing a Ford

A WOMAN'S IDENTITY (*see also* MOTHERS AND CHILDREN)

Boland	Anorexic
Brooks	The Mother
Brooks	Southeast Corner
Clifton	Homage to my hips
Cofer	*Quinceañera*
de los Santos	Perfect Dress
Nelson	A Strange Beautiful Woman
Olds	The One Girl at the Boys' Party
Plath	Daddy
Rich	Aunt Jennifer's Tigers
Rich	Women
Sexton	Cinderella
Sexton	Her Kind
Uyematsu	Deliberate

WORK

Alarcón	The X in my Name
Blake	The Chimney Sweeper
Cleghorn	The Golf Links
Kooser	Abandoned Farmhouse

Poems for Further Reading, Arranged by Elements

Many instructors tell us that they use the poems in Chapter 33, "Poems for Further Reading," as an extra reservoir or second fuel tank of illustrations. Others, to be sure, think the book already offers too many examples; if that is your feeling, don't bother with this section.

If, however, you would like a few more poems (or some different poems) to illustrate matters taken up in the body of the book, then the following list can help you put your finger on them. It classifies only poems in the "Poems for Further Reading" section, and it works through the book chapter by chapter.

For Writing Topics. After your students have studied a chapter of the book, you can direct them to certain poems in the "Poems for Further Reading." Assign a poem or two and a short paper that springs from their reading. (An essay of two or three paragraphs might be enough: at this stage, overlong papers on topics such as figures of speech, rime and meter, stanza form, etc., might be debilitating.) Topics will occur: The Character of the Soliloquist in Browning's "Spanish Cloister" (after studying *The Person in the Poem*); The Attitude of the Daughter in Plath's "Daddy" (*Tone*), and more.

For suggesting that this manual could use such a classification of the "Poems for Further Reading," our thanks to Professor Harvey Birenbaum of San Jose State University.

Chapter 14: *Listening to a Voice*

TONE

Poems in which the poet's attitude is especially clear:

Jonson	On My First Son
Owen	Anthem for Doomed Youth
Plath	Daddy
Shakespeare	My mistress' eyes are nothing like the sun
Tennyson	Dark house, by which once more I stand
Whitman	I Hear America Singing
C. K. Williams	Elms
Wordsworth	Composed upon Westminster Bridge

Poems that express, as Auden says, "a clear expression of mixed feelings":

Bishop	Filling Station
Hardy	The Darkling Thrush
Larkin	Poetry of Departures
Lowell	Skunk Hour
Nelson	A Strange Beautiful Woman
Nemerov	The War in the Air

THE PERSON IN THE POEM

Poems in which the identity of the speaker is interestingly different from the poet's "I":

Boland	Anorexic
R. Browning	Soliloquy of the Spanish Cloister
Chesterton	The Donkey
Gunn	The Man with Night Sweats
Pound	The River Merchant's Wife: A Letter

IRONY

Other kinds besides ironic point of view, as in the poems just listed:

Hardy	The Convergence of the Twain (*irony of fate*)
Reed	Naming of Parts (*a discrepancy between the study of a gun and the study of nature, between the voice of the instructor and the view of the soldier; verbal irony in the pun "easing the spring"*)

Chapter 15: Words

LITERAL MEANING: WHAT A POEM SAYS FIRST

Poems that can be taken at face value, without looking for symbols, endless suggestions, huge significance (not that they won't repay thought and close reading):

Clifton	Homage to my hips
Hall	Names of Horses
Larkin	Poetry of Departures
Millay	Recuerdo
Poe	A Dream within a Dream
Slavitt	Titanic
Updike	Ex-Basketball Player
Whitman	Song of the Open Road
C. K. Williams	Elms

THE VALUE OF A DICTIONARY

Poems containing two or more brief allusions:

Dryden	To the Memory of Mr. Oldham
Hecht	Adam
Nemerov	The War in the Air

Poems with central allusions:

Atwood	Siren Song
Auden	Musée des Beaux Arts
Chesterton	The Donkey
Eliot	Journey of the Magi
Milton	When I consider how my light is spent
Tennyson	Ulysses
Yeats	The Magi

WORD CHOICE AND WORD ORDER

Poems in dialect:

Anonymous	The Twa Corbies

Poems in Middle English:

| Chaucer | Merciless Beauty |

Poems whose diction and syntax depart from those of speech:

Blake	The Tyger
Coleridge	Kubla Khan
Cummings	somewhere i have never travelled
Hardy	The Convergence of the Twain
Hopkins	No worst, there is none
Hopkins	Spring and Fall
Hopkins	The Windhover
Keats	To Autumn
Levine	They Feed They Lion
Moore	Poetry
Thomas	Fern Hill

Poems containing technical words:

| Reed | Naming of Parts |

Poems in colloquial diction:

Frost	Birches
Frost	Stopping by Woods on a Snowy Evening
Olds	The One Girl at the Boys' Party
Updike	Ex-Basketball Player

Poems containing an interesting mix of formal and colloquial diction:

Bishop	Filling Station
Ginsberg	A Supermarket in California
Larkin	Poetry of Departures
Levine	They Feed They Lion
Simpson	American Poetry

Chapter 16: Saying and Suggesting

Poems especially full of words rich in connotations:

Anonymous	The Three Ravens
Anonymous	The Twa Corbies
Coleridge	Kubla Khan
Cummings	somewhere i have never travelled
Keats	To Autumn
Ransom	Piazza Piece
Thomas	Fern Hill

Chapter 17: Imagery

Bishop	Filling Station
Erdrich	Indian Boarding School: The Runaways
Fairchild	A Starlit Night
Keats	To Autumn
Kooser	Abandoned Farmhouse
Randall	A Different Image
Ransom	Piazza Piece
Swift	A Description of the Morning

Tennyson	Dark house, by which once more I stand
Thomas	Fern Hill
W. C. Williams	Spring and All
W. C. Williams	To Waken an Old Lady

Chapter 18: Figures of Speech

METAPHOR AND SIMILE

Poems with central metaphors:

Hopkins	The Windhover
Phillips	Running on Empty
Song	Stamp Collecting
W. C. Williams	To Waken an Old Lady
Wordsworth	Composed upon Westminster Bridge
Wroth	In this strange labyrinth

Other poems with prominent metaphors:

Shakespeare	That time of year thou mayst in me behold
Wilbur	The Writer
Wright	A Blessing

Poem with a prominent simile:

Teasdale	The Flight

OTHER FIGURES OF SPEECH

Blake	The Sick Rose (*apostrophe*)
Donne	A Valediction: Forbidding Mourning (*paradox*)
Frost	Birches (*understatement*)
Keats	To Autumn (*apostrophe, personification*)
Marvell	To His Coy Mistress (*hyperbole*)
Plath	Daddy (*hyperbole*)
Reed	Naming of Parts (*pun*)
Waller	Go, Lovely Rose (*apostrophe, personification*)
W. C. Williams	Spring and All (*personification*)

Chapter 19: Song

BALLADS

Anonymous	Lord Randall
Anonymous	The Three Ravens
Anonymous	The Twa Corbies

A balladlike poem:

Auden	As I Walked Out One Evening

Chapter 20: Sound

ALLITERATION AND ASSONANCE

Blake	The Tyger
Coleridge	Kubla Khan
Hopkins	No worst, there is none

Hopkins	Spring and Fall
Hopkins	The Windhover
Thomas	Fern Hill
Waller	Go, Lovely Rose

RIME

Poems whose rimes may well repay study:

Blake	The Sick Rose
Lowell	Skunk Hour
Owen	Anthem For Doomed Youth
Plath	Daddy

Chapter 21: Rhythm

STRESSES AND PAUSES

In any good metrical poem, rhythms matter, of course, and can't be disentangled from meanings. Here are some poems in open or syllabic forms in which rhythms play strong parts:

Hall	Names of Horses
Levine	They Feed They Lion
Reed	Naming of Parts
Smart	For I will consider my Cat Jeoffry
Thomas	Fern Hill
Whitman	I Hear America Singing

METER

| Wyatt | They flee from me that sometime did me sekë |
| Yeats | The Magi (*worth scanning: irregularities battle with regularity for supremacy*) |

Chapter 22: Closed Form

FORMAL PATTERNS, SONNETS, OTHER FORMS

Poems in blank verse:

Frost	Birches
Justice	On the Death of Friends in Childhood
Tennyson	Ulysses
Updike	Ex-Basketball Player

Poems in closed (heroic) couplets:

Dryden	To the Memory of Mr. Oldham
Jonson	On My First Son
Swift	A Description of the Morning

Poems in tercets:

| Hardy | The Convergence of the Twain |

Poems in tightly structured riming stanzas:

| Donne | The Flea |
| Frost | Stopping by Woods on a Snowy Evening |

Gunn	The Man with Night Sweats
Hardy	The Darkling Thrush
Hecht	Adam
Herbert	Love
Keats	To Autumn

Poems in syllabic stanzas:

Moore	Poetry
Noguchi	Hokku
Thomas	Fern Hill

Sonnets:

E. B. Browning	How Do I Love Thee?
Hopkins	No worst, there is none
Hopkins	The Windhover
Keats	When I have fears that I may cease to be
Milton	How soon hath time
Milton	When I consider how my light is spent
Owen	Anthem for Doomed Youth
Shakespeare	My mistress' eyes are nothing like the sun
Shakespeare	That time of year thou mayst in me behold
Shakespeare	When, in disgrace with Fortune and men's eyes
Wordsworth	Composed upon Westminster Bridge
Wroth	In this strange labyrinth

Villanelles:

Bishop	One Art

Chapter 23: Open Form

Classics of open form poetry:

Cummings	somewhere i have never travelled
Eliot	Journey of the Magi
Ginsberg	A Supermarket in California
Pound	The River Merchant's Wife: A Letter
Roethke	Elegy for Jane
W. C. Williams	Spring and All
W. C. Williams	To Waken an Old Lady
Wright	A Blessing

Chapter 24: Symbol

Ashbery	At North Farm
Blake	The Sick Rose
Lowell	Skunk Hour
Randall	A Different Image

Chapter 25: Myth and Narrative

Atwood	Siren Song
Eliot	Journey of the Magi
Hecht	Adam
Ransom	Piazza Piece
Yeats	The Magi

Chapter 26: *Poetry and Personal Identity*

Boland	Anorexic
Brooks	The Mother
Browning	How Do I Love Thee?
Clifton	Homage to my hips
de los Santos	Perfect Dress
Gunn	The Man with Night Sweats (*gay identity*)
Hayden	Those Winter Sundays (*being a son*)
Heaney	Digging
Hecht	Adam (*fatherhood as an identity*)
Jonson	On My First Son
Larkin	Poetry of Departures
Lowell	Skunk Hour
Milton	When I consider how my light is spent (*Milton on his disability*)
Nelson	A Strange Beautiful Woman
Owen	Anthem for Doomed Youth (*war poem written by a soldier*)
Phillips	Running on Empty
Plath	Daddy
Tennyson	Dark house, by which once more I stand
Thomas	Fern Hill

Poems Students Like Most

At the end of the book is a short student questionnaire that solicits each student's opinion about his or her reactions to the book. The editors read and save each completed questionnaire they receive. These candid student responses often help improve the anthology from edition to edition.

One of the most interesting insights afforded by these questionnaires is a good sense of the poems students like most. (Their favorites often differ from the poems instructors rate most highly, though there is also much overlap.) Significantly, both students and instructors lean heavily toward twentieth-century poems and poets. Instructors might enjoy learning what poems and poets are most frequently chosen by students. Some choices may be surprising.

Students often identify their favorite poets rather than a specific poem. The five poets most frequently named by students are (in order):

FAVORITE POETS

1. William Carlos Williams
2. Robert Frost
3. E. E. Cummings
4. Emily Dickinson
5. Langston Hughes

The individual poems most frequently praised by students are listed below. Some are familiar favorites; others are pleasant surprises. There may be poems high on this list that some instructors do not teach. It might be worthwhile to consider adding them to your reading list.

FAVORITE POEMS (*Student Choices in Rank Order*)

1. Robert Frost, "Fire and Ice"
2. Stevie Smith, "Not Waving but Drowning"
3. Walt Whitman, "O Captain! My Captain!"
4. Margaret Atwood, "You fit into me"
5. Robert Frost, "'Out, Out—'"
6. Elizabeth Bishop, "The Fish"
7. Robert Browning, "My Last Duchess"
8. Robert Frost, "The Road Not Taken"

9. Sylvia Plath, "Metaphors"

10. James Stephens, "A Glass of Beer"

11. W. H. Auden, "The Unknown Citizen"

12. William Blake, "The Tyger"

13. E. E. Cummings, "anyone lived in a pretty how town"

14. Emily Dickinson, "Because I could not stop for Death"

15. Stephen Crane, "The Heart"

16. A. E. Housman, "To an Athlete Dying Young"

17. Robert Frost, "The Secret Sits"

18. Theodore Roethke, "My Papa's Waltz"

19. Lewis Carroll, "Jabberwocky"

20. William Shakespeare, "Shall I compare thee to a summer's day?"

This list of student favorites is not statistically reliable, and it changes slightly with each new batch of responses, but the results are nonetheless interesting to ponder. A purist might blanch at the particular Whitman poem chosen from the many in the book, but if the list indicates anything, it is that the students responding have pretty good taste in poetry. No matter how discouraging some days in the classroom may occasionally feel, you can take heart that you are making a strong impression on many students.

13
Reading a Poem

William Butler Yeats, THE LAKE ISLE OF INNISFREE, page 661

As a young man in London in 1887–1891, Yeats found himself hating the city and yearning for the west of Ireland. He recalled: "I was going along the Strand, and passing a shop window where there was a little ball kept dancing by a jet of water, I remembered waters about Sligo and was moved to a sudden emotion that shaped itself into 'The Lake Isle of Innisfree'" (*Memoirs* [New York: Macmillan, 1972] 31). In London (he recalled in his *Autobiography*), he sometimes imagined himself "living in imitation of Thoreau on Innisfree, a little island in Lough Gill." The nine bean rows of the poem were evidently inspired by Thoreau's bean patch.

Yeats's lines provide rich rows of sound for the student to hoe: assonance (from *I . . . arise* in the first stanza through the o-sounds in the closing stanza), onomatopoeia *(lapping)*, initial alliteration, internal alliteration (*arise, Innisfree; hear, heart's core*). Sound images of bees, cricket, linnet, and lake water are predominate. Whatever noises come from roadway or pavement, however, are left unspecified.

Perhaps, in London, Yeats thought himself one of Ireland's prodigal sons. At least, A. Norman Jeffares has noticed in the first line an echo from the parable of the prodigal son (Luke 15:18): "I will arise and go to my father" (*A Commentary on the Collected Poems of W. B. Yeats* [Stanford: Stanford UP, 1968] 35).

In later years, according to John Unterecker, Yeats was shocked that "The Lake Isle" had become his most popular poem. He had taken a dislike to its "Biblical opening lines." But audiences always demanded it of him, and his sonorous reading of the poem is available on a recording (Spoken Arts, 753).

MLL *MyLiteratureLab Resources.* Biography, critical overview, and bibliography for Yeats. Longman Lecture and critical essay on "The Lake Isle of Innisfree."

LYRIC POETRY

D. H. Lawrence, PIANO, page 664

About the first question: it's really a quick writing assignment. Ten minutes of class time might be enough to let students write their paraphrases. To be sure, you could let them wing it and paraphrase the poem out loud, but the results may not be so thoughtful or accurate. A few of the students might then be asked to read their efforts aloud, for others to agree or disagree with.

Reader response theory, if crudely applied, might claim that every para-phrase is valid. But we think it greatly helps a class discussion to assume that it is possible to find an interpretation of a poem that all or most will agree comes closest to it.

"Piano" isn't a flawless poem. Lawrence was seldom at ease in rime, and the strained juxtaposition of *clamor* and *glamor* indicates his discomfort. Still, *glamor* is an accurate word in its context: the mature man knows that the child's eyes endowed the past with an illusory beauty. The quality of Lawrence's poem may be seen in the specificity of its detail: "the boom of the tingling strings," "the small, poised feet." Lawrence enters into the child's perspective, while able to criticize it from outside. The speaker is resisting his urge to cry, as the connota-tions of his words indicate (the song is *insidious*, it *betrays*). But at last he is unable to hold back his tears and, sensibly, yields to them.

How does Lawrence's poem escape bathos? Robert Pinsky has offered an explanation in "Poetry and Pleasure," in *Threepenny Review* (Fall 1983). The subject of "Piano," Pinsky finds, is a stock source for poems, "as mothers-in-law or airplanes with ethnically various passengers are stock sources for jokes." Yet the poem strikes us with "something fresh, not stock." Its language is vivid, unconventional; its words *insidious* and *betrays* add a "steely spring"; it sets up an energetic tension between present and past.

Adrienne Rich, AUNT JENNIFER'S TIGERS, page 664

Rich's own comments on "Aunt Jennifer's Tigers" (found in this chapter's "Writ-ers on Writing") provide an interesting view of the poem. Rich explains how an artist can put many things into a poem which he or she is not fully conscious of until much later. Today Rich is universally recognized as the chief poet of Amer-ican feminism, but that was neither her public image nor her private identity in 1951. Yet Rich's feminist perspective had already begun to emerge intuitively in her early poems such as "Aunt Jennifer's Tigers."

It is apparent in the poem that the poet perceived something wrong with the passive role assigned to women. The pride, confidence, and fearlessness ("mascu-line" virtues, whatever the sex of the tigers) of Aunt Jennifer's imaginary creations contrast sharply with Aunt Jennifer herself—a frail lady with fluttering fingers, *ter-rified hands*. Worth comment is the poet's use of the word *ringed*—suggesting "encircled"—to refer both to the wedding ring that "sits heavily upon Aunt Jen-nifer's hand" and to "ordeals she was mastered by," specifically marriage and being expected to conform. Although she goes down in defeat, her tigers triumph.

Possible questions for discussion include:

1. In literal terms, what are Aunt Jennifer's tigers? What sort of "panels" does she appear to be making?

2. The speaker depicts Aunt Jennifer mainly through her hands. What specific details characterize these hands?

3. Why are Aunt Jennifer's hands "terrified"?

4. What attributes characterize the tigers?

5. What does Aunt Jennifer express in the panel she weaves that she does not so easily express in her daily life?

Compare Aunt Jennifer with the dead woman who once embroidered fantails in Wallace Stevens's "The Emperor of Ice-Cream." For another contrast between a dull world of reality and the colorful life of the imagination, see Stevens's "Disillusionment of Ten O'Clock," in which:

> Only, here and there, an old sailor,
> Drunk and asleep in his boots,
> Catches tigers
> In red weather.

For an interesting classroom discussion, ask students why this poem is lyric rather than narrative. There is certainly a story implied in the images that describe Aunt Jennifer and her surroundings, and Rich surely intends us to ponder the significance of these images. The poem remains essentially lyric, however, in its brevity, musicality, and evocative emotionality. A lyric poem characteristically focuses on a particular instant in time and explores—usually in subjective and imagistic terms—the emotional, intellectual, and imaginative implications of that instant. (A narrative poem, by contrast, must move from one significant point in time to another.) A good lyric poem, however, will often contain secondary narrative elements, just as a strong narrative poem will incorporate lyric effects to heighten its impact.

Mary Slowik discusses "Aunt Jennifer's Tigers" and other early poems of Rich in "The Friction of the Mind," *Massachusetts Review* (Spring 1984): 142–60.

MLL *MyLiteratureLab Resources.* Biography, critical overview, and bibliography for Rich.

NARRATIVE POETRY

Anonymous, SIR PATRICK SPENCE, page 665

On the questions in the book: We really don't think the king's motive can be known for sure from this bare portrait of him; we ask this question mainly to prompt students to pay attention to what they find on the page and to be wary of deep extrapolations. As far as we see him in the poem, the king sits around drinking wine, leading a life of ease, and (with a deliberate official gesture) sends his best sea-captain and a loyal contingent of naval officers to their doom. Although the poet takes a sour view of the comfortable life at court, he feels for the Scots nobles, and we too are moved by his spare sketch of the bereaved ladies, futilely waiting for their men, who will never return. The great stanza about the new and old moons, apparently an ill omen, serves further to heighten the tension of the story and foreshadow its conclusion.

Here are two more questions:

1. Comment on Sir Patrick's character. What do you make of his abrupt transition from laughter to tears (lines 13–16)? (He is not only brave and loyal to obey the king's order; he is a passionate man with quick, open, unconcealed feelings.)

2. In what lines do you notice a wry comment on the soft life that the nobles led at court? What does this attitude suggest about this anonymous poet? (lines 29–30: The nobles are loath to get their fine shoes wet. Probably the poet wasn't a noble, but a sarcastic commoner.)

In the famous image of the slim new moon, W. D. Snodgrass finds visual reminders of the king's golden crown and of the gold combs in the ladies' hair. For him, withering scorn for the Scottish lords afraid to dampen their fancy French pumps comes naturally to the singer, who probably went barefoot for much of his life. And he concludes: "This ballad, at least partly because of its scorn for the ignorant court, seems superbly successful in recognizing a more genuine nobility. Not that I need agree with its values: personally, I'd prefer (though not expect to find) a captain with more loyalty to his men than to king and office. Yet while the song lasts, I partake of the Scottish singer's world, and am broadened by entrance to another's experience, another's values." See "Shapes Merging and Emerging," *Shenandoah* (Winter 1991): 58–83.

Robert Frost, "Out, Out—," page 667

Like Sir Patrick Spence's, the boy's initial reaction to his terrible realization is to laugh; then, almost at once, dismay sets in. And like the folk ballad, "'Out, Out—'" tells a story of sudden, meaningless death, and does so with spare economy.

Perhaps the "they"—the doctor and the hospital staff—who turn to their own affairs are not merciless. The "watcher at his pulse" grows frightened when the pulse fails; no one wants to believe the boy will die. Radcliffe Squires finds no one to blame for the "faceless accident." In his view, "Simultaneously, one sees the human watchers touched by normal griefs and fears. And yet life must turn to a more important task finally, that of continuing. . . . Only the grand composer could hold together in one poem the two severe and mutually accusing ideas that one must be moved to pity and compassion and that one must coldly and sternly pursue the duty of endurance and survival" (*The Major Themes of Robert Frost* [U of Michigan P, 1963] 46). Frost's poem offers no comfort, but it seems a realistic view of what happens in an emergency ward. Any student interested in a career in medicine might be asked for a response to this poem.

Frost's allusion to *Macbeth* is part of the meaning of the poem, and students may be asked to think about it. Perhaps Frost suggests that the snarling buzz-saw full of sound and fury, reaching out its friendly handshake, just doesn't make sense. This, as Stanley Burnshaw has noticed, is one among several of Frost's poems that seem to question the existence of a benevolent order in the universe. Others include "A Servant to Servants," "The Housekeeper," "Home Burial," and (we would add) "Design" (*Robert Frost Himself* [New York: Braziller, 1986] 298).

Frost based his poem on an actual incident: an accident that had happened in 1910 to a sixteen-year-old boy he knew in Bethlehem, New Hampshire; five years went by before the poem took form (in 1915–1916). See Lawrance Thompson, *Robert Frost: The Early Years* (New York: Holt, 1966) 566–67.

In the article just cited in the previous entry, W. D. Snodgrass contrasts "Sir Patrick Spence" with "'Out, Out—.'" The first poem is about a man who looks unflinchingly at the world's horror ("the buzz-saw of the world"); the second, about a boy who tries to avoid beholding it.

Of Frost's poem, he remarks: "The one thing you must never do while working with machinery is to lift your eyes. The boy does just that—not to count ranges, but perhaps to count time 'saved from work' by his sister's call. A horrifying salvation is granted him: not just a half hour, but a lifetime, saved from work." Why the vision of five mountain ranges on the horizon (lines 4–6)? "To lift one's view from saw to horizon, reveals a terrifying similarity. We are given one glimpse, ironically lovely, of the edged and jagged teeth of a world only too ready to take us for its 'Supper.'" If the poem had a superscription, it ought to come from the old hymn: "Work, for the night is coming when man (or boy) works no more."

Jean Tobin, who teaches at the University of Wisconsin Center in Sheboygan County, reports the powerful effect Frost's poem usually has on students.

> Your discussions of narrative, lyric, and dramatic poetry work well for the kinds of students I have. I read Frost's "'Out, Out—'" and was pleased by absolute silence at the end followed by one student's under-the-breath "Damn." As the discussion roared along, even that first hour, one student remarked how strange it was that the boy's first reaction was to laugh. "Oh, no," said a girl, holding up a hand and keeping it raised until we all saw it had no fingers, "that's exactly what you do." After that I didn't have to convince anybody about the relevance of poetry to daily life.

MLL *MyLiteratureLab Resources.* Biography, critical overview, critical articles, and bibliography for Frost. Interactive reading and critical essay on "'Out, Out—.'"

Dramatic Poetry

Robert Browning, My Last Duchess, *page 668*

We include this famous dramatic monologue in the book because of instructor demand; we received more requests to reinstate the poem after dropping it from a revised edition than any other selection. Students generally find it fascinating, and instructors consider it an invaluable means of teaching the idea of a persona poem.

Some teachers may want to assign this poem in conjunction with Browning's "Soliloquy of the Spanish Cloister," which is in the "Poems for Further Reading" chapter. These two dramatic poems, both uttered by speakers we find unsympathetic, may be taken together as memorable works of character-drawing. In each poem, Browning places us in the midst of a society remote from our own in time and thoroughly undemocratic. Of the two, only "My Last Duchess" is a typical dramatic monologue. "Soliloquy," as its title indicates, addresses no listener.

"My Last Duchess" may be familiar to students from high school literature courses; if a show of hands indicates that they have met it before, we would spend less time with it. Whether or not it is familiar, it makes a useful companion to "Soliloquy." Students may be asked to define their feelings toward the Duke, to point to lines in the poem that helped define those feelings. Browning stresses the Duke's arrogance ("I choose / Never to stoop"; "I gave commands; / Then all smiles stopped together") and engages our sympathies for the poor

Duchess in lines 21–31, despite the Duke's contempt for her facility to be glad-dened. We know one instructor who in teaching this classic takes the tack, "Shouldn't we feel sorry for the Duke, with all his marital troubles?" (Students of both sexes are usually provoked to rise and trounce him.) Another question: to what extent is the Duke's attitude toward women presumably typical of his society? That the Count, the visitor's master, would offer a daughter to a man who had just disposed of his wife, suggests that the Duke is not alone in regard-ing women as chattel. Still, even for a Renaissance duke he seems cold-hearted: wives and works of art seem identified as objects to collect.

What were the Duke's commands that stopped the Duchess's smiles? "That she should be put to death, or he might have had her shut up in a convent," Browning once explained. But lines 2 ("Looking as if she were alive") and 46–47 ("There she stands / As if alive") seem to hint that she was executed. Hypocrisy is still another aspect of the Duke's character: compare his protest that he lacks skill in speech (lines 35–36) with his artful flattery of the Count (49–53).

Instructors should note that this book includes Robert Langbaum's insight-ful commentary on "My Last Duchess" in the "Critical Approaches to Litera-ture" chapter.

MLL *MyLiteratureLab Resources*. Photographs and biographical information for Browning. Longman Lecture, audio clip, student paper, and critical essay on "My Last Duchess."

WRITING EFFECTIVELY

William Stafford, ASK ME, page 672
William Stafford, A PARAPHRASE OF "ASK ME," page 672

The author himself so skillfully paraphrases this poem in the prose excerpt that follows it, that an editor offers further analysis at his own risk. A few comments, however, may provide a departure point for classroom discussions. Notice how the speaker asks several questions in the poem that are never specifically answered. *What* mistakes has the speaker made? *What* difference has love or hate made in his life? *Is* what he has done his life? The speaker answers the questions only with the final enigmatic and imagistic line. Stafford clearly trusts the reader's intuition to understand the ending.

Stafford's paraphrase is a bit freer and more interpretive than we might want from a student, but he proceeds through the poem line by line, image by image. Notice how Stafford spends more time on the final image than on earlier ones. He knows it requires more commentary—and a small imaginative leap—to explain. Stafford's deft paraphrase of "Ask Me" should demonstrate to students that close reading and critical discussion are not antithetical to the spirit of poetry.

14
Listening to a Voice

Tone

Theodore Roethke, My Papa's Waltz, page 674

Theodore Roethke's poem is one of the most widely taught selections in the book, and it usually proves a provocative topic for classroom discussion. We revised the critical discussion of the poem in earlier editions to reflect the broad range of opinion on this powerful poem. We have also included a student essay focused directly on the main issues that usually emerge from classroom discussions.

Many instructors have shared their reactions with us. Steven Hind of Hutchinson Community College disagreed with a previous edition's comments on this poem—"It seems to me that the poem is richer than Professor Kennedy's discussion would allow"—and finds its view of Papa ambivalent. "Kennedy hears a 'playfulness' in the slant rhyme *dizzy* and *easy*. Would it be possible to hear that as a slight dissonance? The only other double rhyme in the poem is *knuckle* and *buckle*, which has a hard edge to it, to my ear, [Mother] doesn't seem to be having such a good time. The involuntary response suggests that this isn't a novel experience. She will be the one who picks up the pans, one supposes. *Scraped* is a harsh verb. The ear is a sensitive organ. Certainly the boy loves his father and relishes the recollection of the dear brute's drunken revelry that included him, but these verbs present an unavoidable tension, it seems to me. The father may, as Professor Kennedy says, be 'happily using his son's head for a drum,' but that doesn't mean the drum is entirely comfortable with the impact."

Hind adds a sobering anecdote:

> Last year in composition class I taught the recovering alcoholic son of an alcoholic father. He wrote papers about the loving and terrible bond he felt with his father, and some of his experiences reminded me of this poem. I saw Rick in the hall two weeks ago and asked how his summer had gone. "It would have been better if I hadn't learned that my father has been molesting his daughter the past four years and I didn't know about it," he said. They are in therapy. "My mother's countenance / Could not unfrown itself."

Ann Barnard of Blackburn College, in a provocative article, also thinks the poem's dark side worth emphasis. She and a colleague had expressed chagrin that half their students had read "My Papa's Waltz" as a poem about child abuse, reducing it to a social tract. But their mutual rediscovery of the poem "included the idea of covert *emotional* abuse." Papa, whose waltz gives the child both pleasure and pain, is a figure of ambivalence. See "'My Papa's Waltz' as a Problem in Pedagogy," *Teaching English in the Two-Year College* 18 (Feb. 1991): 43–47.

Fred Roux of Shippensburg University of Pennsylvania reports that his students' interpretations of "My Papa's Waltz" have differed according to sex. Young men almost unanimously respond to the poem as a happy childhood memory of a loving father's exuberant horseplay. A few young women react negatively. For them, "I hung on like death" and "You beat time on my head," as well as "battered" and "scraped," suggest that the speaker's recollection is unhappy. They also assume that a man with whiskey on his breath must be drunk. None has perceived an ironic parallel between their responses and that of the speaker's frowning mother. "From this," adds Professor Roux, "it would appear that student response to 'My Papa's Waltz' is, to a degree, the result of a difference in socializing experiences during early childhood." Haven't any young women had boisterous fathers? We'd like to hear about other classroom experiences.

As Alan Seager discerns in his biography of Roethke, *The Glass House* (New York: McGraw, 1968) 23, the mature Roethke seems to have felt a certain guilty resentment against his father, a sense of how (as an awkward, chubby, bookish, and sensitive child) the young poet had failed to make the old man proud of him.

"My Papa's Waltz" may have had its genesis in a wish-fulfilling dream. After his father's death Roethke wrote a memoir (calling himself "John"): "Sometimes he dreamed about Papa. Once it seemed Papa came in and danced around with him. John put his feet on top of Papa's and they'd waltz. Hei-dee-dei-dei. Rump-tee-tump. Only babies expected dreams to come true" (qtd. in Seager, 24).

Countee Cullen, FOR A LADY I KNOW, page 675

From Cullen's first book, *Color* (1925), this is one of a series of twenty-nine epitaphs. Compare it with another brief poem that makes a biting social comment: Sarah N. Cleghorn's "The Golf Links." Cleghorn's poem seems angrier; the tone of Cullen's poem seems to be one of wry amusement at stupidity.

Cullen's early biography is sparsely documented. Raised by his grandmother until he was eleven, he was then adopted by the Reverend Frederick A. Cullen, pastor of a Methodist church in Harlem, who gave the future poet not only a name but a new life of books and conversation. Famed as the leading poet of the Harlem Renaissance, Cullen suffered a decline in reputation when militant black critics of the 1960s reevaluated his work and found it wanting in anger and social consciousness. But his wit can bite, as it does in "For a Lady I Know"; and Houston A. Baker has rightly called much of his work an "ironical protest . . . against economic oppression" in his short study of Cullen, *A Many-Colored Coat of Dreams* (Detroit: Broadside, 1974).

Anne Bradstreet, THE AUTHOR TO HER BOOK, page 676

The "rags" (line 5) worn by this bastard brat of a book may have been the first edition's abundance of typographical errors. Although Bradstreet patiently revised her work, she did not live to see her "brat" appear in better dress. This poem prefaced the Boston edition published in 1678, six years after the author's death.

Robert Hutchinson, in the introduction to his edition of *Poems of Anne Bradstreet* (New York: Dover, 1969), gives a concise account of the book's publication. Evidently the author's family, proud of her poetry, felt that it deserved more notice than New England could then give. The Reverend John Wood-bridge, Bradstreet's brother-in-law, took with him to England the manuscript of the collection. London at the time had sixty printers; New England, one—and so it must have been difficult, even then, to print poetry in America. "The fact," notes Hutchinson, "that Herrick's *Hesperides* had just appeared in England while the latest venture of Samuel Green, the Cambridge, Massachusetts, printer, was a revision of *The Bay Psalm Book* to rid it of its crudities, gives an indication of the intellectual distance between the two countries."

Walt Whitman, To a Locomotive in Winter, page 677
Emily Dickinson, I like to see it lap the Miles, page 678

Though both of these great nineteenth-century Americans take almost the same subject, in tone and in form the two poems differ as sharply as opera differs from chamber music. (Some students might argue that the mutual subject isn't a moving locomotive but the poet's praise of it. While seeing a real similarity, they would be missing the distinction between subject and tone.) Whitman addresses his machine in awe and exultation. In lines 14–19 he practically prays to it (almost like Henry Adams on bended knees before the dynamo in *Education*). Dickinson is evidently more playful in her affectionate view of the locomotive as a great beast. It is horselike in that it neighs and has a stable, but it isn't quite a horse: it crawls and hoots. Both poets, incidentally, see not only a locomotive, but a whole train. Dickinson's seeing it "chase itself" suggests cars trying to catch their locomotive as they roll downhill. Dickinson's allusion to Boanerges means no more, we think, than that the locomotive is a servant and is thunderous.

Whitman's poem is full of diction from music: *recitative, beat, ringing bell, notes, chant, harp, piano, trills*. The locomotive embodies poetry, too, in its metrical pant and roar, and in its ability to serve the Muse. The word *recitative* indicates the form the poem will be cast in. In Italian opera, to which Whitman was devoted, Rossini had introduced the use of the full orchestra to accompany the recitative, the passage of half-sung, half-spoken declamation; and it may be that, as Robert D. Faner has argued, such recitative was a basic model for Whitman's poetry. "The recitative, highly rhythmic and emotional, punctuated by instrumental accompaniment with thrilling effect, and in its chanted delivery giving the impression of the rhythms of speech, he found well adapted to the bulk of his work, which he thought of as a sort of bardic chant" (*Walt Whitman and Opera* [Carbondale: Southern Illinois UP, 1951] 234).

MLL *MyLiteratureLab Resources.* Biography, critical overview, and bibliography for Whitman and Dickinson.

Benjamin Alire Sáenz, To the Desert, page 679

Benjamin Alire Sáenz's passionate "To the Desert" is an unrhymed sonnet—fourteen lines of blank verse. (There is also a conscious pattern of assonance at the line ends to suggest rhyme—*night/sky, your/thirst, dios/me*—as well as one slant rhyme, *bend/brand.*) Sáenz's language is both erotic and religious, which is not an unusual situation for Catholic religious poetry, especially in the Spanish tradition. (Sáenz once studied for the priesthood, and the poem's bilingual diction and religious language announce its Latin Catholic heritage.)

"I came to you one rainless August night," the poem begins as it sets up thirst as its central metaphor. In the poem thirst becomes both physical and spiritual, emotional and topographic. Students should be asked to consider how Sáenz's title helps us understand the meaning of the poem. A reader can learn much not only from understanding the speaker of a poem but also from its stated listener. In religious writing, the desert is the place of spiritual self-knowledge, trial, and purification. Sáenz's poem uses that archetype to build a compressed drama of spiritual discovery.

Weldon Kees, FOR MY DAUGHTER, page 679

Weldon Kees, who was born in Beatrice, Nebraska, in 1914, was one of the most talented artists of his generation. In his short life he managed to do distinguished work in poetry, fiction, painting, film, criticism, and music. In 1955, shortly after the breakup of his marriage, Kees disappeared. Most evidence suggests that he killed himself by jumping off the Golden Gate Bridge, but some of his friends believed that Kees faked a suicide so that he could go off to Mexico and start a new life. In either event, Kees was never seen again.

"For My Daughter" usually creates a lively classroom discussion, but the conversation often veers in two different directions—one literary, the other ethical. On the literary side, students are often divided on the question of whether the poet should mislead the reader for thirteen lines and then reveal the truth (that he has no daughter) only in the final line. Some beginning students may feel that the author isn't playing fair with his readers, that he is exploiting their emotions. This discussion can be important for students because it dramatizes the fact that literature isn't necessarily considerate of our emotions—it has more important goals than leaving us at ease. Kees was a particularly savage poet in respect to pointing out the cruel and unjust parts of life that most people *want* to overlook. The important point is that the speaker comes clean in the last line, and that admission changes the meaning of everything said before. The first thirteen lines, therefore, can be read in two different ways—once coming up to the end (a father's worst fears for his daughter) and again retrospectively from the end (a man's reasons for not wanting children, especially on the brink of a world war).

The other discussion of "For My Daughter" concerns the ethical responsibilities faced by any parent bringing children into the world. (It may be worth noting here that Kees is not striking a hollow pose in this poem. He and his wife decided not to have children.)

One small technical note is worth mentioning: "For My Daughter" is a Shakespearean sonnet.

THE PERSON IN THE POEM

Natasha Trethewey, WHITE LIES, page 680

This poem is discussed at some length in the prose paragraph following the text. Once given the biographical information contained in the paragraph, some students may complain that the poem cannot be properly understood—or, worse, cannot be understood at all—without a knowledge of the author's background. It might be better to have the class read and interpret the poem on its own before introducing the biographical material. In this way, you may be better able to emphasize the distinction between a satisfactory engagement with the text itself and a deeper reading based on outside facts, a reading that enhances, but is not necessary to, a full understanding of the poem.

Edwin Arlington Robinson, LUKE HAVERGAL, page 682

Teaching this poem consistently produces some of the most interesting classes that I (DG) have ever conducted. I read the poem aloud in class, then I ask students to answer three questions:

1. Who is the speaker of the poem?

2. What does the speaker ask Luke Havergal to do?

3. Should Luke Havergal follow the speaker's advice?

Students immediately agree that these are sensible questions to ask. In order to answer them, however, they have to learn how to interpret the poem. Have them list on the blackboard everything they know about the speaker (there isn't much to know) in one column. Then have them list in another column essential information they wish they knew but are not told. They will soon discover that the voice speaking claims to be from beyond the grave.

It helps to ask students how many characters are in the poem. There are only three, and each of them—this discovery will show students how much grammar reinforces meaning—is associated with a specific personal pronoun. There is the *I* (the speaker), the *you* (Luke Havergal), and the *she* (Havergal's lost love). Have students collectively put on the blackboard what they can find out about each character.

To figure out what the speaker asks Luke Havergal to do, students must interpret "the western gate." It will help to notice all the imagery of time and seasons in the poem. The *West* in most poetry is often associated with death because the sun sets in the west. (For an illuminating comparison, notice how the aged Ulysses in Tennyson's poem sails west "beyond the sunset, and the baths / Of all the western stars until I die.") Let students spend the time necessary to figure "the western gate" out by themselves. At that point, it will be easy for them to discuss whether Havergal should follow this questionable advisor and his deadly suggestion.

> MLL *MyLiteratureLab Resources*. Critical essay on "Luke Havergal."

Ted Hughes, HAWK ROOSTING, page 683

Hughes's beautifully unnerving "Hawk Roosting" provides an excellent basis for any classroom discussion of poetic voice and persona. The poem is a dramatic monologue spoken by a non-human voice—a powerful antidote to any student who believes all poems are direct autobiographical statements from the author's life. A lesser poet might have settled merely for the basic situation of the poem—the world seen from the hawk's perspective. Hughes explores the deeper implications of his subject. Using human language, he tries to articulate how alien the hawk's worldview is to our own. The effect is quietly astonishing.

When writers treat animals as their subjects, they often become sentimental. They project human emotions and values—often childish ones—on the animals and overly dramatize these situations, especially the vulnerability of creatures in nature. The resulting stories—from *Bambi* and *The Wind in the Willows* to *Watership Down*—are often compelling stories, but they tell us more about the author than the animals because they completely humanize their subjects. Hughes instead emphasizes how differently a hawk might view existence. "Hawk Roosting" reveals a predator's perspective—merciless, efficient, and utterly self-assured. The hawk sits "in the top of the wood" both literally and metaphorically. It rests on the top of the food chain. ("I kill where I please because it is all mine.") Perfectly adapted to its ecological niche, it also sees the world finely suited to its own needs. ("The convenience of the high trees!")

The poem disturbs us not only for its celebration of predation but also because it suggests how many of our own assumptions about the world depend upon our being members of our own species, *homo sapiens*.

Suji Kwock Kim, MONOLOGUE FOR AN ONION, page 684

Archibald MacLeish famously states that "A poem should not mean / But be" ("Ars Poetica"). We might half-seriously state the theme of this poem as "An onion does not mean; it is." Though the onion moves us to tears, it remains cool and detached, and even as it is being chopped to bits, the speaker unsparingly slices through what it sees as the pretension, sentimentality, and self-delusion of the human heart in its quest for "meaning." The onion prides itself on its integrity, the purity of its "union / Of outside and in, surface and secret core," in contrast to the human being "divided at the heart" both physically and emotionally (just as our hearts will "beat [us] to death" both physically and emotionally). From its heartless depths, it sneers at the wreckage that we inflict on ourselves and on everything around us. While it protests humanity's waste and squalor, its disdain for our emotional wallowing is at the furthest remove from "Be gentle with me because I am just like you." We can no doubt take a lesson from the onion's rebuke of some of our worst excesses, but it is difficult to imagine that the author wholly endorses its viewpoint. It is our egg-breaking, omelet-making quest for meaning that makes us most human in the best sense of the term; like the figures depicted on Keats's Grecian urn, the onion, while spared from our worst excesses, is also cut off from our glories and fulfillments.

William Wordsworth, I WANDERED LONELY AS A CLOUD, page 685
Dorothy Wordsworth, JOURNAL ENTRY, page 686

To point out the distance between art and reporting, it may be helpful to read Wordsworth's poem aloud—at least part of it. In their rhythm, lines such as "Fluttering and dancing in the breeze" and "Tossing their heads in sprightly dance" make the motion of the daffodils come alive. By comparison, Dorothy Wordsworth's record of the incident ("the rest tossed and reeled and danced") seems merely excellent prose.

Wordsworth's sister was a distinguished poet in her own right, as Hyman Eigerman demonstrates in *The Poetry of Dorothy Wordsworth* (New York: Columbia UP, 1940), an anthology of passages from her journals arranged into formally open verse.

 MyLiteratureLab Resources. Biography, critical overview, and bibliography for Wordsworth.

James Stephens, A GLASS OF BEER, page 686

The high regard of the Irish for the magical powers of speech has given them a long and glorious tradition of poetic cursing. In the ancient tales of the Ulster saga, we read of kings who wouldn't go to battle without an accompanying druid: a poet-priest charged with pronouncing magnificent metrical curses upon the enemy. Who knows?—in the pubs of Stephens's native Dublin, curses like the one in "A Glass of Beer" may well have seemed ordinary, even mild.

Although the speaker—some frustrated drinker hard up for cash—is in a towering rage at the barmaid who denied him, the tone of the poem is not anger but high amusement. There is irony, too, in the obvious contrast between the speaker's stupendous hyperboles and the puny occasion for them. Save this poem, if you like, for teaching figures of speech.

There is hardly a better modern poem, however, for reminding students that the feelings expressed in poetry aren't always positive. A poem may be written in rage or chagrin, as well as in love or joy. This seems an essential truth and one that XJK has tried to demonstrate at some length in *Tygers of Wrath: Poems of Hate, Anger, and Invective* (Athens: U of Georgia P, 1981), an annotated anthology showing the tradition of dark emotion in British, Irish, and American poetry from the Middle Ages to the present. Naturally, in this tradition, "A Glass of Beer" holds an honored place.

"A Glass of Beer" is a free translation from the Irish of Daíbhí Ó Bruadair (c. 1625–1698). The original with a translation by Thomas Kinsella ("A Shrewish, Barren, Bony, Nosey Servant") is given by Seán Ó Tuama and Kinsella in *An Duanaire: An Irish Anthology* (Philadelphia: U of Pennsylvania P, 1981) 116–17.

Anne Sexton, HER KIND, page 687

This poem was one of Sexton's favorites, and she usually recited it as the opening of her public readings. (She even named a rock performance group with which she was briefly involved "Anne Sexton and Her Kind.") Published in her first collection, *To Bedlam and Part Way Back* (1960), it became her signature poem.

Who is the speaker? It may help to know that, according to Diane Middlebrook's fascinating *Anne Sexton: A Biography* (Boston: Houghton, 1991), the first draft was titled "Night Voice on a Broomstick" and a later draft labeled "Witch." But there really do seem to be two voices in the poem—one a witch, the other a housewife (see lines 9–11 with their "skillets, carvings, shelves, / closets, silks, innumerable goods; / fixed suppers for worms and elves"). Middlebrook calls this technique "the double 'I,'" and she points out how at the end of each stanza, the speaker "steps through the frame of 'like that' to witness, interpret, and affirm her alter ego . . . ."

William Carlos Williams, THE RED WHEELBARROW, page 688

Evidently many readers have found it easy to admire this poem without feeling a need to know the circumstances in which it was written. For an interesting appreciation, see Louis Untermeyer, *The Pursuit of Poetry* (New York: Simon, 1969) 25. Untermeyer views the poem as a kind of haiku that makes us aware of glories in commonplaces. A more sharply critical estimate is that of Roy Harvey Pearce in his fine essay "Williams and the 'New Mode'" in *The Continuity of American Poetry* (Princeton: Princeton UP, 1961) 335–48. Pearce charges the poem with sentimentality: "At its worst this is togetherness in a chickenyard." However, in Pearce's view, the poem also has a better aspect: what "depends" is the poet's vocation as a poet. He needs common objects in order to write poems, and the objects in turn need him to imagine them into poetry.

Direct your students to the first writing topic on page 705 that provides some biographical information on the "inspiration" for this poem. If the librarian is right about the situation in which the poem was written, "The Red Wheelbarrow" seems a better poem than we had realized: a kind of prayer, a work of compassion. However, that the poem fails to give us an intimation of the reasons for the poet's feelings (and of why we ought to share them) does expose it to Pearce's accusation that it is sentimental. Whatever the instructor's opinion, students may be invited to debate the merits and demerits of the poem.

MLL *MyLiteratureLab Resources.* Biography, critical overview, and bibliography for Williams.

IRONY

Robert Creeley, OH NO, page 688

"What interests me about 'Oh No' is its tone," Cynthia Edelberg remarks in an interview with the poet. "How would you describe it?" Creeley replies that he sees it as wry irony, the poem being "self-parody," a comment on his feelings at the time. "As Joel Oppenheimer said, that would qualify me to be a Jew. He really liked that poem. It's that kind of humor" (Edelberg's *Robert Creeley's Poetry: A Critical Introduction* [Albuquerque: U of New Mexico P, 1978] 168).

"Oh No" seems to be another poem about where you arrive when you die. Creeley, we suspect, kids a conventional notion of heaven: he makes it a smug, artificial place where the saved sit around smirking at one another.

W. H. Auden, THE UNKNOWN CITIZEN, page 690

For making students better aware of irony, Auden's familiar satire remains as dependable as any poem we know. Little seems to have dated in it, other than the praise of the citizen for adding five children to the population. Students are usually good at seeing that, unlike the unknown soldier, the citizen is all too thoroughly identified; and that, nevertheless, his true nature and inmost wants remain unknown. Meaty questions for discussion naturally arise: What are the premises of such a society? It seems dedicated to the proposition that to conform to a norm is the highest virtue—any individual traits, of course, being an annoyance to statisticians. What is a "Modern Man?" One with animal needs, but no aspirations. The epitaph, often overlooked, is worth dwelling on: it tells us at once that the unknown citizen is only a number, and that bureaucrats keep track of him—and, incidentally, like the rest of the poem, the epitaph is in rime.

"The Unknown Citizen" is one of six poems in this chapter in which we hear a voice obviously not the poet's. (The others are the ones by Robinson, Hughes, Betjeman, Stephens, and Blake.)

 MyLiteratureLab Resources. Biography, critical overview, and bibliography for Auden.

Sharon Olds, RITES OF PASSAGE, page 691

This poem will not require much explanation. Anyone familiar with six- and seven-year-old boys will understand the situation. The interesting exercise in class is to search out the ironic metaphors and language in the poem ("short men," "small bankers," "celebrating my son's life") and then discuss their effect on our reading of the poem. If some students complain that the poem overstates its case and makes too much of the boys' penchant for mock violence, it will provide a good opportunity to ask if a poem (and one might even classify this short descriptive work as "lyric," since it explores a moment's perception) needs to provide a balanced view of life or if it is acceptable to create the sudden, overwhelming, and perhaps unbalanced emotions we feel in a particular moment or situation.

John Betjeman, IN WESTMINSTER ABBEY, page 692

Cadogan Square was an especially fashionable London address around the turn of the century, and the fact that the reader owns stocks (line 30) also indicates her style of life. Her mind, however, is ordinary: her ideals seem bounded by drugstore novels and by plumbing that works properly.

Students usually have a fine time picking out the easy contradictions in the lady's beliefs: that the Lord may allow bombs to hit German women but not English women; that He protects whites more dutifully than blacks; that it is all very well for the "gallant blacks" to die, but let the Empire remain united; that democracy and class distinction go hand in hand.

The speaker's attitude seems to be: "Let God wait upon my convenience." To call His word a "treat" reduces Scripture to the importance of candy. That Betjeman first printed this ironic blast at smug, hate-mongering chauvinism in the midst of World War II strikes us as a brave and large-minded plea for genuine Christian charity.

Sarah N. Cleghorn, THE GOLF LINKS, page 693

What a great epigram!—no verbal irony in it, just matter-of-fact notation of a social condition that seems ironic in the extreme. As Robert Frost said in his introduction to Cleghorn's autobiography, *Threescore* (1936), "There is more high explosive for righteousness in the least little line of Sarah Cleghorn's poem about the children working in the mill . . . than in all the prose of our radical-bound-boys pressed together under a weight of several atmospheres of revolution." (The conservative Frost didn't like Marxists, but he called Cleghorn "a saint and a reformer" anyway.) For a more recent tribute, see Irving Dilliard, "Four Short Lines," *The Nation* 222 (10 Apr. 1976): 444–45.

Stanley Kunitz and Howard Hayward's *Twentieth Century Authors* (New York: Wilson, 1942), in an article on Cleghorn that she apparently helped write, explains the twenty-year hiatus between her early books and her later ones: "This was caused by the fact that her socialism and pacifism made editors and publishers reluctant to use her later writing, and partly by the fact that in middle age she became a teacher." Among her other works is a novel, *The Spinster* (1916), and a last collection, *Poems of Peace and Freedom* (1945).

Edna St. Vincent Millay, SECOND FIG, page 693

This couplet is the second poem in Millay's volume *A Few Figs from Thistles*, whose title may remind you of A. E. Housman's lines "Out of a stem that scored the hand / I wrung it in a weary land." Like the "First Fig," the universally known quatrain that begins "My candle burns at both ends," this poem celebrates the brief and beautiful in contrast to the substantial and dull. It is of course ironic that the speaker should disdain what is "safe" and "solid" in favor of that which is built upon the sand, but "ugly" in the first line and "shining" in the second should leave us in no doubt regarding the author's intentions.

MLL *MyLiteratureLab Resources.* Biography and photos for Millay.

Joseph Stroud, MISSING, page 694

1. *Is the first line of this poem sarcastic? Why or why not?* Rather than being "conspicuously bitter, heavy-handed, and mocking" (the attributes of sarcasm discussed in the textbook), the tone of the opening line of this poem is gentle and somewhat wistful. The speaker is not mocking anyone, not even himself; he is expressing his feeling of being more and more out of touch with the world and the family he knew (and may have loved—he doesn't really say) when he was nine or ten years old.

2. *What do you make of the poem's last word?* The speaker is now out of touch with that little boy, with whom, as the poem's last word suggests, he no longer seems to identify, perceiving the boy instead as someone completely separate from the man he has become.

Thomas Hardy, THE WORKBOX, page 694

Dramatic irony is present in the discrepancy between the carpenter's limited knowledge and the reader's growing conviction that the wife knew John much better than she cares to admit. Her phrase "mere accidental things" contains verbal irony, and in general the whole speech in lines 25–28 is a verbal irony.

Cosmic irony may be operating too (and one is sure that it is, knowing Hardy) in the Fate or chance that caused the carpenter to select a piece of poor John's coffin out of all pieces of wood in the world.

To us, the situation in the poem had seemed like that in James Joyce's "The Dead": the wife, by remembering a young man who died of love for her, has a bleak realization that she might have known a joyous life had she married him instead. However, Albert Furtwangler and his students at Mount Allison University found other possible levels of irony, as he kindly wrote to report. For Professor Furtwangler, "The Workbox" is marred by an excess of irony that runs too deep: "it remains fascinating in the long run more as a puzzle than as a clear disclosure of character." Among other readings he considered the two following, which he thinks overingenious and yet consistent with the poem.

The husband, aware of his wife's past, has contrived his present as a cunning torture for her. "He seems to offer it in love, but takes pleasure in drawing out his wife's confused replies . . . thus trapping her in her own hypocrisy."

The husband knows his wife's history; and she knows that he knows it. "But they coexist uneasily with each other by exercising an elaborate fiction of ignorance."

What will you and your students decide?

J. O. Bailey sees in this poem the "ballad-like theme of the lover who died of grief when his beloved married another." Like traditional English and Scottish ballads, the poem has a question-and-answer structure and ends in a surprise. (See *The Poetry of Thomas Hardy* [Chapel Hill: U of North Carolina P, 1970].) Compare "The Workbox" in these respects with "Bonny Barbara Allan."

MLL *MyLiteratureLab Resources*. Biography, critical overview, and bibliography for Hardy.

FOR REVIEW AND FURTHER STUDY

William Blake, THE CHIMNEY SWEEPER, page 695

Set next to Cleghorn's "Golf Links," Blake's song will seem larger and more strange; yet the two poets seem comparable in their hatred of adults who enslave children. Though Blake is not a child, he obviously shares Tom Dacre's wish that the chimney sweepers be freed from their coffinlike chimneys, washed clean, and restored to childhood joys. The punning cry "'weep! 'weep! 'weep! 'weep!" is the street cry of the sweepers, sent through London to advertise their services. Compare the tone of this poem to that of Blake's "London"; the anger is similar, but in "The Chimney Sweeper," a poem also touching and compassionate, anger is not stated outright, but only implied.

Tom Dacre's dream has a basis in reality: in Blake's time, sweeps were often sent up chimneys naked, the better to climb through narrow spaces (and thus saving the expense of protective clothing). Martin K. Nurmi points out this fact in his essay "Fact and Symbol in 'The Chimney Sweeper' of Blake's *Songs of Innocence*" (*Bulletin of the New York Public Library* 68 [April 1964] 249–56). "Naked immersion in soot, therefore, is Tom's normal state now, and naked white cleanliness is its natural opposite."

Refer your students to the interesting commentary on "The Chimney Sweeper" by Camille Paglia in the chapter "Critical Approaches to Literature."

Music to "The Chimney Sweeper" has been supplied by Allen Ginsberg, who sings on *Songs of Innocence and Experience* (MGM recording FTS 3083), assisted by Peter Orlovsky.

MLL *MyLiteratureLab Resources.* Photographs and biographical information for Blake. Audio clip and critical essay on "The Chimney Sweeper."

David Lehman, REJECTION SLIP, page 696

The humor here is obvious, as the first four stanzas carry their speaker through increasingly absurd exaggerations on the theme of sour grapes. The final stanza enlarges the frame of reference, and with it enlarges our perspective on what is happening in the poem. For those who know the statement, it is almost impossible to read "Rejection Slip" without being reminded of John Berryman's notorious comment in his *Paris Review* interview, published in 1972 (the year of his suicide, provoked largely by the chaos his alcoholism had made of his life): "The artist is extremely lucky who is presented with the worst possible ordeal which will not actually kill him. At that point, he's in business. . . . I hope to nearly be crucified." Lehman deftly skewers the image, nurtured by the so-called Confessional poets, of the poet as a wounded and self-destructive soul who fashions great art out of extreme states of misery and self-pity; the final stanza indicts as well the audience whose responsiveness encourages such themes and such behavior. Lehman's own attitude would seem to be much more in line with the corrective offered by Lewis Hyde: "In the future it would be nice if it were a little harder for the poet to come to town drunk and have everyone think that it's great fun."

William Stafford, AT THE UN-NATIONAL MONUMENT ALONG THE CANADIAN BORDER, page 697

This is a wonderful poem that celebrates an even more wonderful event—that two neighboring countries have lived in peace for nearly two hundred years. (It may be worthwhile in class to ask the obvious *factual* question about what this poem celebrates.)

Stafford's poem uses language memorably in at least two unusual ways. First, the poem characterizes the scene mainly by what did *not* happen there—no battles, no deaths, no monument, no memorable historical events of any kind. Second, Stafford consciously invokes the central non-event by borrowing the diction of patriotic oratory: heroic, soldier, battle, monument, ground, hallowed, people, celebrate. (One wonders if Lincoln's "Gettysburg Address" was in the back of Stafford's mind.) But Stafford uses these words in exactly the opposite way from an old-fashioned commemorative oration.

H. L. Hix, I LOVE THE WORLD, AS DOES ANY DANCER, page 697

H. L. Hix's exuberant short love poem is actually an individual section of his long, lyrical, and meditative sequence "Orders of Magnitude," which appeared in his second collection, *Rational Numbers* (2000). One remarkable aspect of this richly realized poem is how imaginatively it employs tactile imagery to communicate its effects. The dancer (and the speaker) love the world with the tips of their toes. The twenty digits of his hands and feet "tenders" the many textures of the world. The sensations that naked feet feel are listed: lush wet grass, piles of rose petals, hot summer sidewalks, sand, dirt, and finally the body of the beloved. The poem asserts the delectable continuity of all those phenomena for the speaker, for whom marital love is an extension of his physical joy in the world. Surely the human toes have never been more joyously acknowledged in verse.

Richard Lovelace, To Lucasta, page 698

"To Lucasta" may refer to an actual parting. During the Puritan Revolution of 1642–1645, Lovelace fought in the service of Charles I. Students will readily see the poet's theme that Honor (duty to God and King) takes priority over duty to Lucasta; the tone of the poem may give them greater difficulty. The closing line makes a serious affirmation: Honor for Lovelace is not an "old Lie," but a creed. Neither grim nor smug, the poem has wit and loving tenderness. The witty second stanza seems almost comic in its figures of speech: having renounced Lucasta's nunlike chastity and calm, the speaker will now go and whet his sword upon the body of someone wilder.

Wilfred Owen, Dulce et Decorum Est, page 698

Owen's theme is apparent: death in battle is hideous, no matter what certain ignorant poets say about it. For us, there seems irony in the fact that Owen himself was to be killed in action in France. Although in a wartime letter he called himself "a conscientious objector with a very seared conscience," Owen in this poem does not question that to die for one's country may be necessary. His attitude is overpowering disgust—with the butchery of war, with those who idealize it.

 MyLiteratureLab Resources. Longman Lecture, interactive reading, and critical essay on "Dulce et Decorum Est."

Writers on Writing

Wilfred Owen, War Poetry, pages 699–700

Owen's fragmentary notes toward a preface to his still unpublished book are tremendously eloquent. It is interesting to find that Owen's heightened prose often reads like poetry.

A good classroom question is what Owen sees as the purpose of poetry. He does not see the contemporary poet as having direct political power, although there was a strong political element in the poems he wrote during the Great War. Instead, Owen sees the poet's role as telling the truth. By speaking the truth about difficult and, in this case, tragic events, the poet *warns.* Owen's sense of truth-telling predicts the current concept of poetry as witnessing.

15
Words

LITERAL MEANING: WHAT A POEM SAYS FIRST

Why a whole section on literal meaning? The need first occurred to XJK in a conversation with Robert Reiter and David Anderson of Boston College. Professor Reiter, who had been using the book in a previous edition, pointed out that, while it was well to encourage students to read poetry for its suggestions, his students tended to go too far in that direction and sometimes needed to have their attention bolted down to the denotations of words on a page. Early in a poetry course, the problem seemed especially large—"I try not to let them look for any symbols until after Thanksgiving!" Mr. Anderson had felt the same difficulty. In teaching Donne's "Batter my heart" sonnet, he had had to argue with students who couldn't see how, in a poem of spiritual aspiration, Donne could possibly be referring to anything so grossly physical as rape. They needed to see the plain, literal basis of Donne's tremendous metaphor, that they might then go on to understand the poet's conception of sanctifying grace.

With these comments in mind, the publishers sent a questionnaire to more than one hundred instructors who had used the book, asking them (among other questions) whether they felt the need for more emphasis on denotation. All who replied said that they would welcome such an emphasis (in addition to the emphasis on connotation)—all, that is, except for one instructor (God help him) who reported that he couldn't persuade his students to rise *above* the level of the literal, if indeed he could get them to rise that far.

Most instructors like to discuss imagery fairly early. They will find nothing to hinder them from taking the chapter on imagery ahead of this one. Another procedure would be to defer "Imagery" until after having discussed both denotation and connotation—taking in sequence the present chapter, "Words," and the following chapter, "Saying and Suggesting."

William Carlos Williams, THIS IS JUST TO SAY, page 707

Williams once recalled that this poem was an actual note he had written to his wife—"and she replied very beautifully. Unfortunately, I've lost it. I think what she wrote was quite as good as this" (conversation with John W. Gerber and Emily M. Wallace in *Interviews with William Carlos Williams*, ed. Linda Welshimer Wagner [New York: New Directions, 1976]).

For parodies of this famous poem, see Kenneth Koch's "Variations on a Theme by William Carlos Williams" in *Contemporary American Poetry*, ed. A. Poulin (Boston: Houghton, 1980), and other anthologies.

MyLiteratureLab Resources. Biography, critical overview, and bibliography for Williams.

Marianne Moore, SILENCE, page 708

This poem appears autobiographical on the surface, but the notes that Marianne Moore scrupulously appended to her poems make it clear that it is a composite, imaginary portrait of a father. (Moore barely knew her father, who had suffered a nervous breakdown shortly after her birth; perhaps, for that reason, imaginary fathers were all the more important to her.) The first five lines were adapted from a "Miss A. M. Homans," according to Moore. "Make my house your inn" is a quotation from Edmund Burke, to which Moore added her telling last line. The father in the poem presumably lived in Cambridge, Massachusetts (from references to Longfellow's grave and Harvard), a town in which Moore never resided. We belabor these facts and sources only to demonstrate that poems are often not so autobiographical as they might seem.

A central theme of "Silence" is the eloquence of understatement and restraint. The poet Donald Hall praises this poem in his study *Marianne Moore: The Cage and the Animal* (New York: Pegasus, 1970), saying that by "eschewing the easy words for the ambiguous emotion," Moore displays "a species of honesty and not evidence of lack of depth." Precision is another key term. Notice how important the speaker considers distinctions between related words and situations (*silence/restraint, inn/residence*).

Robert Graves, DOWN, WANTON, DOWN!, page 709

This poem can be an astonisher, especially if students haven't read it in advance. One freshman group XJK sprang it on provided a beautiful gamut of reactions from stunned surprise to hilarity. At first, most didn't know quite what to make of the poem, but they soon saw that its puns and metaphors point to details of male and female anatomy; in catching these, they found themselves looking to literal meanings. After further discussion, they decided that the poem, however witty, makes a serious point about the blindness of lust. To get at this point, students may be asked to sum up the contrast Graves is drawing between Love and Beauty and the wanton's approach to them.

The title (and opening line) echo a phrase from Shakespeare in a passage about eels being rolled into a pie (*King Lear*, II, iv, 118–123):

LEAR: O me, my heart, my rising heart! But down!

FOOL: Cry to it, nuncle, as the cockney did to the eels when she put 'em i' th' paste alive. She knapped 'em o' th' coxcombs with a stick and cried, "Down, wantons, down!" 'Twas her brother that, in pure kindness to his horse, buttered his hay.

One instructor at a community college in New Jersey has reported an embarrassing experience. One morning, not having had time to prepare for class, he introduced this poem without having read it first. "What's it about?" he queried, and someone in the class replied, "An erection." "WHAT?" he exploded. "Come on, now, let's look at it *closely.* . . ." But as he stared at the poem before him, a chill stole over him. Luckily, he was saved by the bell.

John Donne, BATTER MY HEART, THREE-PERSONED GOD, FOR YOU, page 709

On Donne's last line: the literature of mysticism is full of accounts of spiritual experience seen in physical terms; any students who wish to pursue the matter might be directed, for instance, to the poems of St. John of the Cross (which have been splendidly translated by John Frederick Nims).

John E. Parish has shown that Donne's poem incorporates two metaphors, both worn and familiar: the traditional Christian comparison of the soul to a maiden and Christ to a bridegroom, and the Petrarchan conceit of the reluctant woman as a castle and her lover as an invading army. Donne brilliantly combines the two into a new whole. In lines 1 to 4, the sinner's heart is like a walled town fallen to Satan, the enemy. Now God the rightful King approaches and knocks for entrance. But merely to knock won't do—the King must break open the gates with a battering ram. The verbs in these lines all suggest the act of storming a citadel, "and even *blowe* may be intended to suggest the use of gunpowder to blow up the fortress" ("No. 14 of Donne's *Holy Sonnets,*" *College English* 24 [January 1963]: 299–302).

"The paradox of death and rebirth, the central paradox of Christianity" is (according to A. L. Clements in another commentary) the organizing principle of the poem. To illustrate the paradox of destroying in order to revive, Donne employs two sorts of figurative language: one, military and destructive; the other, marital and uniting ("Donne's 'Holy Sonnet XIV,'" *Modern Language Notes* 76 [June 1961]: 484–89).

Both the Clements and the Parish articles are reprinted, together with four other discussions of the poem, in *John Donne's Poetry,* edited by Clements (New York: Norton, 1966).

It is hard to talk for long about rhythm in poetry without citing the opening lines of "Batter my heart." Both in meter and in meaning, they must be among the most powerful lines in English poetry.

MLL *MyLiteratureLab Resources.* Biography, critical overview, and bibliography for Donne.

THE VALUE OF A DICTIONARY

Henry Wadsworth Longfellow, AFTERMATH, page 711

Like many seemingly abstract words, *aftermath* was originally a concrete descriptive term that referred to the usually meager second growth of crop in a field that had already been mowed that season: *after + math* (an obsolete word for *mowing*). Once you read Longfellow's quietly moving poem, you'll never forget the etymology. "Aftermath" shows how poets usually employ words with careful consideration of their histories.

"Aftermath" provides a literal description of mowing the second growth in a winter field, but the treatment suggests a hidden symbolic meaning. Longfellow is careful not to specify exactly what the subtext is and leaves every reader free to project his or her own private meaning into the poem. The structure of Longfellow's insight, however, is painfully clear: to revisit a scene of the past can be devastating.

Fledged means "having feathers" and refers to young birds who are now old enough to have grown feathers and flown from their nests. *Rowen* is a synonym for *aftermath*, a season's second crop, usually of hay.

John Clare, MOUSE'S NEST, page 712

The connection between the final couplet and the rest of the poem is one of metaphor. Small trickles of water that "scarce could run" are newborn mice; "broad old cesspools," their mother.

Milton Klonsky has praised the poem in his anthology of graphic and pictorial poetry, *Speaking Pictures* (New York: Harmony, 1975). He admires "the cinematic flow of Clare's imagery, with each picture flashing by to be replaced by the next before its own afterimage has completely faded." This comment might be discussed—do students agree that Clare's poem seems cinematic and contemporary?

A few facts of Clare's heartbreaking life might interest students. Born into grinding poverty, the son of a field laborer in Northamptonshire, Clare enjoyed brief fame for his *Poems Descriptive of Rural Life* (1820). Lionized by Coleridge and other London literati as an untutored genius, he was then forgotten. The latter half of his life was spent in lunatic asylums, where he wrote some remarkable lyrics and (under the delusion that he was Lord Byron) a continuation of *Don Juan*. Theodore Roethke, whose work shows a similar delight in close-up views of living creatures, has paid tribute (in his poem "Heard in a Violent Ward") to "that sweet man, John Clare."

J. V. Cunningham, FRIEND, ON THIS SCAFFOLD THOMAS MORE LIES DEAD, page 713

Cunningham's epigram states a metaphor: it likens two famous separations decreed by Henry VIII. Separation of the Body (the Church of England) from the Head (the Pope) is like the decapitation of More, who had opposed it. A possible original for Cunningham's epigram, a Latin epigram by John Owen (1606), has been discovered by Charles Clay Doyle:

> Abscindi passus caput est a corpore Morus;
> Abscindi corpus noluit a capite.

In 1659 Thomas Pecke rendered it into English:

> What though Head was from Body severed!
> *More* would not let Body be cut from Head.

Doyle remarks that in fact More played down the role of the Pope as "head" of the Church, preferring the allegorical view (derived from Paul) of Christ as head upon the Church's body ("The Hair and Beard of Thomas More," *Moreana* 18, 71–72 [Nov. 1981]: 5–14).

Kelly Cherry, ADVICE TO A FRIEND WHO PAINTS, page 714

The seemingly incongruous images of this poem are all common subjects in the paintings of Cezanne. The first question to ask the class is "Who is Cezanne?" Then ask how catching that allusion helps us understand the poem. It will also heighten the immediacy of the poem if one brings a book of his paintings into class. Almost any book on the artist will illustrate most if not all of the images in the poem.

Once the role of allusion is understood in the poem, it is interesting to ask students what the final line implies about the speaker's attitude toward the painter-friend in the title. What message does the poem subtly give the "tearing, tugging" painter-friend?

Carl Sandburg, GRASS, page 714

Carl Sandburg's poem, which was written while World War I was still raging, incorporates five place names into its brief length. All five proper nouns are the names of famously bloody battlegrounds. Austerlitz and Waterloo were scenes of major battles in the Napoleonic Wars. Gettysburg refers, of course, to the decisive Civil War battle in Pennsylvania. Ypres and Verdun were the sites of the battles in World War I that still rank among the deadliest military engagements in human history. Since the allusions are all used in parallel ways, a reader should be able to understand the role of any battle he or she does not know from the context as long as he or she recognizes some of the names.

It might be worth asking the class who is speaking in the poem. The speaker is the grass itself, a symbol of the natural world's enduring ability to reassert its power over human history. This aspect of Nature is often viewed in harsh terms, but Sandburg's poem displays it in a gentle, consolatory way. In historical terms, one might consider Sandburg's poem a vision of peace in the final days of World War I.

WORD CHOICE AND WORD ORDER

An exercise to make a class more aware of *le mot juste* is suggested by W. Jackson Bate and David Perkins in *British and American Poets* (San Diego: Harcourt, 1986). Print out several lines of a poem, with an admirably chosen word or words left out. Let students suggest ways to fill in the blank and debate their choices. Then the instructor whips out a trump card: the way the poet filled in the blank—if you're lucky, to "a collective sigh of appreciation."

Robert Herrick, UPON JULIA'S CLOTHES, page 716

This short classic is included in the book by popular demand. The poem deserves inclusion for beauty's sake alone, but it is also mighty useful in the classroom to illustrate the power of diction. *Liquefaction* is an unforgettable word in Herrick's poem—a strong metaphor clothed in suave music. Note that the poem contains only two Latinate words (one in each stanza)—*liquefaction* and *vibration*. Both of them are employed and positioned for their special resonance. Students will also learn something about the history of English by looking up *brave* in a dictionary. Herrick uses it here in a now slightly archaic sense to mean "finely dressed" or "splendidly turned out," though by Shakespeare's time the adjective was also employed, according to the *OED*, as "a general epithet of admiration." Remember Miranda's famous exclamation in *The Tempest*: "O brave new world / That has such people in't."

Kay Ryan, BLANDEUR, page 718

Kay Ryan's witty poem demonstrates that on certain occasions writers can invent the words they need. (Ryan actually coins two related words in her poem—the noun *blandeur* and the verb *blanden*.) Although the poem is in one sense a joke, it also seemingly reflects a sincere desire for the comfortable average rather than the sublime extremes of human experience. The poem states its preference for the undramatic "mean" and not for grand and terrible excess.

Ryan's poem is written in short free verse lines wonderfully interwoven with many irregular rimes. Many rimes occur at the ends of lines—*happen/flatten/blanden/Canyon, fissures/your,* and *hearts/parts*—but others appear elsewhere in the line like *rondure/fissures, hand/remand, calving/halving*. The effect of this intricate and unexpected riming is to slow down our reading and hear the many interconnections of sound and sense.

Thomas Hardy, THE RUINED MAID, page 719

In a London street, an innocent girl from Dorset encounters a friend who has run away from life on the farm. Now a well-paid prostitute, 'Melia calls herself *ruined* with cheerful irony. That this maid has been made, it would seem, has been the making of her. Hardy, of course, is probably less stricken with awe before 'Melia's glamorous clothes than is the first speaker. As the *ain't* in the last line indicates, 'Melia's citified polish doesn't go deep.

For a sequel to "The Ruined Maid," see "A Daughter Returns" in Hardy's last collection of poetry, *Winter Words*. With "Dainty-cut raiment" and "earrings of pearl," a runaway daughter returns to her country home only to be spurned by her father for having lost her innocence.

 MyLiteratureLab Resources. Biography, critical overview, and bibliography for Hardy. Critical essay on "The Ruined Maid."

Richard Eberhart, THE FURY OF AERIAL BOMBARDMENT, page 720

Dr. Johnson said that technical language is inadmissible to poetry, but in the case of Eberhart's poem it is hard to agree. We do not need to know the referents of "belt feed lever" and "belt holding pawl" in order to catch the poet's meaning. Indeed, he evidently chooses these terms as specimens of a jargon barely comprehensible to the unlucky gunnery students who failed to master it. At a reading of his poems in public, Eberhart once remarked that he had added the last stanza as an after-thought. The tone (it seems to us) remains troubled and sorrowful but shifts from loftiness and grandeur to matter-of-fact. This shift takes place in diction as well: from the generality of "infinite spaces," "multitudinous will," "eternal truth," and "the Beast" in man's soul down to "Names on a list," "lever," and "pawl." The poem is a wonderful instance of a poet's writing himself into a fix—getting snarled in unanswerable questions—and then triumphantly saving the day (and his poem) by suddenly returning with a bump to the ordinary, particular world.

Wendy Cope, LONELY HEARTS, page 721

Wendy Cope's bittersweet villanelle demonstrates that old forms can easily accommodate new content, as long as the poet has enough imagination and skill.

Students never seem to have trouble understanding this poem. It is a fun exercise to have students write an additional personal ad in the same rime scheme, but, if you use this idea, be prepared for some odd results.

You might suggest that students read the biographical note on Cope in the "Lives of the Poets" section. Her late-blooming career and personal problems may add a personal dimension to this poem. If she is making gentle fun of the authors of personal ads, she also understands their emotional needs.

FOR REVIEW AND FURTHER STUDY

E. E. Cummings, ANYONE LIVED IN A PRETTY HOW TOWN, page 722

Trained in the classical languages, Cummings borrows from Latin the freedom to place a word in practically any location within a sentence. The first two lines are easy to unscramble: "How pretty a town anyone lived in, with so many bells floating up [and] down." The scrambling is artful, and pedestrian words call attention to themselves by being seen in an unusual order.

The hero and heroine of the poem are anyone and noone, whose names recall the pronoun-designated principals in Cummings's play "Him"—hero Him and heroine Me. Are they Everyman and Everywoman? Not at all: they're different; they're strong, loving individuals whom the poet contrasts with those drab women and men of line 5, "both little and small," who dully sow isn't (negation) and reap same (conformity). Unlike the wise noone and anyone, the everyones of line 17 apparently think they're really somebody.

In tracing the history of anyone and noone from childhood through their mature love to their death and burial, Cummings, we think, gives a brief tour through life in much the way that Thornton Wilder does in Our Town. But not all readers will agree. R. C. Walsh thinks that, in the last two stanzas, anyone and noone do not literally die but grow into loveless and lifeless adults, whose only hope of rejuvenation is to have children (Explicator 22 [May 1964]: item 72). But it seems unlike Cummings to make turncoats of his individualists. Bounded by the passage of the seasons, the rain, and the heavens, the mortal lives of anyone and noone seem concluded in their burial. But in the next-to-last stanza they go on sleeping in love and faith, dreaming of their resurrection.

MyLiteratureLab Resources. Photographs and biographical information for Cummings. Audio clip and critical essay on "anyone lived in a pretty how town."

Billy Collins, THE NAMES, page 723

As Robert Francis observed in *The Satirical Rogue on Poetry* (1968): "Now the chief trouble with writing for and about an occasion is that you become so impressed with the importance of the occasion that you are likely to become impressed with the importance of your writing about it. Something big, obviously, is called for." By contrast, in "The Names" Billy Collins never directly mentions the horrific events of September 11, 2001, or the World Trade Center, or even the name of "this city" (line 22), nor does the speaker call attention to (and implicitly expect to be admired for) his own sensitivity. Instead, Collins achieves a great emotional effect through the quiet presentation of an alphabet of representative names of victims, embedding them in the details of the natural world both to show that our awareness of this event, with its immense human loss, has become permanently intertwined with our perceptions of the world about us, and to remind us that human life, like the natural world, is both fleeting and enduring. The effect is underscored by the simplicity and dignity of the poem's style, which is wholly appropriate to the subject and so restrained that, although every line is heavy with the emotions of pain and loss, there is no overt emotional reference at all until the very last line, which is made all the more powerful by the very modesty of its statement.

 MyLiteratureLab Resources. Biography, critical overview, and bibliography for Collins. Longman Lecture on "The Names."

EXERCISE: *Different Kinds of English*, page 724

Anonymous, CARNATION MILK, page 724
Kenneth Rexroth, VITAMINS AND ROUGHAGE, page 725
Gina Valdés, ENGLISH CON SALSA, page 725

Students won't need much help to see that "Carnation Milk" is unschooled speech; that Rexroth alternates between straightforward diction and more "educated" phrasing; and that Valdés flavors her English with a strong seasoning of Spanish expressions, just as her title suggests.

Rexroth's "Vitamins and Roughage" turns on the conflict that is stated and resolved in line 6, "That nature is still stronger than man." There are two levels of diction employed, reflecting the two sides of the issue. "Reluctant humanists"—reluctant to acknowledge the primacy of instinct over intellect—and their values are characterized by the polysyllabic intellectual diction that predominates in the poem, but that diction is significantly undercut by the more direct and vivid phrasing of lines 1, 4, and 10. There is also meaningful use of straightforward phrasing in line 12, where intellectual systems are called "games"—flimsy artificial constructs that collapse when assaulted by earthy realities.

Like Rhina P. Espaillat's "Bilingual/Bilingüe," Gina Valdés's "English con Salsa" mixes—or, better, flavors—English diction with Spanish to reinforce its thematic preoccupation with the interaction between cultures. This larger point is quite clearly stated and illustrated throughout the text, but a careful reading will reveal some underlying subtleties: the allusion to the Mixtec language and civilization in the last line is a reminder that other cultures long predate both the English and the Spanish on this continent; the place names in line 27 underscore the fact that the interplay between English and Spanish has existed for centuries; and, despite these facts, lines 6–9 ironically point up the limits of the opportunities that await the new Americans in this ESL class.

Lewis Carroll, JABBERWOCKY, page 726

WRITERS ON WRITING

Lewis Carroll, HUMPTY DUMPTY EXPLICATES "JABBERWOCKY," page 727

"Jabberwocky" has to be heard aloud: you might ask a student to read it, alerting him or her in advance to prepare it, and offering tips on pronunciation. ("The *i* in *slithy* is like the *i* in *slime;* the *a* in *wabe,* like the *a* in *wave.*")

Although Carroll added *chortled* to the dictionary, not all his odd words are invented. *Gyre* of course means "to spin or twist about"—it is used as a noun in Yeats's "Sailing to Byzantium" and "The Second Coming." *Slithy* (sleazy or slovenly), *rath* (an earthen wall), *whiffling* (blowing or puffing), and *callooh* (an arctic duck that winters in Scotland, so named for its call) are legitimate words, too, but Carroll uses them in different senses. *Frabjous* probably owes something to *frab,* a dialect word meaning "to scold, harass, or nag," as Myra Cohn Livingston points out in her anthology *O Frabjous Day!* (New York: Atheneum, 1977).

Writing in 1877 to a child who had inquired what the strange words meant, Carroll replied:

> I am afraid I can't explain "vorpal blade" for you—nor yet "tulgey wood"; but I did make an explanation once for "uffish thought"—it seems to suggest a state of mind when the voice is gruffish, the manner roughish, and the temper huffish. Then again, as to "burble" if you take the three verbs "<u>b</u>leat," "<u>mur</u>mur" and "war<u>ble</u>," and select the bits I have underlined, it certainly <u>makes</u> "burble": though I am afraid I can't distinctly remember having made it that way.

Students can have fun unpacking other portmanteau words: *gimble* (*nimble, gambol*); *frumious* (which Carroll said is *fuming* plus *furious*); *vorpal* (*voracious, purple*), *galumphing* (*galloping in triumph*), and so on. (*Uffish* suggests *oafish* too.) Some of these suggestions come from Martin Gardner, who supplies copious notes on the poem (as well as translations of it into French and German) in *The Annotated Alice* (New York: Bramhall, 1960).

All other critics, however, must yield precedence to the estimable Humpty Dumpty, whose definite comments appear in "Writers on Writing" following the poem.

MLL *MyLiteratureLab Resources.* Longman Lecture, interactive reading, and critical essay on "Jabberwocky."

16
Saying and Suggesting

John Masefield, CARGOES, page 732

Much of the effect of Masefield's contrast depends on rhythms and word-sounds, not just on connotations. In stanza 2, the poet strews his lines with dactyls, producing ripples in his rhythm: *diamonds, emeralds, amethysts, cinnamon*. In the third stanza, paired monosyllables (*salt-caked, smoke stack, Tyne coal, roadrails, pig-lead, firewood*) make for a hard-hitting series of spondees. Internal alliteration helps the contrast, too: all those *m*-sounds in the dactyls; and in the harsher lines "Dirty British coaster with a salt-caked smoke stack, / Butting," all the sounds of the *r*, the *t*, and the staccato *k*.

"Cargoes" abounds with lively, meaningful music, yet Masefield is generally dismissed nowadays as a mere balladeer—a jog-trot chronicler of the lives of the poor and unfortunate. In naming him poet laureate, George V (it is said) mistakenly thought him a hero of the working class; unluckily for his later fame, Masefield, like Wordsworth, enjoyed a long senility.

William Blake, LONDON, page 733

Blake's "London" broadens the themes explored in his "The Chimney Sweeper." The personal pathos of "The Chimney Sweeper" becomes a general indictment of a society in which such exploitation is possible. In "London," we see Blake as a prophetic poet—not prophesying the future like a tabloid seer, but speaking as a prophet who declares the moral necessity of just change in a time of evil.

In his essay "On Blake and His Critics" (1934), G. K. Chesterton singled out the third stanza of "London" for special praise. He called the images "two lightning-flashes revealing two separate Visions of Judgment." It is important to remember that Blake was a Londoner born and bred who spent most of his life within the city limits. He is not a country poet describing urban squalor; he is a native morally dissecting his own home town. He knows every image from the inside out.

If Blake were to walk the streets of an American city today, would he find any conditions similar to those he finds in "London"? Is this poem merely an occasional poem, with a protest valid only for its time, or does it have enduring applications?

MLL *MyLiteratureLab Resources.* Photographs and biographical information for Blake.

Wallace Stevens, Disillusionment of Ten O'Clock, page 735

Stevens slings colors with the verve of a Matisse. In this early poem, he paints a suggestive contrast between the pale and colorless homeowners, ghostlike and punctually going to bed at ten, and, on the other hand, the dreams they wouldn't dream of dreaming; and the bizarre and exotic scene inside the drunken head of our disreputable hero, the old seafarer. Who in the world would wear a beaded sash or *ceinture?* (A Barbary pirate? An Arabian harem dancer?) Ronald Sukenick has made a terse statement of the poem's theme: "the vividness of the imagination in the dullness of a pallid reality" (*Wallace Stevens: Musing the Obscure* [New York: New York UP, 1967]). Another critic, Edward Kessler, has offered a good paraphrase: "Only the drunkard, the irrational man ('Poetry must be irrational' [*Opus Posthumous* 162]), who is in touch with the unconscious—represented here, and often elsewhere, by the sea—can awake his own passionate nature until his blood is mirrored in the very weather" (*Images of Wallace Stevens* [New Brunswick: Rutgers UP, 1972]).

While they will need to see the contrast between pallor and color, students might be cautioned against lending every color a particular meaning, as if the poem were an allegory.

Stevens expressed further disappointment with monotonous neighbors in a later poem, "Loneliness in Jersey City," which seems a companion piece to this. In Jersey City, "the steeples are empty and so are the people," who can't tell a dachshund from a deer. Both poems probably owe some of their imagery to Stevens's days as a struggling young lawyer living in rooming houses in East Orange, New Jersey, and Fordham Heights, in New York City.

> **MLL** *MyLiteratureLab Resources.* Biography, critical overview, and bibliography for Stevens.

Gwendolyn Brooks, Southeast Corner, page 735

This short poem first appeared in Brooks's debut volume, *A Street in Bronzeville* (1945). The book centered on a group of interrelated poems, including this one, set in Bronzeville, a fictional African American neighborhood in Chicago. In her autobiography *Report from Part One* (Detroit: Broadside P, 1972), Brooks praised Langston Hughes, whom she met during the time she was composing the poems in *A Street in Bronzeville*:

> Mightily did he use the street. He found its multiple heart, its tastes, smells, alarms, formulas, flowers, garbage, and convulsions. He brought them to his table-top. He crushed them to a writing paste. He himself became the pen . . .

In that passage, Brooks seems to be describing her own method in these early poems. Perhaps the key word in the poem is "tan" in line 11. As in others of her early poems, Brooks is concerned here with issues of intraracial prejudice. The Madam (the term inevitably suggests the mistress of a bordello) had engaged in a kind of prostitution, enriching herself by selling skin-lightening and hair-straightening products to African American girls who had been bred to reject themselves and to aspire to Caucasian standards of beauty. Even in death she is contented and impassive, and her gaudy coffin and monument show the same preoccupation with superficial appearances that was the basis of her fortune. Yet Brooks does not criticize the woman, probably born poor, for posthumously displaying her material success. The poet seems to revel in the tomb's ironic opulence.

 MyLiteratureLab Resources. Biography, critical overview, and bibliography for Brooks.

Timothy Steele, EPITAPH, page 736

"Silence is golden"—but Sir Tact is obviously a coward, afraid to speak his mind. This epigram is included in Steele's first collection of poems, *Uncertainties and Rest* (Baton Rouge: Louisiana State UP, 1979).

E. E. Cummings, NEXT TO OF COURSE GOD AMERICA I, page 736

Even if the last line and the quotation marks around the rest of the text were omitted, it would be hard to miss the satiric intent of this sonnet. From the bland, empty affirmation of religious belief in the first line, through the piling up of stock patriotic phrases rendered meaningless by being pulled out of context (and syntactical wholeness), culminating in the string of idiotic interjections in lines 7 and 8, Cummings's sense of the ridiculousness of the rhetoric and the meritriciousness of the orator is all but palpable. In lines 9–12, the speechmaker plays a particularly nasty kind of moral trump card, manipulating the sacrifices of the war dead to close off debate, followed by the reflexive and hypocritical lip service to liberty in line 13. He is saying, in effect: We honor our heroes for their defense of our freedoms, but anyone who exercises those freedoms to dissent from my views is unpatriotic or worse. And then the entire speech is neatly deflated by the poem's final line.

  You can hear Cummings read "next to of course god america i" and three others of his poems online at *Salon* (search "E. E. Cummings" at <www.salon.com>).

 MyLiteratureLab Resources Photographs and biographical information for Cummings.

Robert Frost, FIRE AND ICE, page 737

In his first line, Frost probably refers to those who accept the Biblical prophecy of a final holocaust; and in his second line, to those who accept scientists' forecasts of the cooling of the earth. We admire that final *suffice;* a magnificent understatement, it further shows the power of a rime to close a poem (as Yeats said) with a click like a closing box.

  When we polled students about their favorite poems in the anthology, their number one choice was Frost's "Fire and Ice." This unforgettably incisive lyric clearly illustrates how the poet's mind works with contradiction. Point out how the poem wonderfully argues its way to an inconclusive but nonetheless apocalyptic finale. And note the darkness of the poet's vision: both of the alternatives he offers are terrifying. No wonder college students love it. How many nine-line poems manage to destroy the world not once but twice?

 MyLiteratureLab Resources. Biography, critical overview, critical articles, and bibliography for Frost.

Clare Rossini, FINAL LOVE NOTE, page 737

Clare Rossini's "Final Love Note" employs the language of love poetry to suggest a profound depth of emotion regarding an elm dying in her yard. Although we are first led to believe that the speaker is addressing a human lover, we find later that "Final Love Note" is a nature poem. We are unaware of the lover's identity through the opening stanza, while the tone becomes erotic at times—"clothes strewn on the floor," "moaned over me at night, never tiring." Not until the second stanza, when the speaker addresses the "you" as elm, do we learn that the object of her affection is a dying tree. Even with that truth revealed, the speaker's diction does not stray from that of love poetry. For her, the tree is greater than a human lover. She attributes her past comfort to the beauty and shade the tree has provided, and her present restlessness and sense of "abandonment" is blamed on the imminent destruction of the elm.

The penultimate stanza shifts time to the present tense, the morning in which she is writing, while in her yard she can "hear the chain saw cry out ecstatically." The personification of the elm is completed in the last stanza: "Your many arms are falling." Rossini closes "Final Love Note" with a stroke of irony— the conventionally romantic image of an open sky is now inappropriate and disquieting in the elm's absence: "garish blue stretch / Or drafty ceiling harshly lit by stars." Even in the tree's absence, the speaker views the elm in terms of domestic space and erotic desire. The open sky now visible becomes the mourning lover's bedroom ceiling.

Jennifer Reeser, WINTER-PROOF, page 738

In the first stanza of this poem (the title piece and first poem in her second collection) the author is clearly *saying* she values the calendula (perhaps so named because it blooms in most months—that is, throughout the calendar—in warm climates, such as Reeser's Louisiana) and the other winter-proof blossoms for their resistance to the ravages of time and adversity. In the second stanza there is more *suggesting*: the flowers named there are traditionally associated with brevity and mortality—think of the tubercular courtesan in Alexandre Dumas's *The Lady of the Camellias* and reread Herrick's "To the Virgins, to Make Much of Time" and Waller's "Go, Lovely Rose." In calling that part of the garden where these fragile flowers are decomposing "the graveyard," Reeser draws the obvious parallel to human existence. She is indebted to the winter-proof blossoms because they help her focus on life and its joys, rather than obsessing over its inevitable end.

Alfred, Lord Tennyson, TEARS, IDLE TEARS, page 738

Tennyson's brooding lyric is a classic example of poetic suggestion. The poem opens with a paradox. The speaker unexpectedly finds himself weeping when "looking on the happy autumn-fields." The tears are declared *idle*, which is to say they seemingly lack any real basis. But are they really mysterious in their origin? The "Writing Assignment" at the end of the chapter asks students to explain why the speaker is weeping.

Tennyson loads the poem with suggestive imagery and situations to answer this question. It might help students to begin by noticing *when* the poem takes place. It is autumn—the time of harvest and completion. The speaker seemingly cannot help but reflect in this season on "the days that are no more." *Where* the poem takes place also reinforces the sense that the speaker is painfully cut off from the past. The speaker weeps while "looking on the happy autumn-fields." Seeing them and remembering the past triggers a series of revealing reveries about "the days that are no more."

The first image associated with the past is light on a sail. First, the sail seems "fresh" and dawn-like—bringing "our friends up from the underworld." The last word of that line, *underworld*, explicitly brings death into the poem. Any reassuring image of the dead returning to us, however, is quickly reversed as the ship sinks "with all we love below the verge." The death imagery becomes more explicit in stanza 3 when the dawn song of the birds falls on "dying ears," and the sun rises to "dying eyes." In the final stanza, the intensity of the speaker's mood heightens appreciably. He speaks explicitly of love—lost love—and the pain of remembering the beloved. By the end of the poem the reader recognizes (at least intuitively) that the speaker weeps from the memory of a dead or lost beloved (*both* circumstances are stated) and the pain of being unable to recapture the past.

The late Cleanth Brooks wrote a penetrating analysis of Tennyson's poem, "The Motivation of Tennyson's Weeper," which is found in his influential critical collection *The Well Wrought Urn* (New York: Harcourt, 1947). Brooks's analysis perfectly illustrates the power of close textual reading. Dean of the New Critics, however, Brooks does not discuss the biographical background of Tennyson's lyric. Although not necessary to understand the poem, the facts of its origin are interesting in themselves. Tennyson wrote the poem in the autumn of 1834 after the death of his closest friend, Arthur Hallam. It was composed—an interesting bit of literary trivia—in the ruins of Tintern Abbey, nearly within sight of Hallam's grave and on the same spot that William Wordsworth had conceived his great ode in 1798.

MLL *MyLiteratureLab Resources.* Biography, photographs, critical overview, and bibliography for Tennyson.

Richard Wilbur, LOVE CALLS US TO THE THINGS OF THIS WORLD, page 739

WRITERS ON WRITING

Richard Wilbur, CONCERNING "LOVE CALLS US TO THE THINGS OF THIS WORLD," page 740

Wilbur suavely explains this richly detailed poem in the "Writers on Writing" that follows "Love Calls Us to the Things of This World" in the book. The poem may seem a bit difficult to students until they catch the extended metaphor in the first twenty lines (laundry on the line as angels). The poem depends on a series of oppositions (laundry and angels, earth and heaven, soul and body, sleep and waking). Even the poetic language mixes the vulgar and the exalted ("the punctual rape of every blessèd day"). Have students find as many oppositions as possible, and you will watch them grasp the larger themes of the poem in the process. (You won't believe how many elegant oppositions blissfully coexist in this quietly visionary poem.)

 MyLiteratureLab Resources. Interactive reading of "Love Calls Us to the Things of This World." Critical essay by Wilbur, "Cold War Poetry."

17
Imagery

Ezra Pound, IN A STATION OF THE METRO, page 743

Pound recalled that at first this poem had come to him "not in speech, but in little splotches of color." His account is reprinted by K. K. Ruthven in *A Guide to Ezra Pound's* Personae, *1926* (Berkeley: U of California P, 1969). Students might like to compare this "hokku-like sentence" (as Pound called the poem) with the more suggestive Japanese haiku freely translated later in this chapter.

For a computer-assisted tribute to this famous poem, see the curious work of James Laughlin and Hugh Kenner, reported in "The Mixpoem Program," *Paris Review* 94 (Winter 1984): 193–98. Following Laughlin's suggestion that the five nouns of "In a Station of the Metro" might interestingly be shuffled, Kenner wrote "A Little Program in Basic" that enabled a computer to grind out 120 scrambled versions of the poem, including these:

> The apparitions of these boughs in the face;
> Crowds on a wet, black petal

> The crowd of these apparitions in the petal;
> Faces on a wet, black bough.

Kenner then wrote a program in Pascal that would shuffle eight words and produce 40,320 different versions. We don't know what it all demonstrates, except that Pound's original version still seems the best possible.

Kenner's historical account of the London literary scene and its influences on the composition of this poem is found in the "Critical Approaches to Literature" section of this book.

Taniguchi Buson, THE PIERCING CHILL I FEEL, page 743

Harold G. Henderson, who translated this haiku, wrote a good terse primer in *An Introduction to Haiku* (Garden City: Anchor, 1958). Most of Henderson's English versions of haiku rime like this one; still, the sense of the originals (as far as the reader ignorant of Japanese can tell from Henderson's glosses) does not seem greatly distorted.

T. S. Eliot, THE WINTER EVENING SETTLES DOWN, page 745

This is the first of the series of four poems called "Preludes," originally published in the July 1915 issue of Wyndham Lewis's *Blast*. It was written during Eliot's days at Harvard. The "Preludes," writes Grover Smith in *T. S. Eliot's Poetry and Plays* (Chicago: U of Chicago P, 1965), belong to the era of "Prufrock." Of "The winter evening settles down," Smith says:

> The first "Prelude" begins with winter nightfall in an urban back street; from indoor gloom and the confined odor of cooking it moves outside into the smoky twilight where gusts of wind whip up leaves and soiled papers, and a shower spatters the housetops. Such adjectives as "burnt out," "smoky," "grimy," "withered," "vacant," "broken," and "lonely" carry the tone.

Some students may point out, though, that the lighting of the lamps seems to end the poem on a note of tranquillity.

 MyLiteratureLab Resources. Biography, critical overview, and bibliography for Eliot.

Theodore Roethke, ROOT CELLAR, page 745

Probably there is little point in spending much time dividing imagery into touches and tastes and smells; perhaps it will be enough to point out that Roethke's knowledgeable poem isn't all picture-imagery. There's that wonderful "congress of stinks," and the "slippery planks" are both tactile and visual. Most of the language in the poem is figurative, most of the vegetation is rendered animal: bulbs like small rodents, shoots like penises, roots like a forgotten can of fishing worms. Roethke doesn't call the roots lovely, but obviously he admires their tough, persistent life.

 MyLiteratureLab Resources. Interactive reading and critical essay on "Root Cellar."

Elizabeth Bishop, THE FISH, page 746

This poem is made almost entirely of concrete imagery. Except for *wisdom* (line 63) and *victory* (66), there is no very abstract diction in it.

Obviously the speaker admires this stout old fighter. The image "medals with their ribbons" (line 61) suggests that he is an old soldier, and the "five-haired beard of wisdom" (line 63) suggests that he is a venerable patriarch, of whom one might seek advice.

The poor, battered boat has become magnificent for having the fish in it. The feeling in these lines is joy: bilge, rust, and cracked thwarts are suddenly revealed to be beautiful. In a way, the attitude seems close to that in Yeats's "Sailing to Byzantium," in which the triumphant soul is one that claps its hands and louder sings for every tatter in its mortal dress. The note of final triumph is sounded in "rainbow, rainbow, rainbow!" (line 75). The connotations of *rainbow* in this poem are not very different from the connotations often given the word by misty-eyed romantic poets such as Rod McKuen, but we believe Bishop because of her absolutely hard-eyed and specific view of the physical world. (She even sees the fish with X-ray imagination in lines 27–33.)

Anne Stevenson says in *Elizabeth Bishop* (New York: Twayne, 1966):

> It is a testimony to Miss Bishop's strength and sensitivity that the end, the revelation or "moment of truth," is described with the same attention to detail as the rest of the poem. The temptation might have been to float off into an airy apotheosis, but Miss Bishop stays right in the boat with the engine and the bailer. Because she does so, she is able to use words like "victory" and "rainbow" without fear of triteness.

Because the fish has provided her with an enormous understanding, the speaker's letting it go at the end seems an act of homage and gratitude.

Compare "The Fish" with the same poet's richly imaged "Filling Station."

The poet reads this poem on a recording, *The Spoken Arts Treasury of 100 Modern American Poets*, vol. 10, SA 1049.

MLL *MyLiteratureLab Resources.* Biography, critical overview, and bibliography for Bishop. Critical essay on "The Fish."

Anne Stevenson, THE VICTORY, page 748

This powerful short poem rejects all of the sentimental versions of childbirth and motherhood. It focuses on the violent physical details and emotional shock of giving birth.

One of the chief strategies of Confessional and Feminist poetry has been to admit personal feelings that conventional "good manners" would consider inappropriate or even shameful. In "The Victory," Stevenson presents a new mother's pain and horror at her newborn son. By admitting these feelings, she implicitly confesses that she is a bad mother in conventional terms. But Stevenson's speaker is unconcerned with keeping up appearances; she is obsessed with getting at the difficult truth of the moment. She is trying to sort through her own unexpected feelings.

It may be worthwhile to stress that as a *lyric* poem, "The Victory" tries to capture the intensity of insight from a particular moment. Stevenson's poem does not imply that the speaker will feel this shocked aversion to her child in the future. In fact, the last two lines of the poem imply that she will—despite her initial reaction—grow to love him.

Charles Simic, FORK, page 748

Simic's surreal, short poem introduces an object familiar to us, a fork, and presents it as strange and threatening. The central image is plainly stated: the fork "resembles a bird's foot." An evil, indeed violent, world begins to take shape as one looks more closely at Simic's word choice. The fork, we are told at the start of the poem, is evidently visiting from hell. An eerie turn comes in the second stanza when the speaker addresses a "you" who may be the reader, another person in the poem, or the speaker himself. In any case, we are pulled into a dark landscape of cannibals, hell, stabbings, and naked bird heads—a scene right out of Hieronymus Bosch. We are perhaps pulled in against our will, through our familiarity with the object. Each of us has held a fork, so it is impossible to avoid identifying with the images. That is the real achievement of "Fork"—its surefire inclusion of the reader.

You might begin class discussion by having students point out the words that equip the fork with evil characteristics. A possible writing exercise is to have students come up with their own poems in which a familiar object is treated as foreign and unknown.

Emily Dickinson, A ROUTE OF EVANESCENCE, page 749

"A Route of Evanescence" will probably inspire a heated guessing contest. Contestants will need to pay attention to Dickinson's exact words.

Enclosing this poem in a letter to Thomas W. Higginson, Dickinson gave it the title "A Humming-Bird."

The poet's report of the hummingbird's arrival from Tunis is fanciful: the creature could hardly fly 4,000 miles nonstop in one morning. And New England hummingbirds don't need to cross the Atlantic; to find a warmer climate, they migrate south. If it was a ruby-throated hummingbird that the poet saw, though, it might indeed have come a long distance from a winter in Mexico or Central America.

The poet's ornithology may be slightly cockeyed, but her imagery is accurate. Hummingbird wings appear to rotate, but they aren't seated in ball joints; they merely flap fast.

> **MLL** *MyLiteratureLab Resources.* Biography, critical overview, and bibliography for Dickinson.

Jean Toomer, REAPERS, page 749

This ominous poem, with its contrasts between sound and silence, possibly contains a metaphor. The black field hands are being destroyed by something indifferent and relentless, much as the trapped rat is slain under the blade. (Or, as in "Scottsboro," as a cat stalks a "nohole mouse"?)

A grandson of P. B. S. Pinchback, the black who served for a short time during Reconstruction as acting governor of Louisiana, Toomer had only a brief public career as a writer. His one book, *Cane* (1923), which experimentally combined passages of fiction with poetry, helped to spearhead the Harlem Renaissance. "Reapers" is taken from it.

That Toomer was a man divided between his profound understanding of blacks and his own desire to pass for white emerges in a recent biography, *The Lives of Jean Toomer: A Hunger for Wholeness*, by Cynthia Earl Kerman and Richard Eldridge (Baton Rouge: Louisiana State UP, 1987). *The Collected Poems of Jean Toomer* (Chapel Hill: U of North Carolina P, 1988) is a slim volume of 55 poems, the best of them from *Cane*.

Gerard Manley Hopkins, PIED BEAUTY, page 750

Sumptuously rich in music (rime, alliteration, assonance), this brief poem demands to be read aloud.

Some students might agree with Robert Frost's objection that the poem "disappoints . . . by not keeping, short as it is, wholly to pied things" (1934 letter to his daughter Lesley, in *Family Letters of Robert and Elinor Frost* [Albany: State U of New York P, 1972] 162). But, as question 4 tries to get at, Hopkins had more in mind than dappled surfaces. Rough paraphrase of the poem: God is to be praised not only for having created variegation, but for creating and sustaining contrasts and opposites. In lines 5–6, tradesmen's tools and gear, like the plow that pierces and cuts the soil, strike through the surfaces of raw materials to reveal inner beauty and order that had lain concealed.

For a convincing argument that Hopkins in "Pied Beauty," like Dickens in *Hard Times*, complains about a drab, mechanical, industrial-age uniformity in Victorian England, see Norman H. MacKenzie, *A Reader's Guide to Gerard Manley Hopkins* (Ithaca: Cornell UP, 1981) 85–86. Few students will crave to fathom the poet's notions of *instress* and *inscape*, but if you do, see John Pick's unsurpassed *Gerard Manley Hopkins, Priest and Poet*, 2nd ed. (London: Oxford UP, 1966) 53–56.

The point of question 5 is that if the images of the poem were subtracted, its statement of theme would also disappear.

Hopkins discovered the form of "Pied Beauty" and called it the *curtal sonnet* (*curtal*, riming with *turtle*: "crop-tailed"). But, remarks MacKenzie, such sonnets are like a small breed of horse: "compressed, not merely cut short." Instead of two quatrains, the form calls for two tercets; then, instead of a sestet, four lines and one brief line more. (Other curtal sonnets by Hopkins: "Peace" and, even more closely cropped, "Ashboughs.")

MLL   *MyLiteratureLab Resources.* Photographs and biographical information for Hopkins. Audio clip and critical essay on "Pied Beauty."

ABOUT HAIKU

We expanded the haiku section in an earlier edition, refreshing the contemporary section with a couple of new selections and adding a group of haiku by Japanese Americans who were confined to internment camps during World War II, in one of the more shameful episodes of modern American history. These poems provide a quietly devastating commentary on the ironies and the injustice of the situation in which these innocent people were placed.

There is also a selection of hokku by Yone Noguchi in "Poems for Further Reading." Please take a look at these early twentieth-century poems; Noguchi was the first Asian American poet, and he was in many ways the person who first helped bring the haiku tradition over into English. He has been neglected by literary historians, and we are proud to give his pioneering work additional attention.

A biographical/critical note on Noguchi is found in this manual (in the commentary on "Poems for Further Reading"). Biographies of the "Three Masters" of classical Japanese haiku (Basho, Buson, and Issa) are found in the anthology in the chapter "Lives of the Poets."

The response to the enlarged haiku coverage has been excellent; the section now allows instructors enough material to make a separate unit on the subject. Lee Gurga, associate editor of *Modern Haiku* and a master of the form in his own right, has praised our coverage of Basho, Buson, and Issa, but he wishes that we had also included work by Shiki (1876–1902), the fourth "Master" of the haiku, who was the originator of the modern haiku in Japan. Shiki was responsible for renaming the form from *hokku* (opening verse) to *haiku* (playful verse). We will take Gurga's suggestion under consideration for future editions, but meanwhile we include one of his own astute examples of the haiku form in our selection of contemporary haiku.

Basho's frogjump poem, "In the old stone pool," may well be the most highly prized gem in Japanese literature: in Japanese there exists a three-volume commentary on it.

For an excellent discussion of the problems of teaching haiku, and of trying to write English ones, see Myra Cohn Livingston's *When You Are Alone / It Keeps You Capone: An Approach to Creative Writing with Children* (New York: Atheneum, 1973) 152–62. Livingston finds it useful to tell students a famous anecdote. Kikaku, a pupil of Basho, once presented his master with this specimen:

Red dragonflies—
Tear off their wings
And you have pepper pods.

As a haiku, said Basho, that's no good. Make it instead:

Red pepper pods—
Add wings
And you have dragonflies.

A moment of triumph, such as all teachers of poetry hope for but seldom realize, has been reported in a letter to XJK from Maurice F. Brown of Oakland University, Rochester, Michigan:

Last year, teaching W. C. Williams in an "invitational" course for a week, I began with "Red Wheelbarrow" . . . and a student hand went up (class of 100): "That's not a poem! That's junk. What if I say, 'Here I sit looking at a blackboard while the sun is shining outside.' Is that a poem?" It was one of those great teaching moments . . . and I did a quick count and wrote it on the board:

Here I sit looking
    At a blackboard while the sun
is shining outside.

Not only a poem . . . a perfect haiku.

A thorough guide to this rocky acre of poetry, by William J. Higginson with Penny Harter, is *The Haiku Handbook: How to Write, Share, and Teach Haiku* (New York: McGraw, 1985).

Several small journals focus on haiku and tanka. If you or your students want to pursue studying (and perhaps even publishing) haiku, you will want to look at some of these magazines. *Modern Haiku* has been in existence for over thirty years. And the Haiku Society of America publishes *Frogpond*. For information, go to <www.modernhaiku.org> and <www.hsa-haiku.org>.

Those interested in the "Three Masters" of the Japanese haiku tradition will want to consult Robert Hass's *The Essential Haiku: Versions of Basho, Buson, and*

Issa (Hopewell, NJ: Ecco, 1994). Hass provides both generous selections from the poets and an informed introductory essay for each writer.

Looking over the eight contemporary haiku, the reader will see that not every poet adheres to the traditional seventeen-syllable pattern. The skillful and illuminating combination of two images or ideas, however, remains central to the haiku's identity in English. The poems are too short to require much commentary, but the title of one poem invites a few remarks.

Why is John Ridland's "The Lazy Man's Haiku" the work of a slothful soul? Because, according to the poet (in a letter), "he's too lazy to write the proper number of syllables in any line—or to get rid of that occidental end-rhyme à la Harold Henderson's ever-unconvincing translations in that old Anchor book." Henderson, in *An Introduction to Haiku* (New York: Anchor, 1956), forced all the haiku to rime like his version from Buson given at the beginning of this chapter. (Reading it as a poem in English, we find it profoundly convincing, and suspect it took work.)

FOR REVIEW AND FURTHER STUDY

John Keats, BRIGHT STAR! WOULD I WERE STEADFAST AS THOU ART, page 754

Unlike Petrarchan poets, Keats isn't making the star into an abstraction (Love); he takes it for a visible celestial body, even though he sees it in terms of other things. His comparisons are so richly laden with suggestions (star as staring eye, waters as priestlike), that sometimes students don't notice his insistent negations. The hermit's all-night vigil is *not* what Keats desires. He wants the comfort of that ripening pillow, and (perhaps aware of his impending death) envies the cold star only its imperishability—oh, for unendurable ecstasy, indefinitely prolonged! Compare this to Keats's "To Autumn" in which the poet finds virtue in change.

Many readers find the last five words of the poem bothersome. Students might be asked, Does Keats lose your sympathy by this ending? If so, why? If not, how would you defend it? We can't defend it; it seems bathetic, almost as self-indulgent as Shelley's lines in "Indian Serenade":

> Oh, lift me from the grass!
>   I die! I faint! I fail!
> Let thy love in kisses rain
>   On my lips and eyelids pale.

Thomas Mauch, of Colorado College, intelligently disagrees, and suggests how "or else swoon to death" may be defended. The *or*, he thinks, is what grammarians call an inclusive *or*, not an exclusive.

> I believe that the speaker is saying, not that if he can't be forever in the close company of the beloved he would rather be dead—sort of like what Patrick Henry said about liberty—but rather that, given the closeness to the woman, dying in that condition would be just as good as experiencing it forever, since in either case he would not undergo a separation from her (and

still retain his consciousness of it). I think it is the same point he makes in the "Ode to a Nightingale":

> Now more than ever seems it rich to die,
>   To cease upon the midnight with no pain,
>   While thou art pouring forth thy soul abroad
>   In such an ecstasy!

The poem, Mr. Mauch concludes, illustrates the kind of closure that Keats admired when he affirmed that a poem should "die grandly."

 MyLiteratureLab Resources. Photographs, biographical information, critical overview, and bibliography for Keats. Longman Lecture on "Bright star!"

EXPERIMENT: *Writing with Images*, page 754

To write a poem full of images, in any form, is probably easier for most students than to write a decent haiku. (On the difficulties of teaching haiku writing, see Myra Cohn Livingston, cited under "About Haiku.") Surprisingly, there is usually at least one student in every class who can't seem to criticize a poem to save his neck, yet who, if invited to be a poet, will bloom or at least bud.

Walt Whitman, THE RUNNER, page 754

Try reading "The Runner" without the adverbs *lightly* and *partially.* Does the poem even exist without those two delicate modifiers?

T. E. Hulme, IMAGE, page 754

Hulme's poems seem always to have been brief. In his own collection *Personae,* Ezra Pound took two pages to include "The Complete Poetical Works of T. E. Hulme" (in which "Image" does not appear). Pound remarked, "In publishing his *Complete Poetical Works* at thirty, Mr. Hulme has set an enviable example to many of his contemporaries who have had less to say."

William Carlos Williams, EL HOMBRE, page 755

This famous little poem engages one of Williams's principal themes, the primacy of the image, and the consequent need to look clearly at things in terms of themselves rather than obscure them with irrelevant comparisons. This concept is also treated in other Williams poems written in the same period, such as "Tract" and "To a Solitary Disciple," and it surfaces again twenty years later in "The Term." Nonetheless, it is almost impossible not to derive from these early poems some sense of Williams's feelings of isolation in the literary landscape of his time. As the critic Steven Gould Axelrod has observed, "Williams troped on his situation in 'El Hombre.'"

In 1918, the year after "El Hombre" appeared in book form, Wallace Stevens published in the *Little Review* a poem called "Nuances of a Theme by

Williams," in which he quotes Williams's text in its entirety and improvises on the phrases "shine alone" and "lend no part." Recalling this tribute many years later, Williams said, "I was deeply touched."

 MyLiteratureLab Resources. Biography, critical overview, and bibliography for Williams.

Chana Bloch, TIRED SEX, page 755

Chana Bloch's brief poem tells its entire story through images (a very discreet thing to do considering the subject). The first image—the damp matchbook—is particularly clever since the poet develops it to represent both male (the match) and female (the matchbook) sexuality. Bloch also carefully avoids depicting the speaker's inner thoughts and focuses instead on the external images (watching "that sparrow the cat / keeps batting around") that suggest a great deal about what is happening both in bed and in the speaker's mind. The final image of joylessly paging through a supposedly great book provides a touch of wit to this ingenious poem.

Robert Bly, DRIVING TO TOWN LATE TO MAIL A LETTER, page 755

No doubt the situation in this poem is real: Bly, who lives in frequently snow-bound Minnesota, emits hundreds of letters. Compare this simple poem to Frost's "Stopping by Woods on a Snowy Evening," which also has a speaker who, instead of going home, prefers to ogle snowscapes.

Note that this poem is examined in the "Writing Critically" section at the end of this chapter in the main book.

Rita Dove, SILOS, page 755

"Silos" is a poem not only *of* images but *about* them as well, and it is particularly about what the silos suggest to those who perceive them. It is interesting to note that the most pleasing and fanciful suggestion is attributed to "a stranger." Those who live with the silos looming over them in their everyday lives, whether adults or children, have more mundane and at best ambiguous interpretations of them.

It is also interesting to note that the postmodern world has apparently transcended its ribs. The poem's silos are those of the Quaker Oats Company, whose factory once dominated the downtown section of Akron, Ohio, the poet's native city (see the prose poem "Quaker Oats" in the first section of Dove's largely autobiographical collection *Grace Notes*, which also contains "Silos"). The factory is now a mall, and its silos have been converted into suites of hotel rooms.

Louise Glück, MOCK ORANGE, page 755

The sensory imagery of Glück's poem is nearly all-encompassing. In the course of the poem the speaker invokes the senses of sight, touch, hearing, and smell. The persistent image of the mock orange becomes associated with sex early in the poem—an association the speaker finds not merely unpleasant but terrifying. She associates sex with suffocation, paralysis, and humiliation. The title image also eventually becomes a pun on *mock* ("Do you see? / We were made fools of.")

Billy Collins, EMBRACE, page 756

Billy Collins has an extraordinary gift for ingenious imagery, and "Embrace" is no exception. Here Collins creates an image and then invites the reader to examine it from two sides. The extended image, which begins so playfully and even romantically, soon proves not only devastatingly lonely but foreboding. This poem contains a lesson every cinematographer knows—the same physical image can elicit a radically different effect depending on the angle from which it is depicted.

A CD of Billy Collins reading his poems, *The Best Cigarette*, has been released by Eric Antonow's small good productions (800-829-7552).

MLL *MyLiteratureLab Resources*. Biography, critical overview, and bibliography for Collins.

John Haines, WINTER NEWS, page 757

We are struck by "the stiffening dogs" in this poem. It is possible both to picture such stiffening and to feel it in one's muscles and bones. Haines appeals mostly to the senses of sight ("clouds of steaming breath," "the white- / haired children") and sound ("Oil tins bang," "the voice of the snowman"). Clearly the children's hair, far from manifesting premature aging, is merely covered with snow. Is that snowman a surreal monster, or is his voice another name for the wind?

In 1947 John Haines went to Alaska as a homesteader and began to write poetry there. This is the title poem from his first collection, *Winter News* (Middletown, CT: Wesleyan UP, 1966).

Stevie Smith, NOT WAVING BUT DROWNING, page 757

Stevie Smith reportedly got the initial inspiration for this poem from a newspaper item that described a man who drowned in full view of his friends; they mistook his signals for help as playful waving. Smith pursued the fatal irony of this freak accident and found a chilling universal message in it. Students have no trouble understanding how a person's desperate signals for help can be misunderstood or ignored by others.

If you share the story of the poem's genesis with students, you might also point out how the poem's title reads like a tabloid headline.

It never hurts to belabor the obvious with students. You might suggest they read the short biographical note on Smith and discover that the poet is a woman. Any student particularly interested in Smith should be directed to the superb 1978 film *Stevie* starring Glenda Jackson, which contains an especially powerful rendition of this poem.

WRITERS ON WRITING

Ezra Pound, THE IMAGE, page 758

Pound's brief paragraphs on the image may be the most influential critical passage about modern poetry. This excerpt from his 1913 essay "A Few Don'ts by an Imagiste" (later retitled and incorporated into "A Retrospect") provided a list of issues and opinions that have helped shape the poetic practice of the last nine decades.

Pound's criticism itself unfolds most effectively in short imagistic bursts. Ask students to share the sentence or pair of sentences that most interest them. Are there any ideas with which they fervently agree or disagree?

One word in Pound's passage may need explanation: as its capitalization indicates, *Mosaic* refers to Moses (and his Ten Commandments).

18
Figures of Speech

WHY SPEAK FIGURATIVELY?

Alfred, Lord Tennyson, THE EAGLE, page 767

For a hostile criticism of this poem, see Robert Graves, "Technique in Poetry," *On Poetry: Collected Talks and Essays* (New York: Doubleday, 1969) 402–405. Graves finds Tennyson's fragment unable to meet the minimal requirement that a poem should make good prose sense. He complains that if the eagle stands on its hands then its wings must be feet, and he ends up by rewriting the poem the way he thinks it ought to be. Though his remarks are fascinating, Graves reads the poem too literally.

Another critic has suggested that this poem is a product of Tennyson's hopeless nearsightedness. Celebrating the eagle's 20–20 zoom-lens vision and ability to see a fish from high up, Tennyson yearns for a goal he could not attain: "optical inclusiveness." (See Gerhard Joseph, "Tennyson's Optics: The Eagle's Gaze," *PMLA* 92 [May 1977]: 420–27.)

 MyLiteratureLab Resources. Biography, photographs, critical overview, and bibliography for Tennyson.

William Shakespeare, SHALL I COMPARE THEE TO A SUMMER'S DAY?, page 767
Howard Moss, SHALL I COMPARE THEE TO A SUMMER'S DAY?, page 768

Shakespeare's original—rich in metaphor, personification, and hyperbole—means more, of course, than Moss's tongue-in-cheek desecration. The only figure of speech in Moss's rewrite is the simile in line 1, and even that is denigrated ("Who says?"). Moss manages to condense 115 great words to 78, a sonnet to a mere thirteen lines. It took a poet skilled in handling rimes to find such dull ones.

Shakespeare's nautical metaphor in line 8 may need explaining: a beautiful young person is a ship in full sail; accident or age can untrim the vessel. Compare this metaphor to "bare ruined choirs where late the sweet birds sang" ("That time of year").

 MyLiteratureLab Resources. Photographs, biographical information, and bibliography for Shakespeare. Audio clip, student essay, and critical essays on "Shall I compare thee to a summer's day?"

METAPHOR AND SIMILE

Emily Dickinson, MY LIFE HAD STOOD – A LOADED GUN, page 770

This astonishing metaphysical poem (another hymnlike work in common meter) can be an excellent provoker of class debate. Before trying to fathom it, students might well examine its diction. *Sovreign Woods* ("sovereign" would be the more usual spelling) suggests an estate owned by a king. How do the Mountains *reply?* By echoing the gun's report. Apparently the *smile* is the flash from the gun's muzzle; and the *Vesuvian face*, a glimpse of the flaming crater of the volcano. The Eider-Duck, a sea duck, has particularly soft and silky down which is used in pillows and quilts. The gun's *Yellow Eye* seems, again, its flash, and the emphatic *Thumb* is presumably the impact of the bullet that flattens its victim. (Some will say the thumb is a trigger finger, but you don't pull a trigger with your thumb.)

Argument over the meaning of the poem will probably divide the class into two camps. One will see the poem, like "Because I could not stop for Death," as an account of resurrection, with the Owner being God or Christ, who carries away the speaker, life and all, to the Happy Hunting Grounds of Paradise. We incline toward the other camp, the view that the Owner seems a mere mortal, perhaps a lover. The last stanza reveals that he can die. So taken, the last two lines make more sense. Not having the power to die, the speaker feels something lacking in herself. She doesn't wish to outlive her huntsman and be a lonely killer.

Philip Larkin admits the possibility of both views: "This is a romantic love in a nutshell, but who is its object? A religious poet—and Emily was this sometimes—might even have meant God" (*Required Writing* [New York: Farrar, 1984] 193).

A third camp has appeared, proclaiming a feminist interpretation. The poem, as summed up by Adalaide Morris, "tells about a life packed with a potential that the self was not empowered to activate," From this point of view, the poem is overtly political and exhilarating to teach because it recognizes long suppressed animosities ("Dick, Jane, and American Literature Fighting with Canons," *College English* 47 [1985]: 477).

But the poem remains tantalizingly ambiguous. You won't know until you go into class what a discussion may reveal.

 MyLiteratureLab Resources. Biography, critical overview, and bibliography for Dickinson.

Alfred, Lord Tennyson, FLOWER IN THE CRANNIED WALL, page 771

Why does Tennyson say "what God and man is" instead of "what God and man *are*"? Apparently, this isn't faulty grammar but higher pantheism. God and man are one.

 MyLiteratureLab Resources. Biography, critical overview, and bibliography for Tennyson.

William Blake, TO SEE A WORLD IN A GRAIN OF SAND, page 771

This famous short poem begins Blake's "Auguries of Innocence." Written around 1803 in a notebook and then carefully transcribed by Blake into another notebook made from discarded sheets from his engraving business, this poem was not published until 1863—35 years after the poet's death.

 MyLiteratureLab Resources. Photographs and biographical information for Blake.

Sylvia Plath, METAPHORS, page 771

Students usually are prompt to see that the central fact of the poem is the speaker's pregnancy. The speaker feels herself to be a walking riddle, posing a question that awaits solution: What person is she carrying? The "nine syllables" are like the nine months of gestation. All the metaphors refer to herself or to her pregnancy, except those in lines 4–5, which refer to the unborn baby: growing round and full like an apple or plum, seeming precious as ivory (and with ivory skin?), fine-timbered in sinew and bone like a well-built house.

The tone of the poem is clear, if complicated. Humor and self-mockery are evident in the images of elephant and strolling melon. In the last line, there is a note of wonder at the inexorability of gestation and birth: "The train there's no getting off."

A lively class might be asked to point out any possible connection between what the poem is saying about the arbitrary, fixed cycle of pregnancy and its own form—the nine nine-syllable lines.

As Plath records in her Boston journal for 20 March 1959, the pregnancy she had hoped for ended in a miscarriage. Grieving and depressed, she went ahead and finished this poem, then explicitly called "Metaphors for a Pregnant Woman" (*Journals*, New York: Ballantine, 1983) 298–99.

 MyLiteratureLab Resources. Interactive reading and critical essay on "Metaphors."

N. Scott Momaday, SIMILE, page 772

Momaday is best known as a novelist and prose writer; his *House Made of Dawn* won the 1969 Pulitzer Prize in fiction. But Momaday is also an accomplished poet whose work often combines a compressed formal style with the natural imagery of his native Southwest. The Oklahoma-born author of Kiowa ancestry also often incorporates tribal legends into his verse.

"Simile," true to its title, gives us a single, extended simile, but it withholds the emotional motivation for the choice of this particular image. The reader is forced to interpret the behavior of the metaphorical deer in order to answer the *what* of the opening line. Those familiar with T. S. Eliot's concept of "an objective correlative" ("a set of objects; a situation, a chain of events which shall be the formula" that unleashes a particular emotion in a reader) will recognize Momaday's "Simile" as a classic example of that technique. Momaday lets his image work on the reader's unconscious rather than specify its emotional meaning.

Emily Dickinson, IT DROPPED SO LOW – IN MY REGARD, page 772

The whole poem sets forth the metaphor that someone or something the speaker had valued too highly proved to be like a silver-plated item (a chafing dish? a cream pitcher?) that she had mistaken for solid silver. Its smash revealed that it was made of cheap stuff.

In another version, lines 5–6 read: "Yet blamed the Fate that fractured—*less* / Than I reviled myself." Students may be asked which version they prefer, and why they prefer it. (We much prefer *reviled* to *denounced* because of its resonance—the sound of the *i*—and its alliteration, the *l* in *reviled* and *self*. Besides, *fractured* seems a more valuable word than *flung*: it gets across the notion of something cracked or shattered, and its *r* sets up an alliterative echo with the words *entertaining, Wares,* and *Silver.)*

Craig Raine, A MARTIAN SENDS A POSTCARD HOME, page 773

When this poem won a 1978 magazine award in England, the judge James Fenton hailed the new "Martian School" of poetry. The name stuck because it referred to a tendency among several young British poets to use strange metaphors and outrageous similes to describe everyday objects.

In Raine's poem a Martian visitor tries to describe objects and activities on Earth. Seen from this alien perspective, everything appears quite strange. Half of what the Martian says is bizarrely wrong, but the other half is often weirdly insightful.

In a 1990 interview on BBC Radio, the poet Clive Wilmer elicited an interesting comment from Raine about the form of the poem:

> [T]he form of "A Martian Sends a Postcard Home" is the form of a postcard. We're all familiar with sonnets and couplets and odes and irregular odes, but it's possible to write a poem in a form that hasn't been used before, in this case the form of a postcard. Everybody writes a postcard saying: "Uncle Willy fell in the sea. Weather's been terrible for days. Lodgings not bad. See you next week. Wish you were here." In other words, it's an excuse for very, very heterogeneous subject-matter.

EXERCISE: *What Is Similar?,* page 774

We'd suggest that this exercise be run through rapidly. We wouldn't give students much time to ponder but would briskly call on people, and if anyone hesitated for long, we would skip to someone else. Give them time to cogitate about these items, and they are likely to dredge up all sorts of brilliant, reached-for similarities in each pair of things—possibly logical, but having nothing to do with the lines. Immediate flashes of understanding are the goal of this exercise, not ponderous explication. Do this one for fun, and so it might be; do it slowly and seriously, and it could be deadly.

OTHER FIGURES OF SPEECH

On the subject of puns, students familiar with *Hamlet* and other classics of the Bard may be asked to recall other puns of Shakespeare (besides the celebrated lines about golden lads and girls). If such a discussion prospers, Dr. Johnson's well-known observation in his preface to Shakespeare's works may provide an assertion to argue with:

> A quibble is to Shakespeare what luminous vapors are to the traveler: he follows it at all adventures; it is sure to lead him out of his way, and sure to engulf him in the mire. . . . A quibble is the golden apple for which he will always turn aside from his career or stoop from his elevation. A quibble, poor and barren as it is, gave him such delight that he was content to purchase it by the sacrifice of reason, propriety, and truth. A quibble was to him the fatal Cleopatra for which he lost the world, and was content to lose it.

James Stephens, THE WIND, page 775

As a birthday present to Stephens, James Joyce once translated this poem into five other languages (French, German, Italian, Latin, and Norwegian). These versions are reprinted in *Letters of James Joyce*, ed. Stuart Gilbert (New York: Viking, 1957) 318–19.

Margaret Atwood, YOU FIT INTO ME, page 778

The first two lines state a simile. In the second couplet, *hook* and *eye* turn out (to our surprise) to be puns.

MLL *MyLiteratureLab Resources.* Critical essay on "You fit into me."

John Ashbery, THE CATHEDRAL IS, page 778

Ashbery's unexpected pun on *slated* inspired student Steven B. Stanley of Metropolitan State University to coin "a more contemporary example of a pun" in a one-line poem of his own, "The Spelling Bee Champion":

> Studied a spell.

His instructor, Cathy Lewis, took a vote in class: Was Stanley better than Ashbery? Not surprisingly, Stanley triumphed. He adds: "I also came up with: 'The library is booked for demolition.' However, that sounded a little too like Ashbery." Perhaps your students might like to try writing one-liners in this vein, and so realize (as Ashbery does) that it is possible to have fun with poetry.

George Herbert, THE PULLEY, page 778

The title may need clarification. Man's need for rest is the pulley by which eventually he is drawn to rest everlasting. The pulley Herbert has in mind is probably not horizontal (like the one with a clothesline) but the vertical kind rigged to hoist a heavy weight. Despite the puns, the tone of the poem is of course devoutly serious, Herbert's concern in it being (in the view of Douglas Bush) "to subdue the wilful or kindle the apathetic self."

Lines 2–10, on the "glass of blessings" and its contents, set forth a different metaphor. As Herbert's editor, F. E. Hutchinson (*Works* [Oxford: Oxford UP, 1941]), and others have remarked, "The Pulley" seems a Christian version of the story of Pandora. At her creation Pandora received gifts from all the gods, mostly virtues and graces—though Hermes gave her perfidy. In some tellings of the myth, Pandora's gift (or vase) held not plagues but further blessings. When she became curious and opened it, they slipped away, all except the one that lay at the bottom—hope.

Herbert's poem, in its fondness for the extended metaphysical conceit, invites comparison with Donne's simile of the compasses in "A Valediction: Forbidding Mourning." If the instructor cares to discuss metaphysical poetry, "The Pulley" may be taken together with Herbert's "Love." ("Easter Wings" raises distracting contradictions and may be left for a discussion of concrete or graphic poetry.) Other poems of Donne and of Dickinson can also be mentioned.

Students might be encouraged to see that poets of the seventeenth century had certain habits of thought strikingly different from our own, but that some of these habits—like the fondness for startling comparisons of physical and spiritual things—haven't become extinct. Perhaps the closest modern equivalent to the conceits of Herbert and Donne may be found in fundamentalist hymns. Two earlier twentieth-century illustrations:

> If you want to watch old Satan run
> Just fire off that Gospel gun!

and

> My soul is like a rusty lock.
> Oh, oil it with thy grace!
> And rub it, rub it, rub it, Lord,
> Until I see thy face!

(The first example is attributed to a black Baptist hymn writer; the second, to the Salvation Army, according to Max Eastman in *Enjoyment of Laughter* [New York: Simon, 1936].) Another illustration, probably influenced by fundamentalist hymns, is a country and western song recorded in 1976 by Bobby Bare, "Dropkick Me, Jesus" ("through the goalposts of life").

Dana Gioia, MONEY, page 779

With a little effort, you should be able to find examples of the following figures of speech in this compendium of common references to our common currency: metaphor, epithet, personification, hyperbole, metonymy, synecdoche, and pun. *Note:* you will find no occurrences of simile or apostrophe.

 *MyLiteratureLab Resources.* Video clip of Dana Gioia reciting "Money."

Charles Simic, MY SHOES, page 779

While the descriptions in the poem seem fanciful or surrealistic throughout, many are expressed in straightforward language that does not employ figures of speech. Among those that do, we would cite metaphors in lines 1 and 2 (and by extension in line 10 and lines 15–16) and personification in line 14 and lines 17–19. In addition, the entire poem is an instance of apostrophe.

FOR REVIEW AND FURTHER STUDY

Robert Frost, THE SILKEN TENT, page 780

Although the word *as* in the opening line might lead us to expect a simile, "The Silken Tent" is clearly an immense metaphor, comparing woman and tent in a multitude of ways. What are the ropes or cords? Not merely commitments (or promises to keep) to friends and family, but generous sympathies, "ties of love and thought," on the part of a woman who cares about everything in the world.

While paying loving tribute to a remarkable woman, the poem is also a shameless bit of showing off by a poet cocksure of his technical mastery. Managing syntax with such grace that the poem hardly seems contrived, Frost has sustained a single sentence into an entire sonnet. "The whole poem is a performance," says Richard Poirier, "a display for the beloved while also being an exemplification of what it is like for a poem, as well as a tent or a person, to exist within the constrictions of space ('a field') and time ('at midday') wherein the greatest possible freedom is consistent with the intricacies of form and inseparable from them" (*Robert Frost: The Work of Knowing* [New York: Oxford UP, 1977] xiv–xv). Poirier points out, too, that the diction of the poem seems Biblical, perhaps echoing "The Song of Songs" (in which the bride is comely "as the tents of Kedar") and Psalm 92 (in which the godly "grow like a cedar in Lebanon"). Not only does the "central cedar pole" signify the woman's spiritual rectitude, it points toward heaven.

In teaching this poem, one can quote Frost's remark to Louis Untermeyer, "I prefer the synecdoche in poetry, that figure of speech in which we use a part for a whole." In 1931 Frost recalled that he had called himself a Synecdochist back when other poets were calling themselves Imagists: "Always, always a larger significance. A little thing touches a larger thing" (qtd. in Elizabeth Shepley Sergeant, *Robert Frost: The Trial by Existence* [New York: Holt, 1960] 325).

MLL *MyLiteratureLab Resources.* Biography, critical overview, critical articles, and bibliography for Frost.

April Lindner, LOW TIDE, page 781

There is personification in the opening sentence (lines 1–4), with its suggestion that as the tide goes out, the ocean performs a sort of mild striptease; the figure is extended with "What's left veiled" in line 11. The simile occurs in the explicit comparison in lines 6–7. The descriptions are never overtly sensual, but throughout the poem the surf is invested with a sensuousness that stimulates and finds its response in the poem's human characters: "Our hands itch / for all they might gather." The very end of the poem, with its reference to silk, likewise intertwines the sensuousness of the natural world with the human.

Jane Kenyon, THE SUITOR, page 781

This economical poem moves from simile to simile: (1) "like the chest of someone sleeping" (steadily rising and falling); (2) "like a school of fish" (flashing their pale bellies), and (3) "like a timid suitor" (hesitant, drawing back, reluctant to arrive).

Until her untimely death from leukemia in 1995, Kenyon lived in Danbury, New Hampshire, with her husband, the poet Donald Hall. *Otherwise: New and Selected Poems* (Graywolf Press) was published posthumously in 1996.

Robert Frost, THE SECRET SITS, page 782

Besides its personification of the sitting Secret, Frost's poem contains an implied metaphor. To dance round in a ring is to make futile efforts to penetrate a secret—merely going around in circles.

A. R. Ammons, COWARD, page 782

Ammons's figure of speech is, of course, a pun, but it is also a pun that underlines the original metaphor of *run* in the expression "runs in my family."

Kay Ryan, TURTLE, page 782

Kay Ryan is one of the most interesting poets of recent years. Born in California in 1945, she was raised in the San Joaquin Valley and the Mojave Desert, but those dry landscapes do not suggest the densely written and lushly detailed imaginative terrain of her poetry. Ryan has a particular gift for evocative compression. Her characteristic poem is short but not small—full of wry observation, weirdly original images, interwoven figures of speech, and magically unpredictable musicality. The first time one reads a Ryan poem is almost always a pleasure, and one soon discovers that her poems not only allow and reward rereading, they insist on it.

Ryan's "Turtle" is so densely packed with image and metaphor that each rereading uncovers interesting details and correspondences. And yet the tone of the poem is wonderfully matter-of-fact as the speaker produces one extravagant metaphor after another. This strange combination of tone and figurative language gives the poem an arresting quality rather reminiscent of certain poems by Marianne Moore or Elizabeth Bishop, though Ryan's style is distinctly her own. Notice how many rimes the poem contains. Few are end-rimes. Many are off-rimes. Most occur mid-line: *graceless/case/places; slope/hopes; skirts/convert; ditch/which;* and so forth. The effect of the intricate wordplay and hidden rimes is to slow readers down and invite them to savor every detail.

Ryan has published six volumes of poetry: *Dragon Acts to Dragon Friends* (Taylor Street Press, 1983), *Strangely Marked Metal* (Copper Beech, 1985), *Flamingo Watching* (Copper Beech, 1994), *Elephant Rocks* (Grove, 1996), *Say Uncle* (Grove, 2000), and *The Niagara River* (Grove, 2005).

Kay Ryan has provided these comments on "Turtle":

> "Turtle" came out of an extended time of the most terrible and absolute frustration. That's why it's so giddy. Everything in it is compressed, image and rhymes jammed too tight, threatening to explode. But it can't explode, because all the pieces are twisted together, and twisted again.

> "Turtle" was written in a single morning, as almost all of my poems are. I began with the first line, "Who would be a turtle who could help it?" It's mysterious how a poem develops out of its beginnings; right now I am thinking that it is like lighting a fuse that came into existence by its own burning, creating the dynamite that it explodes. But now I'm thinking, maybe the dynamite doesn't explode; maybe it just forever threatens. That's even better.

> Rhyme tells me where to go in a poem. It is a big bully, really, and hard to control. A sound listens for companions out in the distance beyond what has been said; it strains the poem forward, calling it into existence. Rhyme is an engine of yearning. It makes me write what I couldn't imagine.

> The internal rhymes in this poem have a range of ridiculousness that I love. I doubt I'll ever do better than rhyming "a four-ore" with "afford." Or on a grander scale, may I point out the achievement of "Her track is graceless . . . / a packing-case places"? I love these dismantled and remantled rhymes, but I also love every other sort of rhyme. I see rhyme as a binding energy in the finished poem, something that generates integrity, making the poem loyal to itself. I could compare rhyme to the glueyness that holds molecules together.

> It was the most exquisite pleasure to write this poem. And it did nothing whatsoever to dissipate my frustration. The truth of that strikes me as funny.

Heather McHugh, LANGUAGE LESSON, 1976, page 782

Throughout her poetic career, Heather McHugh has taken a particular delight in the vagaries and peculiarities of the English language (in which the word *cleave*, for instance, is its own antonym). This poem, set in Philadelphia on the two-hundredth anniversary of that city's becoming the "cradle of liberty," sets its keynote by showing how, in the "American" language, that revered term is also suggestive of presumption and transgression. The poet revels in the drollery of the twin games of tennis and language, "in which love can mean nothing" and in which the rich, who are accustomed to being waited on by others, "prepare to serve." The seventh couplet is particularly ingenious, with its visual and verbal parallelism reinforcing the emphasis on "doubletalk" and setting up the surprisingly affecting conclusion, in which what sounds like its opposite turns out to be a tender declaration of dependence.

Robinson Jeffers, HANDS, *page 783*

This poem can be profitably read with Jeffers's "To the Stone-Cutters." Both poems show his belief in humanity's tenuous position versus nature, and both reveal his interesting view of art—that it is impermanent compared to nature's eternity but that nonetheless it outlives its makers to provide comfort and wisdom to future generations. "Hands," however, is a gentler poem than "To the Stone-Cutters," and it shows Jeffers's deep, lifelong respect for the cultures of Native Americans, whom he admired for living more closely to nature than modern man.

Robert Burns, OH, MY LOVE IS LIKE A RED, RED ROSE, *page 784*

Figures of speech abound in this famous lyric, similes (lines 1–2, 3–4), a metaphor (*sands o' life*, 12), overstatement (8 and 9, 10), and possibly another overstatement in the last line.

See other professions of love couched in hyperbole, among them Marvell's "To His Coy Mistress" and Auden's "As I Walked Out One Evening." Are the speakers in these poems mere throwers of blarney, whom no woman ought to trust?

For a discussion of this poem that finds more in it than figures of speech, see Richard Wilbur, "Explaining the Obvious," in *Responses* (New York: Harcourt, 1976). Burns's poem, says Wilbur, "forsakes the lady to glory in Love itself, and does not really return. We are dealing, in other words, with romantic love, in which the beloved is a means to high emotion, and physical separation can serve as a stimulant to ideal passion." The emotion of the poem is "self-enchanted," the presence or absence of the lady isn't important, and the very idea of parting is mainly an opportunity for the poet to turn his feelings loose. Absurd as this posture may be, however, we ought to forgive a great songwriter almost anything.

WRITERS ON WRITING

Robert Frost, THE IMPORTANCE OF POETIC METAPHOR, *page 784*

Frost made so many insightful and memorable observations about poetry that it is difficult to select just one passage. Rather than reprint one of his more famous comments, we have selected this fascinating but little-known passage from an address he gave at Amherst College in 1930.

In this brief excerpt Frost speculates on the general value of a literary education. He observes how studying poetry trains us to understand metaphors and other figures of speech. Metaphors pervade all types of discourse, Frost says, and they are used in all walks of life. An education in poetry helps us judge metaphors critically—to see how far they apply to a situation truthfully and where they "break down."

 MyLiteratureLab Resources. Biography, critical overview, and bibliography for Frost.

19
Song

SINGING AND SAYING

"Song" is an unusual chapter. It approaches poetry in ways different from most other textbooks. We urge new instructors to try this chapter. Most students who write comments about this book say this chapter is the most appealing. "It shows that poetry isn't all found in books," is a typical comment; and many students are glad to see song lyrics they recognize. Most important, the chapter talks to them about poetry by using songs—a context they know a great deal about. It also encourages them to hear poems in a way that they might never have done before if their entire experience was seeing poems on the printed page.

Even if there is not time for a whole unit on song, the instructor who wishes to build upon this interest can use at least some of this chapter to introduce the more demanding matters of sound, rhythm, and form (treated in the chapters that follow). Some instructors take the tack that lyric poetry begins with song, and they begin their courses with this chapter, supplemented by folk ballads elsewhere in the text.

Besides Ben Jonson's classic nondrinking song, many other famous poems will go to melodies. The tradition of poems set to music by fine composers is old and honorable. For lists of such poems with musical settings (and recordings), see *College English* for February 1985 and December 1985.

Ben Jonson, TO CELIA, page 788

Students may not know that in line 2 *I will pledge* means "I will drink a toast." Also, *I would not change for thine* (line 8) in modern English becomes "I would not take it in exchange for yours."

To demonstrate that "To Celia" is a living song, why not ask the class to sing it? Unfortunately, you can no longer assume that the tune is one that everyone knows, so you may need to start them off.

Anonymous, THE CRUEL MOTHER, page 789

Some versions of this ballad start the narrative at an earlier point in time, with a woman discovering that she is pregnant by the wrong man when she is about to marry another. See Alan Lomax's Notes to *The Child Ballads*, vol. 1, Caedmon TC 1145, an old LP record, which contains an Irish version.

If the instructor cares to discuss the bottomless but student-spellbinding topic of archetypes, this ballad will serve to illustrate an archetype also visible in the stepmother figure of many fairy tales.

William Shakespeare, O MISTRESS MINE, *page 790*

Here Shakespeare wrote in the most popular song form of his era. How many popular song lyrics look this good after four hundred years? Shakespeare had the brevity of the madrigal form working to his advantage; singers busy with elaborate counterpoint didn't need the extended lyrics found in such simpler strophic forms as the ballad. Although this song was presumably sung by a single voice (the clown, Feste, in *Twelfth Night*), it employs the madrigal form usually associated with three or more voices. Madrigals could take flexible forms ranging from four to thirteen lines.

In "Music in Shakespeare," an essay in his collection *The Dyer's Hand*, W. H. Auden says of "O mistress mine": "Taken by themselves, the songs in this play are among the most beautiful Shakespeare wrote. . . . But in the contexts in which Shakespeare places them, they sound shocking. Taken playfully, such lines as [lines 9–12] are charming enough. . . . Taken seriously, these lines are the voice of elderly lust, afraid of its own death. Shakespeare forces this awareness on our consciousness by making the audience to the song a couple of seedy old drunks."

 MyLiteratureLab Resources. Photographs, biographical information, and bibliography for Shakespeare. Longman Lecture on "The Theme of Love in the Sonnets."

Edwin Arlington Robinson, RICHARD CORY, *page 792*
Paul Simon, RICHARD CORY, *page 792*

This pair sometimes provokes lively class discussion, especially if someone in the class maintains that Simon converts Robinson into fresh, modern terms. Further discussion may be necessary to show that Robinson's poem has a starkly different theme.

Robinson's truth, of course, is that we envy others their wealth and prestige and polished manners, but if we could see into their hearts we might not envy them at all. Simon's glib song does not begin to deal with this. The singer wishes that he too could have orgies on a yacht, but even after he learns that Cory died a suicide, his refrain goes right on, "I wish that I could be Richard Cory." (Live rich, die young, and make a handsome corpse!)

Some questions to prompt discussion might include:

1. In making his song, Simon admittedly took liberties with Robinson's poem. Which of these changes seem necessary to make the story singable? What suggestions in the original has Simon picked up and amplified?

2. How has Simon altered the character of Richard Cory? Is his Cory a "gentleman" in Robinson's sense of the word? What is the tone of Simon's line, "He had the common touch"? Compare this with Robinson: "he was always human when he talked." Does Robinson's Cory have anything more than "Power, grace and style"?

3. In the song, what further meaning does the refrain take on with its third hearing, in the end, after the news of Cory's suicide?

4. What truth about life does Robinson's poem help us see? Is it merely "Money can't make you happy" or "If you're poor you're really better off than rich people"? Does Simon's narrator affirm this truth, deny it, or ignore it?

Frank J. D'Angelo has noticed that the name Richard Cory is rich in connotations. It suggests Richard Coeur de Lion, and other words in Robinson's poem also point to royalty: *crown, imperially, arrayed, glittered, richer than a king.*

 MyLiteratureLab Resources. Longman Lecture and critical essay on "Richard Cory."

BALLADS

Anonymous, BONNY BARBARA ALLAN, page 793

Despite the numerous versions of this, the most widespread of all traditional ballads in English, most keep the main elements of the story with remarkable consistency. American versions tend to be longer, with much attention to the lovers' eventual side-by-side burial, and sometimes have Barbara's mother die of remorse, too! Commentators since the coming of Freud have sometimes seen Barbara as sexually frigid, and Robert Graves once suggested that Barbara, a witch, is killing Sir John by sorcery. An Irish version makes Barbara laugh hideously on beholding her lover's corpse.

To show how traditional ballads change and vary in being sung, a useful recording is *The Child Ballads*, vol. 1, Caedmon TC 1145, containing performances collected in the field by Alan Lomax and Peter Kennedy. Six nonprofessional singers are heard in sharply different versions of "Barbara Allan," in dialects of England, Scotland, Ireland, and Wales.

Dudley Randall, BALLAD OF BIRMINGHAM, page 796

Randall's poem is an authentic broadside ballad: it not only deals with a news event, it was once printed and distributed on a single page. "I had noticed how people would carry tattered clippings of their favorite poems in their billfolds," the poet has explained, "and I thought it would be a good idea to publish them in an attractive form as broadsides" (Interview in *Black World*, Dec. 1971). "Ballad of Birmingham" so became the first publication of Randall's Broadside Press, of Detroit, which later expanded to publish books and issue recordings by many leading black poets, including Gwendolyn Brooks, Don L. Lee, and Nikki Giovanni.

The poem seems remarkably fresh and moving, though it shows the traits of many English and Scottish popular ballads (such as the questions and answers, as in "Edward," and the conventional-sounding epithets in stanza 5). Randall presents without comment the horror of the bombing—in the mother's response and in the terrible evidence—but we are clearly left to draw the lesson that if the daughter had been allowed to join the open protest, she would have been spared.

Four black girls were killed in 1963 when a dynamite blast exploded in Birmingham's Sixteenth Street Baptist Church. In September 1977, a Birmingham grand jury finally indicted a former Ku Klux Klansman, aged 73, on four counts of first degree murder.

BLUES

Bessie Smith with Clarence Williams, JAILHOUSE BLUES, page 798

No one knows exactly who wrote this blues song. Authorship is assigned to Smith and Williams because they recorded it in 1923, but their version owes much to a traditional folk blues that survives in several versions. The concept of authorship in a conventional sense has little meaning in an oral tradition like early blues. Singers took songs they heard and transformed them into material for their own performance. One interesting feature of "Jailhouse Blues" is that the singer addresses the *blues* itself and converses with it.

W. H. Auden, FUNERAL BLUES, page 799

Auden's poem not only uses many blues elements (especially hyperbolic figures of speech to depict sadness); these lines were also originally written for music. The first two stanzas (followed by different third and fourth stanzas) appeared in *The Ascent of F6*, a play that Auden wrote with Christopher Isherwood in 1936. Set to music by the young Benjamin Britten, the words lamented the death of the play's visionary hero. A few years later Auden and Britten rewrote both the words and the music as a cabaret song. (The poem was later set to music again by the American composer Ned Rorem.)

In the process of revision, the song changed from a dirge for a lost political savior to a personal lament for a dead lover. A careful reader will note how the imagery becomes less public and civic in the final two stanzas.

Auden keeps the exaggerated imagery of traditional blues and the flamboyant emotionalism. He also rimes in couplets, as blues songs conventionally do, but he drops the standard repetition of the first line. "Funeral Blues" therefore employs the mood and style of traditional blues but varies the metrical form.

"Funeral Blues" has long been one of Auden's more popular "songs" (a category the author used in his *Collected Poems*), but thanks to its inclusion in the film *Four Weddings and a Funeral*, it has become one of the most widely known modern love poems.

RAP

Run D.M.C., from PETER PIPER, page 800

One reason we chose this excerpt from among many rap lyrics was its density of allusion. "Peter Piper" contains as many literary references as Milton's "Lycidas," but most students don't find them intimidating because they come from popular culture and children's literature. It might be helpful to work through the allusions and discuss how they shape the lyrics' effect on the listener; then use this as a model of how allusions to myth and literature work in traditional poetry. (It's nice to see King Midas in a Run D.M.C. lyric.) Rap is a form of oral poetry, and it's interesting to note how these lyrics incorporate many pieces of the central English-language classic of oral poetry—*Mother Goose*.

A metrical note: notice how once the rap settles into its regular rhythm (line 12) it bounces along in a four-stress line, the standard measure of English-language oral poetry from the Anglo-Saxons till today.

FOR REVIEW AND FURTHER STUDY

John Lennon and Paul McCartney, ELEANOR RIGBY, page 801

"Eleanor Rigby," we think, is a poem. Although swayed by the superstition that priests are necessarily lonely because celibate, McCartney's portraits of Father McKenzie and of Eleanor have details that reflect life. Both music and words contain an obvious beat, and if students pick out those syllables in long lines 4 and 7, 14 and 17, and 24 and 27, they will be getting into the subject of meter. (Each of the lines contains a stressed syllable followed by four anapests.)

Bob Dylan, THE TIMES THEY ARE A-CHANGIN', page 802

Bob Dylan's folk song became one of the definitive political anthems of the 1960s, and decades later it holds up extraordinarily well, even on the page. Seen from such a distance, "The Times They Are a-Changin'" is remarkable for its lack of specific topical issues. None of the key political issues of the era is mentioned by name—not even Civil Rights or pacifism. There are a few topical allusions embedded in the text. The lines "Don't stand in the doorway / Don't block up that hall," for example, refer to Governor George Wallace's defiant action to stop school integration in Alabama. But no listener needs to catch that now oblique allusion to get the broader sense of the lines because Dylan has so thoroughly universalized his images. In fact, except for the first line of stanza three with its references to senators and congressmen, there are no specifically American references in the song, which otherwise could apply equally to England, Italy, India, or China.

The song's imagery seems more informed by the Bible than the newspaper. The rising waters, the raging battle, the falling old order have an openly prophetic ring to them. (The lines "And the first one now / will later be last" directly allude to the Gospels—Matthew 19:30, Mark 10:31, Luke 13:30.) The poet/songwriter announces himself as the prophet of a new generation that intends to refashion society in direct confrontation with its elders, but no program of reform is offered by the speaker. The nature of this new order is left almost entirely up to our imagination. Perhaps one reason this song proved so powerful and popular was that each listener could project whatever vision of a new society he or she preferred.

Aimee Mann, DEATHLY, page 804

In the film *Magnolia*, the song "Deathly" is related to Claudia, the adult, drug-addicted daughter of a television quiz-show host, who maintains that she was sexually abused by her father. The song's lyrics describe her reaction—an instinctive defensiveness and unwillingness to be drawn out emotionally—to meeting a lonely, kindhearted police officer who is immediately and protectively attracted to her. The text works fairly successfully on the page (although when separated from its musical setting and forced to stand alone, it is metrically a bit wobbly in places), and lines 30–33 are particularly striking; but the loveliness of the melody—enhanced by the purity of Mann's voice—mitigates the harshness of the statement and adds dimensions of complexity and ambiguity that not only enrich the experience of "Deathly" but are quite appropriate to the character of Claudia and to the film's larger themes.

WRITERS ON WRITING

Paul McCartney, CREATING "ELEANOR RIGBY," page 805

McCartney's comments to the interviewer reveal a great deal about the creative process—how one idea grows unexpectedly out of another. It is interesting to imagine that this song was nearly titled "Daisy Hawkins."

20
Sound

SOUND AS MEANING

Alexander Pope, TRUE EASE IN WRITING COMES FROM ART, NOT CHANCE, page 809

Nowadays, looking at the pages of an eighteenth-century book of poetry, we might think the liberal capitalization and use of italics merely decorative. But perhaps Pope wished to leave his readers little choice in how to sound his lines. Most of his typographical indications seem to us to make sense—like a modern stage or television script with elements underlined or capitalized, lest the actors ignore a nuance.

Line 12 is deliberately long: an alexandrine, or twelve-syllable line, that must be spoken quickly in order to get it said within the time interval established by the other shorter, pentameter lines.

William Butler Yeats, WHO GOES WITH FERGUS?, page 811

Originally a song in Yeats's play *The Countess Cathleen*, this famous lyric overflows with euphony. Take just the opening question (lines 1–3): the assonance of the various o-sounds; the initial alliteration of *w*, *d*, and *sh*; the internal alliteration of the *r* in *Fergus*, *pierce*, and *shore*—musical devices that seem especially meaningful for an invitation to a dance. The harsh phrase *brazen cars* seems introduced to jar the brooding lovers out of their reveries. Unless you come right out and ask what brazen cars are, not all students will realize that they are brass chariots. In ancient Ulster, such chariots were sometimes used for hunting deer—though how you would drive one of them through the deep woods beats us.

If you discuss meter, what better illustration of the power of spondees than "And the WHITE BREAST of the DIM SEA?"

The last line of the poem, while pleasingly mysterious, is also exact. The personification "dishevelled wandering stars" makes us think of beautiful, insane, or distracted women with their hair down: Ophelia in Olivier's film *Hamlet*. That they are wandering recalls the derivation of the word *planet*: Greek for "wanderer." In what literal sense might stars look disheveled? Perhaps in that their light, coming through the atmosphere (and being seen through ocean spray) appears to spread out like wild long hair. For comparable figures of speech, see Blake's "Tyger," in which the personified stars weep and throw spears.

> **MLL** *MyLiteratureLab Resources*. Biography, critical overview, and bibliography for Yeats. Interactive reading of "Who Goes with Fergus?"

EXERCISE: *Listening to Meaning,* page 811
John Updike, RECITAL, page 811
William Wordsworth, A SLUMBER DID MY SPIRIT SEAL, page 812
Emanuel di Pasquale, RAIN, page 812
Aphra Behn, WHEN MAIDENS ARE YOUNG, page 812

"Recital" shows off Updike as one of America's virtuosos of light verse. The whole poem seems written in imitation of the trochaic "oom-pah" of a tuba, and every line ends in a thumping celebration of the near rime between Mr. Bobo's surname and his chosen instrument. Onomatopoeia is heard even more obviously in Behn's *hum-drum.* In di Pasquale's lines, the *s*-sounds fit well with our conception of rain, and *hushes* is an especially beautiful bit of onomatopoeia. By the way, di Pasquale's poem is particularly remarkable in view of the fact that the poet, born in Sicily, did not learn English until he was sixteen. Di Pasquale is now a professor of English at Middlesex Community College in New Jersey; his first collection of poems, *Genesis,* was published in 1989, and he has since published a sequence of love poems, *Escapes the Night* (2001).

In Wordsworth's Lucy poem, sound effects are particularly noticeable in the first line (the soporific *s*'s) and in the last two lines (the droning *r*'s and *n*'s). If students go beyond the sound effects and read the poem more closely, they might find problems in the first stanza. Is the poet's slumber a literal sleep or a figurative one? That is, is Wordsworth recalling some pleasant dream of Lucy (whether the living Lucy he used to know, or the dead Lucy in Eternity), or is he saying that when she was alive he was like a dreamer in his view of her? If so, he was deluded in thinking that she would always remain a child; he had none of the usual human fears of death or of growing old. However we read the poem, there is evidently an ironic contrast between the poet's seeing Lucy (in stanza 1) as invulnerable to earthly years and his later view that she is affected, being helplessly rolled around the sun once a year with the other inanimate objects. And simple though it looks, the poem contains a paradox. The speaker's earlier dream or vision of Lucy has proved to be no illusion but an accurate foreshadowing. Now she is a "thing," like rocks and stones and trees, and she cannot feel and cannot suffer any more from time's ravages.

Aphra Behn was the first English woman to earn a living by her pen. *Oroonoko* (1688), a tale of slavery in Surinam, is sometimes called the first true English novel. Her colorful life, mostly spent in London's literary bohemia, included a hitch in Holland as a spy for the Crown. In her destitute late years she was pilloried in lampoons ("a lewd harlot"), perhaps because she remained faithful to the Stuarts. She was buried in Westminster Abbey under her poetic pen name, Astrea Behn. Nowadays she seems to be enjoying a respectful dusting-off. See the extensive treatment given her in *Kissing the Rod: An Anthology of 17th Century Women's Verse,* ed. Germaine Greer and others (London: Virago, 1988) 240–60.

 MyLiteratureLab Resources. Student paper for "Recital." Biography, critical overview, and bibliography for Wordsworth. Critical essay on "A Slumber Did My Spirit Seal."

ALLITERATION AND ASSONANCE

A. E. Housman, EIGHT O'CLOCK, page 814

The final *struck* is a serious pun, to which patterns of alliteration, begun in the opening line *(st . . . st, r)* and continued through the poem, have led up. The ticking effect of the clock is, of course, most evident in *the clock collected.*

Compare Housman's strapped and noosed lad with the one in Hugh Kingsmill's parody of Housman, "What, still alive at twenty-two?"

 MyLiteratureLab Resources. Biography, critical overview, and bibliography for Housman.

James Joyce, ALL DAY I HEAR, page 814

This poem is the first of two "tailpieces" added to the sequence of love lyrics called *Chamber Music,* Joyce's first book publication. In these early, admittedly minor (but still highly accomplished) verses, Joyce already shows the excellent ear that would produce such stunning aural effects in *Ulysses* and *Finnegans Wake.* The alliterations in the second, third, and fifth lines are all on relatively soft consonants, in keeping with the melancholy and generally muted tone of the poem. All nine of the poem's rime words (at the ends of lines 2, 4, and 6; 3, 7, and 11; and 8, 10, and 12), along with *cold* (line 7), stress the long o sound, knitting the entire text together into an echo of the moan of the waters and the mood they evoke in the speaker.

MyLiteratureLab Resources. Biography, critical overview, and bibliography for Joyce.

Alfred, Lord Tennyson, THE SPLENDOR FALLS ON CASTLE WALLS, page 815

If read aloud rapidly, this famous lyric from Tennyson's *The Princess* will become gibberish; and the phrase *Blow, bugle, blow,* a tongue twister. But if it is read with any attention to its meaning, its long vowels and frequent pauses will compel the reader to slow down. Students may want to regard the poem as mellifluous non-sense, but they may be assured that the poem means something, that it is based on a personal experience of the poet's. Visiting the lakes of Killarney in 1848, Tennyson heard the bugle of a boatman sound across the still water, and he counted eight distinct echoes. "The splendor falls" is the poet's attempt to convey his experience in accurate words.

MyLiteratureLab Resources. Photographs, biography, critical overview, and bibliography for Tennyson. Audio clip for "The splendor falls on castle walls."

RIME

William Cole, ON MY BOAT ON LAKE CAYUGA, page 816

This is one of a series of comic quatrains, "River Rhymes," first printed in *Light Year '85* (Case Western Reserve U: Bits Press, 1984).

James Reeves, ROUGH WEATHER, page 818

This wise and lovely sonnet by the late British poet James Reeves deserves to be better known. (Perhaps it has been anthologized in the UK, but we have not seen it in an American collection.) The poem is technically notable for at least two reasons. First, the entire sonnet consists of a single sentence carefully developed to advance a complex and moving argument about how two lovers survive a difficult separation. Second, "Rough Weather" begins and ends with striking feminine rimes, but it modulates in the middle into masculine rimes.

The theme of the poem is how strongly the speaker's love persists—and indeed thrives—despite the absence of his beloved. The exact circumstance of their separation is never stated. The phrase "this rough, divisive weather" hints perhaps at some problem, and the speaker's later admission "And tell myself I want you to be free" suggests that the lover's absence may be voluntary—perhaps even a desertion. But the speaker stands steadfast in his affection and marvels at how strong memory proves in fostering love. Intelligence, as well as the physical senses, can nourish and sustain genuine love.

Hilaire Belloc, THE HIPPOPOTAMUS, page 819

This amusing short poem requires no commentary. Instructors and students alike might enjoy exploring more of Belloc's light verse, to be found in anthologies such as Kingsley Amis's *The New Oxford Book of English Light Verse* (New York: Oxford UP, 1978).

Ogden Nash, THE PANTHER, page 819

Extremely popular in his day, Nash may now be somewhat of an acquired taste. The first couplet of "The Panther" is clever, but not in a unique way; the second is likely to make the reader say Ouch; but the third exemplifies the kind of linguistic lunacy—exquisite or excruciating, depending on one's point of view—that produced the following complete poems, among many others: "The Bronx? / No, thonx!" and (referring to a risqué revue of the 1920s) "In the Vanities / No one wears panities."

William Butler Yeats, LEDA AND THE SWAN, page 820

The deliberately awful off-rime *up* / *drop* ends the sonnet with an appropriately jarring plop as the God-swan discards the used Leda and sinks into his post-ejaculatory stupor.

Other questions that can be raised:

1. What *knowledge* and *power* does Yeats refer to in line 14?

2. Do the words *staggering* (line 2) and *loosening* (line 6) keep to the basic meter of the poem or depart from it? How does rhythm express meaning in these lines? (It staggers on *staggering* and loosens on *loosening*.)

3. Compare this poem to Donne's sonnet "Batter my heart." Is the tone of Yeats's sonnet—the poet's attitude toward this ravishing—similar or dissimilar?

For an early draft of the poem, see Yeats's *Memoirs*, ed. Denis Donoghue (New York: Macmillan, 1973) 272–74.

MLL　*MyLiteratureLab Resources.* Biography, critical overview, and bibliography for Yeats. Critical essay on "Leda and the Swan."

Gerard Manley Hopkins, GOD'S GRANDEUR, page 820

Students who think Hopkins goes too far in his insistence on rimes and other similar sounds will have good company, including Robert Bridges, William Butler Yeats, and Yvor Winters. Still, it is hard not to admire the euphony of the famous closing lines—that ingenious alternation of *br* and *w*, with a pause for breath at that magical *ah!*—and the cacophony of lines 6–8, with their jangling internal rimes and the alliteration that adds more weight to *smeared*, *smudge*, and *smell*. For Hopkins, of course, sound is one with meaning, and the cacophonous lines just mentioned are also, as John Pick has pointed out, "a summary of the particular sins of the nineteenth century." For a brilliant demonstration that sound effects in Hopkins's poetry have theological meaning, see J. Hillis Miller, *The Disappearance of God* (Cambridge: Harvard UP, 1963) 276–317. Miller finds the poet's theory revealed in his sermons and journals: "Any two things however unlike are in something like"; therefore, "all beauty may by a metaphor be called rhyme."

In the text, it seemed best not to bury the poem under glosses but to let the instructor decide how thoroughly to explicate it. Here are a few more glosses in case they seem necessary:

Line 7, *man's smudge:* the blight of smoke and ugliness cast over the countryside by factories and mines. As a student for the priesthood in North Wales and as a parish priest in London and Liverpool, Hopkins had known the blight intimately. Another suggestion in the phrase: nature is fallen and needs to be redeemed, like man, who wears the smudge of original sin. Line 12, *morning . . . springs:* The risen Christ is like the sun at dawn. Eastward is the direction of Jerusalem, also of Rome. (Hopkins cherished the hope that the Church of England and the Pope would one day be reconciled.) Lines 13–14, *bent* / *World:* Perhaps because of its curvature the earth looks bent at the horizon; or perhaps the phrase is a transferred epithet, attributing to the earth the dove's bent-over solicitude. (And as the world seems to break off at the horizon, line 13 breaks at the word *bent*.) Line 14, *broods:* like a dove, traditional representation of the Holy Ghost.

For still more suggestions, see Pick, *Gerard Manley Hopkins, Priest and Poet*, 2nd ed. (Oxford: Oxford UP, 1966) 62–64; Paul L. Mariani, *Commentary on the Complete Poems of Gerard Manley Hopkins* (Ithaca: Cornell UP, 1970); and (not least) the poet's "Pied Beauty."

A sonnet by Wordsworth also begins "The world is," and Hopkins no doubt knew of it. In their parallel (though different) complaints against trade and commerce, the two deserve to be compared. Both poets find humanity artificially removed from nature: this seems the point of Hopkins's observation in lines 7–8 that once soil was covered (with grass and trees) and feet were bare, and now soil is bare and feet are covered. Clearly we have lost the barefoot bliss of Eden, but in answer to Wordsworth, one almost expects Hopkins to cry, "Great God! I'd rather be a Christian." (Wordsworth by *world* means "worldliness.")

 MyLiteratureLab Resources. Photographs and biographical information for Hopkins.

Fred Chappell, NARCISSUS AND ECHO, page 821

Fred Chappell is best known as a novelist and short story writer, yet his poetry is exceptionally fine. He has often experimented with old verse forms (like Anglo-Saxon stress meter). In "Narcissus and Echo," he revived a virtually defunct form called "Echo Verse," which had not received much attention since the Renaissance. (Note that "Echo Verse" is described in the footnote to the poem.) To complete his *tour de force*, he uses the form to dramatize the plight of the nymph Echo.

Chappell takes the Echo Verse form one difficult step further than most earlier poets and makes his echoes form a vertical poem down the right-hand side of the page. (Students will usually miss that aspect of the poem unless you point it out to them.) Likewise, Narcissus's speech can be read in isolation, so there are essentially three different poems in this text: Narcissus's self-absorbed solo, Echo's plaintive response, and the pair's lopsided dialogue.

Robert Frost, DESERT PLACES, page 822

Possible answers to the questions following the poem:

1. *What are these desert places that the speaker finds in himself? (More than one theory is possible. What is yours?)* Terrible pockets of loneliness.

2. *Notice how many times, within the short space of lines 8–10, Frost says* lonely *(or* loneliness*). What other words in the poem contain similar sounds that reinforce these words?* The word *snow*, occurring three times. Other *o*-sounds occur in *oh, going, showing, no, so,* and *home.* The *l* of *lonely* is echoed by alliteration in *looked, last,* and *lairs*.

3. *In the closing stanza, the feminine rimes* spaces, race is, *and* places *might well occur in light or comic verse. Does "Desert Places" leave you laughing? If not, what does it make you feel?* It makes us feel a psychic chill! Yet the feminine rime lightens the grim effect of what is said and gives it a kind of ironic smirk.

For an intriguing if far-out appreciation of this poem that makes much of the sibilant *s*-sounds, see Marie Boroff, "Sound Symbolism as Drama in the Poetry of Robert Frost," *PMLA* 107 (1992): 131–144.

MLL *MyLiteratureLab Resources.* Biography, critical overview, critical articles, and bibliography for Frost.

READING AND HEARING POEMS ALOUD

Many poets spend their energies in writing poems and are not effective public speakers. Here is a comment by William Stafford on why certain poets read their poems with apparent carelessness. Unlike the Russian poet Andrei Voznesensky, a great performer, Stafford says,

> Most of the poets I know would feel a little guilty about doing an effective job of reading their poems. They throw them away. And I speak as one who does that. It feels fakey enough to be up there reading something as though you were reading it for the first time. And to say it well is just too fakey. So you throw it away. (Interview in *The Literary Monitor* 3.3–4 [1980])

This comment raises provocative questions for discussion. What is the nature of a poetry reading? Should it be regarded as a performance or as a friendly get-together?

For a symposium on poetry readings, with comments by Allen Ginsberg, James Dickey, Denise Levertov, and twenty-nine other poets, see *Poets on Stage* (New York: Some/Release, 1978).

A catalogue of over 800 radio broadcasts on cassette and CD, including a rich variety of programs featuring contemporary poets such as John Ashbery, Gwendolyn Brooks, John Ciardi, Rita Dove, Allen Ginsberg, Anthony Hecht, Colette Inez, Philip Levine, and many others reading and talking about their work, is available from New Letters on the Air, University of Missouri-Kansas City, 5100 Rockhill Road, Kansas City, MO 64110, phone (816) 235–1159. Or, go to <www.newletters.org>.

EXERCISE: *Reading for Sound and Meaning*, page 824
Michael Stillman, IN MEMORIAM JOHN COLTRANE, page 824
William Shakespeare, FULL FATHOM FIVE THY FATHER LIES, page 825
Chryss Yost, LAI WITH SOUNDS OF SKIN, page 825
T. S. Eliot, VIRGINIA, page 825

In Michael Stillman's tribute to the great jazz saxophonist, *coal train* is not only a rich pun on Coltrane's name, it also becomes the poem's central image. The poet has supplied this comment:

One thing about that poem which has always pleased me beyond its elegiac strain—is the way the technique of the lines and phrases corresponds to a musical effect in Coltrane's playing. He was known for his ability to begin with a certain configuration of notes, then play pattern after pattern of variations. The repetition of "Listen to the coal . . . listen to the . . . listen to . . . listen" was one way to capture a feature of his playing. The image of the coal train disappearing into the night comes, particularly, from a place on the James River, west of Richmond, where I happened to be when I heard of Coltrane's death. Like all jazz musicians, I felt the loss very deeply.

Shakespeare's song contains an obvious illustration of onomatopoeia (the bell's sound), obvious alliteration in the *f*-full first line, and (less obviously) internal alliteration (note the *r* and *n* sounds) and assonance galore. Like a drowned man's bones, ordinary language becomes something "rich and strange" in this song.

The central metaphor of Chryss Yost's poem is weaving, and the author has woven an extraordinarily beguiling fabric of sound. Although the poem is only sixteen short lines long, students will be hard-pressed to find devices of sound Yost does not use. Rime, assonance, alliteration, enjambment, stress pattern, syllable count, and repetition are all present. Although the metrical scheme is syllabic, Yost also repeats patterns of stressed and unstressed syllables. Note, for example, how the stress pattern of the first line echoes in the opening line of the second stanza.

The *lai* (or more precisely, *lai nouveau*) is a French form of sixteen lines divided into two eight-line stanzas. Each line has a set syllable count of either two or five syllables. Students can discover the pattern by analyzing Yost's poem. The form is rarely used in English—probably because of the difficulty of rhyming sixteen lines with only three sounds. (The *a* rhyme must be used twelve times!) Amazingly, Yost not only handles the form in the most natural way but creates a gentle yet deeply expressive lyric poem in which the language of weaving becomes a metaphor for the motions of making love.

Chryss Yost has provided the following commentary on her poem:

The lai, while short, is a deceptively difficult beast to master for at least three reasons. First, unlike most metrical forms in English which count the stressed syllables, the lai measures the syllables in each line. Second, the syllable count is extremely short, just five or two syllables per line. Finally, each stanza uses just two rhymes (*aabaabaa*). In combination with the short lines, this means that the poem must depend on relatively few sounds. A poem with short words and lots of repetition risks falling into obvious, overused rhyme (like *love* and *dove*). I wanted the poem to celebrate the interlocking, tightly-woven form, and I couldn't resist the pun on lai. I went hunting for beautiful and unusual words and discovered *weft*—the threads woven to make fabric. *Weft* has a soft, lingering sound and the meaning seemed to fit the form. *Weft* led to *heft*, *warp*, and *skein*. The technical language of weaving gave me the tools I needed to create an untraditionally sensual poem from a rather restrictive traditional form.

Eliot's "Virginia" is an experiment in quantitative verse, according to George Williamson (*A Reader's Guide to T. S. Eliot* [New York: Noonday, 1957]). You might read aloud "Virginia" and Campion's quantitative "Rose-cheeked

Laura" and ask the class to detect any similarity. Ted Hughes has written of "Virginia" with admiration. How is it, he wonders, that Eliot can create so vivid a landscape without specific images? "What the poem does describe is a feeling of slowness, with a prevailing stillness, of suspended time, of heat and dryness, and fatigue, with an undertone of oppressive danger, like a hot afternoon that will turn to thunder and lightning" (*Poetry Is* [New York: Doubleday, 1967]).

 MyLiteratureLab Resources. Photographs, biographical information, and bibliography for Shakespeare. Biography, critical overview, and bibliography for Eliot.

WRITERS ON WRITING

T. S. Eliot, THE MUSIC OF POETRY, page 826

Eliot's remarks on poetic music are full of significant distinctions—most notably his observation that poetic music does not exist apart from poetic meaning. He also bases poetry firmly in speech ("one person talking to another") and assumes that all poetic music will emerge in some way from the sound and rhythms of conversation.

21
Rhythm

STRESSES AND PAUSES

In the first section of this chapter, rhythm is discussed with as few technicalities as possible. For the instructor wishing to go on to the technicalities, the second part of the chapter, "Meter," gives the principles of scansion and the names of the metrical feet.

Except for one teacher at the University of Michigan, James Downer, who would illustrate the rhythms of Old English poetry by banging on his desk for a drum, we have never known anyone able to spend entire classes on meter without etherizing patients. Meter, it would seem, is best dealt with in discussing particular poems.

EXERCISE: *Get with the Beat,* page 831

Browning's four-beat anapestic lines vigorously capture the speed of the scene they describe.

Keeler's loose ballad meter seems suitably rollicking for his down-home subject and tone.

Finch's rhythm is itself an homage to her subject. She has borrowed the hymn stanza that Dickinson used so frequently. Likewise, Finch has deliberately imitated the clear syntax and sonorous cadences of the church hymns to present her images. Although Finch arranges her poem in couplets, the rime scheme and syntax fall into Dickinsonian quatrains.

Eisler's lines describing a newspaper photo of Marilyn Monroe have three strong stresses per line, but Eisler creates a different rhythm in each line by varying the number of unstressed syllables. The effect is a jazz-like syncopation. (The first line also has strong secondary stresses on the compound words *newsprint* and *moonprint* that make this especially evocative line read slowly.)

Shakespeare's songs were sung in the theater. Among other things, they provided a break from the iambic pentameter of most characters' speech. This song from *The Tempest* has a loosely iambic rhythm, but the line lengths differ. They follow a lost melody rather than a strict metrical scheme. The rollicking, unpredictable rhythm seems very appropriate to the mood and setting of the song.

Gwendolyn Brooks, WE REAL COOL, page 833

The poet might have ended every line with a rime, as poets who rime usually do:

We real cool.
We left school.

The effect, then, would have been like a series of hammer blows because there are so many short end-stopped lines and so many rimes in quick succession. But evidently Brooks is after a different rhythm. What is it? How to read the poem aloud? Let members of the class take turns trying, and compare their various oral interpretations. If you stress each final *We*, then every syllable in the poem takes a stress; and if, besides, you make even a split-second pause at every line break, then you give those final *We*'s still more emphasis. What if you don't stress the *We*'s but read them lightly? Then the result is a skipping rhythm, rather like that of some cool cat slapping his thighs.

After the class has mulled this problem, read them Brooks's own note on the poem (from her autobiography, *Report from Part One* [Detroit: Broadside, 1972] 185), which is reprinted in the "Writers on Writing" section at the end of this chapter.

As a student remarked about the tone and theme of this poem, "She doesn't think they're real cool, she thinks they're real fool—to die so young like that."

Brooks recorded her own reading of the poem for *The Spoken Arts Treasury of 100 Modern American Poets*, vol. 13, SA 1052.

MLL *MyLiteratureLab Resources*. Biography, critical overview, and bibliography for Brooks. Interactive reading, student paper, and critical essay on "We Real Cool."

Alfred, Lord Tennyson, BREAK, BREAK, BREAK, page 834

Tennyson's plangent poem displays an interesting rhythmic design. It is written in accentual meter in which the author counts the number of strong stresses per line (rather than in the more conventional accentual-syllabic measure in which one counts both syllables and stresses). The normative line of Tennyson's poem has three strong stresses (though later in the poem, it occasionally broadens to four stresses). By varying the syllable count, Tennyson is able to create all sorts of interesting effects. (It may be worth pointing out to students that Tennyson employs exactly the same technique as Rap in this regard.)

The opening stanza should be scanned as follows:

            /   /   /
    Break, break, break,

        U U   /   U   /   U /
        On thy cold gray stones, O Sea!

        U U /   U U   /   U   /   U
        And I would that my tongue could utter

            U   /   U U / U /
            The thoughts that arise in me.

Note how Tennyson's accentual meter can stretch the line from 3 to 9 syllables.

MyLiteratureLab Resources. Biography, critical overview, and bibliography for Tennyson.

Ben Jonson, SLOW, SLOW, FRESH FOUNT, KEEP TIME WITH MY SALT TEARS, page 834

O sounds slow the opening line, whose every word is a monosyllable. Further slowing the line, eight of the ten monosyllables take heavy beats. "Drop, drop, drop, drop" obviously racks up still more stresses, as do the spondees that begin lines 4, 5, and 6. The entire effect is that we are practically obliged to read or sing the poem slowly and deliberately—as befits a lamentation.

EXERCISE: *Two Kinds of Rhythm,* page 835
Sir Thomas Wyatt, WITH SERVING STILL, page 835
Dorothy Parker, RÉSUMÉ, page 836

These two poems differ in their rhythm: Wyatt compels a heavy pause only at the end of every quatrain, while Parker end-stops every line. Students may be shown that pauses and meanings go together. Both poems are cast in two sentences, but Wyatt develops one uninterrupted statement throughout the entire poem (in sonnet fashion: first the summary of the speaker's problem in the opening three stanzas, then the conclusion beginning with "Wherefore all ye"). "Résumé," as its punctuation indicates, makes a new self-contained statement in every line.

A question on meaning: Must light verse necessarily be trivial in its theme? State Parker's theme in "Résumé." Surely it isn't trivial. At least in theme, the poem seems comparable to Hamlet's soliloquy "To be or not to be . . . ."

After *Not So Deep as a Well,* her collected poems of 1936, Parker brought out no more poetry collections. "My verses," she insisted to an interviewer. "I cannot say poems. Like everybody was then, I was following in the exquisite footsteps of Miss Millay, unhappily in my own horrible sneakers" (*Writers at Work: The Paris Review Interviews,* 1st ser. [New York: Viking, 1959]). Parker's wit, acerbic and sometimes macabre, is as clear from "Résumé" as it is from her celebrated remark on being informed that Calvin Coolidge had just died: "How could they tell?"

 MyLiteratureLab Resources. Photographs and biographical information for Parker. Video clip for "Résumé."

METER

XJK used to think of meter as a platonic ideal norm from which actual lines diverge, but J. V. Cunningham's essay "How Shall the Poem Be Written?"

changed his mind. Metrical patterns (in the abstract) do not exist; there are only lines that poets have written, in which meters may be recognized. "Meter," declares Cunningham, "is perceived in the actual stress-contour, or the line is perceived as unmetrical, or the perceiver doesn't perceive meter at all" (*The Collected Essays of J. V. Cunningham* [Chicago: Swallow, 1976] 262).

Max Beerbohm, ON THE IMPRINT OF THE FIRST ENGLISH EDITION OF *THE WORKS OF MAX BEERBOHM*, page 836

John Updike has paid tribute to this brilliant bit of fluff:

> The effortless a-b-a-b rhyming, the balance of "plain" and "nicely," the need for nicely in pronouncing "Iambically" to scan—this is quintessential light verse, a twitting of the starkest prose into perfect form, a marriage of earth with light, and quite magical. Indeed, were I a high priest of literature, I would have this quatrain made into an amulet and wear it about my neck, for luck. ("Rhyming Max," a review of Beerbohm's collected verse, reprinted in *Assorted Prose* [New York: Knopf, 1965])

Thomas Campion, ROSE-CHEEKED LAURA, COME, page 842

Campion included this famous lyric in his polemic *Observations on the Art of English Poesie* (1602), in which he argued that English poets ought to adopt the quantitative meters of Greek and Latin. "This cannot be done in English," says John Hollander, "with its prominent word stress, save by assigning Latin vowel lengths to the written English, and simply patterning what amounts to a typographical code which cannot be heard as verse. . . . 'Rose-cheekt Laura' is therefore merely an unrhymed English trochaic poem, perfectly plain to the ear" (Introduction to *Selected Songs of Thomas Campion*, selected by W. H. Auden [Boston: Godine, 1973]).

EXERCISE: *Meaningful Variation*, pages 842–843

Aside from minor variations from a metrical norm (such as the substitution of a trochee for an iamb), the most meaningful departures in these passages seem to occur in these words or phrases:

1. Dryden: *deviates*. (Now there's a meaningful deviation!)

2. Pope: the spondees *snakes*, *drags*, and *slow length*.

3. Byron: the last line of Byron's stanza is two syllables (or one iambic foot) longer than the earlier lines. These extra syllables give the stanza a strong sense of closure.

4. Stevens: *spontaneous, casual, ambiguous*.

EXERCISE: *Recognizing Rhythms*, page 843

Edna St. Vincent Millay, COUNTING-OUT RHYME, page 843
Jacqueline Osherow, SONG FOR THE MUSIC IN THE WARSAW
GHETTO, page 844
A. E. Housman, WHEN I WAS ONE-AND-TWENTY, page 844
William Carlos Williams, SMELL!, page 845
Walt Whitman, BEAT! BEAT! DRUMS!, page 845
Langston Hughes, DREAM BOOGIE, page 846

Probably it is more important that students be able to recognize a metrical poem than that they name its meter. The Millay and Housman poems are thoroughly metrical. The Whitman and Williams are not, but they include metrical lines in places: in Whitman's poem, besides the refrain (lines 1, 8, and 15) there are primarily iambic lines that end each stanza; the Williams poem grows rhythmically insistent in places where the speaker berates his nose for its omnivorous and indecorous curiosity. The first and third stanzas of the Osherow poem have a ballad-like near regularity, but the middle of the second stanza contains two lines of iambic pentameter: perhaps the author strives to avoid a repetitive singsong rhythm that might seem to undermine the gravity of the subject. Hughes's "Dream Boogie" starts out with a metrical beat, then (deliberately) departs from it in the italicized interruptions.

 MyLiteratureLab Resources. Biography, critical overview, and bibliography for Millay, Housman, Williams, Whitman, and Hughes. Critical essay on "Dream Boogie."

David Mason, SONG OF THE POWERS, page 846

Another powerful poem written in accentual meters: there are two strong stresses in each line. Since nursery rhymes are usually written in accentual meters, and Mason's poem uses the children's game of Scissors, Paper, Stone as its unifying metaphor, the meter is especially appropriate to the subject. But Mason also uses the rough-edged quality of accentual meter to convey the raw, uncompromising nature of his protagonists. Each character (Stone, Paper, Scissors) speaks in turn, announcing its power, pride, and position. As the poem progresses, these symbolic speakers reveal how unrestrained ambition and desire destroy human relations and community.

WRITERS ON WRITING

Gwendolyn Brooks, HEARING "WE REAL COOL," page 847

Brooks's remarks on her poem suggest how she consciously uses rhythm as an instrument of meaning. By placing *we* at the end of each of the first seven lines—in contrast to a more conventional placement at the beginning of each line—she forces the reader to stop and think more probingly about what the lines mean. In the interview, she also stresses that her lineation was not trying to copy a colloquial rhythm but to express her attitude toward the protagonists in her poem—a significant and provocative distinction.

Kilroy, as students may need to know, was a fictitious—even mythical—character commemorated in graffiti chalked or penciled by U.S. soldiers wherever they traveled in World War II. KILROY WAS HERE was even scrawled in the sands of Anzio, a small testimonial that the graffitist is a person.

22
Closed Form

Beginning students of poetry have often had a hard time appreciating either a sonnet or a poem in open verse because they have yet to distinguish one variety of poetry from the other. On first meeting an unfamiliar poem, the experienced reader probably recognizes it as metrical or nonmetrical from its opening lines—and perhaps can tell at a glance from its look on the page (compact sonnet or spaced-out open verse). Such a reader then settles down to read with appropriate expectations, aware of the rules of the poem, looking forward to seeing how well the poet can play by them. But the inexperienced reader reads mainly for plain prose sense, unaware of the rhythms of a Whitmanic long line or the rewards of a sonnet artfully fulfilling its fourteenth line. Asked to write about poetry, the novice reader may even blame the sonnet for being "too rigid," or blame William Carlos Williams for "lacking music" (that is, lacking a rime scheme) or for "running wild." Such readers may have their preferences, but they say nothing about a poem or the poet's accomplishments.

That is why this chapter and the following one seem to us essential. To put across to students the differences between the two formal varieties, it isn't necessary to deal with every last fixed form, either. One can do much by comparing two poems (closed and open) on the theme of sorrow: Edna St. Vincent Millay's fine sonnet "What lips my lips have kissed" and Stephen Crane's astonishing "The Heart." Before taking up closed form, you might care to teach some song lyrics or a couple of traditional folk ballads. That way, the student isn't likely to regard fixed forms as arbitrary constructions invented by English teachers. A stanza, you can point out, is the form that words naturally take when sung to a tune; that is how stanzas began. Sing a second round of a song, and you will find yourself repeating the pattern of it.

FORMAL PATTERNS

John Keats, THIS LIVING HAND, NOW WARM AND CAPABLE, page 851

After Keats's death, these grim lines were discovered in the margin of one of his manuscripts. Robert Gittings has pointed out that the burden of the poem is much like that of two letters Keats wrote late in life to Fanny Brawne, charging her conscience with his approaching death and blaming her for enjoying good health. "This," says Gittings, "marks the lowest depths of his disease-ridden repudiation of both love and poetry" (*John Keats* [Boston: Atlantic-Little, 1968] 403). To discuss: can a repudiation of poetry nevertheless be a good poem?

MyLiteratureLab Resources. Photographs, biographical information, critical overview, and bibliography for Keats.

Robert Graves, COUNTING THE BEATS, *page 853*

At mid-century, Robert Graves was generally considered one of the major English poets of the Modern era. Then shortly before his death he fell out of critical favor. His work almost vanished from the anthologies. Now his reputation is slowly but surely on the rise. Poet, novelist, critic, autobiographer, Graves stands as a diverse and original (if also often eccentric) literary talent—the one surviving British poet of the First World War to achieve a major literary career.

"Counting the Beats" has received almost no critical attention, but it has been a favorite among poets since its first appearance. The poem has an almost hypnotic rhythm. The stanza pattern of the poem is original. The meter is accentual. Each four-line stanza begins with a short two-beat line. The next line has three beats. The long third line of each stanza has five stresses. The stanza then ends with another short two-beat line.

The rime scheme is equally noteworthy and original. Each stanza ends with an *I*-sound, but the first three lines of each stanza repeat a single word as an end-rime. This gives each stanza the effect of the two speakers repeating, refining, and qualifying their ideas as they converse.

Readers interested in learning more about Graves might want to consult the scholarly journal *Focus on Robert Graves and His Contemporaries*, edited by Richard Schumaker and published by the Department of English at the University of Maryland.

John Donne, SONG ("GO AND CATCH A FALLING STAR"), *page 854*

Maybe it is worth pointing out that, in bringing together short stanzas to make one longer one, Donne hasn't simply joined quatrain, couplet, and tercet like a man making up a freight train by coupling boxcars. In sense and syntax, each long stanza is all one: its units would be incomplete if they were separated.

Phillis Levin, BRIEF BIO, *page 856*

Levin's poem is, of course, an acrostic. The first letter of each line spells out the hidden subject of the poem—*BUTTERFLY.* The title also contains a double pun. First, the poem contains a brief biography of the butterfly's life (*bio* means *life* in Greek); second, the butterfly's life is brief. Levin provides this note about her poem:

> Poetry is intimately bound up with the unknown, and so to write a riddle is to begin from the reverse of our condition, and to mirror the condition of the reader. In a riddle, as in life, we do not know what will follow, what will surprise, and yet we remain engaged, because the riddle catches us. The tension and expectations arise from the encountering of a form—for if it closes, both in time and space, we expect it to disclose itself finally.

If a butterfly always seems to be moving somewhere, we must follow it, as one must follow the lines, the thread of thought and images, to find the answer to the riddle. Thus, the butterfly is an icon of passing, of the ethereal nature of presence. To compose a poem whose answer is the butterfly is to make an encomium to ephemeral beauty and eternal form. To write an acrostic is to commit oneself to a rather arbitrary journey, without rhyme or reason: one must first accept the fact of the letters that form the word, and from there make one's way into the poem, believing one's imagination will flower to meet the pressures and limitations imposed by the pattern accepted from the start.

But the very form of a riddle suggests an answer just out of reach, promising in time to be attainable. A riddle poses the possibility of knowing, of grasping; and in the case of a butterfly, the riddle's answer, when grasped, is the fulfillment of holding in one's mind the image of something that cannot be held in one's hand—without destroying the object. Perhaps the subject of the riddle, which I alighted on by chance, is really a paradigm of the poet's desire: to hold what cannot last, except in memory or in works that create a realm enacting the vividness of memory, and thereby making it possible to share what is usually limited to the boundary of individual consciousness. The poem is in the movement, not the answer, though that need for an answer, heightened by the growing sense of the as-of-yet unrecognized familiar noun, propels the reader, just as the delight in finding associations and clues that bring the reader closer is what moves the poet.

"Brief Bio" is also, of course, my elliptical, elided biographical note—a brief life, or a brief summation of one, an *ars poetica* in miniature. To be what one is, pure movement inseparable from one's form, the unity of rhythm and design—that is what I want my poems to embody, and that is what a butterfly seems to say of itself in its act of being itself. Its being is transitive, subject and object cannot be distinguished.

The profile of the butterfly is inscribed in the poem's shape (whose contours can be traced on the right side), just as the letters spelling its identity are traced on the vertical axis of the left-hand margin. If there is nothing less "concrete" than a butterfly, still we relish its brief moments of stillness, voyeurs to its constant sequence of change, the freedom of its detachment, to suddenly rise and then dip down, sipping nectar from a flower—as if in the same gesture it were eating and praying before passing on.

THE SONNET

William Shakespeare, LET ME NOT TO THE MARRIAGE OF TRUE MINDS, page 857

Shakespeare's enormously popular Sonnet 116 is a meditation on ideal love and romantic fidelity. As one would expect of any famous work by Shakespeare, the meaning of every line in the poem has been debated. Most modern critical discussions have centered on whether the speaker really believes that perfect human constancy is possible or whether the poem is subtly skeptical about its own romantic idealism.

A crucial notion to point out in a classroom discussion is that Shakespeare's poem discusses a spiritual union ("the marriage of true minds," not of bodies). He acknowledges that physical youth and beauty are victim to the ravages of Time. Spiritual love even endures bodily death, the poem asserts, and lasts until Doomsday.

 MyLiteratureLab Resources. Photographs, biographical information, and bibliography for Shakespeare. Critical essay on "Let me not to the marriage of true minds."

Michael Drayton, SINCE THERE'S NO HELP, COME LET US KISS AND PART, page 858

Nay, yea, wouldst, and *mightst* are the only words that couldn't equally well come out of the mouth of a lover in the twenty-first century.

There seems to be an allegorical drama taking place, as Laurence Perrine has pointed out in "A Drayton Sonnet," *CEA Critic* 25 (June 1963): 8. Love is also called Passion, and apparently his death is being urged along by the woman's infernal Innocence.

Edna St. Vincent Millay, WHAT LIPS MY LIPS HAVE KISSED, page 858

Millay's originality has been insufficiently appreciated by critics. Too often she has been portrayed as a sentimental traditionalist removed from the mainstream of Modernist innovation. Millay's diction was very traditional, and her devotion to metrical forms such as the sonnet seemed conservative when compared to the experimentalism of Pound and Williams. And yet Millay's tone and subject matter were revolutionary in their time, and her strong feminist voice remains powerful. The sexual candor and moral freedom of this 1923 sonnet hardly seem reactionary or conservative.

The female speaker of the sonnet recalls her many lovers but—significantly— only in a general sense. They are too numerous for her to individualize. She displays no traditional guilt for her amours. Her only specific remorse concerns her own aging. (By implication, she longs to be young and in love again.)

The sestet of Millay's sonnet explicitly recalls Shakespeare's sonnet "That time of year thou mayst in me behold"—another poem in which an aging lover regrets the passing of youth and the approach of old age. Millay boldly appropriates Shakespeare's metaphor of the winter tree and develops it for her own ends. In her excellent essay "Love's 'Little Day': Time and the Sexual Body in Millay's Sonnets" (in *Millay at 100: A Critical Appraisal,* edited by Diane P. Freedman, Carbondale: Southern Illinois UP, 1995), Stacy Carson Hubarb comments:

> The aging speaker as songless tree is an abject figure, one that we might be tempted to read as a prototype of abandoned womanhood, pathetic and powerless, if it were not for the powerful alliance that such abjectness establishes between Millay's speaker and Shakespeare's. The speaker of Shakespeare's sonnet makes a spectacle of his abjection by way of persuasion; so, too, does Millay's, but with the further motive of authorizing herself through

poetic echo. To read such self-abjection without a view to literary history would be to mistake it for mere self-pity, a sentimental attachment to the figure of woman as victim, rather than the bold poetic affiliation that Millay surely intends it to be.

 MyLiteratureLab Resources. Photographs and biographical information for Millay. Video clip and student paper for "What lips my lips have kissed, and where, and why."

Robert Frost, ACQUAINTED WITH THE NIGHT, page 859

This poem first appeared in *West-Running Brook* (1928), Frost's fifth volume, which some critics felt marked a turning in his work toward dark, personal themes. One might argue whether Frost's turn to dark themes began here, but it is true that many of his grimmer early poems were cast in a seemingly impersonal narrative form.

"Acquainted with the Night" shows many of the features we associate with Frost's darkly introspective side. Not only is the speaker solitary and alienated from the human community surrounding him; he fatalistically accepts this isolation. The poem begins and ends with the same line, which emphasizes the inescapable quality of the speaker's destiny, though by now *night* has acquired a metaphorical as well as a literal meaning.

Although the poem is written in a direct first-person voice, it confides very little to the reader. We know the speaker's desperate isolation but, as William Pritchard observes in his superb study *Frost: A Literary Life Reconsidered* (New York: Oxford UP, 1984), the poem provides "no clues or provocation to significant action." We know what is happening in the poem but not why. Noting that the poem was written in *terza rima*, Randall Jarrell commented that it possessed "Dante's own form . . . with some of Dante's own qualities." We might elaborate on Jarrell's passing remark by saying that one reading of the poem would describe it as the speech of a lost soul wandering in his own private hell.

It is worth noting that the moody Frost was a compulsive walker whose late night rambles were legendary, though he liked them best with friends.

 MyLiteratureLab Resources. Biography, critical overview, critical articles, and bibliography for Frost. Longman Lecture on "Acquainted with the Night."

Kim Addonizio, FIRST POEM FOR YOU, page 860

Anyone who thinks the sonnet form forces a writer into old-fashioned themes should look at this sexy and surprising poem. Addonizio creates a totally contemporary situation and language, and yet she also touches subtly on ancient, indeed primal poetic themes—the impermanence of flesh, the unpredictability of sexual passion, and the mysterious relationship between body and soul.

An interesting question to ask in class: what do the images the speaker's lover has tattooed onto his (or possibly her) body suggest about the person's character? The tattoos depict lightning and blue swirls of water out of which a serpent faces a dragon. These are the only specific images we have of the otherwise unseen lover.

Mark Jarman, UNHOLY SONNET: HANDS FOLDED, page 860

Mark Jarman has provided the following note.

> John Donne's Holy Sonnets are the models for my Unholy Sonnets. His poems are urgent declarations of faith and appeals for mercy, despite the obvious realities of sin and death. Donne applies terrific pressure to form and metaphor, and both at times come close to collapse. Still, he works from Anglo-Catholic, Christian assumptions widely disseminated and shared in his time. It is almost impossible to work from such assumptions today. My aim in the Unholy Sonnets has been to work against any assumption or shared expression of faith, to write a devotional poetry against the grain. At the same time I have tried to write traditional sonnets without sticking to any one traditional form. So far (the project is ongoing) the Unholy Sonnets includes English, Italian, Spenserian, composite, and nonce forms. Calling them Unholy is a way of warding off piety but not, I hope, ultimately, belief.

From the list of sonnet forms that Jarman provides in his comment, the one that fits "Hands Folded" is *composite*: the first eight lines resemble a Petrarchan octave in their *a b a b* rime scheme (though lines 5–8 do not repeat the rime words of the first four lines); the last six lines replicate a Shakespearean quatrain and concluding couplet. "All the people" are, of course, the eight fingers (excluding thumbs) of the two hands clasped together as alluded to in the familiar rhyme this poem is based on: "Here is the church, / Here is the steeple, / Open the doors, / And see all the people." If there is a turn of thought, it comes with the "But" at the beginning of line 11, where the poem moves from a fanciful description of two entangled hands to an implicit comment on human relationships.

Twenty "Unholy Sonnets" appear in Jarman's collection *Questions for Ecclesiastes* (Brownsville: Story Line, 1997).

Timothy Steele, SUMMER, page 861

Steele's sonnet carefully uses language that evokes—to rearrange his own words—the voluptuous plenty of summer. Most of the images are deliberately still or static: windless lakes, dense orchards, slow creeks, and the person "supine" in the meadow grass. The poem also contrasts nature's immense abundance with the poor striving of humankind. Faced with summer's magnificence, the thoughtful person simply surrenders to it. In this sense, Steele's sonnet works in the tradition of the *carpe diem* poem, but in Steele's world the consciousness of death is entirely absent. He suggests that we seize the day simply because it is so beautiful.

Instructors may want to note that Horace's original *carpe diem* ode is found in the "Translation" chapter along with three translations of it.

A. E. Stallings, SINE QUA NON, page 861

Note the ways in which Stallings combines the traditional features of the sonnet form with unusual variations of her own in order to achieve the subtle and moving effects of "Sine Qua Non." The rime scheme presents a variation on the Shakespearean sonnet: there are three quatrains riming *abba*, followed by a concluding couplet, but there are no full stops at the ends of lines 4 and 12; the text presents a linked, flowing set of separate ways of making the same central point, rather than approaching the subject from a different perspective in each four-line unit. In its appearance on the page, "Sine Qua Non" more closely resembles a Petrarchan sonnet, yet the turn, such as it is, at line 9 is actually more of a return to the poem's opening, with its repetition of the poem's first five words. The movement from octave to sestet is perhaps best perceived as a movement from implicit statement in the first eight lines to a more explicit approach in the last six, especially in line 12.

R. S. Gwynn, SHAKESPEAREAN SONNET, page 862

This is a Shakespearean sonnet in both form and content, inspired by newspaper TV-show plot summaries that had, for purposes of satiric inspiration, the double felicity of being laughably insipid and in perfect iambic pentameter. With that line as his *donnée*, Gwynn proceeds to perform similarly banal reductions of *Romeo and Juliet; Macbeth; A Midsummer Night's Dream; Richard III; Julius Caesar; Henry IV, Part 1; Othello; Henry V; Twelfth Night; As You Like It; King Lear; Coriolanus;* and *Antony and Cleopatra.*

Of the prominent formalist poets writing today, Gwynn may be the keenest satirist. He has written a wonderful extended satire on contemporary poets and poetry in the great tradition of Pope's *Dunciad: The Narcissiad* (New Braunfels, TX: Cedar Rock P, 1981). He frequently reviews poetry for *Texas Review, Sewanee Review,* and other literary journals, and he is currently a professor of English at Lamar University in Beaumont, Texas.

THE EPIGRAM

Alexander Pope, EPIGRAM ENGRAVED ON THE COLLAR OF A DOG, page 863

Students may be asked: What's the point? Pope makes a devastating comment on society. With few exceptions (such as His Royal Highness), every man is a dog: owned by somebody, accepting handouts, licking his master's hand, learning to heel.

Sir John Harrington, Robert Herrick, William Blake, E. E. Cummings, Langston Hughes, J. V. Cunningham, John Frederick Nims, Stevie Smith, Brad Leithauser, Dick Davis, Anonymous, Hilaire Belloc, Wendy Cope, A SELECTION OF EPIGRAMS, pages 863–865

Highly various, these thirteen examples illustrate the persistence of the epigram. Whether the form of an epigram is closed or open, its essence consists of brevity and a final dash of wit.

Besides writing "Of Treason," called the best epigram in English, Harrington has another claim to immortality: he invented the water closet.

Blake offers a definition of the epigram, written as epigrams.

Cunningham, the American master of the verse epigram in our time, has had few recent rivals. Instructors who seek further examples of this fixed form will find many to quote in his *Collected Poems and Epigrams* (Chicago: Swallow, 1971).

Nims, the closest rival to Cunningham, collected his epigrams, including "Contemplation," in *Of Flesh and Bone* (New Brunswick: Rutgers UP, 1967). When first printed, in the *New Yorker*, this poem was called "A Thought for Tristram"—suggesting that *you* means Isolde, betrothed of King Mark, with whom Tristan/Tristram shares a love potion.

If the haiku-like brevity of epigrams tempts you to ask your class to write a few, resist the temptation. Even from a bright class the results are likely to depress you. A successful epigrammatist needs, besides the ability to condense, the ability to deliver that final rapier thrust of nastiness. A talented creative writing class, after tackling poems in a few of the less demanding forms (ballads, villanelles, sestinas), might try epigrams, either rimed or rimeless.

If you do decide to challenge your class with writing an epigram, you might suggest they try the Wendy Cope approach and either update or revise an existing epigram. You'll be surprised how personal some revisions can become.

THE CLERIHEW

As for the "conventional subject matter" of the clerihew, you should find a hint in the following example by E. C. Bentley:

> The Art of Biography
> Is different from Geography.
> Geography is about Maps,
> But Biography is about Chaps.

OTHER FORMS

Robert Pinsky, ABC, page 866

The title of Robert Pinsky's short poem suggests its form: an abecediary, a poem which uses the order of the alphabet as its structural principle. Exactly twenty-six words long (not counting the equal sign in the last line), the poem offers one word for each letter of the alphabet in strict order from A to Z. Pinsky turns what might merely be a word game into a concise and evocative meditation on death. The meditation acquires a strange force because it seems to push against the arbitrary limitations of the form. Each new word feels hard-won, a fragment of meaning achieved against the odds. Without the poem's demanding form, Pinsky could easily achieve a more fluent statement of his theme, but that difficult articulation and urgent economy would vanish.

Dylan Thomas, Do not go gentle into that good night, page 867

No mere trivial exercise (as a villanelle tends to be), Thomas's poem voices his distress at the decline and approaching death of his father. At the time, the elder Thomas was a semi-invalid, going blind, and suffering from the effects of tongue cancer. As a teacher of English at Swansea Grammar School, the poet's father had ruled his class with authority; but those who knew him only in his last years knew a different, humbled man. (See Constantine FitzGibbon, *The Life of Dylan Thomas* [Boston: Atlantic-Little, 1965] 294–95.)

Like many other Thomas poems, this one contains serious puns: *good night, grave.* "Another assumption in this poem," says Amy Mulvahill (in a student paper written at Tufts), "may be Thomas's own self-destructive drive that led him to drink himself to death. It's possible that he preferred to taunt death with his boisterous life—to go down unrepentant and brawling."

Repetitious as a villanelle is, the form suits this poem, making its refrains sound like prayers said over and over. If you have any student poets, you might challenge them to write villanelles of their own. The hard part is to make the repeated lines occur naturally, to make them happen in places where there *is* something to be said. But the repetitious form is helpful; write the two refrain lines and already your labors are eight-nineteenths over.

For another instance of Thomas's fondness for arbitrary, demanding forms, see the poem "Prologue" at the beginning of Daniel Jones's edition of *The Poems of Dylan Thomas* (New York: New Directions, 1971). A poem of 102 lines, its first and last lines rime with each other, as do lines 2 and 101, 3 and 100, 4 and 99, and so on, until two riming lines collide at the poem's exact center. Except for that inmost pair of lines, however, no reader is likely to notice the elaborate rime scheme—rimes so far apart they can't be heard; but apparently it supplied the poet with obstacles to overcome and a gamelike pleasure.

MLL *MyLiteratureLab Resources.* Interactive reading and critical essay on "Do not go gentle into that good night."

Robert Bridges, Triolet, page 867

The triolet is a form usually associated with light verse, but Bridges's poem demonstrates that it can convey heavier emotional loads if used with sufficient skill. Bridges's triolet could be offered as an example of a short lyric—compressed, evocative, musical, and personal. He also manages to make the opening lines acquire considerable additional force by the end of the poem. We now know both that the couple fell into their passion unawares (they "did not guess") and that their love was not only difficult but irretrievably disastrous. Is there a more moving triolet in English?

Elizabeth Bishop, Sestina, page 868

We would answer the questions following the poem like this:

1. That some terrible loss—a death in the family?—causes the grandmother to weep seems a guess that fits the poem. The old woman tries to hide her grief from the child (lines 6, 10, 31–32); she thinks it was somehow foretold (9).

2. We have no authority to read this poem as autobiography, but the figure of the grandmother—the most important person in Bishop's early life—and the stormy setting (such as we might find in a village on the Nova Scotia coast) invite us to do so. The source of grief may have been the death of the poet's father (hence, an irony that the child draws a man with tear-shaped buttons) or it may have been the illness of her mother, hospitalized several times for a mental disorder. When Bishop was eight months old her father died, and according to Robert Giroux, "The first real home Elizabeth knew was in the coastal town of Great Village, Nova Scotia, where her widowed mother returned in order to be with her parents" (Introduction to Bishop's *Collected Prose* [New York: Farrar, 1984]). When the poet was five, her mother had a final breakdown, leaving the girl in the care of her grandmother. Apparently Bishop looked back to her days in Nova Scotia with affectionate yearning. When she was six, her father's wealthy parents moved her to Worcester, Massachusetts, for a less happy stay.

3. Small round pieces of paper. Almanacs (such as *The Old Farmer's*) come with punched holes to make them easy to string and hang on a hook or a nail.

4. The playful ingenuity of the sestina, like that of the villanelle, tempts a poet to wax clever; yet Bishop is writing a deeply felt, moving poem in it. The tone is lightly serious, compassionate—yet with touches of gentle humor: the Little Marvel Stove, the child's drawings. Irony, too, informs the poem: a contrast between the grandmother's sorrow and the child's innocent ignorance.

5. Nims's comment seems an apt description of "Sestina." In the six repeated words, we are given the setting (*house*) the characters (*grandmother, child*), and key symbols (*Stove, almanac, tears*). "Sestina" weaves all six into a subtle relationship. This poem is full of things that suggest magic: the prophetic almanac, the teacup (with which fortune-tellers divine), the "marvellous stove." It also is full of secret-keepers: the grandmother, the almanac with its powers of prophecy, the concluding reference to the "inscrutable house." The repetitions are worth tracing: *tears*, in particular, accumulates an effect. In stanza 2 the tears arrive like an equinoctial storm; in 3, the kettle also weeps; in 4, tea is tears; in 5, the man in the child's drawing wears tears; in 6, the almanac weeps paper tears; and finally, in the envoy, tears are flowers. "Time to plant tears" may be a literal quotation from the almanac, *tears* being (if memory serves) the name of a small white flower favored by rock gardeners.

Bishop's *Complete Poems* contains another intriguing sestina, "A Miracle for Breakfast." At the time it was written Bishop remarked (in a 1937 letter to Marianne Moore):

It seems to me that there are two ways possible for a sestina—one is to use unusual words as terminations, in which case they would have to be used differently as often as possible—as you say, "change, of scale." That would make a very highly seasoned kind of poem. And the other way is to use as colorless words as possible—like Sidney, so that it becomes less of a trick and more of a natural theme and variations. I guess I have tried to do both at once. (Quoted by Nims in his essay cited in question 5.)

In the later "Sestina," the terminal words seem to be deliberately usual ones.

For the poet Eavan Boland's insightful comparison of "Sestina" and Bishop's poem "One Art," please see the notes on the latter poem in this manual.

MLL   *MyLiteratureLab Resources.* Biography, critical overview, and bibliography for Bishop.

EXERCISE: *Urgent Repetition*, page 869

This experiment just might leave you surprised at the quality of some of its results. Whoever writes a sestina has a powerful ally—the form—on his or her side.

In a *tour de force*, a student in a poetry workshop at Tufts once wrote a fairly successful sestina taking *one, two, three, four, five,* and *six* for its repeated words. The result seemed only mildly boring and mechanical!

WRITERS ON WRITING

A. E. Stallings, ON FORM AND ARTIFICE, page 870

Stallings makes the important observation that *artificial* is not a dirty word; *art, artifice,* and *artificial,* after all, are all linguistically related. A true artist works— with insight, discipline, and skill—to create the desired effect, which is far from the same thing as spontaneously setting down one's thoughts and feelings. A writer wishing, for example, to communicate the thrill and ache of first love could hardly do worse than transcribe an actual phone conversation, in all of its tedium and banality, between two smitten teenagers. "It seems an obvious point for art," as she says, but these days it also seems to be a point that needs to be made.

23
Open Form

Denise Levertov, Ancient Stairway, page 873

This poem is discussed fairly extensively in the text. It may be a useful piece to use to generate a discussion about the nature of poetry. Particularly if you have just spent class time emphasizing the conventions of closed forms as they are discussed and illustrated in the previous chapter, you might begin by asking something like, "Given the absence of rime and meter, and of all the conventions of traditional poetical form, what is particularly poetic about this piece? What makes it a poem?"

E. E. Cummings, Buffalo Bill 's, page 877

Cleanth Brooks and Robert Penn Warren have taken this poem to be an admiring tribute to William Cody (*Understanding Poetry*, 3rd ed. [New York: Holt, 1960]). But Louis J. Budd, in an interesting dissent, thinks Cummings is satirizing the theatricality of the old sideshow straight-shooter and finds Mister Death "a cosmic corporal gathering up defunct tin-gods and stuffed effigies" (*The Explicator* 11 [June 1953]: item 55).

MLL *MyLiteratureLab Resources.* Photographs and biographical information for Cummings. Audio clip and critical essay on "Buffalo Bill 's."

W. S. Merwin, For the Anniversary of My Death, page 877

W. S. Merwin's poem is written in unpunctuated free verse. The lines tend to end on natural speech pauses, but without conventional punctuation the reader cannot know if a phrase or sentence ends until he or she says the line aloud (or reads it carefully) and proceeds to the next line. The effect is one of discovering the full meaning of the lines only as they unfold. The phase "Tireless traveler," for example, is initially ambiguous in syntactical terms. Does it refer to the speaker or the silence of death? Only by going on to the next line ("Like the beam of a lightless star") does the reader understand that the phrase stands in apposition to *silence*. Merwin's lack of punctuation, therefore, both slows down one's reading of the poem and endows its language with an appropriate sense of mystery.

The central idea of the poem is itself a mystery—the exact date of the speaker's death. This question is a universal one because it is a mystery that every human faces. Merwin uses the occasion of his quandary to meditate on his mortality and to praise the beauty of the world in religious terms, though his spiritual impulse reflects the mystery of existence. The speaker bows "not knowing to what." Ultimately, Merwin's "For the Anniversary of My Death" is a contemporary version of the Roman poet Horace's *carpe diem* ode, in which the speaker acknowledges the impossibility of knowing the exact time of one's inevitable death and so resolves to seize the day by living fully.

William Carlos Williams, THE DANCE, page 878

Scanned, the poem is seen to abound in pairs of unstressed syllables. The result is a bouncing rhythm—anapestic or dactylic, depending on where one wishes to slice the lines into feet. This rhythm seems appropriate to a description of frolicking dancers and helps establish the tone of the poem, which is light, however serious. Williams severs his units of sense again and again in midphrase, placing his line breaks after *and, the, about, thick, those, such*. In this poem run-on lines predominate, and this is not only a technical device but a way of underlining the poem's meaning. Williams conveys a sense of continuous movement in a syntax that keeps overflowing line units.

By repeating its opening line, the poem, like Brueghel's dancers, comes round in a circle to where it began. Another metaphor is possible: like a painting enclosed in a frame, the poem encloses its central scene in a frame of words.

Williams first saw Brueghel's painting in Vienna in 1924, but he wrote this poem in 1942, some eighteen years later. A French critic, Jacqueline Saunier-Ollier, has speculated on the curious fact that the poem, in describing a vividly colorful tableau, omits all color images. Her work on Williams's Brueghel poems is summed up in *William Carlos Williams: Man and Poet*, ed. Carroll F. Terrell (Orono: National Poetry Foundation, 1983) 528–29.

 MyLiteratureLab Resources. Biography, critical overview, and bibliography for Williams.

Stephen Crane, THE HEART, page 879
Walt Whitman, CAVALRY CROSSING A FORD, page 879

These two nineteenth-century American poems seem comparable mainly in their brevity and use of narration. The assonance and internal alliteration in Whitman's phrase *silvery river* are echoed in the poem's opening line: the assonance of the *i*-sound in *line, wind, islands;* the internal alliteration of the *r* in *array, where, green*. But any line of this short poem will repay such inspection. Crane's "The Heart" is obviously less heavy on verbal music, although *Held his heart in his hands* is heavily alliterative; and the second stanza favors the letter *b*. There is rime, too: *it/bitter, bitter/heart*.

Whitman seems to lambaste his poem with sound effects in his enthusiasm for his grand military spectacle. Crane cares for music, too, and yet his is a subtler, harsher one. Although longer in words, Whitman's "Cavalry" contains fewer pauses than "The Heart" (fifteen compared to Crane's seventeen, if every comma and line-end counts as a pause). The result is, in Crane's poem, a much more hesitant, start-and-stop movement—appropriate, perhaps, to a study of self-immolation. Whitman apparently wants an expansive, continuous progress in his syntax, as in his cavalry.

 MyLiteratureLab Resources. Biography, critical overview, and bibliography for Whitman. Interactive reading and critical essay on "Cavalry Crossing a Ford." Biography, critical overview, and bibliography for Crane.

Ezra Pound, SALUTATION, page 880

Ezra Pound is best known for his formidably allusive Modernist epic, *The Cantos,* which he worked on for over fifty years. Less well known are Pound's early London poems, which are often funny, tender, and direct. This poem from *Lustra* (1915) attacks the bourgeoisie for its snobbery, materialism, and concern with appearance. In the poem's hierarchy of values, the fish, who are furthest from these failings, are the happiest. This celebration of simplicity may seem a bit odd coming from so fiercely cultured and mannered a figure as Pound, but you will notice that, in this context, the speaker is canny enough to rank himself near the bottom of the happiness scale.

Wallace Stevens, THIRTEEN WAYS OF LOOKING AT A BLACKBIRD, page 880

Suggestive as blackbirds may be, the theme of the poem is, "Pay attention to physical reality." Stevens chides the thin ascetic men of Haddam who would ignore good blackbirds and actual women for golden phantasms. He also chides that asinine aristocrat who rides about Connecticut (of all places) in a glass coach as if thinking himself Prince Charming. The poem ends in a section whose tone is matter-of-fact flatness, rather as though Stevens were saying, "Well, here's the way the world is; if you don't like it, go read newspapers." Taken as a series of notes for an argument for literalism, this much-discussed poem seems to have unity and to lead to a definite conclusion. For another (and more complicated) view of it, see Helen Vendler, *On Extended Wings* (Cambridge: Harvard UP, 1969).

Way-of-looking number 5 recalls Keats's "Grecian Urn": "Heard melodies are sweet. . . ."

Way number 10 eludes final paraphrase. Are the "bawds of euphony" supposed to be, perhaps, crass ex-poets who have sold out their Muses, who utter music to please the box office instead of truth? But blackbirds flying in a green light are so strikingly beautiful that even those dull bawds would be moved to exclaim at the sight of them.

 MyLiteratureLab Resources. Biography, critical overview, and bibliography for Stevens.

Prose Poetry

Carolyn Forché, The Colonel, page 883

It is possible to argue either way on whether "The Colonel" is a prose poem or a short prose piece, but the stronger case is that it is a poem in prose. Why? First, "The Colonel" displays the compression we usually associate with poetry (prose fiction would unfold more leisurely). Second, by the end of the piece, it becomes apparent that the organization is as much lyric as narrative (the image of the ears pressed to the ground harks back to the *heard* in the opening line and to the auditory images throughout). Third, the density of literary effect (imagery, description, metaphor) has the feel of poetic language. The absence of poetic rhythms and lineation isn't enough to offset these qualities.

The rhetoric of Forché's piece deserves some attention. The effect of the poem depends heavily on the opening sentence ("What you have heard is true."). If we do not—at least initially—accept Forché's piece as reportage, then the poem loses a great deal of its impact. Forché understands this assumption clearly: notice how she dates the incident at the end to increase its verisimilitude. Some critics have questioned whether the episode truly happened as Forché presents it. That is a legitimate historical query, but, in poetic terms, it hardly matters; she has convincingly created the appearance of reality. The exaggerations seem no less credible than the bizarre incidents that fill the newspapers because Forché has captured the tone of factuality.

MLL *MyLiteratureLab Resources.* Student paper for "The Colonel."

Charles Simic, The Magic Study of Happiness, page 883

This piece takes its title from a poem by the great nineteenth-century French poet Arthur Rimbaud (1854–1891), who was himself a pioneer in the art of the prose poem, and whose work—unsurprisingly, given the fact that all his poetry was written while he was still in his teens—deals frequently with themes of childhood and youth. Rimbaud's lines (from "Ô saisons, ô châteaux!") are: "J'ai fait la magique étude / Du bonheur, qu'aucun n'élude" ("I have made the magic study / Of happiness, which no one escapes"). Rimbaud biographer Graham Robb says of this and other, related poems: "Rimbaud attaches his songs to a concept which had fascinated him in the works of nineteenth-century illuminists: that behind the stage-set of sensory impressions lies a pure, absolute reality. . . . This ultimate truth can be glimpsed only in fleeting moments when the senses are no longer separate from the objects of perception, when the personality evaporates. . . ."

"The Magic Study of Happiness" appears in Simic's *Dime-Store Alchemy* (1992), a book about the reclusive American collage artist Joseph Cornell (1903–1972) that is itself a collage of sorts, combining biography, analysis, and Simic's own imaginative responses to Cornell's work. Cornell's miniature boxes often contain startling juxtapositions of objects and photographs through which he seeks, not unlike Rimbaud, to transcend rational perception and evoke a childlike sense of wonder. In an interview with the journal *Artful Dodge* shortly after the publication of *Dime-Store Alchemy*, Simic said:

> I really think that language cannot say or produce or convey the complexity, the depth of an experience, of heightened consciousness. When you feel exceptionally lucid, when you feel truly present to yourself and you see the world and you see yourself watching the world, there's a kind of plenitude of consciousness. So you step away from yourself and say "My God, I exist!" But, saying I exist is an impoverishment. There is so much more there; the experience itself is much larger than whatever words you have uttered. So I always feel that language does not quite equal the intensity of experience—that words are approximations. But this is a very complicated subject. The paradox that occurs is that attempts through words, through language, cannot instantly, simultaneously convey experience. One attempts by manipulating words in some fashion to find a way in a poem to recreate what the experience felt like originally. But it's no longer the same thing. It's coming to it in a very different way.

In that same interview, Simic rejects the interviewer's description of the pieces in *Dime-Store Alchemy* as prose poems; nonetheless, he allowed "The Magic Study of Happiness" to be included in David Lehman's anthology *Great American Prose Poems: From Poe to the Present* (2003). It is also worth noting that Simic is far from dismissive of the concept of the prose poem, either in general or in his own work: in 1989 he published *The World Doesn't End: Prose Poems*, which was awarded the 1990 Pulitzer Prize for poetry.

VISUAL POETRY

For more examples of graphic poetry, see the anthologies edited by Klonsky and Kostelanetz cited in footnotes to this chapter. Other useful anthologies include Emmett Williams's *Anthology of Concrete Poetry* (New York: Something Else, 1967), Eugene Wildman's *Chicago Review Anthology of Concretism* (Chicago: Chicago Review, 1967), Mary Ellen Solt's *Concrete Poetry: A World View* (Bloomington: Indiana UP, 1969), and Emmett Williams's selection of "Language Happenings" in *Open Poetry: Four Anthologies of Expanded Poems*, ed. Ronald Gross and George Quasha (New York: Simon, 1973).

George Herbert, EASTER WINGS, page 884
John Hollander, SWAN AND SHADOW, page 885

The tradition of the shaped poem, or *Carmen figuratum*, seems to have begun in Renaissance Italy, and the form flourished throughout Western Europe in the seventeenth century. English practitioners of the form, besides Herbert, included Robert Herrick (in "The Pillar of Fame") and George Puttenham.

Of "Easter Wings," Joan Bennett has remarked, "The shape of the wings on the page may have nothing but ingenuity to recommend it, but the diminuendo and crescendo that bring it about are expressive both of the rise and fall of the lark's song and flight (Herbert's image) and also the fall of man and his resurrection in Christ (the subject that the image represents)" (qtd. by F. E.

Hutchinson in his edition of Herbert's *Works* [Oxford: Oxford UP, 1941]). Visual shape and verbal meaning coincide strikingly when the second stanza dwindles to *Most thin*.

Like Herbert, Hollander clearly assumes that a word-shape has to have a meaningful relation to what is said in it. His reflected swan is one of twenty-five shaped poems collected in *Types of Shape* (New York: Atheneum, 1969). Other graphic poems in the book include a car key, a goblet, a beach umbrella, an Eskimo Pie, and the outline of New York State. Paul Fussell, Jr., discussing "Easter Wings" and Hollander's shaped poems, expresses reservations about this kind of poetry. Most shaped poems, he finds, are directed more to eyes than ears—"or better, we feel that the two dimensions are not married: one is simply in command of the other." But the greatest limitation in the genre is that there are few objects that shaped poems can effectively represent: "their shapes can reflect the silhouettes of wings, bottles, hourglasses, and altars, but where do we go from there?" (*Poetic Meter and Poetic Form* [New York: Random, 1965] 185–87). Students might be told of Fussell's view and asked to comment. A further disadvantage of most shaped poetry is that it cannot be heard aloud without loss.

 MyLiteratureLab Resources. Critical essay on "Easter Wings."

Terry Ehret, from PAPYRUS, page 886

Terry Ehret comments on her poem:

Why the hieroglyph?

I had felt provoked for some time to do a mistranslation, or free-associative translation, of the Papyrus Harris 500 Text, and in January of 1991, busy with a new house, new town, two small children and a newborn, while the jets bombed Iraq and Rodney King took his serial beatings, I sat down each night after the household was asleep to find out what I was thinking. I'd pull out the text, select a glyph (or sometimes a sequence of glyphs) that suited my mood, and then free-associated from the image toward some part of my life I couldn't directly see.

I often suspect my native language isn't language at all, at least not words, but rather rhythm and image. Most poems arise out of these impulses. Pictograms and hieroglyphs, being close to their origins in gesture and object, seem to speak very directly to that place where feelings lie but where words can't entirely go.

During the Middle Kingdom when the original Papyrus text was written, the hieroglyphs had come to represent phonetic sounds. The particular glyph I was working with for this poem was a combination of T (breadloaf) and TH (unknown). Studying it awakened in me a haunting grief, a feeling of exile, of someone stirring uneasily in sleep, and I tried to catch these feelings/images in the words of the prose poem. As the series grew each night, a narrative evolved, each glyph revealing a different part of the drama. I stopped writing when I felt I had come to the end of the story, and selected 18 of them to arrange in the sequence *Papyrus: A Temporary Journey*. The glyph serves as title, or more accurately, as parallel text. I think of them as two versions of the same thing.

Dorthi Charles, CONCRETE CAT, page 887

This trifle first appeared in the second edition of *An Introduction to Poetry* and has been retained out of loyalty to the past. While hunting for an illustration of the sillier kind of concrete poem that simply and unfeelingly arranges words like so many Lincoln Logs, XJK found the very thing in one of William Cole's anthologies of humorous poetry: "Concrete Poem" by the British wit Anthony Mundy. Mundy's work repeats *miniskirt* several times in the form of a miniskirt and tacks on a couple of *legleglegleglegs*. No doubt he was parodying concrete poetry, too. But the cheapskate in XJK rebelled at the thought of paying for permission to reprint such a simple doodad, so he decided to cut and paste together a homemade specimen. While constructing the cat, he had some fun with it, making the tongue a *U*, and so on. As far as we know, however, the pun in the cat's middle stripe (tripes) is the only place where language aspires toward poetry and becomes figurative.

FOUND POETRY

Ronald Gross, YIELD, page 888

Fitting together drab and prosaic materials, Gross leaves them practically unaltered. What he lends them are patterns that seem meaningful. By combining traffic-sign messages in "Yield," he implies that the signs insistently pressure us with their yips and barks. "Yield" states its theme implicitly: we are continually being ordered to conform, to give in, to go along with laws laid down for us. We must heed the signs in order to drive a car, but perhaps it is chilling to find their commands so starkly abstracted. Students might want to discuss whether it is reading too much into the poem to suspect that this theme applies to other areas of our lives, not only to driving.

A discussion of Gross's work may be one of those rare sessions that end with the students' realization that to remove speech from its workaday contexts and to place it into lines is, after all, what most poets do. Many poems, not only found poems, reveal meanings by arranging familiar things into fresh orders.

Nancy Adams Malone of Mattatuck Community College in Waterbury, Connecticut, contributes an insight about "Yield": "Everybody seems to think it's a comment on social conformity, but it seems to me easier and more fun to read it as a seduction."

Jacob Korg of the University of Washington passes on a class assignment that enjoyably makes its point. He asks his students to bring in whatever found poems they can discover. "The best one," he reports, "was the juxtaposition of two shop signs: ADULT ENTERTAINMENT and LIVE BAIT."

EXPERIMENT: *Finding a Poem*, page 889

Timothy F. Walsh, of Otero Junior College in Colorado, discovered another found poem in an earlier edition of this book:

"The sonnet,"
quipped Robert Bly,

"is where old professors
go to die."

"It was fun," he writes, "to discuss found poems following my students' reading about them and then point to one I found in the previous chapter." (The Bly quotation is on page 859 of the current edition.)

SEEING THE LOGIC OF OPEN FORM VERSE

E. E. Cummings, IN JUST-, page 889

Cummings's poem is one of his "Chansons Innocentes," little songs for children. In it, however, we meet a poet who is familiar with the classics and who naturally associates spring with goat-footed Pan. In Greek mythology, the god's pipes heralded the return of Persephone and caused birds and beasts to start up at his call. In Cummings's view, he seems a kind of Pied Piper who brings children running.

Line breaks and capital letters in the poem seem designed to emphasize particulars. *Just-spring*, capitalized, is the name of a holiday: the moment when spring begins. Dividing its name with a line break gives it more importance, perhaps; and *mud - / luscious* similarly takes emphasis. Why are the children's names telescoped (*eddieandbill, bettyandisbel*)? So that these names will be spoken rapidly, pell-mell, the way their owners run and the way children speak about their friends. And when the lame balloonman completes his transformation into Pan, the word *goat-footed* is framed with white space on a line by itself. Except by putting it in capitals, the poet could hardly have thrown more weight on it.

MLL *MyLiteratureLab Resources.* Photographs and biographical information for Cummings. Audio clip for "in Just-."

Carole Satyamurti, I SHALL PAINT MY NAILS RED, page 890

Satyamurti's poem demonstrates that there are other means than meter for organizing poetic language. In this case, syntax gives the poem a linguistic structure as formal as that of a sonnet. One might also say the poem has another structure—that of a list, a common genre but not one we usually associate with poetry (though we can upgrade it to the venerable literary device of the *catalogue*, as in Homer's catalogue of Greek ships in *The Iliad*). Notice that Satyamurti's lines are grammatically incomplete, unless we read them in conjunction with the title.

All this formal discussion shouldn't blind us to Satyamurti's provocative content. "I Shall Paint My Nails Red" does something that poetry should: it makes us think deeply about a part of our everyday world. It asks questions about something we might otherwise take for granted.

Alice Fulton, FAILURE, page 890

In an interview that appeared in the Spring 2005 issue of the journal *Folio*, Alice Fulton says:

> We're so used to the gentle, fringed appearance of the right margin in poems that a right-justified margin seems hard-edged, obdurate. The silence of the margin is formalized; the white space seems to solidify. . . . My poem "Failure". . . uses right-justified stanzas to suggest a sense of being up against It.

The layout on the page reinforces the poem's thematic commitment—bred by repeated, frustrating attempts to attain the unattainable—to "the dung / and starspit of what-is."

Another of Fulton's comments in that interview provides an interesting perspective on an earlier section of this chapter: "Poets are so lucky to have the line as a way of making meaning. I think it's why I've never been interested in writing 'prose poetry.' I don't want to give up the possibilities of the line."

WRITERS ON WRITING

Walt Whitman, THE POETRY OF THE FUTURE, page 891

Although Whitman created one of the main traditions of American free verse, he had surprisingly little to say about the verse technique he fostered. In this interesting passage from the 1876 preface to the reissue of *Leaves of Grass*, Whitman focuses on two different sorts of innovation—free expression of emotion and direct presentation of character. He sees these features of attitude, tone, and subject leading American poetry into the future.

24
Symbol

T. S. Eliot, THE BOSTON EVENING TRANSCRIPT, page 895

To help a class see the humor of Eliot's poem, try reading it aloud and pronouncing the name of the newspaper slowly and deliberately, in the dullest tones you can muster. This small gem can serve effectively to introduce an early, longer Eliot poem of spiritual desolation, "The Love Song of J. Alfred Prufrock."

 MyLiteratureLab Resources. Biography, critical overview, and bibliography for Eliot.

Emily Dickinson, THE LIGHTNING IS A YELLOW FORK, page 896

Perhaps the poet would have added more punctuation to this poem had she worked longer on it; a rough penciled draft is its only surviving manuscript. Students may ask, Isn't the fork a symbol? No, it is the other half of a metaphor: what the lightning is like. The lightning (like most literary symbols) is a physical thing or event, reportedly seen. The Apparatus of the Dark (neither fork nor lightning) is whatever dimly glimpsed furniture this cosmic house may hold. The fork seems too simple an instrument to deserve the name of Apparatus. The lightning is doing the revealing, not itself being revealed.

 MyLiteratureLab Resources. Biography, critical overview, and bibliography for Dickinson.

Thomas Hardy, NEUTRAL TONES, page 897

Students usually like to sort out the poem's white, gray, washed-out, and ashy things. Can anyone think of a more awful description of a smile than that in lines 9–10? The God in line 2 seems angry and awe-inspiring. He has chided or reproved the sun and caused it to turn pale in fear (like a schoolboy before a stern headmaster).

Line 8 is a stickler. In Hardy's first draft it read, "On which was more wrecked by our love." Both versions of the line seem awkward, and the present version is obscure, but probably the sense of this and the previous line goes: we exchanged a few words about the question, Which one of us had lost (suffered) the more by our love affair? (That is, after *which* we should mentally insert "of the two of us.")

For speculation about the facts behind "Neutral Tones," see Robert Gittings's fine biography *Young Thomas Hardy* (Boston: Little, 1975) 86–93. Much has been guessed about the possible love affair between young Hardy and his cousin Tryphena Sparks; but if the woman in "Neutral Tones" was indeed real, no one has identified her for sure.

Similar in imagery to "Neutral Tones" is this horrific line from Hardy's novel *The Woodlanders*, chapter 4, when a poverty-stricken woman, Marty South, sees her last hopes expire: "The bleared white visage of a sunless winter day emerged like a deadborn child" (cited by F. B. Pinion in *A Commentary on the Poems of Thomas Hardy* [New York: Barnes, 1977]).

MLL *MyLiteratureLab Resources.* Biography, critical overview, and bibliography for Hardy. Critical essay on "Neutral Tones."

Matthew, THE PARABLE OF THE GOOD SEED, page 898

"The Parable of the Good Seed" is one of three parables that Jesus tells to the crowd describing the "kingdom of heaven" in the thirteenth chapter of Matthew. After Jesus and the disciples leave the crowd and go into a house, the disciples ask him to explain this particular parable. Jesus obliges them with an explication. (We paraphrase the reply in the book following the text of the parable.) Here is his answer from Matthew:

> He answered and said unto them, "He that soweth the good seed is the Son of Man; the field is the world; the good seeds are the children of the kingdom; but the tares are the children of the wicked one; the enemy that sowed them is the devil; the harvest is the end of the world; and the reapers are the angels. As therefore the tares are gathered and burned in the fire; so shall it be in the end of this world. The Son of Man shall send forth his angels, and they shall gather out of his kingdom all things that offend, and them which do iniquity; and shall cast them into a furnace of fire; there shall be wailing and gnashing of teeth. Then shall the righteous shine forth as the sun in the kingdom of their Father. Who hath ears to hear, let him hear." (Matthew 13:37–43)

The special importance of this parable is that Jesus clearly states his own interpretation of the tale. He intends it, therefore, as an allegory with one consistent equivalent meaning assigned to each narrative element. Not all Gospel parables can be so easily allegorized. Some, such as "The Parable of the Prodigal Son," are so subtly complex as to allow multiple interpretations. Jesus himself told the disciples that his parables allowed two interpretations—one purely narrative reading open to the general public and another, deeper allegorical interpretation available to those who have been initiated in "the mysteries of the kingdom of heaven" (Matthew 13:10–23).

George Herbert, THE WORLD, page 899

The controlling image is established in the poem's opening phrase, "Love built a stately house"; we might liken this house, as the title suggests, to the world itself, with particular emphasis on our earthly existence and the soul's tenure in the body. In each of the poem's first three stanzas, a bad builder—Fortune, Pleasure, and Sin, respectively—causes the house to be flimsy and in danger of collapse, until the damage is repaired by a better craftsman. The razing of the house in the last stanza signifies the end of the world, and the "braver Palace" is, of course, heaven.

Edwin Markham, OUTWITTED, page 900

Broadly speaking, the circle in this poem symbolizes a fence or a barrier that draws a distinction between what it encloses and what it excludes. The symbol functions the same way both times; the difference lies in what is enclosed or excluded in each instance. So precise and traditional is Markham's use of the circle that we can describe it as a conventional symbol, perhaps even as an allegory—except, of course, for the poem's extreme brevity and lack of narrative.

The Wagner College Library has a large Edwin Markham Archive, some of which is available online. You can access the archive and hear a recording of Markham reading this poem by starting a search at <http://www.wagner.edu/library/embio>.

John Ciardi, A BOX COMES HOME, page 900

As a gunner on a B-29, John Ciardi flew 16 combat missions over Japan during the Second World War. Then, through the recommendation of a friend who knew that Ciardi was a widely published poet, he was appointed in April 1945 to write applications for awards and decorations, as well as letters of condolence to the families of men killed or missing in action. According to Ciardi's biographer, Edward Cifelli,

> The challenge was to make each letter sound as though the general had personally known each soldier, and Ciardi agonized over the work: "I did the best I could. But it was a bland kind of tinkering with tragedy. It tore me up. Some woman somewhere might treasure that lousy manufactured letter for the rest of her life . . . . " Then, in one of those ironic, not to say grisly, twists of fate that Ciardi was so aware of, his former plane and crew went down over Tokyo Bay on the third mission they flew without him. They took a direct hit in the wing gas tank, "and the plane just blew up, disintegrated in midair." In the incredible chanciness of war, Ciardi had been spared because he had been called upon to write letters of condolence—which he then had to write to the families of his own crew.

For many people, the phrase "the United States of America" might immediately call up an image of the symbol of the nation, the American flag. For the speaker of "A Box Comes Home" the phrase seems to link immediately to an image of that flag draped over the coffin of a serviceman, Arthur—whose relationship to the speaker is unspecified—who was killed in battle. From its title on, the poem is informed by the attitude expressed by Ciardi in the above passage—that our official rites and commemorations are "a bland kind of tinkering with tragedy," gestures thoroughly inadequate to the demands made of these young men by their country and the totality of their sacrifice in response to those demands. The fourth stanza implies that Arthur in life, his uniform, represented his country more nobly than it has represented him in death—although, of course, the United States is hardly singled out in this regard, as the second and third stanzas make clear. The last two stanzas call for an America that will not fail or betray Arthur and so many others like him, but will live up to its own ideals as heroically as Arthur did. Even so, the speaker has a sufficiently strong sense of history that he states this wish as a hope, not an expectation.

A great deal of scholarship on Ciardi was published in the nineties, much of it done by Edward Cifelli of the County College of Morris, New Jersey. Cifelli published *The Selected Letters of John Ciardi* (Fayetteville: U Arkansas P, 1991). His full-length biography, *John Ciardi*, appeared in 1997 along with a new edition of *The Collected Poems* (both from Akansas). These books present the life and work of the first major Italian American poet.

Robert Frost, THE ROAD NOT TAKEN, page 901

Stanley Burnshaw writes, in *Robert Frost Himself* (New York: Braziller, 1986), that Frost often said "The Road Not Taken" was about himself combined with Edward Thomas, a Welsh poet and good friend. Knowing this, Burnshaw confessed, didn't contribute much to his understanding of the poem. Still, the story is tantalizing. In *Robert Frost: The Years of Triumph* (New York: Holt, 1970) biographer Lawrance Thompson tells about the "excruciations through which this dour Welshman [Thomas] went each time he was required to make a choice." This amused Frost, who once said to Thomas, "No matter which road you take, you'll always sigh, and wish you'd taken another." "The Road Not Taken" (originally called "Two Roads") was apparently written to poke quiet fun at this failing. When Frost sent the poem in a letter to Thomas, the Welshman apparently missed the joke. He assumed, as have many readers since, that the speaker in the poem was Frost himself. Disappointed, Frost (according to Thompson) "could never bear to tell the truth about the failure of this lyric to perform as he intended it."

Despite the ambiguity that surrounds the poet's intent, the poem succeeds. The two roads are aptly symbolic of the choices we have to make almost every day of our lives. Still, perhaps the poem's essential playfulness is evident in the dramatic "sigh" with which the speaker expects some day to talk about his choice, and in the portentousness of the last line, which seems a bit exaggerated considering that the two roads were "really about the same."

A hardworking introduction to symbolism in poetry is that of Paul Hawkes of East Stroudsburg University. In a published article, he describes his classroom version of the TV game show "Family Feud," in which teams of students try to guess which meanings of certain symbols have occurred to most of the class. His aim is to show that a symbol, which may have widely familiar and traditional associations, can mean more or less the same to everyone; its meanings aren't the property of one reader alone. Then, to put this insight to use, he takes up "The Road Not Taken."

"I use this poem," he explains, "because it is simple and straightforward, offering little resistance to any student I may ask to summarize the paraphrasable content of the poem." He asks, "What statements in the poem, what choices of diction, suggest that the two roads are to be understood as something more than literal paths in the woods?" And students tend to reply, "A person wouldn't 'sigh' about a choice made years ago unless it was important," or, "The speaker wouldn't regret it 'ages hence' if it were only a path," or, "Why else would he say the decision 'has made all the difference' unless that decision were life-changing?" (We're paraphrasing and condensing Mr. Hawkes's examples.)

Someone will usually guess that the choice of roads suggests Frost's personal choice of careers: Should he or should he not become a poet? Hawkes then encourages the class to speculate on other possible life choices: marriage, children, a job, relocation. Perhaps this poem is about decision-making; perhaps the nature of the roads need not be specified. As in *Pilgrim's Progress*, a road or a journey on it is a traditional and conventional symbol for life; a fork or crossroads, a decision or turning-point. "The poem," he concludes, "suggests regret not for the way life has turned out but for the severe limitations life imposes on our desire to explore its possibilities." (See "Fire, Flag, Feud, and Frost: Teaching the Interpretation of Symbols," *Exercise Exchange* [Spring 1991] 6–11.)

 MyLiteratureLab Resources. Biography, critical overview, critical articles, and bibliography for Frost. Critical essay on "The Road Not Taken."

Christina Rossetti, UPHILL, page 902

This allegorical poem develops a conventional simile: life is like a journey (shades of *Pilgrim's Progress*!). The road is the path of life; the day, a lifespan; the inn at the end of the road, the grave; other wayfarers, the dead; the door, the mouth of the grave (or perhaps the gate of Heaven); the beds, cold clay (or perhaps Heavenly rest). The title suggests another familiar notion: that life is a struggle all the way.

One possible way to paraphrase line 14: "You'll find the end result of your life-long strivings: namely, death and the comfort of extinction." A more happily Christian paraphrase is possible, for Rossetti professed herself a believer: "Your labor shall bring you to your goal, the sight of the Lord." Without admitting the possibility of such a faith, the poem will seem grimmer and more cynical than it is.

Do these two characters seem individual persons? Not in the least. This is a straight question-and-answer poem, a dialogue between two stick figures.

Christian Wiman, POŠTOLKA, page 902

As the speaker is in Prague, the words he is learning are presumably words of the Czech language. The kestrel, a reddish-gray falcon, seems to him to be "a concentration of its light" willed by "the red dusk"; this sense of there being something willed or even fated in the falcon's arrival is underlined by the fact that "pane by pane it eyed / the stories facing ours / but never looked inside," but later it directly meets the speaker's gaze. Among innumerable superstitions, the appearance of a red bird may signify good luck, or the arrival of any bird at one's window might be an evil omen—which would seem to be the case here, to judge by the shiver that seizes the speaker's companion. Either way, one should make a wish on it, whether to take advantage of the opportunity or to neutralize the foreboding. He is urged to do so by his companion, in whose cheek a reddish "bloom of blood" appears and then disappears, coming and going like the moment, like the bird itself, and like the "almost love" that the bird symbolizes.

FOR REVIEW AND FURTHER STUDY

EXERCISE: *Symbol Hunting*, page 903

William Carlos Williams, THE TERM, page 903
Ted Kooser, CARRIE, page 904
Jane Hirshfield, TREE, page 904
Jon Stallworthy, AN EVENING WALK, page 905
Lorine Niedecker, POPCORN-CAN COVER, page 905
Wallace Stevens, ANECDOTE OF THE JAR, page 906

"The Term" should be taken literally; its key phrase is "Unlike a man," suggesting that it would be pointless to look for symbolic meaning in the sheet of paper, since its resemblance to a man is superficial and irrelevant. "Carrie" presents dust in its traditional role as a symbol for human mortality (although Kooser uses the symbol in a charmingly original way). Jane Hirshfield's "Tree" spells out its symbolism fairly directly: the "house" contains "your life," which is represented by "this clutter of soup cans and books"; in contrast, the "great calm being" of the redwood tree embodies "immensity"; will you attune yourself to this larger life spirit or lose yourself in the petty details of day-to-day existence? In "An Evening Walk," the author explicitly makes the unanswered ringing telephone, with "[i]ts dark voice welling up," a symbol of "animal grief," a grief intensified by the pain and frustration of trying and failing to connect with someone else; all of these feelings are compounded by the simile in the poem's last line. "Popcorn-can cover" uses literal language in a manner reminiscent of Williams, but the title image of the popcorn-can cover screwed to the wall can be taken as a symbol of the house dweller's poverty and pragmatism. Niedecker does not force the symbolism of the image, yet it is there for our notice. "Anecdote of the Jar" contains central symbols.

Students familiar with Stevens sometimes reason, "The jar is a thing of the imagination, that's why it's superior to the wilderness—it makes order out of formless nature, the way Stevens thinks art is supposed to do." But Stevens is constantly warning us of the dangers of the mind divorced from the physical world, and we think he means this gray, bare, dominion-taking jar to be ominous. Who could think a wilderness *slovenly* before it came along? Some critics take the phrase *of a port in air* to mean a portal, "an evanescent entry . . . to order in a scene of disorder" (Ronald Sukenick, *Wallace Stevens: Musing the Obscure* [New York: New York UP, 1967]). We read it differently: *portly*, imposing, pompous. Although it is true that Stevens frequently raises the same philosophic or aesthetic questions, from poem to poem he keeps supplying very different answers. See the brilliant essay on Stevens by J. Hillis Miller in *Poets of Reality* (Cambridge: Harvard UP, 1965).

Jerald Bullis has written an intriguing poem in response to "Anecdote of the Jar." Thanks to Peter A. Fritzell of Lawrence University for discovering it.

Buck It

Take a shot-up bucket in a swale of woods—
For years "things" have been adjusting to it:
The deer have had to warp their whylom way
Through the fern to honor the order in their blood
That says not to kick it; the visiting woodcock

Probably take it for some kind of newfangled stump,
And doubtless welcome any addition that offers
Additional cover—especially if its imposition
Provides a shelving stay for worm-rich mulch;
A rivulet of breeze low-eddying the swale
Breaks around it much the way a stress's
Flow gets an increment of curvature
From encounter with an old Singer
Sewing machine; the ferns thereabout have turned
A bit more plagiotropic; if it's upright
And the lid's off it's an urn for leaves, bark-bits,
Bird droppings; but in the scope of the whole
Forty-acre woodpatch is it likely
To take dominion everywhere? no more
Than a barbed-wire tangle of words or a good jar.

MLL *MyLiteratureLab Resources.* Biography, critical overview, and bibliography for Stevens. Interactive reading of "Anecdote of the Jar."

WRITERS ON WRITING

W. B. *Yeats*, POETIC SYMBOLS, page 906

Symbols are central to Yeats's poetics. They are not arbitrary creations of the writer but primal forms of human communications—arising like Carl Jung's universal archetypes from the unconscious. For Yeats, therefore, the symbol is in some sense independent of the poet and carries "numberless meanings" beyond the often narrow intentions of the author.

25
Myth and Narrative

This chapter was revised in recent editions to make it more accessible to students. Although the chapter still begins with a discussion of what constitutes myth, there is now an attempt to relate the idea of myth to students' experience with popular culture, especially movies and television. This shift may initially annoy some instructors, but we hope that, if they stick with the chapter, they will discover that we have tried to show how similar myths permeate popular and literary culture. We want to make the material of this chapter less threatening to beginning students while still useful to instructors excited by the prospect of teaching Lawrence, Yeats, and Wordsworth.

Besides the poems in this chapter, other poems in the text will readily lend themselves to the study of myth and its pervasiveness in literature.

The story of Adam and Eve which figures in Frost's "Nothing Gold Can Stay" might be supplemented with Anthony Hecht's "Adam" (in "Poems for Further Reading").

Personal myths may be found in the poems of Blake, in Hardy's "Convergence of the Twain," and in certain poems of Yeats outside this chapter, such as "Leda and the Swan" and "Sailing to Byzantium."

Poems containing central references to familiar classical myths are Cummings's "in Just-," with its reincarnation of the Great God Pan, and Allen Ginsberg's "A Supermarket in California." Christian mythos is of course inseparable from the devotional poems of Donne and Herbert, from Hopkins's poems and G. K. Chesterton's "The Donkey," from Eliot's "Journey of the Magi" and Yeats's "The Magi," from Milton's sonnet on his blindness, and from many more.

In this chapter, Thomas Hardy (in "The Oxen") and William Wordsworth (in "The World Is Too Much with Us") sadly contemplate myths in decline.

Robert Frost, NOTHING GOLD CAN STAY, page 911

Many of your students may already be familiar with this popular poem. The relevant detail of the poem in this context is how much narrower its meaning would be if the reference to Eden were dropped. This single mythic allusion expands the resonance of the poem from the transience of spring's beauty to the transience of all perfection.

In his excellent study *Robert Frost: A Literary Life Reconsidered* (reissued with a new preface in 1993 by the University Press of New England), William Pritchard savors the poem's remarkable compression in the following way:

> The poem is striking for the way it combines the easy delicacy of "Her early leaf's a flower" with monumentalities about Eden and the transient fading

of all such golden things, all stated in a manner that feels inevitable. It is as if in writing "Nothing Gold Can Stay," Frost had in mind his later definition of poetry as a momentary stay against confusion. The poem's last word proclaims the momentariness of the "gold" that things like flowers and Eden, dawn and poems share. So the shortness of the poem is also expressive of its sense. (Quoted by permission of the author)

MLL *MyLiteratureLab Resources.* Biography, critical overview, critical articles, and bibliography for Frost. Critical essays for "Nothing Gold Can Stay."

D. H. Lawrence, BAVARIAN GENTIANS, page 911

Written in 1929 when Lawrence was ill and nearing death, this splendid poem has been read as a kind of testament. As Keith Sagar has paraphrased it, "the poet's soul has been invited to the nuptials and accepts with joy." Dissolution offers not mere oblivion but the promise of renewed life, the cyclical rebirth of both the gentians and Persephone (*The Art of D. H. Lawrence* [Cambridge: Cambridge UP, 1966], 244–45). Another famous poem of Lawrence's last months, "The Ship of Death," may be read as a companion to this.

Why is "Bavarian Gentians" a better title for the poem than Lawrence's first thought, "Glory of Darkness"?

William Wordsworth, THE WORLD IS TOO MUCH WITH US, page 912

As its sense and its iambic meter indicate, the opening line calls for a full stress on the *with*.

Wordsworth isn't arguing for a return to pagan nature worship. Rather, like Gerard Manley Hopkins's blasting tirade in "God's Grandeur," he is dismayed that Christians, given to business and banking, have lost sight of sea and vernal woods. They should pay less heed to the world, more to the earth. What "powers" have they laid waste? The ability to open themselves to nature's benevolent inspirations. Modestly, the poet includes himself in the *us* who deserve reproof. The impatient outburst ("Great God!") is startlingly unbookish and locates the break in sense between octave and sestet in an unconventional place.

Compare Wordsworth's "Composed upon Westminster Bridge" for a somewhat similar theme.

MLL *MyLiteratureLab Resources.* Biography, critical overview, and bibliography for Wordsworth.

H. D. [Hilda Doolittle], HELEN, page 913

What a cold, hate-inspiring queen H. D. portrays! She makes a sharp contrast with the lovable image of Helen as a child in Yeats's "Long-legged Fly."

Heather Burke's student essay on "Helen" at the end of this chapter provides an intelligent and fairly comprehensive close reading of the poem. For a few notes on recent scholarly activity on H. D., see the note on her poem "Heat" in this manual.

ARCHETYPE

Louise Bogan, MEDUSA, page 914

Bogan's chilling poem is a perfect example of how modern poets have used classical myths to new ends. Bogan presents Medusa quite faithfully to the Greek legend, but she employs the myth for distinctively modern psychological purposes—to portray a state of spiritual and emotional paralysis. The speaker is literally petrified in an eternal moment. Nothing will ever change. One curious feature of "Medusa" is that the speaker shows no surprise, no bitterness, no anger at the paralyzing Gorgon—only total resignation.

Bogan's biographer, Elizabeth Frank, believes the poem portrays the poet's mother as the paralyzing female monster. While there is no specific textual evidence for this interpretation, it is not inconsistent with the facts of Bogan's troubled past. This psychoanalytical/biographical interpretation, however, is not especially useful in reading "Medusa" as poetry. In fact, to reduce the poem to any single allegorical interpretation limits the powerful symbolic resonance of the central situation. The speaker's paralysis can be read with equal validity as emotional, spiritual, imaginative, or artistic. The poem invites us to interpret the speaker's dilemma beyond its literal narrative meaning, but the text does not demand any single construction.

John Keats, LA BELLE DAME SANS MERCI, page 915

This poem, unpublished in Keats's lifetime, was written in 1819, and some of its phrasing was later revised by Keats. While it is customary to accept an author's final version of a work as definitive, it is generally agreed that the original text of "La Belle Dame sans Merci" is fresher and more effective, and it is that text which we have printed here. The poem's title and basic situation are derived from a long French poem by Alain Chartier (c.1385–c.1433), translated into English by Sir Richard Ros around 1640.

Predilections for the ballad form, for medieval settings, and for supernatural themes were all characteristic of one strain of English Romanticism, as exemplified earlier (at about the time of Keats's birth) in the work of Samuel Taylor Coleridge, most notably in "Christabel" and "The Rime of the Ancient Mariner," and Robert Southey. Notice how many of the attributes of the medieval folk ballad Keats imitates here: lack of rime in the first and third lines of each quatrain; occasional metrical irregularities; pointless specificity ("kisses four"—compare "Nine bean-rows will I have there" in Yeats's "The Lake Isle of Innisfree"); shifting (and unidentified) speakers; and elliptical narration.

The season is clearly autumn, a time traditionally depicted as one of melancholy and decline, as is made clear through the descriptions provided by the unidentified speaker of the first three stanzas. Some have seen an autobiographical dimension in this melancholy and decline, speculating that Keats used the myth of the succubus-like fairy creature who enchants and seduces men, only to abandon them, as a way of expressing his complex feelings toward his fiancée, Fanny Brawne. The historical record, however, shows her to have been an intelligent young woman who reciprocated the depth and tenderness of his love—a far cry from the shallow and heartless flirt of legend toying with the affections of the tormented, dying poet.

 MyLiteratureLab Resources. Photographs, biographical information, critical overview, and bibliography for Keats.

PERSONAL MYTH

William Butler Yeats, THE SECOND COMING, page 917

The brief discussion in the book leaves several points untouched. Students may be asked to explain Yeats's opening image of the falcon and the falconer; to discuss the meaning of the *Blood-dimmed tide* and the *ceremony of innocence*; to explain how the rocking cradle at Bethlehem can be said to "vex" twenty centuries to nightmare; and to recall what they know about the sphinx.

In *A Vision*, Yeats sets forth his notion of the two eras of history (old and new) as two intertwined conelike gyres, revolving inside each other in opposing directions. He puts it succinctly in a note for a limited edition of his poem *Michael Robartes and the Dancer* (1921):

> The end of an age, which always receives the revelation of the character of the next age, is represented by the coming of one gyre to its place of greatest expansion and of the other to that of its greatest contraction. At the present moment the life gyre is sweeping outward, unlike that before the birth of Christ which was narrowing, and has almost reached its greatest expansion. The revelation which approaches will however take its character from the contrary movement of the interior gyre.

Students can be asked to apply this explanation to "The Second Coming." (In fact, this might be a writing assignment.)

For other evidence of Yeats's personal mythology, direct students to "Leda and the Swan" and "Sailing to Byzantium." For alternative versions of "The Second Coming," see Yeats's worksheets for the poem as transcribed by John Stallworthy in *Between the Lines: Yeats's Poetry in the Making* (Oxford: Oxford UP, 1963).

 MyLiteratureLab Resources. Biography, critical overview, and bibliography for Yeats.

Gregory Orr, TWO LINES FROM THE BROTHERS GRIMM, page 918

When he was twelve years old, Gregory Orr shot and killed his younger brother in a hunting accident. As he recounts in his memoir *The Blessing*, this event left him emotionally devastated and near-suicidal, and it had a severely damaging effect on the surviving members of his family, whose customary method of dealing with tragedy was silence and emotional detachment. Once one knows this history, it is almost impossible not to interpret the poem in light of it, and to see the "Hansel and Gretel"-like opening of the poem (and the horror-movie-like image in line 4) as Orr's response to the accident and its traumatic effect on his family and their relationships with one another. The poem also exemplifies—not through its content, but by virtue of its very existence—a central theme of Orr's memoir, the healing and transformative power of art.

If you choose to incorporate this information in your presentation of the poem, you might wish first to determine the most effective way of doing so; in this connection, you may find it helpful to reread Natasha Trethewey's poem "White Lies" and the discussion of it in both the anthology itself and this manual.

Diane Thiel, MEMENTO MORI IN MIDDLE SCHOOL, page 918

Diane Thiel has provided this note about her poem:

> For years, I wanted to write about this memory of an odd middle school project I presented on Dante's *Inferno*. The piece existed only as notes for some years. About twenty years after the childhood incident described in the piece, the poem finally came together and found its form as *terza rima* (the form Dante invented in the Middle Ages). I chose a rather loose interpretation of *terza rima* for the poem (varying the end-rhymes between exact rhymes, slant rhymes, and assonance) because the variation seemed to best suit the conversational diction and tone of the poem.
>
> I think of "*Memento Mori* in Middle School" as an echo-location, a multilayered term I invented in the book, *Echolocations* (2001), which contains the poem, to refer to conversations with the past. In the case of this poem, the conversation is with both this work of art from a distant medieval past and the more immediate echoes of a childhood interpretation of the piece. The union of the *Inferno* with that trial-filled middle school age becomes a reflection of threshold crossings that burn themselves into our memories.

An Exercise for Students:
In my writing guide, *Writing Your Rhythm*, I include an exercise which asks students to respond to a poem (preferably choosing from a more distant century) using the form of the chosen piece. This approach helped "*Memento Mori* in Middle School" find its form.

MYTH AND POPULAR CULTURE

Charles Martin, TAKEN UP, page 921

"Taken Up" illustrates how a good poet can borrow potentially hackneyed material from popular culture and, by linking it to the underlying myth, transform it into genuine poetry.

Martin links the popular myth of flying saucers with the eternal human need for the divine. His golden aliens (whose bodies are so fine as to seem incorporeal) are almost godlike. What they offer the humans who waited for them is a version of heaven. (Notice that the aliens mention angels in factual terms; the spiritual and divine are real to them.) The situation of the poem on a hill deliberately recalls the Transfiguration and Ascension episodes of the Gospels. The aliens are science fiction versions of angels—perhaps even gods.

One way to start a classroom discussion on the poem is to ask if anyone has seen Spielberg's *Close Encounters of the Third Kind* and encourage someone to describe the film's ending. Then compare it to the poem and discuss from what mythic sources they both draw their inspiration.

Andrea Hollander Budy, SNOW WHITE, page 922

"The story of the prince" makes Snow White's experience seem unique and inaccessible, and thus it serves as a convenient cover story to keep other, frustrated women from trying to horn in on her good thing. The reference to "the footprints of your own / children" calls up images of women with gangs of children underfoot, a detail suggestive of a life whose grind and "plainness" they would be only too glad to escape by fleeing into the forest to be made much of by seven attentive little men.

Anne Sexton, CINDERELLA, page 923
WRITERS ON WRITING
Anne Sexton, TRANSFORMING FAIRY TALES, page 926

"Cinderella" was part of Sexton's fifth collection, *Transformations* (Boston: Houghton, 1971). This volume consisted of seventeen long poems that retold fairy tales in idiosyncratic versions. Although earlier poets such as Auden and Jarrell had published revisionist fairy tale poems, Sexton's book proved extremely influential by claiming the fairy tale as the special territory of feminist poets. Some critics (as well as Sexton's editor, Paul Brooks) felt these poems represented a falling off from her more compressed earlier poetry, and there is some truth in that criticism. But the poems have remarkable narrative energy and originality.

"Cinderella" begins like a lyric poem with a series of four rags-to-riches stories that seem gleaned from the tabloids. But just when it might seem that Sexton would wrap up her short poem, she leaps into an extended narrative. Her version of Cinderella is very close to the Perrault original, although she spices it up with contemporary images and large doses of irony. Then, as the story comes to its conclusion, Sexton emphasizes the violent aspects of the original so that it overwhelms the romance. In the last stanza, Sexton resumes the original structure of the poem with a bitterly ironic version of "happily ever after."

To use an overworked term, Sexton "deconstructs" the happy ending of a fairy tale; marriage, in her view, is no solution to Cinderella's problems but the beginning of new ones.

The two letters included in "Writers on Writing"—one to her publisher, the other to a fellow writer—describe Sexton's intentions in turning popular fairy tales to her own ends. She wants to make the stories "as wholly personal as my most intimate poems." This attitude may surprise students who don't yet understand how an artist's treatment can transform borrowed material (like myth or legend) into something unique and idiosyncratic.

26
Poetry and Personal Identity

"Poetry and Personal Identity" provides students with an introduction to the ways in which a poet's race, gender, cultural background, age, and other factors influence his or her writing. The chapter explores the different ways that poets have defined their personal, social, sexual, and ethnic identities. It also examines the problematic relationship between the author and the poem.

The first section focuses on autobiography and explores the idea of "confessional" poetry. Having drilled students earlier in this book that poems cannot be read as direct autobiography, we now relax a bit and let them think about the tricky relationship between life and art through Sylvia Plath's brilliant but harrowing "Lady Lazarus." This issue usually generates lively classroom discussion. The challenge will be to keep the discussion on track by focusing on the specific text under examination.

We then broaden the discussion by showing how autobiography includes issues of culture, race, age, and gender. Two compelling poems on minority identity—by Rhina Espaillat and Claude McKay—show different approaches toward ethnic writing. With Samuel Menashe and Francisco X. Alarcón we see poems about Jewish and Mexican American identity. The coming-of-age poems by Judith Ortiz Cofer and Amy Uyematsu draw on their authors' Hispanic and Asian backgrounds.

Anne Stevenson's short poem "Sous-Entendu" focuses on gender in terms that students should understand from their everyday life, while Adrienne Rich's poem explores it in more general, archetypal terms. Yusef Komunyakaa's powerful Vietnam poem raises questions of identity that transcend racial categories; he is a black veteran, but he seems to speak for all Vietnam vets without losing his personal identity (reflected in the Vietnam Veterans Memorial's black stone). With Donald Justice's striking "Men at Forty," we begin looking at issues of age; these questions are explored—with merciless honesty—in Philip Larkin's "Aubade," a poem that will disturb everyone. Andrew Hudgins's poem explores both religion and the gap between generations. Shirley Geok-lin Lim's poem portrays the ambivalent emotions of the immigrant caught between cultures.

Sylvia Plath, LADY LAZARUS, page 934

This poem was written over seven days in late October 1962 about two weeks after the composition of "Daddy" (in the "Poems for Further Reading" chapter). On February 11, 1963, Plath committed suicide by putting her head in a gas oven.

In her 1989 biography of Plath, *Bitter Fame*, Anne Stevenson describes "Lady Lazarus" as a "merciless" self-projection of the author, who cast herself as "the central figure of her mythic world." Considering several of the poems written that final October, Stevenson continues:

The poems are extraordinary *performances*—not only in their consummate poetic skill, but in that their central figure is giving a performance as though before a single quelled spectator or in a fairground . . .

Stevenson concludes:

These poems, penetrating the furthest reaches of disdain and rage, are bereft of all normal "human" feeling. Hurt has hardened to hate, and death is omnipresent.

Surely the dark anger and aching death-wish are tangible in "Lady Lazarus." This poem is spoken by a voice beyond hope. If Plath is a performer, she performs only a script of her own merciless invention.

One stylistic note: "Lady Lazarus" (like "Daddy") is full of German tags. You might ask students why she uses German so much in these late poems. The Nazi connection will be easy for them to see, but it may be worthwhile to mention that Plath's father, Doctor Otto Plath (Ph.D. in entomology), was a German immigrant who spoke with a heavy accent. In other words, there is something to interest both formalist and biographical critics in this chilling late poem.

MLL *MyLiteratureLab Resources.* Longman Lecture on "Lady Lazarus."

Rhina Espaillat, BILINGUAL / BILINGÜE, page 937

Espaillat's poem is an excellent demonstration of the famous dictum of William Carlos Williams, "No ideas but in things." How better to demonstrate the challenges and frustrations of shuttling between two languages (and two cultures) than to employ both languages in the statement itself? The use of both English and Spanish also vividly underscores the daughter's inability to maintain the divisions that her father insists on, divisions that he hopes will prevent his daughter from becoming Americanized to the point where she will be alienated from their heritage and even from him. Removing the Spanish phrases would indeed change the poem, and significantly for the worse. The speaker's heart is one in its ability to cherish both parts of her identity, but the strain of doing so is evident throughout the text.

CULTURE, RACE, AND ETHNICITY

Claude McKay, AMERICA, page 938

McKay was one of the first of many black American writers who emigrated from the West Indies. (Students might write an interesting comparison between McKay's sonnet and the later Caribbean poet Derek Walcott's "The Virgins," to be found in the "Poems for Further Reading" chapter.) McKay was born in Jamaica in 1891 and immigrated to the United States in 1912. Although shaped by black experience, "America" reaches for—and indeed achieves—universality of expression; it articulates the frustrated dreams and overpowering desires of any young immigrant. The speaker in this poem defines himself not by his ethnic identity but by his existential identity—as an outsider—in a heartless, if vital society.

Samuel Menashe, THE SHRINE WHOSE SHAPE I AM, page 939

Menashe's poem defines Jewishness in a mystical biological way. "Breathed in flesh by shameless love," he was born from his parents' bodies, and his body contains the history of his people. "There is no Jerusalem but this" means, among other things, that his Jewishness is not found in a geographical place but in himself: his body is the lost temple ("the shrine") of his people, his bones the hills of Zion. This poem may seem difficult to students at first, but once they understand the central metaphor, they usually find it fascinating. A good place to start discussing the poem is its title, which contains the central idea.

Menashe's short, compressed poems have been repeatedly praised by leading critics such as Stephen Spender, Donald Davie, Kathleen Raine, and Hugh Kenner, but his work remains little known. Menashe lives in New York City in a cold-water flat. His most recent work is *New and Selected Poems* (2005), for which he won the first Neglected Masters Award from the Poetry Foundation.

Francisco X. Alarcón, THE X IN MY NAME, page 940

Alarcón's poem is about the relation between one's name and one's identity. On a literal level, the X in Alarcón's name stands presumably as an abbreviation for Xavier (a name that almost always identifies one as being of Catholic background and most commonly Hispanic descent, though many an Irishman bears it, too). But Alarcón sees the letter as a symbol for the X an illiterate peasant must sign on the legal documents that control his or her life. Ultimately, Alarcón also implicitly uses the X (in a way perhaps influenced by Malcolm X) as an algebraic symbol for the elements of his identity lost or repressed in America.

Francisco X. Alarcón teaches at the University of California at Davis. He publishes poetry in both Spanish and English.

Judith Ortiz Cofer, QUINCEAÑERA, page 940

Cofer creates a wonderfully detailed speaker for this coming-of-age poem—a young woman on the brink of adulthood only half cognizant of the mysteries of her new identities. Still partly a child, the speaker embraces her new self with a mixture of awe, fear, and pride. Her childhood is symbolized by the dolls put in the chest "like dead / children." The fifteen-year-old now stands in a middle ground between childhood and marriage. Her new status is represented most clearly by the menstrual blood that privately confirms her new status as an adult woman at least partially independent from her mother (who will no longer wash her clothes and sheets). Although on one level the poem presents a universal female situation, the title, images, and mythology are distinctly Latin Catholic. Cofer's poem demonstrates that a poem does not necessarily lose universality by being embodied in a specific cultural framework. As William Stafford observed, "All events and experiences are local, somewhere."

Amy Uyematsu, DELIBERATE, page 941

Without knowing that the author is a sansei (third-generation Japanese American), one might assume, from the Los Angeles setting and other details, that the speaker—who, along with her friends, dreads being mistaken for white, the quintessence of the uncool—is Hispanic. Awareness of the author's (and presumably the speaker's) Asian heritage gives another layer of meaning to the title, with its implication of assuming styles of dress and behavior that do not come out of one's own culture. The reference to "Daddy's muddy gardening shoes," which evokes traditional mainstream American attitudes toward the Japanese and suggests how badly these girls wish to escape the burden of those attitudes, also stirs the intriguing possibility that what they are doing, essentially, is exchanging one stereotype for another.

Yusef Komunyakaa, FACING IT, page 942

This powerful poem requires little commentary. One feature of the poem wants special mention because students may overlook it: the *entire* poem describes what the speaker sees on the polished black granite of the Vietnam Veterans Memorial. What he witnesses there is the combination of the memorial itself and what the mirror-like stone reflects. *Reflection* (line 6) is therefore the key word in the poem, a word the author uses in both senses, for, as the speaker studies the name on the stone, he reflects on his wartime experience and flashes back to the death of a fellow soldier. The way the stone both mirrors and transforms the reality around it is the external symbol for the speaker's internal experience.

GENDER

Anne Stevenson, SOUS-ENTENDU, page 943

Students will have no trouble understanding the situation of this poem, but you may need to push them to explore the role of language between the two people. Not only does everything the people say (and don't say) have two meanings— one literal, the other sexual—but the words they speak metaphorically become part of the clothes they remove.

Emily Grosholz, LISTENING, page 944

The speaker of Emily Grosholz's poem is an expectant mother. The listener is the unborn child in her womb. The speaker develops the idea of how words connect mother and child in a series of metaphors and allusions. She will weave her new son "a birthplace" out of words. Likewise, language will "re-create the gardens of the world," including perhaps the original Garden of Eden, a landscape of pure grace and innocence. Language is also called a "cradle" for the child. All of these images are positive and sustaining. The unborn son "still on his stalk" is implicitly compared to a flower—a part of creation that lacks language. (The stalk is also perhaps a more specific metaphor for the umbilical cord that connects mother and son.) The mother will give him the gift of language "to draw him out" into his full being.

Students might enjoy comparing Grosholz's images and metaphors with those in Sylvia Plath's "Metaphors," which addresses a similar subject.

EXERCISE: *Donald Justice*, MEN AT FORTY, page 945
           Adrienne Rich, WOMEN, page 945

As anyone who tries to translate the images and metaphors of either poem into the voice of the opposite gender discovers, both of these poems are embedded in the sexual identity of the speaker. But the experiences they describe still speak to the opposite sex. The poems' structures do survive the translation, which demonstrates that good art can be both specific and universal.

For an example of how a skilled poet translated one set of these images across genders, here is a poem by Andrea Hollander Budy from her award-winning *House Without a Dreamer* (Brownsville: Story Line, 1993):

Women at Fifty
after Donald Justice

All of their doors
Have closed and their daughters'
Rooms betray a familiar faint perfume
That says *I'll not be back.*

They pause sometimes
At the top of the stairs
To stroke the bannister,
Its perfect knots.

They invite other women now
Only to clean. And like queens in fairy tales
They turn their heads from mirrors
That hold secrets they've kept

Even from themselves,
As they look into their husbands' faces
When their husbands say
They only look.

Women at fifty
Corner a cricket with a broom
And do not kill it, but shoo it out of the house
Into the abundant silence.

(Poem reprinted by permission of the author and Story Line Press.)

For Review and Further Study

Shirley Geok-lin Lim, Learning to love America, page 946

The title of this poem may immediately suggest the speaker's ambivalence about her situation: her love for America is not immediate and instinctive, but must be acquired through a learning process. Complex feelings are shown throughout the text. Lines 2–4 suggest the necessity of letting go of what is past and cannot be regained, along with an acceptance of the newfound land that sounds grudging at best; lines 15–16 also point to the immense difficulties involved in uprooting oneself and one's family and trying to put down roots in a new place. Many other details point to more positive aspects of the experience of assimilation: a sense of inclusion (line 5), personal integration and wholeness (lines 9–11), and freedom (line 12). The last five lines reinforce the complexity of the speaker's responses, telling us that while the love of a new country, or the sense of belonging in the place where one has come, may not be a spontaneous and rapturous response, it is in the end a necessary and inevitable one.

Lim, who was born and educated in Malacca, Malaysia, earned her Ph.D. in English at Brandeis. For years she taught at Westchester Community College in New York. She is currently a professor at the University of California at Santa Barbara.

Andrew Hudgins, Elegy for My Father, Who Is Not Dead, page 946

Hudgins's poem explores religious identity—and, by extension, a generation gap. He and his father see death differently. The father has a devout Christian's faith in an afterlife; the speaker, by contrast, is not sure. The son is not against his father's religion, he simply doesn't share its consolations.

Students can compare the father's vision of death in this poem with the bleak view of the speaker in Philip Larkin's "Aubade" at the end of the chapter.

Alastair Reid, Speaking a Foreign Language, page 947

Alastair Reid is a Scottish poet who has lived all of his adult life abroad—in Spain, the United States, and now the Dominican Republic. Although he is best known as a translator of Neruda, Borges, and other Latin American authors and as a *New Yorker* contributor, Reid is a superb poet. "Speaking a Foreign Language" brings a double perspective to the challenge of communicating in a second tongue: Reid portrays the roles of both speaker and listener. "What faith / we rest in one sentence," Reid writes, "hoping a smile will follow," as he portrays the role of the speaker. Then in the second stanza he shifts perspective from the speaker to the listener ("And yet, to hear . . .") and affirms how our common humanity helps translate "syntax into love."

Philip Larkin, AUBADE, page 948

"Aubade" was the last substantial poem that Philip Larkin wrote. Except for a few minor short poems and occasional verses, he produced no more poetry in his remaining eight years. "I didn't abandon poetry," he later remarked, "it abandoned me." In this context, it's hard not to see "Aubade" as a kind of summing up—and if so, what a chilling summation!

"Aubade" is a confessional poem about old age and the fear of death. Larkin's poems often begin in observation and only midway move into a personal tone. "Aubade" begins with a surprising personal confession ("I work all day and get half drunk at night"). Waking alone in bed in the middle of the night, the speaker confronts his own mortality and discovers he has no defenses—neither philosophical ("No rational being / Can fear a thing it will not feel" he notes ironically) nor religious ("That vast moth-eaten musical brocade / Created to pretend we never die"). Larkin sees death without any illusions and can barely survive the vision. Ultimately, he can only resolve to meet it when he must ("Death is no different whined at than withstood").

The British critic John Bayley sees Larkin's ability to confront this frightening subject so candidly in poetry as a kind of moral victory. Larkin, Bayley claims, "goes on to descant with an almost joyful eloquence on the fear of death and the terror of extinction. The fear is all too genuine but the fact of the poetry overcomes it."

Students may want to compare this poem to Andrew Hudgins's "Elegy for My Father, Who Is Not Dead." In Hudgins's poem, religious faith banishes the fear of death for the father. It would be hard to find a starker contrast in tone or images between the two visions of death.

WRITERS ON WRITING

Rhina Espaillat, BEING A BILINGUAL WRITER, page 949

This passage from the Afterword to *Where Horizons Go* (1998), Rhina Espaillat's second book of poems, is not only an excellent gloss on her poem "Bilingual / Bilingüe" but also an intriguing and enlightening discussion of the dilemma of the bilingual writer. Espaillat shows us how the choice of a language involves so many other, larger choices between cultures and even loved ones, leading to difficulties that are made even more complex by the fact that pure choice—the father's insistence on an absolute division between the world inside the family's apartment and the larger alien world that surrounds it—is impossible when one lives in a foreign culture. Instead, one must endlessly negotiate between the two worlds, in a process that brings inevitable stress, confusion, and pain. But in this excerpt, as in the poem, Espaillat stresses her ultimate reconciliation of her two cultures, along with deeper discoveries that this reconciliation provides. As she says elsewhere in the Afterword, "There is a sense in which every poet is bilingual, and those of us who are more overtly so are only living metaphors for the condition that applies to us all."

27
Translation

IS POETIC TRANSLATION POSSIBLE?

WORLD POETRY

Li Po, DRINKING ALONE BENEATH THE MOON, pages 954–956

The small unit on Li Po (pronounced Lee-Bo) offers a brief introduction to the pleasures and challenges of Chinese poetry, perhaps humanity's longest thriving poetic tradition. The T'ang Dynasty writer Li Po is traditionally considered, with his contemporary Tu Fu, one of China's two greatest poets. We have presented one of his most famous poems in four versions—Chinese characters, phonetic transcription, literal translation, and literary translation. (Note how the original Chinese rhymes, with a regular number of syllables and characters per line.) The central image of the lonely drinker and the moon has a special poignancy in the Chinese literary tradition since the hard-drinking Li Po legendarily died trying to embrace the reflection of the moon in a river.

There are a great many English translations of Li Po. Having read through many alternatives, we chose Arthur Waley's famous version, "Drinking Alone by Moonlight." Quietly lyrical and deftly modulated, Waley's translation reads beautifully as a poem in English. No other translation seems equally faithful to the original or so expressively realized in English. This translation also has a substantial claim to historical importance because Waley (1889–1966), who worked in the Oriental Prints and Drawings department of the British Museum, was perhaps the most influential translator of Chinese poetry in the twentieth century. More even than Ezra Pound, Waley created the English-language conventions by which most subsequent work has been translated.

COMPARING TRANSLATIONS

Horace, "CARPE DIEM" ODE, page 956

Quintus Horatius Flaccus, whom we remember as Horace, was the son of a freed slave. Although his father was a poor man, he sacrificed a great deal to give his talented son an excellent education in Rome and Athens. Having served as a soldier on the losing side of the Roman civil wars, Horace returned to find his father dead and their small farm confiscated. He managed to find work as a minor financial clerk and gradually established his reputation as a poet. By the end of his life in 8 B.C. he was one of the most honored authors in the Roman empire. He has never lacked readers since.

This famous short ode created a tradition of lyrics we call *carpe diem* poems. Although later poets often use the *carpe diem* line to woo their reluctant lovers, Horace's original is more strictly philosophical. We do not know how long our lives will last, and death is inevitable, so let us enjoy the time we have. (Horace's clear-eyed stoic acceptance of death contrasts interestingly with Larkin's nihilistic terror in "Aubade" in the preceding chapter.) Horace finds joy and meaning in life's uncertainty. No wonder it became the framework for later playful poems such as Marvell's "To His Coy Mistress" and Herrick's "To the Virgins, to Make Much of Time."

Edwin Arlington Robinson, James Michie, A. E. Stallings, TRANSLATIONS FROM HORACE, pages 957–958

All three translations are excellent—but in different ways. The Robinson (done when he was barely out of school) is straightforward and classical in its approach. The Michie emphasizes the lyric and intimate elements of the Latin. A. E. Stallings's recent version of Horace updates the ancient Roman images into *au courant* equivalents with Psychic Friends, the millennium, and the purported Y2K computer crash all making appearances in her wittily rhymed lines.

Some of the best student poems ever seen by one of the editors of this anthology came from an assignment to "translate this poem into a contemporary American setting, preferably somewhere where you yourself have lived." (None of the students knew Latin, so they worked with a literal translation plus two poetic versions.) The results were outstanding, and the students were astounded at how many settings appeared to work equally well.

Omar Khayyam, RUBAI, page 958

The phonetic transcription of the Persian may confuse students slightly, if they study the rime scheme, because in this poem all four lines rime (rather than the usual *aaba* scheme).

But it seems worthwhile to let them study the original of the best-known rubai in English (and almost equally famous in Persian). You might point out to the class the poem's final word in Persian—*soltani*, a word that exists virtually unaltered in English as *sultan*.

Edward FitzGerald, Robert Graves and Omar Ali-Shah, Dick Davis, TRANSLATIONS FROM OMAR KHAYYAM, pages 959–960

FitzGerald's rubaiyat are so intoxicating that we couldn't resist including a few more at the end. But their music should not distract you entirely from Dick Davis's ingeniously faithful version, which even duplicates the original's quadruple rime. (Davis teaches Persian literature at Ohio State University and is a considerable poet in his own right.) By comparison, the Graves/Ali-Shah version seems stiff and unidiomatic.

Parody

Ezra Pound, in his *ABC of Reading*, urges students of poetry to write parodies of any poems they find ridiculous, then submit their parodies to other students to be judged. "The gauging pupil should be asked to recognize what author is parodied. And whether the joke is on the parodied or the parodist. Whether the parody exposes a real defect, or merely makes use of an author's mechanism to expose a more trivial content."

Anonymous, We four lads from Liverpool are, page 961

The origin of this jingle among children who sang it (to the familiar tune of "We Three Kings of Orient Are") on the streets of Edinburgh, about 1963 when the Beatles became popular, is attested to by the folklorist James T. R. Ritchie in *The Singing Street* (Edinburgh and London: Oliver & Boyd, 1964). Clearly, even Christmas carols are fair game to jejune British parodists. Another classic, current at the time of the abdication of Edward VIII in 1936, goes, "Hark, the herald angels sing: / Missus Simpson's pinched our king!"

Wendy Cope, from Strugnell's Rubaiyat, page 961

Wendy Cope has written about how her father would recite FitzGerald's *Rubaiyat* to his family. Having loved the poems since childhood, Cope turned her considerable powers of parody to exorcising these resonant poems from her psyche. To parody the old song, "You always hurt the poems you love."

Jason Strugnell is a second-rate poet invented by Cope. Strugnell leaps on every fashionable and unfashionable bandwagon—thereby allowing Cope endless opportunities for parody. All of the FitzGerald originals parodied by Cope can be found in the translation section of this chapter.

Hugh Kingsmill, What, still alive at twenty-two?, page 962

Kingsmill's insistence on dying young suggests "To an Athlete Dying Young," but the parodist grossly exaggerates Housman's hint of nihilism. Like bacon, Kingsmill's lad will be "cured"—of the disease of life. (And how often Housman himself says *lad* by the way.) His metaphysical conceit of ink and blotting pad coarsens Housman's usual view of night and day. (Some comparable Housman lines, from "Reveille": "Wake: the silver dusk returning / Up the beach of darkness brims, / And the ship of sunrise burning / Strands upon the eastern rims.")

Bruce Bennett, The Lady Speaks Again, page 962

Bennett's quatrain shows students a different use of parody. Bennett is not making fun of Emma Lazarus's sonnet (the original appears in the next chapter, "Recognizing Excellence"); instead, he uses Lazarus's poem as a departure point for his own satire on how contemporary America has fallen short of the ideals articulated by Lazarus's democratic vision.

Gene Fehler, IF RICHARD LOVELACE BECAME A FREE AGENT, page 962

The target of Fehler's satire has only become more vulnerable since 1984. Professional baseball has lost its innocence. Although there is no less joy in Mudville, a baseball-addicted poetry lover will find much pleasure in the work of Gene Fehler, the poet laureate of American baseball, whose work often appears in baseball journals and anthologies. His collection *Center Field Grasses: Poems from Baseball* (Jefferson, NC: McFarland, 1991) is especially delightful for its parodies of sixty classic poems, including "A Certain Slant of Curve," "On First Looking at a Mantle Homer," "A Noiseless Patient Owner," "The Lead Rises, the League Falls," and "Song of the Open Base."

Aaron Abeyta, THIRTEEN WAYS OF LOOKING AT A TORTILLA, page 963

Abeyta's Latino parody of Wallace Stevens's Modernist classic may invite your students to try their hand at a similar revision—perhaps even as an in-class writing assignment. One thing Abeyta's parody demonstrates is the strength of great syntax and form. Even rewritten with entirely new images, Stevens's original form carries the new meanings strongly along.

WRITERS ON WRITING

Arthur Waley, THE METHOD OF TRANSLATION, page 965

Waley's comments, like those of many another translator, provide for the rest of us—who might otherwise tend to assume that translation is a simple matter of word-by-word substitution—an interesting glimpse into the actual complexities of translation, especially of poetry. After reading the translations in this chapter, would you agree with Waley that "the restrictions of rhyme necessarily injure either the vigor of one's language or the literalness of one's version"?

28
Poetry in Spanish: Literature of Latin America

Sor Juana, ASEGURA LA CONFIANZA DE QUE OCULTURÁ DE TODO UN SECRETO (SHE PROMISES TO HOLD A SECRET IN CONFIDENCE), translated by *Diane Thiel*, page 970

One might find it surprising that Sor Juana, a Catholic sister, wrote such a great volume of love poetry. As discussed in the prose excerpt by Stephanie Merrim at the end of the chapter, there are a variety of conjectures about her choice of this subject matter. The intensity of the passion in these poems is extraordinarily memorable, though.

In "She Promises to Hold a Secret in Confidence," one feels the passion of the speaker and also the weight of the confidence which must be kept. The speaker's passion is especially evident in the fact that she not only tears up the secret, but swallows it. She doesn't want it taken from her chest. The secret has become literally a part of her.

Sor Juana's poetry often uses elaborate wordplay, as can be seen in the play of "tore" and "be torn" in this poem and in the husk and the chestnut in "A Simple Gift Made Rich by Affection." This wordplay, as well as the tight rimes, is common to the baroque style of her era. But while much poetry in this style can feel stilted or outdated, Sor Juana's verse has an intensity of emotion brimming beneath the surface.

Sor Juana, PRESENTE EN QUE EL CARIÑO HACE REGALO LA LLANEZA (A SIMPLE GIFT MADE RICH BY AFFECTION), translated by *Diane Thiel*, page 970

As noted in the discussion of the preceding poem, Sor Juana's characteristic wordplay is also quite evident in this text. The husk in the poem seems to be the thorny self, the exterior that contains the chestnut. Perhaps the chestnut is the love the speaker has to give, or the speaker's spirit, while the husk represents the difficult aspects of the speaker's nature, of which she is well aware. Both Sor Juana poems included here feel like correspondences, either missives actually sent or love poems with a specific recipient.

Note that in both of these poems, the translator has chosen to re-create the wordplay in English and has also re-created the tight rhyme schemes characteristic of Sor Juana's work and her era. One might ask students about different translators' choices throughout the chapter.

Pablo Neruda, Muchos Somos (We Are Many), translated by *Alastair Reid,* page 971

"Muchos Somos" is not merely one of Neruda's most famous poems, it is also among his most deeply characteristic. It reveals his open, exuberant, and personable poetic voice. One can see the influence of Walt Whitman in this poem. Compare Neruda's multiple personalities to Whitman's famous confession in *Song of Myself:* "Do I contradict myself? / Very well then I contradict myself / (I am large, I contain multitudes.)"

Alastair Reid's translation wonderfully captures the verve of the Spanish, but it remains important that we hear the poem in the original language. For classroom discussion, ask a student to read the Spanish aloud. (If you have native Spanish speakers in class, don't miss the chance to let them recite it.) The sonorous resonance of Neruda's language will be obvious even to students who have no Spanish.

It might also be worthwhile to ask if students have seen the Italian film *Il Postino (The Postman),* an Academy Award nominee for best film in 1995. Although fictionalized, the film presents Neruda's political exile in Italy. Students may well have seen the film without remembering the poet's name. *Il Postino* did a marvelous job of portraying Neruda's life-affirming, imaginative exuberance.

Pablo Neruda, Cien Sonetos de Amor (V) (One Hundred Love Sonnets (V)), translated by *Stephen Tapscott,* page 973

Pablo Neruda, though known for the politics in his poetry, is perhaps best known for his love poetry. In this love poem, the merging of images of the body with images of the land is particularly potent: "you are my dark familiar clay: touching your hips, / I touch the wheat in its fields again." The end of the poem continues this connection: Love is a land of "kisses and volcanoes." The last line reverberates with the intensity of "volcanoes" and surprises somewhat in the poem. It leaves the reader shaken by the assertion.

Jorge Luis Borges, Amorosa Anticipación (Anticipation of Love), translated by *Robert Fitzgerald,* pages 974–975

The premise of Borges's poem is both simple and ingenious. His speaker imagines his beloved (whom he has not yet known—and perhaps never will know—physically as a lover) after they have made love. As he imagines her sleeping, his thoughts are hardly carnal, but instead deeply emotional and in the end virtually spiritual in his love. As Neruda does in "One Hundred Love Sonnets (V)," Borges uses the landscape to speak about love. In this poem, the speaker, addressing his love, refers to the "shore of your life" and "that ultimate beach of your being" which he will see for the first time if they ever become lovers in a physical sense. The poem is one of renewal, of seeing one's love with new eyes. The reference to becoming "virgin again" in sleep supports this reading of renewal. The end of the poem has a note of sadness, however, as the speaker thinks of his love "free from love," free from himself.

Jorge Luis Borges, LOS ENIGMAS (THE ENIGMAS), translated by *John Updike*, pages 975–976

The poem itself feels like the subject matter—puzzling, enigmatic. The speaker looks to the day of his own death, which he sees as a kind of immortality but also as a condition of never having existed. The rimes of the sonnet form lend themselves to the subject matter as well. One might ask students about Updike's translation, which doesn't carry over many of the rimes. Is anything lost in this choice of a way of translating the poem? Note that Updike does retain some of the lyricism and ends the poem on an eloquent rime: "oblivion" and "been."

Octavio Paz, CON LOS OJOS CERRADOS (WITH EYES CLOSED), translated by *Eliot Weinberger*, page 977

This short poem by the Nobel laureate Octavio Paz is simple enough that anyone with basic Spanish can follow it in the original. (The original text will also give any native Spanish speakers in your class a chance to show off their bilingual abilities.) The poem explores a paradoxical conceit: in shutting oneself off from physical light, one can experience an inner light. Becoming a "blind stone" to the outside, "you light up within." The second stanza turns the metaphor erotic, although Paz is deliberately ambiguous about whether the lovers are together or apart. "Night after night" the speaker recreates his love with his eyes shut—perhaps carving her features from memory or perhaps touching her with his hands. The final stanza celebrates how the lovers enlarge their existence by knowing one another "with eyes closed".

Octavio Paz, CERTEZA (CERTAINTY), translated by *Charles Tomlinson*, page 977

This short poem by Paz speaks simultaneously about his consideration of the artistic process and about the fleeting nature of our lives, where what is said vanishes as it is spoken. Why "parentheses," one might wonder. Are the words captured there, in their cage of parentheses? Parentheses seem to be a symbol for what is written/recorded, as opposed to what vanishes in speech.

SURREALISM IN LATIN AMERICAN POETRY

César Vallejo, LA CÓLERA QUE QUIEBRA AL HOMBRE EN NIÑOS (ANGER), translated by *Thomas Merton*, pages 979–980

Vallejo's poem is an extraordinary example of surrealism, where sense is made by that which doesn't make sense. The progression of anger breaking a man into children, which break into birds and then eggs, sets up the reader's expectations in the poem. One feels the intensity of "anger," the manifestation of which often has precisely such a surreal quality; it breaks a person down into pieces.

Students might be asked what kind of meaning they glean from such bizarre, surreal images and assertions. Do they "feel" the poem even as they struggle to make sense of it?

CONTEMPORARY MEXICAN POETRY

José Emilio Pacheco, ALTA TRAICIÓN (HIGH TREASON), translated by *Alastair Reid*, page 981

Pacheco is a Mexican poet who has chosen to work in the United States, and he currently teaches at the University of Maryland. He writes in Spanish, but he collaborated with the noted poet-translator Alastair Reid (himself an immigrant from Scotland) on the English versions of his poems. Pacheco's presence in the anthology (along with the inclusion of writers such as Octavio Paz, Rhina Espaillat, Emanuel di Pasquale, Derek Walcott, and Claude McKay—not to mention Alastair Reid) highlights the importance of immigrants and foreign expatriates in our literary culture.

Pacheco's poem should require little gloss, but the effective and subtle irony of the opening probably deserves a moment's consideration in class to show how irony can be used rhetorically. By saying "I do not love my country" in a poem that celebrates his love for his homeland, Pacheco effectively qualifies the nature of his affection. It is not conventional patriotism but love for its particulars.

It is worth noting that although the poem presumably celebrates Mexico, its images are deliberately universal. It could be describing Finland or China. The title of this poem is also ironic: Pacheco's treason is a personal love for his country.

Francisco Hernández, BAJO CERO (BELOW ZERO), translated by *Carolyn Forché*, pages 981–982

The portrait of the mind of a suicide that this poem presents could be described as chilling in both the physical and the emotional connotations of the term. In the opening lines, Hernández rejects the common assumption that a person on the verge of self-destruction suffers from a mind that is feverishly spinning out of control. The feeling of icy emptiness is conveyed not only by the sensory descriptions, but also by the constant recurrence of negative terms (*not, nor, never, nothing, neither, no one*), patiently fashioning the sense of a mind beyond any claim life can make—whether in the form of a lover, one's children, or any other earthly attachment or emotion—and coldly sealed in its own focused isolation.

It may seem odd at first that a Mexican poet would invest a text with such wintry imagery, but as we read we come to realize that heat and passion are here implicitly associated with life, a connection that is memorably reinforced in the poem's last two lines.

Tedi López Mills, CONVALECENCIA/CONVALESCENCE, page 982

"Convalescence" comes closer than most of the poems in the anthology to the condition of "pure poetry"—that is, poetry which essentially uses imagery to create a mood or convey a sensation with little, if anything, in the way of larger thematic intent, thus fulfilling Archibald MacLeish's famous dictum that begins his "Ars Poetica": "A poem should not mean / But be." With a series of auditory images intended to produce an effect equivalent to that of chalk screeching on a blackboard, López Mills conveys the heightened sensitivity and irritability of someone recovering from an illness, for whom the common noises of the daily round—as hinted at by the epigraph from the great Spanish poet Antonio Machado—become almost unendurable assaults. The insistently repeated *first* is intended, of course, to communicate the raw newness of each offense to the nerves, before the senses have an opportunity to accommodate and adjust to the intrusion.

WRITERS ON WRITING

Octavio Paz, IN SEARCH OF THE PRESENT, page 983

In this excerpt from Paz's 1990 Nobel Lecture, he focuses on the influence of different cultures that affects writers, with Latin American writers as a vital example. The very language has been "transplanted," and Latin American writers feel simultaneously European yet not European. Languages grow and are transformed over the years and via their different uses. Paz is interested in the dialogue that is formed as a result of the recognition of this multilayered history.

WRITERS ON TRANSLATING

Alastair Reid, TRANSLATING NERUDA, page 983

Reid's illuminating memoir of translating Neruda gives us an intimate glimpse of how one poet translates another. Reid's entire memoir, which also discusses his long working relationship as a translator of Jorge Luis Borges, is well worth reading. It originally appeared in the June 24, 1996, issue of the *New Yorker*.

29
Recognizing Excellence

Ezra Pound long argued for the value of bad poetry in pedagogy. In his *ABC of Reading*, Pound declared that literary education needs to concentrate on revealing what is sham so that the student may be led to discover what is valid. It is a healthy gesture to let the student see that we don't believe everything contained in a textbook to be admirable. Begin with a poem or two so outrageously awful that the least sophisticated student hardly can take it seriously—some sentimental claptrap such as Cook's "The Old Arm-Chair." From these, you can proceed to subtler examples. It is a mistake to be too snide or too self-righteous toward bad poems, and it is well to turn quickly to some excellent poetry if the classroom starts smelling like a mortuary. There is a certain sadness inherent in much bad poetry; one can readily choke on it. As Allen Tate has said, the best attack upon the bad is the loving understanding of the good. The aim in teaching bad poetry has to be the admiration of good poetry, not the diffusion of mockery.

One further suggestion on bad poetry: a program of really execrable verse orated with straight faces by a few students and members of the faculty can be, with any luck, a fine occasion. For bad poems to work on besides those offered in this chapter, see the dustier stacks in a library for the following anthologies: *Heart Throbs* and *More Heart Throbs*, ed. Joe Mitchell Chapple (New York: Grosset, 1905 and 1911, respectively; many later editions); *The Stuffed Owl: An Anthology of Bad Verse*, ed. D. B. Wyndham Lewis and Charles Lee (London: Dent, 1930; reprinted in the United States by Capricorn paperbacks); *Nematodes in My Garden of Verse*, ed. Richard Walser (Winston-Salem: Blair, 1959); *The Worst English Poets*, ed. Christopher Adams (London: Wingate, 1958); *Pegasus Descending: A Book of the Best Bad Verse*, ed. James Camp, X. J. Kennedy, and Keith Waldrop (New York: Macmillan, 1971); and *The Joy of Bad Verse*, ed. Nicholas T. Parsons (London: Collins, 1988).

Anonymous, O MOON, WHEN I GAZE ON THY BEAUTIFUL FACE, page 987

Glorious behind seems inexact, and so does *boundaries* for "boundlessness."

Grace Treasone, LIFE, page 987

Treasone's poem develops a central metaphor, but its language is wildly imprecise. Is the tooth "that cuts into your heart" one's own or somebody else's? (It is probable that the poet means not tooth but "toothache.") Anatomically, the image seems on a par with the "heart's leg" of the tradesman poet quoted by

318

Coleridge. Through the murk of her expression, however, the poet makes clear her theme: the familiar and sentimental notion that life is really all right if you see it through (or have a competent dentist).

Treasone's item first adorned a Dover, New Jersey, newspaper column of local poets called "This Way to Parnassus."

Emily Dickinson, A DYING TIGER – MOANED FOR DRINK, page 987

This is not, by any stretch of the critical imagination, a good poem. Besides the poet's innocent lack of perception that *His Mighty Balls* suggests not eyeballs but testicles, the concluding statement (that the fact that the tiger was dead is to blame) seems an un-Dickinsonian failure of invention. Perhaps the poet intended a religious allegory (Christ the Tiger). Her capitalization of *He* in the last line doesn't seem sufficient proof of such intent, for her habits of capitalization cannot be trusted for consistency.

The failures of splendid poets are fascinating. As in this case, they often seem to result from some tremendous leap that sails over and beyond its object, with the poet crashing to earth on the other side.

EXERCISE: *Ten Terrible Moments in Poetry*, pages 988–989

J. Gordon Coogler, a printer by trade, was said to have displayed a sign in the window of his print shop in Columbia, South Carolina: "POEMS WRITTEN WHILE YOU WAIT."

For Byron's rousing lines, we have to thank Walter H. Bishop of Atlanta, for whom this discovery won first prize in a contest to find the worst lame verse by a well-known poet, conducted by John Shelton Reed in *Chronicles*. (The results were reported in the magazine's issue of November 1986.)

Mattie J. Peterson has attracted fierce partisans, some of whom see her battling Julia A. Moore for the crown of Queen of American Bad Verse. Richard Walser has brought out a modern facsimile of her 1890 book, *Little Pansy, A Novel, and Miscellaneous Poetry* (Charlotte: McNally & Loftin, 1967).

Francis Saltus Saltus is the rediscovery of Nicholas T. Parsons in *The Joy of Bad Verse* (London: Collins, 1988). We lifted the two excerpts from Parsons's splendid anthology, and it was a temptation to lift a third:

> Oh! such a past can not be mute,
>   Such bliss can not be crushed in sorrow,
> Although thou art a prostitute
>   And I am to be hanged tomorrow.

Saltus regarded himself as a rakehell. As C. T. Kindilien has observed, "Although he idealized cigarette-smoking women, looked for pornography in the Bible, and honored Baudelaire, Gerard de Nerval, and Le Marquis de Sade, he never escaped the tone of the boy who expected any moment to be caught smoking behind the barn" (*American Poetry in the Eighteen-Nineties* [Brown UP, 1956] 188–89).

Rod McKuen, THOUGHTS ON CAPITAL PUNISHMENT, page 990
William Stafford, TRAVELING THROUGH THE DARK, page 991

McKuen is still popular with some students, and any dogmatic attempt to blast him may be held against you. There may be value in such a confrontation, of course; or you can leave evaluation of these two works up to the class. Just work through McKuen's effusion and Stafford's fine poem, detail by detail, in a non-committal way, and chances are good that Stafford will win the contest.

It may not be apparent that Stafford's poem is ordered by a rime scheme from beginning to end: *abcb* stanzas and a final couplet. Stafford avoids obvious rimes in favor of the off-rimes *road / dead* and *engine / listen* and the cutoff rimes *killing / belly, waiting / hesitated,* and *swerving / river*—this last a device found in some folk ballads. McKuen's poem announces an obvious rime scheme but fails to complete it. Unlike Stafford, he throws rime out the window in the end, with the effect that his poem stops with a painful inconclusiveness.

Stafford contributes a long comment on his poem to *Reading Modern Poetry: A Critical Introduction,* Paul Engle and Warren Carrier, eds. (Glenview: Scott, 1968).

Wallace McRae, REINCARNATION, page 992

If any recent cowboy poem deserves the name of classic, it's "Reincarnation," probably the most widely recited work by one of the best-known poets of the cowboy school. McRae is a cattle rancher from Forsyth, in eastern Montana, an area where his family settled five generations ago.

"Reincarnation" is no simple thing to evaluate. Its theme of the organic continuity of life seems straight out of *Hamlet:* "Thus may a king pass through the guts of a beggar." But the poem turns out to be a shaggy-dog meditation that leads up to an insulting joke: "Slim, you always were a horse's turd, and you still are." Still, most of us will probably enjoy being taken in. Perhaps we feel relief when a ponderous meditation on life and death turns into a mere comic kick in the teeth.

The poem's language wavers inconsistently between plain speech and bookishness: "life's travails," "rendered mound," "yer vegetative bower." In retrospect, McRae's bookish, ornate phrasings may seem ironic, for apparently even the poet doesn't take them in earnest. They exist only to be punctured with a bang in the last line.

Short of attending the annual Cowboy Poetry Gathering in Elko, Nevada (if you can get a room), the next-best introduction to the field may be two anthologies edited by Hal Cannon: *Cowboy Poetry* and *New Cowboy Poetry* (Salt Lake City: Peregrine Smith Books, 1985 and 1990). *American Cowboy Poetry,* published in Idaho, is a magazine whose motto might well be "Git along, little doggerel, git along." (We are grateful for the advice and a bibliography provided by Jim Hoy of Emporia State University.)

RECOGNIZING EXCELLENCE

William Butler Yeats, SAILING TO BYZANTIUM, page 994

Has XJK implied that this poem is a masterpiece so far beyond reproach that no one in his right mind can find fault with it? That is, of course, not the truth. If the instructor wishes to provoke students to argument, he or she might read them the withering attack on Yeats's poem by Yvor Winters (*Forms of Discovery* [Chicago: Swallow, 1967] 215–16).

This attack really needs to be read in its entirety. Winters is wrong, we believe, but no one can begin to answer his hardheaded objections to the poem without being challenged and illuminated.

Other discussions of the poem, different from XJK's and also short, appear in Richard Ellmann's *Yeats: The Man and the Masks* (New York: Macmillan, 1949) and John Unterecker's *A Reader's Guide to William Butler Yeats* (New York: Noonday, 1959). Those who wish to go deeper still and to read a searching examination (informed by study of Yeats's manuscripts) can be directed to Curtis Bradford, "Yeats's Byzantium Poems," *PMLA* 75 (Mar. 1960): 100–25. For those interested in alternatives, John Stallworthy reprints nearly all the legible manuscript versions in *Between the Lines: Yeats's Poetry in the Making* (Oxford: Clarendon, 1963) 87–112.

A deconstructionist reading of "Sailing to Byzantium," subjecting the poem to relentless questioning, showing where it fails to make sense and how it doesn't work, is offered by Lawrence I. Lipking in "The Practice of Theory" (in *Profession 83: Selected Articles from the Bulletins of the Association of Departments of English and the Association of Departments of Foreign Languages*, MLA, 1983). But in his role as a poststructuralist, Lipking confesses himself "a sheep commissioned to say something sympathetic about wolves." He finds that deconstructionist tactics offend his students, especially the bright, idealistic ones who expect their teachers to show them why certain works are great, and who wish poems to "make sense" and to relate to their own lives.

Jean Bauso has used a writing assignment to introduce this challenging poem. "I want you to pretend that you're an old person—someone in his or her eighties," she tells a class. "You've got arthritis, so buttoning or zipping your clothes is slow. Now you will write for ten minutes nonstop in the voice of this old person that you've made yourself into. You want to follow your person's stream of consciousness as he or she sits there thinking about the human condition, about the fact that we human beings have to die." After the students free-write for ten minutes, they read a few of the results, and she picks up on any comments about wishing for immortality. Then she asks for responses to the name "Byzantium," perhaps holding up pictures of the Santa Sophia mosaics. She then reads "Sailing to Byzantium" aloud, gives out reading sheets with points for reading it alone, and dismisses the class. For Bauso's detailed account of this lesson plan and her reading sheets, see "The Use of Free-Writing and Guided Writing to Make Students Amenable to Poems," *Exercise Exchange* (Spring 1988).

MLL *MyLiteratureLab Resources.* Biography, critical overview, and bibliography for Yeats. Critical excerpts on "Sailing to Byzantium."

EXERCISE: *Two Poems to Compare,* page 996

Arthur Guiterman, ON THE VANITY OF EARTHLY GREATNESS, page 996
Percy Bysshe Shelley, OZYMANDIAS, page 996

The title of Guiterman's bagatelle playfully echoes that of a longer, more ambitious poem: Samuel Johnson's "The Vanity of Human Wishes." If Guiterman's achievement seems smaller than that of Shelley's "Ozymandias," still, it is flaw-less. "Ozymandias," although one of the monuments of English poetry, has a few cracks in it. Many readers find line 8 incomplete in sense: the heart that fed what, or fed on what? From its rime scheme, we might think the poem a would-be Italian sonnet that refused to work out.

Nevertheless, Shelley's vision stretches further than Guiterman's. Ozymandias and his works are placed at an incredibly distant remove from us. The structure of the poem helps establish this remoteness: Ozymandias's words were dictated to the sculptor, then carved in stone, then read by a traveler, then told to the first-person speaker, then relayed to us. Ironies abound, more subtle than Guiterman's. A single work of art has outlasted Ozymandias's whole empire. Does that mean that works of art endure (as in "Not marble nor the gilded monuments")? No, this work of art itself has seen better days, and soon (we infer) the sands will finish covering it. Obviously, the king's proud boast has been deflated, and yet, in another sense, Ozymandias is right. The Mighty (or any traveler) may well despair for themselves and their own works, as they gaze on the wreckage of his one surviving project and realize that, cruel as Ozymandias may have been, time is even more remorseless.

What are the facts behind Shelley's poem? According to the Greek historian Diodorus Siculus, Ozymandias was apparently a grand, poeticized name claimed for himself by the Egyptian pharaoh Rameses II. Diodorus Siculus saw the king's ninety-foot-tall statue of himself, carved by the sculptor Memnon, in the first century B.C. when it was still standing at the Ramesseum in Thebes, a mortuary temple. Shelley and his friend Horatio Smith had read a description of the shattered statue in Richard Pococke's *Description of the East* (1742). Smith and Shelley wrote sonnets expressing their imagined views of the wreckage, both of which Leigh Hunt printed in his periodical the *Examiner* in 1818. This is Smith's effort, and students might care to compare it with Shelley's:

On a Stupendous Leg of Granite, Discovered Standing by Itself in the Deserts of Egypt

In Egypt's sandy silence, all alone,
    Stands a gigantic leg, which far off throws
    The only shadow that the desert knows.
'I am great Ozymandias,' saith the stone,
    'The king of kings: this mighty city shows
The wonders of my hand.' The city's gone!—
    Nought but the leg remaining to disclose
The site of that forgotten Babylon.

We wonder, and some hunter may express
Wonder like ours, when through the wilderness,
    Where London stood, holding the wolf in chase,
He meets some fragment huge, and stops to guess
    What powerful but unrecorded race
    Once dwelt in that annihilated place.

For more background to the poem, see H. M. Richmond, "Ozymandias and the Travelers," *Keats-Shelley Journal* 11 (1962): 65–71.

MLL
   MyLiteratureLab Resources. Audio clip for "Ozymandias."

Robert Hayden, THE WHIPPING, page 997

Hayden's poem chillingly depicts the cycles of family and social violence. The old woman beats the boy to avenge the "lifelong hidings / she has had to bear." The narrator stands outside the action of the poem, but the boy's tears trigger his own memories of being beaten by—in a frightening synecdoche—"the face that I / no longer knew or loved." Notice that Hayden deliberately leaves the relationship between "the boy" and "the old woman" unstated. Is she mother, grandmother, aunt, babysitter, foster mother? It doesn't matter in the poem. She is large and powerful while the boy is small and helpless. One might assign this poem together with Hayden's "Those Winter Sundays," for contrasting views of domestic life.

 MyLiteratureLab Resources. Biography, critical overview, and bibliography for Hayden.

Elizabeth Bishop, ONE ART, page 998

Like Thomas's "Do not go gentle," this villanelle manages to say something that matters while observing the rules of a tricky French courtly form. (For remarks on the villanelle and on writing it, see the entry on Thomas's poem in this manual.) A similar feat is performed in Bishop's ingenious recollection of childhood, "Sestina."

Question: What varieties of loss does the poet mention? (She goes from trivial loss—lost door keys—to lost time, to losing beloved places and homes, to loss of love.)

In recalling that she has lost a continent, the poet may be speaking personally: she lived in Brazil for many years, and wrote this poem after returning to America. Early in life, Bishop knew severe losses. Her father died when she was eight months old; when she was five, her mother was confined to an institution.

Perceptively, the Irish poet and critic Eavan Boland has likened "One Art" to Bishop's "Sestina," remarking that "it is obvious that [the poet] entrusted some of her deepest implications of loss to two of the most intricate game forms in poetry." However, she finds differences between the two works: "'Sestina' is packed with desolate halftones, dropped hints, and the incantatory shadows of nursery rhymes. It manages to convey, at one and the same time, that there is sorrow, yes, and loss, yes, but that they are imperfectly understood. Therefore the poem operates at two different levels. Within it a terrible sorrow is happening. But the teakettle keeps boiling, the cup is full of tea, the stove is warm. Only we, outside the poem, get the full meaning of it all. 'One Art' is quite different. . . . The tone, which is both casual and direct, is deliberately worked against the form, as it is not in 'Sestina.' Once again, Bishop shows that she is best able to display feeling when she can constrain it most." (We quote from her fine essay on Bishop's work, "Time, Memory, and Obsession," *PN Review* [Nov.–Dec. 1991] 18–24.)

 MyLiteratureLab Resources. Biography, critical overview, and bibliography for Bishop. Longman Lecture on "One Art."

W. H. Auden, SEPTEMBER 1, 1939, page 999

It seems fitting that only months before writing "September 1, 1939," W. H. Auden composed his justly celebrated elegy for William Butler Yeats, since this poem, like Yeats's "Easter 1916," shows a magnificent poet working at the height of his powers, writing with sureness and authority, creating a profound meditation on the relationship between our private natures and our public life. The speaker sits "Uncertain and afraid" as years of compromise and appeasement have reached their inevitable end in the unleashing of a war that is certain to have catastrophic effects for the world (although few could have predicted the full horror of that catastrophe). Some have understood the reference to Linz (line 16) to ascribe the roots of Nazism to Hitler's unhappiness and isolation as a child. Some have understood lines 21–22 to refer to the punitive terms of the Treaty of Versailles or to the inevitable response by the Allies to the German invasion of Poland; whatever specific application of these lines one may make in the context of 1939, it can hardly be doubted that every day's newspapers furnish new proofs, on both the global level and the personal, of the general truth of Auden's observation.

The third and fourth stanzas address "the lie of Authority / Whose buildings grope the sky" (lines 82–83), just as the fourth, fifth, and sixth stanzas analyze "The romantic lie in the brain / Of the sensual man-in-the-street" (lines 80–81). As the poet and critic John Fuller points out, "September 1, 1939" is "centered upon the need to establish the Just Society. . . . The basis of such a society is a universal love, the Christian Agape indeed, which appears to be denied by the Eros of the individual corrupted by sin." While seemingly impervious himself to "[t]he windiest militant trash / Important Persons shout" (lines 56–57), the speaker nonetheless recognizes that he, like all others, must rise above the Eros and the dust that constitute the lower part of his nature, so that he may approach and, he hopes, attain the universal love which he sees as the only possible salvation for a morally diseased world. Only on this basis can we show the "affirming flame" that is needed as desperately now as in 1939.

 MyLiteratureLab Resources. Biography, critical overview, and bibliography for Auden.

Walt Whitman, O CAPTAIN! MY CAPTAIN!, page 1002

This formerly overrated poem is uncharacteristic of Whitman in its neatly shaped riming stanzas and in its monotonously swinging observation of iambic meter, so inappropriate to a somber elegy. The one indication that an excellent poet wrote it is the sudden shift of rhythm in the short lines that end each stanza—particularly in line 5, with the unexpected turning-on of heavy stresses: "Oh heart! heart! heart!"

MyLiteratureLab Resources. Biography, critical overview, and bibliography for Whitman.

EXERCISE: *Reevaluating Popular Classics*, page 1004

Paul Laurence Dunbar, WE WEAR THE MASK, page 1004

Nowadays, Paul Laurence Dunbar is perhaps most frequently perceived as the author of a great deal of conventional and undistinguished verse in standard English and of ballads in African American dialect that are sometimes labored, often mawkish, and, to some, cringe-inducing. According to this view, his popularity in his own time was inflated by shallow standards and by allowances made for him because of his race, and contemporary interest in him is based more on historical and ethnic considerations than on aesthetic ones.

While there may be some truth to this (admittedly exaggerated) characterization, it is ultimately unfair to Dunbar. His 1902 novel, *The Sport of the Gods*, is a strong, well-written book which, though it has been reprinted several times, is still underappreciated. And amid the mass of his verse are some genuinely solid achievements—including, most notably, the poem at hand. There may be a couple of small blemishes in "We Wear the Mask": "torn and bleeding hearts" in line 4 is a bit of a cliché, and "guile" might not have been used in the preceding line if not for the necessity of the rime. But these slight weaknesses are far outweighed by the poem's strengths: Dunbar adheres strictly to a very demanding form —the rondeau—with almost no visible strain, and in doing so he displays a great deal of organization, control, and, for the most part, restraint. The artistry shown here is satisfying in itself, and it persuades the reader that the treatment has done justice to the theme.

Emma Lazarus, THE NEW COLOSSUS, page 1005

Most Americans know at least a line or two of this famous sonnet carved on the pedestal of the Statue of Liberty, but surprisingly few can name the author of the poem. The poem and its author have vanished from most anthologies and textbooks. Yet Lazarus's sonnet seems that rare thing—a truly successful public poem. The images are clear and powerful, the language is memorable, and the sonnet avoids the chief danger of public poetry—prolixity. The contrast between the original colossus of the ancient world, which represented might, and the new colossus, which represents freedom, is both an original and effective means of dramatizing the difference between the Old World of European despotism and the New World of American democracy, a popular theme of nineteenth-century patriotic poetry, but one rarely so well expressed.

Edgar Allan Poe, ANNABEL LEE, page 1006

Students usually adore this poem. Most modern critics hate it. There is some truth in both camps.

Let's catalogue the faults of the poem first. The poem is sentimental: it asks the reader to be sad while reveling in the beauty of the sadness. The poem is also heavy-handed. When Poe gets a nice line or image going, he can't resist repeating it—more often for the sake of sound than sense. (These repetitions make most of the stanza patterns go awry.) The language is abstract and literary (*angels, kingdom, highborn kinsmen, sepulcher, maiden,* etc.). It may be unfair to say that these are not authentic *American* images, but, more to the point, the words seem borrowed from a book rather than observed from life.

And yet, with all its faults neatly noted, the poem remains weirdly beautiful. The very irregularity of the stanzas keeps the form of the poem subtly surprising, despite the bouncy anapestic meter. The abstract quality of the language used in this hypnotic meter—all drenched in emotion—eventually gives the poem a dreamlike reality. That placeless "kingdom by the sea" now begins to resemble the world of memory, and the poem lures us back into our own emotion-drenched childhood memories. (*"I* was a child and *she* was a child," as more than one psychological critic has noted, places the poem in a presexual stage; Annabel Lee is a bride only in the future tense.) The childlike innocence of the language and emotions somehow carry the poem into a sphere where adult critical concerns seem less relevant. "Annabel Lee" somehow marries the style and meter of light verse to the themes of elegiac, if not quite tragic, poetry. Whatever its faults, American poetry would be poorer without it.

When told we were including this poem in a new edition, one instructor (a highly regarded critic adept in literary theory) said, "Be gentle. I love that poem. Critics keep showing me why it's awful, but I love it anyway." We hope she feels we've been gentle enough.

MLL *MyLiteratureLab Resources.* Photographs, biographical information, critical comments, bibliography for Poe.

WRITERS ON WRITING

Edgar Allan Poe on Writing, A LONG POEM DOES NOT EXIST, page 1007

Do you agree or disagree? If Poe is right, should we discard *The Odyssey, The Divine Comedy,* and "Lycidas"? If he is wrong, then how do you account for the fact that certain long poems contain patches of deadly dullness?

30
What Is Poetry?

This chapter is not designed to answer the question of its title in any definitive sense. Instead, we have attempted to create an occasion for reflection and discussion after all the material covered earlier in the book. We have compiled a small anthology of quotations by writers on the nature of poetry. You may want to supplement our list with others you have discovered.

Archibald MacLeish, ARS POETICA, page 1009

This compressed and vividly drawn Modernist manifesto rewards careful reading couplet by couplet. Many people remember the famous closing lines—probably the most widely quoted formulation of modern poetry in English—but forget how finely realized the rest of the poem is. MacLeish manages a difficult trick in "Ars Poetica"—he creates a didactic poem in lyric form. Each rimed *vers libre* couplet contains an idea which is expressed in evocative lyric terms.

MacLeish plays upon a number of verbal paradoxes which students sometimes like to point out. He says a poem ought to be "mute," "dumb," and "wordless"; yet he is obviously writing a poem in speakable, audible words. As in some of the definitions of poetry quoted elsewhere in this chapter, MacLeish's poem understands that some truths can be expressed only as dynamic tensions between opposing forces or ideas. (Note, for example, Auden's definition of poetry— "the clear expression of mixed feelings.")

The poem contains a larger paradox, a potential topic for class argument. "A poem should not mean / But be," declares the poet. But is his poem pure being? Is it not heavy on meaning?—a tendency that an *ars poetica*, a poem that tells us how poetry should be written, can hardly be expected to avoid.

Ha Jin, MISSED TIME, page 1012

We end the pedagogic portion of the poetry book with Ha Jin's simple, direct, and moving "Missed Time," a poem the average reader can appreciate on first hearing. Poems need not be complex or challenging to matter. What they need be is expressive, true, and beautiful—though no lover of literature will confuse the beautiful with the merely pretty or decorous.

31
Two Critical Casebooks: Emily Dickinson and Langston Hughes

This chapter offers a representative cross-section of two major American poets, Emily Dickinson and Langston Hughes—one author drawn from the nineteenth century, the other from the twentieth. The selections found in this chapter can be supplemented by additional poems from these two writers elsewhere in the text. There are now 21 Dickinson poems and 17 Hughes poems in the volume as well as substantial prose passages from each author. We have also incorporated visual information into the book, with author and documentary photographs relevant to the poems and the historical periods. Finally, a critical casebook on each poet's work provides a variety of analytical approaches for the student.

This chapter gives instructors the additional flexibility of using the material for in-depth classroom examinations of the individual poets. The casebooks provide students with some background—including author biographies and criticism—to prepare essays and term papers, though many instructors may want students to supplement their reading and research in the library or on our textbook Web site.

EMILY DICKINSON

This selection of Dickinson's poems spans her entire career. We have presented many of her most famous poems because students should know these classic works, but we have also included a few lesser-known ones to add variety and, we hope, surprise.

 MyLiteratureLab Resources. Biography, critical overview, and bibliography for Dickinson.

Emily Dickinson, SUCCESS IS COUNTED SWEETEST, page 1014

When the first collection of Dickinson's *Poems* (1890) was published—four years after her death—by Mabel Loomis Todd and T. W. Higginson, they placed this poem on the first page. The editors implicitly saw that it represents an important theme in the poet's work. They may also have used the poem to symbolize Dickinson's lifelong obscurity. Ironically, this was one of only seven poems Dickinson actually published in her lifetime. It appeared anonymously in 1878 (two decades after its inception) in Helen Hunt Jackson's anthology, *A Masque of Poets*.

The poem articulates one of Dickinson's central themes—how suffering heightens perception and understanding. The nature of success, the poem argues, is best "comprehended" by someone who has tried to secure it but failed. The central image of the poem is the defeated, dying soldier who hears the distant sounds of a victory he will never share. (Some critics— even the learned Judith Farr—comment that the military image is borrowed from the Civil War, which inspired so many poems from Dickinson, but the dating of the poem's first appearance in two manuscripts from 1859 makes such a connection impossible.)

In a lecture on Dickinson delivered in 1959 at the bicentennial celebration of the town of Amherst, Richard Wilbur made a cogent case that the poem goes beyond the conventional ideas of compensation ("the idea that every evil confers some balancing good, that through bitterness we learn to appreciate the sweet"). Wilbur speculated that Dickinson's poem

> is arguing for the *superiority* of defeat to victory, of frustration to satisfaction, and of anguished comprehension to mere possession. What do victors have but victory, a victory which they cannot fully savor or clearly define? They have paid for their triumph by a sacrifice of awareness; a material gain has cost them a spiritual loss. ("Sumptuous Destitution," reprinted in *Responses: Prose Pieces 1953–1976* [New York: Harcourt, 1976])

Emily Dickinson, I TASTE A LIQUOR NEVER BREWED, page 1014

This joyful lyric is a most unusual nature poem—a hymn to the world's beauty in a form reminiscent of a drinking song. The first stanza celebrates a liquor that doesn't exist in the literal sense—it is never brewed but definitely intoxicating. An "Inebriate of Air" (what a gorgeous phrase!) and "Debauchee of Dew," the speaker draws her ecstasy from the everyday world around her rather than from the distant and seemingly romantic "Vats upon the Rhine." As in a good drinking song, the speaker brags about her great capacity to drink in the third and fourth stanzas. She cannot stop imbibing this "liquor never brewed."

In his superb essay on Dickinson, "Sorting Out," J. V. Cunningham quarrels with the traditional efforts to read the poet's work biographically. So much Dickinson criticism and textual scholarship, he observes, tries to create "a reconstructed history of the poet's emotional life." Such an approach obscures the actual surface meaning of the poem—"History would destroy the text to attain the fact." Cunningham then remarks:

> And so it is amusing that one of the best known poems of these [supposedly autobiographical works], "I taste a liquor never brewed" (214), has been until quite recently read as a self-portrait of Legendary Emily, that

"Debauchee of Dew," that "little Tippler / Leaning against the – Sun." But it seems more likely that the speaker is not Emily at all, but a hummingbird; that the poem is, as many similar nature poems are, a riddle; and we have long missed the answer, not knowing "Guess Who?" was being asked. (*The Collected Essays of J. V. Cunningham* [Chicago: Swallow, 1976])

Questions the class might ask include whether the poem is indeed a riddle and whether Cunningham's interpretation is entirely inconsistent with traditional readings. Could the speaker not be both a hummingbird and the poet herself—or, more precisely, be the hummingbird as an allegory for the poet?

"I taste a liquor never brewed," one of the very few of her nearly 1800 poems to be published in her lifetime, appeared in a newspaper, the Springfield (Massachusetts) *Republican*, on Saturday, May 4, 1861. Here is the text of the poem as first printed, which is of interest for its demonstration of the ways in which Dickinson's earliest editors "normalized" her work to make it acceptable to the taste of the times. The poem is supplied with a (somewhat misleading) title; the first stanza is rewritten to provide an exact rhyme (though "Frankfort berries" is Dickinson's own phrase, from an alternative draft); and, most damaging of all, the extraordinary concluding image is flattened out to something quite conventional.

The May-Wine

I taste a liquor never brewed,
From tankards scooped in pearl;
Not Frankfort berries yield the sense—
Such a delirious whirl.

Inebriate of air am I,
And debauchee of dew;—
Reeling through endless summer days,
From inns of molten blue.

When landlords turn the drunken bee
Out of the Fox-glove's door,
When butterflies renounce their drams,
I shall but drink the more;

Till seraphs swing their snowy hats,
And saints to windows run,
To see the little tippler
Come staggering toward the sun.

Emily Dickinson, WILD NIGHTS – WILD NIGHTS!, page 1015

It is worth noting that this famous love poem contains almost nothing explicitly about romantic love. And yet the text radiates erotic passions—mostly through suggestive word choice and imagery.

The first stanza begins with a fantasy of the "wild nights" the speaker would enjoy if she were with her beloved. (We know she speaks to her beloved because of the "Heart" metaphor in the second stanza.) The sexual element of the fantasy is also suggested by the associations of *luxury*, which originally meant *lust* or *lasciviousness*. (Remember the ghost of Hamlet's father admonishing his son: "Let not the royal bed of Denmark be / A couch for luxury and damnèd incest.") Although the word had also acquired its modern meaning by Dickinson's time, the echo of the original sense still remained. Finally, the nocturnal setting of the poem also suggests the obvious setting for the consummation of sexual love.

The second stanza introduces a metaphorical situation that continues through the rest of the poem—a boat in port. The speaker, however, realizes that this metaphor is still fantasy. She both imagines herself a boat in harbor (lines 6–9) and sees herself in her real situation (lines 11–12) as merely longing to "moor" herself to her beloved.

One more interesting word in this poem is *Eden*. The image of "Rowing in Eden" suggests that fulfillment of the speaker's romantic longings is paradisiacal. The metaphor of Eden further suggests that the speaker's longings—however erotic—are innocent of sin. Eden, the lost paradise, permitted a sexual freedom unknown to the post-lapsarian world. (Dickinson knew her Milton.) The speaker, therefore, longs for erotic fulfillment in a way that harmonizes body and soul in an idealistic, Edenic fashion.

MLL *MyLiteratureLab Resources.* Audio clip for "Wild Nights—Wild Nights!"

Emily Dickinson, I FELT A FUNERAL, IN MY BRAIN, page 1015

There are at least two ways of approaching this stark and powerful poem. We can read it either as a poem about death—the speaker's mental vision of her own extinction—or as a poem that uses death as the central metaphor in an allegory of an unstated psychological anguish.

The poem has an explicit narrative structure. It describes a funeral service and burial. The speaker describes the event simultaneously from two different but related perspectives (a characteristic Dickinsonian device). She places the funeral inside her brain, but she also experiences the ceremony as if she were inside the coffin at the service. Trapped in the coffin, she cannot see the events, only hear them. To borrow a phrase from Judith Farr (whose 1992 study, *The Passions of Emily Dickinson*, places the poet in the context of mid-nineteenth-century American sensibility), the poem is "staged to describe the sensations of lost perception."

Emily Dickinson, I'M NOBODY! WHO ARE YOU?, page 1016

Small and simple, this poem is nonetheless memorable. It illustrates some classic Dickinsonian verbal devices—especially her gift of using everyday words (like *nobody* and *somebody*) in unusual but revelatory ways. Students might enjoy comparing this poem to E. E. Cummings's "anyone lived in a pretty how town," which uses the same verbal device in a more elaborately sustained manner.

Emily Dickinson, I DWELL IN POSSIBILITY, page 1016

Given the fact that its keynote is "Possibility," this little poem makes very effective use of contrast and ambiguity in its treatment of the theme. From the first two lines, it is clear that if it is in contrast to "Prose," then "Possibility" must signify poetry and/or the imagination. It makes sense that there would be more windows in the house of Possibility, and one might at first assume that the superiority of its doors would also mean that there are more of them; but then we see that this house, however limitless its roof may be, is solidly constructed and "Impregnable of Eye," which would suggest that the life of poetry and the imagination is an exclusive, even hermetic one—which it certainly was, as practiced by Dickinson herself. After the nice play on the word "Occupation"—suggesting both residency and employment—the last two lines are suitably rich in possibility: the speaker seems to say that the poet's art will be both her way of comprehending the mysteries of existence and her means of achieving salvation.

Emily Dickinson, THE SOUL SELECTS HER OWN SOCIETY, page 1016

"The Soul selects her own Society" is about both solitude and companionship. It is ultimately a love poem, though it does not initially seem so. The first two stanzas are written in the third person. The speaker views the "Soul" from a distance, though it will eventually seem it is her own soul she describes. The "Soul" chooses her "Society," which proves in the final stanza (now spoken in the first person) to be a single other person. This "divine Majority" of two suffices for the speaker, who then cares little for the rest of the world. She becomes "Like Stone." Even an Emperor kneeling at her doorstep leaves her unmoved.

Emily Dickinson, SOME KEEP THE SABBATH GOING TO CHURCH, page 1017

This celebration of natural religion was one of the seven poems Dickinson actually published during her lifetime. It appeared in the March 12, 1864, issue of *The Round Table*, a New York weekly published by a relation. (It appeared there under the title "My Sabbath," which may have been Dickinson's own suggestion.)

In the original Massachusetts colony, Sunday church attendance was legally mandatory. By Dickinson's time it was merely a social obligation—but a serious one. Although Dickinson was deeply (if also unconventionally) religious, she stopped attending church by her thirtieth birthday. This poem was published a few years thereafter. The poem makes a clear and cogent case for worshipping God not by attending a church service but by being attentive to God's creation. The poem has a simple rhetorical structure: the speaker contrasts her own practices (what the *I* does) with the customs of *some*. A useful question for class discussion is to ask how each of Dickinson's natural images suitably matches (or exceeds) the ecclesiastic person or object it replaces—chorister, dome, surplice, bell, sexton, and clergyman.

Emily Dickinson, AFTER GREAT PAIN, A FORMAL FEELING COMES, page 1017

The meaning of the poem depends heavily on the first three words, "After great pain." All of the subsequent description and rationale originate as consequences of this suffering. If "outlived," the poem suggests, great pain transforms one.

Like many other Dickinson poems, "After great pain" contains images and suggestions of death—tombs, the "hour of Lead," the "Freezing persons" losing consciousness in the snow. In this poem, however, the implied protagonist has survived the possible brush with death. (It is, in fact, possible to interpret the poem as describing a sort of spiritual resurrection—in contrast to the metaphorical reading of "I felt a Funeral, in my Brain" as describing a spiritual or emotional death and disintegration.)

The style and form of the poem are worth noting. Although it feels intimately personal, the poem is spoken in the third person. The speaker seemingly distances herself from the intensity of emotion she has painfully lived through. The middle stanza is arranged as irregular (5 lines versus the two 4-line stanzas that surround it). Heard aloud, however, the two irregular lines (7 and 8) combine into a metrically standard tetrameter line. Dickinson probably arranged the written text in an irregular fashion to slow the reader down and to emphasize the ideas presented in the lines.

Emily Dickinson, THIS IS MY LETTER TO THE WORLD, page 1017

This memorable short poem begins with a characteristic Dickinsonian twist, "This is my letter to the World / That never wrote to Me." As Richard B. Sewall remarks in his detailed volume *The Life of Emily Dickinson* (Cambridge: Harvard UP, 1980), this poem "too often regarded as a tearful complaint about being neglected is actually a statement . . . of the difficulty of conveying what she calls the 'Message' of Nature." The "Her" in line 5 is clearly nature, but to whom do the "Hands" belong in line 6? It is possible to interpret these hands as belonging to posterity—probably the "countrymen" of line 7 whose tender judgment she implores.

If this poem is not specifically a complaint about being neglected, it is nonetheless a call to posterity. Whatever else it might mean, the poem is also an address to her posthumous audience. She may humbly position herself merely as Nature's messenger, but she does claim authorship as the transcriber of that message. She also implicitly confides an uncertainty about her own achievement and hopes that her audience will be tender in its judgment.

Emily Dickinson, I HEARD A FLY BUZZ – WHEN I DIED, page 1018

Plump with suggestions, this celebrated fly well demonstrates a symbol's indefiniteness. The fly appears in the room—on time, like the Angel of Death—and yet it is decidedly ordinary. A final visitor from the natural world, it brings to mind an assortment of suggestions, some of them offensive (filth, stenches, rotting meat, offal, and so forth). But a natural fly is a minor annoyance, and so is death, if one is certain of Eternity. Unsure and hesitant in its flight, the fly buzzes as though faltering. It is another failing thing, like the light that comes through the windows and through the eyes (which are, as a trite phrase calls them, "the windows of the soul").

Most students will easily identify "Eyes around" as those of surrounding friends or relatives, and "that last Onset" as death throes. Is "the King" Death or Jesus? It seems more likely that the friends and relatives will behold death. What is the speaker's assignable portion? Physical things: keepsakes bequeathed to friends and relatives; body, to the earth.

Discussion will probably focus on the final line. It may help students to remember that the speaker is, at the present moment of the poem, in Eternity. The scene she describes is therefore a vision within a vision. Perhaps all the last line means is (as John Ciardi has argued), "And then there was no more of me, and nothing to see with." But the last line suddenly thrusts the speaker to Heaven. For one terrible moment she finds herself, with immortal eyes, looking back through her mortal eyes at a blackness where there used to be light.

 MyLiteratureLab Resources. Audio clip for "I heard a Fly buzz—when I died."

Emily Dickinson, I STARTED EARLY – TOOK MY DOG, *page 1018*

It would be unfortunate if students were to regard this poem as nothing more than a sexual fantasy. Handled with frankness and tact, it can be an excellent class-awakener. The poet expresses feelings for the natural world so intense that, like a mystic choosing erotic imagery to speak of the Beatific Vision, she can report her walk on the beach only in the language of a ravishing. The humor of the poem is essential: the basement-dwelling mermaids, the poet's picturing herself as a mouse.

Emily Dickinson, BECAUSE I COULD NOT STOP FOR DEATH, *page 1019*

QUESTIONS FOR DISCUSSION

1. *What qualities does Dickinson attribute to death? Why is Immortality going along on this carriage ride?* For the poet, death and immortality go together. Besides, Dickinson is amplifying her metaphor of Death as a gentleman taking a woman for a drive: Immortality, as would have been proper in Amherst, is their chaperone.

2. *Is the poem, as the poet wrote it, in some ways superior to the version first printed? Is* strove *perhaps a richer word than* played? *What is interesting in the phrase* Gazing Grain? *How can grain "gaze"?* Grain has kernels like eyes at the tips of its stalks. As the speaker dies, the natural world—like the fly in "I heard a Fly buzz"—is watching. *What is memorable in the rhythm and meaning of the line "The Dews drew quivering and chill"?* At *quivering,* the rhythm quivers loose from its iambic tetrameter. The image of cold dampness foreshadows the next stanza, with its images of the grave.

3. *What is the Carriage? What is the House?*

4. *Where is the speaker at the present moment of the poem? Why is time said to pass more quickly where she is now?* Eternity is timeless.

5. *What is the tone of the poem?* Complicated!—seriousness enlivened with delicate macabre humor? Surely she kids her own worldly busyness in the opening line.

William Galperin reads the poem as a feminist affirmation. Not death, he finds, but immortality is Dickinson's subject. In the end the poet asserts a triumph possible only because she has renounced the proposal of Death, that threatening gentleman caller who might have married her ("Emily Dickinson's Marriage Hearse," *Denver Quarterly* Winter 1984: 62–73).

Emily Dickinson, THE BUSTLE IN A HOUSE, page 1019

This evocative short poem perfectly illustrates one of Dickinson's greatest imaginative methods—the interpenetration of the domestic and the religious realms. The first stanza describes in clinical terms the busy activity in a house after the death of a loved one. The activity is "solemnest," but the living continue their work. The second stanza, however, reveals a radical shift—first into a symbolic mode and then into a religious one. The domestic activities of the first stanza are now allegorized into emotional symbols—the Heart and Love. The last two lines affirm trust in Eternity (not always the case in Dickinson's work) and close the poem with an epigrammatic click.

Emily Dickinson, TELL ALL THE TRUTH BUT TELL IT SLANT, page 1019

Critics have traditionally seen this poem as Dickinson's clearest explanation of her poetic method, and it does remind us of her indirect procedures. Note that the *Truth* is associated with images of light. The poet's job is to make the light illuminating rather than blinding, to ease the viewer into seeing truth gradually. (Even the word *Delight*, which Dickinson wonderfully qualifies with *infirm* to describe the human capacity for truth, contains a possible play on the word *light*.) Likewise, the inability to grasp the truth—to see the light, in the metaphoric world of this poem—is characterized as blindness.

EMILY DICKINSON ON EMILY DICKINSON

Emily Dickinson, RECOGNIZING POETRY, page 1020

It may be worth pointing out to students that this famous passage from Dickinson does not exist in any of her writing. It comes from a letter that T. W. Higginson, a critic and novelist who befriended Dickinson after she wrote him, mailed to his wife during a visit to Amherst. Higginson took notes on his conversation with the poet to share with his wife; these brief notes provide a vivid description of both her genius and her eccentricity. (We have reprinted the statement in its full original context in the "Critics on Emily Dickinson" section which follows.)

QUESTIONS FOR DISCUSSSION

1. Is Dickinson right about recognizing poetry? Is there any other way to recognize it than by experiencing physical sensation?

2. What poem in the anthology affects you in the way that Dickinson describes? Can you relate the sensations you experience to any particular words or images in the poem?

Emily Dickinson, SELF-DESCRIPTION, page 1021

Few letters in literature have generated more commentary—and wild speculation—than Dickinson's April 25, 1862, response to Thomas Wentworth Higginson. Virtually every sentence has been offered several interpretations. The letter is often excerpted, but we have included the whole text to give an accurate impression of Dickinson's unique epistolary style.

Here Dickinson lists her poetic influences—Keats and the two Brownings. For prose she lists Ruskin and Browne, two notably gorgeous and ornate stylists, as well as Revelation, a revealing choice among the books of the Bible. It is worth noting that all of these choices remain respectable a century and a half later. Dickinson recognized truly good writing in both verse and prose. And amusingly she admits she has never read Whitman because she has been "told that he was disgraceful."

CRITICS ON EMILY DICKINSON, pages 1023–1029

We have offered five interesting and diverse critical views of Emily Dickinson. The first is **Thomas Wentworth Higginson**'s extensive account of meeting her in 1870. He not only provides a number of superb observations, he also quotes her remarks extensively. Students will note that Dickinson's famous statement on recognizing poetry ("I feel physically as if the top of my head were taken off") came not from the poet's own letters but from Higginson's account. "I never was with any one who drained my nerve power so much," Higginson remarks at the end of his letter.

Thomas H. Johnson provides an account of discovering Dickinson's manuscripts—one of which we have reproduced. This background will help students understand the unusual nature of the texts of her poems—not an unimportant aspect of interpreting her work. **Richard Wilbur** offers a compelling psychological and biographical portrait of the poet. **Cynthia Griffin Wolff** discusses Dickinson's obsessive central theme, death, and provides a reading of "Because I could not stop for Death," while **Judith Farr** gives a reading of "My Life had stood – a Loaded Gun" that addresses issues of power, gender, and love.

LANGSTON HUGHES

Our selection of Hughes's poetry tries to represent the considerable range of his work—in mood, form, and genre. His special gift of combining traditional and innovational impulses is especially apparent. The juxtaposition with Dickinson's work in this chapter also opens up some interesting comparisons in style and approach that might be used for student essays.

 MyLiteratureLab Resources. Biography, critical overview, and bibliography for Hughes.

Langston Hughes, THE NEGRO SPEAKS OF RIVERS, page 1030

This remarkable poem was written by Hughes while still in his teens. The influence of Walt Whitman and Carl Sandburg, two early models, is evident, but the poem already demonstrates Hughes's characteristic voice. A good discussion question to ask is why Hughes chooses each of the four specific rivers to tell his story of the Negro race. The Euphrates is traditionally seen as the original center of human civilization. By invoking it, Hughes places the Negro at the dawn of humanity. The Congo is the center of black African culture. The Nile represents the source of the most celebrated African culture, and Hughes claims for the Negro a role in building this great civilization. Finally, the Mississippi becomes a symbol of the Negro in America, though Hughes selects a joyous moment to represent the race's turbulent place in our history.

Langston Hughes, MOTHER TO SON, page 1031

This stark, naturalistic poem contains (and half conceals) a transcendent central symbol—a stairway. While the mother has not spent her life climbing a "crystal stair," she has nonetheless felt confident she was ascending a stairwell. This more mundane stairway is badly maintained, poorly lit, and slightly dangerous, but the mother has had the drive and courage to climb it. And she insists that her son show the determination to do so, too.

The spare, conversational free verse of "Mother to Son" provides an interesting contrast to the extravagantly syncopated jazz rhythm of "The Weary Blues" or the rich formal measures of "Song for a Dark Girl." Hughes's poems show a wonderful prosodic range.

Langston Hughes, DREAM VARIATIONS, page 1031

This poem, according to Hughes's biographer, Arnold Rampersad, was written in response to the poet's 1923 trip to Africa. Presenting a vision of racial harmony, the poem contrasts the "white day" and the gentle dark night in a dream of joyous and unproblematic co-existence. The poem's now famous last line served as the title of John Howard Griffin's *Black Like Me* (1961), an exposé of American racial prejudice and discrimination.

Langston Hughes, I, Too, page 1032

This poem represents Hughes's admirable ability to critique American race relations and yet maintain a hopeful tone. The speaker's identity is crucial to the symbolic structure of the poem. He is a brother, a spurned darker brother but nonetheless a member of the family who knows he has an unquestioned right to live in the home. The symbolic segregation of being forced to eat in the kitchen obviously reflects the social realities of Southern segregation in that era. The speaker, however, knows his day will come soon—"tomorrow" in line 8—when he will claim his rightful place at the table, confident of his strength and beauty. But, as the last stanza reminds us, it isn't only the threat of the speaker's strength that will intimidate the others but the justice of his cause. They will "be ashamed" of their previous oppression.

The title and opening line is probably an allusion to Walt Whitman's famous passage in part 52 of "Song of Myself":

I too am not a bit tamed . . . I too am untranslatable,
I sound my barbaric yawp over the roofs of the world.

Langston Hughes, The Weary Blues, page 1032

"The Weary Blues" is a poem of rhythmic bravado. Hughes starts with a basic four-beat line ("Droning a drowsy syncopated tune"). He then flamboyantly varies it with jazz-like syncopations and contrasts it with interpolated short lines. As in "Song for a Dark Girl," he also incorporates allusive quotations from a traditional song—in this case the blues song of the poem's title. ("The Weary Blues" was published, after all, in the twenties—the same decade as T. S. Eliot's allusive *The Waste Land* and Ezra Pound's *A Draft of XVI Cantos*. Hughes was a populist Modernist but a Modernist nonetheless.)

There are two key characters in "The Weary Blues"—the speaker and the piano-playing blues singer. The poem is a recollection by the speaker of the performance he recently heard in Harlem. (Lenox Avenue was one of the main streets of Harlem nightlife in the twenties. It has since been renamed Malcolm X Boulevard, so Hughes's once famous setting has become a historical footnote.) The speaker is of unstated race, but the blues singer is repeatedly identified as a Negro. The singer and his song ultimately become a symbol for the sorrows of the modern African American. ("Sweet Blues! / Coming from a black man's soul. / O Blues!") The expression of the blues seems not only cathartic to the singer but almost annihilating. After singing all night, he goes home to sleep "like a rock or a man that's dead."

Hughes's biographer, Arnold Rampersad, has called "The Weary Blues" a work "virtually unprecedented in American poetry in its blending of black and white rhythms and forms." In his autobiographical book *The Big Sea* (1940), Hughes commented, "It was a poem about a working man who sang the blues all night and then went to bed and slept like a rock. That was all." Most readers will find much more in the poem than that summary suggests.

MLL *MyLiteratureLab Resources.* Longman Lecture on "The Weary Blues."

Langston Hughes, SONG FOR A DARK GIRL, page 1033

One of the most impressive things about Hughes's massive *Collected Poems* is the stylistic diversity of his work. Written in regular rimed quatrains, "Song for a Dark Girl" shows the tight formal but evocatively modernist side of Hughes's style. The poem uses an ironic, allusive refrain borrowed from Daniel Decatur Emmet's famous minstrel song "Dixie's Land," which during the Civil War became a marching song for Confederate troops and then a nostalgic rallying cry for the lost Southern cause. Hughes quotes the song lyric, which is spoken in the faux-black voice of the minstrel, to underscore the reality that the black experience in "de land ob cotton" is not so joyful. The Christ-like imagery associated with the lynched young man is important to note.

Langston Hughes, PRAYER ("GATHER UP"), page 1033

This lovely little poem shimmers with the compassion for the downtrodden that is so large a component of Hughes's work. Notice the movement in the second stanza from "pity" (which inherently suggests a distance between those who pity and the objects of their pity) to the much more intimate "love." Notice too the nice ambiguity of the poem's last word: it is not only God's mercy that "All the scum / Of our weary city" have despaired of, but also the mercy of those who foolishly regard themselves as superior.

Langston Hughes, BALLAD OF THE LANDLORD, page 1034

This ingenious ballad begins to tell its story in the traditional way but then presents an innovative turn midway. The ballad starts in the voice of a black tenant who complains about his negligent landlord. As the poem progresses, the reader realizes that the speaker is arguing with his landlord, who is actually present. The argument heats up until the speaker threatens to hit the landlord (in line 20). Suddenly and unexpectedly, the voice of the poem shifts to outside observers, who condemn and overtly misrepresent the tenant. (Note how Hughes also abruptly shifts his meter and lineation once the voices change.) The poem ends with three isolated but sequential newspaper headlines in all capital letters. Hughes's mixture of auditory prosody and visual prosody in this poem is extremely interesting and demonstrates his use of Modernist techniques in seemingly populist works.

Langston Hughes, KU KLUX, page 1034

In his discussion of its concluding stanza, the critic Bart Brinkman offers an interesting interpretation of the larger implications of this seemingly simple poem:

> In order for the black man to look in the white man's face, the latter must remove his KKK hood—his sustaining marker of whiteness—and reveal himself as an individual. The white man's demand becomes a desperate

plea: he is begging for the black man to acknowledge some essential white-ness that is not dependent on an oppressive dialectic, but is biologically inherent and assured. We do not get the black man's response to this last question (unless we consider it to be the poem itself) and we do not know his fate. But we are left with an impression of "whiteness" as fragile and poorly constructed, to be questioned even by a man under torture. Hughes's poem interrogates the history of oppression based on race and calls into question the very category of race itself.

Langston Hughes, END, page 1035

This unusually stark poem presents a chilling vision of death. Hughes's images of death go one step beyond the conventional depictions. Time has not merely stopped; there is no time. Shadows have not fallen; there are no shadows. There is not only no light but also no dark. There is not even a door to exit. There is, by implication, nothing at all. This free verse, imagistic, and consciously imper-sonal poem demonstrates a different side of Hughes's talent—a darker and colder side—yet its immediacy and accessibility remain characteristic.

Langston Hughes, THEME FOR ENGLISH B, page 1035

This poem demonstrates how a great writer in his maturity can turn a routine homework assignment into a memorable piece of literature. If youth is wasted on the young, so perhaps are writing assignments.

Hughes is so convincing a storyteller that you will probably have to remind students—repeatedly—that this poem is not autobiographical. Hughes was not born in Winston-Salem, but in Joplin, Missouri. He did not go to school in Durham, but in Lawrence, Kansas, and Cleveland, Ohio. He did attend Columbia (where, by implication, the poem takes place), but he left after a year to travel. (He later completed his college education at Lincoln University in Pennsylvania.) He was nearly fifty when he wrote this poem, not twenty-two as the narrator is.

Langston Hughes, SUBWAY RUSH HOUR, page 1036

In this compressed but vivid depiction of rush hour in the subway, the poet seems to send an optimistic message: that were blacks and whites ever to mingle closely with one another on equal terms, there would be "no room for fear." Notable in the poem is Hughes's imagery. Within his sixteen-word limit he evokes three of the five senses: smell, touch, and sight.

Langston Hughes, SLIVER, page 1036

"Sliver" provides another example of how Hughes employs a direct, song-like structure to create a richly evocative lyric. Hughes enjoyed contrasting the visual arrangement of his poems to the auditory shape. In "Sliver" he prints the two rhymed quatrains as a single, eight-line stanza to underscore the tight imagistic unity of the poem. Note, for example, how the "sliver of the moon" unexpectedly becomes the weapon to slit the man's throat.

Langston Hughes, HARLEM [DREAM DEFERRED], page 1037

Simile by simile, Hughes shows different attitudes, including violent protest, that blacks might possibly take toward the long deferral of their dream of equality. Students might be asked what meaning they find in each comparison. Also worth noting are the strong, largely unpleasant verbs used to characterize the types of decay caused by deferring the dream: *dry up*, *fester*, *run*, *stink*, *crust and sugar over*, and *sags*. No wonder an explosion is likely to follow.

Hughes's poem supplied the title for Lorraine Hansberry's long-running Broadway play, *A Raisin in the Sun* (1958), in which the Youngers, a family descended from five generations of slaves, seek to move out of a Chicago ghetto in hopes of fulfilling their dream.

Donald Ritzhein has written a moving account of what the poem has meant to him, starting when his mother cut it out of a newspaper and pasted it to his bedroom door. "By the time I got to high school . . . I still didn't know a lot about the misery of deferred dreams . . . I knew a little more about them when I heard Martin Luther King, Jr. talk about dreams in Washington. I finally felt a little of what it's like to defer dreams when John F. Kennedy was killed" ("Langston Hughes: A Look Backwards and Forwards," *Steppingstones*, Harlem, Winter 1984: 55–56). Have you any student who would care to write about what the poem has meant to her or him?

Langston Hughes, AS BEFITS A MAN, page 1037

Each of the poem's first two stanzas begins with the line "I don't mind dying." The speaker, unlike a great many others, is calmly reconciled to the inevitable end of his own existence. What does concern him is not how or when he will die, or even how much he will suffer, but how he will be remembered and mourned—and, "as befits a man," what that means to him is how he will be remembered and mourned by the women in his life. As shown in the third stanza, he wants the richness and fullness of his life to be commemorated by appropriate fanfare and display at his funeral.

You may find it useful to have your students compare and contrast this poem with Gwendolyn Brooks's "Southeast Corner": while Brooks seems disapproving of the Madam's superficiality and complacency, there is no sense here that Hughes is anything but admiring of his speaker's gusto and *joie de vivre*.

LANGSTON HUGHES ON LANGSTON HUGHES

Langston Hughes, THE NEGRO ARTIST AND THE RACIAL MOUNTAIN, page 1038

Hughes's essay "The Negro Artist and the Racial Mountain" was the key manifesto of the younger African American artists associated with the Harlem

Renaissance. This crucial article originally appeared in the *Nation* as a response to George Schuyler's dismissive article "The Negro-Art Hokum." Hughes's proud assertion of black identity and the unabashed celebration of jazz and the blues struck a responsive chord among many members of the new generation of African American artists and intellectuals. The new artists saw their role, in the words of Arnold Rampersad, "to assert racial pride and racial truth in the face of either black or white censure or criticism."

Langston Hughes, THE HARLEM RENAISSANCE, page 1039

In his autobiography, *The Big Sea* (1940), Hughes gave a vivid account of the Harlem Renaissance. This passage describes both the cultural excitement and the racial tension of Harlem's nightlife after white people began patronizing the local clubs. This profitable influx of white customers led to bizarre situations such as the famous Cotton Club and other nightspots, banning African Americans except as performers and staff—"barring their own race," as Hughes indignantly puts it. But Hughes also celebrates the talent and vitality of the club scene in a way that conveys the African American side of the Jazz Age.

CRITICS ON LANGSTON HUGHES, pages 1041–1048

The critical selections on Langston Hughes offer a range of approaches. **Arnold Rampersad**, Hughes's most distinguished biographer, discusses the innovative aspects of the early poetry, which blended both black and white literary traditions. **Rita Dove** and **Marilyn Nelson** examine Hughes's role as spokesman for African Americans. **Darryl Pinckney** analyzes in both historical and reader-response terms how Hughes connected with his early African American readers. **Peter Townsend** analyzes how Hughes used jazz influences and speculates on the social impact of his jazz poetry during his long career. Finally, **Onwuchekwa Jemie** provides a highly sensitive reading of Hughes's most famous poem, "Dream Deferred" (also published under the title "Harlem").

32
Critical Casebook: T. S. Eliot's "The Love Song of J. Alfred Prufrock"

As the first poem in T. S. Eliot's first published volume, and therefore the first poem in every subsequent selected and collected edition of his poetry, "The Love Song of J. Alfred Prufrock" has been the introduction to Eliot's work for many readers over the nearly one hundred years since it was first published. To this day, "Prufrock" remains an ideal text for young people to make their first acquaintance with Eliot. It is substantial enough to communicate some of his major themes and techniques, without being daunting in its length or complexity. It can still seem strange and in places even shocking to those who have not encountered it before, and thus it can still suggest to contemporary readers the radical innovations of Modernism, while proving at the same time to be absorbing and accessible. And, despite all indications to the contrary, many adolescents and young adults will still sympathize, and even empathize, with the poem's preoccupation with such concerns as loneliness, self-consciousness, fear of the opposite sex, the desire to live meaningfully in a trivializing culture, and pervasive feelings of futility and failure.

The poem's enduring popularity with readers has recently been reaffirmed in an extraordinary fashion. David Lehman, editor of the new *Oxford Book of American Poetry* (2006), selected the ten poems from that anthology that he considered the most popular, and readers were asked to vote for their favorite from the list. "Prufrock" was the clear winner, beating out such warhorses as Walt Whitman's "Song of Myself," Robert Frost's "Stopping by Woods on a Snowy Evening," Edgar Allan Poe's "The Raven," and Emma Lazarus's "The New Colossus."

In addition to "The Love Song of J. Alfred Prufrock," this chapter presents a number of supplemental texts and images selected to enrich your students' understanding of the poem, to enable them to view it in the context of its own time, and to help them understand why it is a work for all time. "Publishing 'Prufrock'" recounts—with excerpts from Ezra Pound's letters to Harriet Monroe, the editor of *Poetry* magazine—Pound's often frustrating but untiring efforts to get "Prufrock" into print. A selection of excerpts from the reviews, in both Britain and America, of *Prufrock and Other Observations* (1917) gives a vivid sense of both the dismissive incomprehension and the discerning appreciation of some of the poem's earliest readers. Passages from Eliot's own critical writings communicate some of his poetic theories and techniques as they bear directly on the poem. A cross-section of some of the best critical discussions of the poem over the last several decades helps to illuminate some difficult passages and other significant aspects of the text—and concludes with observations by two distinguished poet-critics, John Berryman and M. L. Rosenthal. Rosenthal's reminiscence of what

"Prufrock" meant to him in his own adolescence should prove to be of particular interest to young readers involved in their own first encounter with Eliot's poem.

T. S. Eliot, THE LOVE SONG OF J. ALFRED PRUFROCK, page 1051

Given the wealth of supplemental material presented in the chapter, an extended commentary on the poem seems superfluous, if not presumptuous. But we would like to offer a few questions to start the classroom discussion.

QUESTIONS FOR DISCUSSION

1. *Why the epigraph from Dante? What expectations does it arouse?* Perhaps that this "song" will be the private confession of someone who thinks himself trapped and unredeemable, and thinks it of his hearer, too; also, that he is emboldened to speak only because he feels that his secrets will be kept.

2. *What facts about J. Alfred can we be sure of? His age, his manner of dress, his social circles? What does his name suggest? Can you detect any puns in it?* A prude in a frock—a formal coat.

3. *What do you make of the simile in lines 2–3? What does it tell us about this particular evening?* Etherized suggests fog, also submission, waiting for something grim to happen—his insides are going to be exposed and examined. *What does it tell you about Prufrock's way of seeing things?* "A little sick," some students may say, and with reason.

4. *What gnaws at Prufrock?* Not just his sense of growing old, not just his inability to act. He suffers from Prufrock's Complaint: dissociation of sensibility. In line 105, unable to join thought and feeling, he sees his own nerves existing at one remove from him, as if thrown on a screen by a projector.

5. *Who are "you and I" in the opening line? Who are "we" at the end?* Some possibilities: Prufrock and the woman he is attending. Prufrock and the reader. Prufrock and Prufrock—he's talking to himself, "you" being the repressive self, "I" being the timid or repressed self. Prufrock and the other eggheads of the Western world—in this view, the poem is Eliot's satire on the intelligentsia.

6. *What symbols do you find and what do they suggest? Notice those that relate to the sea,* even oyster-shells (line 7). XJK points out blatantly that water has connotations of sexual fulfillment, and quotes "Western Wind." Eliot hints that, unlike Prufrock, the vulgar types who inhabit cheap hotels and fish shops have a love life.

7. *Try to explain the last three lines.*

8. *Now summarize the story of the poem. What parts does it fall into?* Part one: Prufrock prepares to try to ask the overwhelming question. Then in lines 84–86 we learn that he has failed to ask it. In 87–110 he tries to justify himself for chickening out. From 111 to the end he sums up his static present and hollow future.

A few other points worth making:

That Eliot may have taken the bones of his plot from Henry James's "Crapy Cornelia" (1909) is Grover Smith's convincing theory. "This is the story of White-Mason, a middle-aged bachelor of nostalgic temperament, who visits a young Mrs. Worthington to propose marriage but reconsiders owing to the difference in their worlds" (*T. S. Eliot's Poetry and Plays* [Chicago: U of Chicago P, 1960] 15).

"The meter of 'Prufrock' is peculiar," observes John Heath-Stubbs. "It is not simply free verse, as in [Eliot's] earlier Laforgueian pieces, but in its lines of irregular length, many but not all of which rhyme, suggests a free version of the Dantesque Canzone." This suggestion, and the poem's epigraph from the *Inferno*, point to Eliot's growing preoccupation with Dante ("Structure and Source in Eliot's Major Poetry," *Agenda* [Spring-Summer 1985]: 24).

Cleanth Brooks has written an essay full of wisdom and practical advice, "Teaching 'The Love Song of J. Alfred Prufrock,'" which you can find in *Eliot's Poetry and Plays*, one of the MLA's valuable "Approaches to Teaching" series (1988).

T. S. Eliot Reading His Poetry (Caedmon recording TC 1045) includes the poet's rendition of "Prufrock." There are also recordings of the poem spoken by Alec Guinness (*Sir Alec Guinness Reads T. S. Eliot*) and Ted Hughes (*T. S. Eliot: The Waste Land and Other Poems*).

[MLL] *MyLiteratureLab Resources*. Biography, critical overview, and bibliography for Eliot. Student paper on "The Love Song of J. Alfred Prufrock."

PUBLISHING "PRUFROCK," page 1055

This selection is intended to give some sense of the poem's original appearances—including the tangled bibliography of Eliot's first three poetry chapbooks—and to demonstrate the eternal nature of the issues involved. The excerpts from Ezra Pound's letters to Harriet Monroe convey the flavor of Pound's explosive and often arrogant personality, especially in defense of the writers and the artistic principles that he strongly believed in, and they illustrate the age-old clash between the artist's uncompromising integrity and the editor's audience-pleasing instincts. Pound's expostulations, in his letter of January 31, 1915, against what he perceived as Monroe's desire to have "Prufrock" end "on a note of triumph" may put you in mind of the famous witticism about "the ultimate *Reader's Digest* article: 'New Hope for the Dead.'" It should interest students to discover that many works now regarded as classics encountered a good deal of difficulty in achieving publication, and to learn how much perseverance is often needed in the face of obstacles to success.

THE REVIEWERS ON *PRUFROCK AND OTHER OBSERVATIONS*: 1917–1918, page 1057

The three British reviews excerpted here were all published anonymously, as was the custom of the times with such publications. The judgments expressed were no doubt intended to sound magisterial and absolute, rather than being presented for what they were, the opinions of fallible—and at times, it would seem from the internal evidence, unqualified—individuals. From the tone of these passages it can be seen how seriously those publications took themselves as "guardians of the faith," to borrow a sarcastic phrase from another of the poems in the *Prufrock* volume. The reviewer for the *Times Literary Supplement* (who was F. T. Dalton, an assistant editor of the *TLS* from 1902 to 1923) seems serene in his conviction that what he considers trivial and unenjoyable will strike most others in the same way; rather more surprising is his description of Eliot's poems as "untouched by any genuine rush of feeling," until one considers the gush of hyperbolic sentiment displayed in so much of the verse of that period. The author of the notice in the *Literary World* assumes, as was common in such circumstances, that what he cannot understand is deliberate nonsense, intended as a hoax by its author; his astuteness in maintaining that "[a]ll beauty has in it an element of strangeness" makes his overall obtuseness all the more peculiar. The writer in the *New Statesman* seems considerably more discerning than his colleagues, but his tone is somewhat patronizing overall, and, as May Sinclair suggests, it is uncomprehending, if not offensive, to exalt "The *Boston Evening Transcript*" at the expense of "Prufrock."

More perceptive were the reactions of Eliot's fellow Americans (and fellow poets). One would expect a favorable review from **Conrad Aiken,** given his friendship with Eliot; less expected, perhaps, is the mingling of a bit of blame ("the trivial") with the praise, showing Aiken's concern to demonstrate the objectivity of his judgment—though the phrase "the adorers of free verse" shows his own commitment to traditional verse techniques. Like Aiken, **Babette Deutsch** emphasizes Eliot's great technical skill and his cleverness. Of the three, it is **Marianne Moore** who most clearly communicates the depth and seriousness of Eliot's achievement in the *Prufrock* volume.

This recognition of Eliot's true value is even more directly displayed in the review by the British novelist **May Sinclair**. In the midst of excoriating the *New Statesman* review, she uses the word "masterpieces" to describe the poems and refers several times to Eliot's "genius." Among all the reviewers represented in this sampling, she is the one who shows the greatest awareness of the implications of Eliot's work for the future development of poetry.

T. S. ELIOT ON WRITING

T. S. *Eliot*, POETRY AND EMOTION, page 1061

This passage from the seminal essay "Tradition and the Individual Talent" addresses a number of concerns. In taking issue with William Wordsworth's classic definition of poetry as "the spontaneous overflow of powerful emotion recollected in tranquility," Eliot is a bit puckish in describing it as "an inexact formula," since he disputes every term of the phrase he quotes—and surely would have disputed "spontaneous" as well, had he quoted the entire comment. Eliot also supplies a useful corrective to some strivers after novelty when he says that it is not poetry's mission "to seek for new human emotions to express." The most famous passage in the excerpt is the last two sentences; in the light of facts about Eliot's personal life revealed after his death, it is fashionable among some to interpret these remarks in a narrowly personal manner—an unavoidable and, to some extent, valid response, but ultimately an insufficient engagement of the full implications of what Eliot is saying.

T. S. *Eliot*, THE OBJECTIVE CORRELATIVE, page 1062

Here is Eliot's famous definition of a term of his own devising, a formulation that has become as much a part of the critical discourse as Keats's "negative capability" and Coleridge's "willing suspension of disbelief."

T. S. *Eliot*, THE DIFFICULTY OF POETRY, page 1062

Eliot's remarks on the subject of difficulty in poetry are well worth attending to, not only because his own poetry is frequently branded "difficult," but especially because of the good sense in what he has to say. As he points out, there are different ways in which a poem can be difficult and different reasons for such difficulty, and some of these are more worthy of respect than others. Two points made in this excerpt are particularly worth emphasizing to students: (1) there are times when a poem must be difficult, when its being otherwise would entail an injustice to the complexity or even the intractability of the material and/or the author's vision; (2) one should read poetry, especially difficult poetry, not in a state of anxiety to determine "what the author is trying to bring out"—that is, to impose an understanding on the text, sum up the theme, and move on as quickly as possible—but, instead, with a relaxed openness and receptivity, to experience the poem on all of its levels, not just that of paraphrasable content.

CRITICS ON "PRUFROCK," page 1064

We begin with the commentary by **Denis Donoghue,** even though it is the most recent of our critical excerpts, because his speculations on the possible meanings of the epigraph provide an entranceway into discussion of the text. Your students may also appreciate Donoghue's description of his discovery of "Prufrock" in his adolescence and his immediate awareness that it was "memorable" and "fully achieved," without any concern for what critics had to say on the subject.

Speaking of speculations and entrances into the poem, **Christopher Ricks** considers a range of implications arising from the poem's title—not only the odd coupling of its two halves, but especially the speaker's name and the assumptions that it provokes; then, having done this, he is just deconstructionist enough to question the legitimacy of the procedure.

In his comments on the referents of the pronouns in "Prufrock," **Philip R. Headings** understandably gives most of his attention to the unidentified "you" of line 1; he valuably supplies the source for Eliot's well-known coy observations on the subject, though Headings's own conclusion about the identity of "you" is certainly open to challenge.

By considering the ways in which time functions in the poem, **Maud Ellmann** provides an illuminating analysis of Prufrock's use of tenses; from there, she addresses the larger issue of what it is that he is expressing when he expresses himself.

Burton Raffel employs the word "indeterminacy" to describe Eliot's frequent use of allusions that are not fully explained in context. He takes up two instances—Prufrock's intention to "wear the bottoms of my trousers rolled" and the "overwhelming question"—and decides that, while these references may not be presented with pinpoint precision, they are clear enough in context to satisfy all but the most insecure readers.

As a poet, **John Berryman** cultivated a notoriously compressed and difficult style, and his prose can also be demanding. But it is worth grappling with here for the illuminations that it affords regarding four central historical and fictional figures that Prufrock invokes in the course of his monologue. Especially rewarding is Berryman's analysis of one of the strangest and most difficult passages in the poem, the "pair of ragged claws" couplet.

Bringing us full circle, **M. L. Rosenthal** recalls his own discovery of "Prufrock" in the 1930s and muses on the reasons why Eliot's early poetry has a perpetual appeal for adolescents.

33
Poems for Further Reading

Anonymous, LORD RANDALL, page 1075

Students might be asked to read the information about ballads in the chapter "Song," either before or after reading this ballad. "Lord Randall" exhibits many of the qualities of the traditional folk ballad, including a certain roughness in places, as with the meter in line 19. But, as demonstrated by the shift in the refrain halfway through, it demonstrates a certain degree of literary sophistication as well.

QUESTIONS FOR DISCUSSION

1. The basic situation in this ballad is slow to unfold. Is this an effective technique here, or do you think that the poem would have benefited by opening with more of a "grabber"?

2. Do you find the repetitiousness of the refrain a hindrance to your enjoyment of the poem? What is gained (or lost) by changing the refrain in the sixth stanza?

3. What is the value to the poem of the question-and-answer method of storytelling? Is the ending of the poem surprising, or do you see it coming from a long way off?

4. What else could the author have told us about Lord Randall's "true-love" and their relationship? Do you find it troublesome that she does what she does without our knowing why? Might the poem have suffered if the author had more deeply explored her motivations?

Anonymous, THE THREE RAVENS, page 1076
Anonymous, THE TWA CORBIES, page 1077

QUESTIONS FOR DISCUSSION

1. In "The Three Ravens," what is suggestive about the ravens and their conversation? How are the ravens opposed in the poem by the hawks and the hounds? (The ravens are selfish eaters of carrion, but the hawks and hounds are loyally standing guard over their dead master's body. Their faithfulness also suggests that of the fallow doe.)

2. Are you persuaded by Friedman's suggestion (quoted in the note under "The Three Ravens") that the doe is a woman who is under some enchantment? What other familiar fairy tales or stories of lovers transformed into animals do you recall?

3. Do you agree that "The Twa Corbies" is "a cynical variation of 'The Three Ravens,'" as it has been called? Compare the two poems in their comments on love and faithfulness.

4. For all the fantasy of "The Three Ravens," what details in the ballad seem realistic reflections of the natural world?

Anonymous, LAST WORDS OF THE PROPHET (NAVAJO MOUNTAIN CHANT), page 1077

This valediction is part of the Mountain Chant of the Navajo translated by Washington Matthews, one of the pioneering linguistic anthropologists. His work helped broaden appreciation for the genius of Native American poetry. The Mountain Chants were performed by the Navajo under the direction of a shaman and contain many archaic words whose meanings were lost even to the priesthood.

Matthew Arnold, DOVER BEACH, page 1078

Arnold and his family did such an efficient job of expunging the facts of his early romances that the genesis of "Dover Beach" is hard to know. Arnold may (or may not) have been in love with a French girl whom he called Marguerite, whose egotistic gaiety made her difficult. See Lionel Trilling's discussion of the poem and of Arnold's Marguerite poems in his biography *Matthew Arnold* (New York: Columbia UP, 1949). Marguerite, Trilling suspects, viewed the world as much more various, beautiful, and new than young Arnold did.

A sympathetic reading of "Dover Beach" might include some attention to the music of its assonance and alliteration, especially the s-sounds in the description of the tide (lines 12–14). Line 21 introduces the central metaphor, the Sea of Faith. Students will probably be helped by a few minutes of discussion of the historical background of the poem. Why, when the poem appeared in 1867, was religious faith under attack? Darwin, Herbert Spencer, and Victorian industrialism may be worth mention. Ignorant armies (line 37) are still with us. Arnold probably had in mind those involved in the Crimean War of 1853–1856, perhaps also those in the American Civil War. For sources of the poem, see C. B. Tinker and H. F. Lowry, *The Poetry of Matthew Arnold* (New York: Oxford UP, 1940) 173–78.

A dour view of the poem is taken by Donald Hall in "Ah, Love, Let Us Be True" (*American Scholar*, Summer 1959). Hall finds "love invoked as a compensation for the losses that history has forced us to sustain," and adds, "I hope there are better reasons for fidelity than disillusion. . . . Like so many Victorian poems, its negation is beautiful and its affirmation repulsive." This comment can be used to provoke discussion. A useful counterfoil to "Dover Beach" is Anthony Hecht's satiric poem "The Dover Bitch," in his collection *The Hard Hours* (New

York: Atheneum, 1960) and in many anthologies. For other critical comment, see William E. Cadbury, "Coming to Terms with 'Dover Beach,'" *Criticism* 8 (Spring 1966): 126–38; James Dickey, *Babel to Byzantium* (New York: Farrar, 1968) 235–38 (a good concise general essay); and A. Dwight Culler, *Imaginative Reason: The Poetry of Matthew Arnold* (New Haven: Yale UP, 1966).

John Ashbery, AT NORTH FARM, page 1079

It is never easy to decide what an Ashbery poem "means." This one is rich with suggestions about which students may be invited to speculate. Who is this threatening catlike "someone" for whom we set out milk at night and about whom we think "sometimes, / Sometimes and always, with mixed feelings"? Is it the grim reaper? And yet Death always knows where to find the person he's looking for. And what are we to make of lines 7–11? How can the granaries be "bursting with meal, / The sacks of meal piled to the rafters" if "Hardly anything grows here"? The poet hints at a terrible sterility underlying the visible abundance at North Farm. Perhaps the farm can be regarded as, among other things, a paradigm of the world, rich in material things but spiritually empty. But that is to reduce the poem to flat words. Because such paraphrases tend to slip from Ashbery's poems like seals from icebergs, this poet's work is a favorite of critics. It challenges them to make subtler and stickier paraphrases.

Margaret Atwood, SIREN SONG, page 1079

Atwood's "Siren Song" is a wonderfully tricky poem that seduces the reader as cleverly as it does its doomed listener. The reader doesn't realize that he or she has been taken in, until it is too late.

The poem is in three parts. The first section (lines 1–9) recounts the sirens and their deadly songs. Many readers will recognize the legendary monsters (half bird, half woman) from Book XII of *The Odyssey*. "Siren" has become a synonym for a dangerously alluring woman. The second section (lines 10–24) switches gears suddenly, as one of the sirens confesses to us her unhappy plight. She offers to tell us the secret of her irresistible song, but mainly she talks about herself and cries for our help. Then, without knowing it until too late, we are in the final section (the last three lines), where we realize that we have been lured into the siren's emotional grasp.

Feminist poets have often retold famous myths and legends with a twist; Atwood's "Siren Song" is surely a model of this genre.

You can listen to a recording of Margaret Atwood reading "Siren Song" at <http://www.poetryarchive.co.uk/poetryarchive/trackListing.do?poetId=96> and watch a video clip in which Atwood discusses the significance of myth at <http://www.pbs.org./moyers/faithandreason/media_players/atwoodpreview.html>.

W. H. Auden, AS I WALKED OUT ONE EVENING, page 1081

This literary ballad, with its stark contrast between the innocent song of the lover and the more knowing song of the clocks, affords opportunities to pay close attention to the poet's choice of words. Auden selects words rich in connotations: the *brimming* of the river (which suggests also the lover's feelings), the *crooked* neighbor (with its hint of dishonesty and corruption as well as the denotation of being warped or bent by Time, like the "diver's brilliant bow"). Figures of speech abound: the opening metaphor of the crowds like wheat (ripe and ready to be scythed by Time the Reaper), the lover's extended use of hyperbole in lines 9–20, the personifications of Time and Justice, the serious pun on *appalling* in line 34 (both awe-inspiring and like a pall or shroud, as in Blake's "London"), the final reconciliation in metaphor between the original "brimming river" and the flow of passing Time. Auden's theme appears to be that as young lovers grow old, their innocent vision is smudged and begrimed by contact with realities—and yet "Life remains a blessing" after all.

The lover's huge promises in stanzas 3 and 4 ("I'll love you Till China and Africa meet . . .") have reminded Richard Wilbur of the hyperbolic boasts of the speaker in Burns's "Oh, my love is like a red, red rose." Burns speaks for the romantic lover, wrapped in his own emotions, but Auden's view of romantic love is skeptical. "The poem then proceeds to rebut [the lover's] lines, saying that the human heart is too selfish and perverse to make such promises" (*Responses* [New York: Harcourt, 1976] 144).

This poem may appear to have too little action in it to resemble folk ballads in more than a few touches. Auden himself, according to Monroe K. Spears, did not call this a ballad but referred to it as "a pastiche of folk-song."

"As I Walked Out One Evening" is one of the "Five Lyrics" included in *W. H. Auden Reading* (Caedmon recording TC 1019). For comparison with the poet's own modest delivery, *Dylan Thomas Reading*, vol. 4 (Caedmon TC 1061), offers a more dramatic rendition.

MLL *MyLiteratureLab Resources.* Biography, critical overview, and bibliography for Auden.

W. H. Auden, Musée des Beaux Arts, page 1083

In Breughel's *Landscape with the Fall of Icarus* (reproduced with this poem), students may need to have their attention directed to the legs disappearing in a splash, one quarter inch below the bow of the ship. One story (probably apocryphal) is that Breughel's patron had ordered a painting on a subject from mythology, but the artist had only this landscape painting completed. To fill the order quickly, Breughel touched in the little splash, gave the picture a mythological name, and sent it on its way. Question: How does that story (if true) make Breughel seem a shallower man than Auden thinks he is?

Besides the *Landscape,* Auden apparently has in mind two other paintings of Pieter Breughel the Elder: *The Census,* also called *The Numbering at Bethlehem* (Auden's lines 5–8), and *The Massacre of the Innocents* (lines 9–13). If the instructor has access to reproductions, these works might be worth bringing in; however, the *Landscape* seems central to the poem. This painting seems indebted to Ovid's *Metamorphoses,* but in Ovid the plowman, shepherd, and fisherman looked on the fall of Icarus with amazement. The title of Auden's poem, incidentally, is close to the name of the Brussels museum housing the *Landscape*: the Musées Royaux des Beaux Arts.

Edward Mendelson has remarked on the poem in *Early Auden* (New York: Viking, 1981):

> The poetic imagination that seeks out grandeur and sublimity could scarcely be bothered with those insignificant figures lost in the background or in the crowd. But Auden sees in them an example of Christianity's great and enduring transformation of classical rhetoric: its inversion of the principle that the most important subjects require the highest style. If the sufferings of a carpenter turned preacher mattered more to the world than the doom of princes, then the high style, for all its splendor, was a limited instrument. . . . These casually irregular lines make none of the demands for action and attention that marked Auden's earlier harangues on the urgency of the times, yet beneath the apparent surface disorder a deeper pattern of connectedness gradually makes itself felt. The unassertive rhymes, easily overlooked on a first reading, hold the poem together.

Yet another device of language helps bring unity to Auden's meditation, in P. K. Saha's view. Four clauses begin with *how*, and one phrase begins with *anyhow* (line 11). These *hows* vary in meaning; still, the repeated *how* is the crucial word in the linguistic pattern of the poem ("Style, Stylistic Transformations, and Incorporators," *Style* 12 [1978]: 18–22).

 MyLiteratureLab Resources. Biography, critical overview, and bibliography for Auden.

Elizabeth Bishop, FILLING STATION, page 1084

QUESTIONS FOR DISCUSSION

1. *What is the poet's attitude toward the feeble attempts at beautification detailed in lines 23–33? Sympathy, contempt, or what? How is the attitude indicated?* The attempts are doomed, not only by the gas station's being saturated with oil, but by the limitations of the family, whose only reading appears to be comic books and whose tastes run to hairy plants and daisy-covered doilies. In line 20, *comfy* is their word, not the poet's own. But the tone of the poem seems to be good-humored amusement. The sons are "quick and saucy"—likable traits. The gas station can't be beautiful, but at least its owners have tried. In a futile gesture toward neatness, they have even arranged the oil cans in symmetry.

2. *What meanings do you find in the last line?* Somebody has shown love for all motorists by arranging the oil cans so beautifully that they spell out a soothing croon, such as what one might say over and over to an agitated child. But the somebody also suggests Somebody Up There, whose love enfolds all human beings—even this oil-soaked crew.

3. *Do you find any similarity between "ESSO—SO—SO—SO" in "Filling Station" and "rainbow, rainbow, rainbow!" in "The Fish"?* Both lines stand late in their poems and sound similar; both express the speaker's glimpse of beauty—or at least, in "Filling Station," the only beauty the people can muster and the poet can perceive.

Helen Vendler, discussing the poem in *Part of Nature, Part of Us* (Cambridge: Harvard UP, 1980), takes the closing statement to mean "God loves us all." But Irvin Ehrenpreis disagrees: "The '—SO—SO—SO' of overlapping labels on stacked cans is supposed to comfort automobiles as if they were highstrung horses, i.e., like a mother, not a god." Doily and begonia indicate that some absent woman has tried to brighten up this gas station for her husband and her sons (review of Vendler's book in *New York Review of Books*, 29 Apr. 1980).

Edward Cifelli, County College of Morris, passes along an insight from his student Joseph Grana. The message "ESSO—SO—SO—SO" may be an SOS from the same "somebody" who embroidered the doily and waters the plant. Professor Cifelli adds, "The pitiable woman who tries to put traces of beauty into a filthy filling station is unconsciously calling out for help, for rescue. Now *that* engages me!"

Robert Pinsky has also written of "Filling Station" with high esteem. He calls the poem a kind of contest between "the meticulous vigor of the writer" and "the sloppy vigor of the family," both filling a dull moment and scene with "an unexpected, crazy, deceptively off-hand kind of elegance or ornament." He particularly admires the poet's choice of modifiers—including the direct, honest-seeming *dirty*. "Adjectives," he notes, "according to a sound rule of thumb for writing classes, do not make 'good descriptions.' By writing almost as though she were too plain and straightforward to have heard of such a rule, Bishop loads characterizations of herself and her subject into the *comfy* dog, the *dim* doily, the *hirsute* begonia; the quietest possible virtuoso strokes" (*The Situation of Poetry* [Princeton: Princeton UP, 1976] 75–77).

"I've sometimes thought 'Filling Station' would make a good exercise for acting students," observes critic and teacher David Walker, "given the number of different ways the first line—and much of the rest—might be stressed. Is the opening exclamation solemn and childlike, or prissy and fastidious, or enthusiastic? All we can identify with certainty, I think, is the quality of fascination, the intent gaze on the filling station's pure oiliness." Walker is reminded of Frost's "Design" in that both poets seek to discover "a meaningful pattern in apparently random details"—but while Frost points toward a sinister architecture in what he observes, Bishop finds beauty and harmony ("Elizabeth Bishop and the Ordinary," *Field* [Fall 1984]).

Brad Leithauser has admired the poem's ingenious sound effects. At its end, "the cans of oil are arranged like cue cards to prompt that concluding sentence, the SO—SO—SO grading toward that 'Somebody loves us all.' Neatly, the message in the oil cans is reinforced by both the 'so' and the 'softly' in the fourth line from the end" ("The 'Complete' Elizabeth Bishop," *New Criterion* [Mar. 1983]: 38).

MLL *MyLiteratureLab Resources.* Biography, critical overview, and bibliography for Bishop.

William Blake, THE TYGER, page 1086
William Blake, THE SICK ROSE, page 1087

"The Tyger," from *Songs of Experience*, is a companion piece to "The Lamb" in *Songs of Innocence*. But while "The Lamb" poses a relatively easy question ("Little lamb, who made thee?") and soon answers it, "The Tyger" poses questions that remain unanswerable. Alert students may complain that some of Blake's questions have no verbs—what dread hand and what dread feet did *what?* While the incompleteness has been explained by some critics as reflecting the agitated tone of the poem, it may have been due to the poet's agitated habits of composition. Drafts of the poem in Blake's notebook show that, after writing the first three stanzas, he began the fourth stanza with the line "Could fetch it from the furnace deep," which would have completed the question in line 12. But then he deleted it and wrote stanza four almost as it stands now. (See Martin K. Nurmi, "Blake's Revision of 'The Tyger,'" *PMLA 71* [1956]: 669–85.) Other useful discussions include that of E. D. Hirsch, Jr., *Innocence and Experience* (New Haven: Yale UP, 1964), who thinks the stars are the rebel angels who threw down their spears when they surrendered; and John E. Grant, "The Art and Argument of 'The Tyger'" in *Texas Studies in Literature and Language 2* (1960): 38–60.

In "The Sick Rose," why is the worm, whose love is rape, *invisible?* Not just because it is hidden in the rose, but also because it is some supernatural dweller in night and storm. Perhaps the worm is unseen Time, that familiar destroyer— is the rose then mortal beauty? Those are usual guesses. For an unusual guess, see E. D. Hirsch, Jr.: "The rose's sickness, like syphilis, is the internal result of love enjoyed secretly and illicitly instead of purely and openly." In Hirsch's view, the poem is social criticism. Blake is satirizing the repressive order, whose hypocrisy and sham corrupt the woman who accepts it. Still, like all the best symbols, Blake's rose and worm give off hints endlessly, and no one interpretation covers all of them. We noted with interest that "The Sick Rose" is rightly included in *The Faber Book of Seduction* (London, 1988).

[MLL] *MyLiteratureLab Resources.* Photographs and biographical information for Blake. Audio clip for "The Tyger."

Eavan Boland, ANOREXIC, page 1088

Boland's poem is spoken in the voice of an anorexic. Although self-inflicted starvation is the controlling idea, the anorexia is expressed in two clusters of images. The first set of images evokes a witch being burned at the stake (her flesh consumed away in punishment for her heresy). The second set of images relates to claustrophobia and presents a series of small enclosures. Boland counterpoints these two sets of images in a feverishly quick pace. The speaker aspires to be "sinless, foodless," though she destroys her body in the process.

The image of the witch also appears in Anne Sexton's poem "Her Kind." Sexton's use of the witch affords interesting parallels to Boland's poem. Both speakers assume the witch's identity to express forbidden aspects of their troubled selves.

Gwendolyn Brooks, THE MOTHER, page 1089

This powerful, direct poem is controversial for many readers, but it so memorably addresses an important contemporary issue that it is worth risking an overheated classroom discussion. Students will easily become polarized according to their moral positions on abortion, so it will help if you focus the discussion on the poem itself rather than broader social, legal, and theological issues. What does this troubling poem say?

First of all, point out that the poem is not spoken by Brooks about herself, that it employs two voices—first a narrator who speaks to another character ("The Mother" of the title), then the Mother's voice itself. Recognizing this literary distancing device will in itself depoliticize the discussion and allow you to focus on the poem's complex and at times almost contradictory argument. Second, point out the crucial division in the poem. In the first stanza the mother is the *you*. Another voice describes her situation. (This voice can be seen as either an outsider or part of the mother's divided self.) In the second stanza, however, the mother suddenly becomes the *I* and describes her own thoughts, fears, and memories. The *you* now becomes the unborn children. This switch is quiet but startling.

The form of "The Mother" is interesting and unusual—rimed free verse. Brooks usually rimes her free verse lines in couplets, but in a few places she varies the pattern. A good question to ask students is what effect does the form have on the poem's tone?

 MyLiteratureLab Resources. Biography, critical overview, and bibliography for Brooks. Longman Lecture on "The Mother."

Gwendolyn Brooks, THE PREACHER: RUMINATES BEHIND THE SERMON, page 1090

In reading this poem, one might be reminded of the quip attributed to Voltaire and others, "God created man in his own image, and man returned the favor." As he ruminates in his heart of hearts, expressing private thoughts that do not find their way into his sermon, Brooks's preacher imagines an anthropomorphic God, one, he thinks, whose exalted position, and the barriers that that position creates between him and all others, may very well create feelings of loneliness and emptiness within. But of course we understand God to be all-sufficient unto himself, never to suffer such human afflictions as loneliness and need. Preachers, however, might feel isolated by their exalted positions and by expectations that they are superior beings who do not have to contend with the same weaknesses and problems that others do, and such preachers may very well unconsciously identify with a God onto whom they project their own longings and needs.

For an interesting comparison, you might read your class "Was He Married?" by Stevie Smith, a poem that explores the God-man relationship from a different—one might say opposite—perspective: the principal speaker in Smith's poem sees the humanly imagined Christ as an inadequate model because, as God, he cannot understand or feel the doubts and fears that lie at the heart of the human experience.

 MyLiteratureLab Resources. Biography, critical overview, and bibliography for Brooks.

Elizabeth Barrett Browning, HOW DO I LOVE THEE? LET ME COUNT THE WAYS, page 1091

Dropping this famous sonnet from a previous edition broke more than one teacher's heart. The many requests for this poem, "My Last Duchess," "Mending Wall," "Death be not proud," and Poe's work remind us how much students enjoy reading famous poems—works that an educational theorist like E. D. Hirsch would claim have "cultural utility." They are poems that are still frequently quoted in newspapers, conversation, and electronic media. Anthologists eager for novelty too often forget that these famous poems are novel to every new generation.

This is the penultimate sonnet of forty-four constituting Elizabeth Barrett Browning's *Sonnets from the Portuguese,* a book that Ezra Pound once called "The second: that is, a sonnet sequence surpassed in English by one other alone. I would argue for that." The sonnets document the poet's growing love for Robert Browning, whom she married, in defiance of her father's wishes, in her fortieth year. "My little Portuguese" was a pet name Robert often used for Elizabeth: hence the title of her book.

Teachers not opposed to biographical interpretations might direct their students to the notes on both Brownings in the "Lives of the Poets" chapter.

MLL *MyLiteratureLab Resources.* Audio clip for "How Do I Love Thee? Let Me Count the Ways."

Robert Browning, SOLILOQUY OF THE SPANISH CLOISTER, page 1091

The "Soliloquy" is a poem especially valuable for combating the notion that poetry can deal only in love and gladness. Here the subject is a hatred so intense that the speaker seems practically demented. In the last stanza, he almost would sell his soul to the Devil in order to blight a flowering shrub. A little background information on abbeys, their organization, and the strictness of their rules may help some class members. From the internal evidence, it is hard to say whether this is a sixteenth-century cloister or a nineteenth-century one; Barbary corsairs (line 31) plied their trade from about 1550 until 1816. The business about drinking in three sips (lines 37–39) may need explaining: evidently it refers to a symbolic observance, like crossing knife and fork.

It might be stressed that the person in this poem is not the poet: the tone isn't one of bitterness but of merriment. Comedy is evident not only from the speaker's blindness to his own faults, but from the rollicking rhythm and multi-syllable comic rimes *(abhorrence/Lawrence; horsehairs/corsairs; Galatians/damnations; rose-acacia/Plena gratia).*

Questions: With what sins does the speaker charge Brother Lawrence? (Pride, line 23—monogrammed tableware belonging to a monk!; lust, 25–32; and gluttony, 40.) What sins do we detect in the speaker himself? (Envy, clearly, and pride—see his holier-than-thou attitude in stanza 5. How persuasive are his claims to piety when we learn he secretly owns a pornographic novel?) "Soliloquy" abounds in ironies, and class members can spend a lively few minutes in pointing them out.

MLL *MyLiteratureLab Resources.* Photographs and biographical information for Browning.

Geoffrey Chaucer, MERCILESS BEAUTY, page 1093

It can be great fun for students to learn (well, more or less) how to pronounce Chaucer's English, provided one has the time and strength to help them make the attempt. One does much better by Chaucer's lines if one puts on an Irish brogue. (A couple of Guinness stouts before class usually help.)

Some scholars doubt that Chaucer himself wrote this poem, but if he did not, someone who thoroughly knew Chaucer's work probably did.

"Since I escaped from love, I've grown so fat . . ." is a crude modernization of another poem from the "Merciles Beaute" series. Carlos Baker offers another modern American version of it in his book of poems *A Year and a Day* (Nashville: Vanderbilt UP, 1963).

G. K. Chesterton, THE DONKEY, page 1094

QUESTIONS FOR DISCUSSION

1. *Who is the speaker—some particular donkey?* No, the generic donkey, looking back over the history of his kind.

2. *To what prehistoric era does Chesterton refer in lines 1–3?* To the original chaos out of which the world was made. The poet apparently imagines it in bizarre, dreamlike imagery: fish with wings, walking forests, fig-bearing thorn. Chesterton was fascinated by the book of Genesis "because of its beginning in chaos," comments Garry Wills in his introduction to a reprint edition of Chesterton's novel of 1908, *The Man Who Was Thursday* (New York: Sheed, 1975). The novel hints at a playful God who enjoys returning things to chaos every now and then. Writing about the world of dream in a newspaper article in 1904, Chesterton remarked, "A world in which donkeys come in twos is clearly very near to the wild ultimate world where donkeys are made."

3. *Whose "ancient crooked will" is meant? The will of the devil in perversely designing the donkey, or the donkey's own venerable stubbornness?* We're not certain.

4. *What fools does the donkey chide in the last stanza?* Anybody who ever abused a donkey, or who thinks donkeys contemptible.

5. *Explain how the allusion in the last stanza is essential to the meaning of the poem.*

6. *What devices of sound contribute to the poem's effectiveness?*

Lucille Clifton, HOMAGE TO MY HIPS, page 1095

Lucille Clifton's poetry exults in everyday images—often viewed from an unusual angle that reveals some transcendent aspect. Her work is also terse and compressed, as in this short but definitely not petite poem. Clifton's exuberant poem is, first of all, a dramatic monologue. The speaker celebrates her own hips ("*these* hips" is a repeated phrase). Written in free verse, the poem divides its lines into natural speech units, often short declarative sentences. Another interesting feature of the poem is Clifton's personification of the hips: "They go where they want to go / they do what they want to do." The poem is so conversational that students may easily miss Clifton's sly figures of speech.

Samuel Taylor Coleridge, KUBLA KHAN, page 1096

The circumstances of this poem's composition are almost as famous as the poem itself, and, for the convenience of instructors who wish to read to their students Coleridge's prefatory note, here it is:

> In the summer of the year 1797, the author, then in ill health, had retired to a lonely farmhouse between Porlock and Linton, on the Exmoor confines of Somerset and Devonshire. In consequence of a slight indisposition, an anodyne had been prescribed, from the effects of which he fell asleep in his chair at the moment that he was reading the following sentence, or words of the same substance, in *Purchas's Pilgrimage*: "Here the Khan Kubla commanded a palace to be built, and a stately garden thereunto. And thus ten miles of fertile ground were inclosed with a wall." The author continued for about three hours in a profound sleep, at least of the external sense, during which time he had the most vivid confidence that he could not have composed less than from two to three hundred lines; if that indeed can be called composition in which all the images rose up before him as *things*, with a parallel production of the correspondent expressions, without any sensation or consciousness of effort. On awaking he appeared to himself to have a distinct recollection of the whole, and taking his pen, ink, and paper, instantly and eagerly wrote down the lines that are here preserved. At this moment he was unfortunately called out by a person on business from Porlock, and detained by him above an hour, and on his return to his room, found, to his no small surprise and mortification, that though he still retained some vague and dim recollection of the general purport of his vision, yet, with the exception of some eight or ten scattered lines and images, all the rest had passed away like the images on the surface of a stream into which a stone has been cast, but, alas! without the after restoration of the latter!

It is clearly a vulgar error to think the poem a mere pipe dream which anyone could have written with the aid of opium. The profound symbolism of "Kubla Khan" has continued to intrigue critics, most of whom find that the pleasure-dome suggests poetry, the sacred river, the flow of inspiration, or instinctual life. About the *ancestral voices* and the *caves of ice* there seems less agreement, and students might be invited to venture their guesses. For a valuable modern reading of the poem, see Humphry House, "Kubla Khan, Christabel and Dejection" in *Coleridge* (London: Hart-Davis, 1953), also reprinted in *Romanticism and Consciousness*, ed. Harold Bloom (New York: Norton, 1970).

Some instructors may wish to bring in "The Rime of the Ancient Mariner" as well—in which case it may be a temptation to go on to Jung's theory of archetypes and to other dreamlike poems such as Yeats's "The Second Coming." A fine topic for a term paper might be, after reading John Livingston Lowes's classic source study *The Road to Xanadu* (Boston: Houghton, 1927), to argue whether it is worth trying to find out everything that may have been going on in the back of a poet's mind, and to what extent such investigations can end in certainty.

MLL *MyLiteratureLab Resources.* Audio clip, student essay, and critical essay on "Kubla Khan."

Billy Collins, CARE AND FEEDING, page 1097

The equation that this poem turns on—that one year of a human being's life is equal to seven years in the life of a dog—is usually expressed the other way around, as when, in answering a friend's question about the age of a pet dog, we might say something like: "Harlow is nine, which makes her sixty-three in human years." Here, on the eve of his sixtieth birthday, the speaker begins by calculating his age in dog years, and through the rest of the poem he imagines himself as both dog and master. He is an adult human being who is mature and responsible, as befits both the dignity of his age and his status as a higher being; at the same time, he sees himself as a dog in the simple, playful side of his nature, prompted entirely by instinct and affection. As the title suggests, he must see to the care and feeding of his inner dog (which, thanks to such care, has become "venerable") and must nurture that side of himself in order to stay as fully alive, in every sense of the word, as he can.

 MyLiteratureLab Resources. Biography, critical overview, and bibliography for Collins.

Hart Crane, MY GRANDMOTHER'S LOVE LETTERS, page 1098

Diane Thiel, a poet and professor of English, has contributed this commentary:

> In his correspondence, Hart Crane speaks of the trials of writing this early poem after the initial inspiration. He longs for the "silence" he feels is necessary to properly address his subject. The poem becomes a poignant example of the poet's process, of the surprising turns a work might take, and of the possible inability to fully embrace certain endeavors at various points in one's life.
>
> Early in the poem, the speaker tries to chart the constellation of his grandmother's life, via love letters discovered in the "corner of the roof." Yet already in the first two stanzas, the images suggest that the speaker feels the tug of impermanence: the old letters "are brown and soft / And liable to melt as snow." Crane continues to evoke an elegiac tone with such images in the third stanza: "It is all hung by an invisible white hair." In contrast to the impermanence is the rain, constant throughout the space of the poem.
>
> It is "the loose girdle of soft rain" that helps to create the music of the poem. The piece has a generally iambic current, but it is indeed "loose" and "soft," with an "echo" of meter, rather than a tight pattern. The rhymes as well are "gentle" and "soft": these two words themselves are repeated in the poem. In Crane's music, the words "enough," "Elizabeth," "roof" and "soft" provide a light touch of rhyme. Such delicacy makes his exact rhymes all the more intense when they appear: "the invisible white hair" alongside the "birch limbs webbing the air." He leads his "grandmother by the hand / Through much of what she would not understand."
>
> The poem ends with the rain on the "roof" gently rhyming its "laughter" at the poet's attempts to inhabit the past, via his grandmother's love life. The poem, which initially tried to explore the world of those letters, now recognizes the difficulty of the poet's role as translator of certain experiences. In

his correspondence, after recounting his difficulties with the subject matter, Crane states that the finished poem was "shorter than [he] had planned."

When the speaker asks himself if his fingers are "long enough to play / Old keys that are but echoes" and longs for the silence to be able to hear the music, one senses not only the longing for his grandmother's experience, but a longing to feel such a love himself. The speaker seems to wonder at his own ability to love. The poem becomes a quiet harbinger of his later "Voyages": "Permit me voyage, love, into your hands." The rain's "gently pitying laughter" suggests a realization of the distance the speaker feels, not only from the grandmother's experience, but from his own ability to inhabit the "greatness of such space." In its longing, the poem, itself, feels like a love letter—to his grandmother, to her life, and to his own desire to "carry back the music to its source."

E. E. Cummings, SOMEWHERE I HAVE NEVER TRAVELLED,GLADLY BEYOND, page 1099

Why is this exquisite love poem so rarely anthologized? Cummings surely ranks as one of the great love poets in American literature, and this evocative lyric is one of his finest efforts. Many readers prize it greatly. We recently received a wedding announcement that reprinted the poem, and Woody Allen included the entire poem at a pivotal moment in *Hannah and Her Sisters*. The striking last line is one of the most famous in modern American poetry, and it serves as epigraph to Tennessee Williams's *The Glass Menagerie*.

The central image of the poem is a rose which the speaker equates with himself. (If one adopts a biographical strategy by which to interpret the text, it is worthwhile to note that Cummings wrote the poem for Anne Barton, an artist's model, whom he married in 1929 and divorced in 1932 after she left him for a wealthy New York surgeon. The interesting aspect of a biographical view is that Cummings's speaker uses the flower image, traditionally a female image, for himself, and it becomes a symbol of sexual and emotional awakening in the presence of his beloved.)

The poem moves via paradox and synesthesia. Eyes are "silent." The speaker cannot touch things because "they are too near." Fragility is portrayed as "intense." The effect is to endow the situation with strangeness and mystery. Words are used oddly, the lover's looks *unclose* the speaker. Punctuation is employed for expressive purposes, and normal word order is changed to heighten its musical and semantic effect, as in the lovely lines "you open always petal by petal myself as Spring opens / (touching skilfully,mysteriously)her first rose." All of these effects are used subtly and unexpectedly. Cummings carefully avoids repeating any verbal trick too often in this poem. Even the form of the poem is alluringly elusive. Many lines slip into iambic pentameter, but the poem never falls into a predictable rhythmic pattern. There are also rhymes hidden throughout the poem, but only in the last stanza do they appear conventionally at the ends of the lines. The sheer density of beautifully employed poetic effects and the constant shifting from one effect to another create an intoxicating, almost hypnotic spell on the listener.

MLL *MyLiteratureLab Resources.* Photographs and biographical information for Cummings.

Marisa de los Santos, PERFECT DRESS, page 1100

Dr. Johnson famously described remarriage as "the perpetual triumph of hope over experience," an adage with some applicability to "Perfect Dress." "Today in the checkout line," says the speaker, "I felt the old pull, flare / of the pilgrim's twin flames, desire and faith." Everyone, of course, feels desires of one kind or another, but it is faith—the belief that these desires can be fulfilled in just the ways that we want them to be—that distinguishes the speaker of this poem, and faith that the speaker finds impossible to relinquish. When she was fifteen, she "reached for poly-ester satin, / machine-made lace, petunia- and Easter-egg-colored, / brilliant and flammable. Nothing *haute* about this / *couture* but my hopes for it"—and yet those hopes are enough for the believer, "despite all we know." Even toward the end of the poem, she is still willing to credit at least the possibility that such hopes may be realized: "Silly maybe or maybe // I was right, that there's no limit to the ways eternity / suggests itself . . ." Despite the occasional ruefulness of tone earlier in the poem, this commitment seems, on the surface at least, uncomplicated by irony.

It might be interesting to read and discuss this poem in the context of sev-eral other texts in the anthology: Jane Martin's play *Beauty* (for the theme that physical beauty is everyone's secret desire) and Margaret Atwood's poem "Siren Song" (for the suggestion that, despite knowing better, we can't help falling for the same old lures every single time).

John Donne, DEATH BE NOT PROUD, page 1101

During the Renaissance, when life was short, a man of the cloth like Donne would have surprised no one by being on familiar terms with death. Still, "Death be not proud," one of Donne's "Holy Sonnets," is an almost startling put-down of "poor death." Staunchly Christian in its sure expectation of the Resurrection, Donne's poem personifies death as an adversary swollen with false pride and unworthy of being called "mighty and dreadful." (For another bold personifica-tion, see "Batter my heart, three-personed God," another of the "Holy Sonnets," in which Donne sees God as ravisher.)

In "Death be not proud" the poet accuses death of being little more than a slave bossed around by "fate, chance, kings and desperate men"—a craven thing that keeps bad company, such as "poison, war, and sickness," and is itself power-less without their assistance. Finally Donne taunts death with a paradox: "death, thou shalt die."

Of interest, though perhaps of less than immediate usefulness in the class-room, are the articles on Donne's religious poetry by Helen Gardner, Louis L. Martz, and Stanley Archer in *John Donne's Poetry: Authoritative Texts, Criticism*, ed. A. L. Clements (New York: Norton, 1966). All three explore the extent to which Jesuit methods of meditation might have influenced the "Holy Sonnets."

It might be instructive for students to compare two personifications of death: Donne's and Emily Dickinson's in "Because I could not stop for Death," where death appears in the guise of a courtly gentleman who stops by to take the poet for a pleasant ride.

MLL *MyLiteratureLab Resources.* Biography, critical overview, and bibliography for Donne. Audio clip for "Death be not proud."

John Donne, THE FLEA, page 1102

This outrageous poem is a good class-rouser on a dull day, but we don't urge you to use it unless the class seems friendly. (Some women students tend to be offended by Donne's levity; men tend to be put off by his ingenuity.)

A little familiarity with a seventeenth-century medical notion may help make Donne's metaphor clear. Conception, it was thought, took place when the blood of men and women mingled during intercourse. That is why Donne declares in line 11 that "we almost, yea more than married are." Bitten by the flea containing his blood, the woman may already be pregnant.

Instructors fond of Donne's knotty poems will be grateful for Theodore Redpath's valuable crib-book *The Songs and Sonets of John Donne* (London: Methuen, 1956; also New York: University Paperbacks, 1967). Redpath works through the poems line by line, explicating difficulties. He explains line 18: The woman would commit "three sins in killing three" in that she'd commit murder in killing him, suicide in killing herself, and sacrilege in killing the flea. Why sacrilege? Because she would be attacking a "marriage temple" and symbol of the Trinity.

Patricia Meyer Spacks has treated the poem to scrutiny in *College English* 29 (1968): 593–94.

 MyLiteratureLab Resources. Biography, critical overview, and bibliography for Donne.

John Donne, A VALEDICTION: FORBIDDING MOURNING, page 1102

In his *Life of Donne*, Izaak Walton tells us that Donne wrote this poem for his wife in 1611, when he was about to depart on a diplomatic mission to France.

Much of the meaning of the poem depends upon the simile of the compasses in the last three stanzas. There is probably no better way to make sure students understand it clearly than to bring in a draftsman's compass—even the Wal-Mart variety—and to demonstrate the metaphor with it. There'll always be someone who thinks Donne means the kind of compass that indicates north.

QUESTIONS FOR DISCUSSION

1. *What is a* valediction *anyway? What is a high school "valedictorian"?*

2. *Why does the speaker forbid mourning? Do lines 1–4 mean that he is dying? Explain this simile about the passing away of virtuous men.* As saints take leave of this world—so sweetly and calmly that one hardly knows they're gone— let us take leave of each other.

3. *In lines 7–8, what is suggested by the words with religious denotations?* Profanation *(the desecration of a sacred thing)*, the laity. *What is the idea?* Love seems to the speaker a holy mystery. He and his wife are its priests or ministers.

4. *Explain the reference to astronomy in the third stanza.* Earthquakes shake, rattle, and roll; Ptolemaic spheres revolve gently and harmlessly. This takes us to the notion of *sublunary* lovers in stanza 4. In the medieval cosmos, the heavenly bodies are fixed and permanent, while everything under the moon is subject to change.

5. *Paraphrase stanza 4.* Unlike common lovers, bound to their earthly passions, we have less need of those things that serve sensual love: namely, bodies.

6. *Why is beaten gold an appropriate image in the sixth stanza? What connotations does gold have?* Refined, precious, durable, capable of being extended without breaking.

7. *Comment on the word* hearkens, *line 31.* As a draftsman's compass will illustrate, the fixed central foot leans forward when the compass is extended, as if, in Donne's comparison, eager for its mate's return.

 MyLiteratureLab Resources. Biography, critical overview, and bibliography for Donne.

John Dryden, To the Memory of Mr. Oldham, page 1104

With the aid of Dryden's great short poem (and the selections in the book from Swift, Pope, and Johnson), one at least can acquaint students with a little neoclassical poetry. The directness and plainness of Dryden's poem are clear from its very opening, and in teaching it one can question the assumption that neoclassical poetry is written only in bookish and Latinate words.

In teaching Dryden's poem, one can also mention (and define) the elegy and refer students to other famous elegies in the text.

A. E. Housman's "To an Athlete Dying Young" may be likened to Dryden's poem in that both poets favor classical conventions: footraces with laurels as crowns and the dead hero's descent into the underworld. Both poets find that premature death can confer benefits. What would Oldham have gained had he survived? More polish as a poet, yet he would have lost much of his force. In reading Housman's poem, students can be helped to recognize its metaphors: the comparison in the first two stanzas of victor's chair and dead lad's coffin, the comparison in line 5 of all human life to a footrace with death at the finish line. Students might be asked if they know of any living proof of Housman's observation that sometimes the name dies before the man (a truth often shown by the wistfulness of old football players at alumni weekends).

T. S. Eliot, Journey of the Magi, page 1104

The speaker is a very old man ("All this was a long time ago . . .") looking forward to his death. As his mind roves back over the past, it is mainly the discomforts and frustrations of his journey that he remembers, and when he comes to the part we have been waiting for, his account of the Nativity, he seems still mystified, as though uncertainly trying to figure out what had happened—"There was a Birth, certainly." Apparently the whole experience was so devastating that he prefers to omit all further details. His plight was to recognize Christ as God and yet to be unable to accept Christ as his savior. Being a king, he did not renounce his people, but they henceforth seemed alien to him, clutching their discredited gods like useless dolls.

The passage beginning "Then at dawn" (lines 21–28) is full of foreshadowings, both hopeful and sinister. Besides the symbolic white horse, the vine leaves suggest Christ, who said to his disciples, "I am the vine, ye are the branches" (John 15:5). The tavern customers suggest the Roman soldiers who will drink and cast dice at the cross.

Although Eliot's dissatisfied Magus isn't one of the kings portrayed by Yeats in "The Magi"—being dissatisfied for different reasons—it is curious that Eliot may have taken the dramatic situation of his poem from one of Yeats's stories. In "The Adoration of the Magi" in Yeats's prose collection *Mythologies* (reprinted in 1925, two years before Eliot first published his poem), three old men call on the storyteller and, drawing close to his fire, insist on telling him of a journey they had made when young, and of a vision of Bethlehem. Like Eliot's speaker, who repeats "set down / This set down / This," they demand that their story be taken down word for word.

Among the useful discussions of Eliot's poem are Elizabeth Drew's in *T. S. Eliot: The Design of His Poetry* (New York: Scribner, 1949) 118–22, and Grover Smith's in *T. S. Eliot's Poetry and Plays* (Chicago: U of Chicago P, 1960) 121–25. More recently, Daniel A. Harris has characterized the Magus as a primitive Christian with a "baffled consciousness of mystery." See his article "Language, History, and Text in Eliot's 'Journey of the Magi,'" *PMLA* 95 (1980): 838–56. But Harris's opinions are questioned by William Skaff in a letter in *PMLA* 96: (1981) 420–22: "In 'Journey' Eliot adopts the dramatic mask of the Magus in order to express his own struggles with literal belief, his real 'religious position of 1927.'"

MLL *MyLiteratureLab Resources.* Biography, critical overview, and bibliography for Eliot.

Louise Erdrich, INDIAN BOARDING SCHOOL: THE RUNAWAYS, page 1106

For discussion: Have you ever been somewhere you wanted to run away from? If so, how does your memory of that experience compare with that of the speaker in this poem?

This poem is long on wounds: the railroad tracks are scars (6), the runaways' old welts are like roads (15), the names they wrote in wet cement and the leaves they pressed into the sidewalk before it dried recall "delicate old injuries" (22–24). All these things carry powerful connotations of being wounded, mistreated, beaten down—like the runaways themselves.

Jacklight (New York: Holt, 1984), the collection in which this poem appears, contains several other realistic poems of Indian life. Since the success of *Love Medicine* (1984), *The Beet Queen* (1986), and *Tracks* (1988), Louise Erdrich is best known as a novelist, but we think her poetry warrants attention too.

Erdrich, born in Little Falls, Minnesota, grew up in Wahpeton, North Dakota, and now lives in New Hampshire.

B. H. Fairchild, A STARLIT NIGHT, page 1107

The opening stanza of "A Starlit Night" (the first three words of the poem, actually) establishes the universality, as Fairchild sees it, of the theme he is developing.

All over America, at what is perhaps that part of the day most likely to lead us into reflectiveness and longing, men pause and think in the middle of a totally mundane activity. The equation of the memory of one's first sexual experience with taxes and broken faucets may seem a bit odd at first: why would such recollections have the same nagging, insistent quality as the other two more obvious irritants? As is suggested by the phrase "the stars rushing, rushing away," the answer might be a pervasive feeling of disappointment, a feeling that nothing—including the very things we thought would do so—has ever really healed the emptiness inside us.

The remaining three stanzas focus on a particular couple, especially the wife lying in bed watching her husband, who presumably stands at the closet with his pants over his arm, as examples of that universal condition. The details of her life—unmade bed, piled dishes in the sink, great gray sea of the kitchen's linoleum floor—surround her and threaten to overwhelm her, while the music coming from the radio downstairs takes her back to her own childhood and her father's constant praise and encouragement of her playing despite the fact, significant in the larger context of the poem, that she never quite got the piece right. The lovely, ghostly image of the moon sliding over the lacquered piano top "as if it were something / that lived underwater, something from far below," very effectively knits the poem's two main strands, as it symbolizes both the subterranean longings of the human soul (compare the "board games / with missing pieces" of lines 20–21) and the relentless passage of time (the "sunburst clocks in the kitchen / that made them, each morning, a little sad" in lines 21–22).

The last two lines are quite striking, especially the last five words. On the surface, "and now they have it" would seem to suggest a state of satisfaction, and yet, in the context of everything that has gone before, the couple in "A Starlit Night" seem in the end to be as isolated and unfulfilled as the people in an Edward Hopper painting.

Robert Frost, BIRCHES, page 1107

"Birches," according to Lawrance Thompson, was written during a spell of homesickness in 1913–1914, when Frost and his family were living in Beaconsfield, Buckinghamshire, England (*Robert Frost: The Years of Triumph* [New York: Holt, 1970] 37, 541).

Students may be led to see the poem as much more than a nostalgic picture of boyhood play. From line 43 on, the poem develops a flamboyant metaphor. Richard Poirier has given us a good summary of the poem's theme: "While there are times when the speaker [of "Birches"] would 'like to get away from earth awhile,' his aspiration for escape to something 'larger' is safely controlled by the recognition that birch trees will only bear so much climbing before returning you, under the pressure of human weight, back home" (*Robert Frost: The Work of Knowing* [Oxford: Oxford UP, 1977] 172).

One line in "Birches" meant most to Frost, the line about feeling lost in the woods, facing too many decisions about which way to go. He pointed it out to audiences on several occasions: "It's when I'm weary of considerations" (line 43). Reading the poem at Bread Loaf in July 1954, he remarked of the line, "That's when you get older. It didn't mean so much to me when I wrote it as it does now" (*Robert Frost: A Living Voice*, ed. Reginald Cook [Boston: U of Massachusetts P, 1974] 51). Radcliffe Squires has written interestingly of the birch tree as a path toward heaven fraught with risk, suspense, even a kind of terror. The climbing boy performs his act of birch-bending gracefully, but in doing so goes almost too far, like one filling a cup "even above the brim" (*The Major Themes of Robert Frost* [Ann Arbor: U of Michigan P, 1963] 55–56).

Sidelights on the poem: Frost wrote to his friend Charles Madison in 1950, "'Birches' is two fragments soldered together so long ago I have forgotten where the joint is." Can anybody find it? . . . A particular word he congratulated himself on finding was *crazes* in line 9: "cracks and crazes their enamel" (Cook, 230). Frost's concern for scientific accuracy is well known. He sought evidence to confirm his claim that birches bend to left and right. "With disarming slyness, he said: 'I never go down the shoreline [from Boston] to New York without watching the birches to see if they live up to what I say about them in the poem.' His birches, he insisted, were *not* the white mountain or paper birch of northern New England (*Betula papyrifera*); they were the gray birch (*Betula populifolia*)" (Cook, 232).

 MyLiteratureLab Resources. Biography, critical overview, critical articles, and bibliography for Frost. Audio clip for "Birches."

Robert Frost, MENDING WALL, *page 1109*

This familiar poem is often misread or loaded with needless symbolism. Some possible notions you might meet:

1. That the poem is an allegory: the wall stands for some political barrier such as segregation, immigration quotas, or the Iron Curtain. But can the text of the poem lend such a notion any support? Frost, according to Louis Untermeyer, frowned on all attempts to add to the wall's meaning: "He denies that the poem says anything more than it seems to say" (Note in *Robert Frost's Poems* [New York: Washington Square P, 1964]).

2. Frost's theme is that fences should be destroyed. Up with communal land, away with private property! But as Radcliffe Squires points out, none of Frost's other poetry supports such a left-wing view. Neither does "Mending Wall" support it, "for the poet-narrator himself cooperates with the wall-builder, replacing the stones in the spring even as he protests in spirit" (*The Major Themes of Robert Frost* [Ann Arbor: U of Michigan P, 1963]).

3. The maxim "Good fences make good neighbors" is just a smug platitude for which the speaker has only contempt. This view would make him out to be a cynic. Yet, by cooperating in the wall-mending, the speaker lends the maxim some truth. Although limited in imagination, the neighbor isn't an idiot. (Frost is portraying, by the way, an actual farmer he liked: the cheerful Napoleon Guay, owner of the farm next door to the Frosts' farm in Derry, New Hampshire. See *New Hampshire's Child: The Derry Journals of Leslie Frost* [Albany: State U of New York P, 1969].)

At the center of the poem is a contrast between two ways to regard mending a wall. The speaker's view is announced in the first line; the neighbor's is repeated in the last. "The opposing statements," says Untermeyer, "are uttered by two different types of people—and both are right." Students may be asked to define the very different temperaments of speaker and neighbor. A hard-working farmer to whom spring means walls to mend, the neighbor lacks fancy and frivolity. Spring is all around him, yet he *moves in darkness,* as though blind. Lines 30–40 compare him to a man of the Stone Age. A conservative from habit, he mends walls mainly because his father did. The speaker, full of mischief and imagination, is presumably a poet who wants to do no more hard labor than he can help. The speaker enjoys having some fun with the neighbor, telling him that apple trees won't invade pines. Mending walls is a kind of spring ritual, and the speaker likes to pretend there is magic in it: using a spell to make stones balance, blaming the wear-and-tear of winter upon elves—or more exactly, upon some Something not to be offended.

 MyLiteratureLab Resources. Biography, critical overview, critical articles, and bibliography for Frost. Longman Lecture on "Mending Wall."

Robert Frost, STOPPING BY WOODS ON A SNOWY EVENING, page 1110

Students will think they know this poem from their elementary school text-books, in which it is usually illustrated as though it were about a little horse, but they may need to have its darker suggestions underlined for them. Although one can present a powerful case for seeing Frost as a spokesman for the death wish, quoting other Frost poems such as "Come In," "To Earthward," and "Into My Own," we think it best to concentrate on this familiar poem and to draw the class to state what it implies. The last stanza holds the gist of it. What would he do if he *didn't* keep his promises? There is sense, however, in an objection a student once made: maybe he'd just stay admiring the snow for another fifteen minutes and be late for milking. "People are always trying to find a death wish in that poem," Frost told an audience at the Bread Loaf Writers' Conference in 1960. "But there's a life wish there—he goes on, doesn't he?"

Ask students if they see anything unusual about the rime scheme of the poem (rimes linking the stanzas as in *terza rima* or as in Shelley's "Ode to the West Wind"), and then ask what problem this rime scheme created for the poet as the poem neared its end. How else would Frost have ended it if he hadn't hit upon that magnificent repetition? In 1950 Frost wrote to a friend, "I might confess the trade secret that I wrote the third line of the last stanza of 'Stopping by Woods' in such a way as to call for another stanza when I didn't want another stanza and didn't have another stanza in me, but with great presence of mind and a sense of what a good boy I was I instantly struck the line out and made my exit with a repeat end" (qtd. in Lawrance Thompson, *Robert Frost: The Years of Triumph* [New York: Holt, 1970] 597–98). On another occasion Frost declared that to have a line in the last stanza that didn't rime with anything would have seemed a flaw. "I considered for a moment winding up with a three line stanza. The repetend was the only logical way to end such a poem" (letter of 1923 to Sylvester Baxter, given by R. C. Townsend, *New England Quarterly* 36 [June 1963]: 243).

That this famous poem may be sung to the old show tune "Hernando's Hideaway" (from *The Pajama Game*) was discovered by college students working as waiters at the Bread Loaf Writers' Conference in 1960.

Paper topic: Read Lionel Trilling's speech at Frost's eighty-fifth birthday dinner, in which Trilling maintained, "I think of Robert Frost as a terrifying poet" ("A Speech on Robert Frost: A Cultural Episode," *Partisan Review* 26 [Summer 1959]: 445–52; also reprinted in *Robert Frost: A Collection of Critical Essays*, ed. James M. Cox [Englewood Cliffs: Prentice, 1962]). Referring to "Stopping by Woods" and other Frost poems, state to what extent you agree or disagree with Trilling's view.

Frost reads the poem on *An Album of Modern Poetry* (Library of Congress, PL 20) and on *Robert Frost Reading His Own Poems*, record no. 1 (EL LCB 1941, obtainable from the National Council of Teachers of English, 1211 Kenyon Road, Urbana, IL 61801). Both recordings also include "Fire and Ice."

 MyLiteratureLab Resources. Biography, critical overview, critical articles, and bibliography for Frost.

Allen Ginsberg, A SUPERMARKET IN CALIFORNIA, page 1110

A comparison of this poem with Walt Whitman's work (e.g. "To a Locomotive in Winter") demonstrates the extent to which Ginsberg, in his tribute to Whitman, uses very Whitmanlike "enumerations." Ginsberg's long sentences, his use of free verse, parentheses, and fulsome phrases ("childless, lonely old grubber," "lonely old courage-teacher," etc.) are further indications that he is paying tribute to Whitman in part by echoing his style.

There is in "A Supermarket in California" as well a quality of surrealism that is Ginsberg's own. The existence of a "Neon fruit supermarket," the juxtaposition of past and present, the inclusion of the Spanish poet García Lorca (like Ginsberg and Whitman, a homosexual) "down by the watermelons," and the references to Charon and to the River Lethe all hover at the edges of dream.

Questions for discussion: What does Ginsberg mean when he speaks of "the lost America of love"? What does the poem say about loneliness? About death? (Whitman's death, in the poem, is as lonely a journey as Ginsberg imagines his life to have been.)

Thom Gunn, THE MAN WITH NIGHT SWEATS, page 1111

Thom Gunn's particular genius was to embody the human and artistic contradictions of his age. Reading his extravagantly diverse *Collected Poems* (1994), one finds poems on LSD and San Francisco street hustlers next to lyrics on Catholic saints and Caravaggio—all of them recognizably drawn from the same imagination. Gunn is the crown prince of incongruity, a Romantic entranced by classical control, an experimentalist who never renounced rime and meter, and an anti-authoritarian ruled by mandarin standards.

When Gunn first came to California from England in 1954, he was only twenty-five but had already published a celebrated book of poems. Having won a writing fellowship to Stanford, the young gay poet with "a promiscuous love of experience" studied with the famously rigorous Yvor Winters. Gunn's already incisive style sharpened under Winters's formalist tutelage, yet his tone and subjects kept their rebellious edge. His second book may have begun with rimed iambic stanzas, but they described a motorcycle gang on the move.

Gunn's greatest moment as a poet came at his most difficult time—the AIDS epidemic. In a single month he lost four close friends. Out of this personal and public crisis grew *The Man with Night Sweats* (1992), which will probably stand as the finest poetic testament of those plague years. While most AIDS poetry relied on naked grief and raw emotion, Gunn's lucid but lyric meditations were simultaneously realistic and transcendent. He did not merely give voice to the lost—he gave them poetry, as in the title piece, which begins: "I wake up cold, I who / Prospered through dreams of heat / Wake to their residue, / Sweat, and a clinging sheet."

The speaker in Gunn's poem faces the certainty of his own impending death. The language is precisely phrased and classically balanced in the tradition of English death poems such as John Keats's "When I have fears that I may cease to be." This earlier poem would provide illuminating contrast for class discussion or possible student essays. What words would suffice to face one's own death?

Donald Hall, NAMES OF HORSES, page 1112

Hall is apparently eulogizing not one horse but a long succession of them, each taking on its predecessors' duties through the years. The poem enumerates the everyday chores the horses had to do, "generation on generation," Sundays included. The "man, who fed you and kept you, and harnessed you every morning" represents not a single farmer, apparently, but all those on this New Hampshire farm who cared for and finally buried their horses in the time-honored way "for a hundred and fifty years." Like all dead animals (including people), the horses when they die become "soil makers," useful even in their graves.

The wonderful list in the poem's last line delivers what the title has promised, names of horses. The last one, Lady Ghost, is the most connotative. You might wish to have students explore its suggestions.

First published in the *New Yorker*, this poem later appeared in Hall's seventh book of poems, *Kicking the Leaves* (New York: Harper, 1978). The farm in New Hampshire where Hall lives was once a working farm run by his grandparents and, before them, his great-grandparents. Hall has written a prose memoir, *String Too Short to Be Saved* (Boston: Godine, 1981), about the boyhood summers he spent there with his grandmother and grandfather. "Names of Horses," too, seems to depend heavily on the poet's fond memories of the farm he still loves.

Thomas Hardy, THE CONVERGENCE OF THE TWAIN, page 1113

The discovery in September 1985 of the well-preserved wreck of the *Titanic* in the North Atlantic, and the subsequent squabble over possession of it, gave this old favorite poem a certain immediacy. Most students will be familiar with the history of this great disaster from news reports or from the many popular films and books. Still, a few facts may need to be recalled. The fateful day was April 15, 1912. The pride of the British White Star lines, the *Titanic* was the world's largest ship in its day, celebrated for luxurious trappings (including Turkish baths and a fully equipped gym). Many of the unlucky passengers were wealthy and famous. One reason the *Titanic* sank with such cost of life was that the builders, smugly assuming the ship to be unsinkable, had provided lifeboats for fewer than half the 2,200 passengers. (Only 705 people survived.) Hardy wrote the poem for the souvenir program of a benefit show for the *Titanic* Disaster Fund (to aid survivors and the bereaved) given at Covent Garden, May 14, 1912.

Hardy has been seen as an enemy of science and industrialism, those spoilers of rural England, but Donald Davie argues that "The Convergence of the Twain" shows no such animosity. The poem censures vanity and luxury, "but not the technology which built the great ship and navigated her" (*Thomas Hardy and British Poetry* [Oxford: Oxford UP, 1972]). Although Hardy personally knew two victims of the disaster, the "Convergence," as J. O. Bailey points out, is not a personal lament; indeed, the drowned are hardly mentioned. The poem is a philosophic argument, with the Immanent Will punishing man for pride: "It acts like the Greek concept of Fate that rebukes *hubris*" (*The Poetry of Thomas Hardy* [Chapel Hill: U of North Carolina P, 1970]). Fate, however, seems personified in the poem as the Spinner of the Years, a mere agent of the Will.

Students can concentrate profitably on the poet's choice of words: those that suggest the exotic unnaturalness of the *Titanic's* furnishings (*salamandrine, opulent, jewels . . . to ravish the sensuous mind, gilded*). Diction will also point to the metaphor of the marriage between ship and iceberg: the *intimate welding* and the *consummation*. The late Allen Tate was fond of reading this poem aloud to his friends, with mingled affection and contempt, and remarking (according to Robert Kent) that it held "too many dead words, dead then as now, and all the more obtuse for having been long dead in Shelley. 'Stilly,' for example." From Hardy's original printed version of the poem, as given in *The Variorum Edition of the Complete Poems of Thomas Hardy*, ed. James Gibson (New York: Macmillan, 1979), it appears that he originally cast line 6: "The cold, calm currents strike their rhythmic tidal lyres." Isn't *thrid* an improvement, even though it is stiltedly archaic?

MLL   *MyLiteratureLab Resources.* Biography, critical overview, and bibliography for Hardy.

Thomas Hardy, THE DARKLING THRUSH, page 1115

"The Darkling Thrush" comes out of the Romantic pastoral tradition, and through its first two stanzas Hardy pulls out all the stops in displaying the connection between the bleakness of the landscape and the bleakness of the speaker's mood. Virtually every line yields a word indicative of enervation and hopelessness: note "spectre," "dregs," "desolate," "weakening," "broken," and "haunted" in the first eight lines alone.

It is at the poem's midpoint that the thrush of the title makes his sudden and surprising appearance, a bird who is described as being as "frail, gaunt, and small" (line 21) as the speaker feels himself to be, and thus is presented as a figure with whom the speaker may readily identify, and with whose values and reactions he may therefore be willing to associate himself. And so a reader may be tempted—a temptation to which many students will almost certainly succumb—to characterize the poem's theme along these lines: I was suffering from gloom induced by the winter-afternoon dying-of-the-light blahs, until the joyous song of this little bird showed me how silly I was to feel that way.

But notice how muted the conclusion of the poem actually is. The speaker says that "I could think" (line 29) that the thrush knew something that he didn't, not "I *did* think." And the very end of the poem reminds us that, if there is any basis for hope, the speaker remains "unaware" of it. You might find it useful to have your students compare "The Darkling Thrush" with Hardy's own "The Oxen," in which the speaker describes his attitude to the pious legend of his youth as "hoping," not "persuaded." You might also discuss "The Darkling Thrush" in terms of Robert Frost's "The Road Not Taken," another poem whose subtleties are often overlooked by consolation-seekers who would reduce it to a sort of national anthem of rugged individualism.

MLL *MyLiteratureLab Resources.* Biography, critical overview, and bibliography for Hardy.

Thomas Hardy, HAP, page 1116

This early poem summarizes Hardy's bleak view of existence. A lesser artist might have been crushed by this sense of hopelessness, but Hardy filled the theological gap with love, compassion, and humor. Students might compare this bitterly atheistic poem with the gentler "The Oxen." In "The Oxen" Hardy longs for the Christian faith he had as a child.

Two things are worth noting in the poem (since students sometimes over-look them). First, Hardy would rather have a cruel deity than none at all. It is not the pain of existence he bemoans, it is the meaninglessness of life without some guiding divine plan. Second, Hardy's worldview is so deeply religious that even when he claims there is no God, he ends up personifying the nothingness under which he suffers ("Crass Casualty" and "dicing Time," which he then groups as "purblind Doomsters").

The vocabulary of "Hap" is interesting. The title word means both a "hap-pening" and "chance." *Hap* is not used much today but is still alive in common terms in "happenstance" and "hapless." *Casualty* is a word we are used to seeing primarily in accident reports and insurance forms. Hardy uses it here in its broader original sense of "chance" in the same way we still use "accident" in the neutral sense of a "chance event." Detective novel fans may know *Doomsters* from the title of Ross Macdonald's compelling novel; *doomster* is an archaic word for a judge (that survives in the family name Dempster). In Scottish courts the doomster not only read the sentence but also carried out the execution. Finally, you might quiz the class on *purblind*, a perfectly modern term that many of them won't know.

"Hap" is, by the way, a sonnet. Notice how neatly the meaning turns at the beginning of the sestet ("But not so."). Hardy uses the form so naturally that one might overlook it entirely.

MLL *MyLiteratureLab Resources.* Biography, critical overview, and bibliography for Hardy.

Robert Hayden, THOSE WINTER SUNDAYS, page 1117

QUESTIONS FOR DISCUSSION

1. Is the speaker a boy or a man? How do you know?

2. Summarize the poem's theme—its main idea.

3. What do you understand from "the chronic angers of that house"?

4. How does this poet's choice of words differ from that of most writers of prose? Suggestion: Read the opening five lines aloud.

This brief poem, simple in the word's best sense, has a depth that rewards close reading. It appears that years have intervened between the speaker today and his previous self, the observing child. Now the speaker understands his father better, looks back on himself, and asks, "What did I know?"

The poem states its theme in its wonderful last line (worth quoting to anyone who distrusts abstract words in poetry). Students can miss Hayden's point unless they understand its vocabulary. *Austere* can mean stern, forbidding, somber, but it can also mean (as it does here) ascetic, disciplined, self-denying. To rise in the freezing house takes steely self-discipline. That the father's life is built on austerity we get from his labor-worn hands. What is an *office*? A duty, task, or ceremony that someone assumes (or has conferred on him): the tasks of shining shoes, of stirring banked fires in a furnace (or a coal-burning stove?). James Wright, a keen admirer of Hayden's poem, has spoken of it in an interview:

> The word *offices* is the great word here. *Office*, they say in French. It is a religious service after dark. Its formality, its combination of distance and immediacy, is appropriate. In my experience uneducated people and people who are driven by brute circumstance to work terribly hard for a living, the living of their families, are very big on formality. (*The Pure Clear Word: Essays on the Poetry of James Wright*, ed. Dave Smith [Urbana: U of Illinois P, 1982] 10)

Perhaps the "chronic angers" belong to the father: the boy gets up slowly and fearfully as though in dread of a tongue-lashing. Yet this reading does not seem quite in keeping with the character of the father as he emerges: stoic, patient, long-suffering, loving. Hayden does not invest these angers in the father exclusively. Perhaps any tenant of this bitterly cold house has reason to dread getting up in it.

When read aloud, the opening stanza reveals strong patterns of sound: the internal alliteration of the *k*-sound in *blueblack, cracked, ached, weekday, banked, thanked* (and, in the next stanza, in *wake, breaking, chronic*)—staccato bursts of hard consonants. Rather than using exact rime at the ends of lines, Hayden strengthens lines by using it internally: *banked/thanked* (line 5), *wake/breaking* (6); perhaps off-rime, too: *labor/weather* (4), *rise/dress* (8). Alliteration and assonance occur in *clothes . . . cold* (2), *weekday weather* (4). If you assign this poem early in your investigation of poetry, probably it matters more that students hear and respond to the rich interplay of repeated sounds than that they be able to give these devices labels.

"Those Winter Sundays" is the most often reprinted poem of Robert Hayden. A black poet who grew up in Detroit and who for many years was an English professor at the University of Michigan, he has written other poems apparently drawn from childhood and memory, among them "Obituary," another moving tribute to his father. Hayden's posthumous *Collected Poems* (New York: Norton/Liveright, 1985) belongs, we think, in every library.

MyLiteratureLab Resources. Biography, critical overview, and bibliography for Hayden.

Seamus Heaney, DIGGING, page 1118

When Irish poet Seamus Heaney went to Lewiston, Maine, in 1986 to receive an honorary degree at Bates College, he read "Digging" aloud to the assembled graduates, parents, and friends. It seemed an appropriate choice. Some of the Maine students in his audience must have found expressed in Heaney's poem their own admiration for hardworking forebears whose course through life they had decided not to follow. Is the speaker in the poem uneasy about choosing instead to be a poet? It is clear that he admires the skill and strength his father and grandfather displayed in their work. But the poem ends on a positive note. The poet accepts himself for what he is.

In "Feeling into Words," an essay in his *Preoccupations* (New York: Farrar, 1980), Heaney likens the writing of poetry to digging up archaeological finds. Apparently it is a matter of digging a spade into one's past and unearthing something forgotten. "Digging," written in 1964, was his earliest poem in which it seemed that his feelings had found words. "The pen/spade analogy," he adds, "was the simple heart of the matter and *that* was simply a matter of almost proverbial common sense." As a schoolboy, he was often told to keep studying "because 'learning's easily carried' and 'the pen is lighter than the spade.'"

 MyLiteratureLab Resources. Longman Lecture on "Digging."

Anthony Hecht, ADAM, page 1119

"Adam" was the title poem (see line 26) of Anthony Hecht's Pulitzer Prize-winning collection, *The Hard Hours* (1967). The book is dedicated to Hecht's two sons, Jason and Adam. The poem's title, therefore, has a double resonance—one religious, the other personal. The poem memorably embodies one of the central teachings of the Judeo-Christian tradition, namely that human love emulates God's love for mankind. Hecht parallels God's love for His first "son," Adam, with the poet's love for his own son Adam.

The first stanza is spoken by the God of Genesis to Adam, who has been created but not yet awakened to find the world fashioned for him. The divine voice announces that "These very words you hear / Compose the fish and starlight." God's word, as the Judeo-Christian tradition believes, becomes reality. While not claiming divine power for his own words, the speaker of "Adam" asserts his right as a poet and father to use the power of language to bless and comfort his son.

It may be worth asking students about the dramatic situation of the poem. Where is the speaker's son when these fatherly words are spoken? (In the beginning of the third stanza, we learn that the son is in a foreign country and the poet speaks "to the empty air.")

Several other poems can be profitably compared to "Adam." To explore the human dimension, "Adam" can be compared to the two Robert Hayden poems in the book. "Those Winter Sundays," especially, provides a son's glimpse of a father to contrast with this father's view of a son. Finally, a dramatic contrast could be made with Weldon Kees's "For My Daughter," which is spoken by a man who feels he has no power to bless or protect his child.

George Herbert, LOVE, page 1121

Herbert's poem is often read as an account of a person's reception into the Church; the eaten *meat*, as the Eucharist. Herbert's extended conceits or metaphors are also evident in "The Pulley."

For discussion: compare "Love" with another seventeenth-century devotional poem, Donne's "Batter my heart." What is the tone of each poem? Herbert may seem less intense, almost reticent by comparison. Douglas Bush comments, "Herbert does not attempt the high pitch of Donne's 'Divine Poems.' His great effects are all the greater for rising out of a homely, colloquial quietness of tone; and peace brings quiet endings—'So I did sit and eat'" (*English Literature in the Earlier Seventeenth Century* [New York: Oxford UP, 1945] 139).

Herbert, by the way, is an Anglican saint—the only one who does not also appear in the Roman Catholic calendar.

Robert Herrick, TO THE VIRGINS, TO MAKE MUCH OF TIME, page 1122

Roses would have suited Herrick's iambic meter—why is *rose-buds* richer? Rosebuds are flowers not yet mature and therefore suggest virgins, not matrons. There may be a sexual hint besides: rosebuds more resemble private parts than roses. But in this poem, time flies, the rosebuds of line 1 bloom in line 3. *Rose-buds* is also rhythmically stronger than *roses*, as Austin Warren has pointed out: it has a secondary stress as well as a primary. Warren has recalled that when he first read the poem in college in 1917, he misread *rose-buds* as *roses*, kept misreading it ever after, and only a half-century later realized his mistake and found a new poem in front of him. "In untutored youth, the sentiment and the rhythm suffice: the exactness of the language goes unnoticed. And in later life a remembered favorite escapes exact attention because we think we know it so well" ("Herrick Revisited," *Michigan Quarterly Review* 15 [Summer 1976]: 245–67).

Question for discussion: What do you think of Herrick's advice? Are there any perils in it?

Gerard Manley Hopkins, SPRING AND FALL, page 1122

Hopkins's tightly wrought syntax may need a little unraveling. Students may be asked to reword lines 3–4 in a more usual sequence ("Can you, with your fresh thoughts, care for leaves like the things of man?") and then to put the statement into more usual words. (An attempt: "Do you, young and innocent as you are, feel as sorry for falling leaves as for dying people?") Lines 12–13 may need a similar going over and rough paraphrase. ("Neither any human mouth nor any human mind has previously formed the truth that the heart and spirit have intuited.") "Sorrow's springs are the same"—that is, all human sorrows have the same cause: the fact that all things pass away. A world of constant change is "the blight man was born for": an earth subject to death, having fallen from its original state of a changeless Eden. The difficulties of a Hopkins poem result from a swiftly thoughtful mind's trying to jam all possible meaning into a brief space (and into words that are musical).

Wanwood is evidently a term the poet coined for pale autumn woods. W. H. Gardner, the editor of Hopkins's poems, finds in it also the suggestion of "wormwood"—bitter gall, also wood that is worm-eaten. The term *leafmeal* reminds him of "piecemeal," and he paraphrases line 8: "One by one the leaves fall, and then rot into mealy fragments."

MLL *MyLiteratureLab Resources.* Photographs and biographical information for Hopkins.

Gerard Manley Hopkins, NO WORST, THERE IS NONE, page 1123

Just from reading the title (and opening phrase) of this Petrarchan sonnet, one might get the impression that the thrust of the poem is consolatory, but as we read on, we come to see that the theme here is reflective of Edgar's famous aside in Shakespeare's great tragedy *King Lear*, "And worse I may be yet: the worst is not / So long as we can say 'This is the worst'"—in effect, that there is no conceivable limit to the depths of human suffering. As lines 2–4 suggest, earlier pangs of grief ("forepangs") do not cushion later ones by teaching us to cope with suffering; instead, deeper pains only make us suffer more deeply, and these sufferings are not alleviated or even diminished by the traditional consolations of religious belief.

As seen in line 6, the angst that the speaker suffers from is not merely particular to himself and his circumstances; it is a "world-sorrow," and his cries resound "on an age-old anvil": the suffering that he describes is universal, an unavoidable condition of being human. In keeping with the recurring motif of giving a momentary illusion of hope only to snatch it away a moment later, "Then lull, then leave off" at the beginning of line 7 seems at first to refer to the woe itself, but as we read on we come to see that it is only the cries themselves that leave off, not the griefs that cause them.

The beginning of the sestet follows the previously established pattern: "O the mind, mind has mountains" might seem to suggest an intellectual grandeur that can combat and perhaps overcome suffering; but no, Hopkins's point is that from such elevations steep falls are possible, even likely. The superficially baffling statement in lines 10–11 can be unknotted by straightening out the word order: "who ne'er hung there may hold them cheap," i.e., those lucky enough to have never experienced these terrors may not fully grasp how terrible such feelings are.

The ending of "No worst, there is none" may put you in mind of the conclusion of another famous sonnet by a religiously oriented British poet, John Donne's "Death be not proud." What chiefly distinguishes the two is the distance between them. Donne's witty argument is intended as a refutation of death's power over us, whereas Hopkins presents with us with comparatively scant consolation, the realization that just as sleep brings respite from pain at the end of every day, so death will bring us the peace of oblivion at the end of life. The near-despair of this poem is especially striking given the fact that Hopkins was a Jesuit priest, a man of profound religious sentiment and conviction; it serves to remind us that even the truest of believers are not exempt from the dark night of the soul.

 MyLiteratureLab Resources. Photographs and biographical information for Hopkins.

Gerard Manley Hopkins, THE WINDHOVER, page 1123

"The best thing I ever wrote," said Hopkins. If your students have enjoyed "Pied Beauty" or "God's Grandeur" without too much difficulty, then why not try "The Windhover," despite its famous ambiguities? Some students may go afield in reading the opening line, taking *I caught* to mean that the poet trapped the bird; but they can be told that Hopkins, a great condenser, probably means "I caught a glimpse of."

Dispute over the poem often revolves around whether or not the windhover is Christ and around the meaning of *Buckle!* Most commentators seem to agree that the bird is indeed Christ, or else that Christ is like the bird. (Yvor Winters, who thought the poem "minor and imperfect," once complained, "To describe a bird, however beautifully, and to imply that Christ is like him but greater, is to do very little toward indicating the greatness of Christ.") Some read *Buckle!* as a plea to the bird to descend to earth; others, as a plea to all the qualities and things mentioned in line 9 *(Brute beauty, valor, act)* to buckle themselves together into one. Still others find the statement ending in *Buckle!* no plea at all, but just an emphatic observation of what the poet beholds. If Christ is the windhover (other arguments run), in what sense can he be said to buckle? Two of the answers: (1) in buckling on human nature and becoming man, as a knight buckles on armor; (2) in having his body broken on the cross. Students can be asked to seek all the words in the poem with connotations of royalty or chivalry—suggestive, perhaps, of Christ as King and Christ as noble knight or chevalier. Why the *sheer plod?* Hopkins reflects (it would seem) that if men will only buckle down to their lowly duties they will become more Christ-like, and their spiritual plowshares will shine instead of collecting rust. Hopkins preached a sermon that expressed a similar idea: "Through poverty, through labor, through crucifixion His majesty of nature more shines." The *embers,* we think, are a metaphor: moist clods thrown by the plow going down the sillion. Hopkins likes to compare things to hearth fire: for instance, the "fresh-firecoal chestnut-falls" in "Pied Beauty."

For detailed criticism, one might start with Norman H. MacKenzie, *A Reader's Guide to Gerard Manley Hopkins* (Ithaca: Cornell UP, 1981). MacKenzie provides facts from ornithology and his own kestrel-watching: no other birds are so expert in hovering, body horizontal, tail and head pointing down as they study the ground for prey. To hang stationary in the air over one spot, they must fly into the wind "with rapidly quivering (*wimpling,* line 4) wings, missing a few beats as gusts die, accelerating as they freshen"—responding to variations in the wind with nearly computer speed. Once in about every eight hovers, the kestrel will dive, not inertly but with wings held tense and high—it doesn't "buckle" in the sense of *collapse*. If it finds no victim, the bird swings and banks and takes an upward "stride," to hover once more. Hopkins's "how he rung upon the rein" doesn't mean that the kestrel climbs in a spiral. No gyring Yeats-bird, he.

An interesting view of the religious imagery informing this poem can be found in James Finn Cotter's study *Inscape: The Christology and Poetry of Gerard Manley Hopkins* (Pittsburgh: U of Pittsburgh P, 1972). Cotter, who is formidably learned in theology, examines traditional Christian writings to discover how they shaped Hopkins's sense of imagery. Cotter maintains that "Hopkins fashioned a myth of his own making," but that his private vision drew from a wide variety of philosophical and theological sources. In his long, careful reading of "The Windhover" Cotter observes:

> Circular motion and form dominate "The Windhover": the kestrel moves in slow, wide, sharp, and gliding circles which the rhythm and language perfectly mimic. Christ is present here as throughout the other sonnets, in the sun illuminating the scene; he is the dawn drawing the bird to a brilliant expression of itself and hence of its Lord.

Despite his fondness for Old and Middle English, Hopkins luckily refrained from calling the windhover by its obsolete name: *fuckwind* or *windfucker*. (No, that *f* is not a long *s*.) Thomas Nashe in *Lenten Stuffe* (1599) speaks of the "Kistrilles or windfuckers that filling themselves with winde, fly against the winde evermore." See *windfucker* in the *Oxford English Dictionary*. (For this dumbfounding discovery, thanks to David Lynch, who copyedited *Literature*, 4th ed.)

MLL *MyLiteratureLab Resources*. Photographs and biographical information for Hopkins.

A. E. *Housman*, LOVELIEST OF TREES, THE CHERRY NOW, page 1124

What is Housman's theme? Good old *carpe diem*. If you ask students to paraphrase this poem (it's not hard), a paraphrase might add, to catch the deeper implication, "Life is brief—time flies—I'd better enjoy beauty now."

Not part of the rough poem Housman began with, the second stanza was added last. Lines 9–10 originally read: "And since to look at things you love / Fifty times is not enough." What can be said for Housman's additions and changes? (These and other manuscript variations are given by Tom Burns Haber in *The Making of "A Shropshire Lad"* [Seattle: U of Washington P, 1966].)

MLL *MyLiteratureLab Resources*. Biography, critical overview, and bibliography for Housman.

A. E. *Housman*, TO AN ATHLETE DYING YOUNG, page 1124

For a comment on this poem, see the note earlier in this chapter on Dryden's "To the Memory of Mr. Oldham."

Randall Jarrell, THE DEATH OF THE BALL TURRET GUNNER, page 1125

The speaker seems to be an unknown citizen like Auden's. Jarrell's laconic war poem is complex in its metaphors. The womb is sleep; the outside world, waking; and the speaker has passed from one womb to another—from his mother into the belly of a bomber. His existence inside the ball turret was only a dream, and in truth he has had no mature life between his childhood and his death. Waking from the dream, he wakes only to nightmare. In another irony, the matter-of-fact battle-report language of the last line contrasts horribly with what is said in it. How can the dead gunner address us? Clearly the poet had written his epitaph for him—and has done so as Jarrell said he wrote "The Woman at the Washington Zoo," "acting as next friend."

Robinson Jeffers, TO THE STONE-CUTTERS, page 1126

If students will compare this poem with Shakespeare's sonnet "Not marble nor the gilded monuments," they'll be struck by a sharp difference of view. Shakespeare, evidently, is the optimist. For him, a poem can confer immortality and inspire love until doomsday. For Jeffers, poems will merely bring a little respite to "pained thoughts"— much as a spoonful of honey helps a hangover, according to one popular belief.

For a short assignment: Write a paraphrase of each of these two poems. Bring your work to class, ready to read it aloud. We'll discuss the poems, taking off from your work on them.

For another pessimistic view of monuments, direct students to Shelley's "Ozymandias." You might ask them to compare its theme with those of Shakespeare and Jeffers.

A sidelight on this poem: Any doubt he may have had that stone monuments last long didn't prevent Jeffers from building, with his own hands, a stone tower next to his home at the ocean's edge in Carmel, California.

Ben Jonson, ON MY FIRST SON, page 1126

This heartbreaking poem from Jonson's *Epigrammes*, requested by several instructors, repays close reading. What is "the state he should envy"? Death. Why the dead child should be envied is made clear in the lines that immediately follow (7–8). The final couplet is difficult in its syntax, and it contains a pun on *like* in a sense now obsolete. The speaker vows, or prays (*vow*, along with *votive*, comes from the Greek *euchesthai*: "to pray"), that anyone whom he loves may not live too long. The seriousness of Jonson's wit is shown in this colossal pun: *like* meaning "thrive, do well, get on" as well as "to be fond." See *like* in the *OED* for other illustrations:

SHALLOW TO FALSTAFF: "By my troth, you like well and bear your years very well." (*Henry IV, Part 2*, 3.2.92)

"Trees generally do like best that stand to the Northeast wind." (Holland's Pliny, 1600)

"Poems Arranged by Subject and Theme" in this manual lists the book's other poems about fathers and children. In this section, see especially the father-and-son poems by Anthony Hecht, Robert Phillips, and James Wright ("Autumn Begins in Martins Ferry, Ohio").

Donald Justice, ON THE DEATH OF FRIENDS IN CHILDHOOD, page 1127

There is more emotional distance and less grief in this poem than in Ben Jonson's. Nor does the speaker in "On the Death of Friends in Childhood" seem to be mourning one specific loss. The "Friends" he mentions suggests friends in general, perhaps other people's as well as his own. Yet, though time has softened the impact of long-ago losses, the narrator urges that we remember dead childhood friends and what was shared with them.

Brief as it is, this poem by one of the finest modern American poets displays the hallmarks of his work—the unerring sense of rhythm, the quiet beauty of the phrasing, the communication of powerful emotion through restrained statement. In its chiseled perfection, it would not be out of place in the *Greek Anthology*.

John Keats, ODE ON A GRECIAN URN, page 1127

Why is the symbol of the urn so endlessly suggestive? It may help students to recall that Grecian urns are vessels for the ashes of the dead, and that their carved or painted figures (*Of deities or mortal, or of both*) depict a joyous afterlife in the Elysian fields. The urn being round, its design appears to continue endlessly. What greater image for eternity, or for the seamlessness of perfected art?

Most good discussions of the "Urn" confront a few of the poem's celebrated difficulties. Some questions to help speed the confrontation:

1. *Assuming that the urn is said to be* sylvan *because it displays woodland scenes, in what sense is it a* historian? *What history or histories does it contain, or represent?*

2. *How can unheard melodies be sweeter than heard ones?*

3. *Why are youth, lover and loved one, trees, and musicians so lucky to exist upon the urn?* (Lines 15–27.)

4. *What disadvantages do living lovers labor under?* (Lines 28–30.)

5. *In stanza four, the procession of thought turns in a new direction. What additional insight occurs to the poet?* That the urn, whose world had seemed perfect, is in some ways limited and desolate. The altar cannot be reached nor sacrifice fulfilled, nor can the unseen little town ever be returned to.

6. *Paraphrase the statement that the urn "dost tease us out of thought / As doth Eternity."* The urn lures us out of our habit of useless cogitation. Eternity also stops us from thinking because, for us mere mortals, it too is incomprehensible.

7. *How is the urn a "Cold Pastoral"?* Literally, it's lifeless clay; figuratively, it stands aloof from human change and suffering. Compare Stevens's "Jar."

8. *How then can a Cold Pastoral be called "a friend to man"?* It provides a resting place for human ashes; it inspires and delights; and, as the last lines attest, it teaches us.

MLL *MyLiteratureLab Resources.* Photographs, biographical information, critical overview, and bibliography for Keats. Audio clip and student essay on "Ode on a Grecian Urn."

John Keats, WHEN I HAVE FEARS THAT I MAY CEASE TO BE, page 1129

Students will see right away that the poem expresses fear of death, but don't let them stop there: there's more to it. Why does the poet fear death? Because it will end his writing and his loving. The poem states what both loving and writing poetry have in common: both are magical and miraculous acts when they are spontaneous. Besides favoring "unreflecting love" for its "fairy power," Keats would write "with the magic hand of chance." And—if you care to open up a profundity—what might the poet mean by those "huge cloudy symbols of a high romance"? Literal cloud shapes that look like Tristram and Isolde's beaker of love-potion, or what?

Note that this poem addresses not Keats's beloved Fanny Brawne, but "the memory of the mysterious lady seen in adolescence one brief moment at Vauxhall long ago in the summer of 1814," according to Robert Gittings in *John Keats* (Boston: Atlantic, 1968) 188. The poem is about a "creature of an hour." (Fanny, of course, occupied not one hour but many.)

Gittings has found in the poem echoes of two sonnets of Shakespeare, both about devouring time: #60 ("Like as the waves make towards the pebbled shore, / So do our minutes hasten to their end") and #64 ("When I have seen by Time's fell hand defaced"). In the copy of the *Sonnets* that Keats co-owned with his friend Reynolds, these two were the most heavily marked.

This poem has had a hefty impact on later poets, notably John Berryman, who took from it the title for an autobiographical collection of his own poems on ambition and desire: *Love and Fame* (1972).

MLL *MyLiteratureLab Resources.* Photographs, biographical information, critical overview, and bibliography for Keats.

John Keats, TO AUTUMN, page 1130

Although "To Autumn" proved to be the last of the poet's great lyrics, we have no evidence that Keats (full of plans and projects at the time) was consciously taking leave of the world. On September 21, 1819, three days after writing the poem, Keats in a letter to his friend John Hamilton Reynolds spoke of his delight in the season: "I never lik'd stubble fields so much as now—Aye better than the chilly green of the Spring. Somehow a stubble plain looks warm—in the same way that some pictures look warm—this strikes me so much in my Sunday's walk that I composed upon it."

QUESTIONS FOR DISCUSSION

1. *In the opening stanza, what aspects of autumn receive most emphasis? To what senses do the images appeal?*

2. *In the first two stanzas, autumn is several times personified (lines 2–3, 12–15, 16–18, 19–20, 21–22). Who are its different persons?* Conspiring crony, careless landowner, reaper, gleaner, cider presser.

3. *In the third stanza, how does the tone change? Has there been any progression in scene or in idea throughout the poem?* Tone: calm serenity. In the first stanza, autumn is being prepared for; in the second, busily enjoyed, in the third, calmly and serenely contemplated. There is another stanza-by-stanza progression: from morning to noon to oncoming night. Like the *soft-dying day*, the light wind sometimes dies. The gnats in *wailful choir* also have funereal, mourning suggestions, but the stanza as a whole cannot be called gloomy.

4. *What words in stanza 3 convey sounds?* Songs, music, wailful choir, mourn, loud bleat, sing, treble, whistles, twitter. What an abundance of verbs! The lines convey a sense of active music making.

5. *Do you see any case for reading the poem as a statement of the poet's acceptance of the facts that beauty on earth is transitory and death is inevitable?* Surely such themes are present; the poem does not have to be taken to mean that the poet knows he himself will soon perish.

For an unusually grim reading of the poem, see Annabel M. Patterson, "'How to load . . . and bend': Syntax and Interpretation in Keats's 'To Autumn,'" *PMLA* 94 (1979): 449–58. Finding that the poem "undermines" our traditional notion of Autumn, Patterson argues that Keats subversively portrays the goddess as deceptive, careless, and demanding. Her proffered ripeness leads only to *last oozings* and *stubble-plains*—dead ends not to be desired. In the poet's view (as she interprets it), "Nature is amoral and not to be depended upon." Try this argument on the class. Do students agree? Whether or not they side with Patterson, they will have to examine the poem closely in order to comment.

For a good discussion of ways to approach Keats's poem with a class, see Bruce E. Miller, *Teaching the Art of Literature* (Urbana: NCTE, 1980) 75–84. Miller points out that not all students will know how cider is made, and he suggests asking someone to explain Keats's reference to the cider-press in stanza 2. He recommends, too, borrowing from your nearest art department some reproductions of landscape paintings: "Constable's work, which was contemporary with Keats, to my mind almost catches the spirit to 'To Autumn,' but it is a little more literal and photographic. . . ."

With this rich poem, you might well start a discussion of imagery, or review this topic if students have met it earlier. "The students," remarks Miller, "need not ask themselves as they read, 'What does it mean?' Rather they should continually ask, 'What do I see?' 'What do I hear and touch?' 'What do I feel?'"

 MyLiteratureLab Resources. Photographs, biographical information, critical overview, and bibliography for Keats.

Ted Kooser, ABANDONED FARMHOUSE, page 1131

In the first major essay on Ted Kooser's poetry, Dana Gioia wrote in 1983:

> He offers no blinding flashes of inspiration, no mystic moments of transcendence. He creates no private mythologies or fantasy worlds. Instead he provides small but genuine insights into the world of everyday experience. His work strikes the difficult balance between profundity and accessibility, just as his style manages to be personal without being idiosyncratic. It is simple without becoming shallow, striking without going to extremes. He has achieved the most difficult kind of originality. He has transformed the common idiom and experience into fresh and distinctive poetry.

"Abandoned Farmhouse" is an excellent illustration of this analysis. Grounded thoroughly in common details and presented in straightforward statements, it captures the poignancy of failed efforts and ruined hopes by expressing it through the objects left behind. This poignancy is heightened by the consistent use of the past tense in describing the lives lived in the farmhouse and the present tense in communicating what each of the mute details "says": the people and their hopes and dreams are gone, but the sadness continues. Inevitably, one is reminded of certain poems by Robert Frost, most notably "The Need of Being Versed in Country Things," which also chronicle the difficulty and the desolation of life in rural America.

Also worth noting is the subtle artistry of "Abandoned Farmhouse." At first approach it seems to be written in free verse, and several readings may be required to perceive its underlying iambic rhythm and its use of mixed tetrameter and pentameter lines. The very bareness of statement and description throughout the poem gives added force to its single simile—"Its toys are strewn in the yard / like branches after a storm" (lines 21–22)—which itself reinforces the larger theme of living things ripped apart by the harshness of nature. Coupled with the poem's only rime, it creates what in this hushed context is virtually a crescendo effect, which is immediately resolved by the diminuendo of the poem's last sentence.

—Michael Palma

Philip Larkin, HOME IS SO SAD, page 1132

Larkin's considerable achievement in "Home is so Sad" is that he so beautifully captures the ring of ordinary speech within the confines of a tight *a b a b a* rime scheme and iambic pentameter. Note the slant rimes in the second stanza: *as, was,* and *vase.*

In an interview, Larkin recalled a letter he received from a middle-aged mother who had read his poem: "She wrote to say her children had grown up and gone, and she felt precisely this emotion I was trying to express in the poem" ("Speaking of Writing XIII: Philip Larkin," [London] *Times* 20 Feb. 1964: 16). Bruce Martin finds the poem written not from a mother's point of view, but from that of a son who used to live in this house himself. The speaker projects his own sadness into it: it has remained pathetically changeless. What has changed is himself and others who once lived here (*Philip Larkin* [Boston: Twayne, 1978] 52).

DMK, taking a different view, thinks it quite possible to read the poem as though (as in Larkin's well-known "Mr. Bleaney" from the same collection, *The*

Whitsun Weddings) the former inhabitants of this house have died. The speaker is left unidentified, an impersonal seeing-eye. Your students, too, will probably come up with differing interpretations.

Is Larkin's poem sentimental? Hard-eyed and exact in its observations, aided by the colloquialism of line 7, "A joyous shot at how things ought to be," it successfully skirts the danger. Students might like to discuss the three words that follow: "Long fallen wide." Does Larkin mean that the home was an unhappy one, or merely ordinary in its deviation from the idea? Or is it that the arrow—the "joyous shot"—has fallen merely in the sense that, meant to be full of life, the home is now "bereft / Of anyone to please"?

Philip Larkin, POETRY OF DEPARTURES, page 1133

The speaker wonders why he doesn't break with his dull, tame life, just walk out, chuck everything, launch into the Romantic unknown like a highwayman. What an appealing notion! Question: Have you ever yearned to do that very thing? (Who hasn't?)

Well, why doesn't he take off? Because he sees all too clearly and painfully that such a grandiose gesture would be ridiculous. Commenting on lines 25–27, in which the speaker imagines himself swaggering nut-strewn roads and crouching in the fo'c'sle, David Timms finds him "unconvinced by such daydreams, though sympathetic to the dreamers, for he is one himself." And so he dismisses his Romantic urge as too studied and belabored, ultimately false. Still, just because he sees through those dreams, he won't let himself feel superior. The dreams may be artificial, but so is his own tame life, his room, his specially chosen junk. As he is well aware at the end, his greatest danger is to be trapped in owning things and neatly arranging them: books, china, all fixed on shelves in an order "reprehensibly perfect." (We have somewhat expanded on Timms's paraphrase, from *Philip Larkin* [Edinburgh: Oliver & Boyd, 1973] 87.)

William H. Pritchard has remarked that Larkin himself expunged Romantic possibilities from his life, the better to entertain them in his writing ("Larkin's Presence," in *Philip Larkin: The Man and His Work*, ed. Dale Salwak [Iowa City: U of Iowa P, 1989] 74–75).

Irving Layton, THE BULL CALF, page 1134

Sentimental poets frequently shed tears over concrete objects while (in their imagery and diction) failing to open their eyes to the physical world. Such is not the case of Layton's "The Bull Calf," in which the poet tells us that he weeps only after having portrayed the dead calf in exact detail ("one foreleg over the other").

Layton's poem develops a series of contrasts. In the first section, the calf's look of nobility ("the promise of sovereignty," "Richard II") is set against his immaturity. The "fierce sunlight," in an implied metaphor, is compared to the calf's mother: taking in maize, licking her baby. In line 14, the "empty sky," suggestive of the calf's coming death, seems the turning point of the poem. In the remainder, the calf, which had been portrayed at first as full of life and pride, becomes an inanimate object, "a block of wood," a numb mass that emits ugly sounds when handled ("a sepulchral gurgle"). But in the closing lines, introducing still another contrast, Layton seems to show the calf as a living sleeper, or perhaps a statue or finished work of art.

Probably the best-known living poet in Canada at the end of the twentieth century, Layton was born in Rumania and came to Montreal early in life. Situated outside both British and French communities, Layton often had the perspective of an outsider, a Jew, a satirist, and a revolutionary. *The Selected Poems of Irving Layton,* with an introduction by Hugh Kenner (New York: New Directions, 1977), was an attempt to widen his audience south of the border.

Denise Levertov, THE ACHE OF MARRIAGE, page 1135

Despite its brevity, "The Ache of Marriage" gets at the heart of one of the most rewarding, demanding, and frustrating relationships that the majority of us ever experience. The speaker is clearly committed to this relationship, committed by vows, by love (the spouse is twice addressed as "beloved" in the first six lines), and by the desire to make the relationship work and to experience all that it has to offer ("looking for joy, some joy / not to be known outside it"). But as this desire is defeated, commitment comes to feel more like entrapment ("It is leviathan and we / in its belly"). This sense of confinement is somewhat moderated as the metaphor changes from the belly of the beast to an ark, with its suggestion of the voyage of survival and the search for a landfall where a better life may be found. Note the artistry of the poem, as echoes of phrasing and sound reinforce the complexities of theme: the isolation of "each and each" softens to the attempted communion of "two by two," but then "ark" immediately blends into "ache," bringing us back to the poem's title and first line and principal theme, underlining the circular and ultimately static nature of the situation.

Philip Levine, THEY FEED THEY LION, page 1136

As with many another poet, the poem for which Philip Levine is best known is in many ways his least characteristic work. Levine's poems are customarily written in a straightforward, conversational style, and they often concern themselves with the lives of blue-collar workers, especially those in the automobile factories of his native Detroit. Its symbolic details, its multileveled use of language, and its almost apocalyptic urgency make "They Feed They Lion," the title poem of Levine's fifth collection, published in 1972, all but unique in his canon.

Levine has said that this poem was inspired by his return to Detroit after the race riots of 1967: "I had to go back to see what the city was like, and one of the things that I discovered was that it wasn't mine anymore." He has also said that "They Feed They Lion" takes its structure from a poem by Christopher Smart (an excerpt from Smart's poem is included later in this chapter under the title "For I Will Consider My Cat Jeoffry").

There is an especially interesting piece by Joe Jackson on "They Feed They Lion" in the *Explicator* 41:4 (Summer 1983) 56–58. Here are provocative thoughts from its opening and closing paragraphs:

> On a gloomy, greyly monochromatic night in a time and place deliberately left unspecified, the speaker is driving his car from "West Virginia to Kiss

My Ass" through the Appalachian wastelands of tin-roofed huts, junked autos, "black bean and wet slate bread." As he drives, his thoughts become a catalogue of both what he sees and what, through inference, he knows is outside the car window. . . . These observations pass in a frenzied rush, and the sense is that of pressure building at a threatening rate. The speaker does not understand this pressure on a conscious level. . . . As the poem ends, this building pressure finally bursts, and he knows.

. . .

Thus the poem is a litany for the oppressed, in the voice of the oppressed, as told by one of the threatened oppressors. . . . [There] is a constant switching between inanimate and animate, between the dead and the living. This becomes most important in the two stalled strophes on the butchered hog. Through his sacrifice, this hog almost assumes a property of rebirth ("From 'Bow Down' come 'Rise Up'"), which immediately transfigures into the image of a common laborer with a shovel at the end of strophe 4 ("The grained arm that pulls the hands"). Thus, the hog becomes an extended metaphor for the rising poor. . . . At the end of strophe 4, we finally discover what the poem is about; it is here, too, that the voice changes to first person. There is a minor, though pregnant pause. The speaker has also realized the poem's meaning and hurriedly leaves the scene before the threat becomes too real.

Shirley Geok-lin Lim, RIDING INTO CALIFORNIA, page 1137

In "Riding into California," Shirley Geok-lin Lim emphasizes the isolation and alienation that are so much a part of the immigrant experience—although she is quick to make clear ("The veterans in the mobile home / park don't want to be there") that such feelings are not unique to immigrants. What is exclusive to the newcomer from a very different culture is a pervasive sense of dislocation, which can lead to some surprising attitudes (surprising, perhaps, even to their possessor): "So you're / grateful for familiarity, and Bruce Lee / becomes your hero"). In the last three lines, just as she does in "Learning to love America," Lim simultaneously stresses both the positive and—especially—the negative aspects of the experience.

You can see Shirley Geok-lin Lim read "Riding into California"—and briefly discuss the power and pleasure that can come from the writing of poetry—at <http://www.pbs.org/wnet/foolingwithwords/main_video.html>.

Robert Lowell, SKUNK HOUR, page 1138

Students should have no trouble in coming up with the usual connotations of skunk, but they may need help in seeing that the title is a concise expression of Lowell's theme. This is an evil-smelling hour in the speaker's life; and yet, paradoxically, it is the skunks themselves who affirm that life ought to go on. After the procession of dying and decadent people and objects in the first four stanzas, the mother skunk and her kittens form a triumph: bold, fecund, hungry, impossible to scare. Although they too are outcasts (surrounded by their aroma as the poet is surrounded by his madness and isolation?), they stick up for their right to survival.

The poem is rich in visual imagery. In the mind's eye, there are resemblances between the things contained in stanza 5 (the Ford car and the hill's skull), and also between the objects set in fixed rows (love-cars, tombstones, beached hulls). Water and the sea (by their decline or absence) are to this poem what they are to Eliot's *Waste Land*. Even the Church is "chalk-dry"; its spire has become a spar like that of a stranded vessel.

This poem is intensively analyzed in *The Contemporary Poet as Artist and Critic: Eight Symposia*, ed. Anthony Ostroff (Boston: Little, 1964). Richard Wilbur, John Frederick Nims, and John Berryman comment on the poem, after which Lowell comments on their comments. Lowell calls the opening of the poem "a dawdling, more or less amiable picture of a declining Maine sea town. . . . Sterility howls through the scenery, but I try to give a tone of tolerance, humor, and randomness to the sad prospect." He sees the skunk hour itself as a sort of dark night of the soul and refers readers to the poem by St. John of the Cross. Lowell's night, however, is "secular, puritan, and agnostical." Lowell notes that the phrase *red fox stain* was intended only to describe the color of vegetation in the fall on Blue Hill, a mountain in Maine.

Elizabeth Hardwick, Lowell's wife when "Skunk Hour" was written, has affirmed that all the characters in the poem were actual—"were living, more or less as he sees them, in Castine [Maine] that summer. The details, not the feeling, were rather alarmingly precise, I thought. But fortunately it was not read in town for some time" (quoted by Ian Hamilton, *Robert Lowell: A Biography* [New York: Random, 1982] 267).

Sandra M. Gilbert, who sees the poem as "richly magical," reads it for its embodiment of myth. She explores it as a vision of Hell, pointing out that its events happen not on Halloween, but "somewhere in Hallowe'en's ritually black and orange vicinity." (The decorator's shop is "sacramentally orange.") The summer millionaire has departed in fall, like a vegetation deity—Osiris or Attis. Nautilus Island's witchlike hermit heiress is Circe, Hecate, Ishtar, Venus, "the goddess of love turned goddess of death in an All Soul's Night world" ("Mephistopheles in Maine: Rereading Lowell's 'Skunk Hour,'" *A Book of Rereadings*, ed. Greg Kuzma [Lincoln, NE: Pebble and Best Cellar, 1979] 254–64).

Andrew Marvell, To His Coy Mistress, page 1139

Questions for Discussion

1. *"All this poet does is feed some woman a big line. There's no time for romance, so he says, 'Quick, let's hit the bed before we hit the dirt.'" Discuss this summary. Then try making your own, more accurate one. Suggestion: The poem is divided into three parts, each beginning with an indented line. Take these parts one at a time, putting the speaker's main thoughts into your own words.* There's a grain of truth to this paraphrase, rude though it be. We might question, however, whether Marvell's speaker is trying to hoodwink his loved one. Perhaps he only sums up the terrible truth he knows: that time lays waste to youth, that life passes before we know it. He makes no mention of "romance," by the way—that's the paraphraser's invention. A more nearly accurate paraphrase, taking the three divisions of the poem one by one, might go like this:

Lines 1–20: If we had all the room in the world and if we were immortal, then our courtship might range across the globe. My love for you could expand till it filled the whole world and I could spend centuries in praising your every feature (saving your heart for last). After all, such treatment is only what you deserve.

Lines 21–32: But time runs on. Soon we'll be dead and gone, all my passion and all your innocence vanished.

Lines 33–46: And so, while you're still young and willing, let's seize the day. Let's concentrate our pleasure into the present moment. Although we can't make the sun stand still (like Joshua in the Bible), we'll do the next best thing: we'll joyously make time fly.

Now, obviously, any such rewording of this matchless poem must seem a piddling thing. But if students will just work through Marvell's argument part by part, they may grasp better the whole of it.

2. *In part one, how much space would be "world enough" for the lovers? Exactly how much time would be enough time?* To point out the approximate location of the Humber and the Ganges on a globe (or a simple circle drawn on a blackboard) can drive home the fact that when the poet says *world enough,* he spells out exactly what he means. A little discussion may be needed to show that in defining "enough" time, Marvell bounds it by events (the conversion of the Jews), numbers the years, and blocks out his piecemeal adoration. Two hundred years per breast is a delectable statistic! Clearly, the lover doesn't take the notion of such slow and infinitely patient devotion seriously.

3. *What is the main idea of part two? How is this theme similar to that of Housman's "Loveliest of trees"?* Both Marvell and Housman in "Loveliest of trees" are concerned with the passage of time; they differ on what needs to be done about it. Marvell urges action; Housman urges filling one's youth with observed beauty. Of these two expressions of the *carpe diem* theme, Housman's seems the more calm and disinterested.

4. *Paraphrase with special care lines 37–44. Is Marvell urging violence?* In lines 37–44, Marvell's point seems to be that time works a gradual, insidious violence. It is like a devouring beast (*slow-chapped*), holding us in its inexorable jaws. Some students will find the imagery odd, even offensive in a love poem: *birds of prey* (who want to eat, not be eaten), the cannonball of strength and sweetness that batters life's iron gates. Violence is not the speaker's counsel, but urgency. His harsh images lend his argument intensity and force.

5. *Considering the poem as a whole, does the speaker seem playful, or serious?* This fifth question presents an easy dichotomy, but of course Marvell's speaker is both playful and serious. In making clear the tone of the poem, a useful poem for comparison is Marlowe's "Passionate Shepherd." What are the two speakers' attitudes toward love? Marvell's seems more down-to-earth, skeptical, and passion-driven: a lover in a fallen world, not (like Marlowe's shepherd) a lover in a pastoral Eden.

If later on, in teaching figures of speech, you want some great lines for illustrations, turn back to this inexhaustible poem. There's hyperbole in lines 7–20, understatement ("But none, I think, do there embrace"), metaphor, simile, and of course the great personification of chariot-driving time.

Telling a class that Marvell was a Puritan usually shakes up their overly neat assumptions. Some may be surprised to learn that one can be a Puritan and not necessarily be puritanical.

Defending the poem against charges that its logic is fallacious, a recent critic, Richard Crider, has shown that "the speaker's appeal is not merely to the lady's passion, . . . but to a more inclusive and compelling value—completion and wholeness." A good student of Aristotle's logic as well as Aristotle's ethics, Marvell's speaker calls on his listener to exercise all her human powers, among them reason. "Although no single net will capture all the resonances of the final couplet, near the heart of the passage is the thought of living life completely, in accordance with natural law" ("Marvell's Valid Logic," *College Literature* [Spring 1985]: 113–211).

Edna St. Vincent Millay, RECUERDO, page 1140

There is probably not much to do with this delightful poem but leave it alone and let students discover it for themselves. The only thing we would find in it to discuss: Would that newspaper vendor really break down into tears of gratitude? We bet she is a mere literary convention here, and in real life would probably be one tough old egg.

Would this highly musical lyric make a good song? Might it be sung?

MLL *MyLiteratureLab Resources.* Photographs and biographical information for Millay.

John Milton, HOW SOON HATH TIME, page 1141

Traditionally this sonnet had been dated December 1631, the month of Milton's twenty-third birthday and therefore the end of his twenty-third year, but contemporary scholars—one of them stating "Simply put, Milton was no mathematician"—tend to see the poem as having been composed a year later. Whatever the date of its composition, "How soon hath time" is a true Petrarchan sonnet, not only by following the prescribed stanzaic structure and rime scheme but also by including a *volta*, a "turn" or thematic shift, at the beginning of the sestet. In the octave, the speaker laments the swift passage of time and his own failure meanwhile to achieve any accomplishment of note: "But my late spring no bud or blossom show'th" (line 4).

Lines 5–6 are customarily understood to refer to Milton's youthful appearance; it is elsewhere documented that in early and middle life he did in fact look much younger than his actual age. There has been considerable speculation as to the identities of the "timely-happy spirits," that is, those who have achieved more in their early careers than the speaker has: in addition to such obvious candidates as Edmund Spenser and Sir Philip Sidney, the names of several of Milton's contemporaries have been advanced, including Thomas Randolph, a fellow student at Cambridge University who wrote several highly admired verse dramas and died young, and the even more precocious Abraham Cowley, several years younger than Milton, who published his first collection of poetry at the age of fifteen. (Perhaps taking their cue from a presumed play on "measure"—that is, poetic meter—in line 10, most commentators have assumed that the true subject of the poem is achievement, or the lack thereof, in the field of poetry.)

After the seeming anxiety expressed in the octave, Milton resolves his theme with a sort of anti-*carpe diem* approach, maintaining in the last six lines that, however his destiny unfolds, whatever the level or amount of his achievement, it will all be in accordance with the will of God, who is of course the "great task-Master" of line 14, "if I have grace to use it so." The similarity of theme should be obvious between this sonnet and the following one, "When I consider how my light is spent."

John Milton, WHEN I CONSIDER HOW MY LIGHT IS SPENT, page 1142

While this famous sonnet is usually taken to refer to the poet's lost eyesight, some critics have argued that it is not about blindness at all. The familiar title "On His Blindness" was given not by Milton, but by a printer a century later.

QUESTIONS FOR DISCUSSION

1. *If the poem is not about blindness, what might it be about?* Possible suggestions: Milton's declining powers of poetry; Milton's fame as a Puritan apologist.

2. *Is "talent" a pun referring to Milton's talent for writing poetry? What other meanings of the word seem appropriate in this poem?* In the New Testament parable (Matthew 25:14–30), the hidden talent is money that should have been earning interest. That Milton is thinking primarily of work and business can be plausibly argued; other words in the poem convey such connotations— *spent*, *true account*, *day-labor*, and perhaps *useless*, which suggests the Medieval Latin word for interest, *usura*.

The theme of frustration in life (and reconciliation to one's lot) is dealt with differently in Shakespeare's "When, in disgrace with Fortune and men's eyes."

Marianne Moore, POETRY, page 1142

Marianne Moore was a singular poet both on the page and in real life. Her elaborate verse style, complex syllabic meters, and penchant for collage and quotation mirror in some mysterious way her carefully cultivated eccentricity and wry personal reticence. One peculiar feature of her work is that most of her poems— directly or indirectly—explore aesthetics, especially the nature of literary art. In this respect, "Poetry" occupies an important position in her work. This superbly observed and intellectually provocative poem also illustrates a central irony of her work—the more overtly abstract her poem appears, the more covertly personal it proves to be.

"Poetry" appears in several versions in Moore's various collections. Hardly had she first published the poem in 1921 than she began revising it. By the time she published her *Complete Poems* in 1967, Moore had grotesquely cut the poem down to only three lines. For this anthology we have reprinted her original version, which seems to us the finest and fullest one. (Instructors should make sure they compare our version to others they may have in different books.)

"Poetry" is both a defense of poetry as an important human enterprise and—to quote critic Helen Vendler—Moore's "indirect self-reproach for her painstaking absorption in 'all this fiddle.'" While eventually justifying the art of poetry for its heightened attention to genuine phenomena, the poem also admits its own skepticism about the elaborate "fiddle" of poetry and its recognition of the failure of "half poets" and "derivative" writers. Moore's aesthetic ideal is best summarized in her famous (and wondrously oxymoronic) image "imaginary gardens with real toads in them." Boldly the poet affirms the utility of poetry. Poetry is "useful" to Moore when it genuinely encompasses both external and internal reality.

The poet Donald Hall, who knew Moore, has commented in similar terms on the poem:

> In her well-known poem "Poetry," Miss Moore begins, "I too, dislike it." This line has been interpreted as ironic, as an attempt to disarm, or as evidence that she practices her art only half-seriously. Quite obviously, however, her reasoning is serious. She refers to a kind of poetry that is neither honest nor sincere but that has found fashionable approval by virtue of its very obscurity. (*Marianne Moore: The Cage and the Animal* [New York: Pegasus: 1970] 40)

The form of "Poetry" is also worth discussing. It might help to ask the class if the poem has a form—to see what features they discover on their own. Moore shaped the version of "Poetry" reprinted here into five complex syllabic stanzas of six lines each. Students can count out the syllables in each line to determine the stanza pattern. The stanzas also rime—although the rimes are more visible to the eye than audible in her run-on enjambed lines. The rime scheme is *abbccd*. The poem unfolds in the manner of an impassioned, learned conversation, and it employs prose rhythms in its elaborate syllabic pattern. Spoken aloud, it sounds like free verse; on the page, however, the reader sees how carefully wrought it is as formal verse.

Frederick Morgan, THE MASTER, *page 1143*

Morgan's poem describes an actual painting, Han Kan's "Nightshining White," which is owned by the Metropolitan Museum of Art in New York. The painting is so fragile that it is not always on display, but it is so striking that, once seen, it is never forgotten.

Morgan's poem retells the legendary account of the painting's creation. Han Kan (who was active between 742 and 756) was a painter of the T'ang dynasty. His depiction of the Emperor Ming-huang's favorite charger is probably the most famous horse painting in Chinese art, considered a masterpiece since its creation. The actual painted scroll is covered with seals and commentaries by scholars.

The theme of Morgan's poem is the artist's dependence on actual experience. Arriving in the capital, Han Kan is invited to study with the imperial court painter. He chooses instead to study from nature itself in the emperor's stables.

Poetry, then, tends to inhere not in abstract editorial stands but in particulars. William Carlos Williams's brief poem about eating the plums in the ice box may not be great, but it is human and hard to forget. Sources of poems may lie before your eyes. Although poets can learn from reading other poets' work, they can also learn from the testimony of their own senses. In the best poems, as Morgan's poem reminds us, there is always a quality that cannot be distilled from schools and libraries: a freshness that comes only from contact with the living world.

Frederick Morgan was a well-known editor as well as a poet. In 1948 he was one of the founders of the *Hudson Review*, the distinguished journal which has been called "the last of the great quarterlies."

Marilyn Nelson, A Strange Beautiful Woman, page 1144

This strange and beautiful short poem has the simplicity of a haiku—a single image doubled in a mirror followed by a single question also doubled. The poem's power rests in its suggestiveness, and it works—like the mirror—in two ways at once. The poem is affirmative in the speaker's recognition of her own beauty, but it is also subtly self-critical in noting that the speaker is insufficiently familiar with admitting her own beauty, which initially seems "strange" to her. In the same way, the speaker's surprised question—"Hey, / I said, / what you doing here?"—acquires a more disturbing existential quality when the reflection repeats it. What is the speaker doing, the image seems to ask, in and with her own life?

Howard Nemerov, The War in the Air, page 1145

This poem can be understood by students who know very little about World War II, but explaining the many allusions will enrich their appreciation. During World War II, air force pilots and crew members suffered the highest mortality rates of any Allied service branch. Sometimes every member of a squadron would be killed in a single engagement. Nemerov, who served in both the Royal Canadian and American air forces, memorializes those who usually died far away and sometimes vanished into the sea or enemy territory.

Here are the major allusions woven into the poem—all of which would be familiar to veterans of the conflict. In praising the contributions of Allied pilots during the Battle of Britain, Winston Churchill famously told Parliament, "Never in the field of human conflict was so much owed by so many to so few." The inspirational Latin tag *per ardua ad astra* ("through difficult things to the stars") served as the motto of England's Royal Air Force. Mars is, of course, the god of war. "The Good War" was an Allied nickname for World War II. The pun on "for goodness' sake" (in line 14) is also worth noting to students. This seemingly straightforward elegy is full of wordplay, allusion, and wit.

Lorine Niedecker, Poet's Work, page 1145

Though she published five collections here and in Britain, Niedecker's work has seldom appeared in anthologies. But here and there, her life and distinctive work have won recognition. In 1985 the Jargon Society published her collected writing, *From This Condensery*. In 1989 *Niedecker*, a biographical play by Kristine Thatcher, had a successful Off-Broadway production.

The poet, who spent most of her quiet life on remote Blackhawk Island, Wisconsin, worked for a time as a cleaning person in a hospital. While far from literary capitals, she kept up a lively correspondence with Basil Bunting, Cid Corman, William Carlos Williams, Louis Zukofsky, and other innovative nonacademic poets of her day.

"Poet's Work" exemplifies its own content. Like much of Niedecker's work, it is a very short poem written in very short lines, condensed to its essence, with everything extraneous—including "a," "the," or "my" before "desk"—squeezed out (a condensery is a place for making condensed or evaporated milk). Equating the writing of poetry with a trade suggests her practical approach to her work, but the last three lines of the poem, especially "No layoff," will likely put you in mind of William Butler Yeats's "Adam's Curse": "Yet if it does not seem a moment's thought, / Our stitching and unstitching has been naught. / . . . / For to articulate sweet sounds together / Is to work harder than all these, and yet / Be thought an idler. . . . " The ironies inherent in Yeats's observation are no doubt fully endorsed by Niedecker.

Yone Noguchi, A SELECTION OF HOKKU, page 1146

Yone Noguchi, the first Asian American poet of significant influence, was born in Tsushima, a small town near Nagaya, Japan. He became interested in English language and literature in public school. He later studied English at Keio University in Tokyo, but after two years he decided to immigrate to America. He arrived in San Francisco in December 1893, where he worked for a Japanese-language paper while studying American poetry. In 1896 he met the popular Western poet Joaquin Miller, who encouraged his literary ambitions. For three years Noguchi lived in a hut on Miller's hillside property above Oakland, and he associated with *Les Jeunes*, a group of young San Francisco writers including Gelett Burgess. Noguchi soon published two books, *Seen & Unseen* (1897) and *The Voice of the Valley* (1897), which showed the influence of Miller and Walt Whitman. Although written in slightly odd English, these early books were praised for their freshness. His next two collections of poetry, *From the Eastern Sea* (1903) and *The Summer Cloud* (1906), not only display more confidence and originality, they also incorporate more traditional Japanese elements of style and structure. *The Summer Cloud*, which presented sixty-two prose poems, also demonstrated Noguchi's early interest in literary modernism. In 1904 Noguchi returned to Japan—leaving behind his American lover, Leonie Gilmour, and their newborn son, Isamu Noguchi (who would become an internationally celebrated sculptor).

Noguchi corresponded with Ezra Pound and William Butler Yeats about Japanese literary aesthetics. He, therefore, played an important but little-known role in influencing the development of Imagism. He also helped popularize haiku as an English-language form. His volume *Japanese Hokkus* (1920), which was dedicated to Yeats, stills stands as a major early milestone in the American haiku tradition. Noguchi understood his unique role as a conduit between the Japanese and English-language literary traditions. "We must lose our insularity," he wrote hopefully of Japanese literature, but he could certainly have claimed to have helped broaden the perspective of American letters.

Sharon Olds, THE ONE GIRL AT THE BOYS' PARTY, page 1147

This poem whimsically describes a talented little girl, "her math scores unfolding in the air around her," during a pool party at which all the other guests are boys. *They* in lines 2 and 15, *their* in lines 18 and 19 seem to refer only to the boys. In lines 5, 7, and 11, the word *they* apparently includes the girl. You might ask students to note the pairs of adjectives that affirm the child's strength and composure: she is "smooth and sleek" (line 3), her body is "hard and / indivisible as a prime number" (lines 5–6), her face is "solemn and / sealed" (lines 16–17). The adjectives make clear the narrator-mother's respect for her brilliant daughter. Notable too is the metaphor of wet ponytail (itself a by-now-dead metaphor!) as pencil (line 12). That and the "narrow silk suit / with hamburgers and french fries printed on it" remind us that she is in some ways a very typical little girl.

It is the mathematical figures of speech that make this poem unique. Why not ask students to point out and discuss them? Are they apt? Do they ever appear forced? Which ones succeed best?

Wilfred Owen, ANTHEM FOR DOOMED YOUTH, page 1148

Metaphorically, this sonnet draws a contrast between traditional funeral trappings and the actual conditions under which the dead lie on the field of battle: with cannon fire instead of tolling bells, rifle bursts instead of the patter of prayers, the whine of shells instead of choirs' songs, the last lights in dying eyes instead of candle-shine, pale brows (of mourning girls, at home?) instead of shrouds or palls, the tenderness of onlookers (such as the poet?) instead of flowers—an early draft of the poem reads, "Your flowers, the tenderness of comrades' minds"—and the fall of night instead of the conventional drawing down of blinds in a house where someone has died.

For another Owen war poem, see "Dulce et Decorum Est." For other war poems, see in this manual "Poems Arranged by Subject and Theme."

The poet's revisions for this poem, in four drafts, may be studied in the appendix to C. Day Lewis's edition of Owen's *Collected Poems* (London: Chatto, 1963). In its first draft, the poem was called "Anthem for Dead [not Doomed] Youth," and it went, in our reading of the photographed manuscript:

> What minute bells for these who die so fast?
> Only the monstrous anger of our guns.
> Let the majestic insults of their iron mouths
> Be as the priest-words of their burials.
> Of choristers and holy music, none;
> Not any voice of mourning, save the wail
> The long-drawn wail of high, far-sailing shells.
> What candles may we hold for these lost souls?
> Not in the hands of boys, but in their eyes

Shall many candles shine, and [?] will light them.
Women's wide-spreaded arms shall be their wreaths,
And pallor of girls' cheeks shall be their palls.
Their flowers, the tenderness of all men's minds,
And every dusk, a drawing-down of blinds.

Linda Pastan, ETHICS, page 1148

As a student, the narrator, like others in her class, found her teacher's ethical puzzler irrelevant. Now the mature woman pondering the "real Rembrandt" in the museum finds the question still remote from her vital concerns, but for different reasons. The approach of her own old age has shown her that nothing lasts, that with the onflow of years our choices, whatever they may be, fade into insignificance.

One way of entering the poem: students may be asked to sum up its theme. Is it *carpe diem*? Is the poet saying, with Housman in "Loveliest of trees," "Life is fleeting; I'd better enjoy beauty while I can"? No, for the poet seems not to believe in day-seizing. Is it *ars longa, vita brevis est*? No, for both art and life seem pitifully brief and temporary. The point, rather, is that all things pass away despite our efforts to hold on to them. But instead of telling them what the point is, you might ask students to paraphrase the poem's conclusion that "woman / and painting and season are almost one / and all beyond saving by children."

To discuss: In what ways does "Ethics" differ from prose? Pastan's language seems far more musical. She makes beautiful music of alliteration and assonance. Read the poem aloud. And central to "Ethics" is a huge metaphor: old woman, season, earth, painting, and poet become one—all caught in time's resistless fire.

In a previous Instructor's Manual, we wondered: How many times did the speaker have to repeat that ethics course? To our relief, on a recent visit to the University of Arizona in Tucson, Linda Pastan supplied an answer, reported to us by Ila Abernathy of the Poetry Center. Pastan went to the Ethical Culture School in New York City, a private school run by the Ethical Culture Society and serving both elementary and high school students. The school's curriculum hits ethics hard: the poet was required to take once-a-week ethics classes for twelve years.

Linda Pastan chose "Ethics" to represent her in *The Poet's Choice*, an anthology of poets' own favorite poems, edited by George E. Murphy, Jr. (Green Harbor, MA: Tendril, 1980).

Robert Phillips, RUNNING ON EMPTY, page 1149

Robert Phillips was born in Delaware. For many years he worked on Madison Avenue as a copywriter. During his advertising career, Phillips published over a dozen volumes of poetry, short stories, and criticism, and he edited several volumes by his late teacher, Delmore Schwartz. Phillips then joined the Creative Writing Department at the University of Houston. He has provided the following comment about his poem:

> "Running on Empty" is fairly autobiographical. I was stunned at how grudgingly my father let me use the family car once I'd obtained my driver's

license at age 16. It seemed to me he withheld this symbol of my new freedom and attainment just as he withheld his affection. So when I finally had
use of the car, I went hog-wild in celebration and release.

The landscape is Sussex County, Delaware—extremely flat country
bisected by Route 13 (nicknamed "The Dual" because it is composed of
twin lanes dually parallel in an inexorable straight line). I was pushing
my luck speeding and refusing to refuel in an act of rebellion against my
father's strictness (which may explain why the 12th line reads "defying
chemistry" rather than the more accurate "defying physics"—my father
taught high school chemistry, and even in the classroom I was subject to
his discipline).

I'm rather pleased with the way the poem picks up rhythm and begins
to speed when the car does (5th–7th stanzas). And I hope students relate to
the central images of car and boy, one of which can be mechanically refu-
eled and replenished, one of which cannot.

For us the word *chemistry* in line 12 carries additional meaning, as in "behavior or functioning, as of a complex of emotions" (*The American Heritage Dictionary*).
In this sense, too, the narrator was surely in defiance of his father's chemistry.

Sylvia Plath, DADDY, page 1150

There are worse ways to begin teaching this astonishing poem than to ask students to recall what they know of Dachau, Auschwitz, Belsen (line 33), and other
Nazi atrocities. "Every woman adores a Fascist"—what does Plath mean? Is she
sympathizing with the machismo ideal of the domineering male, lashing his whip
upon subjugated womankind? (No way.) For an exchange of letters about the
rightness or wrongness of Plath's identifying with Jewish victims of World War II,
see *Commentary* (July and October 1974). Irving Howe accuses Plath of "a failure
in judgment" in using genocide as an emblem of her personal traumas.

Incredible as it seems, some students possess an alarming fund of ignorance about the Nazis, and some might not even recognize the cloven foot of
Satan (line 53); so be prepared, sadly, to supply glosses. They will be familiar
with the story of Dracula, however, and probably won't need much help with
lines 71–79. Plath may be thinking of *Nosferatu*, F. W. Murnau's silent screen
adaptation of Bram Stoker's novel *Dracula*, filmed in Germany in 1922.
Hitler's propagandists seized on the Nosferatu theme and claimed that the old
democratic order was drinking the country's blood. Plath sees Daddy as doing
the same to his daughter.

Edgar Allan Poe, A DREAM WITHIN A DREAM, page 1153

"A Dream within a Dream" is a poem that Poe kept coming back to; earlier versions of it, substantially different from the final one printed here, were published
in 1827 and 1829. And the theme is certainly one that recurs frequently in Poe's
verse; in a body of work that contains fewer than fifty completed poems, there
are texts titled "A Dream," "Dreams," and "Dream-Land," as well as a number of
other poems that treat the concept without using the word in their titles.

In his classic edition of Poe's complete poems, which inaugurated the Dell Laurel Poetry Series in 1959, the poet Richard Wilbur writes of "A Dream within a Dream":

The hero of these poems is always separated from his love through betrayal, death, or "destiny." This poem begins with a farewell to a woman of the real world by a hero whose incompatible destiny it is to dream. His dreams are of his lost visionary past—of a past that was itself a dream; and he argues that the loss of a dream is as painful as the loss of a "reality," reality itself being only an "insubstantial pageant." . . . What appalls the poet in the last two lines is that dreams, though seemingly beyond time, are yet as subject to change, loss, and oblivion as any temporal thing.

MLL *MyLiteratureLab Resources.* Photographs, biographical information, critical comments, bibliography for Poe.

Alexander Pope, A LITTLE LEARNING IS A DANG'ROUS THING, page 1153

This passage is an excerpt (lines 215–232) from Pope's "An Essay on Criticism," which he published when he was only twenty-three years old. It was this poem, which Joseph Addison immediately proclaimed "a Master-piece in its kind," that made Pope a literary celebrity.

Many teachers object to using excerpts from long works; such selections, they feel, betray the author's original intentions. In general, we agree; we favor including complete poems, so that each part of the work may be seen in relation to the whole. Pope, however, provides a special case. All of his greatest poems are too long to include in total. But it would seem too cruel to deny both teachers and students alike the pleasures of Pope's verse, so we have bent the rules several times to introduce this satiric master's work to a new generation. As every teacher knows, one sometimes needs to bend critical rules a bit.

As long as we are bending the rules, we should point out how much this excerpt from a long didactic poem looks like a self-standing lyric in its new form. Examining these eighteen lines in isolation, we see how carefully Pope arranged the images in each line to build toward a cumulative poetic as well as an intellectual effect. The final image of the weary traveler looking over the mountaintop at the endless Alps rising ahead is a brilliant stroke that seems closer to a romantic sensibility than a neoclassical one.

Ezra Pound, THE RIVER-MERCHANT'S WIFE: A LETTER, page 1154

After the death of Ernest Fenollosa, a scholar devoted to Chinese language and literature, Pound inherited Fenollosa's manuscripts containing rough prose versions of many Chinese poems. From one such draft, Pound finished his own version of "The River Merchant's Wife." Fenollosa's wording of the first line was:

My hair was at first covering my brows (child's method of wearing hair)

Arthur Waley, apparently contemptuous of Pound for ignoring dictionary meanings of some of the words of the poem, made a translation that began:

> Soon after I wore my hair covering my forehead . . .

Pound's version begins:

> While my hair was still cut straight across my forehead . . .

Pound, says the critic Waj-lim Yip, has understood Chinese culture while Waley has not, even though he understands his dictionary. "The characters for 'hair/first/cover/forehead' conjure up in the mind of a Chinese reader exactly this picture. All little Chinese girls normally have their hair cut straight across the forehead." Yip goes on to show that Pound, ignorant of Chinese as he was, comes close in sense and feeling to the Li Po original. (*Ezra Pound's Cathay* [Princeton: Princeton UP, 1969] 88–92.)

What is the tone of the poem? What details make it seem moving and true, even for a reader who knows nothing of Chinese culture?

Dudley Randall, A DIFFERENT IMAGE, page 1155

Randall's memorable and concise poem bears examination from several angles. The poem is in two short stanzas. The first states the challenge in largely abstract terms (the need to create a new image of identity); the second stanza offers a specific solution (to replace a false slave-era stereotype with a majestic African image). Notice that there is nothing specifically African American in the first stanza, but the concluding stanza particularizes the abstract challenge of the opening. Don't forget to point out (or elicit from the class) the fact that a burnt-cork face minstrel would have been a white man wearing blackface in contrast to the authentic African face of a Benin sculpture. The form of the poem is also very interesting. The lines are iambic, but their length is not constant. (They range from two to eleven syllables.) Every line is also rimed but in no regular pattern. Randall's rimed iambic lines, therefore, resemble open form in some key respects.

Finally, there is one literary allusion embedded in "A Different Image." Randall's opening stanza deliberately echoes Ezra Pound's famous lines from *Hugh Selwyn Mauberly* (1921):

> The age demanded an image
> Of its accelerated grimace,
> Something for the modern stage,
> Not, at any rate, an Attic grace.

Randall refashions Pound's search for a meaningful vision of modern beauty in African American terms. Consequently, he returns not to classical Greece but to classical West Africa. Randall's lucidity and immediacy often lead critics to underestimate the sophistication and complexity of his work. He had a classical sensibility that prizes unity of design, economy of means, clarity of intention, and a governing sense of form. The poems contain intense emotion, but it is always held in balance by the total design.

John Crowe Ransom, PIAZZA PIECE, *page 1156*

This weird and wonderful sonnet is both funny and disturbing. The old man by the rose trellis is hardly a model senior citizen but the proverbial dirty old man given an existential twist. The fun of the poem is how well it operates simultaneously on a mundane and mythic level. If the man in the dustcoat is an elderly masher, he is also a death figure who has wandered into the beautiful young lady's moonlit rose garden. The idyllic setting is a classic poetic and artistic archetype for youthful female sexuality and virginity (pervasive in love poetry from "The Song of Songs" to the present). There she waits until her "truelove" comes. In Renaissance painting one also sees this situation frequently—an Edenic pastoral landscape populated by young lovers. These pictures often have a skull hidden in the vines or bushes, bearing the Latin inscription "*Et in Arcadia ego,*" which means "Even in Arcadia, am I [i.e. Death]."

The old man inhabits the same physical space as the young lady, but he sees the lovely setting as proof of their shared mortality. The roses on the trellis are "dying" and the moon's song is "spectral." He will "have [his] lovely lady soon" not because he will rape her in the mundane sense, but because, as Death, he will eventually possess her—no matter how much she ignores his words.

Since "Piazza Piece" is a sonnet, the sestet represents the turn of attitude and perspective. The young lady responds appropriately, affirming life and hope. She considers the old man's warnings and threats as "dry and faint as in a dream." By ordering him away, she also rightly asserts that for the time being at least, the garden belongs to her. Whatever her ultimate fate, she is for the present "a lady young in beauty waiting."

Southerners will probably be familiar with the slightly old-fashioned architectural term *piazza,* which means an open porch or balcony adjacent to a garden; but Yankees, Midwesterners, and Westerners may need some remedial instruction.

Henry Reed, NAMING OF PARTS, *page 1156*

This is one of the most teachable poems ever written. There are two voices: the voice of the riflery instructor, droning on with his spiel, and the voice of the reluctant inductee, distracted by the springtime. Two varieties of diction and imagery clash and contrast: technical terms opposed to imagery of blossoming nature. Note the fine pun in line 24, prepared for by the rapist bees in the previous line. Note also the connotations of the ambiguous phrase *point of balance* (line 27)—a kind of balance lacking in the recruits' lives?

Students need to be shown the dramatic situation of the poem: the poor inductee, sitting through a lecture he doesn't want to hear. One would think that sort of experience would be familiar to students, but a troublesome instructors have met in teaching this poem is the yearning to make out of it a vast comment about Modern Civilization.

The poet himself has recorded the poem for *An Album of Modern Poets,* 1 (Library of Congress, PL 20). Dylan Thomas reads "Naming of Parts" even more impressively in his *Reading, Vol. IV: A Visit to America and Poems* (Caedmon, TC 1061).

Adrienne Rich, LIVING IN SIN, page 1157

The title of Adrienne Rich's powerfully pensive poem may need explaining to some students nowadays, and it is essential that they understand the phrase because it sets up the narrative situation of the poem. As the title indicates, Rich's pair of lovers (who are referred to only as "he" and "she") are living together but not married—a bolder lifestyle in 1955 than today. The woman has expected their life together to be romantic and carefree—"no dust upon the furniture of love"—but the daily reality of housework and habitual intimacy proves dull and disillusioning. This deflation of romantic fantasy suggests the secondary meaning of the title—the Adam and Eve of her hoped-for lover's Eden have fallen from grace into the humdrum world of everyday disappointment.

Rich has neatly divided the two worlds of the protagonists' experience into night and day. The night remains romantic—if also diminished from the woman's original expectations—but the dawn brings only disappointment. The poem never directly states whether the woman's vacillating feelings will bring matters to a crisis, but the relative impact of each emotional state is suggested by the fact that the evening world of love receives three lines of treatment, whereas the daylight world of disillusionment gets twenty-three. These proportions give "Living in Sin" the feel of an Anton Chekhov short story in which the final outcome remains unstated but the narrative situation has been so carefully presented as to make the conclusion inevitable.

For this reason, "Living in Sin" would be a good poem to use in a classroom discussion of "Saying and Suggesting." Rich's poem leaves a great many important things unsaid but implicit. The images suggest conclusions the protagonist seems not yet able to articulate—like the "beetle-eyes" staring at her from the shelf. The poem also has an interesting point of view. Although narrated in the third person, the poem adopts the subjective point of view of the woman.

"Living in Sin" is an early Rich poem (published in 1955 in her second collection, *The Diamond Cutters*). It is tempting, therefore, to read the poem as a narrative that prefigures Rich's turn to feminism. "Living in Sin" certainly responds to such interpretation. The woman in the poem has mistakenly sought fulfillment by creating a domestic world designed to please her male lover. (The particulars of the apartment "had risen at his urging.") Now she begins to understand the mistaken idealism and unintentional subjugation of that decision. Some changes—some escape—must happen, even if the particular course of action has not yet been imagined. What must come next, to quote the title of a subsequent Rich volume, is "the will to change."

Edwin Arlington Robinson, MINIVER CHEEVY, page 1158

"Miniver Cheevy" is one of Robinson's great character portraits. These miniature character studies (see also "Richard Cory") are a genre that Robinson perfected. Influenced by the dramatic and narrative poems of poets such as George Crabbe and Robert Browning, Robinson compressed the portrait poem into tighter, often lyric structures. His work, with its stark realism, bitter antiromanticism, and concise form, marks the true beginning of modern (but not Modernist) American poetry.

Mr. Cheevy of the title is a man unable to face reality. He lives in a fantasy world of "the days of old." Cheevy imagines he would have lived a more exciting and fulfilling life in an earlier age, but Robinson makes it clear that Cheevy's fantasies are pure self-deception. Robinson undercuts Cheevy's delusions with irony ("He missed the medieval grace / Of iron clothing").

Writing the introduction to Robinson's posthumous *King Jasper* in 1935, Robert Frost reminisced about reading "Miniver Cheevy" in London in 1913 with Ezra Pound. They laughed over the fourth *thought* in "Miniver thought, and thought, and thought / And thought about it." "Three 'thoughts' would have been 'adequate' as the critical praise-word then was," Frost remembered ". . . The fourth made the intolerable touch of poetry. With the fourth the fun began."

Theodore Roethke, ELEGY FOR JANE, page 1159

By piling up figures of speech from the natural world, Roethke in "Elegy for Jane" portrays his student as a child of nature, quick, thin, and birdlike. A *wren*, a *sparrow*, a *skittery pigeon*, Jane has a *pickerel smile* and neck curls *limp and damp as tendrils*. She waits *like a fern, making a spiny shadow*. She has the power to make shade trees and (even more surprising) mold burst into song. For her, leaves change their whispers into kisses.

Then she dies. The poet acknowledges that for him there is no consolation in nature, in the "sides of wet stones" or the moss; his grief is not assuaged. Because he mourns the girl as teacher and friend, no more, he recognizes a faint awkwardness in his grief as he speaks over her grave:

> I, with no rights in this matter,
> Neither father nor lover.

Roethke, writing about this poem in *On the Poet and His Craft* (Seattle: U of Washington P, 1965) 81–83, reminds the reader that it was John Crowe Ransom (to whose "Bells for John Whiteside's Daughter" this poem has often been compared) who first printed "Elegy for Jane." Roethke discusses his use of enumeration, calling it "the favorite device of the more irregular poem." He calls attention to one "of the strategies for the poet writing without the support of a formal pattern," a strategy he uses in "Elegy for Jane": the "lengthening out" of the last three lines in the first stanza, balanced by the progressive shortening of the three lines at the poem's end.

Some readers have interpreted "Elegy for Jane" as the work of a man who never had children of his own; but in fact Roethke as a young man had fathered a daughter, for whom he felt great affection. Although "neither father nor lover" of Jane, he at least could well imagine a father's feelings.

Mary Jo Salter, WELCOME TO HIROSHIMA, page 1160

Salter's poem is a meditation on the tragedy of Hiroshima that admits the foreigner's difficulty in understanding the exact nature of the event as the Japanese themselves experienced it. The speaker looks to understand the past cataclysm but repeatedly finds that the contemporary commercial reality impedes her comprehension. The ironic title is made even more mordant by being in English on a sign sponsored by Toshiba. One touristic observation after another distracts, surprises, dismays, or confuses the speaker, until an exhibit of a glass shard trapped in a woman's arm for three decades finally provides the mute but eloquent testimony of suffering and redemption on a tangibly human scale.

 MyLiteratureLab Resources. Longman Lecture on "Welcome to Hiroshima."

William Shakespeare, WHEN, IN DISGRACE WITH FORTUNE AND MEN'S EYES, page 1162

Figures of speech are central to many Shakespearean sonnets, but they hardly enter into "When, in disgrace" until line 11, when the simile of the lark is introduced. The lark's burst of joy suggests that heaven, called *deaf* in line 3, has suddenly become keener of hearing. Critical discussion of the sonnets goes on: *Shakespeare's Sonnets*, edited with analytic commentary by Stephen Booth (New Haven: Yale UP, 1977) is especially valuable.

 MyLiteratureLab Resources. Photographs, biographical information, and bibliography for Shakespeare.

William Shakespeare, NOT MARBLE NOR THE GILDED MONUMENTS, page 1163

To discuss: Is Shakespeare making a wild boast, or does the claim in lines 1–8 seem at all justified? (Time has proved him right. Here we are, still reading his lines, 500 years after they were written! Of course, the fact that he happened to be Shakespeare helped his prediction come true.)

For teaching this poem in tandem with Robinson Jeffers's "To the Stone-Cutters," see the entry on Jeffers in this manual.

 MyLiteratureLab Resources. Photographs, biographical information, and bibliography for Shakespeare.

William Shakespeare, THAT TIME OF YEAR THOU MAYST IN ME BEHOLD, page 1163

Shakespeare's magnificent metaphors will probably take some brief explaining. How is a body like boughs, and how are the bare boughs like a ruined choir loft? Students will get the general import, but they can be helped to visualize the images. "Consumed with that which it was nourished by" will surely require some discussion. Youth, that had fed life's fire, now provides only smothering ashes. The poet's attitude toward age and approaching death stands in contrast to the attitudes of poets (or speakers) in other poems of similar theme: admiration for the exultant sparrows in William Carlos Williams's "To Waken an Old Lady"; defiance in Yeats's "Sailing to Byzantium."

MLL   *MyLiteratureLab Resources.* Photographs, biographical information, and bibliography for Shakespeare. Longman Lecture on "That time of year thou mayst in me behold."

William Shakespeare, MY MISTRESS' EYES ARE NOTHING LIKE THE SUN, page 1164

Have students state positively each simile that Shakespeare states negatively, and they will make a fair catalog of trite Petrarchan imagery. Poking fun at such excessive flattery is a source of humor even today, as in an old wheeze: "Your teeth are like the stars—they come out at night."

MLL   *MyLiteratureLab Resources.* Photographs, biographical information, and bibliography for Shakespeare. Longman Lecture on "The Theme of Love in the Sonnets."

Louis Simpson, AMERICAN POETRY, page 1164

Simpson's brilliant short poem would make an excellent classroom assignment in a discussion that could also include Archibald MacLeish's "Ars Poetica" and Marianne Moore's "Poetry." All three are classic statements of modern poetics. Simpson's is both the most recent work (1963) and the only one specifically focused on what makes American poetry different from other literatures. The short imagistic poem combines odd and usually seemingly unpoetic items (rubber, coal, uranium) with more traditional literary elements (moons, poems). The final stanza develops this principle of contradictory assemblage into the surreal extended simile of the shark-like poem swimming through the desert uttering cries that are almost human. Clearly Simpson's poem is not conceptual and discursive but suggestive and symbolic. What does the shark symbolize? At the very least, the image suggests the restless, untamed, omnivorous, and even dangerous nature of American poetry. How does this vision of the art compare to Moore's or MacLeish's?

David R. Slavitt, TITANIC, page 1164

In "The Convergence of the Twain," Hardy censures the vanity, luxury, and pride that prompted Fate to ram the *Titanic* into an iceberg. Slavitt's poem about the same tragedy takes another tack. He makes dying on the *Titanic* sound almost like fun—all aboard!

If they sold passage tomorrow for that same crossing, who would not buy?

Slavitt's point is that, since we all have to die, it's certainly more glamorous, more desirable to do it "first-class" (note the double meaning of "go" in the last line) than to die less comfortably, in more mundane ways, and soon be forgotten.

Christopher Smart, FOR I WILL CONSIDER MY CAT JEOFFRY, page 1165

Telling us more about cats than Carl Sandburg and T. S. Eliot (in "Prufrock," lines 15–22) put together, Smart salutes Jeoffry in one of several passages in *Jubilate Agno* that fall for a little while into some continuity. This fascinating poem, and the whole work that contained it, have come down to us in a jumble of manuscripts retrieved from the asylum, sorted out brilliantly by W. H. Bond in his edition of Smart's work (Cambridge: Harvard UP, 1954). Some of Smart's gorgeous lines seem quite loony, such as the command to Moses concerning cats (lines 34–35) and the patriotic boast about misinformation: the ichneumon (or *Icneumon*, line 63) is not a pernicious rat, but a weasel-like, rat-killing mammal.

Talking with Boswell of Smart's confinement, Dr. Johnson observed:

> I did not think he ought to be shut up. His infirmities were not noxious to society. He insisted on people praying with him; and I'd as lief pray with Kit Smart as with any one else. Another charge was, that he did not love clean linen; and I have no passion for it.

A possible paper topic: "Smart's Cat Jeoffry and Blake's Tyger: How Are These Poems Similar in View?"

William Jay Smith, AMERICAN PRIMITIVE, page 1167

We might expect a painter called an American primitive to be naive, unsophisticated, and childlike in his view. So is the speaker who draws this verbal scene. Not only do the references to Daddy seem juvenile, but so does the line "the screen door bangs, and it sounds so funny." (Smith, incidentally, has written much fine verse for children in addition to his more serious poetry, and he understands the way a child thinks and speaks.) There is, of course, an ironic distance between the speaker's point of view and the poet's. Irony is enforced, too, in the contrast between the grim event and the bouncy rhythm and use of feminine rimes.

Another possible way of looking at the poem is that Daddy himself is the primitive: the primal dollar-worshipping American. The capitalization of *Dollar* (as in the familiar phrase "the Almighty Dollar") may support this view. We are not told why Daddy died, an apparent suicide, but it is evident that riches did not buy him life. Besides inviting comparison with Sylvia Plath's ironic poem about the death of a terrible "Daddy," Smith's mock-elegy may be set beside Wallace Stevens's "The Emperor of Ice-Cream," with students asked to compare the two in tone and in subject matter.

Cathy Song, STAMP COLLECTING, page 1168

Song's poem depends upon an original and illuminating conceit: the speaker views the countries of the world through the stamps they issue. Understanding that the subject of each stamp reflects in some way the culture and geography that produced it, the speaker speculates on the national vision and self-image behind her stamps. "Stamp Collecting" is a political poem, but it unfolds with such delicate observations and employs such ingenious language that it may be easy for students to miss the political content. Moreover, the poem has no specific ideological ax to grind. "Stamp Collecting" explains the concept of national self-identity rather than any particular political cause.

William Stafford, THE FARM ON THE GREAT PLAINS, page 1169

In 1962—when Stafford still had three decades of life and poetry before him— he selected this poem, "The Farm on the Great Plains," for Paul Engle and Joseph Langland's *Poet's Choice* (New York: Dial, 1962), an anthology in which one hundred or so English-language poets selected their favorite among their own works and supplied a (usually) brief explanation of their choice. Stafford wrote the following note to accompany his poem:

> A glance at "The Farm on the Great Plains" jolts me with a succession of regrets about it, but these regrets link with reassurances as I confront and accept something of my portion in writing: an appearance of moral commitment mixed with a deliberate—even a flaunted—nonsophistication; an organized form cavalierly treated; a trace of narrative for company amid too many feelings. There are emergences of consciousness in the poem, and some outlandish lunges for communication; but I can stand quite a bit of this sort of thing if a total poem gives evidence of locating itself.
>
> And the *things* here—plains, farm, home, winter, lavished all over the page—these command my allegiance in a way that is beyond my power to analyze at the moment. Might I hazard that they signal something like austere hope? At any rate, they possess me. I continue to be a willing participant in the feelings and contradictions that led me to write the poem.

Wallace Stevens, THE EMPEROR OF ICE-CREAM, page 1170

Choosing this poem to represent him in an anthology, Stevens once remarked, "This wears a deliberately commonplace costume, and yet seems to me to contain something of the essential gaudiness of poetry; that is the reason why I like it." (His statement appears in *Fifty Poets: An American Auto-Anthology*, ed. William Rose Benet [New York: Diffield, 1933].)

Some students will at once relish the poet's humor; others may discover it in class discussion. Try to gather the literal facts of the situation before getting into the poem's suggestions. The wake or funeral of a poor old woman is taking place in her home. The funeral flowers come in old newspapers, not in florists' fancy wrappings; the mourners don't dress up, but wear their usual street clothes; the refreshments aren't catered but are whipped up in the kitchen by a neighbor, a cigar-roller. Like ice cream, the refreshments are a dairy product. Nowadays it would probably be a sour cream chip-dip; perhaps in 1923 they were blocks of Philadelphia cream cheese squashed into cups for spreading on soda crackers. To a correspondent, Stevens wrote that *fantails* refers not to fans but to fantail pigeons (*Letters* [New York: Knopf, 1966] 341). Such embroidery seems a low-brow pursuit: the poor old woman's pathetic aspiration toward beauty. *Deal* furniture is cheap. Everything points to a run-down neighborhood, and to a woman about whose passing nobody very much cares.

Who is the Emperor? The usual guess is Death. Some students will probably see that the Emperor and the muscular cigar-roller (with his creamy curds) suggest each other. (Stevens does not say that they are identical.) Ice cream suggests the chill of the grave—and what besides? Today some of its connotations will be commonplace: supermarkets, Baskin-Robbins. To the generation of Stevens, ice cream must have meant more: something luxurious and scarce, costly, hard-to-keep, requiring quick consumption. Other present-day connotations may come to mind: sweetness, deliciousness, childhood pleasure. Stevens's personal view of the icecream in the poem was positive. "The true sense of 'Let be be finale of seem' is let being become the conclusion or denouement of appearing to be: in short, ice cream is an absolute good" (*Letters* 341). An absolute good! The statement is worth quoting to students who have doubts about the poet's attitude toward ice cream—as did an executive of the Amalgamated Ice Cream Association, who once wrote to the poet in perplexity (see *Letters* 501–2). If ice cream recalls sweet death, still (like curds) it also contains hints of mother's milk, life, and vitality.

On a visit to Mount Holyoke, XJK was told that, as part of an annual celebration, it is customary for the trustees and the seniors to serve ice cream (in Dixie cups) to the freshman class at the grave of Mary Lyon, founder of the college. In a flash he remembered Stevens's poem and embraced Jung's theory of archetypes.

 MyLiteratureLab Resources. Biography, critical overview, and bibliography for Stevens.

Jonathan Swift, A DESCRIPTION OF THE MORNING, page 1171

This slice of eighteenth-century London life seems replete with human failings: Betty (a conventional name for a servant) sleeping with her master and trying to hide the evidence, prisoners released from jail in order to steal. Swift's couplets describe not the highborn but the common people, for whom a hackney coach heralded dawn in place of mythology's grander chariot driven across the sky by Phoebus Apollo. Although Swift crams his lines with images of city dirt and human corruption, the humor of his poem implies considerable affection for London's streets and sinners. If students see no humor in his view, let them compare this poem with another poem about eighteenth-century streets, Blake's angry "London," or a rhapsodic, Romantic description of a London morning, Wordsworth's "Composed upon Westminster Bridge."

Larissa Szporluk, VERTIGO, page 1172

In 2001, Larissa Szporluk told an interviewer: "I want readers to feel I am opening something from the unknown. I want my poems to show the uncertainty that lies in where I'm going and what I'm seeing." Her work has been described as "hypnotic" and "incantatory," and reading "Vertigo" aloud will help to demonstrate why. The poem is divided into two sentences: the first one is two words long; the second, twenty-seven lines. From the second line on, we are carried dizzily forward by the swirl of images as our footing is undermined by the systematic denial of certainties—*maybe* in lines 6, 9, and 10; "and the stars that you think / . . . / there should be / aren't even stars / . . . / and don't serve as guides" (lines 13, 15–16, 19); "they don't know who you are" (line 23). The effect is heightened by sound patterns of assonance and internal rime: from the summit of *high, tiny, mite, light, find,* and *height* in the first half of the poem, to the swoop of *don't, below, know, droves,* and *fold* as it rushes toward its seemingly inevitable (but still open-ended) conclusion.

Sara Teasdale, THE FLIGHT, page 1173

Just as romantic love was Sara Teasdale's great theme, the concept of flight was clearly one of great significance to her in the working out of this theme, since she published no fewer than three poems titled "The Flight." Our text of that title appeared in her 1926 collection, *Dark of the Moon.* In this poem, Teasdale's eagles never seem to be entirely real birds of prey: a metaphor in the first stanza, a simile in the second, they are purely symbolic from the opening lines, representing the adventurous love and passionate union of two people. Their spirits are so closely united that the speaker wishes that when one of them dies, the other will follow, a highly romantic aspiration that strongly contrasts with the behavior of eagles—as well as, for that matter, the behavior of most human beings.

Alfred, Lord Tennyson, DARK HOUSE, BY WHICH ONCE MORE I STAND, page 1173

In Memoriam, section 7. "This is great poetry," wrote T. S. Eliot, "economical of words, a universal emotion related to a particular place; and it gives me the shudder that I fail to get from anything in *Maud*" (Introduction to *Poems of Tennyson* [London: Nelson, 1936]). The dark house was indeed a particular place— "67, Wimpole Street," as Tennyson noted—the house of Henry Hallam. The poem contains at least two allusions, whether or not we are expected to pick them up: "And then it started, like a guilty thing" (Horatio describing the ghost in *Hamlet,* I, i, 148); and "He is not here, but is risen" (Luke 24:6). In line 11 of one manuscript version, Tennyson wrote *dripping* instead of *drizzling.* Why is *drizzling* superior? The highest moment in the poem occurs in the last line in the two spondees, at least equal in their effect to Yeats's "And the *white breast* of the *dim sea*" ("Who Goes with Fergus?").

For some of these notes we are indebted to Christopher Ricks's matchless edition of *The Poems of Tennyson* (New York: Norton, 1969).

MLL *MyLiteratureLab Resources.* Biography, critical overview, and bibliography for Tennyson.

Alfred, Lord Tennyson, ULYSSES, page 1174

The following inadequate précis, meant to make lovers of Tennyson's poem irate, might be quoted to students to see whether they agree with it: A hardy old futzer can't stand life in the old folks' home and calls on his cronies to join him in an escape, even though the whole lot of them are going to break their necks.

For criticism, see Paul F. Baum, *Tennyson Sixty Years After* (Chapel Hill: U of North Carolina P, 1948) 92–94; and John Pettigrew, "Tennyson's 'Ulysses': A Reconciliation of Opposites," *Victorian Poetry* 1 (Jan. 1963): 27–45.

 MyLiteratureLab Resources. Biography, critical overview, and bibliography for Tennyson.

Dylan Thomas, FERN HILL, page 1176

Fern Hill is the farm of Thomas's aunt, Ann Jones, with whom he spent boyhood holidays. In line 2 the poet cites a favorite saying of his father's, "Happy as the grass is green." The saying is echoed again in line 38. As students may notice, Thomas likes to play upon familiar phrases and transform them, as in line 7, "once *below* [not *upon*] a time."

It came as a great shock when we first realized that this poem, which XJK had thought a quite spontaneous burst of lyric energy, is shaped into a silhouette, and that the poet contrived its form by counting syllables. Such laborious working methods were customary for Thomas. John Malcolm Brinnin has recalled seeing more than 200 separate and distinct versions of "Fern Hill"—a fact worth conveying to students who think poets simply overflow.

We take the closing line to express Thomas's view of his own poetry, lyrical and rule-bound at the same time: a song uttered in chains. Of course, the last line also means that the boy in the poem was held in chains by Time, the villain, who informs the whole poem (except for stanzas 3 and 4, which see childhood as Eden). Students may be asked to trace all the mentions of Time throughout the poem, then to sum up the poet's theme. William York Tindall, who offers a line-by-line commentary, makes a fine distinction: "Not how it feels to be young, the theme of 'Fern Hill' is how it feels to have been young" (*A Reader's Guide to Dylan Thomas* [New York: Noonday, 1962]). And we'd add, "how it would have felt to grow old, if the boy had realized he wouldn't live forever."

According to Tindall (in a lecture), Thomas used to grow huffy whenever asked if he were an admirer of Gerard Manley Hopkins. Still, to hear aloud both "Fern Hill" and Hopkins's "Pied Beauty" is to notice much similarity of sound and imagery. Hopkins studied Welsh for a time, while Thomas never did learn the language; but both at least knew of ancient Welsh poetry and its ingeniously woven sound patterns.

Thomas's magnificent (or, some would say, magnificently hammy) reading of this poem can be heard on Caedmon recording TC 1002, cassette 51002, compact disk Z1002. The recording, *A Child's Christmas in Wales and Other Poems*, also contains "Do not go gentle into that good night."

John Updike, Ex-Basketball Player, page 1177

Updike's ex-basketball player suffers the fate that Housman's athlete escapes by dying young. Flick Webb has to live on, unsung, in "fields where glory does not stay." The man whose "hands were like wild birds" now uses those hands to pump gas, check oil, and change flat tires. "Once in a while, / As a gag, he dribbles an inner tube." In his spare time, he sits in Mae's luncheonette and "just nods / Beyond her face toward bright applauding tiers / Of Necco Wafers, Nibs, and Juju Beads." (Are today's students familiar with those brand names?)

Updike's light tone does not obscure the pathos of Flick's situation. (Students might be asked if they know anyone like Flick Webb.) Though Updike has written notable light verse, he says of this early poem, his second to be accepted by the *New Yorker*, that it "is 'serious' and has enjoyed a healthy anthology life, though its second stanza now reads strangely to students. . . . That is, they have never seen glass-headed pumps, or gas stations with a medley of brands of gasoline, or the word *Esso*" (foreword to a new edition of Updike's first book, *The Carpentered Hen* [New York: Knopf, 1982]).

See how quickly your class can identify the poem's form as blank verse.

> **MLL** *MyLiteratureLab Resources.* Biography, photos, critical overview, and bibliography for Updike.

Derek Walcott, The Virgins, page 1178

Walcott provides an ironic view of the main seaport of the Virgin Islands. The irony begins with the title, in which the islands seem waiting to be raped or seduced by outsiders. The sun is like a drug ("sun-stoned"), and the term *free port* is used sarcastically to underscore how little of any worth freedom has brought this city. The dense images and careful rhetoric of the poem create the impression of a dead place where no genuine life is possible.

Edmund Waller, Go, Lovely Rose, page 1179

In some ways quieter than Marvell's "To His Coy Mistress" or Herrick's "To the Virgins, to Make Much of Time," this poem has the same theme: *carpe diem.* "Go, Lovely Rose" merits admiration for its seemingly effortless grace and for the sudden, gently shocking focus on our mortality in the poem's final stanza.

Students may enjoy reading Ezra Pound's imitative tribute to Waller: the "Envoi" to *Hugh Selwyn Mauberley*, beginning "Go, dumb-born book . . . ," in *Personae*, Pound's collected shorter poems (New York: New Directions, 1949).

Walt Whitman, from Song of the Open Road, page 1180

This is the fifteenth and concluding section of a poem that first appeared (as "Poem of the Road") in the second edition of *Leaves of Grass*. It was retitled for the 1867 edition and thereafter underwent only slight revision, mainly the elimination of a few lines. Thus it belongs to the early part of Whitman's mature

career, and it reflects the themes of universal oneness and transcendental opti-
mism that characterize that phase of his work.

In his freewheeling and quirky but often shrewdly insightful *Studies in Classic American Literature* (1923), the great British novelist D. H. Lawrence observes:

> This is Whitman's message of American democracy.
> The true democracy, where soul meets soul, in the open road. Democracy.
> American democracy where all journey down the open road, and where a soul
> is known at once in its going. Not by its clothes or appearance. . . . Not by its
> family name. Not even by its reputation. . . . Not by a progression of piety, or
> by works of Charity. Not by works at all. Not by anything, but just itself. . . .
>
> The love of man and woman: a recognition of souls, and a communion
> of worship. The love of comrades: a recognition of souls, and a communion
> of worship. Democracy: a recognition of souls, all down the open road, and
> a great soul seen in its greatness, as it travels on foot among the rest, down
> the common way of the living. A glad recognition of souls, and a gladder
> worship of great and greater souls, because they are the only riches. . . .
>
> The only riches, the great souls.

 MyLiteratureLab Resources. Biography, critical overview, and bibliography
for Whitman.

Walt Whitman, I HEAR AMERICA SINGING, page 1181

In "I Hear America Singing," the twentieth of twenty-one "Inscriptions" with
which he began the third edition of his *Leaves of Grass,* Walt Whitman presents
a vision of America in which people of varied trades and walks of life each sing
his or her own individual song ("what belongs to him or her and to none else"),
and these individual songs somehow blend to form a harmonious whole, reflective of Whitman's vision of, and for, America itself. Whitman biographer David
S. Reynolds observes that this "picture . . . was more than just a metaphor. It
reflected a pre-mass-media culture in which Americans often entertained themselves and each other" (*Walt Whitman's America: A Cultural Biography,* [New
York: Knopf, 1995]).

Even if the image is grounded in fact, we cannot help but wonder how realistic a depiction it was of Whitman's society, as opposed to an idealistic vision of
what America could and, Whitman no doubt hoped, would be. "I Hear America Singing" was first published, after all, in 1860, the year before the beginning
of the Civil War, hardly the most harmonious moment in American history.
And it may also be worth pointing out that it was the title piece of a British
selection of Whitman's most idealistic and affirmative verses about American
society that was rushed into print in the wake of the terrorist attacks of September 11, 2001 (*I Hear America Singing: Poems of Democracy, Manhattan, and
the Future* [London: Anvil, 2001]).

 MyLiteratureLab Resources. Biography, critical overview, and bibliography
for Whitman.

Richard Wilbur, THE WRITER, page 1181

A searching criticism of Wilbur's work, and this poem, is offered by Andrew Hudgins (*Hudson Review*, Winter 1989). Sometimes Wilbur implies that it is possible to master the world and its complicated problems in much the same way that a poet, in a successful poem, masters the language—but it isn't, of course. Wilbur thus places himself in a dilemma, one he is aware of. Hudgins summarizes "The Writer" and interprets it:

> Hearing his daughter as she types a story in her room, he compares the house to a ship and the sound of the typewriter keys to "a chain hauled over a gunwale," while the "stuff" of his daughter's life is "a great cargo and some of it heavy." Then, rather glibly, he wishes her a "lucky passage." As soon as he's completed the metaphor, however, he rejects the "easy figure" because he remembers how difficult the life of a writer can be. The next metaphor he advances is embedded in the anecdote of a "dazed starling" that once became trapped in the same room his daughter is now working in. . . . Though the poem is touching and even powerful, the implied final metaphor, and the ending of the poem, while infinitely better than the rejected first metaphor of the ship, still have a bit of its premeditated neatness about them.

Whether or not the poem is autobiographical, Wilbur does have a daughter, Ellen Wilbur, a widely published fiction writer and the author of *Wind and Birds and Human Voices*, a collection of short stories (Stuart Wright, 1984: NAL paperback, 1985).

MLL *MyLiteratureLab Resources.* Critical essay by Wilbur, "Cold War Poetry."

C. K. Williams, ELMS, page 1182

There is perhaps little for the instructor to add for students to achieve an understanding of "Elms." The poem's basic situation is clear, and it is described clearly, in a focused presentation that avoids all distractions. Modifiers constantly supply us with the qualities we are to associate with the various components of the poem: "stricken elms," "pitiless electric chain saws," "diesel choppers . . . shredding . . . feverishly, incessantly," and so on. In line 5 we are told overtly that "it is as though illusions of reality were stripped," and in the last line, in "the unhealing evening" the refrain of "'Insolent, unconscionable, the winds of time. . . .'"

With little or nothing to interpret in the face of such direct communication, you might ask your students how well they relate to the presentation. Does the poem describe something that they themselves have witnessed at one time or another? If so, does the description seem apt? And, ultimately, do they agree that the sentiments with which the author has invested the situation are appropriate and are supported by his description?

William Carlos Williams, SPRING AND ALL, page 1183

QUESTIONS FOR DISCUSSION

1. *Why cannot Williams's attitude toward spring be called "poetic" and "conventional"? What is his attitude toward the approaching season? By what means is it indicated? Consider especially lines 14–15 and 24–25, and the suggestion of contagious in the opening line.* Spring is stealing over the land as a contagious disease infects a victim. But spring is not a disease: it has a "stark dignity."

2. *An opinion: "This poem clearly draws from the poet's experience as a pediatrician who had attended hundreds of newborns, and whose work was often to describe with clinical exactness the symptoms of his patients." Discuss.* Lines 16–18 especially seem to contain a metaphor of newborn infants. The adjectives *mottled, dried, sluggish* could occur in a physician's report. In lines 9–13 also, the description of bushes, trees, and vines seems painstakingly exact in its detail.

   Recalling his life as writer and physician in an article for a popular magazine, Williams once told how poems would come to him while driving on his daily rounds. "When the phrasing of a passage suddenly hits me, knowing how quickly such things are lost, I find myself at the side of the road frantically searching in my medical bag for a prescription blank" ("Seventy Years Deep," *Holiday* [Nov. 1954]: 78). "By the road to the contagious hospital" was one such poem, originally recorded on prescription blanks (Roy Miki, "Driving and Writing," *William Carlos Williams: Man and Poet*, ed. Carroll F. Terrell [Orono: National Poetry Foundation, 1983] 113).

   Scholars have speculated that the brief lines of many of Williams's poems may have been decreed by the narrow width of a prescription blank, but we don't buy that guess. Had he wanted longer lines Williams would have turned the blanks sideways or composed in smaller handwriting.

MLL   *MyLiteratureLab Resources.* Biography, critical overview, and bibliography for Williams.

William Carlos Williams, TO WAKEN AN OLD LADY, page 1184

QUESTIONS FOR DISCUSSION

1. *By which words or phrases does Williams suggest the physical ravages of old age? What very different connotations do the phrases* broken / seedhusks *and* shrill / piping *carry, as well as the suggestions of feeble and broken senility?* Broken husks suggest a feast, piping suggests merriment.

2. *What is the* dark wind? *Can a wind be literally dark?* No, it can't; Williams means dark in the sense of sinister or menacing. This wind is like the passage of time that buffets or punishes.

3. *What is the dictionary definition of* tempered? *What does the word mean in this poem?*

 MyLiteratureLab Resources. Biography, critical overview, and bibliography for Williams.

William Wordsworth, COMPOSED UPON WESTMINSTER BRIDGE, page 1185

Imaginary conversation:

> *Instructor:* What do you make of the title? Is this a poem composed upon the subject of a bridge, or a poem composed while standing on a bridge's sidewalk?
> *Student:* The latter, obviously.
> *Instructor:* How do you know?
> *Student:* His eye is located up on the bridge. Otherwise he wouldn't see with such a wide-angle lens.
> *Instructor:* You genius! To the head of the class!

Whose is the "mighty heart"? Wordsworth is describing the city as a sleeping beauty about to awaken. Of course, the brightness of the scene is increased by the poet's being out for his stroll before a hundred thousand chimneys have begun to smoke from coal fires preparing kippers for breakfast. Charles Lamb, in a letter to Wordsworth, had chided the poet that the urban emotions must be unknown to him, so perhaps this famous sonnet is an answer to the charge.

Compare "The World Is Too Much with Us" for a different Wordsworth attitude toward commerce; or compare Wordsworth's London of 1807 with Blake's "London" of 1794—practically the same city, but seen from a different perspective. (Wordsworth up on the bridge at dawn, letting distance lend enchantment; Blake down in the city streets by night, with the chimney sweep, the teenage whore, and the maimed veteran.)

 MyLiteratureLab Resources. Biography, critical overview, and bibliography for Wordsworth. Audio clip for "Composed upon Westminster Bridge."

James Wright, A BLESSING, page 1186

At first, students are likely to regard "A Blessing" as "a delicate poem about the kinship between men and horses," as Ralph J. Mills sees it (*Contemporary American Poetry* [New York: Random, 1965]). They will be right, of course; but to take them a step further, they can be asked what *blessing* the poem refers to, and to ponder especially its last three lines. In a sense, the image of stepping over barbed wire into an open pasture (line 7) anticipates the idea of stepping out of one's body into—what? Any paraphrase is going to be clumsy; but Wright hints at nothing less than the loneliness of every creature alive. Although they are together, the two ponies are lonely to an extreme and are apparently overjoyed to see people. By implication, maybe the speaker and his friend are lonely together as well. In lines 15–21 the speaker, to his astonishment, finds himself falling in love with one of the ponies; he sees her beauty as that of a girl. At this point, we might expect him to recoil and cry, "Good grief! what's the matter with me?"—but he persists and becomes enlightened, at least for a moment. Only his physical body, he realizes, keeps him alone and separated. What if he were to shed it? He'd bloom.

A master of open form, Wright knows how to break off a line at a moment when a pause will throw weight upon sense: "Suddenly I realize / That if I stepped out of my body I would break / Into blossom."

Maybe the best way to teach "A Blessing" is just to read it aloud and then say nothing at all.

James Wright, Autumn Begins in Martins Ferry, Ohio, page 1186

Martins Ferry was Wright's home town. The speaker of the poem describes the men of Martins Ferry sitting in the high school stadium, the only place in the vicinity where heroes are likely to appear. Certainly these working-class men have given up dreams of heroism in their own lives. Grey-faced, ruptured, worn out by their jobs in heavy industry, they sit in taverns over their beer, "ashamed to go home" to their wives. Unable even to satisfy the romantic or sexual longings of their wives, who are "dying for love," these men turn to their sons for inspiration. In October, as the year begins to die, they watch the heroic spectacle of their sons' football games. While there is something gloriously primal about Wright's scene, there is also something darkly ironic. Will the sons of Martins Ferry achieve true heroism on the gridiron? Or will they just bang up their knees and dislocate their shoulders for a season or two before they go on to equally unheroic adult lives? The poem masterfully has it both ways—both heroic and doomed.

Perhaps the fathers were once football heroes themselves, as George S. Lensing and Ronald Moran point out in *Four Poets and the Emotive Imagination* (Baton Rouge: Louisiana State UP, 1976), a study that discusses nearly the whole of Wright's work. "From this there is the suggestion that the futures of the current community heroes may be as bleak as the present time assuredly is for the fathers."

Did Wright mean to protest the violence of football—at least, football of the Martins Ferry kind? Not according to the poet himself, who once played on an Ohio River Valley semipro team. Although the high school games were "ritualized, formalized violence," they had positive qualities: "the expression of physical grace," "terrific aesthetic appeal." Wright's own high school produced not just lads doomed to frustration (like their fathers), but at least one football hero—Lou Groza, placekicker for the Cleveland Browns. (Wright made his remarks in an interview reprinted in *The Pure Clear Word: Essays on the Poetry of James Wright*, ed. Dave Smith [Urbana: U of Illinois P, 1982] 3–4.)

In the same critical anthology, Robert Hass sees football in the poem as a harvest ritual, which, like all good harvest rituals, celebrates sexual potency and the fruitfulness of the earth (two positive qualities apparently not conspicuous in Martins Ferry). "Even the stanzaic structure of the poem participates in the ritual. The first two stanzas separate the bodies of the men from the bodies of the women, and the third stanza gives us the boys pounding against each other, as if they could, out of their wills, effect a merging" (210).

Jan Hodge, of Morningside College in Sioux City, Iowa, wrote us a long letter full of insights about this poem. (We have incorporated a few of his remarks into our comments above.) He ends his reading of the poem with some especially interesting observations:

> Isn't the third stanza (introduced by that powerful placement of "Therefore" on a line by itself) the logical culmination of the first *two* stanzas—the point being that it is because of *both* the larger community's need for heroes *and* their fathers' need to find (vicarious) pride in them that the sons give themselves so suicidally (and so beautifully?) to football? The speaker understands the harshness of the lives around him and why therefore football becomes so important. He is also I think compassionate, but refuses to sentimentalize either the game or the failures he sees so accurately. I find Wright's use of the two oxymorons—"suicidally beautiful" and "gallop terribly"—particularly effective to express his ambiguous attitude toward football, the sons, the fathers, and the workers. If there is violence, there is also a kind of grace in their sacrifice—all the more poignant because (as you and others have pointed out) it is almost certainly futile.
>
> "Does Wright mean to protest the violence of football?" you ask. A majority of my students argue so—but less I think because of the poem than because they think (wrongly) I am opposed to football and assign the poem for that reason. I end up in discussion defending the poem against their second-guessing of it. I had assumed for years that such a protest was not Wright's intent; your notes confirm my view.

Finally, some comments by poet William Virgil Davis of Baylor University, who considers "Autumn Begins in Martins Ferry" to be the key poem in Wright's work. In an article on "James Wright's *Cogito*" in *Notes on Contemporary Literature* (Jan. 1993), Davis describes the structure of the poem:

> The poem follows the pattern of a logical argument, the three stanzas paralleling the arrangement of a syllogism. Indeed, the first stanza asserts, "I think it" (1. 2), and the third begins, "Therefore" (1. 9). The two "terms" of the argument are defined at the conclusions of stanzas one and two in the parallel phrases, "Dreaming of heroes" (1. 5) and "Dying for love" (1. 8). These are respectively associated with men (fathers) and women (mothers), and the results of these kinds of "deaths" create situations in which the "sons" of such parents "grow suicidally beautiful / At the beginning of October, / And gallop terribly against each other's bodies" (11. 10–12). This conclusion, following the "Therefore" of line 9, is more than the "*sum*" of Descartes's principle, but, like it, it defines a being born of the realization of a logical argument: what one is is what he believes and feels, based upon his past experiences and his personal history. Still, the "essence," although born of "existence," exceeds it. This is, then, beauty born out of the death of self for the sake of self-realization.
>
> Therefore, what the poem "means" is what the speaker reads or feels at the end of it; and, even if the argument is invalid, it is true.

Mary Sidney Wroth, IN THIS STRANGE LABYRINTH, page 1187

Feminist scholarship has uncovered many unjustly neglected works by women, but surely Mary Sidney Wroth must rank among the most interesting—and most overdue—additions to the canon. The niece of Sir Philip Sidney and Lady Mary Herbert, the Countess of Pembroke, Mary Sidney grew up in a talented and cultivated family. An arranged marriage to Sir Robert Wroth, however, proved unhappy during his lifetime and financially precarious after his death.

Wroth's sonnets were added to her prose romance *Urania* (1621), which she boldly published under her own name. Titled *Pamphilia to Amphilanthus*, the poems (which constitute the first sonnet sequence by an Englishwoman) speak in the voices of the prose romance's two main characters, but the poems also reflect her personal experience after her husband's death, especially her romantic liaison with her married cousin, the Earl of Pembroke, by whom she had two children.

"In this strange labyrinth" employs the image of the labyrinth as a symbol for erotic confusion. Each direction the speaker contemplates taking poses some danger or disappointment. This conceit is developed for thirteen lines until a detail from the myth—Ariadne's thread—is introduced in the final line. As Ariadne's thread guided her lover through the dangers of the labyrinth, so will "the thread of love" guide the speaker.

Sir Thomas Wyatt, THEY FLEE FROM ME THAT SOMETIME DID ME SEKË, page 1188

Surely Wyatt knew what he was about. Sounding the final *e*'s helps to fulfill the expectations of iambic pentameter in lines 2, 12, 15, 17, 20, and 21, lines that otherwise would seem to fall short. In other lines, however, Wyatt appears to make the rhythm deliberately swift or hesitant in order to fit the sense. Line 7 ("Busily seeking with a continual change") seems busy with extra syllables and has to be read quickly to fit the time allotted it. Such a metrical feast seems worthy of Yeats, as does line 11, in which two spondees ("loose gown," "did fall") cast great stress upon that suddenly falling garment.

What line in English love poetry, by the way, is more engaging than "Dear heart, how like you this?" And when have a lover's extended arms ever been more nicely depicted? (This line may be thrown into the teeth of anyone who thinks that, in descriptive writing, adjectives are bad things.)

William Butler Yeats, CRAZY JANE TALKS WITH THE BISHOP, page 1189

Piecing together a history from this Crazy Jane poem and others, John Unterecker has identified the Bishop as a divinity student who had courted Jane in his youth. She rejected him in favor of a wild, disreputable lover: Jack the journeyman. As soon as he got enough authority, the Bishop-to-be had Jack banished, but Jane has remained faithful to her lover (at least in spirit). (See *A Reader's Guide to William Butler Yeats* [New York: Noonday, 1959].) In this poem, the Bishop's former interest in Jane has dwindled to a concern for her soul alone.

Or has it? Perhaps the Bishop, no doubt a handsome figure in his surplice, may be demonstrating Yeats's contention that fair needs foul. Jane is living in lonely squalor. The grave, she says, can affirm the truth that her friends are gone, for it holds many of them; and her own empty bed can affirm that Jack is gone, too. Still, she firmly renounces the Bishop and his advice.

Each word of the poem is exact. Love has *pitched* his mansion as one would pitch a tent. The next-to-last line ends in two immense puns: *sole or whole*. The Bishop thinks that soul is all that counts, but Jane knows that both soul and hole are needed. Such puns may be why Yeats declared (in a letter) that he wanted to stop writing the Crazy Jane series: "I want to exorcise that slut, Crazy Jane, whose language has become unendurable."

What does Yeats mean by the paradoxical statement in the last two lines? Perhaps (1) that a woman cannot be fulfilled and remain a virgin—that, since fair and foul are near of kin, one cannot know Love, the platonic ideal, without going through the door of the physical body; and (2) that the universe is by nature a yin/yang combination of fair and foul (or, as Yeats would have it in *A Vision*, a pair of intertwining gyres). Crazy Jane may be crazy, but in Yeats's view she is a soothsayer.

MLL   *MyLiteratureLab Resources.* Biography, critical overview, and bibliography for Yeats.

William Butler Yeats, THE MAGI, page 1190

After writing a lesser poem than this—"The Dolls," in which dolls hurl resentment at a "noisy and filthy thing," a human baby—Yeats had a better idea. "I looked up one day into the blue of the sky, and suddenly imagined, as if lost in the blue of the sky, stiff figures in procession" (Yeats's note at the back of his *Collected Poems*). Like dolls, the Magi seem frozen, somewhat inhuman ("rain-beaten stones"), unfulfilled. They are apparently troubled that Christ, whose birth was a miracle, died as a man. In hopes of regaining the peace of the Nativity, they pursue a second journey.

Bestial will seem to students an odd word to apply to a stable floor, unless they catch its literal sense: "belonging to beasts." But they will also need to see that its connotations of brutality fit the poem and interact with *Calvary's turbulence*. Compare "The Magi" with the rough beast in "The Second Coming," a poem written after Yeats had more fully worked out his notion that historical events move in a cycle of endless return. ("Leda and the Swan" can be brought in, too, if there is time for it.)

If comparing Yeats's unsatisfied wise men to Eliot's in "Journey of the Magi," good questions to ask include, Which poet writes as a Christian? How can you tell?

MLL   *MyLiteratureLab Resources.* Biography, critical overview, and bibliography for Yeats.

William Butler Yeats, WHEN YOU ARE OLD, page 1190

Yeats wrote this poem to the actress Maud Gonne in October 1891. It is based very loosely on Ronsard's sonnet "Quand Vous Serez Bien Vielle," but it is not a translation. Yeats merely took Ronsard's premise (an old woman rereading the verses a poet wrote to her in their youth) and developed it in his own way.

In this gentlest of love poems, the speaker is resigned to not winning the woman he loves. He is merely one of many men who love her. His claim, however, is that his love was not for the surface charms of her grace or beauty; he alone loved her for her searching soul. And he has the satisfaction of being able to preserve the unique quality of his devotion in words. Yeats's lyric, therefore, celebrates the ennobling power of both love and poetry.

To be candidly emotional risks seeming sentimental, but as we approach the end of the notes to the "Poems for Further Reading," we hope that many years from now a few of our students will take down this book to reread a few of the poems we taught them and realize that we spoke to "the pilgrim soul" in them.

MLL *MyLiteratureLab Resources.* Biography, critical overview, and bibliography for Yeats.

Bernice Zamora, PENITENTS, page 1191

Bernice Zamora was born and raised in Colorado. Though she came from a Spanish-speaking family, she was given an education that stressed assimilation into the mainstream American culture—a process which, as an adult, she came to resent. *Restless Serpents* (1976), her first—and for a long time, only—volume of poetry, has had a great deal of influence, especially in the Chicano community, and has been praised for the power and fierceness of its writing and for its uncompromising confrontation of the world's injustices.

"Penitents" describes a secret ritual that seeks to replicate the passion and suffering of Christ, in order that its enacters may mortify their flesh, achieve humility of spirit, and come to a deeper understanding of the magnitude of Christ's sacrifice on behalf of their souls. Class discussion of this poem might provoke a lively response: it should prove interesting to sample the students' reactions to the values and the behavior of the *penitentes,* and interesting as well to gauge their sense of Zamora's own attitude toward the material. Despite the seemingly clear statements of the poem's last five lines, critic Juan Bruce-Novoa has written of Zamora's "alienation from the male rituals in 'Penitents.'" Is this, do you think, a view imposed on the text from his wider reading in Zamora's work, or can it be discovered and defended through a careful, objective reading of the poem itself?

34
Lives of the Poets

Instead of being strewn throughout the poetry section, biographical notes on the poets are collected in this chapter. The intent is to make them easy to find and to keep them from interrupting the poetry. Biographies are supplied for poets represented by two or more poems.

Envoi

Let us end this section with another poem about teaching poetry—one by Paul Lake, a professor at Arkansas Technical University in Russellville. Lake's "Introduction to Poetry" appears in his collection *Another Kind of Travel* (Chicago: U of Chicago P, 1988).

Introduction to Poetry

She comes in late, then settles like a sigh
On the first day, returning every week
Promptly at ten, each Monday Wednesday Friday,
To study Shakespeare, Jonson, Donne, and Blake;

Enters the room to an approving murmur,
Straightens her dress, then, brushing back her hair,
Arches her body with the slightest tremor,
And sits, while the room grows breathless, in her chair;

Sits for an hour, while busy sophomores worry
Each turgid line, a Botticellian smile
On her rapt face, who's learned how little study
Love involves; who, walking down the aisle,

Knows in her bones how little poetry
Words breathe, and how—on turning to go home—
All eyes will watch her rise above her "C"
And walk off, like a goddess on the foam.

DRAMA

35
Reading a Play

In many parts of the country, students rarely if ever see plays other than school or other amateur productions, and the instructor may encounter some resistance to the idea of studying drama. But all students are steeped in film and television drama, and it may be useful to point out that such drama begins with playscripts. One might reason somewhat like this: Movies and television, it's true, give plays hard competition in our society, and a camera does have advantages. In moments, film can present whole panoramas and can show details in close-up that theaters (with their cumbersome sets and machinery) cannot duplicate. Movies used to be called "photoplays," but the name implies an unnecessary limitation, for there is no point in confining the camera to recording the contents of a picture-frame stage. Yet a play—whether staged in a proscenium theater or in a parking lot—has its own distinct advantages. It is a medium that makes possible things a camera cannot do. Unlike movies and television, a play gives us living actors, and it involves living audiences who supply it with their presences (and who can move one another to laughter or to tears). Compared, say, to the laughter of live spectators at a comedy, the "canned" laughter often dubbed into television programs is a weak attempt to persuade television viewers that they are not alone.

A PLAY IN ITS ELEMENTS

Susan Glaspell, TRIFLES, page 1225

The comeback of *Trifles* may be due, we think, not only to Glaspell's pioneering feminist views but also to its being such a gripping, tightly structured play. Whether or not you have much time to spend on the elements of a play, we think you will find *Trifles* worth teaching; students respond to it.

The Provincetown Players, who performed in a theater on an abandoned wharf, had a fertile summer in 1916. Besides *Trifles*, with Glaspell herself playing Mrs. Hale, their season included the first Eugene O'Neill play to be produced, *Bound East for Cardiff*. Glaspell has said that she derived the plot of *Trifles* from a murder case she had investigated as a reporter in Des Moines.

Ruth E. Zehfuss of DeKalb College has pointed out a meaningful way to compare *Trifles* with another classic drama in this book:

> The key idea in *Trifles*, the conflict between outer or legal authority and inner or moral law, was . . . more than simply a feminist statement. The universality

423

of the question Glaspell poses can be compared to Sophocles' *Antigonê*. In each play, the question is whether individuals have a right to follow their own moral beliefs when their beliefs conflict with the law of the state. ("The Law and the Ladies in *Trifles*," *Teaching English in the Two-Year College* [Feb. 1992], 42–44)

To compare the themes of *Trifles* and *Antigonê*, and how the characters of the two plays embody them, might be a rewarding topic either for class discussion or for a term paper. (See also the entry on *Antigonê* in this manual for more ways to set the two plays side by side.)

MLL   *MyLiteratureLab Resources.* Biography, critical overview, and bibliography for Glaspell.

WRITERS ON WRITING

Susan Glaspell, CREATING TRIFLES, page 1241

Over the past quarter century Susan Glaspell has slowly regained her rightful position as an important innovator in modern American drama. *Trifles* is now securely in the twentieth-century canon, but the rest of Glaspell's work remains too little known; despite some fine recent work, her critical coverage is still incommensurate with her achievement. (Glaspell wrote thirteen plays, ten novels, and nearly fifty short stories.) There is also not yet a comprehensive, full-length modern biography. Much important scholarship needs to be done.

Given the lack of critical and biographical commentary, it is puzzling that Glaspell's 1927 autobiography, *The Road to the Temple*, is not better known. The excerpt from her autobiography in the "Writer's Perspective" has never appeared in any textbook before (though surely some other enterprising editor will soon lift it—with our compliments).

In this section of *The Road to the Temple*, Glaspell provides a first-hand account of two important events in the history of American drama—the creation of the Provincetown Players and the unusual genesis of her first play, *Trifles*, in 1916. As her autobiography makes abundantly clear, Glaspell and George Cram "Jig" Cook's marriage was deeply fulfilling for both partners. It is a gentle irony that Glaspell's feminist play was written at the prompting of her supportive husband. (He also helped create the Provincetown Players to spur her talent.) American literature has had few nicer moments than this one.

The Road to the Temple (New York: Stokes, 1927) is now long out of print. It took me (DG) several months to search out a copy by canvassing major dealers in modern literature, but most large university libraries will have a copy. Glaspell's style is very casual, and the book is fun to read. In addition to her own life story, she provides interesting accounts of American theatrical and bohemian life in the first three decades of the twentieth century. Cambridge's edition of Susan Glaspell's *Plays* (1987), edited by C. W. E. Bigsby, reprints four one-act plays and has excellent scholarly apparatus and a fine introduction. It is indispensable for students of this pioneering playwright.

36
Modes of Drama: Tragedy and Comedy

Christopher Marlowe, DOCTOR FAUSTUS (ACT 2, SCENE 1), page 1251

Of all the components that make up the complex definition of tragedy, perhaps the most hotly debated is that of the protagonist's tragic flaw. While there is a fairly general consensus that the protagonist is customarily undone by some form of **hubris**, one can find significant exceptions to this rule. Our two tragedies by Sophocles would seem to present both the rule and the exception. Clearly, the arrogance and self-importance of Oedipus play a large part in his undoing, from his original actions in defiance of the prophecy—killing any man old enough to be his father and marrying any woman old enough to be his mother—to his very publicly expressed scorn of the power of the gods when he believes that the prophecy has turned out to be false. On the other hand, despite her defiance of Creon's edict, Antigonê's behavior strikes us as blameless and even noble; much more than her father, she seems the innocent victim of cruel circumstances.

We find a similar situation with our two Shakespeare tragedies: Othello's fierce jealousy and failure to trust in Desdemona's love are failings in his otherwise noble nature for which he must be held accountable; but can we truly say that Hamlet's over-intellectualization and hesitancy to act are weaknesses of sufficient gravity that his destruction seems a proper retribution for them?

No such subtleties and complications need concern us in the case of Christopher Marlowe's *Doctor Faustus*. It would be hard to imagine a clearer case of cause and effect—of self-destruction engineered by overweening self-assertion and the deliberate spurning of higher values—than the actions of Faustus in the scene that we have presented here. In the very first speech of the scene, he uses the word "Despair" to characterize his attitude toward God: "Despair in God and trust in Belzebub!" He maintains—because of his failure to penetrate the mysteries of existence—that God does not love him: even Job, in the depths of his anguish, never questioned God's right to dispose of him as He saw fit, but Faustus in his frustration and his pride appears to have decided that only an unloving God would withhold from him the power and knowledge that He alone possesses. When Faustus says, "The god thou serv'st is thine owe appetite," it is not intended as the self-castigation that such a statement obviously ought to be, but is instead a summation of his attitude and his intentions.

Despite God's attempts to deflect him from this course by means of the Good Angel, the congealing of his blood, and the warning of *Homo fuge* upon his arm, Faustus sails through every red light in his mad rush to drive himself over the cliff. Mephistophilis does at one point conjure devils for Faustus to "delight his mind" and distract him from his momentary qualms, but he is uncompromisingly direct and honest in answering Faustus's inquiries and reminding him of the magnitude and the inevitable consequences of what he is doing, despite Faustus's blithe "I think that hell's a fable."

In the final scene of the play, Faustus's twenty-four years have elapsed and, accompanied by a group of friends and fellow scholars, he waits in terror and useless, belated repentance for the fulfillment of the contract. It is a truly harrowing moment when, at the very end, the devils arrive at the stroke of twelve to take the agonized Faustus off to hell. The moral code exhibited in *Doctor Faustus* is quite straightforward: we are judged entirely by our actions, irrespective of motives. Nothing could be simpler, or more terrible. (As indicated in the chapter in the discussion of tragedy, things are quite otherwise at the conclusion of Goethe's *Faust* 250 years later. Although Faust has inadvertently destroyed the lives of everyone he has come in contact with—from Gretchen to the old couple whose land he needs for his ambitious building project—he is saved in the end because of his motivations, his refusal to live dully and unquestioningly like the beasts of the field and the greater mass of humanity.)

From what is known of Marlowe's unorthodox life and opinions, the opening speech of this scene may very possibly embody his own attitudes. Are the conclusion and the whole tenor of the play intended, then, as a sop to conventional morality (provoked not merely by the desire for commercial success but by the urge to avoid arrest and condemnation)? Perhaps so. And if so, there is a point to made here, one that is put forward not at all cynically but simply as a reflection of the facts of life: literary masterpieces are created not merely by the revelation of the heart's deepest needs, however sincere, but by imaginative projection and patiently honed craft applied to the perennial questions of human existence.

COMEDY

David Ives, SURE THING, page 1259

In 1993 I (DG) attended the original off-Broadway production of David Ives's six one-act comedies, *All in the Timing*. By the end of the evening I knew that one of these little comic gems would have to go into the next edition of *Literature*. When *All in the Timing* opened, Ives was a relative unknown in American theater. Soon he became a minor celebrity. A shy but witty man, Ives wore his newfound fame with comic nonchalance. When *New York* magazine listed him as one of the "100 Smartest New Yorkers," Ives told a reporter from the *Columbia University Record* that he didn't approve. "Lists," he explained, "are antidemocratic, discriminatory, elitist, and sometimes the print is too small." Audiences of all kinds respond to Ives's work. *All in the Timing* has gradually become one of the most widely produced contemporary plays in America.

Sure Thing demonstrates how quickly innovative theatrical technique is incorporated into mainstream drama. Ives bases his play in equal parts on modernist experimental theater and popular comedy—half Luigi Pirandello, one might say, and half Groucho Marx. One might add that Ives uses the modernist techniques of dramatic distancing, stylization, and fragmentation to tell the most traditional story possible—a young man and woman meet and fall in love. (Youthful romance has been a central subject of comedy since Menander and Plautus.) The resulting work is both surprising and familiar. The best new art often works exactly as Ives's *Sure Thing* does, by creating a meaningful conversation between the ancient and the new.

If the fragmentary technique of *Sure Thing* isn't just a clever theatrical gimmick, what meaningful conversations does it open up? By dramatizing every moment of mutual attraction and rejection, Ives's disjointed narrative structure provides a candid and detailed anatomy of modern romance. It also shows how individuals both speak and listen in social code. *Sure Thing* is as much about language as romance. Ives embodies the mutual exploration of these two characters entirely in language. There is no physical comedy in the play. The only non-verbal element is the bell that punctuates the action to announce that one of the characters has lost interest in the other. (The bell editorializes only once, with multiple rings after Betty begins to talk about astrological signs, but this auditory gag is merely an intensification of its normal role.)

Perhaps the most interesting idea found in *Sure Thing* is the notion that human personalities are so changeable that the timing of an experience is critical to its proper reception. (And, of course, in no mode of human communication is timing more important than in comedy.) When Betty says that she can't believe she has waited so long to read Faulkner, she initiates a crucial exchange that comments on both the theme and style of the play:

BILL. You never know. You might not have liked him before.

BETTY. That's true.

BILL. You might not have been ready for him. You have to hit these things at the right moment or it's not good.

BETTY. That's happened to me.

BILL. It's all in the timing.

Bill's final phrase became the title of Ives's award-winning night of comedies as well as the title for his collection of fourteen one-act plays, *All in the Timing* (New York: Vintage, 1995). One suspects it wasn't just the theatrical pun that made the phrase so attractive but also the aesthetic it suggests.

Instructors should remember how easy it is to produce *Sure Thing* in the classroom. All one needs is two actors, two chairs, and a bell (or whistle or buzzer). The play takes less than fifteen minutes to perform. Students can also be asked to write and perform additional scenes of their own.

Students interested in writing on Ives should be directed to the other plays in *All in the Timing*, among them two short plays that provide interesting parallels to *Sure Thing*. This first is *Words, Words, Words*, which presents three monkeys (named Milton, Swift, and Kafka) who have been placed in a laboratory at Columbia University with three typewriters to produce the text of *Hamlet*. The second play is *The Universal Language*, in which a young woman takes an introductory lesson in a phony universal language (a parody of Esperanto) that proves to be an educational scam. Both plays are not only hilarious, they offer an insightful critique of language. Ives's preface to *All in the Timing* is in itself a brilliant comic performance.

Jane Martin, BEAUTY, page 1269

No one knows for certain who Jane Martin really is, but everyone familiar with her work knows that she is a steely-eyed observer of the contemporary American scene, with a sharp ear for dialogue and a sharp eye for the foibles and excesses of human nature. The brief one-act play *Beauty* showcases not only her wit and her mimetic skills, but her inventiveness as well: even after she seems to have exhausted all the possibilities of her theme, the play's very last line of dialogue forces us to think again about everything that has gone before.

QUESTIONS

1. *Reread the discussion of* high *and* low comedy *on page 1258. Which of the two terms, in your view, better applies to* Beauty? *Explain and support your choice.* The play's satiric treatment of cultural shallowness and its occasionally witty turns of phrase are reminiscent of high comedy, but overall it fits more comfortably into the genre of low comedy. Carla and Bethany are not especially sophisticated: their dialogue would sound much more at home in *Seinfeld* than in *The Importance of Being Earnest*, and their cultural references are to mass culture—not *The Arabian Nights* but the animated Disney film *Aladdin*. Also, the on-stage explosion at the end of the play is quite farcical in nature.

2. *Much of the point of the play depends on Carla and Bethany seeing one another as opposites. But do they also have any important traits in common?* Despite their perceptions of one another, their differences seem far outweighed by their similarities: both of them are totally self-absorbed; the first half of the play is largely a struggle between them to be the center of attention; and Bethany has lied to her employer about her uncle so that she can go to the beach, even though her uncle actually is in the hospital in intensive care. Each one also claims to be deeply dissatisfied with her own life and envious of the other.

3. *Is Bethany's unhappiness with herself a demonstration of her own superficiality, or is it a commentary on the superficiality of our culture? Can it be both at the same time?* At first, the phrase "my entire bitch of a life" is a bit shocking in the mouth of someone who went straight from college to a high-paying job, has published several short stories, and is very attractive. And yet virtually every one of us, even the most privileged, has at one time or another begun a pessimistic forecast by saying, "With my luck. . . ." As Abraham Mazlow's famous "hierarchy of needs" might suggest, discontent and feelings of wanting—perhaps even deserving—more are fairly universal; satisfaction is fleeting and quickly replaced by new desires. One commentator, assessing the perceived sour mood in the nation during the 2000 election campaign, said something to the effect that, if someone had told you in 1975 that in the year

2000 the Soviet Union will have collapsed and Eastern Europe will be free, South Africa will have ended apartheid and established black majority rule without a civil war, and the Dow will be over 10,000, you would expect that there would be dancing in the streets.

4. *Do Carla's claims of unhappiness with her appearance and her life seem genuine, or are they more accurately described by Bethany's reactions to them?* The thrust of the play, with its emphasis on the theme of "the grass is always greener," would seem to suggest that Carla's complaint is genuine. Remember also that Bethany admits to being "jealous" of Carla, and that Bethany is given to exaggeration; one wonders, for instance, where she manages to find so many men who want to spend a long time getting to know her as a person before they will have sex with her. And just as the play uses the plot device of Aladdin's three magic wishes, we might think here of another legendary character, one whose situation was not nearly as enviable as it seemed from the outside—King Midas.

5. *Reread Bethany's speech, beginning "But it's what everybody wants," just before she makes her final wish. How validly, in your view, does she speak for "everybody" here?* On a superficial level (which is, perhaps, the only level on which Bethany operates), we might see some truth in this statement. Everyone wants to be attractive to others, to be fussed over and made much of, and to enjoy the confidence and self-assurance that we assume the beautiful possess. But further class discussion will no doubt lead to the conclusion that she is way over the top in suggesting that it is a universal, all-consuming desire churning just below the surface of every human interaction. There are many other things that some people want more than beauty—love, wealth, career advancement, personal fulfillment, and so on. One does not have to be beautiful already to agree with Carla's immediate response: "Well, it's not what I want."

6. *What elements of tone and characterization help make* Beauty *an effective comedy?* Tonally, the play is an effective comedy because of the rapid pace of the dialogue, the author's accurate ear for contemporary speech rhythms and phrasing (" . . . and I'm like nuts so I say, you know . . ."), the occasional one-liners ("Dealing what, I've even given up chocolate"), and the on-target pop culture references. In terms of characterization, as discussed above, Martin is quite effective in pointing out the narcissism and superficiality that are pervasive in contemporary American society—and so pervasive in these two young women that these qualities come through a sudden and stunning mind swap almost totally intact, with Carla/Bethany exulting over her acquisition of Carla's legs and Bethany/Carla lamenting that "I can't meet Ralph Lauren wearing these shoes!"

WRITERS ON WRITING

David Ives, ON THE ONE-ACT PLAY, page 1274

Here is a packet of shrewd observations, vivid metaphors, and pungent phrases on the nature of the one-act play, from a—perhaps *the*—contemporary master of the genre. In his colorful way, Ives reconfirms the truth of the old saying, "I didn't have time to write an essay, so I wrote a book instead."

37
Critical Casebook: Sophocles

Sophocles, OEDIPUS THE KING, page 1285

One problem in teaching this masterpiece is that students often want to see Oedipus as a pitiable fool, helplessly crushed by the gods, thus stripping him of heroism and tragic dignity. (A classic bepiddlement of the play once turned up on a freshman paper: "At the end, Oedipus goes off blinded into exile, but that's the way the cookie crumbles.") It can be argued that Oedipus showed himself to be no fool in solving the riddle of the Sphinx or in deciding to leave Corinth; that no god forced him to kill Laïos or to marry Iocastê.

Another problem in teaching this play is that some students want to make Oedipus into an Everyman, an abstract figure representing all humanity. But Oedipus's circumstances are, to say the least, novel and individual. "Oedipus is not 'man,' but Oedipus," as S. M. Adams argues in *Sophocles the Playwright* (Toronto: U of Toronto P, 1957). On the other hand, Freud's reading of the play does suggest that Oedipus is Everyman—or, better, that every man is Oedipus and like Oedipus wishes to kill his father and marry his mother. A passage from Freud's celebrated remarks about the play is included in the casebook.

Despite Freud's views, which usually fascinate students, critical consensus appears to be that Oedipus himself did not have an Oedipus complex. Sophocles does not portray Oedipus and Iocastê as impassioned lovers; their marriage was (as Philip Wheelwright says) "a matter of civic duty: having rid the Thebans of the baleful Sphinx by answering her riddle correctly, he received the throne of Thebes and the widowed queen as his due reward" (*The Burning Fountain* [Bloomington: Indiana University Press, 1954]). Wheelwright also notes, incidentally, that the title *Oedipus Tyrannus* might be translated more accurately as "Oedipus the Usurper"—a usurper being (to the Greeks) anyone who gains a throne by means other than by blood succession. Actually, of course, Oedipus had a hereditary right to the throne. (Another interpretation of the play sees Laïos and Iocastê as having incurred the original guilt: by leaving a royal prince to die in the wilderness, they defied natural order and the will of the gods.)

For the nonspecialist, a convenient gathering of views will be found in *Oedipus Tyrannus*, ed. Luci Berkowitz and Theodore F. Brunner (New York: Norton, 1970). Along with a prose translation of the play by the editors, the book includes the classic comments by Aristotle, Nietzsche, and Freud, and discussions by later critics and psychologists. Seth Bernardete offers a detailed, passage-by-passage commentary in *Sophocles: A Collection of Critical Essays*, ed. Thomas Woodard (Englewood Cliffs, NJ: Prentice, 1966). Francis Fergusson has pointed out that the play may be read (on one level) as a murder mystery: "Oedipus takes the role of District Attorney; and when he at last convicts himself, we have a twist, a *coup de théâtre*, of unparalleled excitement." But Fergusson distrusts any reading so literal, and he questions attempts to make the play entirely coherent and rational. Sophocles "preserves the ultimate mystery by focusing upon [Oedipus] at a level beneath, or prior to any rationalization whatever" (*The Idea of a Theatre* [Princeton: Princeton UP, 1949]). Refreshing, after you read many myth critics, is A. J. A. Waldock's *Sophocles the Dramatist* (Cambridge: Cambridge UP, 1951; reprinted in part by Berkowitz and Brunner). According to Waldock, the play is sheer entertainment, a spectacular piece of shock, containing no message. "There is no meaning in the *Oedipus Tyrannus*. There is merely the terror of coincidence, and then, at the end of it all, our impression of man's power to suffer, and of his greatness because of this power." Pointing out how little we know of Sophocles' religion, Waldock finds the dramatist's beliefs "meagre in number and depressingly commonplace."

Although the religious assumptions of the play may not be surprising to Waldock, students may want to have them stated. A good summing up is that of E. R. Dodds, who maintains that Sophocles did not always believe that the gods are in any human sense "just," but that he did always believe that the gods exist and that man should revere them ("On Misunderstanding the *Oedipus Rex*," *Greece and Rome* [Oxford: Oxford UP, 1966] Vol. 13).

"Possibly the best service the critic can render the *Oedipus Rex*," says Waldock, "is to leave it alone." If, however, other criticism can help, there are especially valuable discussions in H. D. F. Kitto, *Greek Tragedy*, 3rd ed. (London: Methuen, 1961), and *Poiesis* (Berkeley: U of California P, 1966); Richmond Lattimore, *The Poetry of Greek Tragedy* (Baltimore: Johns Hopkins UP, 1958); and Patrick Mullahy, *Oedipus, Myth and Complex* (New York: Grove, 1948).

In the "More Topics for Writing" at the end of the chapter there is one especially challenging topic (number 3): to compare translations of the play. For any student willing to pick up the challenge, we think this topic might produce a great term paper. The differences between versions, of course, are considerable. Sheppard's rendition, or Kitto's, is more nearly literal than that of Fagles and much more so than that of Berg and Clay. In the last team's version of 1978, the persons of the tragedy all speak like formally open lyrics in little magazines of the eighties. Lots of monosyllables. Frequent pauses. Understatement. Lush imagery. Berg and Clay perform this service brilliantly, and it might be argued: why shouldn't each generation remake the classics in its own tongue?

Still impressive is the film *Oedipus Rex* (1957), directed by Tyrone Guthrie, a record of a performance given in Stratford, Canada. Although the theater of the play is more Stratfordian than Athenian, the actors wear splendid masks. The text is the Yeats version.

In 1984, the Greek National Theater presented a much-discussed *Oedipus Rex* at the Kennedy Center in Washington. Bernard Knox offers an admiring account of it in *Grand Street* for Winter 1985. The director, Minos Volankis, staged the play on a "circular, dark brown plate, tilted toward the audience" and etched with a labyrinth pattern. In Volankis's version, Oedipus and Iocastê cannot see the pattern and ignore it as they move about the stage, but the chorus and Teiresias are aware of the labyrinth and respectfully trace its curves in their movements. Oedipus is a clean-shaven youth, the only young person in the play, "caught in a web spun by his elders."

In a useful recent article on teaching *Oedipus,* W. A. Senior of Broward Community College suggests ways to present the play as meaningful to freshmen who wonder how anything so ancient and esoteric as classical drama can help them in their lives today and advance their pursuit of a C.P.A. degree. His approach is to demythify the character of Oedipus, stressing that the protagonist is no god or superman, but a confused, deceived human being at the center of a web of family relationships (to put it mildly) and political responsibilities. Like a business executive or professional today, Oedipus has to interrogate others, determine facts, and overcome his natural reluctance to face painful realities.

To help students come to terms with the central character, Senior has used specific writing assignments. "I have them compose a letter to Oedipus," he reports, "individually or at times in groups, at the height of the action in the third act to advise him on what to do or to explain to him what he has done wrong so far. In a related essay taking a page from *Antigonê* and its theme of public versus private good, which is foreshadowed in *Oedipus Rex,* I ask them to write an editorial on Oedipus as politician; each student must adopt a position and defend it" ("Teaching Oedipus: The Hero and Multiplicity," *Teaching English in the Two-Year College* [Dec. 1992], 274–79).

MLL MyLiteratureLab Resources. Biography, critical overview, and bibliography for Sophocles. Longman Lecture, critical excerpts on *Oedipus.*

Sophocles, ANTIGONÊ, page 1324

QUESTIONS

1. *Some critics argue that the main character of the play is not Antigonê, but Creon. How can this view possibly be justified? Do you agree?* Antigonê disappears from the play in its last third, and we are then shown Creon in conflict with himself. Creon suffers a tragic downfall: his earlier decision has cost him his wife and his son; Eurydicê has cursed him; and in the end, he is reduced to a pitiable figure praying for his own death. Still, without Antigonê the play would have no conflict; surely she suffers a tragic downfall as well.

2. *Why is it so important to Antigonê that the body of Polyneicês be given a proper burial?* "I say this crime is holy." (See Prologue, lines 55–61. See also the footnote on line 3.)

3. *Modern critics often see the play as centering on a theme: the authority of the state conflicts with the religious duty of an individual. Try this interpretation on the play and decide how well it fits. Does the playwright seem to favor one side or the other?* The pious Sophocles clearly favors Antigonê and sees divine law taking precedence over human law; but Creon's principles (most fully articulated in Scene 1, lines 28–41 and 98–124) are given fair hearing.

4. *Comment from a student paper:* "Antigonê is a stubborn fool, bent on her own destruction. Her insistence on giving a corpse burial causes nothing but harm to herself, to Haimon, Eurydicê, and all Thebes. She does not accomplish anything that Creon wouldn't eventually have agreed to do." *Discuss this view.*

5. *Explain the idea of good government implied in the exchange between Creon and Haimon:*

CREON. *Am I to rule this land for others—or myself?*

HAIMON. *It's no city at all, owned by one man alone. (823–24)*

6. *What doubts wrack Creon? For what reasons does he waver in his resolve to punish Antigonê and deny burial to the body of Polyneicês? In changing his mind, does he seem to you weak and indecisive?* Not at all; he has good reason to pull down his vanity and to listen to the wise Haimon and his counselors.

7. *In not giving us a love scene in the tomb between Antigonê and Haimon, does Sophocles miss a golden opportunity? Or would you argue that, as a playwright, he knows his craft?*

David Grene has pointed out that the plots of the *Antigonê* and the *Oedipus* have close similarities. In both, we meet a king whose unknowing violation of divine law results in his own destruction. In both, the ruler has an encounter with Teiresias, whom he refuses to heed. Creon relents and belatedly tries to take the priest's advice—Oedipus, however, defies all wise counsel (introduction to "The Theban Plays" in *Complete Greek Tragedies*, ed. David Grene and Richard Lattimore [Chicago: U of Chicago P, 1959] II: 2–3).

Charles Paul Segal views the clash between Creon and Antigonê as the result of two conflicting worldviews—one female, the other male:

> It is again among the tragic paradoxes of Antigonê's position that she who accepts the absolutes of death has a far fuller sense of the complexities of life. Creon, who lacks a true "reverence" for the gods, the powers beyond human life, also lacks a deep awareness of the complexities within the human realm. Hence he tends to see the world in terms of harshly opposed categories, right and wrong, reason and folly, youth and age, male and female. He scornfully joins old age with foolishness in speaking to the chorus (267–68) and refuses to listen to his son's advice because he is younger (684–85). . . .
>
> All these categories imply the relation of superior and inferior, stronger and weaker. This highly structured and aggressive view of the world Creon expresses perhaps most strikingly in repeatedly formulating the conflict between Antigonê and himself in terms of the woman trying to conquer the man. He sees in Antigonê a challenge to his whole way of living and his basic attitudes toward the world. And of course he is right, for Antigonê's full acceptance of her womanly nature, her absolute valuation of the bonds of blood and affection, is a total denial of Creon's obsessively masculine rationality. ("Sophocles' Praise of Man and the Conflicts of the *Antigonê*," in *Sophocles: A Collection of Critical Essays*, ed. Bernard Knox [Twentieth-Century Views Series: Englewood Cliffs, NJ: Prentice, 1966])

Students with experience in play production might be asked to suggest strategies for staging *Antigonê* today. In their commentary on the play, translators Dudley Fitts and Robert Fitzgerald make interesting suggestions. The

Chorus had better not chant the Odes in unison, or the words will probably be unintelligible; let single voices in the Chorus take turns speaking lines. The solemn parados might be spoken to the accompaniment of a slow drumbeat. No dancing should be included; no attempt should be made to use larger-than-life Greek masks with megaphone mouths. More effective might be lifelike Benda-type masks, closely fitting the face. "If masks are used at all, they might be well allotted only to those characters who are somewhat depersonalized by official position or discipline: Creon, Teiresias, the Chorus and Choragos, possibly the Messenger. By this rule, Antigonê has no mask; neither has Ismenê, Haimon, nor Eurydicê" (*The Oedipus Cycle: An English Version* [New York: Harcourt, 1949] 242–43).

Entertaining scraps from our sparse knowledge of the life of Sophocles are gathered by Moses Hadas in *An Ancilla to Classical Reading* (New York: Columbia UP, 1954). The immense popular success of *Antigonê* led to the playwright's being elected a general, although, as he himself admitted, he was incompetent in battle. Many reports attest to his piety, his fondness for courtesans and boys, and his defeat of an attempt by his sons to have him declared an imbecile. Plutarch relates that when Sophocles, then past ninety, read to the jury from his latest work, *Oedipus at Colonus*, he "was escorted from the lawcourt as from a theater, amid the applause and shouts of all." One account of the playwright's death is that he strangled while reading aloud a long, breathless sentence from *Antigonê*.

Suggestions for Writing. Compare and contrast the character of Creon in the two plays. (In *Oedipus the King* he is the reasonable man, the foil for the headstrong Oedipus.)

How important to the play is Haimon? Ismenê? Eurydicê?

How visibly does the family curse that brought down Oedipus operate in *Antigonê*? Does fate seem a motivating force behind Antigonê's story? (In *Antigonê* fate plays a much less prominent part; the main characters—Creon, Antigonê, and Haimon—seem to decide for themselves their courses of action.)

Ruth E. Zehfuss has noticed that *Antigonê* cries out for comparison with Susan Glaspell's *Trifles*: both are plays in which the protagonists find their moral convictions at odds with the law of the state. Interestingly, Zehfuss sees other parallels. "The settings of both *Trifles* and *Antigonê* emphasize the relative positions of authority figures and those whose lives they control. *Antigonê* is played out in front of the palace, the locus of authority." Similarly, in the stage directions for the beginning of *Trifles*, the Sheriff and the County Attorney are in charge: as guardians of the law, they occupy center stage, near the warm stove, while the women stand off near the cold door. Like Creon, they represent officialdom. Other characters in both plays also reveal similarities. Sophocles' Ismenê, like Glaspell's Mrs. Peters, is a weak character reluctant to challenge the authority of the law. But both Antigonê and Mrs. Hale have the strength to question it and finally to defy it ("The Law and the Ladies in *Trifles*," *Teaching English in the Two-Year College* [Feb. 1992], 42–44).

 MyLiteratureLab Resources. Biography, critical overview, and bibliography for Sophocles.

CRITICS ON SOPHOCLES, pages 1353–1360

This critical casebook on Sophocles tries to provide a representative sampling of the many opinions on the tragedian. We begin with two indispensable critiques of *Oedipus the King*—the celebrated commentaries of Aristotle and Freud. **Aristotle**'s discussion of *Oedipus the King* in his *Poetics* is undoubtedly the single most influential statement in Western drama criticism. In his analysis he tries to define the special psychological and artistic effects of tragic theater. In investigating these questions, the philosopher examines the nature of tragic plotting and characterization.

The father of modern psychology, **Sigmund Freud,** was also, by nature if not by occupation, a literary critic. Many of his major psychoanalytic concepts came from his close reading of texts—from Sophocles and the Old Testament to Shakespeare and da Vinci. In this short passage from *The Interpretation of Dreams* (1900) Freud expounds one of his most influential ideas, the Oedipus complex. Trying to account for the powerful effect Sophocles' tragedy has on modern audiences, Freud hypothesizes that both the Oedipus myth and the ancient Greek play must touch something universal within the audience—namely "our first sexual impulse towards our mother and first hatred and our first murderous wish against our father." The importance of introducing students to these two texts can hardly be overestimated. They are necessary components of cultural literacy as well as illuminating contributions to any discussion of Sophocles.

E. R. Dodds, one of the great Greek scholars of modern times, provides a provocative reading about the nature of Oedipus's character. Taking a critical rather than a scholarly perspective (discussing his own reaction, that is, rather than trying to ascertain Sophocles' original intention), Dodds sees Oedipus as a great tragic character not because of his powerful worldly position as king but because of his interior and intellectual qualities. Oedipus seems great, Dodds maintains, as a symbol of restless human intelligence.

By contrast, **A. E. Haigh** discusses a more general topic, the pervasive role of irony in Sophocles' plays. The concept of irony is difficult for many students to grasp, but they need to understand it in order to approach either *Oedipus* or *Antigonê*. Haigh's treatment is so clear and well organized—with its helpful categories of "conscious" and "unconscious" irony—that his explanation will be very useful to assign to students, especially in introductory courses.

David Wiles provides a succinct summation of the complex role of the Chorus in *Oedipus the King*, emphasizing its function both as dynamic performer in the unfolding events that make up the action of the play and as *raisonneur*, standing apart to comment on those events and to express the larger values that the work seeks to affirm.

Patricia M. Lines's "Antigonê's Flaw" is a brilliant but accessible analysis of Antigonê as a tragic heroine. We thought we knew the play well, but Lines's perspective greatly enhanced our understanding of the complexity of Antigonê's moral position. Antigonê is such a powerfully persuasive figure on stage that the audience is apt to overlook her subtle tragic flaw. As Lines cogently argues, Antigonê is, as the Greek would term it, *autonomos*, a law unto herself, and she acts at the expense of the rest of the *polis*. Any student planning to do a paper on *Antigonê* should read this essay.

WRITERS ON WRITING

Robert Fitzgerald, TRANSLATING SOPHOCLES INTO ENGLISH, page 1361

In an afterword to his 1941 solo translation of *Oedipus at Colonus*, Robert Fitzgerald offered a commentary on the challenges of translating Sophocles. His remarks examine the issue of finding poetic language that was neither too elevated nor too common.

Instructors may be interested to know that Dudley Fitts was the young Robert Fitzgerald's Latin master at the Choate School. They became lifelong friends and collaborated on three celebrated translations of Greek tragedies. When they corresponded, they usually wrote their letters in Latin. Fitts's mentorship helped guide Fitzgerald to his career as the most distinguished American translator of Greek and Roman classical poetry, including *The Iliad*, *The Odyssey*, and *The Aeneid*. Fitzgerald later became the Boylston Professor at Harvard. For an account of Fitzgerald's teaching methods, see Dana Gioia's memoir "Learning from Robert Fitzgerald" in the Spring 1998 issue of the *Hudson Review*.

38
Critical Casebook: Shakespeare

William Shakespeare, OTHELLO, THE MOOR OF VENICE, page 1368

For commentary on the play, some outstanding sources of insight still include A. C. Bradley's discussion in *Shakespearean Tragedy* (1904; rpt. ed. [New York: St. Martin's, 1965]) and Harley Granville-Barker, "Preface to *Othello*," in *Prefaces to Shakespeare*, II (Princeton UP, 1947), also available separately from the same publisher (1958). See also Leo Kirschbaum, "The Modern *Othello*," *Journal of English Literary History 2* (1944), 233–96, and Marvin Rosenberg, *The Masks of "Othello"* (Berkeley: U of California P, 1961). A convenient gathering of short studies will be found in *A Casebook on Othello*, ed. Leonard Dean (New York: Crowell, 1961). For a fresh reading of the play, see Michael Black, who in *The Literature of Fidelity* (London: Chatto, 1975) argues that the familiar view of Othello as a noble figure manipulated by the evil Iago is wrong and sentimental. According to Black, we see ourselves and our destructive impulses mirrored in both characters; hence, we are disturbed.

Lynda E. Boose has closely read the confrontation scene between Othello and Brabantio, the father of Desdemona, in front of the Duke (I, iii), and has found in it an ironic parody of the traditional giving away of the bride at a marriage ceremony. Instead of presenting his daughter to Othello as a gift, the thwarted Brabantio practically hurls her across the stage at the Moor. (The scene resembles Lear's casting away of Cordelia in *King Lear*, I, i.) In most of Shakespeare's plays, the father of the bride wants to retain and possess his daughter. Prevented by law and custom from doing so, he does the next best thing: tries to choose her husband, usually insisting on someone she does not desire. But Shakespeare, in both comedy and tragedy, always stages the old man's defeat ("The Father and the Bride in Shakespeare," *PMLA* 97 [May 1982]: 325–47).

Still another opinion that students might care to discuss: "No actress could credibly play the role of Desdemona if the character's name were changed to, say, Sally" (Frank Trippett, "The Game of the Name," *Time*, 14 Aug. 1978).

General question 3: "How essential to the play is the fact that Othello is a black man, a Moor, and not a native of Venice?" That Othello is an outsider, a stranger unfamiliar with the ways of the Venetians, makes it easier for Iago to stir up Othello's own self-doubts; and so the fact seems essential to the plot. (See especially III, iii, 215–23, 244–47, 274–84.) Venice in the Renaissance had no commerce with black Africa, but Shakespeare's many references to Othello's blackness (and Roderigo's mention of the Moor's "thick lips," I, i, 68) have suggested to some interpreters that Othello could even be a coastal African from below the Senegal. On the modern stage, Othello has been memorably played by African American actor Paul Robeson and by Laurence Olivier, who carefully studied African American speech and body language for his performance at the Old Vic (and in the movie version). A critic wrote of Olivier's interpretation:

He came on smelling a rose, laughing softly with a private delight; bare-footed, ankleted, black. . . . He sauntered downstage, with a loose, bare-heeled roll of the buttocks; came to rest feet splayed apart, hips lounging outward. . . . The hands hung big and graceful. The whole voice was char-acterized, the o's and the a's deepened, the consonants thickened with faint, guttural deliberation. "Put up yo' bright swords, or de dew will rus' dem": not quite so crude, but in that direction. It could have been caricature, an embarrassment. Instead, after the second performance, a well-known Negro actor rose in the stalls bravoing. For obviously it was done with love; with the main purpose of substituting for the dead grandeur of the Moorish empire one modern audiences could respond to. (Ronald Bryden, *New Statesman*, I May 1964)

For a fascinating study of the play by a white teacher of African American stu-dents at Howard University, see Doris Adler, "The Rhetoric of *Black* and *White* in *Othello*," in *Shakespeare Quarterly* 25 (Spring 1974): 248–57. Iago, Roderigo, and Brabantio hold negative and stereotyped views of black Africans which uncomfortably recall modern racial prejudices. In their view, Othello is "lasciv-ious" (I, i, 126), an unnatural mate for a white woman (III, iii, 245–49), a prac-titioner of black magic (I, ii, 74–75). Under the influence of Iago's wiles, Othello so doubts himself that he almost comes to accept the stereotype forced on him, to reflect that in marrying him Desdemona has strayed from her own nature (III, iii, 243). Such, of course, is not the truth Shakespeare reveals to us, and the tragedy of Othello stems from a man's tragic inability to recognize good or evil by sight alone. "Eyes cannot see that the black Othello is not the devil," Adler observes, "or that the white and honest Iago is."

In answer to general question 4 ("Besides Desdemona and Iago, what other pairs of characters seem to strike balances?"): Alvin Kernan in his introduction to the Signet edition of *Othello* comments,

> The true and loyal soldier Cassio balances the false and traitorous soldier Iago. . . . The essential purity of Desdemona stands in contrast to the more "practical" view of chastity held by Emilia, and her view in turn is illumi-nated by the workaday view of sensuality held by the courtesan Bianca. . . . Iago's success in fooling Othello is but the culmination of a series of such betrayals that includes the duping of Roderigo, Brabantio, and Cassio.

The last general question ("Does the downfall of Othello proceed from any flaw in his nature, or is his downfall entirely the work of Iago?") is a classic (or cliché) problem, and perhaps there is no better answer than Coleridge's in his *Lectures on Shakspere:*

> Othello does not kill Desdemona in jealousy, but in a conviction forced upon him by the almost superhuman art of Iago—such a conviction as any man would and must have entertained who had believed in Iago's honesty as Oth-ello did. We, the audience, know that Iago is a villain from the beginning; but in considering the essence of the Shaksperian Othello, we must perseveringly place ourselves in his situation, and under his circumstances. Then we shall immediately feel the fundamental difference between the solemn agony of the noble Moor, and the wretched fishing jealousies of Leontes. . . . Othello had

no life but in Desdemona: the belief that she, his angel, had fallen from the heaven of her native innocence, wrought a civil war in his heart. She is his counterpart; and, like him, is almost sanctified in our eyes by her absolute unsuspiciousness, and holy entireness of love. As the curtain drops, which do we pity the most?

On the suggestion for writing: Thomas Rymer's famous objections to the play will not be easy to refute. At least, no less a critic than T. S. Eliot once declared that he had never seen Rymer's points cogently refuted. Perhaps students will enjoy siding with the attack or coming to the play's defense.

Was the Othello-Desdemona match a wedding of April and September? R. S. Gwynn of Lamar University writes: "Has anyone ever mentioned the age difference between Othello and Desdemona? Othello speaks of his arms as 'now some nine moons wasted.' Assuming that this metaphor means that his life is almost 9/12 spent, he would be over 50! Now if a Venetian girl would have normally married in her teens (think of the film version of *Romeo and Juliet*), that would make about 30 years difference between him and his bride." This gulf, Othello's radically different culture, his outraged father-in-law, and Iago's sly insinuations all throw tall obstacles before the marriage.

"If we are to read the play that Shakespeare wrote," maintains Bruce E. Miller, "we must acknowledge that Othello as well as Iago commits great evil." In *Teaching the Art of Literature* (Urbana, IL: NCTE, 1980), Miller takes *Othello* for his illustration of teaching drama and stresses that Othello went wrong by yielding to his gross impulses. In demonstrating why the play is a classic example of tragedy, Miller takes advantage of students' previously having read Willa Cather's "Paul's Case." That story illustrates "the difference between sadness and tragedy. Paul's death is sad because it cuts off a life that has never been fulfilled. Yet it is not tragic, for Paul lives and dies in this world of human affairs." But Othello's death has the grandeur of tragedy. Realizing at last that Desdemona has been true and that in slaying her he has destroyed his own hopes of happiness, the Moor attains a final clarity of spirit, intuiting the true order of things.

MLL   *MyLiteratureLab Resources.* Photographs, biographical information, critical overview, and bibliography for Shakespeare. Video clip, audio clip, interactive reading, student essay, and critical essay for *Othello*.

TEACHING SHAKESPEARE

Grace Haddox, of El Paso Community College, has written us to share a teaching method she uses with great success to help students understand and appreciate Shakespeare.

Here at community college, many of my students are returning students, older students, GED students, high school dropouts—well, you get the picture. Most are not interested in Shakespeare in the least because they have never experienced Shakespeare, or they read it in high school and thought the texts were boring. So, when presenting Shakespeare to my college students, I have them bring their textbook to class and we listen to an audiotape as the students follow along and annotate their texts. I use a wonderful series from Arkangel—the texts are unabridged, professional actors are used from the Royal Academy of Dramatic Arts and the Royal Shakespeare Company, and music and sound effects are utilized. We start and stop the tape often to discuss the text and language and work out any problems in understanding or interpretation. After we listen to Act I, we take a short quiz, and then we watch a film version of Act I. Then, we go on to Act II, listen to it, quiz, then the film, and so on and so on.

I can't tell you the success I've had with this method. The students are able to really discuss the text in depth because we can go as fast or as slow as we choose with the tape. Moreover, the students develop "an ear" for the language. They always complain that Act I is very difficult because they cannot understand what's going on, but by Act VI, if I try to stop the tape for discussion, I get yelled at because the students are following the action perfectly, and they don't want to be interrupted. Frankly, it's very gratifying to be yelled at for trying to interrupt Shakespeare. Lastly, the students are presented with two versions of the same Shakespeare play—the taped version and the film version. They are extremely critical of the way both are presented, and they discuss the delivery of lines, the settings, and actors who play each part, motivations, director choices, etc. The general reaction at the end of the semester is always favorable, and students realize Shakespeare is not so bad. Incidentally, I had a lot of success with this method at the high school level too.

On a last note, I'd like to share just a few student stories regarding *Othello*. I had a college student a few years ago, Jesus, who was a mediocre student. He barely did the minimum and his attendance was not great. His average was a D moving into the end of the semester, and I anticipated he would have to retake the course. However, when we got to *Othello*, something happened to him. He began discussing the text, and, often, he led the class discussions. His attendance became regular because he "had to see what was going to happen next," and one day he said to me and the whole class, "You know, Ms. Haddox, I really like *Othello*, and I keep trying to talk to my friends about the play and Shakespeare, but all they want to do is kick my a**." Clearly, this was a young man who was transformed by the power of Shakespeare. He earned a B for the course.

This last semester, I had another student, Martin, a brilliant young man actually. I felt that the tape and film method might be too slow or tedious for him, but he told me on the last day of class that the class discussions sparked from the tape really opened up the world of Shakespeare to him. He said to me, "I never really liked Shakespeare, but some of the things we talked about really interested me. I bought a copy of *Macbeth*, and I'm reading that now." Again, I can't tell you how happy I was to hear that.

William Shakespeare, HAMLET, PRINCE OF DENMARK, page 1472

In 1964 on the quadricentennial anniversary of Shakespeare's birth, the celebrated Polish critic Jan Kott observed, "The bibliography of dissertations and studies devoted to *Hamlet* is twice the size of Warsaw's telephone directory. No Dane of flesh and blood has been written about so extensively as Hamlet." A few years earlier, Harry Levin of Harvard computed from A. A. Raven's 1953

Hamlet Bibliography that, over a sixty-year period, a new discussion of *Hamlet* had been published every twelve days. No work of world literature has generated as much commentary as this play.

The key to teaching *Hamlet* is not to be intimidated by this Mount Everest of scholarship. Familiarity with some of the criticism will enrich your teaching, but *Hamlet* has never needed commentary to win over an audience. For more than four hundred years, it has been Shakespeare's most popular tragedy. Nonetheless, it might be worthwhile to review some of the best critical works, especially those that can be recommended to students.

Still indispensable is A. C. Bradley's *Shakespearean Tragedy* (1904), which is available in several inexpensive editions, including a Penguin paperback (1991) with a new introduction by John Bayley. This classic book contains Bradley's general observations on Shakespeare's tragedies along with detailed examinations of *Hamlet, Othello, King Lear,* and *Macbeth.* If you have never read this volume, you are in for a treat: there has never been a better general introduction written to these plays. Bradley was not only a superb scholar and critic; he remains an engaging and lucid writer. The book grew out of Bradley's lectures to undergraduates at the University of Glasgow, and in them we see a great teacher in action.

Most libraries will have David Bevington's excellent critical collection, *Twentieth Century Interpretations of Hamlet* (Englewood Cliffs, NJ: Prentice, 1968). This volume will probably be more useful to students than some later compilations because it presents essays written before the rise of literary theory made them too complicated for most undergraduates to follow easily. We use Professor Bevington's authoritative text and notes for *Hamlet* in the current edition of *Literature*.

Jan Kott's influential *Shakespeare Our Contemporary* (New York: Norton, 1964) is a great pleasure to read. Kott writes about Shakespeare from the perspective of an Eastern European and emphasizes the political nature of the plays. His chapter "*Hamlet* of the Mid-Century" describes how Polish productions of the play reflected the social and political environment around them. "*Hamlet* is like a sponge . . . it immediately absorbs all the problems of our time." Although he grounds his discussion in the history of modern totalitarian states, his comments are extremely illuminating. Describing a performance in Cracow in 1956, he captures a central aspect of *Hamlet* that has eluded most critics (an excerpt from this essay is in our Shakespeare casebook):

> In this performance everybody, without exception, was being constantly watched. Polonius, minister to the royal murderer, sends a man to France even after his own son. . . . At Elsinore castle someone is hidden behind every curtain. The good minister does not even trust the Queen. . . .
>
> Everything at Elsinore has been corroded by fear: marriage, love, and friendship. . . . The murderous uncle keeps a constant watchful eye on Hamlet. Why does he not want him to leave Denmark? His presence at court is inconvenient, reminding everybody of what they would like to forget. Perhaps he suspects something? . . .
>
> Ophelia, too, has been drawn into the big game. They listen in to her conversations, ask questions, read her letters. It is true that she gives them up herself. She is at the same time part of the Mechanism, and its victim. Politics hangs here over every feeling, and there is no getting away from it. All the characters are poisoned by it. (60–61)

The most useful recent study of the play is probably Paul Cantor's *Shakespeare: Hamlet* (Cambridge: Cambridge UP, 1989), which is part of Cambridge's generally distinguished "Landmarks of World Literature" series. Cantor's volume provides a concise, informed introduction to the tragedy. (The entire text is only 106 pages, including the notes and bibliography.) Taking recent scholarship into account, Cantor places the tragedy in a historical context and examines the central critical problems raised by the drama. It is a savvy, sophisticated volume that both instructors and students will find interesting.

The best way of teaching Shakespeare is through performance—not just watching one, but doing one. The more the instructor encourages, entices, cajoles, or compels students to perform scenes from the plays, the more deeply they will become involved in Shakespeare's drama. Memorization remains unfashionable in some circles, but few students will regret having to memorize all or part of a famous soliloquy from *Hamlet*. Memorization helps accommodate a contemporary student's ear to Elizabethan speech more quickly than any other method. Most long-term teachers of Shakespeare will have their own stories of classroom productions, but one particularly interesting account can be found in Frederick Turner's fascinating book *Rebirth of Value: Meditation on Beauty, Ecology, Religion, and Education* (Albany: SUNY Press, 1991). Turner uses his experiences teaching a "Shakespeare in Performance" course to develop a broader theory of education. Turner's discussion (pp. 151–70) focuses on *Hamlet*, but his procedures can be applied to any play:

> The class method was as follows. Each student was assigned to direct a scene from Shakespeare, casting it from the class, and recording the rehearsal process for an essay that would be due later. The rest of the class voted on the performance, and the actors, the director, and any other stage personnel would all get the same grade. In other words, the performing group stood or fell together, and the reward system demanded that it please, move, and inspire a real, experienced, and perceptive audience. As the year went on the productions became more and more elaborate, daring, polished (and time-consuming in rehearsal). The students were addicted and some performed many times more than I had required. They began to use costumes, scenery, makeup, even lights and special effects, improvising with great ingenuity in our drab little classroom, and decorating it festively when appropriate. The grading system was soon forgotten, and we had to remind ourselves to keep it going. Some students even protested their own grades when they thought them too high! (164–65)

Not all classes can afford the luxury of time to perform parts of *Hamlet*, but students should be encouraged to see or hear the play performed. There are several excellent film versions available on video. Laurence Olivier's classic 1948 version won him Academy Awards for best picture and best actor. Olivier's version is heavily cut and highly interpretive (very Freudian), but it remains compelling. Tony Richardson's *Hamlet* (1969) has Nicol Williamson as one of the most celebrated contemporary Hamlets, but it never comes entirely alive. Franco Zeffirelli's 1991 version stars Mel Gibson. Anyone who has not seen the film has the right to be skeptical, but Gibson works surprisingly well. Zeffirelli's lushly realistic production occasionally threatens to overwhelm his superb cast (including Glenn Close, Alan Bates, and Paul Scofield), but he trusts Shakespeare's drama. Casting an actor such as Gibson, best known for action-hero roles like *Road Warrior* or *Lethal Weapon*, seems very Elizabethan. His cinematic associations as a man of action underscore the divided character of the Danish prince, a hero who hesitates to begin.

There is also an excellent BBC audio recording of the complete text of *Hamlet* (distributed in the United States by Bantam Doubleday Dell Audio publishing, available on four cassettes or three compact discs). This performance lavishly parades the wealth of British theater: Kenneth Branagh takes the title role, with Judi Dench as Gertrude and Derek Jacobi as Claudius. Even the minor roles are superbly cast: John Gielgud is the Ghost; Michael Horden the Player King; and Emma Thompson the Player Queen.

Hamlet has one of the most complex plots of any Shakespeare play. There is a large cast. Many characters have different private and public personalities, and Hamlet himself is probably the most multifaceted protagonist in Shakespeare. It is always helpful in class to ask questions that make students think through the basic situation, actions, and characters of the drama. Here are a few possible questions.

QUESTIONS

1. By what means does Shakespeare build suspense before the Ghost's appearances? Why is Hamlet so unwilling to trust what the Ghost tells him? Is it possible to interpret the play so that the Ghost is just a projection of Hamlet's disturbed imagination?

2. What is the play's major dramatic question? At what point is the question formulated? Does the play have a crisis, or turning point?

3. How early in the play, and from what passages, do you perceive that Claudius is a villain?

4. What comic elements does the play contain—what scenes, what characters, what exchanges or dialogue? What is their value to a play that, as a whole, is a tragedy?

5. A familiar kind of behavior is showing one face to the world and another to oneself. What characters in *Hamlet* do so? Is their deception ever justified?

6. How guilty is Gertrude? With what offenses does Hamlet charge her (see III, iv)? Is our attitude toward her the same as Hamlet's, or different? Does our sympathy for her grow as the play goes on, or diminish?

7. If the characters of Rosencrantz and Guildenstern are cut from the play, as is the case in some productions, what is lost?

8. Consider Hamlet's soliloquies, especially those beginning "O that this too too sullied [or *solid*] flesh would melt" (I, ii, 129–159); "O, what a rogue and peasant slave am I!" (II, ii, 477–533); and "To be, or not to be" (III, i, 56–89). How do these meditations round out the character of Hamlet? How do they also serve to advance the story?

9. Discuss how Shakespeare differently portrays Hamlet's feigned madness and Ophelia's real madness.

10. Is Laertes a villain like Claudius, or is there reason to feel that his contrived duel with Hamlet is justified?

11. How is Hamlet shown to be a noble and extraordinary person, not merely by birth, but by nature? See Ophelia's praise of Hamlet as "The glass of fashion, and the mold of form" (III, i, 142–153). Are we to take Ophelia's speech as the prejudiced view of a lover, or does Shakespeare demonstrate that her opinion of Hamlet is trustworthy?

12. Discuss Hamlet's treatment of Ophelia (see especially Act III, Scene i). Does his behavior seem cruel, in conflict with his supposed nobility and sensitivity?

13. In what respects does *Hamlet* resemble a classical tragedy such as *Oedipus Rex*? In what ways is Shakespeare's play different? Is Hamlet, like Oedipus, driven to his death by some inexorable force (Fate, the gods, the nature of things)?

For a classroom discussion of Hamlet's character, you might present the poet-critic Jack Foley's radical notion of the character's individuality (written especially for this handbook):

At the beginning of Sir Laurence Olivier's acclaimed film production of *Hamlet*, a disembodied voice, speaking above an image of clouds, says *"This is the story of a man who could not make up his mind."* Someone in the theater at which I saw it answered ironically, "Oh, so *that's* what it's about." The meaning of *Hamlet* and the nature of the central character are by no means as clear as Olivier wished his audience to believe. To call a play *Hamlet* or *King Lear* or *Richard III* or *Othello* is not so different from calling a television program *The Johnny Carson Show* or *The Bill Cosby Show* or *Roseanne*. The title implies *The Interesting Individual Show*. The Renaissance, the period in which Shakespeare wrote his plays, is often described as the great age of individuality and self-assertion.

Plays with titles like *Hamlet* implicitly promise to "tell all" about some central, charismatic character—someone usually portrayed by the most famous actor in the company—to give us a powerful psychological portrait of a fascinating "individual." Hamlet the character is, we know from hundreds of performances, just such a fascinating "individual"—and he is overwhelmingly real. Yet the moment we try to "explain" his reality—even to explain his essential *problem*—we find ourselves confused, uncertain. The reason for this is that Shakespeare's extremely memorable characters do not behave consistently according to *any* system of psychology, whether Renaissance or Modern. Freud was right. There are moments in the play when Hamlet is exhibiting clear Oedipal characteristics. But not *throughout* the play. Hamlet himself suggests that he is "melancholy"—a psychological condition exhaustively studied by Shakespeare's contemporary, Robert Burton, in *The Anatomy of Melancholy*. It's true, Hamlet is melancholy, but not *throughout* the play. Hamlet also functions as the figure of the Avenger—as in Thomas Kyd's famous revenge drama, *The Spanish Tragedy*. But, again, not *throughout* the play.

The same character who tells his mother that he "knows not seems" displays a considerable interest in theater (an art of "seeming") and announces that he will put on an "antic disposition" and *pretend* to be mad—"seeming" to the max. On the other hand, there are several moments in the play when Hamlet really does appear to be crazy. Nor are such contradictions limited to the character of Hamlet. Polonius is throughout the play nothing but an old fool. Yet his diagnosis of Hamlet as mad for the love of Ophelia is not without some justification in Hamlet's behavior, and his "This above all: to thine own self be true" speech is one of the great set pieces of the play, something far beyond the powers of the foolish old man he is everywhere else. . . . The fact is that Hamlet seems real not because he is a coherent character of "self" or because there is some discoverable "essence" to him but because *he actively and amazingly inhabits so many diverse, interconnecting, potentially contradictory contexts.*

Hamlet is one of the most famous fictional characters ever created. Why is this so? Foley asserts that Hamlet's reality as a character derives from his multiplicity and inconsistency as a character: Hamlet is as difficult to comprehend with a single explanation as a real person. What do your students think?

 MyLiteratureLab Resources. Photographs, biographical information, critical overview, and bibliography for Shakespeare. Longman Lecture, critical essay on *Hamlet*.

William Shakespeare, A MIDSUMMER NIGHT'S DREAM, page 1592

"Wild and fantastical as this play is," said the notoriously sensible Samuel Johnson about *A Midsummer Night's Dream* in 1773, "all the parts in their various modes are well written and give the kind of pleasure which the author designed." In 1904 another paragon of English common sense, G. K. Chesterton, argued the work's merits more emphatically: "The greatest of Shakespeare's comedies is also," he wrote, "from a certain point of view, the greatest of his plays." Chesterton goes on to explain what that "certain point of view" is—psychological complexity and dreamlike verisimilitude—but the first part of his assertion strikes the editors of this volume as eminently plausible. Even amid the varied splendors of Shakespeare's major comedies, *A Midsummer Night's Dream* stands out as a joyously special achievement. The most complexly plotted, fancifully conceived, and overtly erotic of his comedies, it has cast a magic spell on audiences and artists—including Felix Mendelssohn, George Balanchine, Max Reinhardt, and Benjamin Britten—for four centuries.

Shakespeare had no known source for *A Midsummer Night's Dream*, though he borrowed details from various earlier works. He purposefully created an ingeniously intricate plot with four sets of characters—royal, aristocratic, plebeian, and supernatural. Each group is associated with a certain mood or attitude—noble, romantic, farcical, or magical. The playwright hilariously—and sometimes tenderly—interweaves these four plotlines and casts of characters with magisterial ease, creating a work that is simultaneously his most romantic and his zaniest comedy. The elements of magic in the play and the central metaphor of the dream combine to give the comedy a specially lyric atmosphere. Important issues of power and responsibility, love and obsession, and identity and illusion are investigated, but above and beyond those specific themes is the unifying vision of love as a transformative and redemptive emo-tion, with marriage as its proper human institution. It is nearly impossible to read or watch the comedy without being touched by the luminous magic of Shakespeare's affirmation.

In considerably more mundane terms, the comedy also provides broader cov-erage in *Literature* of Shakespeare's achievement. *A Midsummer Night's Dream* offers a more generous and inclusive view of love and marriage than *Othello* or *Hamlet*, and Shakespeare's comic vision both qualifies and illuminates his tragic works. (Instructors should also note the many poems by Shakespeare that appear in the Poetry section of *Literature*.) One obvious question for the classroom is whether the comic or tragic vision of existence captures more of life's experience. This is, of course, an impossible question to answer conclusively, but it is nonetheless worth asking for the discussion it might generate. Students may at first be inclined to favor tragedy since dark and serious art seems more important, but upon reflection they may start to explore the inclusive nature of comedy.

Although Shakespeare's Bottom offers cautionary advice to would-be critics of the play, "Man is but an ass if he go about to expound this dream," we offer a few discussion topics for students. Here are ten questions about the play, pro-vided by Ellen Mease of Grinnell College, that you may want to use in class to clarify a few of its major themes.

QUESTIONS

1. *What event does the play's action look forward to?* The play focuses on the wedding of Theseus and Hippolyta, announced in the opening scene and cele-brated in the final one. In some sense every major action in the play suggests, illuminates, or contrasts with this event. The entire play can be read as an explo-ration of the nature of marital love and union. The reasonable and conciliatory behavior of the two royal lovers, who overcome their previous animosity to marry, also provides perspective on the comic adventures and misadventures of the other couples.

2. *What unifies the play?* Its plotlines converge on the unifying theme of love consummated in marriage, its focal point the ducal wedding, later to include the lovers, with the supernatural blessings of the reconciled fairy king and queen. The general theme of appearance vs. reality highlights the alternative reality of the dream, whether conceived as a path to transcendence or as a conduit of the (Freudian) unconscious. The midsummer night's confusions make concrete the transformative power of imagination, not only in the lover and the lunatic, but also in the poet of the theater. Art, magic, and metamorphosis link the mortal and the fairy worlds. Central to most of these themes are Oberon and Puck, who as "masters of revels" complicate and then unravel the story lines of the fairies (Titania), the lovers, and the mechanicals (Bottom's "translation").

3. *How is the fairy plot linked to the celebratory marital theme of the play?* The language, action, characterization, and imagery of the fairy world combine to cre-ate a festival atmosphere in the play. In Elizabethan times the festival was a spe-cial period when normal social customs were relaxed or reversed—like modern *Mardi Gras* in New Orleans. C. L. Barber, in "May Games and Metamorphoses on a Midsummer Night," chapter 6 of his *Shakespeare's Festive Comedy: A Study*

of Dramatic Form and Its Relation to Social Custom (1959), links the play's action to social customs, festivals, and pageantry familiar to Shakespeare's audience. The May game, for example, mirrors the play's central social action. A May game would begin in town then move into a grove before returning to town:

> The Maying is completed when Oberon and Titania with their trains come into the great chamber to bring the blessings of fertility. They are at once special, a May king and queen making their good luck visit to the manor house, and a pair of country gods, half-English and half-Ovid, come to bring their powers in tribute to great lords and ladies. (119–120)

The spring festival, like the ancient saturnalia, releases energies and transformative powers that are necessary for procreation and social renewal, but are ultimately controlled within the formal bonds of marriage. Shakespeare's dramatic art, in similar fashion, conjures up and gives civilizing shape to the passions, in a pattern of release and transformation:

> Shakespeare, in developing a May-game action at length to express the will in nature that is consummated in marriage, brings out underlying magical meanings of the ritual while keeping always a sense of what it is humanly, as an experience. The woods are a region of passionate excitement [realized in the poetry]. Poetry conveys the experience of amorous tendency diffused in nature; and poetry, dance, gesture, dramatic fiction, combine to create, in the fairies, creatures who embody the passionate mind's elated sense of its own omnipotence. The woods are established as a region of metamorphosis, where in liquid moonlight or glimmering starlight, things can change, merge and melt into each other. Metamorphosis expresses what love sees and what it seeks to do. (132–133)

4. *How does the play exemplify the holiday spirit of revels?* In many of his early romantic comedies and late romances, Shakespeare uses an escape to a "green world," the world of nature, or in this case magic and nature, as a release or holiday revel. As C. L. Barber wrote, "The clarification achieved by the festive comedies corresponds to the release they dramatize: a heightened awareness of the relation between man and 'nature'"—a holiday in celebration of an elemental natural force like summer or harvest. In the alternative reality of the green world, essential human values are rediscovered and secured. Holiday rescues us from everyday.

5. *How does the play use sleep and dream as a central theme?* In sleep our fantasy perceives the wider truths of human experience—both dark and transcendent—denied to it when we are awake. However, the night's accidents befalling the lovers are not the "fierce vexations of a dream" (IV.i.61–62). The fierce passions unleashed by the love juice are endured and safely subdued. The murderous jealousy that erupts into dangerous swordplay is disarmed by Oberon and Puck. The rivalry that threatened the "double cherry on one stem" of Hermia and Helena's girlhood friendship is banished with the dawn that sees them sleeping side by side in the woods. Titania is disabused of her folly with no apparent injury to her dignity. Bottom is restored to his friends trailing clouds of glory ("a most rare vision" [IV.i.193–205]) with no lasting resentment of class differences that would bar him from the bed of a mortal queen. He takes the gift of transitory

joy as his due. Indeed, he addresses Theseus as an equal when he breaks character to correct the Duke's apparent confusion over the role of Wall (V.i.178–180). Of the lovers' seeming "dream and fruitless vision," the lasting fruit will be unions "whose date till death shall never end" (III.2.371–373). Midsummer folly exorcises and dispels the potential dangers of excessive passion.

6. *How do the four sets of lovers, in their respective plotlines, contribute to the play's romantic comedy?*

- *Theseus and Hippolyta*: Theseus appears to have won Hippolyta's love despite having defeated her in battle. Pay attention to their scenes together, especially as he is called upon to mediate in the conflict between Egeus and Hermia (I.i.1–126), the morning hunt scene (IV.i.94–176), and their important exchange in V.i. on fantasy and real experience, reason, and imagination. (Hippolyta's "something of great constancy" at V.i.26 comes close to expressing our sense of the ultimate coherence and plausibility of what Theseus would dismiss as "antique fables" or "fairy toys." Watching the play, we have actually seen how the "airy nothing" of the fairy world has been given "a local habitation and a name" in the midsummer night's confusions and unraveling.) A less obvious theme of the play is the growing sympathy between the two former enemies. They set a moral example of proper marital love for all the other couples.

- *The Young Lovers*: The romantic nature of the young aristocrats is both central and obvious—they are the new generation who are about to enter their procreative period. Their health and happiness suggests the future fate of the city. The younger aristocratic lovers, in their patterned encounters of pursuit and avoidance, also illustrate well one of the most famous principles of comedy, what the French philosopher Henri Bergson called "the mechanical encrusted on the living," when the human being (capable beyond all creatures of adapting flexibly to changing circumstances) behaves more like a thing or machine in rote reflex. The automatism of the inconstant, aberrant men in their sudden about-faces is a rich source of comedy: "What fools these mortals be."

- *The Artisans (including both Bottom's "translation" and the play-within-a-play)*: Bottom's romance with Titania provides a parodic version of the aristocratic romances. It also offers subtle commentary on the social order of the play. Bottom's sudden elevation in social status and his democratic union with the fairy queen leaves him totally unfazed; he regards it as his natural right. The love tragedy of *Pyramus and Thisbe* burlesques the tragic potential of the rendezvous of "star-crossed" lovers like Hermia and Lysander.

- *Oberon and Titania*: These elemental nature gods have upset the balance of nature through their marital quarrels. Their reconciliation dance sets the stage for the final act's royal wedding in Athens and the mechanicals' wedding performance.

7. *How is love presented and critiqued in the play?* Among the many varieties of love and relationship treated in the play (parent-child, ruler-ruled, god-

mortal, friends, sexual lovers), there seems to be a distinction between right relationship and dangerous sexual obsession. The play implicitly recommends due proportion and balanced obligations as the proper order of our affective relations with others. Dotage, obsession, and fixation are important sources of the play's comedy. (Ask students to identify and discuss major instances.) The correction of mistaken or excessive attachment is an important part of the play's resolution.

8. *Does the love juice have a similar effect on all the characters?* The love juice has similar effects on Lysander and Titania (compelling them to dote on love objects not of their choice), but the juice does not appear to work in the same way on Demetrius. Originally in love with Helena and betrothed to her (which technically bars him from contracting a marriage with Hermia, according to Elizabethan law), he has betrayed his true love, swayed either by male inconstancy or by Egeus to pursue a woman who cannot be his. It may bode ill for Helena that Demetrius is still under the influence of the love drug (having received no antidote, unlike Titania and Lysander), but it may also be that the drug merely restores his affection to its proper place.

9. *How is the female role in marital love portrayed in the play? What does it suggest about gender roles in a traditional, custom-bound society?* The theme of "unruly women" and the threat of matriarchal misrule emerges in the adult love relationships, in the first scene's allusion to Theseus's legendary defeat of the Amazons threatening his new city, Athens. Titania's fixation on the orphaned Indian boy has alienated her from her husband, though her devotion to her votaress wins our sympathy. (We might think of Freud's Victorian "family romance," in which the mother/child bond threatens the privileges of the marital bed and requires regulation.) The quarrel between fairy king and queen in turn has brought about an upheaval in the natural order of things. Is Oberon's desire to raise the boy among men, as his page of honor, necessarily a violation of Titania's desire to raise the boy as her own? (Think about rites of passage in patriarchal societies, in which boys are ceremonially removed from the sphere of their mother's influence and inducted into male activities and tribal customs. Such rites preserve traditional gender distinctions and are part of the cultural process by which order is maintained in traditional societies.) In what other ways does the play explore the problem of gender hierarchy?

10. *Do the women truly achieve free choice at the end of the play when they marry their beloveds?* Feminist critics have noticed that of the three brides, only Hippolyta has any lines in Act V. Hermia and Helena are silent. (Their husbands, meanwhile, are wittily engaged in one-upmanship with Theseus.) Either the young women are politely enjoying themselves in the midst of an otherwise very animated scene (no specifically assigned lines being necessary), or once married, they are "barred from discourse." Hippolyta's role in Act V can be read in counterpoint to their silence.

Professor Mease of Grinnell College, an experienced director and actor, has selected passages in the play as performance assignments for the classroom. She recommends the following monologues and scenes for analysis, memorization, and performance.

Women:
Helena: I.i.226–251 ("How happy some o'er other some can be!")
Titania: II.i.81–117 ("These are the forgeries of jealousy.")
Helena: III.ii.192–219 ("Lo, she is one of this confederacy")

Men:
Robin: II.i.43–57; III.ii.6–34 ("My mistress with a monster is in love")
Oberon: II.i.146–185 (cut Robin's brief lines); II.i.249–67 ("I know a bank where the wild thyme blows"); IV.i.40–68
Bottom: IV.i.193–205 ("When my cue comes, call me . . .")

Scene-work:
I.i.128–179, Lysander and Hermia ("How now, my love?")
I.i.180–251, Hermia, Helena, Lysander ("Godspeed, fair Helena.")
I.ii.1–82, the mechanicals' first meeting
II.i.60–145, Oberon and Titania ("Ill met by moonlight, Proud Titania.")
II.i.188–244, Demetrius and Helena ("I love thee not, therefore, pursue me not.")
III.i.1–93, Mechanicals, through Bottom's translation up to his song
III.ii.43–87, Demetrius and Hermia ("O why rebuke you him that loves you so?")
III.ii.345–399, Oberon and Robin ("This is thy negligence. . . .")

Shakespeare's Sources
There is no major source for *A Midsummer Night's Dream*. The plot appears to be Shakespeare's own creation, though he borrows details from many sources. Of the many generally accepted sources for this most original play, Ovid's *Metamorphoses*, *The Golden Ass* of Apuleius, and Chaucer's "The Knight's Tale" and "The Merchant's Tale" may be familiar to students. Pyramus and Thisbe appear in Ovid or Golding's translation (1567) and in Chaucer's "The Legend of Good Women." The lovers derive generally from romances such as Sidney's *Arcadia* and Cinthio's tales in the *Hecatommithi*. In "the most lamentable comedy," Shakespeare may have parodied his own "most excellent and lamentable Tragedie of Romeo and Juliet," written around the same period. Seneca's *Medea* and *Hippolytus* were favorites with Shakespeare; Seneca's seascape with the armed Cupid (*Hipp.*) is the source for the vision Oberon relates to Puck (II.i.149–157). Erasmus's "Praise of Folly" links asses and folly in ways pertinent to Bottom's situation as the wise fool vouchsafed "a most rare vision."

Video
Elijah Moshinsky directed *A Midsummer Night's Dream* in 1980 for BBC Television's Shakespeare Series, distributed by Time/Life in the United States. The BBC Shakespeare Series, produced by Jonathan Miller, is a reliable starting-point for students unfamiliar with the plays. The acting is low-key and realistic, with solid line-work. Directors and designers do their research and take few risks. An uncontroversial production, Moshinsky's *Dream* is beautifully designed and shot, the aristocrats dressed in seventeenth-century Cavalier costume, the Tudor manor house interiors and woodland inspired by Dutch masters. The mechanicals' first scene is set in a tavern a la Frans Hals. The woods are in the Romantic Arcadian style of Claude Lorrain, with an obviously painted though luminous moon reflected in the realistic watery pools where the lovers finally sprawl, wet and muddy from their brawling. Oberon (Peter McEnery), bare-chested, long-haired,

on a black horse, is handsome and sensuous. Titania (Helen Mirren) enters with the "changeling" Indian boy as a vulnerable toddler-in-arms; she is surrounded by a small army of fairies of various ages, male and female, vaguely Celtic and wild. Bottom (Brian Glover) in his hairy ass's head is not fearsome but endearing; and he takes in stride his elevation to the fairy queen's bed. Hermia's "Egypt" or dark gypsy look is transferred to an angry, ethnic Hippolyta; Theseus (Nigel Davenport) wears armor in his first scene with her, but he quickly becomes the mature states-man, man of reason, and affable host.

Productions
Ellen Mease, Professor of Theatre at Grinnell College, has also provided this appre-ciation of Peter Brook's celebrated production of A *Midsummer Night's Dream*.

Shakespeare's romantic comedy A *Midsummer Night's Dream* has become, since Peter Brook's Royal Shakespeare production (1970–1973), the bar exam for ambitious directors. Fitting the protean energies and complexities of the play into the Procrustean bed of a fashionable directorial concept has not killed the patient, but liberated the play's latent dream materials and manifold meanings, as varied as the audiences that respond to them. As Gary Jay Williams observes in *Our Moonlight Revels:* A Midsummer Night's Dream *in the Theater*, "The play comes to the stage as an anthology of gender and class wars, as a critique of state oppression, as a celebration of Third World cultures, and as an exploration of the Victorian or Edwar-dian past in postmodern angst" (204). Darker visions in this recent theatre history may have cramped the play's playfulness and threatened its joyous-ness, but the dyes seem not to take for long. The play is self-renewing in every performance, given the vigor and range of the play's nature images, the ultimate beneficence of its aims, the dignity of its principals (the mor-tal and the fairy royals), the wonder seizing its lovers bent on happiness, and the earnest naiveté of the workmen, even Bottom as an ass in the arms of the fairy queen.

The artistic and commercial success of the Academy Award-winning film *Shakespeare in Love*, with a loving, exuberant, and smart script by Tom Stoppard and Mark Norman, has perhaps done more to make Shakespeare fans out of a mass audience than any single live production of the Bard in the four hundred years since he wrote. The wide availability of good pro-ductions of many of the plays on videotape has also made serious converts. However, those of us—and there were many of us—fortunate enough to have seen Brook's *Midsummer Night's Dream* (hereafter *MND*) knew that we were not only *seeing* but actively *making* the single most innovative produc-tion of the play in the twentieth century. Experiencing a great production can transform a dutiful apprentice into a serious student of drama. Not a local phenomenon but an international one, Brook's *MND* was probably seen by more theatre audiences than any single theatrical production of a Shakespearean play before or since.

Brook's actors made me listen to a living language, speaking the play's enormously varied verse with an emotional and imaginative immediacy that overrode four hundred years of flattening out and dumbing down of the Queen's English. Fleeting as they are in performance, every word, every intention, every verbal image and idea contributed to the "something of great constancy" Hippolyta identifies in the lovers' dream accounts (V.i.26). The crystal-clear intelligence of every character's line delivery, the crisp articulation and pointing of the lines, the brightness and energy of the play-ing—these were stunning gifts for all of us, not just the conservative spec-tator setting the bar high for Royal Shakespeare performers.

However, Shakespeare is not just in the language. The play is in its dra-matic situation, the story told in pictures and concrete stage action. For anyone who knew the history of MND's staging, Brook's visual spectacle was a wonder. The production swept away the elaborate pictorial illusions of nineteenth-century productions set in the antiquary's Athens or Arcadian Salvator Rosa woodlands with real bunnies, and providing an even more "blank" blank slate than the modernist "Shakespearean open stage" (inno-vated by Granville-Barker and popularized by Guthrie at Stratford [Ontario] and in Minneapolis during the regional repertory movement of the 1950s). Brook's staging gave us a startling white trapezoidal handball court, the atmos-phere of circus (trapezes and swings for the fairies and lovers' hi-jinks, Puck's Chinese circus yellow jumpsuit in loose silk) and magic (Cupid's flower a sil-ver plate spinning on a Lucite rod, soaring from Puck to Oberon as they swung in space), the breathtaking, lush eroticism of Sarah Kestelman's Tita-nia on her swinging bower of immense red feathers, the exposed stage machine (metal catwalk above the set walls, for the stage manager, flying technicians, and musicians), and the woods created out of coils of wire like gigantic Slinkies, which the fairies manipulated with fishing poles from the catwalk. There was no moonlit obscurity in any moment of the performance, only the brilliant white light on the clean white walls. (This anti-illusionist theatricality was influenced by the example of Bertolt Brecht's Berliner Ensemble international tour in the mid 1950s.)

The visual magic was embodied in the performers, especially in their colorful costumes (white and pale tie-dye tunics for the lovers, the bright colors of the royals' billowing robes) and kinetic movement. Long months of preparation in acrobatics, gymnastics, aikido, magic routines, and aerial artistry made the performers athletes of the play's passions (recalling Mey-erhold's bio-mechanical training for Russian actors in the 1920s). At the ribald climax (just before intermission), Bottom was buoyed up, a beefy ple-beian Dionysus, on the shoulders of the fairies, their phallic good humor in the best tradition of the old-fashioned bachelor party, as they danced him to his aerial bower. Later the lovers ricocheted like handballs off the walls and hurled themselves like projectiles through the swinging doors upstage. Tiny Hermia leaped into the air to plaster herself spider-like horizontally across a door exit, suspended five feet off the floor, barring Lysander's way. The whooping exuberance of the lovers' huge quarrel modulated to another key as the play tried to wind down to the after-dinner entertainment, the burlesque of Pyramus and Thisbe performed by blue-collar working stiffs. A magnanimous host, Theseus (who doubled as Oberon) insured that the giddy courtiers' remarks did not upset the dignity of his earnest amateurs. His democratic sensitivities left the audience free to laugh with the mechanicals, rather than worry about class snobbery and self-regarding wit.

Accounts and photographs of Brook's production are numerous. The authorized acting version of the production (based on the RSC promptbook) is available. It includes abundant photos, design sketches, and interviews or contributions from Brook, Alan Howard (Theseus/Oberon), composer Richard Peaslee, designer Sally Jacobs, technicians and the stage manager. See Glenn Loney, ed., *Peter Brook's Production of William Shakespeare's "A Midsummer Night's Dream" for the Royal Shakespeare Company* (1974). Succinct accounts appear in Williams (222–233), Griffiths (66-70), Foakes (21–24) and Holland (72 and *passim*).

 MyLiteratureLab Resources. Photographs, biographical information, critical overview, and bibliography for Shakespeare. Longman lecture, critical essay on *A Midsummer Night's Dream.*

CRITICS ON SHAKESPEARE, pages 1658–1669

The large selection of Shakespeare criticism we have reprinted in the casebook hardly touches the surface of the vast scholarship available, but it does provide students with a broad cross-section of critical opinion. It is easy for students to become intimidated by the mountains of material in Shakespeare studies. The important thing is to get them *started* somewhere engaging and reliable. We strove to put together an informed but accessible set of selections that both students and instructors could find useful.

Probably no modern novelist thought more deeply about William Shakespeare than **Anthony Burgess.** His 1964 novel, *Nothing Like the Sun*, is generally considered the most compelling fictional work about the enigmatic Bard of Avon. His late novel *Enderby's Dark Lady* (1984) also begins and ends with brilliant short stories about Shakespeare. Burgess also wrote a full-length critical study of the dramatist as well as a novel about Christopher Marlowe in which Shakespeare appears. Before he began writing fiction (at the age of 38), Burgess worked for the British government as a cultural officer in Asia. The selection that appears in *Literature* comes from a talk the polyglot Burgess gave at an international conference on translation. He addresses several interesting issues about how literary works travel across languages and cultures. He also speculates on why Shakespeare's work has proved nearly universal in its appeal. Finally, he reminds us that literary translation involves far more than finding equivalent words. Two questions you might ask students to start discussion:

1. In Burgess's experience, who seemed to be the only British author with universal appeal in Malaysia? How does Burgess account for this fact?

2. According to Burgess, what does translation involve besides words?

A. C. Bradley's classic discussion of Shakespeare's major tragedies remains interesting a century after its composition. Bradley provides a careful examination of the Danish prince's mental state—his melancholy or madness—read from a realist perspective. In doing so, the critic addresses what is often considered the central dramatic problem of the play, Hamlet's inaction and delay in avenging his father's murder.

Rebecca West's view of Ophelia is not so well known as Bradley's, but it is equally interesting and far more revisionist. In a feminist reading of the play, West views Ophelia as an expendable pawn in Polonius's quest for influence and power in the Danish court. Consequently, Ophelia is not a virgin martyr but a poor girl "sacrificed for family ambition in the days when a court was a cat's cradle of conspiracies." Her connecting Shakespeare's portrait of Ophelia with the situation of young women in the court of Henry VIII is particularly insightful.

Jan Kott's account of producing *Hamlet* in Cracow in 1956 offers brilliant insight into the political aspects of Shakespeare's tragedy. Kott catches something of the importance *Hamlet* has had for post-World War II drama, which understood the play's absurdist and existentialist qualities. The notion of Elsinore as a small totalitarian state full of informers is particularly useful and original.

Joel Wingard provides a reader-response perspective on *Hamlet*. He emphasizes the gaps in the narrative into which the reader projects his or her own meanings. Each reader develops a "reading strategy" for the play to explain away the questions raised by those gaps. Used in conjunction with the "Reader-Response" section in "Critical Approaches to Literature," Wingard's commentary provides students a substantial but manageable introduction to this critical strategy.

Poet **W. H. Auden** was fascinated with Shakespeare. He wrote and lectured fascinatingly on a substantial number of the plays. In Auden's posthumously published *Lectures on Shakespeare* (2000) alone, he discussed thirty-five of the plays as well as *The Sonnets*.

This discussion of Iago comes from Auden's 1961 essay "The Joker in the Pack," reprinted in his critical collection *The Dyer's Hand* (1962). In analyzing *Othello*, Auden notes how differently the villain operates in the play compared to Shakespeare's other tragedies. Iago and not the title character stands at the center of *Othello*, Auden observes, since he motivates the crucial dramatic actions. It is not Fate that dooms Othello; it is another human being. Auden's view of Iago neatly complements Maud Bodkin's identification of Iago as a diabolical figure. The devil, after all, leads persons to voluntary doom by evil advice.

Anyone interested in Auden's relation to Shakespeare should read his superb introduction to *The Sonnets*, which is reprinted in *Forewords & Afterwords* (New York: Random, 1973). Auden also wrote a sequel to *The Tempest*—his 1944 dramatic poem, *The Sea and the Mirror*.

Three questions you may ask students about Auden's analysis are:

1. What aspects of *Othello* does Auden consider unique?

2. What character does Auden assert stands at the center of Shakespeare's play? What is unusual about this character?

3. What is peculiar about Othello's fall in relation to the fall of most tragic heroes?

Maud Bodkin's *Archetypal Patterns in Poetry* (1958) remains a useful guide to mythological criticism as a perspective on English poetry. In the volume she analyzes both *Hamlet* and *Othello* (among many other classics). Her examination of Iago as a satanic figure is persuasive and revealing. She expands on this central insight to explicate Shakespeare's tragedy as a conflict between heroic values (embodied by Othello) and diabolic chaos (expressed by Iago). Her psychoanalytical/mythic reading of Iago places him both as a mythic devil and as the internal mental force that can deny or destroy a person's ideal values.

Even taking into account her cautionary comment at the beginning of the last paragraph—"The markers are morally neutral"—the fact is that **Clare Asquith**'s *Shadowplay* advances a highly controversial and even startling thesis: that William Shakespeare was a passionately committed Catholic in a Protestant England where Catholicism was suppressed and its adherents punished, and that his plays constitute a vast, intricate code that communicates his Catholic values and sympathies. Needless to say, most Shakespeare scholars question her thesis, though a growing number now accept the Bard of Avon's Catholic sympathies. The question is whether there are actually coded messages in the texts of his plays. Asquith has found admirers in Britain among such noted figures as the poet and critic Tom Paulin and the novelist Piers Paul Read, and even many who dispute her conclusions admit that her book is impressively researched. Reviewer Francis Phillips, himself a Catholic, offers a reservation worth noting: "But somehow I feel that this strict, though highly ingenious 'translation' of his deeper meaning, is reductive of its subject. To think of Shakespeare at all times deliberately seeking plots and stories through which to convey one insistent undercover message seems to undermine his prodigality, his life-enhancing bounty, his inventiveness. Although the author insists on his universality, the portrait that emerges from her book is of a man wholly bound up, indeed obsessed, with one theme only."

An interesting, indeed remarkable, aspect of Asquith's writing is that she uses postmodernist critical techniques to reach her traditionalist conclusions. (Her brand of traditionalism, however, is also contrarian, since it rejects the conventional readings of Shakespeare as either Anglican or religiously indifferent.) She deconstructs the texts of the plays to demonstrate that the surface arguments contain contradictory elements; she then uses New Historicist, Reader-response, and Queer Studies techniques to analyze those elements against the political, economic, and ideological background of Shakespeare's age to decipher covert messages as they might have been understood by a persecuted minority of the Elizabethan audience. One may well quibble with particular elements of her ultimate interpretations—and Asquith often seems to go too far—but her overall thesis remains provocative and insightful.

Virginia Mason Vaughan's "Black and White in *Othello*" offers the insight of both historical criticism and cultural studies. She places Shakespeare's characterization within the social and cultural context of the early Jacobean period, especially the assumptions of the "predominately white audience" that viewed the play. Othello is, in her analysis, the Other, and his darkness is "the visual signifier of his Otherness." Whether that Otherness is portrayed as an "African" or "Moor" does not matter; Othello stands perpetually as alien to the other characters and the audience.

Germaine Greer adds to our understanding of and delight in the play-within-the-play of *A Midsummer Night's Dream* by providing historical insight about the kinds of criticism theater faced in Elizabethan England. Her observations about Shakespeare's using the Rustics to gently mock and answer his critics add to our enjoyment of the dialogue.

Linda Bamber analyzes *A Midsummer Night's Dream* as a battle between male and female power. The play begins with a series of female rebellions against male authority (Hermia, Titania, and, perhaps more subtly and implicitly, Hippolyta). The action of the play reveals how these upsets are resolved, according to the Elizabethan view of natural order, in favor of men. Bamber also relates the gentle comic nature of this disruption of gender roles to the "temporary subversion of social order" allowed in holiday festivals.

Writers on Writing

Ben Jonson, On His Friend and Rival William Shakespeare, page 1669

Anyone who claims that William Shakespeare did not write the plays that bear his name must reckon with the testimony of the poet and dramatist Ben Jonson, who left two accounts of the Bard of Avon—one in verse, the other (reprinted here) in conversation with the poet and nobleman William Drummond of Hawthornden, who entertained Jonson and kept detailed notes. (The selection we reprint is the closest thing Jacobean literature has to a literary interview.) Jonson, who did not enjoy consistent box-office success in commercial theater, had a jealous but affectionate relationship with his immensely popular rival. Here in conversation we overhear Jonson grumbling about the man he claimed to love "on this side idolatry." Students interested in pursuing the relationship between the two playwright-poets should also read Jonson's magnificent verse "To the Memory of My Beloved, The Author, Mr. William Shakespeare, and What He Hath Left Us," which appeared as the dedication to the First Folio of Shakespeare's works in 1623. The poem begins:

> To draw no envy, Shakespeare, on thy name,
>   Am I thus ample to thy book and fame;
> While I confess thy writing to be such
>   As neither man nor muse can praise too much.

(Note, too, that three poems by Jonson appear in the Poetry section of *Literature*.)

39
The Modern Theater

Henrik Ibsen, A DOLL'S HOUSE, *page 1679*

At the heart of the play, as its title indicates, is the metaphor of a house of make-believe. In the play's visible symbols we see Ibsen the poet. In Act I, there is the Christmas tree that Nora orders the maid to place in the middle of the room—a gesture of defiance after Krogstad had threatened her domestic peace and happiness. In the Christmas gifts Nora has bought for the children—sword, toy horse, and trumpet for the boys, a doll and a doll's bed for the girl, Emmy—Nora seems to assign boys and girls traditional emblems of masculinity and femininity and (in Rolf Fjelde's phrasing) is "unthinkingly transmitting her doll-identity to her own daughter." When the curtain goes up on Act II, we see the unfortunate Christmas tree again: stripped, burned out, shoved back into a corner—and its ruin speaks eloquently for Nora's misery. Richly suggestive, too, is Nora's wild tarantella to merry music played by the diseased and dying Rank. Like a victim of a tarantula bite, Nora feels a kind of poison working in her; and it is ironic that Rank has a literal poison working in him as well. (The play's imagery of poison and disease is traced in an article by John Northam included in Rolf Fjelde's *Ibsen: A Collection of Critical Essays* [Englewood Cliffs, NJ: Prentice, 1965]). Significant, too, is Nora's change of costume: taking off her fancy dress, she divests herself of the frivolous nonsense she had once believed and puts on everyday street attire.

Ibsen's play was first performed in Copenhagen on December 21, 1879; no doubt many a male chauvinist found it a disquieting Christmas present. Within a few years, *A Doll's House* had been translated into fourteen languages. James Gibbons Huneker has described its fame: when Nora walked out on Helmer, "that slammed door reverberated across the roofs of the world." With the rise of feminism, *A Doll's House* gradually became Ibsen's most frequently performed play—not only on the stage but in television and film adaptations. In 1973 two screen versions were issued almost simultaneously: Joseph Losey's overly solemn version starring Jane Fonda, and Hilliard Elkin's superior adaptation featuring Claire Bloom (expertly assisted by Anthony Hopkins, Ralph Richardson, Denholm Elliott, and Edith Evans).

Ibsen, to be sure, was conscious of sexual injustice. In preliminary notes written in 1878, he declared what he wanted his play to express:

A woman cannot be herself in contemporary society; it is an exclusively male society with laws drafted by men, and with counsel and judges who

457

judge feminine conduct from the male point of view. She has committed a crime and she is proud of it because she did it for love of her husband and to save his life. But the husband, with his conventional views of honor, stands on the side of the law and looks at the affair with male eyes.

Clearly that is what the finished play expresses, but perhaps it expresses much more besides. A temptation in teaching Ibsen is to want to reduce his plays to theses. As Richard Gilman says, the very name of Henrik Ibsen calls to mind "cold light, problems, living rooms, instruction" (*The Making of Modern Drama* [New York: Farrar, 1964]).

But is the play totally concerned with the problems of the "new woman"? Ibsen didn't think so. At a banquet given in his honor by the Norwegian Society for Women's Rights in 1898, he frankly admitted,

> I have been more of a poet and less of a social philosopher than people have generally been inclined to believe. I thank you for the toast, but I must decline the honor of consciously having worked for women's rights. I am not even quite sure what women's rights really are. To me it has been a question of human rights.

Elizabeth Hardwick thinks Ibsen made this statement because he had "choler in his bloodstream" and couldn't resist making a put-down before his admirers. She finds Ibsen nevertheless admirable: alone among male writers in having pondered the situation of being born a woman—"To be female: What does it mean?" (*Seduction and Betrayal* [New York: Random, 1974]). Perhaps there is no contradiction in arguing that Ibsen's play is about both women's rights and the rights of all humanity.

Another critic, Norris Houghton, suggests a different reason for the play's timeliness. "Our generation has been much concerned with what it calls the 'identity crisis.' This play anticipates that theme: Ibsen was there ahead of us by ninety years" (*The Exploding Stage* [New York: Weybright, 1971]). Houghton's view may be supported by Nora's declared reasons for leaving Torvald: "If I'm ever to reach any understanding of myself and the things around me, I must learn to stand alone."

The play is structured with classic severity. Its first crisis occurs in Krogstad's initial threat to Nora, but its greatest crisis—the climax—occurs when Helmer stands with the revealing letter open in his hand. We take the major dramatic question to be posed early in Act I, in Nora's admission to Mrs. Linde that she herself financed the trip to Italy. The question is larger than "Will Nora's husband find out her secret?"—for that question is answered at the climax, when Helmer finds out. Taking in more of the play, we might put it, "Will Nora's happy doll house existence be shattered?"—or a still larger question (answered only in the final door slam), "Will Nora's marriage be saved?"

Ibsen's magnificent door slam has influenced many a later dramatist. Have any students seen Stephen Sondheim and Hugh Wheeler's musical *Sweeney Todd, The Demon Barber of Fleet Street* (1979) on stage or on television? At the end, Todd slams a door in the faces of the audience, suggesting that he would gladly cut their throats.

For a dissenting interpretation of Ibsen's play, see Hermann J. Weigand, *The Modern Ibsen* (New York: Dutton, 1960). Weigand thinks Nora at the end unchanged and unregenerate—still a wily coquette who will probably return home the next day to make Torvald toe the line.

A topic for class debate: Is *A Doll's House* a tragedy or a comedy? Much will depend on how students interpret Nora's final exit. Critics disagree: Dorothea Krook thinks the play contains all the requisite tragic ingredients (*Elements of Tragedy* [New Haven: Yale UP, 1969]). Elizabeth Hardwick (cited earlier) calls the play "a comedy, a happy ending—except for the matter of the children."

To prevent North German theater managers from rewriting the play's ending, Ibsen supplied an alternative ending of his own "for use in an emergency." In this alternative version, Nora does not leave the house; instead, Helmer makes her gaze upon their sleeping children. "Oh, this is a sin against myself, but I cannot leave them," says Nora, sinking to the floor in defeat as the curtain falls. Ibsen, however, thought such a change a "barbarous outrage" and urged that it not be used. Students might be told of this alternative ending and be asked to give reasons for its outrageousness.

Citing evidence from the play and from Ibsen's biography, Joan Templeton argues that those critics who fail to see *A Doll's House* as a serious feminist statement have distorted its meaning and unintentionally diminished its worth ("*The Doll House* Backlash: Criticism, Feminism, and Ibsen," PMLA: January 1989).

For a cornucopia of stimulating ideas, see *Approaches to Teaching Ibsen's* A Doll's House, edited by Yvonne Shafer (New York: Modern Language Association, 1985), in the MLA's likable paperback series "Approaches to Teaching Masterpieces of World Literature." June Schlueter writes on using the play as an introduction to drama and notes that, unlike *Oedipus*, the play does not create an inexorable progress toward disaster. "At any point, we feel, justifiably, that disaster might be avoided." Irving Deer recommends approaching the play by considering "how it deals with decaying values and conventions." J. L. Styan urges instructors to have a class act out the play's opening moments, before and after discussing them, so that Ibsen's wealth of suggestive detail will emerge, which students might otherwise ignore. Other commentators supply advice for teaching the play in a freshman honors course, in a course on women's literature, and in a community college. Joanne Gray Kashdan, author of this last essay, reports that one woman student exclaimed on reading the play: "I realized I had been married to Torvald for seven years before I divorced him!"

 MyLiteratureLab Resources. Biography, critical overview, and bibliography for Ibsen. Longman Lecture on *A Doll's House.*

WRITERS ON WRITING

Henrik Ibsen, CORRESPONDENCE ON THE FINAL SCENE OF *A* DOLL'S HOUSE, page 1735

Ibsen's letters are a striking reminder of the great pressure that can be exerted upon even the greatest works of art by a deadly combination of middle-class morality, the profit motive, and an utter lack of imagination. The 1880 letter poignantly reflects his frustration and helplessness in his efforts to protect the integrity of *A Doll's House*, as he is forced to butcher the ending of his own play as the only way to fend off a much greater desecration. The 1891 letter, written from a position of much greater control, is more satisfying, especially in its last two sentences.

Ibsen, of course, is far from being the only author to have been subjected to such treatment, but most writers are lucky enough to be in their graves when it occurs. A century after Shakespeare, a hack called Nahum Tate—who also happened to be the Poet Laureate of Great Britain—rewrote *King Lear* with an ending in which Cordelia survived and married Edgar; a century after that, Charles Lamb charitably referred to Tate's version as "ribald trash." In our own time, there is the 1991 film travesty of *The Scarlet Letter*, in which Demi Moore's Hester Prynne flaunts her independence and cavorts merrily in the forest with Dimmesdale, unrecognizable as the anguished and guilt-ridden protagonist of Hawthorne's classic novel. At the time of the film's release, a cartoon in the *New Yorker* showed a peg-legged sea captain standing on a dock holding a harpoon, with a white whale hanging beside him; the caption read: "The Demi Moore version of *Moby-Dick*."

TRAGICOMEDY AND THE ABSURD

Milcha Sanchez-Scott, THE CUBAN SWIMMER, page 1739

Very little criticism has been written about Milcha Sanchez-Scott, but she is a genuine dramatic talent. *The Cuban Swimmer* is one of the most interesting experimental plays in recent American theater. Sanchez-Scott is also one of the most talented Hispanic playwrights now active. She is not a prolific writer, but her best work is richly conceived and brilliantly executed. Her plays such as *Latina* (1980), *The Cuban Swimmer* (1984), and *Roosters* (1987) are important additions to contemporary American drama.

The Cuban Swimmer is an experimental play in both form and style, but, unlike most experimental drama, it succeeds. This play requires no critical intervention to clarify its aims. Audiences intuitively follow Sanchez-Scott's innovative devices, and the play's cumulative impact is considerable. *The Cuban Swimmer* creates three distinct but interdependent worlds—the swimmer in the water, her family in the boat behind her, and the radio newscasters in the helicopter. Obviously, none of these worlds can be presented realistically on stage. They must be stylized in some way by the director and the designer. This factor highlights the symbolic—almost allegorical—atmosphere of the play, a quality the author both indulges and satirizes.

Perhaps the most interesting aspect of *The Cuban Swimmer* is the bilingual texture of the dialogue. Sanchez-Scott creates two separate linguistic worlds—the mixture of Spanish and English spoken by the Suárez family and the cliché-ridden media English of the newscasters. These two "dialects" also differ in another crucial sense—one is the private language of love, duty, and tradition; the other is the public language of hyperbole and manipulation. Although *The Cuban Swimmer* brilliantly employs the visual potential of theatrical spectacle, the play centers on language. Significantly, one does not need to know Spanish to enjoy the play (although a sizable portion of the text is *en Español*). Sanchez-

Scott carefully positions the Spanish so that a monolingual English-speaker can guess most of it from context while still experiencing the cultural richness of the characters' bilingual existence.

There is so much family drama going on in *The Cuban Swimmer* that an attentive reader might meaningfully examine almost every relationship—across generations, across genders, across cultures. At the center of the family drama is Eduardo Suárez, whose driving ambition is for his daughter Margarita to achieve athletic fame and success. As both coach and father, he projects his own complex set of needs and desires (as father, immigrant, and exile) on Margarita. The play signals some of his desires overtly and others indirectly. His boat, for instance, is named *La Havana*, an ironic moniker for a political exile who runs a salvage yard. His wife is—Sanchez-Scott revels in symbolic possibilities—the former Miss Cuba. His nineteen-year-old daughter is the "Cinderella entry" in the "Wrigley Invitational Women's Swim to Catalina" and probably the only amateur among the professional swimmers.

The ending of *The Cuban Swimmer* deserves commentary. The play has flirted with symbolism from the opening (in a dozen details from the generically named *Abuela* to the religious prayers and oaths spoken by the family), but now it unfolds into a sort of Magic Realism reminiscent of García Márquez. Pushed by her father past endurance, Margarita seems to drown. She certainly disappears. Then she miraculously reappears on the breakers off Santa Catalina to win the race. The radio announcers call her upset victory in language that bespeaks not only media hype but also the Latin Catholic imagery that is woven through the play. Here are the play's final words:

> This is indeed a miracle! It's a resurrection! Margarita Suárez, with a flotilla of boats to meet her, is now walking on the waters, through the breakers . . . onto the beach, with crowds of people cheering her on. What a jubilation! This is a miracle!

Shakespeare's *The Tempest* and Milton's "Lycidas" also seem to be hovering around the play's climax—or, at the very least, the traditional myths of death, sea-change, and resurrection. Sanchez-Scott has so carefully prepared us for the magical final tableau that it seems simultaneously both surprising and inevitable for this daughter of Miss Cuba and the head usher of the Holy Name Society to be reborn miraculously out of the sea to *Santa* Catalina—like Jesus walking on the waves. *The Cuban Swimmer*'s comic tone allows us to view this final scene ironically, but the play's tight symbolic structure also suggests we should take it seriously. That so complex and ambitious an ending could work testifies to Sanchez-Scott's imaginative power.

Sandra Santa Cruz directed a production of *The Cuban Swimmer* in 1997 at the University of Colorado, Boulder. (The photo for *The Cuban Swimmer* that appears in the book was taken from this production.) She wrote an interesting account of her experiences selecting, producing, and directing the play, from which we offer excerpts:

> In selecting a play, I began to search for a work that would look at the Hispanic experience, a community we are not normally accustomed to seeing in American theater. I was disappointed to encounter a number of one-act plays written by Hispanic playwrights whose stories seemed to focus negatively on

Hispanic life. While I am not particularly interested in a one-sided, idealized portrait of the Hispanic experience, I don't agree with those works which portray Hispanics, or any other community, from a demoralizing, degrading perspective. In my opinion, this negative imagery only serves to reinforce and perpetuate harmful stereotypes. Rather, I am interested in works that present a range of choices. I found Milcha Sanchez-Scott's *The Cuban Swimmer* to represent a realistic portrait of a family who oscillates between adversity and triumph; frustration and hope.

From the outset, *The Cuban Swimmer* seemed to capture the imagination, interest and excitement of people throughout the Theater department. It presented a unique set of challenges, the most obvious of which is the setting—the ocean! How would that environment be created? Secondly, it portrays the experience of a Cuban family. How would a cast who was largely unfamiliar with this particular culture and language relate to the language and characterization? Although only a seemingly short one-act play, the events of *The Cuban Swimmer* range from stasis to crisis, from calm to fury. The external world imposes itself through the television media and the natural world through calamity. . . .

In my opinion, *The Cuban Swimmer* explores the fundamental question of identity; one's own image of "self," how that "self" is defined and how that self-identity is tested. It's about the loss of dignity and confidence in oneself and how that affects self-image. The play is driven by the emotional, physical, and spiritual survival of a family whose hopes and dreams have been undermined by a callous external world. Despite the dangers and hardships of the open sea, the real battle lies within the family itself; especially when their image of "self" is shattered.

. . . Ultimately, Margarita finds the inner strength to emerge triumphant; transcending limitations imposed by an external world and in full possession of her self—"self-possessed," so to speak.

WRITERS ON WRITING

Milcha Sanchez-Scott, WRITING THE CUBAN SWIMMER, page 1752

Milcha Sanchez-Scott provides an extremely interesting account of her life and literary development in M. Elizabeth Osborn's valuable anthology *On New Ground: Contemporary Hispanic-American Plays* (New York: Theater Communications Group, 1987). This book also reprints Sanchez-Scott's *Roosters*. The excerpt reprinted in *Literature* describes the author's discovery of herself as a writer as well as the initial inspiration for *The Cuban Swimmer*.

40
Evaluating a Play

This chapter may be particularly useful for students to read before they tackle a play about whose greatness or inferiority you have urgent convictions. The chapter probably doesn't deserve to be dealt with for long in class, but it might lead to a writing assignment: to comment on the merits of any play in the book.

If you assign students to write a play review (see "Reviewing a Play" in the chapter "Writing About a Play"), you might like to have them read this chapter first.

41
Plays for Further Reading

Arthur Miller, DEATH OF A SALESMAN, page 1763

QUESTIONS

1. Miller's opening stage directions call for actors to observe imaginary walls when the action is in the present, and to step freely through walls when the scene is in the past. Do you find this technique of staging effective? Why or why not?

2. Miller has professed himself fascinated by the "agony of someone who has some driving, implacable wish in him" (*Paris Review* interview). What—as we learn in the opening scene—are Willy Loman's obsessions?

3. What case can be made for seeing Linda as the center of the play: the character around whom all events revolve? Sum up the kind of person she is.

4. Seeing his father's Boston side-girl has a profound effect on Biff. How would you sum it up?

5. Apparently Biff's discovery of Willy's infidelity took place before World War II, about 1939. In this respect, does *Death of a Salesman* seem at all dated? Do you think it possible, in the present day, for a son to be so greatly shocked by his father's sexual foibles that the son's whole career would be ruined?

6. How is it possible to read the play as the story of Biff's eventual triumph? Why does Biff, at the funeral, give his brother a "hopeless" look?

7. How are we supposed to feel about Willy's suicide? In what way is Willy, in killing himself, self-deluded to the end?

8. What meanings do you find in the flute music? In stockings—those that Willy gives to the Boston girlfriend and those he doesn't like to see Linda mending? In Biff's sneakers with "University of Virginia" lettered on them (which he later burns)? In seeds and gardening?

9. Of what importance to the play are Charley and his son Bernard? How is their father-son relationship different from the relationship between Willy and Biff?

10. What do you understand Bernard to mean in telling Willy, "sometimes . . . it's better for a man just to walk away"?

11. Explain Charley's point when he argues, "The only thing you got in this world is what you can sell. And the funny thing is that you're a salesman, and you don't know that." (Miller, in his introduction to the play, makes an applicable comment: "When asked what Willy was selling, what was in his bags, I could only reply, 'Himself.'")

12. What do you make of the character of Ben? Do you see him as a realistic character? As a figment of Willy's imagination?

13. Suppose Miller had told the story of Willy and Biff in chronological order. If the incident in the Boston hotel had come early in the play, instead of late, what would have been lost?

14. Another death of another salesman is mentioned in this play: that of Dave Singleman. How does Willy view Singleman's death? Is Willy's attitude our attitude?

15. In a famous speech in the final Requiem, Charley calls a salesman a man who "don't put a bolt to a nut," and Charley recalls that Willy "was a happy man with a batch of cement." Sum up the theme or general truth that Charley states. At what other moments in the play does this theme emerge? Why is Willy, near death, so desperately eager to garden?

16. When the play first appeared in 1949, some reviewers thought it a bitter attack upon the capitalist system. Others found in it social criticism by a writer committed to a faith in democracy and free enterprise. What do you think? Does the play make any specific criticism of society?

17. Miller has stated his admiration for Henrik Ibsen: "One is constantly aware, in watching his plays, of process, change, development." How does this comment apply to *A Doll's House*? Who or what changes or develops in the course of *Death of a Salesman*?

Directed by Elia Kazan, with Lee J. Cobb superbly cast as Willy Loman, *Death of a Salesman* was first performed on Broadway on February 10, 1949. Originally, Miller had wanted to call the play *The Inside of a Head*, and he had planned to begin it with "an enormous face the height of the proscenium arch which would appear and then open up." Fortunately, he settled upon less mechanical methods to reveal Willy's psychology. In later describing what he thought he had done, Miller said he tried to dramatize "a disintegrating personality at that terrible moment when the voice of the past is no longer distant but quite as loud as the voice of the present." *Death of a Salesman* has often been called "poetic" despite its mostly drab speech. At first, Miller had planned to make its language more obviously that of poetry, and in an early draft of the play he wrote much of it in verse. He then turned it into prose on deciding that American actors wouldn't feel at home in verse or wouldn't be able to speak it properly. Miller's account of the genesis of the play is given in his introduction to his *Collected Plays* (New York: Viking, 1959).

In the same introduction, Miller tells why he thinks the play proved effective in the theater but did not make an effective film. Among other reasons, the movie version transferred Willy to actual scenes that in the play he had only imagined, and thus destroyed the play's dramatic tension. It seems more effective—and more disturbing—to show a man losing touch with his surroundings, holding conversations with people who still exist only in his mind. Keeping Willy fixed to the same place throughout the play, while his mind wanders, objectifies Willy's terror. "The screen," says Miller, "is time-bound and earth-bound compared to the stage, if only because its preponderant emphasis is on the visual image. . . . The movie's tendency is always to wipe out what has gone before, and it is thus in constant danger of transforming the dramatic into narrative." Film buffs may care to dispute this observation.

Miller's play is clearly indebted to naturalism. Willy's deepening failure parallels that of his environment: the house increasingly constricted by the city whose growth has killed the elms, prevented anything from thriving, and blotted out human hope—"Gotta break your neck to see a star in this yard." Heredity also works against Willy. As in a Zola novel, one generation repeats patterns of behavior established by its parent. Both Willy and Biff have been less successful than their brothers; presumably both Willy and his "wild-hearted" father were philanderers; both fathers failed their sons and left them insecure. Willy explains, "Dad left when I was such a baby . . . I still feel—kind of temporary about myself."

The play derives also from expressionism. Miller has acknowledged this debt in an interview:

> I know that I was very moved in many ways by German expressionism when I was in school: . . . I learned a great deal from it. I used elements of it that were fused into *Death of a Salesman.* For instance, I purposefully would not give Ben any character, because for Willy he *has* no character—which is, psychologically, expressionist because so many memories come back with a simple tag on them: something represents a threat to you, or a promise. (*Paris Review* 38 [Summer 1966])

Ben is supposed to embody Willy's visions of success, but some students may find him a perplexing character. Some attention to Ben's speeches will show that Ben does not give a realistic account of his career, or an actual portrait of his father, but voices Willy's dream versions. In the last scene before the Requiem, Ben keeps voicing Willy's hopes for Biff and goads Willy on to self-sacrifice. Willy dies full of illusions. Unable to recognize the truth of Biff's self-estimate ("I am not a leader of men"), Willy still believes that Biff will become a business tycoon if only he has $20,000 of insurance money behind him. One truth gets through to Willy: Biff loves him.

Class discussion will probably elicit that Willy Loman is far from being an Oedipus. Compared with an ancient Greek king, Willy is unheroic, a low man as his name suggests. In his mistaken ideals, his language of stale jokes and clichés, his petty infidelity, and his deceptions, he suffers from the smallness of his mind and seems only partially to understand his situation. In killing himself for an insurance payoff that Biff doesn't need, is Willy just a pitiable fool? Pitiable, perhaps, but no mere fool: he rises to dignity through self-sacrifice. "It seems to me," notes Miller (in his introduction to his *Collected Plays*), "that there is of necessity a severe limitation of self-awareness in any character, even the most knowing . . . and more, that this very limit serves to complete the tragedy and, indeed, to make it all possible." (Miller's introduction also protests measuring *Death of a Salesman* by the standards of classical tragedy and finding it a failure.)

In 1983 Miller directed a successful production in Beijing, with Chinese actors. In 1984 the Broadway revival with Dustin Hoffman as Willy, later shown on PBS television, brought the play new currency. Hoffman's performance is available on videocassette from Teacher's Video Company at (800) 262-8837. Miller added lines to fit the short-statured Hoffman: buyers laughing at Willy call him "a shrimp." The revival drew a provocative comment from Mimi Kramer in the *New Criterion* for June 1984: she was persuaded that Miller does not sympathize with Willy Loman and never did.

> Since 1949 certain liberal attitudes—towards aggression, ambition, and competitiveness—have moved from the periphery of our culture to its cen-ter, so that the views of the average middle class Broadway audience are now actually in harmony with what I take to have been Miller's views all along. In 1949 it might have been possible to view Willy as only the victim of a big, bad commercial system. In 1984, it is impossible not to see Miller's own distaste for all Willy's attitudes and petty bourgeois concerns, impossible not to come away from the play feeling that Miller's real judgment of his hero is that he has no soul.

For a remarkable short story inspired by the play, see George Garrett's "The Lion Hunter" in *King of the Mountain* (New York: Scribner, 1957).

A natural topic for writing and discussion, especially for students who have also read *Othello* and a play by Sophocles: How well does Miller succeed in mak-ing the decline and fall of Willy Loman into a tragedy? Is tragedy still possible today? For Miller's arguments in favor of the ordinary citizen as tragic hero, stu-dents may read his brief essay "Tragedy and the Common Man" in the "Writer's Perspective" following the play.

For other comments by Miller and a selection of criticism by various hands, see *Death of a Salesman: Text and Criticism*, ed. Gerald Weales (New York: Viking, 1967). Also useful is *Arthur Miller: A Collection of Critical Essays*, ed. Robert W. Corrigan (Englewood Cliffs, NJ: Prentice, 1969). In *Arthur Miller* (London: Macmillan, 1982), Neil Carson seeks to relate *Death of a Salesman* to the playwright's early life.

> **MLL** *MyLiteratureLab Resources.* Biography, critical overview, and bibliography for Miller. Critical essay on *Death of a Salesman*.

WRITERS ON WRITING

Arthur Miller, TRAGEDY AND THE COMMON MAN, page 1833

QUESTIONS

1. *In arguing that a tragedy can portray an ordinary man, how does Miller find an ally in Sigmund Freud?* See Miller's second paragraph and Freud's comments on Oedipus, page 1354.

2. *According to Miller, what evokes in us "the tragic feeling"? Compare his view with Aristotle's view found on page 1353.* Unlike the Greek theorist, Miller finds the sense of tragedy arising not from pity and fear, but from contemplating a character who would give his life for personal dignity.

3. *In Miller's view, why is tragedy not an expression of pessimism? What outlook does a tragedy express?*

4. *Consider what Miller says about pathos, and try to apply it to* Death of a Salesman. *Does the play persuade you that Willy Loman would have won his battle? That he isn't witless and insensitive? Or is the play (in Miller's terms) not tragic but only pathetic?*

Tennessee Williams, THE GLASS MENAGERIE, page 1836

QUESTIONS

1. How do Amanda's dreams for her daughter contrast with the realities of the Wingfields' day-to-day existence?

2. What suggestions do you find in Laura's glass menagerie? In the glass unicorn?

3. In the cast of characters, Jim O'Connor is listed as "a nice, ordinary, young man." Why does his coming to dinner have such earthshaking implications for Amanda? For Laura?

4. Try to describe Jim's feelings toward Laura during their long conversation in Scene VII. After he kisses her, how do his feelings seem to change?

5. Near the end of the play, Amanda tells Tom, "You live in a dream; you manufacture illusions!" What is ironic about her speech? Is there any truth in it?

6. Who is the main character in *The Glass Menagerie?* Tom? Laura? Amanda? (It may be helpful to review the definition of a protagonist.)

7. Has Tom, at the conclusion of the play, successfully made his escape from home? Does he appear to have fulfilled his dreams?

8. How effective is the device of accompanying the action by projecting slides on a screen, bearing titles and images? Do you think most producers of the play are wise to leave it out?

For Williams's instructions for using the slide projector, see "How to Stage *The Glass Menagerie*" in the "Writers on Writing" following the play. Personally, we think the slide projector a mistake. In trying to justify it, Williams underestimates the quality of his play's spoken lines—but what do your students think?

The gracious world of the old South lives on in Amanda's memories. No doubt its glories shine brighter as the years go by, but all three members of the

Wingfield family, in their drab little apartment, live at several removes from the real world. Laura is so shy that she cannot face strangers, yet her mother enrolls her in a business school where she is, of course, doomed to failure. Next, quite ignoring the fact that Laura has no contact with anyone outside her own family, Amanda decides that her daughter ought to marry and cheerfully sets about finding her a gentleman caller. Some students will want to see Amanda as a silly biddy and nothing more, so it may help to ask: In what ways is she admirable? (See Williams's initial, partially admiring description of her in the cast of characters.)

A kindly, well-intentioned young man, Jim O'Connor is a self-styled go-getter, a pop psychologist. Like Biff Loman in *Death of a Salesman*, Jim is a high school hero whose early promise hasn't materialized. He was acquainted with Laura in school but now remembers her only when prompted. Laura's wide-eyed admiration for him flatters Jim's vanity, and in her presence he grows expansive. Gradually, Laura awakens in him feelings of warmth and protectiveness, as well as a sense that her fragility bespeaks something as precious and rare as her glass unicorn. It is with genuine regret that he shatters her tremulous, newly risen hopes with the revelation that he is engaged to be married to Betty, a young woman as unremarkable as himself.

Laura's collection of glass animals objectifies her fragility, her differentness, her removal from active life. Significantly, the unicorn is her favorite. "Unicorns, aren't they extinct in the modern world?" asks Jim; and he adds, a few lines later, "I'm not made out of glass." When Jim dances with Laura and accidentally breaks off the unicorn's horn, the mythical creature becomes more like the common horses that surround him, just as Laura, by the very act of dancing, comes a few steps closer to being like everyone else. Although Jim can accept the broken unicorn from Laura as a souvenir, he cannot make room in his life for her. Her fleeting brush with reality does not in the end alter her uniqueness or release her from her imprisonment.

Amanda's charge that Tom manufactures illusions seems a case of the pot calling the kettle black. As we know from Amanda's flighty talk and far-fetched plans for Laura, the mother herself lives in a dream world. But she is right about Tom. A would-be poet, a romantic whose imagination has been fired by Hollywood adventure movies, Tom pays dues to the Merchant Seamen's union instead of paying the light bill. So desperate is he to make his dreams come true, he finally runs away to distant places, like his father before him. In truth, each character in the play has illusions—even Jim, who dreams of stepping from his warehouse job into a future as a millionaire television executive. And as Tom's commentaries point out, at the time of the play's action all Americans seemed to be dazzled by illusions, ignoring the gathering threat of World War II. "In Spain, there was Guernica! But here there was only hot swing music and liquor, dance halls, bars, and movies, and sex that hung in the gloom like a chandelier and flooded the world with brief, deceptive rainbows."

For a challenging study of the play, see Roger B. Stein, "*The Glass Menagerie* Revisited: Catastrophe without Violence," *Western Humanities Review* 18 (Spring 1964):141–53. (It is also available in *Tennessee Williams: A Collection of Critical Essays,* ed. Stephen S. Stanton [Englewood Cliffs, NJ: Prentice, 1977].) Stein finds in the play themes of both social and spiritual catastrophe: the failure of both Christianity and the American dream. Although some of the play's abundant Christian symbolism and imagery would seem just decoration, students may enjoy looking for it. Scene V, in which Tom tells his mother that Laura will have a gentleman caller, is titled on the screen "Annunciation." Laura says she has dreaded to confess she has left business school because her mother, when disappointed, wears a look "like the picture of Jesus' mother." Amanda is also identified with the music of "Ave Maria." When Tom comes home drunk, he tells Laura of seeing the stage magician Malvolio, an Antichrist who can escape from a nailed coffin and can transform water to wine (also to beer and whiskey). Jim O'Connor is another unsatisfactory Savior: he comes to supper on a Friday night and (symbolically?) is given fish, but unlike the Christ, he can work no deliverance. Laura is described as if she were a saint, or at least a contemplative. When she learns that Jim is engaged to Betty, "the holy candles in the altar of Laura's face have been snuffed out." Compare Williams's instructions to lighting technicians in his production notes:

> Shafts of light are focused on selected areas or actors, sometimes in contradistinction to what is the apparent center. For instance, in the quarrel scene between Tom and Amanda, in which Laura has no active part, the clearest pool of light is on her figure. This is also true of the supper scene. The light upon Laura should be distinct from the others, having a peculiar pristine clarity such as light used in early religious portraits of female saints or madonnas.

Most suggestive of all, Williams keeps associating candles with lightning. Amanda's candelabrum, from the altar of the Church of the Heavenly Rest, had been warped when the church was struck by lightning. And when Tom, in his final speech, calls on Laura to blow her candles out, he declares that "nowadays the world is lit by lightning." The playwright suggests, according to Stein, that a hard, antireligious materialism now prevails. (At least, this line of reasoning may be worth an argument.)

The character of Laura apparently contains traits of Williams's sister, Rose. Although the painfully shy Laura is not an exact portrait of his sister (Laura "was like Miss Rose only in her inescapable 'difference,'" Williams has written), the name of Rose suggests Laura's nickname, "Blue Roses." A young woman with "lovely, heartbreaking eyes," Rose felt acute anxiety in male company. She was pressed by her mother to make a painful social debut at the Knoxville Country Club. For a time she was courted by a junior executive, an ambitious young man who soon suspended his attentions. After the breakup, Rose suffered from mysterious illnesses, showed symptoms of withdrawal, and eventually was committed to the Missouri State Asylum. Williams tells her story in his *Memoirs* (New York: Doubleday, 1975) 116–28. Like Tom Wingfield, apparently Williams as a young man was a restless dreamer and aspiring writer who left home to wander the country.

In his own memoir, William Jay Smith, who knew Williams in St. Louis as a fellow college student at Washington University, remarks on the background of the play:

> I am frequently amused by those who take Tom's autobiographical projection of his family in *The Glass Menagerie* literally and picture him as having inhabited a run-down, seedy old house, if not a downright hovel. The house on Arundel Place, with its Oriental rugs, silver, and comfortable, if not lux-

urious furniture, was located in an affluent neighborhood. . . . Our entire bungalow on Telegraph Road would have fitted comfortably into one or two of its rooms. Mrs. Williams presided over it as if it were an antebellum mansion. (*Army Brat* [New York: Persea, 1980] 190)

An excellent reading of the complete play with Montgomery Clift, Julie Harris, and Jessica Tandy is available on audio cassette from Caedmon (A-301). Additionally, Paul Newman's 1987 version of *The Glass Menagerie*, starring Joanne Woodward and John Malkovich, with Karen Allen and James Naughton, is available on DVD.

 MyLiteratureLab Resources. Biography, critical overview, and bibliography for Williams.

WRITERS ON WRITING

Tennessee Williams, HOW TO STAGE *THE GLASS MENAGERIE*, page 1883

QUESTIONS

1. How does Williams feel about theatrical "realism"?

2. How does Williams argue for his use of the slide projector? If you were producing *The Glass Menagerie*, would you follow the playwright's instructions and use the projector, or leave it out?

3. What other antirealistic devices would Williams employ? Would you expect them to be effective?

42
New Voices in American Drama

This chapter presents a small cross-section of contemporary American plays to supplement the main selections in the book. The section can be taught as a unit to present new developments in American theater, or instructors can use individual plays to illustrate themes discussed elsewhere in the Drama section. Rita Dove's reimagining of the Oedipus myth in *The Darker Face of the Earth* shows both the timelessness of the great stories and their inexhaustible freshness. Beth Henley's *Am I Blue* is a funny and touching depiction of two vulnerable young people in which, like Williams's *The Glass Menagerie*, many students will see themselves. David Hwang's one-act play *The Sound of a Voice* provides an additional selection for "The Modern Theater," especially in demonstrating contemporary alternatives to realistic theater. Terrence McNally's *Andre's Mother* could serve as an ideal vehicle for an additional discussion on the elements of a play in Chapter 35, "Reading a Play." Less than three pages long, this powerful vignette is guaranteed to provoke a lively classroom discussion, and its brevity permits it to be read aloud in class without taking up more than a few minutes. August Wilson's *Fences* also makes an excellent text for a discussion of "Modern Theater," since, like Miller's *Death of Salesman*, it shows that tragic grandeur can be found in the humblest of lives. Critical statements by the playwrights appear in the "Writers on Writing" feature that follows each play. Finally, these plays provide students with potential subjects for research papers. Possible paper topics are suggested in the notes on individual plays.

Rita Dove, THE DARKER FACE OF THE EARTH, page 1886

This writer (Michael Palma) recalls a college classmate, years ago, who was astounded to discover that Johann Wolfgang von Goethe had written a play on the Faust theme despite the fact that Christopher Marlowe's *Doctor Faustus* had been in existence for more than two centuries. He was unable to wrap his mind around the idea that someone would come along and write a play that someone else had already written. He might have had an easier time with the concept nowadays, when movie remakes are common and there is a tradition, stretching from *All in the Family* to *The Office*, of British television series being refashioned for the American market. Needless to say, the tradition of adapting existing plots is much older than that. After all, virtually every one of Shakespeare's plays was derived from some other written source, just as his own works have been the basis for many adaptations, ranging from Jane Smiley's variation on *King Lear* in her Pulitzer Prize-winning novel *A Thousand Acres* to the highly imaginative recasting of *The Tempest* in the 1956 science fiction film *Forbidden Planet*. In fact, it is only in the last couple of centuries that originality—as we understand the term to mean the creation of one's characters and plots totally out of one's own imagination—has come to be expected, and even demanded, in works of literature.

There is a kind of fitness in the fact that Rita Dove chose Sophocles' *Oedipus the King* as a model for her verse drama *The Darker Face of the Earth*, in that Sophocles, like his contemporaries, based his own dramas on myths and legends that would already have been familiar to the Athenian play-going public. In fact, the story goes that Euripides, fearing that the material of his new drama was not as familiar to the audience as was customary, once sent an actor onto the stage to tell the audience the entire plot of the play it was about to watch. Needless to say, any performer doing that today, given contemporary ticket prices, would be taking his life in his hands. But earlier audiences were less concerned with the mere details of *what* was happening than they were with the larger issues of *why* it was happening, of what the protagonists' actions revealed about their personalities and their value systems, and about human nature and experience, human possibility and limitation. A sophisticated audience will take each new reworking of a classic plot as a challenge: What can *this* writer do to make the old tale new again, how can he or she use the story to mine new insights?

The relationship between *Oedipus the King* and *The Darker Face of the Earth* is a fruitful and illuminating one. The moral pollution of the Theban ruling family, externalized by the plague that has afflicted the city, is an apt template for the social and moral enormity of slavery and the degradation that it inflicted upon everyone it touched. The familial violence and sexual transgression of *Oedipus* are reflected in the brutal treatment and predatory exploitation that were all but built into the slave system. And in both plays the concept of doom is an inextricable combination of personal failings and the individual's helplessness in the grip of larger forces he cannot control or even fully comprehend; as the Doctor tells Amalia very early in Dove's play, "Some mistakes you live with until you die" (Prologue).

The Darker Face of the Earth is not a "retelling" of *Oedipus the King* in the strict sense of providing a one-to-one correspondence in which every character and action in the one play are reproduced in the other. There are notable differences between the two works, perhaps most notably in their endings: at the conclusion of Dove's play, Augustus is carried off in triumph (of a sort), rather than being banished in disgrace. At the beginning of Act II, Dove gives us what might be seen as a sly justification for the many changes called for in retrofitting *Oedipus* for an antebellum milieu, when she has Louis, who has long since sealed himself in his astronomical pursuits, make the following observation:

> Every night at the same hour, each star appears
> slightly to the west of its previous position.
> Scientists calculate that the 12 houses of the zodiac
> have shifted so radically since ancient times,
> their relation to each other
> may now signify completely different portents.
>
> (Act I, Scene i, page 1926)

In addition to differences, however, there are of course some very significant similarities between the two works. Dove hints at this connection at the outset, in the stage directions at the beginning of her play: "On occasion, the slaves comment upon the play somewhat in the manner of a Greek chorus." And the backbone of her narrative is of course the broad outline of the Oedipus story— her protagonist is maimed and taken away shortly after his birth, is raised in ignorance of his true parentage, and returns to unwittingly kill his father and cohabit with his mother.

Admittedly, Augustus Newcastle, despite his dignity, his regal bearing, and his sometimes lordly manner, is a slave, not a ruler. Nonetheless, Dove does a great deal to establish parallels between the two protagonists:

> *Scipio:* ... Au-gus-tus?
> Ain't never heard that one before.
> What kind of name is that?
> *Augustus:* The name of a king.　　　　(Act I, Scene iii, page 1904)

Like Oedipus—and with the same element of dramatic irony—Augustus regards himself as a child of fortune and a favorite of the gods:

> *Augustus:* ... Why, your Scylla's a baby
> compared to the voodoo chiefs in the islands.
> They can kill you with a puff of smoke
> from their pipes—if you believe in them.
> Take me: I've been cursed enough times
> to bring down a whole fleet of ships
> around me—but here I sit, high and dry.
> So I guess they must be saving me
> for something special.　　(Act I, Scene iv, pages 1910–1911)

Notice especially in the above passage the phrase "if you believe in them": again like Oedipus, Augustus is sufficiently proud, sufficiently persuaded of his own majesty and exceptionalism, to flirt with the notion that the laws of destiny that govern ordinary human beings need not concern him.

Perhaps the most important difference between the two plays lies in the emphasis placed on passion and romantic love in *The Darker Face of the Earth*, which is reflective of the much greater emphasis placed on these values in our culture than in that of ancient Greece. In *Oedipus the King*, Iocastê's thematic function (as opposed to her significance to the plot) does not go much beyond abetting and instigating Oedipus's blasphemous assertions. Amalia is a much richer and more complex personality, and she has a correspondingly greater role to play. She is both a symbol of and a commentator on the endless intricacies of the master-slave relationship, and in her erotic dance of death with Augustus she contributes much more meaningfully than Iocastê to the play's central crisis.

Where Oedipus is largely concerned with unfolding and understanding long-ago events he is now powerless to change, Augustus finds himself in a very fluid situation in which he still has the ability—despite the baleful destiny that has hung over him since his birth—to make self-defining choices. In his case, those choices are severely complicated by his emotions, not only in his tangled relationship with Amalia, but also because of his feelings for Phebe (and hers for him)—issues that are given their most direct engagement in the dialogue between Augustus and Phebe at the beginning of Act II, Scene vii. A bit later, just before he is all but swept away by the play's climactic revelations and events, Augustus states his dilemma starkly:

> Everything was so simple before!
> Hate and be hated!
> But this—love or freedom—
> is the devil's choice.   (Act II, Scene vii, page 1950)

"Reading the Scars: Rita Dove's *The Darker Face of the Earth*," a long and detailed essay by Theodora Carlisle, appeared in the Spring 2000 issue of *African American Review*; it can be read on the Internet at <www.findarticles.com>. The entire program for the 2001 production of the play at the University of South Carolina is available by searching the play title at <www. cas.sc.edu/thea>. And you can see a number of full-color production stills from its 2006 presentation at Pierce College by searching the play title at <www.pierce.ctc.edu>.

—Michael Palma

Rita Dove, THE INSPIRATION FOR *THE DARKER FACE OF THE EARTH*, page 1958

In this interview with the publisher of *The Darker Face of the Earth*, Rita Dove gives an absorbing insight into the circumstances that led to the creation of the play. Her innately poetic sensibility is on full display as she vividly re-creates her view of Jerusalem in late-afternoon light and her sense of the majesty and the tragedy of the ancient world. As she makes clear, what drew her to the theme—and what she sought to communicate in her own text—was the feeling of overwhelming and all-pervading doom, an inexorable destiny that crushes all possibilities of love, happiness, and fulfillment.

Beth Henley, AM I BLUE, page 1959

It is no wonder that Beth Henley's *Am I Blue* has been extremely popular with high school and college drama groups, not only because of its brevity, small cast, and relatively uncomplicated sets, but especially because in its developing relationship between an extroverted, needy high school girl and an awkward, defensive college boy, students can easily see themselves and their own most intimate and often unspoken concerns. Henley's first play, written when she herself was an undergraduate, *Am I Blue* has proved to be a template for many of her subsequent plays and film scripts, in which quirky and outrageous characters clash as they grope toward understanding, and tart and often cutting observations mask an underlying tenderness and longing for acceptance.

For such a young writer, and one who had not written a play before, Henley shows a remarkable sureness and economy in presenting her two main characters. From the very outset of the play, even before a line of dialogue has been spoken, everything about Ashbe—the way she is dressed, her sitting down at a stranger's table and covering herself with his raincoat, even her name—suggests a flamboyant (and somewhat forced) unconventionality and a desperate desire for attention. Her remarks about Miss Marcey and Mr. Groves establish her affinity for (one might say, identification with) odd and outcast individuals. John Polk seems to be her total opposite, not only withdrawn and hostile but also strongly resistant to the concept of individuality. Notice how frequently, in the first page or so of the play, he resorts to generalizations: "any thief"; "one of those kleptomaniacs"; "most infants"; "some slum kid"; "Everyone knows." At some level, he seems to be trying to make sense of the unfamiliar by fitting it into familiar categories and trying to find acceptance through his own acceptance of the values that have been passed on to him. Her conclusions about the bars and bordellos of the neighborhood seem based on experience and observation; his, about her as well as about how one is supposed to live in this world, are mostly received opinions.

Ashbe seems imaginative and expansive in contrast to his literal-mindedness and reserve. Their differences are neatly pointed out by their separate reactions to finding a hat in the street. When Ashbe suggests that John Polk wear it, he says, "No, thanks, you don't know who's worn it before"; her response is: "That makes it all the more exciting." When she makes extravagant guesses about the previous owner and invites him to join in, he refuses, adding, "Anyway what's the good of guessing? I mean you'll never really know." Later, when Ashbe tells John Polk that food coloring "makes a drink all the more aesthetic," he responds: "No thank you, just plain water." One should be careful, however, not to overemphasize this detail to the point of idealizing her character. What Henley is doing in *Am I Blue* is psychologically richer and thematically more complex than the usual *Pretty Woman* sort of plot in which a charming free spirit transforms an unlikable stiff. She is, after all, an adolescent, and her romanticizing is at least in part a function of her immaturity; nowhere is this more clearly shown than when she says that "it really wouldn't be bad" if he got her pregnant and then goes on about what "wonderful fun" it would be to raise the baby.

In an earlier exchange, when John Polk tells her, "You're mixed up. You're probably one of those people that live in a fantasy world," Ashbe replies: "I do not. I accept reality as well as anyone." How we interpret this comment of hers may prove to be a key to much of what is happening in the play. It seems insufficient to write it off simply as a demonstration of her lack of self-awareness. With "as well as anyone" Henley may very well be suggesting that every human being's ability to accept reality is a tricky and precarious business, that we all need to dream, and even at times to fantasize. Obviously, Ashbe goes a bit far in this direction, but, just as obviously, John Polk doesn't go nearly far enough:

JOHN POLK. . . . Dad feels I should go to business school first; you know, so I'll become, well, management-minded. . . .

ASHBE. Is that what you really want to do?

JOHN POLK. I don't know. It would probably be as good as anything else I could do. . . . Sure, it'll be a ball.

ASHBE. I'd hate to have to be management-minded. (1968)

While they are drawing and cutting paper hats earlier on, John Polk says, with some irony and perhaps a bit of condescension, "It's kind of you to give my creative drives such freedom." Irony aside, this is of course exactly what Ashbe is doing throughout the play, giving John Polk the freedom to acknowledge his real self, as opposed to the expectations of his father, his fraternity brothers, and just about everyone else. Henley keeps this process credible as the play unfolds, with plenty of bickering, backtracking, and name-calling between the two even as they continue to reveal more of their true feelings to one another. The turning point comes when Ashbe's father telephones just as John Polk is about to storm out of the apartment. Hearing the hurt and vulnerability expressed in her half of the phone conversation arouses his sympathy as well as an awareness that his problems and confusions are not unique to him (a theme that students will likely be responsive to, and one well worth stressing to them). From this point on, they become much more open with one another, both confessing their lack of sexual experience, and more accepting of one another. When she says, "I've probably been put in the wrong world. I can see that now," he tells her that "You're fine in this world." Both characters have moved from their original extremes and met happily in the middle ground where their communicating and coming together must take place. His culminating admission, that his refusal to make love to her is not rejection but a deeper acceptance, is telling: his own natural instincts are much more decent and sensitive than the values he has been pressured to affirm.

WRITERS ON WRITING

Beth Henley, A PLAYWRIGHT IS BORN, page 1975

Beth Henley's introduction to her *Collected Plays* provides many noteworthy observations about her work and her characters. This brief reminiscence about *Am I Blue* will be interesting to any student considering becoming a writer. It may particularly intrigue students that Henley originally wrote the work, her first play, in a college playwriting class.

David Henry Hwang, THE SOUND OF A VOICE, page 1976

David Hwang's short play *The Sound of a Voice* is simple, direct, and deeply mysterious. The play unfolds like an eerie folktale. A nameless man visits an enigmatic female hermit who is reputed to be a witch. Although they both recognize that they are potential foes, they fall into a doomed love affair. Eventually, one of them is destroyed. Hwang's treatment combines elements from both Eastern and Western traditions. *The Sound of a Voice* borrows many features from Nō drama, the courtly theater of Japan. Despite their elaborate and allusive language, Nō plays have simple narrative structures and focus mostly on the interaction of two principal characters (one of whom is usually a ghost haunting a mysterious locale). Like Nō drama, *The Sound of a Voice* prominently deploys music to build a brooding atmosphere rife with emotive impact and symbolic significance. *The Sound of a Voice* also resembles the short symbolist plays of William Butler Yeats, J. M. Synge, and August Strindberg. Yeats's plays, which masterfully combine elements of Nō drama with English verse tragedy to create a poetic form for folk material, seem particularly influential on *The Sound of a Voice*.

The main reason to outline the rich literary background of *The Sound of a Voice* is not that the play needs such explication. Hwang's play wears its learning lightly; the influences have all been assimilated into a remarkably straightforward and accessibly contemporary style. The importance of Hwang's diverse sources is to demonstrate the complex heritage of an Asian American playwright. There is sometimes a temptation to reduce the work of minority writers to mere autobiography, but in this short play Hwang consciously draws from a Japanese genre that has nothing directly to do with either the Chinese heritage of his family or the historical traditions of the author's native language, English. Hwang himself has complained about how narrowly he has been stereotyped as a writer:

> I first became aware of the simplistic nature of this stereotyping when I did the two Japanese plays *The Sound of a Voice* and *The House of Sleeping Beauties*. I thought this work was a departure because these were the first plays I'd written that didn't deal with being Chinese American, with race and assimilation; I felt that they were tragic love stories. Yet they were not perceived as being a departure, because they had Asian actors. (*Contemporary Authors*, ed. Susan M. Trosky, vol. 132 [Detroit: Gale Research])

While *The Sound of a Voice* draws from Hwang's consciousness as an Asian writer, it is also a work that grows out of the traditions of American experimental theater.

QUESTIONS

1. *How does Hwang's names for his two characters ("Man" and "Woman") affect our reading of the play?* Although the author lets the woman's name (Hanako) slip into the stage directions, he otherwise refers to them only by their generic titles of Man and Woman. The two characters never give one another their true names but only self-evident fictions (Yokiko, Man Who Fears Silence, and Man Who Fears Women). By refusing to name them, Hwang encourages us to see them as archetypal or symbolic characters. The visitor is all men, and Hanako is, implicitly, womankind. Their story, by extension, bears some symbolic significance to all male-female relations. When the Woman suggests "Man Who Fears Women" as a name for her visitor, she underscores the symbolic nature of their relationship. The action generally seems not to be realistic in detail but symbolic in import. Hwang is not trying to recreate the texture of daily reality as a naturalistic dramatist might; instead, he attempts to portray a mythic drama—a folk legend come to life. Although the action of Hwang's play takes place in Japan, one could easily imagine a staged production of it set in rural New England or on the Louisiana bayou. All you would have to change is to substitute a Vermont fiddle or Cajun violin for the *shakuhachi*.

2. *Why does the man visit the woman in her remote house?* We never know *exactly* why he visits, but we gradually learn that he came on a quest or dare to kill her. The woman tells of other men who arrived because "great glory was to be had by killing the witch in the woods." He initially believes (as do the nearby villagers) that she is a witch who enchants and destroys the men who visit her home. He even imagines (scene 7) that her flowers contain the

trapped spirits of her previous lovers. As the man falls in love with her, his desire to kill her disappears, but he is nonetheless plagued by guilt at his failure to keep to his quest.

3. *The woman is unsure of the length of time since her last visitor. What effect does that uncertainty have on our sense of the dramatic situation?* This detail contributes to the mythic quality of the action. It seems possible that she is a supernatural being unaffected by human mortality; or, perhaps more to the point, that this particular plot is played again and again between her and generations of young men. Moreover, at the very least, it adds to the sense of mystery that pervades the play.

4. *Does this play have a central conflict?* Like Japanese etiquette, the action of Hwang's play is understated; the real drama is implied mostly in the details. Both the man and the woman understand from the opening scene that they are locked in a potentially mortal combat, but neither of them directly admits that knowledge. Everything concerning the central conflict emerges slowly—and often indirectly—at least insofar as the audience is concerned. But Hwang's deliberately low-key style eventually intensifies the dramatic tension as it creates a heavy sense of mystery we become anxious to resolve. The central dramatic conflict is the symbolic battle that the man and woman play out. The woman seems to win by removing the man's fears and arousing love in him. Ironically, however, the man, who could not defeat her by force, manages to destroy her by love. His decision to abandon her after their professions of devotion drives her to suicide.

5. *When we read a play, we focus mostly on the text. When we see a play in the theater, however, we experience it visually as well as verbally. What nonverbal elements play important roles in Hwang's play? The Sound of a Voice* illustrates the importance of nonverbal elements in achieving theatrical effects. Two complete scenes (4 and 6), as well as the conclusion, are played without words. Another episode (scene 8) depends on a visual trick (the man balancing his chin on the point of a sword) to create dramatic tension. Likewise, one of the central contests between the two characters is a physical fight with wooden sticks. The play's finale is a visual tableau. Music also plays an important role in establishing and maintaining the mood of the play. Students will be able to find other nonverbal elements of the play. Hwang reminds us of the importance of spectacle, even in a modest, two-character play. A play works by total representation of a drama, not by the words alone.

There are a great many possible topics for papers based on Hwang's play. Students could trace a single image from the play (flowers would be an obvious candidate) and discuss its significance. Another interesting notion would be to discuss the use of music in the play: what does it contribute to the atmosphere and tone that words could not? Another good subject would be to examine the two scenes in the play (4 and 6) that are played without words: what effect do they have on the structure and feeling of the drama? Students could also discuss the end of *The Sound of a Voice*: is the woman's death tragic? The theme of suicide would be an illuminating topic because both characters contemplate the idea, and the woman hangs herself at the end of the play. Finally, students could compare and contrast *The Sound of a Voice* with one of its models—either a Nō drama or one of Yeats's short plays. Nō plays are generally very brief (around ten pages). Arthur Waley's classic *The Nō Plays of Japan* (New York: Grove, 1957) provides an excellent starting point. Any play by the most celebrated master of the form, Seami, such as *Tsunemasa* or *Kumasaka* (both in the Waley book), would work well. Several of Yeats's short plays provide excellent contrasts to Hwang's piece, most notably *Deidre*, *The Only Jealousy of Emer*, and *Purgatory*.

 MyLiteratureLab Resources. Biography, critical overview, and bibliography for Hwang. Critical essay on *The Sound of a Voice*.

WRITERS ON WRITING

David Henry Hwang, MULTICULTURAL THEATER, page 1991

QUESTIONS

1. What events contributed to Hwang's heightened consciousness of his Asian roots?

2. What importance does Hwang feel mythology has in drama?

3. On what does Hwang think the notion of "ethnic theater" depends?

Terrence McNally, ANDRE'S MOTHER, page 1992

One of the major genres of contemporary American theater has been the AIDS play—a drama that explores the painful social, moral, and personal issues that came into public prominence in the epidemic of Acquired Immune Deficiency Syndrome. Terrence McNally examines these issues with his characteristic mixture of humor and humanity in *Andre's Mother,* a dramatic vignette of extraordinary compression. At the center of this compelling scene is the title character, a role without words. Students find this play provocative. Not only does it address a highly visible public issue, but the play's literary structure focuses the reader's attention on puzzling out what goes on inside Andre's Mother's mind.

QUESTIONS

1. *What relation does Andre's Mother have to the other characters in the play?* Her only connection is through her dead son, but they come from a part of his life she never knew—or at least never acknowledged. She has never met the other three people, although they played important roles in her son's life. She seems to be isolated in her grief and her unspoken disapproval of her son's homosexuality. Arthur, Penny, and Cal are articulate, sophisticated, witty people. Andre's Mother is neither urbane nor worldly (Andre is described by Cal as a "country boy"). There is a social distance between her and them. McNally portrays her intense isolation, confusion, and initial resentment through her silence.

2. *Andre's Mother, the title character of this piece, never says a word in the course of the play. What thoughts and emotions do you think she experiences in the final scene? Give reasons for your opinions.* The dramatic point of this vignette is to make the audience project their feelings onto the silent, suffering mother. McNally does not portray her in an entirely positive light. She refuses to speak, even as Cal desperately begs her for some response. She has also apparently never acknowledged that her son was gay. Her presumed disapproval made it impossible for Andre to speak to her either about his homosexuality or illness, and yet we feel the intensity and isolation of her grief. All we know about her feelings, however, are her external actions, which in the final scene appear understandably ambiguous. She wants to hold on to the balloon. She starts to let it go, then pulls it back to kiss it before finally letting it sail away. Her fixed stare on the balloon, however, suggests she cannot let go of her son or break his "last earthly ties" with her. However harshly we may have judged her earlier in the play, we are probably touched by her evident love and pain in this final moment.

3. *Is the balloon a symbol in* Andre's Mother? *If so, what does it represent?* This becomes the dominant symbol of McNally's vignette. Cal explains what he considers the balloons' significance. "They represent the soul," he explains. "When you let go, it means you're letting his soul ascend to Heaven. That you're willing to let go. Breaking the last earthly ties." It seems uncertain, however, whether Andre's Mother would share Cal's interpretation. When she finally lets go of her balloon, her slow, agonized gestures seem to confirm the permanence of her earthly ties. A more focused interpretation of the balloon is probably in order. The balloons may be intended to represent all the things that Cal claims, but they also come to symbolize the relationship each character has with the deceased. Arthur and Penny let go first; they knew him least well. Each expresses his or her personal perspective on him. Cal's farewell is more deeply complicated, especially since he speaks it to Andre's silent Mother. One might even suggest that the Mother's painful silence suggests all that went unspoken between her and her son. The balloons also become surrogates for Andre, whose presence haunts the play he never enters. Can your students suggest other symbolic associations of the balloons?

A good writing exercise would be to have students create a final speech for Andre's Mother. Ask them to write 500 words for her character to speak alone on the stage about her reactions to Andre's death. An alternative version of the assignment would be to have her speak to Andre's spirit, as if he could hear her.

MLL *MyLiteratureLab Resources.* Video clip of *Andre's Mother.*

WRITERS ON WRITING

Terrence McNally, HOW TO WRITE A PLAY, page 1995

McNally offers invaluable advice to all aspiring authors: the best way to become a writer is to write. He expresses himself with a light touch, but he puts forward important ideas. Writing is a process, McNally asserts, that does not fully begin until one writes. Many students labor under the misconception that inspiration happens entirely away from one's desk or keyboard. McNally's sensible comments not only illuminate his own creative process, they provide students with a helpful perspective on their own writing.

August Wilson, FENCES, page 1996

Shortly after August Wilson's death in October 2005, the political commentator and sportswriter Dave Zirin published a tribute to Wilson that included these observations:

> [I]n 1988 when I saw *Fences* on Broadway, all I knew was that I was 14 years old and thought going to a play would be as much fun as a shot glass of morphine. At the time, I was far more interested in [New York Mets Centerfielder] Mookie Wilson than August Wilson. I settled into my seat and assumed what anthropologists call "the slouch of the sulking brat." I had no idea that my every conception of theater, sports, and racism, was about to be turned on its head. . . .
>
> Eventually Troy, an absolute black hole of bitterness, almost swallows the Maxson family whole, pushing away his wife, child and friends. Troy can't overcome the contradiction in his life: the journey from superstar to picking up trash for nickels and dimes. He can't stand the thought of Cory getting abused by the athletic industrial complex in the same way. But he also can't stand the thought of Cory succeeding where he failed—just because he happened to be born "twenty years too early." He also cheats on his wife Rose because he hates the idea that she could love him for who he is—and that she is the best he could do, describing his marriage to her as "living for eighteen years on first base."
>
> The title of the play is illustrative of Wilson's brilliance. Troy spends considerable time on stage building a fence for their modest home at the constant prodding of Rose. Her desire to see it built becomes an openly symbolic issue that the characters comment on with insight and sadness which rescues it from being a ham-handed symbolic device. His friend Bono remarks that "Some people build fences to keep people out. Others build fences to keep people in. Rose wants to hold onto you all. She loves you." Troy also makes direct reference to the fence. To him it's the last line of defense against the hellhounds nipping at his heels.
>
> But the word "fences" recalls something else, never mentioned explicitly in the play. "Fences" is baseball slang for the outfield wall that must be cleared for a home run. The phrase "swing for the fences" or "clear the fences" is derived from this. Troy, who could clear the fences with ease on the field, feels trapped by them in his life. Sports, which held the promise of escape, instead fenced him in and swallowed him whole, and he attempts to take his family with him. In the play's final scenes, we see that his family has more strength than Troy ever gave them credit for—strength to withstand even his pull toward self-destruction. ("Tribute to August Wilson: Breaking Down Fences," *Common Dreams News Center*, 15 Oct. 2005 <http://www.commondreams.org/views05/1014-21.htm>)

Zirin begins by touching on something that we hope—and expect—will be reflected in your experience of teaching *Fences*—that the universality of Wilson's themes, his genius for character creation, and the sheer emotional power of the play will, in the end, win over even the most resistant and unsophisticated of adolescents. Zirin gives a succinct discussion of the meaning of the play's title and the varied layers of its function and symbolic resonance in the course of the drama; we may add to his examples the very beginning of Act 1, Scene 2, when Rose stands in the yard hanging the laundry on the line and singing, "Jesus, be a fence all around me every day / Jesus, I want you to protect me as I travel on my way."

Also noteworthy is Zirin's observation that "his family has more strength than Troy ever gave them credit for—strength to withstand even his pull toward self-destruction." Troy is far from being the only character in the play who has had to deal with disappointment, frustration, or adversity in his life: Rose speaks quite eloquently, both to Troy and after his death, about her own loneliness and the limited choices in her life; Lyons tells of the emptiness inside him that can only be eased by his music; and Bono offers a moving reminiscence of how he has tried throughout his life to compensate for the absence of his father. Yet each of them remains gentle-souled and compassionate throughout the play, and none of them lets unhappiness or thwarted hopes congeal into bitterness and anger, as Troy increasingly does. (We might also mention, however, as others have pointed out, that at the end of the play every adult member of Troy's family has either been swallowed up by or sought refuge in some sort of institution— Gabriel in the mental hospital, Lyons in the workhouse, Rose in the church, and Cory in the Marines; quite clearly, Troy has played a major role in driving them into these situations, either through active intervention, in the case of Gabriel, or in his treatment of them.)

In the second paragraph of the excerpt, Zirin addresses the play's central concern—the frustrations of Troy Maxson's life and the effect of those frustrations on his attitudes, his behavior, and his dealings with everyone around him. And, given the terms in which he casts his brief discussion, Zirin also touches on what may be the central issue of *Fences* as far as class presentation is concerned—the great, perhaps even insuperable difficulty of trying to make Troy seem an admirable or even sympathetic character in the eyes of your students. Cory is the character that students are most likely to identify with, and Troy's treatment of his younger son will almost certainly strike them as arbitrary, mean-spirited, and willfully cruel—and never more so than in the climax of the exchange between them in Act 1, Scene 3, when Troy angrily cries out, "Who the hell say I got to like you?" and says that in caring for his son he is motivated exclusively by responsibility. Given his fury and his refusal to throw the boy even the slightest crumb of affection, his claim to Rose at the end of the scene— that he is trying to toughen Cory so that he'll be able to face the cruel world out there—comes across as only a partial truth as well as being rather disingenuous. (He displays much less self-awareness than, say, the doctor-narrator of William Carlos Williams's memorable short story "The Use of Force," who recognizes that he has used his authority and good intentions as a cover for his angrily overpowering a little girl who obstinately refuses treatment.)

There seems to be no end to Troy's unpleasant and off-putting qualities. He is irritated a good deal of the time, and he disputes virtually everything that is said to him; when he has no more substantive rejoinder, he'll resort to saying "I ain't talking about no" whatever the subject happens to be. Given the play's baseball motif, his attitude is reminiscent of Yankees manager Casey Stengel's response to reporters who second-guessed him: "You're full of shit, and I'll tell you why." Troy constantly complains about others disregarding his wishes, while he constantly and categorically refuses to do anything that anyone else wants him to, such as going to hear Lyons play; he even goes so far as to refuse Lyons's repayment of his loans so that he can continue to grouse about how Lyons never pays him back. He also feels free to find fault with everyone while denying everyone else the same right in return: as Lyons tells him near the end of the play's first scene, "Now I don't come criticizing you and how you live. I just come by to ask you for ten dollars. I don't wanna hear all that about how I live."

This hypocrisy that accompanies his unending self-righteousness is perhaps Troy's most grating characteristic. He complains that all the garbage-truck drivers are white and demands to be made a driver himself, even though, as it turns out, he has no driver's license and no experience driving a truck—as well as no concern whatsoever about his lack of those basic qualifications. As with his treatment of Cory, his betrayal of Rose is quite alienating, and our alienation is compounded by his lame-sounding excuses and justifications. After sidestepping Bono's frequent questions and warnings about Alberta, Troy finally tells his friend, in Act 2, Scene 1, that "As long as it sets right in my heart . . . then I'm okay. Cause that's all I listen to. It'll tell me right from wrong every time." Later in that same scene, when he breaks the news to Rose with the explanation that "after eighteen years I wanted to steal second," it's hard not to cheer her on when she uses his own rhetorical device on him—with much greater justification than he ever had—and says, "We're not talking about baseball! We're talking about you going off to lay in bed with another woman . . . and then bring it home to me." And after everything, he can still say (in Act 2, Scene 3): "A man's got to do what's right for him. I ain't sorry for nothing I done. It felt right in my heart."

So, in the light of all this, how do you persuade students that such a man is worthy of their understanding and sympathy, let alone that he has the dignity and stature of a tragic protagonist? To start with, we might establish a context for the discussion by recalling a sentence in Rita Dove's "The Inspiration for *The Darker Face of the Earth*": "In a different world, Amalia might have been a woman of independent means and Augustus a poet; instead, both are doomed to be crushed when their emotions run counter to the ruling status quo." At least those two had the consolation—if it is a consolation—of believing that the ruling status quo that crushed them was unchanging and unchangeable. But Troy Maxson, who in a different world would have been a superstar with a major-league baseball team and would have enjoyed all the fame and wealth that his talent and achievements entitled him to, must toil every day at a physically demanding and socially disdained job (remind students that Troy did not have the option of saying the equivalent of "I'm not going to flip burgers"). And he is forced to watch as the world changes around him, tasting the gall—or, more precisely, denying the changes and refusing to taste it—that the ruination of his dreams and his life was caused, as much as anything, by his bad luck in being born too soon.

A great deal of Troy's energy is consumed by his shielding himself from this insupportable awareness. Wilson hints at this element of his nature early in the opening scene, when Rose complains about Troy's continuing to shop at the local grocery store despite the lower prices and greater selection at the A&P; she tells him: "There's a lot of people don't know they can do no better than they doing now. That's just something you got to learn." But of course that is something that Troy absolutely refuses to learn, because to do so would bring his entire belief system—and his ability to cope with reality as he understands it—crashing down. The point comes up again at the end of Act 1, Scene 3, when he tells Rose that he decided at the time of Cory's birth that "that boy wasn't getting involved in no sports. Not after what they did to me in the sports," to which Rose replies, "Times have changed from when you was young, Troy. People change. The world's changing around you and you can't even see it." There are depths to Troy: while it is true that he wants to protect Cory from the hurts he has endured, there is also truth in Rose's observations, and truth as well in Cory's statement at the very end of Act 1 that Troy is thwarting his dreams "Just cause you didn't have a chance! You just scared I'm gonna be better than you, that's all!"

Very early in Act 2, as cited above in Dave Zirin's comments, Bono tells Troy that "Some people build fences to keep people out . . . and other people build fences to keep people in." While our instinctive reaction to that statement is to class Troy exclusively with the first group, a case might be made that he is actually in both camps, building a fence around himself and excluding everyone, yet at the same time trying to keep his loved ones safe from the threatening world outside—as we see in the passionate soliloquy that ends Act 2, Scene 2, when, having just learned of Alberta's death in giving birth to their daughter, he defiantly asserts to "Mr. Death" that he intends to build a fence around what belongs to him to keep it safe until the two of them fight their final battle. The complexity of Troy's character is shown also in his attitude toward his father, whom he admires—and strives to emulate—for his sense of responsibility in working hard and taking care of his family, but whom he rejects for his meanness of spirit and lack of feeling for his family. (In this respect, Troy may put you in mind of Eugene O'Neill's powerful 1924 tragedy, *Desire Under the Elms*, in which Eben Cabot fails to see that his hatred of his father is based more on their similarities than on their differences.) And we see too how this relationship is passed on to the next generation: Cory resents his father deeply, and then he replicates his father's experience by fighting with him and leaving home while still in his teens to make his own way in the world, feeling rejected and undefended despite his father's vaunted sense of responsibility.

In Troy Maxson, August Wilson has given us a portrait of a proud and honorable spirit repeatedly and severely damaged by life, one whose accumulated hurts ultimately prove too much for him. His story is unique to—and unimaginable outside of—the African American experience in mid-twentieth-century America, as Wilson himself would have been the first to point out. Yet there is something timeless and universal about it as well. Like Oedipus or Othello or any other truly tragic figure, Troy compels our sympathy and our admiration even as we watch him buckle under the pressures of his existence. In the play's final scene—which will no doubt suggest the Requiem at the conclusion of Arthur Miller's *Death of a Salesman*, just as Troy himself will in some ways remind you of Willy Loman—Troy's loved ones gather for his funeral in what turns out to be a powerful moment of healing and reconciliation. Lyons says of him: "He wasn't satisfied hitting in the seats . . . he want to hit it over everything! . . . Yeah, Papa was something else." Cory, having at first declared that he will not attend the funeral, then relents and joins Raynell in singing Troy's father's song about Old Blue. And Rose tells Cory: "Your daddy wanted you to be everything he wasn't . . . and at the same time he tried to make you into everything he was. I don't know if he was right or wrong . . . but I do know he meant to do more good than he meant to do harm." These are the people closest to Troy, but they are also the ones most deeply hurt by him, and if in the end they can forgive him his trespasses, if they can see the decency in his heart and remember him at his best, then so should we.

Shortly after Wilson received a second Pulitzer Prize for *The Piano Lesson* in April 1990 (his first had been for *Fences* in 1987), he made a few revealing comments to an interviewer. Nothing in his work is autobiographical, he declared; nothing he had written had been taken from his own experience. He had successfully avoided studying other playwrights and claimed to have read nothing by Shakespeare except *The Merchant of Venice* (in high school), nothing by Ibsen, Miller, or Tennessee Williams. The only other playwrights whose work he acknowledged an acquaintance with were Amiri Baraka, Ed Bullins, and Athol Fugard. He claimed that he never attended the theater himself and hadn't been to a movie in ten years. "Part of this creative isolation is self-protective fear," explained the interviewer, Kevin Kelly. "Wilson is afraid of tampering with those chaotically rich and whimsically independent forces in his head, terrified of confusing their voices and stories with the voices and stories of other writers" ("August Wilson's True Stories," *Boston Globe*, 29 April 1990).

MLL *MyLiteratureLab Resources.* Biography, critical overview, and bibliography for Wilson.

WRITERS ON WRITING

August Wilson, A LOOK INTO BLACK AMERICA, page 2047

As brief as this excerpt is, in it Wilson makes several trenchant observations. He makes clear that his own stance is not primarily social or political, but aesthetic, yet he acknowledges the power of art to generate social and political effects. For those to whom its characters and subject matter are alien, a work of art can be a window into new experience and a bridge to awareness of a shared humanity. For those to whom the characters and subject are familiar, the work can be a surprising affirmation of the value and the dignity of their lives.

WRITING

43
Writing About Literature

This chapter is a brief guide to informal and formal writing about literature, with emphasis on writing short critical essays. As succinctly as we can, we escort the student through the various procedures of reading and thinking about a piece of literature; doing pre-writing exercises to discover writing ideas; finding a topic; developing a literary argument; and organizing, drafting, revising, correctly formatting, and finishing a paper. (In the chapter "Writing a Research Paper," we present material appropriate to gathering information and writing and documenting a long, well-researched critical essay.)

If these writing chapters fulfill their purpose, they will save you some breath and spare you from reading many innocent (and perhaps not-so-innocent) plagiarisms, floating unidentified quotations (of the kind that suddenly interrupt the student's prose with Harold Bloom's prose in quotation marks), and displays of ill-fitting critical terminology.

PREPARING TO WRITE: DISCOVERING IDEAS

The section "Preparing to Write" quickly covers a number of tried-and-true prewriting methods and, using Frost's "Nothing Gold Can Stay" as a text, provides student samples of each one. You may also wish to dedicate some class time to invention exercises that help students generate writing topics. Asking and answering questions is always an excellent way to generate material for an essay. Questions and answers can help students clarify their views on a subject, identify patterns, and make connections. You might develop questions on different elements of a text: plot, theme, point of view, style, setting, character. Students can work in small groups on one element and then come together as a class to discuss their "findings" and brainstorm to generate specific topics. Individually, they can then generate a working thesis.

DEVELOPING A LITERARY ARGUMENT

Some of your students may do most of their reading on the Internet, where the majority of blogs and posts—with their unfounded assertions, *ad hominem* attacks, and illogical rants—will only reinforce in their minds the popular meaning of the word *argument*. In this section, we emphasize points such as a clear thesis, logical development, a thoughtful and measured tone, and the use of textual evidence to back up one's claims. This discussion seeks not only to make clear to students what is meant by argument in the intellectual sense, but also to assist them in formulating a successful argument and developing it in a focused and persuasive manner.

Anonymous, A LITTLE POEM REGARDING COMPUTER SPELL
CHECKERS, page 2073

This poem, which was first shown to us by Cara Nusinov, of Miami, Florida, has
long circulated on the Internet. The version reprinted in our book seems to be
based on a longer piece of light verse by Jerrold H. Zar, who is Associate Provost
for Graduate Studies at Northern Illinois University. His original poem was
titled "Candidate for a Pullet Surprise" (note the pun) and was first published in
the *Journal of Irreproducible Results* (39.1, Jan./Feb. 1994). The Internet seems to
have worked rather like the old oral tradition in compressing and modifying his
text into a new collective and anonymous version, but Professor Zar deserves
proper credit for its early version.

Once—at the end of a class in which argument had waxed over the question "Is 'Naming of Parts' an antiwar poem or isn't it?"—XJK made the mistake
of cutting off the discussion and telling students to go home and write their
opinions down on paper. The result was to cool future class discussions: students
were afraid that if they talked animatedly, they would be told to write. A different approach is that of the instructor who would halt a class discussion that had
grown driveling, or bad-tempered, or without heart, and cry, "For God's sake,
let's all stop talking! Now get out your pencils and write me a paragraph. . . ."
He claims that in the next class the discussion improved markedly.

44
Writing About a Story

If your students complain, "I've never written about stories before—what am I supposed to do?" you can have them read this section. We can't imagine spending whole class hours with this material; it is supplied here mainly to provide students with illustrations of acceptable papers written by each of three usual methods, and a few pointers on format and mechanics. If you like, you can assign this section for outside reading when you first make a writing assignment.

A GIFT TO INSTRUCTORS: THE CARD REPORT

XJK comments: The card report (pages 2092–2094) may well be God's gift to the instructor overwhelmed with papers to grade. At least, I can't take credit for its creation. This demanding exercise first impressed me as a student in the one course I took at Teachers College, Columbia. The professor, Lennox Grey, assigned us aspiring literature teachers to pick ten great novels we hadn't read and to write card reports on them. Among the novels were *War and Peace* and *Les Misérables*, and although Grey allowed us as many as two cards to encompass them, I must have spoiled a pack of cards for every novel I encompassed. But the task was an agreeable challenge, and I felt it obliged me to look more closely at fiction than I ever had. Later, as a graduate student in Ann Arbor, I found the same device heavily worked by Kenneth Rowe, Arthur Miller's teacher of playwriting, in a popular course in modern drama. Every week, students were expected to read two full-length plays and to turn in two card reports. Nearly a hundred students swelled the course, and Rowe employed two teaching assistants to do the grading. As one of them, I soon realized the beauty of the method. Even a novice like me could do a decent job of grading a hundred card reports each week without being crushed under the toil, either. For an hour a week Rowe met with the other assistant and me and superintended our labors a little, and we thrashed out any problem cases.

If you care to give such an assignment a try, don't feel obliged to write a card report of your own as a Platonic ideal to hold your students' reports up to. When you gather in the sheaves, you can compare a few of them (looking hard at the reports of any students whom you know to be intelligent and conscientious) and probably will quickly see what a better than average report on a story might encompass. In grading, it isn't necessary to read every item on every card: you may read the plot summaries with intermittent attention and concentrate on the subtler elements: symbol, theme, evaluation. Because extensive remarks by the instructor don't seem called for (and, anyway, wouldn't fit on the card), your comments may be short and pointed. If a student reporting on "The Tell-Tale Heart" has omitted a crucial symbol, you may simply query, "The eye?" or "The heartbeat?" One can probably grade thirty card reports in less than an hour and do an honest job; whereas a set of thirty essays, even brief ones, will take at least four hours.

By asking students to produce so few words, you need not feel that their writing skills are being slighted. To get the report to fit the card, a good student has to do several drafts and revisions, none of which the instructor has to read. A shoddy job by a student who hasn't thoroughly read the story is painfully obvious. Once in a while, after a surfeit of expansive essays, I have asked a class for a card report just to rest my eyes and to remind them of the virtues of concision. Some students inevitably grumble, but most are in for a reward, and some will even be delighted that the assignment is so clearly defined and limited!

Warn your students to allow plenty of time to do this job right. Stephen Marcus, of the University of California, Santa Barbara, tells us that some of his students were appalled to find it took them two or three hours to write one card report. That sounds about par for the assignment; if you want to abbreviate it, you can omit some of the required elements.

TOPICS FOR WRITING

In choosing an essay topic, when given a choice, many students have trouble deciding how large a topic to attempt in an assigned word length, and many are tempted to choose a topic larger than they can handle. Some want to make sure they'll have enough ideas to meet the word length. Even if you don't care to assign any of the topics suggested in the text, having students read the lists in the "Topics for Writing" section in this chapter may give them a clearer notion of the right amplitude of topics on Fiction for papers of various lengths.

If this list, the writing assignment, "More Topics for Writing" at the end of most chapters, and your own inspiration don't suffice, additional suggestions for writing may be quarried from the questions that follow the stories.

45
Writing About a Poem

Here are notes on the poems contained in "Writing About a Poem."

Robert Frost, DESIGN, page 2102

If you wish to deal with this section in class, you might have students read "Design," the two student papers that follow the poem, and Randall Jarrell's explication. What did these writers notice about the poem that you didn't notice? What did you notice about it that they left out?

Besides Jarrell's classic explication, many other good discussions of the poem can be consulted. Elizabeth Drew has a succinct explication in *Poetry: A Modern Guide to Its Understanding and Enjoyment* (New York: Norton, 1959), and there is a more detailed reading by Richard Ohmann in *College English* 28 (Feb. 1967): 359–67.

Also of interest is Frost's early draft of this poem, titled "In White," found on page 2124 of the text. What is the theme of each version? Is it more difficult to tell from the vaguer, more general draft? In rewriting, Frost seems to have made his details more specific and also to have defined the central idea.

MLL *MyLiteratureLab Resources*. Biography, critical overview, critical articles, and bibliography for Frost.

Abbie Huston Evans, WING-SPREAD, page 2118

The student's evaluation seems just to us. While "Wing-Spread" is not so vivid a cameo as "Design," nor so troubling in its theme, and while it contains trite rimes (except for *beryl/peril*), we think it a decent poem and admirably terse.

Insufficiently recognized (like most poets), Evans (1881–1979) had a long, productive life. Her *Collected Poems* was published in 1970 by the University of Pittsburgh Press. It contains dozens of poems better than "Wing-Spread."

SUGGESTIONS FOR WRITING

Here are a few more topics for paper assignments to supplement the list at the end of the chapter.

Topics for Brief Papers (250–500 words)

1. A *précis* (French, from Latin: "to cut short") is a short abstract or condensation of a literary work that tries to sum up the work's most essential elements. Although a précis, like a paraphrase, states the poet's thought in the writer's own words, a paraphrase is sometimes as long as the original poem, if not longer. A précis, while it tends to be much briefer than a poem, also takes in the essentials: theme, subject, tone, character, events (in a narrative poem), and anything else that strikes the writer as important. A précis might range in length from one ample sentence to a few hundred words (if, say, it were condensing a long play or novel, or a complex longer poem). Here, for instance, is an acceptable précis of Robert Browning's "Soliloquy of the Spanish Cloister":

   > The speaker, a monk in a religious community, voices to himself while gardening the bitter grudge he has against Brother Lawrence, one of his fellow monks. He charges Lawrence with boring him with dull talk at mealtime, sporting monogrammed tableware, ogling women, drinking greedily, ignoring rituals (unlike the speaker, who after a meal lays knife and fork in a cross—which seems overly scrupulous). Having vented his grudge by slyly scissoring Lawrence's favorite flowering shrubs, the speaker is now determined to go further, and plots to work Lawrence's damnation. Perhaps he will lure Lawrence into misinterpreting a text in Scripture, or plant a pornographic volume on him. So far gone is the speaker in his hatred that he is even willing to sell his soul to the devil if the devil will carry off Lawrence's; and so proud is the speaker in his own wiles that he thinks he can cheat the devil in the bargain. Vespers ring, ending the meditation, but his terrible grudge seems sure to go on.

   As the detailed précis makes clear, Browning's poem contains a chronicle of events and a study in character. The précis also indicates the tone of the poem and (another essential) its point of view.

   Students might be supplied with a copy of the above material to guide them and be asked to write précis of four or five poems, chosen from a list the instructor compiles of six or eight poems in the "Poems for Further Reading."

2. Find a poem that you like, one not in this book so that it may be unfamiliar to other members of the class. Insert into it a passage of five or six lines that you yourself write in imitation of it. Your object is to lengthen the poem by a bit of forgery that will go undetected. Type out the whole poem afresh, inserted lines and all, and have copies duplicated for the others in the class. Then let them try to tell your forged lines from those of the original. A successful forgery will be hard to detect, since you will have imitated the poet's language, handling of form, and imagery—indeed, the poet's voice.

Topics for More Extensive Papers (600–1,000 words)

1. Relate a personal experience of poetry: a brief history of your attempts to read it or to write it; a memoir of your experience in reading poetry aloud; a report of a poetry reading you attended; an account of how reading a poem

brought a realization that affected you personally (no instructor-pleasing pieties!); or an account of an effort to foist a favorite poem upon your friends, or to introduce young children to poetry. Don't make up any fabulous experiences or lay claim to profound emotions you haven't had; the result could be blatantly artificial ("How I Read Housman's 'Loveliest of trees' and Found the Meaning of Life"). But if you can honestly sum up what you learned from your experience, then do so, by all means.

2. Write an imitation or a parody of any poem in the book. This and the following topic may result in a paper of fewer words than the essay topics, but the amount of work required is likely to be slightly more.

    (*Note:* This assignment will be too much of a challenge for some students, and not all ought to be required to do it. But those who possess the necessary skills may find themselves viewing the poet's work as if they were insiders.) The instructor has to insist that the student observe the minimal formal requirements of a good imitation. A convincing imitation of, say, Thomas Hardy can hardly be written in Whitmanic free verse. Students may be urged to read entire collections of work in order to soak up a better sense of the poet. This assignment asks much, but the quality of the results is often surprising. Honestly attempted, such an exercise requires far more effort from students than the writing of most critical essays, and it probably teaches them more.

3. After you have read several ballads (both folk ballads and literary ballads), write a ballad of your own, one at least twenty lines long. If you need a subject, consider some event recently in the news: an act of bravery, a wedding that took place despite obstacles, a murder or a catastrophe, a report of spooky or mysterious happenings. Then, in a prose paragraph, state what you learned from your reading of traditional or literary ballads that proved useful to you as a ballad composer yourself.

Topics for Longer Papers (1,500 words or more)

1. Leslie Fiedler, the critic and novelist, once wrote an essay in which he pretended to be a critic of the nineteenth century ("A Review of *Leaves of Grass* and *Hiawatha* as of 1855," *American Poetry Review* 2 [Mar.–Apr. 1973]). Writing as though he subscribed to the tastes of that age, Fiedler declared Whitman's book shaggy and shocking and awarded Professor Longfellow all the praise. If you can steep yourself in the literature of a former age (or a recent year) deeply enough to feel confident, such an essay might be fun to write (and to read). Write about some poem once fashionable and now forgotten; or about some poem once spurned and now esteemed. Your instructor might have some suggestions.

2. For a month (or some other assigned period of time), keep a personal journal of your reading of poetry and your thinking about it. To give direction to your journal, you might confine it to the work of, say, half a dozen poets who interest you; or you might concentrate on a theme common to a few poems by various poets.

46
Writing About a Play

In an introductory literature course that saves drama for last, there seems never enough time to be fair to the plays available. That is why many instructors tell us that they like to have students read at least two or three plays on their own and write short papers about at least one or two of them.

If you decide to assign such critical writing but find your time for paper-grading all the more limited as your course nears its end, you might consider assigning a card report (discussed and illustrated on pages 2128–2131). Earlier in this manual (in "Writing About a Story"), we trumpet the virtues of card reports—which aren't every instructor's salvation, but which we have found to work especially well for teaching plays. The card report shown in the book—on Glaspell's *Trifles*—manages to cover a one-act play in two card faces. For a longer and more involved play, you might want to limit the students' obligation to just a few of that play's elements (leaving out, say, *Symbols* and *Evaluation*). Otherwise, they'll need more than one card.

Among the "Topics for More Extended Papers" (page 2136), number 5 invites the student to imagine the problems of staging a classic play in modern dress and in a contemporary setting. If you prefer, this topic could be more general: Make recommendations for the production of any play. In getting ready to write on this topic, students might first decide whether or not the play is a work of realism. Ask them: Should sets, lighting, and costumes be closely detailed and lifelike, or should they be extravagant or expressionistic? Would a picture-frame stage or an arena better suit the play? What advice would you offer the actors for interpreting their roles? What exactly would you emphasize in the play if you were directing it? (For a few insights into methods of staging, they might read Tennessee Williams's "How to Stage *The Glass Menagerie*" on page 1883.)

47
Writing a Research Paper

This chapter builds on the information presented in Chapter 43, "Writing About Literature." (As students prepare to embark on a research essay, you might encourage them to review those sections in Chapter 43 that talk about discovering writing ideas, developing a literary argument, defining a thesis, and outlining.) This chapter focuses on the essential aspects of a research paper:

- **Doing Research for an Essay: Print, Electronic, and Web Resources**—finding research resources, recording information, analyzing research material.

- **Evaluating and Using Internet Sources**—conducting worthwhile Internet searches, determining reliable resources.

- **Guarding Academic Integrity**—covering both intentional and unintentional plagiarism. Includes the disconcerting issue of plagiarized term papers (note that in the short section "A Warning Against Internet Plagiarism," we detail how professors can now use software and services to identify plagiarized work—our token contribution to your ongoing battle).

- **Acknowledging and Documenting Sources**—acknowledging others' ideas and words, using citations within an essay, preparing a Works Cited list based on MLA standards.

- **Using Visual Images**—finding, integrating, and documenting visual images into a research paper.

For many students, the Internet is their primary research tool, and too often there is only cursory evaluation of the source of the accessed material. We have given specific examples of reliable Web sites and why those sites can be regarded as trustworthy. We have also provided a checklist for judging the reliability of both print and Web resources. Some instructors report that they like to spend a class session in the school's computer lab exploring both reliable and unreliable sites. They identify topics pertaining to a story or poem from the syllabus, and then search out a number of sites for students to consider in advance of the class session. This hands-on exercise can help students learn to differentiate between reliable sites and questionable sites as they do their own research.

When developing your research paper assignment, determine the number and type of Internet sources that you will allow students to use. Students should understand that they need to use printed as well as electronic sources. Obviously, search engines such as *Google* have transformed the landscape of research and the Internet should never be banned out of hand as a place to find research material, yet much valuable scholarship is still not available online. To reduce the chance of plagiarism (unintended or blatant) from the Web, and to ensure that Internet referenced material is from a reliable source, you might require students to turn in a printed copy of the Internet source material with their final papers.

If you want to encourage students to begin their research in their own college library, you might consider having the Reference Librarian conduct a class session devoted to doing literary research. Many students do not know how to use all the resources available in their college library. An introduction tailored to their needs for your specific assignment may help make them efficient academic researchers.

Documenting sources, especially Internet sources, is challenging for most students. We have provided detailed information for citing print and Internet sources, a sample Works Cited list, and a comprehensive guide to the types of citations that students will likely use in their papers. Encourage students to allow sufficient time to prepare their Works Cited page, and review their papers for scrupulous documentation.

Because students are human and we humans procrastinate, it is advisable to break the task of generating a research essay into dated steps. Establish a calendar of due dates when you issue your assignment: topic with working thesis statement; working list of reference material; outline; first draft; revised draft; peer review session; final draft. Our goal should be to have students engage in the real writing process—that process by which writing, thinking, rewriting, and rethinking lead to real re-vision. We want our students to realize the depths of meaning present in the literature that they read and the depths of their own responses and ideas through continued exploration.

48
Writing as Discovery: Keeping a Journal

A Comment on Student Journals

In "Keeping a Journal," we establish the value of student writing as a key component in the active process of understanding and making meaning of a piece of literature. Directed journal responses (specific questions that you pose) can allow students to come prepared to take part in a class discussion. Open responses (a subject of interest chosen by the student) can foster the discovery and exploration of ideas and interpretations. Ideally, journal writing should offer students the chance to sharpen their skills of literary analysis, and it may provide the seed of an idea that can be nurtured into a formal essay.

To ensure that students keep up to date with assignments, we recommend that you collect journal responses every few weeks. Read the responses and comment on whether the work is meeting your expectations. If you allow and encourage students to revise or expand their journal entries, they should staple the revised entry to the original; this way, when you collect the journal as a whole, you can readily see whether additional work has been done.

49
Writing an Essay Exam

As a student, you may have written your essay exams the way most of us did—frantically spewing out whatever came into your head, no matter how repetitious or off the main point it might have been, as you listened to the ever-louder rumble of Time's wingéd chariot. The intent of this chapter is to provide your students with valuable insights and reminders that will help them to sharpen their awareness of what exam questions actually ask of them and to answer the questions as effectively as possible. The few extra minutes taken in following these suggestions will save them many more minutes that might otherwise be spent in writing sentences and paragraphs of unresponsive comments.

We constantly remind our students to express themselves in such a way as to be certain that their intended meaning is clearly communicated to the reader, but it's very easy to forget that the same rule applies to us as well. One of the most useful features of this chapter is a listing, with concise definitions, of the imperative verbs that we tend to favor in writing essay questions, so that students will understand precisely what is expected of them when we ask them to *analyze* or *contrast* or *explain*.

50
Critical Approaches to Literature

PURPOSE OF CRITICAL APPROACHES

This chapter is designed to introduce students to the variety of possible approaches they can take in analyzing literature. Theory and criticism have become such important aspects of undergraduate literary study that many instructors have asked for an informed beginner's guide to the subject. Our objective has been to cover the area intelligently without overwhelming or con-fusing the beginning student.

This section presents overviews of ten critical approaches. While these ten methods do not exhaust the total possibilities of literary criticism, they represent the most influential and widely used contemporary approaches. Each approach is introduced with an overview designed to explain to beginning students the central ideas of the critical method. The general note does not try to explain every aspect of a critical school or to summarize its history; instead, it focuses on explaining the fundamental insights that motivate each approach. While many contemporary critics combine methodologies, it seemed wisest to keep the cat-egories as simple and separate as possible because students may be wrestling with these ideas for the first time.

CRITICAL SELECTIONS

After the introductory note, each critical school is illustrated by three critical excerpts. The first excerpt is usually a theoretical statement explaining the gen-eral principles of the approach. In each case, we have selected a passage from one of the methodology's leading practitioners that summarizes its central ideas in an accessible way. There is, for example, **Cleanth Brooks** listing the princi-ples of Formalist Criticism, **Elaine Showalter** outlining the issues of Feminist Poetics, **Northrop Frye** explaining the concept of Mythic Archetypes, and **Stanley Fish** presenting the parameters of the Reader-Response method. These selections reinforce and broaden the ideas found earlier in the introductory notes. They also familiarize the student with a major figure in each school.

This general statement is then followed by two more critical excerpts that discuss actual works in the book. These critical analyses have been selected with great care to provide illuminating but accessible examples of each school. The excerpts are not only well argued and informed analyses, they are also clearly written, with a minimum of theoretical jargon. Footnotes have been added to explain any references that might be unfamiliar to students.

It was not always possible to find critical excerpts that could do the double duty of illustrating a school of thought and analyzing a text at hand. Sometimes, as in **Harold Bloom**'s discussion of poetic influence or **Roland Barthes**'s announcement of "the death of the author," we chose the clearest exposition available of an influential critical concept. (We also felt that students would profit by seeing where these influential ideas originated.) Some of these critical texts are challenging because the ideas are subtle and complex, but—once again—we have always tried to find the most accessible excerpt.

LITERARY WORKS DISCUSSED

Critical methods are always easier to understand when they discuss a poem, play, or story you know. Consequently, we have tried to find noteworthy excerpts that illustrate a particular critical approach and *that also focus on a literary text found in the book.* This feature allows the instructor the possibility of assigning many of these critical texts as ancillary readings.

The criticism on fiction lends itself well to classroom use. **Daniel Watkins's Marxist reading of D. H. Lawrence's "The Rocking-Horse Winner,"** for example, would surely help students understand the symbolic structure of that arresting story. **Nina Pelikan Straus's "Transformations in *The Metamorphosis*"** suggests that the sibling relationship has been neglected in favor of the father-son struggle, and it offers a provocative discussion of the gender role reversal that occurs between Gregor and Grete. **Edmond Volpe's analysis of "Barn Burning"** illuminates the mythic structure that underlies Faulkner's story. **Emily Toth's biographical study of Kate Chopin** shows how the circumstances of Chopin's early widowhood and subsequent romances provide the template for her themes and even more specifically for her character Alcée in "The Storm." **Gretchen Schulz and R. J. R. Rockwood give a persuasive psychological reading of Joyce Carol Oates's "Where Are You Going, Where Have You Been?"** with a detailed analysis of fairy tale motifs in the story. In **"The Economics of 'Sweat,'" Kathryn Lee Seidel** provides rich historical background information on the unique black town of Eatonville, Florida, and its symbiotic relationship to its white "twin" of Winter Park, the sturdy social platform on which Zora Neale Hurston constructed her artistic achievement in that story. **Michael Clark's formalist analysis of "Sonny's Blues"** examines the interplay of symbol and meaning in James Baldwin's story. Examining Chekhov's own love life, **Virginia Llewellyn Smith's biographical reading of "The Lady with the Pet Dog"** opens up interesting parallels between an author's life and his work.

In poetry, **Robert Langbaum's formalist analysis of "My Last Duchess"** makes a good supplementary assignment to reading Browning's poem. **Brett Millier's biographical comment on Elizabeth Bishop's "One Art"** might broaden a discussion of the villanelle into other issues. **Hugh Kenner places Ezra Pound's "In a Station of the Metro" in a historical context** by recreating the heady atmosphere of Modernist London. **Joseph Moldenhauer provides students with an informed but accessible historical account** of how Andrew Marvell used elements of the Renaissance tradition in **"To His Coy Mistress,"** while **Geoffrey Hartman deconstructs Wordsworth's "A Slumber Did My Spirit Seal." Camille Paglia uses the perspectives of Cultural Studies** to provide a reading of **William Blake's "The Chimney Sweeper."**

Using the Chapter

Some instructors may want to use "Critical Approaches to Literature" as a formal part of the course, but more, we suspect, will prefer to use it in a less systematic way as a resource that can be tailored to whatever occasion seems suitable. An excellent way to introduce students to the section is to assign a short paper analyzing a single poem according to the critical approach of their choice. This method allows them to explore the introductory material for each critical school and then learn one approach in depth by trying it out on a specific text.

Many poems in the book lend themselves to this assignment. Some likely choices (from the first few Poetry chapters) would include: D. H. Lawrence's "Piano," Robert Browning's "My Last Duchess," Theodore Roethke's "My Papa's Waltz," Anne Bradstreet's "The Author to Her Book," Anne Sexton's "Her Kind," Wilfred Owen's "Dulce et Decorum Est," Langston Hughes's "Theme for English B," and Alfred Tennyson's "Tears, Idle Tears." All of these poems invite multiple readings from a variety of perspectives.

Certain stories naturally suggest multiple readings. Poe's "The Tell-Tale Heart," for instance, allows formalist, biographical, psychological, mythological, reader-response, and deconstructionist readings. Charlotte Perkins Gilman's "The Yellow Wallpaper" is similarly open to multiple interpretations; openly autobiographical, it directly addresses issues of gender, sociology, psychology, and myth. Other stories that invite wide approaches include Faulkner's "A Rose for Emily," Cheever's "The Five-Forty-Eight," Tan's "A Pair of Tickets," Joyce's "Araby," Hawthorne's "Young Goodman Brown," Walker's "Everyday Use," O'Connor's "A Good Man Is Hard to Find," and Cather's "Paul's Case." If you want to assign a single work for students to try out the critical approach of their choice, you could probably not do better than Kafka's *The Metamorphosis*.

Plays such as *Oedipus the King, Antigonê, Othello,* and *Hamlet* have already been analyzed from every conceivable critical perspective, but there's no reason why a student shouldn't try his or her own hand at them. A *Doll's House, Trifles,* and *Death of a Salesman* are naturally open to multiple approaches. Milcha Sanchez-Scott's *The Cuban Swimmer* profitably invites mythic, psychological, sociological, formal, and biographical readings. Finally, a particularly interesting comparison might be made between Rita Dove's resetting of the Oedipus myth, *The Darker Face of the Earth,* and Sophocles' play.

Other Resources

If any of your brighter students should start writing papers following any of these critical approaches, and you should want to provide them with models longer than the brief illustrative samples we supply, a new series of paperbacks may be helpful to them. It will be still more helpful if they are familiar with a classic such as *Frankenstein, The Scarlet Letter, Wuthering Heights, Heart of Darkness, Hamlet, A Portrait of the Artist as a Young Man, Gulliver's Travels, The Awakening,* or *The House of Mirth.* Titles dealing with each of these classics and others have appeared, or will appear shortly, in the series "Case Studies in Contemporary Criticism," whose general editor is Ross C. Murfin of the

University of Miami (Bedford Books and St. Martin's Press). Each book contains five essays on its novel or play, illustrating five different approaches: Psychoanalytic criticism, Reader-Response criticism, Feminist criticism, Deconstruction, and the New Historicism. There are also readable essays that explain each critical school, and bibliographies of critical books representing each of them.

Appendix 1
Teaching Creative Writing

WRITING A POEM (*Some notes by XJK*)

These notes are provided mainly for the instructor who employs this anthology in a creative writing course. Some may be of interest, however, to anyone who in teaching composition includes a unit on writing poems. Such an instructor will probably have firm persuasions about poetry and about the teaching of poets. Instead of trying to trumpet any persuasions of my own, let me just set down some hunches that, from teaching poetry workshops, I have come to feel are mostly true.

In reading a student's poem, you have to look at it with your mind a blank, reserving judgment for as long as possible. Try to see what the student is doing, being slow to compare a fledgling effort to the classics. There's no use in merely reading the poem and spotting the influences you find in it—"Ha, I see you've been reading Williams!" You can, however, praise any virtues you discover and you can tell the student firmly, kindly, and honestly of any adverse reactions you feel. Point to anything in the poem that causes you to respond toward it or against it. Instead of coldly damning the poem's faults, you can inquire why the writer said something in such-and-such a way rather than in some other. You can ask to have anything you don't understand explained. If a line or a passage doesn't tell you anything, you can ask the student to suggest a fresh way of wording it. Perhaps the most valuable service you can perform for a student poet is to be hard to please. Suggest that the student not settle for the first words that flash to mind, but reach deeper, going after the word or phrase or line that will be not merely adequate but memorable.

The greatest method of teaching poetry writing I have ever heard of was that of the late John Holmes. Former students at Tufts remember that Holmes seldom made comments on a poem but would often just lay a finger next to a suspect passage and fix the student with a look of expectancy until the silence became unendurable and the student began to explain what the passage meant and how it could be put better. (I have never made the Holmes method succeed for me; I can't keep from talking too much.)

Most workshop courses in poetry fall into a classic ritual. Students make copies of their poems, bring them in, and show them to the class. This method of procedure is hard to improve upon. Some instructors find that the effort of screening the work themselves first and deciding what to spend time on in class makes for more cogent class sessions, with less time squandered on boring or inferior material. In general, class sessions won't be any more lively or valuable than the poems that are on hand. (An exception was a workshop I once visited years ago at MIT. The poems were literal, boring stuff, but the quality of the students' impromptu critical analyses was sensational.) Often a great class discussion will revolve around a fine poem with deep faults in it.

The severest challenge for the instructor, incidentally, isn't a *bad* poem. A bad poem is easy to deal with; it always gives you plenty of work to do—passages to delete, purple adjectives to question. The challenge comes in dealing with a truly surprising, original, and competent poem. This is risky and sensitive work because genuine poets usually know what they are doing to a greater degree than you or any other outsider does; and you don't want to confuse them with reactions you don't trust. For such rare students, all a poetry workshop probably does is to supply an audience, a little encouragement, and sometimes even an insight.

There are natural temptations, of course, to which teachers of poets fall prey. Like coin collectors, they keep wanting to overvalue the talents they have on hand, to convince themselves that a student is a Gem Mint Condition poet, when a less personal opinion might find the student just an average specimen, although uncirculated. It's better to be too slow than too quick to encourage a student to seek nationwide publication. It is another temptation, if you have a class with a competent poet in it, to devote most of each session to that poet's latest work, causing grumblings of discontent (sometimes) among the other paying customers. I believe that a more competent poet deserves more time, but you have to conduct a class and not a tutorial.

Poetry workshops can become hideously intimate. They are bound to produce confessional or diary poems that, sometimes behind the thinnest of fictive screens, confide in painful detail the writer's sexual, psychic, and religious hangups. I have known poetry workshops where, by semester's end, the participants feel toward one another like the members of a hostile therapy group. That is why I believe in stressing that a poem is not merely the poet's self-revelation. It usually helps to insist at the start of the course that poems aren't necessarily to be taken personally. (See "Poetry and Personal Identity" if you need ammunition.) Everybody will know, of course, that some poets in the class aren't capable of detached art and that a poem about a seduction may well be blatant autobiography; but believe me, you and your students will be happier if you can blow the trumpet in favor of the Imagination. There is no point in circulating poems in class anonymously, pretending that nobody knows who wrote them. Somebody will know, and I think that the sooner the members of the class freely admit their identities, the more easy and relaxed and open the situation will be. To know each one personally, as soon as you can, is essential.

As the workshop goes on, I don't always stick to a faithful conference schedule. Some will need (and wish for) more of your time than others, but I like to schedule at least one conference right away, at the beginning of the course. This is a chance to meet with students in private and get a sense of their needs. I tell them to bring in a few poems they've already written, if they've written any. But I make it clear that class sessions will deal only with brand-new poems. At the end of the course, I program another such conference (instead of a final exam), sit down with each student, and ask, "Well, where are you now?"

Some students will lean on you for guidance ("What shall I write about?"); others will spurn all your brilliant suggestions and want to roar away in their own directions. Fine. I believe in offering the widest possible latitude in making assignments—but in giving *some* assignments. Even the most inner-directed poet can learn something from being expected to move in a new direction. Having a few assignments will discourage the customers who think they can get through any number of creative writing courses by using the same old yellowed sheaf of poems. Encourage revision. Now and then, suggest a revision as an assignment instead of a new poem.

In "Writing a Poem" I offer a radical suggestion: that the students memorize excellent poems. Feeling like a curmudgeon for making this recommendation, I was happy to find support for it in the view of Robert Bly, who remarked in *Coda* (June/July 1981):

> I won't even read a single manuscript now, when I visit a university workshop, unless the poet in advance agrees to memorize fifty lines of Yeats. At the first workshop I visited last fall it cut the number of graduate-student writers who wanted to see me from 15 to 2. Next year I'm changing that to fifty lines of *Beowulf*.

Bly may seem unreasonably stern, but he and I agree on the value of memorization. I believe it helps coax the writing of poetry down out of the forebrain and helps it unite with the pulse.

Bly has sane things to say, in the same article, about the folly of thirsting for publication too early. And here's one of his unorthodox exercises for a writing workshop (imparted in an interview in the *Boston Globe Magazine* for April 10, 1988):

> One workshop, I brought in an onion for each of the students. I asked everybody to spend 10 to 15 minutes describing the exterior of the onion, using all of their senses. That requires every bit of observation you have, to remain looking at the onion. Then, in the second part of the exercise, I said, "Now I want you to compare the onion to your mother."

That must have rocked 'em! I wonder if it produced any good results.

CREATIVE WRITING RESOURCES IN *LITERATURE*

Although knowing something about any element of poetry may benefit a poet-in-training, here is a list, chapter by chapter, of material in *Literature* that may be particularly useful in a creative writing class.

Chapter 14, Listening to a Voice: THE PERSON IN THE POEM, page 680
Novice poets often think of their poems as faithful diary accounts of actual experiences. This section may be useful to suggest to them that, in the process of becoming art, the raw material of a poem may be expected to undergo change.

Chapter 17, Imagery: ABOUT HAIKU, page 750
Assignment: Write some haiku, either original or in imitation of classic Japanese haiku.

Chapter 17, Imagery: EXPERIMENT: *Writing with Images*, page 754
A poetry writing assignment with possible examples.

Chapter 18, Figures of Speech: *Howard Moss*, SHALL I COMPARE THEE TO A SUMMER'S DAY?, page 768
Assignment: Choosing a different famous poem, write a Moss-like version of it. Then try to indicate what, in making your takeoff, was most painful to leave out.

Chapter 18, Figures of Speech: *Jane Kenyon*, THE SUITOR, page 781
Assignment: Write a poem similarly constructed of similes or metaphors.

Chapter 19, Song: *Paul Simon*, RICHARD CORY, page 792
Assignment: In somewhat the fashion of Simon's treatment of Robinson, take a well-known poem and rewrite it as a song lyric. Try singing the result to a tune.

Chapter 20, Sound: EXERCISE: *Listening to Meaning*, page 811
Assignment: After reading these examples, write a brief poem of your own, one heavy with sound effects.

Chapter 20, Sound: READING AND HEARING POEMS ALOUD, page 823
Assignment: Ponder this section before reading your own poems aloud in class.

Chapter 21, Rhythm: METER, page 836
Assignment: After working through this section on your own, write a poem in meter.

Chapter 22, Closed Form: page 850
This chapter may be of particular value to a poetry writing class. Not only does it analyze some traditional forms, it also suggests a rationale for formally open verse.
Assignment: After considering the definition of *syllabic verse* given in this chapter, carefully read Dylan Thomas's "Fern Hill." Work out the form of the Thomas poem with pencil and paper, then try writing a syllabic poem of your own.

Chapter 23, Open Form: page 873
This chapter is important for students to read and consider because it tries to suggest why competent verse is seldom entirely "free." It also helps students who are enamored of traditional, formal notions of poetry to open themselves up to new possibilities.
Assignment: Ponder, not too seriously, Wallace Stevens's "Thirteen Ways of Looking at a Blackbird." Then, as the spirit moves you, write a unified series of small poems. Or, on a more modest scale, write a fourteenth way of looking at this poetic fowl.

Chapter 25, Myth and Narrative: MYTH AND POPULAR CULTURE, page 920

Assignment: Read the final section of the chapter, "Myth and Popular Culture." Retell a popular story (from the Bible, folklore, or the movies) in the form of a poem, but give the story some new twist that allows the reader to see the familiar tale in a novel way.

Chapter 27, Translation: pages 953–959

Assignment: Consider the translations in this section and decide what you admire or dislike in each of them. Translate a poem of your choice, from any language with which you are familiar or can follow in a bilingual edition.

Chapter 27, Translation: PARODY, page 960

Assignment: Read these parodists, comparing their work with the originals. Then, choosing some poet whose work you know thoroughly, write a parody yourself.

Appendix 2
Notes on Teaching Poetry by XJK

These notes are offered in response to the wishes of several instructors for additional practical suggestions for teaching poetry. They are, however, mere descriptions of a few strategies that have proved useful in my own teaching. For others, I can neither prescribe nor proscribe.

1. To a greater extent than in teaching prose, the instructor may find it necessary to have poems read aloud. It is best if students do this reading. Since to read a poem aloud effectively requires that the reader understand what is said in it, students will need advance warning so that they can prepare their spoken interpretations. Sometimes I assign particular poems to certain people, or I ask each person to take his or her choice. Some advice on how to read poetry aloud is given in the chapter "Sound." I usually suggest only that students beware of waxing overemotional or rhetorical, and I urge them to read aloud outside of class as often as possible. If the student or the instructor has access to a tape recorder, it may be especially helpful.

2. It is good to recall occasionally that poems may be put back together as well as taken apart. Sometimes I call on a student to read a previously prepared poem just before opening a discussion of the poem. Then, the discussion over and the poem lying all around in intelligible shreds, I ask the same student to read it over again. It is often startling how the reading improves from the student's realizing more clearly what the poet is saying.

3. I believe in asking students to do a certain amount of memorization. Many groan that rote learning is mindless and grade-schoolish, but it seems to me one way to defeat the intellectualizations that students (and the rest of us) tend to make of poetry. It is also a way to suggest that we do not read a poem primarily for its ideas: to learn a poem by heart is one way to engrave oneself with the sound and weight of it. I ask for twenty or thirty lines at a time, of the student's choice, then have them write the lines out in class. Some students have reported unexpected illuminations. Some people, of course, can't memorize a poem to save their souls, and I try to encourage but not to pressure them. These written memorizations take very little of the instructor's time to check, and they need not be returned to the students unless there are flagrant lacunae in them.

4. The instructor has to sense when a discussion has gone on long enough. It is a matter of watching each student's face for the first sign of that fixed set of the mouth. Elizabeth Bishop once wisely declared that, while she was not opposed to all close analysis and criticism, she was against "making poetry monstrous and boring and proceeding to talk the very life out of it." I used to be afraid of classroom silences. Now, I find it helps sometimes to stop a discussion that is getting lost, and say, "Let's all take three minutes and read this poem again and think about it silently." When the discussion resumes, it is usually improved.

Some of the finest, most provocative essays on teaching poetry in college I have seen are these:

Alice Bloom, "On the Experience of Unteaching Poetry," *Hudson Review* (Spring 1979): 7–30. Bloom: "I am interested in the conditions of education that would lead a student to remark, early in a term, as one of mine did, that 'I wish we didn't know these were poems. Then it seems like it would be a lot easier.'"

Clara Clairborne Park, "Rejoicing to Concur with the Common Reader" in her volume *Rejoining the Common Reader: Essays, 1962–1990* (Evanston: Northwestern, 1991). Park is now a professor at Williams College, but for many years she taught in a community college. This essay recounts the joys and disappointments of working with students who were just discovering literature. Park is most concerned by how to relate literature to the lives of her students without condescending to them. She praises a kind of simplicity in approaching literature that "need not mean narrowness." Discussing the teacher's realization that he or she participates "in a process that changes lives," Park writes an essay that proves both moving and enlightening.

Appendix 3
Integrating Poetry and Composition

How do you teach students to read poetry and, at the same time, to write good prose? Instructors who face this task may find some useful advice in the following article, first published in The English Record, bulletin of the New York State English Council. It is reprinted here by the kind permission of the author, Irwin Weiser, director of developmental writing, Purdue University.

THE PROSE PARAPHRASE:
INTEGRATING POETRY AND COMPOSITION

Irwin Weiser

Many of us teach composition courses which demand that we not only instruct our students in writing but that we also present literature to them as well. Such courses often frustrate us, since a quarter or a semester seems too brief to allow us to teach fundamentals of composition alone. How are we to integrate the teaching of literature with the teaching of writing? What are we to do with a fat anthology of essays, fiction, poetry, or drama and a rhetoric text and, in some cases, a separate handbook of grammar and usage?

Recently, I tried an approach that seemed to provide more integration of reading and writing than I previously had felt I attained in similar courses. The course was the third quarter of a required freshman composition sequence; the departmental course description specifies the teaching of poetry and drama, but also states "English 103 is, however, primarily a composition, not a literature, course. Major emphasis of the course should be on writing." The approach I will describe concerns the study of poetry.

Because this is a writing course, I explained to my students that we would approach poetry primarily as a study of the way writers can use language, and thus our work on denotation and connotation, tone, irony, image, and symbol should help them learn to make conscious language choices when they write. Chapters in Kennedy/Gioia's *Literature* entitled "Words," "Saying and Suggesting," and "Listening to a Voice" fit nicely with this approach. Further, because this is a writing course, I wanted my students to have frequent opportunities to write without burying myself under an even greater number of formal, longish papers than I already required. An appropriate solution seemed to be to have my students write prose paraphrases of one or two poems from those assigned for each discussion class.

During the first week of the course, we discussed and practiced the paraphrase technique, looking first at Kennedy's explanation of paraphrasing and then at his paraphrase of Housman's "Loveliest of trees, the cherry now." By reading my own paraphrase, not among the ablest in the class, I was able to place myself in the position of co-inquirer into these poems, most of which I had not previously taught. This helped establish a classroom atmosphere similar to that of a creative writing workshop, one conducive to the discussion of both the poetry in the text and the writing of the students. In fact, while the primary purpose of assigning the paraphrases was to give my students extra writing practice, an important additional result was that throughout the quarter their paraphrases, not the teacher's opinions and interpretations, formed the basis for class discussion. There was rarely a need for the teacher to *explain* a poem or a passage: someone, and frequently several people, had an interpretation, which satisfied most questions and resolved most difficulties.

At the end of this essay are examples of the prose paraphrases students wrote of Emily Dickinson's "I heard a Fly buzz—when I died." Two of the paraphrases, at 90 and 112 words, are approximately as long as Dickinson's 92-word poem; the 160-word third paraphrase is over 75% longer because this student interpreted as she paraphrased, explaining, for example, that the narrator willed her earthly possessions in a futile attempt to hasten death. Such interpretation, while welcome, is not at all necessary, as the two shorter, yet also successful, paraphrases indicate. In fact I had to remind students that paraphrases are not the same as analyses, and that while they might have to interpret a symbol—as these students variously explained what the fly or the King meant—or unweave a metaphor, their major task was to rewrite the poem as clear prose.

The first paraphrase is perhaps the most straightforward of this group. The author's voice is nearly inaudible. He has stripped the poem of its literary qualities—no "Heaves of Storm," only "the air before a storm"; no personification; the author is only present in the choice of the word "sad" to describe the final buzz of the fly. His paraphrase is a prose rendering of the poem with no obvious attempt to interpret it.

Paraphrase II seems to ignore the symbolic importance of the fly, and perhaps in the very casualness of the phrase "and the last thing I was aware of was this fly and its buzz" suggests the same insignificance of death from the perspective of the hereafter that Dickinson does. More interesting is this student's treatment of the willing of the keepsakes: the formal diction of "proper recipients," "standard fashion," and "officially ready to die" suggests death as a ritual. Unexpected interpretations like this appear frequently in the paraphrases, demonstrating the flexibility and richness of language, emphasizing the error in assuming that there is one right way to interpret a poem, and sometimes, when the interpretations are less plausible, leading to discussions of what constitutes valid interpretation and how one finds support for interpretations of what one reads.

The third paraphrase, as I suggested before, offers more interpretation as well as a stronger authorial voice than the previous two. The author adds a simile of her own, "as if the winds had ceased temporarily to catch their breaths," and more obviously than the other students uses the fly as a metaphor for death in her final sentence.

I will not take the space for a thorough analysis of these paraphrases, but I think that they suggest what a teacher might expect from this kind of assignment. Clearly, these three students have read this poem carefully and understand what it says, the first step towards understanding what it means. Small group and classroom discussions would allow us to consider these paraphrases individually and comparatively, to point out their merits and weaknesses, and then to return to the original verse with new perspectives.

Most heartening were the comments of several students during the quarter who told me that they felt more confident about reading poetry than they previously had. Though I doubt that my students are any more ardently devoted to poetry now than they were before the course began, they are not intimidated by verse on the page. They have an approach, a simple heuristic, for dealing with any unfamiliar writing. Ideally, my students will remember and use their ability to paraphrase and their ability to use their paraphrases to understand and evaluate what they read when they come upon a particularly difficult passage in their chemistry or history texts during the next three years or in the quarterly reports or technical manuals or journals they will read when they leave the university and begin their careers.

Appendix: Sample Paraphrases

Paraphrase I

I heard death coming on. The stillness in the room was like the stillness in the air before a storm. The people around me had wiped their eyes dry, and they held their breaths waiting for that moment when death could be witnessed in the room. I wrote a will which gave away my possessions—that being the only part of me I could give away. A fly then flew between the light and me making a sad, uncertain buzz. My eyesight faded and I could not see to see.

Paraphrase II

I heard a fly buzz as I was about to die. The sound of the fly broke the quietness in the room which was like the calm before a storm. The people sitting around waiting for me to die cried until they could not cry anymore. They began to breathe uneasily in anticipation of my death when God would come down to the room to take me away. I had willed all of my valuables to the proper recipients in the standard fashion. I was officially ready to die, going through the final dramatic moments of my life, and the last thing I was aware of was this fly and its buzz.

Paraphrase III

I could feel the approach of death just as I could hear the buzz of an approaching fly. I knew death was buzzing around, but I did not know when and where it would land. The stillness of death was like the calmness that exists between storms, as if the winds had ceased temporarily to catch their breaths.

I was aware of the sorrow in the room. There were those who had cried because death was near, and they waited for death to stalk into the room like a king and claim its subject.

I willed all of my earthly possessions, all that could legally be assigned to a new owner, in an attempt to hasten death. But there was no way to control death; I was at the mercy of its timing. And then like the fly that finally lands on its choice place, death fell upon me, and shut my eyes, and I could no longer see.

* * *

Mr. Weiser reported in a letter that, once again, he had used the method of poetry paraphrase in his writing course, and remained pleased with it. "My students," he remarked, "no longer treat poems as holy scripts written in some mystical code, but attack them fearlessly." The course had proved fun both for them and for him, and he felt he was paying his dues to both writing and literature.

Index of Authors
with Titles